LINCOLN'S FORGOTTEN ALLY

CIVIL WAR AMERICA

Gary W. Gallagher, editor

Lincoln's Forgotten Ally

JUDGE ADVOCATE GENERAL

JOSEPH HOLT OF KENTUCKY

ELIZABETH D. LEONARD

THE UNIVERSITY OF

NORTH CAROLINA PRESS

Chapel Hill

*Publication of this book was supported in part by a generous
gift from Eric Papenfuse and Catherine Lawrence.*

Designed by Richard Hendel
Set in Arnhem and TheSerif types
by Tseng Information Systems, Inc.

The paper in this book meets the guidelines for permanence
and durability of the Committee on Production Guidelines for
Book Longevity of the Council on Library Resources.

The University of North Carolina Press has been a member of
the Green Press Initiative since 2003.

Frontispiece: Portrait of the young Joseph Holt, ca. 1845.
Courtesy of Dr. Joseph Holt Rose and Halaine Rose, Pasadena, California.

Library of Congress Cataloging-in-Publication Data
Leonard, Elizabeth D.
Lincoln's forgotten ally : Judge Advocate General Joseph Holt of Kentucky /
Elizabeth D. Leonard.
p. cm. — (Civil War America)
Includes bibliographical references and index.
ISBN 978-0-8078-3500-5 (cloth : alk. paper)
1. Holt, Joseph, 1807–1894. 2. United States. Army. Judge Advocate General's
Dept.—History. 3. Judges—United States—Biography. 4. United States—
Politics and government—1849–1877. I. Title.
KF368.H586L46 2011
355.0092—dc22   2011011687
[B]

To Catherine Rose,
Margaret Rose Badger,
and Joseph Holt Rose,
friends and keepers of
the flame

CONTENTS

ILLUSTRATIONS

My first encounter with Joseph Holt came in the late 1980s when I was working on my first book, *Yankee Women: Gender Battles in the Civil War*. In this book I examined the wartime contributions of Northern women, including Dr. Mary Walker, a homeopath who had earned her M.D. at Syracuse Medical College in the mid-1850s and who, during the war, sought to put her training to use as a Federal army surgeon. For much of the war Walker's efforts were in vain. But in 1864 she received an appointment as a contract surgeon for the army, a position she held until the war's end, after which she hoped to parlay her wartime employment into a permanent position as a U.S. Army physician. Unfortunately, a number of the key figures to whom she proposed this idea remained opposed to the notion of a woman doctor serving in the army except in cases of extreme emergency. Among these was Joseph Holt who, as the army's judge advocate general, crafted a brief in the fall of 1865 explaining why President Andrew Johnson should turn down Walker's request. By way of compromise, Holt suggested that Johnson award Dr. Walker the Congressional Medal of Honor instead and send her on her way. Johnson took Holt's advice, with the result that Walker became the first woman to earn the Medal of Honor in American history, but she was out of a job.[1]

I confess that for a number of years after I completed *Yankee Women* I thought about Holt only grudgingly and with resentment because of the way he had handled Mary Walker's case. However, in the course of my research on the aftermath of the Lincoln assassination for *Lincoln's Avengers: Justice, Revenge, and Reunion after the Civil War*, I came to know a good deal more about Holt's rich and complex life story that diminished my rage and evoked instead a degree of respect and sympathy that grew over time. In addition, my research quite unexpectedly led me to a series of letters Holt received from Mary Walker herself beginning in August 1890, when she was fifty-seven and he was eighty-three. In these letters Walker wrote to Holt with genuine admiration and affection, thanking him for the gifts of melon—and cash—that he had sent when she was sick, providing him with advice for managing his rheumatism—she suggested bathing his joints every day in olive oil—and indicating that, should she ever return to her hometown of Oswego, New York, and open the retirement community she had been planning, he would be more than welcome to spend his remaining years there. (On one occasion Walker firmly, but fondly, reminded Holt to address her not as "Mrs. Walker," but as "Dr. Walker.") Half a year before he died, Walker—who was then sixty-one and had in fact relocated to Oswego—even offered to return to Washington to serve as Holt's private doctor, *free of charge*, she insisted, so that she could demonstrate her gratitude for all the many kindnesses he had shown her, and so that she might have "the satisfaction of being able to throw a little sunshine into your room" in the final phase of his life.[2]

Realizing that Mary Walker had forgiven Holt, I knew that I must forgive him, too. Then, something truly amazing happened: in August 2004, thanks to James M. McPherson's generous review of *Lincoln's Avengers* in the *New York Review of Books*—and sometime after I had already decided that it was now my professional task to flesh out the biography of Joseph Holt in full—I received a letter from Catherine Rose, who lives in California and is a direct descendant of Joseph Holt's brother, Thomas, and Thomas's wife, Rosina; Cathy is Joseph Holt's great-great-great-grandniece. "My grandmother," Cathy wrote in her letter to me, "venerated Joseph Holt and spoke of him frequently." Indeed, she explained, Holt "was a hero" to her grandmother, Mary Holt Rose, and a source of inspiration for all of his brother Thomas's descendants, and her father, Joseph Holt Rose Sr., and her brother were both named after him. "In his own life and in what he tried to teach us," Cathy went on, "my father emphasized the importance of honor, integrity, fairness, and responsibility," qualities he associated with Joseph Holt, for whom his "admiration . . . became a part of his own character."[3]

In the years since Cathy Rose first wrote to me, she and I have maintained a warm and regular correspondence, as I have done, as well, with her younger sister, Margaret Rose Badger, who also lives in California. In January 2009 the three of us finally met for the first time, having committed ourselves, sight unseen, to an adventurous week in freezing-cold Kentucky, where we toured a myriad of sites that were relevant to the lives of Joseph Holt and Abraham Lincoln. There we visited the old Holt mansion in Stephensport, where we wandered through the badly vandalized old structure imagining its former magnificence, and paid our respects in the family graveyard that Cathy, Margaret, and their brother still pay to maintain. While in Kentucky, the three of us met most of the very few people in the state who are doing their part to bring Joseph Holt's full story back into the light. Most notably, we met the wonderful local book collector Norvelle Wathen and his wife Cindy, who welcomed us into their home and introduced us to all of their seventeen cats. We also met Susan Dyer, whose courageous drive to preserve and restore the old Holt family mansion deserves enormous praise. Later, in the spring of 2009 I traveled to

California for a conference and had the pleasure of meeting Joseph Holt Jr., who goes by the name "Holt," and his wife, Halaine. Holt and Halaine graciously allowed me to bring back to Maine several large manila envelopes full of family documents relevant to the Holt family's long history, which have been invaluable in helping me get to know and understand their ancestor. This biography of Joseph Holt is dedicated to Cathy, Margaret, and Holt, who grew up with the spirit—and a magnificent portrait—of their great-great-great-uncle in their home, and who have so generously shared their family history, their insights, and their friendship with me.

There are many others who deserve my thanks for making this biography possible, not least Norvelle Wathen, who arranged for me to have access to the Holt house, who has been an unwavering and enthusiastic supporter of this project, who sent me a huge file folder of several decades' worth of extremely useful clippings from Kentucky newspapers that touched on the Holt story, and who provided the lovely pictures of the house and Holt's gravestone that I have included here. Also important in terms of my ability to locate and collect images for the book were Paul Hogroian (Library of Congress); Martin Kelly (Colby College); Jennifer Duplaga (Kentucky Historical Society); Robin Wallace (The Filson Historical Society); and Halaine Rose, whose excellent photograph of the Holt portrait is the book's frontispiece.

I would also like to thank the many librarians and archivists who have helped me along the way, including the wonderful people at the Library of Congress Manuscripts Division—especially Lincoln curator John Sellers (now retired) and archivist Bruce Kirby—and at the National Archives. I am grateful as well to John Rhodehamel at the Huntington Library, who many years ago had the Huntington's collection of Holt material microfilmed expressly for my use. My thanks, too, to the librarians at the Kentucky Historical Society, the Filson Historical Society, and the Louisville Public Library, who assisted me so ably during my visits to their institutions to tease out some of the more obscure details of Holt's life; to Susan Lintleman at the U.S. Military Academy at West Point for helping me to find my way through the academy's digital archives; and to the librarians here at Colby College, who have been so helpful with my extensive interlibrary loan needs and who made various important databases—especially the *U.S. Congressional Serial Set* and the *Official Records of the Union and Confederate Armies*—available online. I also want to thank the folks at the Kentucky Historical Society in Frankfort—especially Nelson Dawson and Kent Whitworth—who encouraged my work and, in Dr. Dawson's case, published my first article on Joseph Holt in *The Register of the Kentucky*

Historical Society. A number of scholars have been unusually generous in sharing with me their encounters with Holt in the context of their own research, especially Jonathan W. White of Christopher Newport University; Stephen Engle of Florida Atlantic University; and John Quist of Shippensburg University. J. Matthew Gallman of the University of Florida has also been most instrumental in making this a much better book.[4]

Special thanks go to my excellent research assistant, Daniel J. Franklin (Colby College, '09), who not only photocopied hundreds of documents for me but also gave me the great benefit of his shrewd analysis of those documents as well as of the text of this book as it slowly took shape. I thank my good friend Christiane Guillois for translating portions of the French-language letters Holt received from two of his correspondents, for sharing her wisdom about the human heart in the nineteenth century (and the twenty-first), and, when I had to be out of town, for making a loving home away from home for my sons with her dear husband, Arthur Greenspan.

These acknowledgments would be woefully incomplete without an expression of my tremendous appreciation to historians Joan Waugh of the University of California, Los Angeles, and Gary Gallagher of the University of Virginia, who invited me to speak about Holt at the Huntington Library's Lincoln Bicentennial Symposium in 2009, and who have been unfailingly supportive of the biography—and of me as a scholar—as far back as I can remember. I especially want to thank Gary for welcoming my work into his excellent Civil War America series, for giving the manuscript the good, tough read it needed, and for conveying all of his suggestions in the most humane and diplomatic way. I am also extremely grateful to David Perry and the top-notch staff at the University of North Carolina Press for being willing to give Joseph Holt's story the attention it deserves. And finally, I thank my sons, Anthony and Joseph, for their companionship, trust, humor, intelligence, patience, and love. You make it all worth doing.

LINCOLN'S FORGOTTEN ALLY

INTRODUCTION

Today, Stephensport, Kentucky, which is located on the Ohio River in Breckinridge County, in the northwestern portion of the state, is an easy drive from the bustling city of Louisville. The sixty-mile trip takes about an hour and a half by car. It is hardly obvious, of course, why a traveler would choose to take the time to visit Stephensport (population 400 in 2000) unless he or she had family or friends living there. Why not visit Hodgenville, seventy miles to the southeast and the birthplace of Abraham Lincoln, or the Lincoln Boyhood National Memorial, just sixty miles northwest, across the river in Indiana? Or travel to Fairview, about 125 miles southwest in Todd (formerly Christian) County, to see where Jefferson Davis was born? Individuals interested in the history of the American Civil War in particular would surely find any of these places more interesting, or so they might assume.

But Stephensport has a treasure of its own worth seeing: a sadly neglected but still impressive and moving architectural artifact that links the town to the nineteenth-century world that Abraham Lincoln and Jefferson Davis inhabited and the terrible national crisis over which they presided from 1861 to 1865. Stephensport's tattered treasure, which rises quite suddenly and apparently out of nowhere as one drives along Route 144, is the imposing three-story brick mansion that once belonged to the family of a man named Joseph Holt. Although the Holt House has been badly weather-beaten and even vandalized over the course of the half-century it has stood unoccupied, its former grandeur is unmistakable: fourteen rooms, a number of them with huge fireplaces and eight-foot-high slots for windows, elegant ironwork, as well as sturdy staircases that still refuse to creak when climbed. Clearly it was once a magnificent place with a lovely yard, some of whose trees—including a beautiful, unexpected gingko— have grown enormous over time.

Whether the Holt House and its surrounding property can ever be restored to even a semblance of their former glory is a question that remains to be answered. As for Joseph Holt, his story is not entirely unlike that of his family's home in Stephensport. For Holt, too, is barely remembered today, although he was once a highly respected person of enormous prestige, fame, and influence in his community, his state, his region, and across the nation. Indeed, as I argue in this book, no member of Abraham Lincoln's administration or the postwar federal government—indeed, no Civil War–era political figure—has been more unjustly neglected by historians, more misrepresented by Americans' collective historical "memory," and, in the end, more completely forgotten than Joseph Holt. This biography seeks to redress that wrong.

Born in 1807 not far from where the dilapidated mansion stands, Joseph Holt spent his earliest years as the quiet, deeply reserved but extremely bright and bookish second son of a slaveholding lawyer/farmer and his wife. By 1860, though, the fifty-three-year-old Holt had gone far. A wealthy and highly accomplished attorney living and working in the nation's capital, he was considered a serious contender to oppose Lincoln for the nation's highest office by many of the leading lights in the Democratic Party, of which he and his family had long been loyal supporters.

By that time, Holt had already served in James Buchanan's administration for three years, first as commissioner of patents and then in the president's cabinet as postmaster general. For reasons that had to do with both his fundamental nature and his sense of where his duty lay, Holt dismissed his supporters' encouragement to seek the presidency himself. Then, in the wake Lincoln's election, as Buchanan's cabinet began to crumble, Holt accepted an emergency appointment as secretary of war. In this post, he strove courageously from December 31, 1860, to March 6, 1861, to hold the collapsing nation and the federal government together.

On March 4, 1861, Abraham Lincoln became president. Just over a month later war erupted in Charleston Harbor. Although Lincoln's April 15 call for troops to put down the rebellion drove four previously undecided states into the Confederacy, four other states that lay along the border between slavery and freedom remained ambivalent. Among these, perhaps the most important was resource-rich Kentucky, which Lincoln and Holt agreed *must* be held. Over the course of the next several months they worked together—successfully—to sustain their native state's loyalty to the Union and then transform that loyalty into armed support. Profoundly grateful for all of Holt's efforts on behalf of the nation thus far, Lincoln was also impressed by Holt's brilliant legal mind, his sense of personal and national honor, and his stern commitment to duty. Moreover, he was certain that Holt would both endorse and enforce his administration's war policies. And so, in September 1862, Lincoln appointed Holt judge advocate general of the U.S. Army. *Lincoln's Forgotten Ally* is, in part, the story of Holt's dedicated wartime collaboration with Lincoln—not least on the question of emancipation. For although he had grown up with slavery and even, for a time, became a slave owner in his own right, Holt eventually— and decisively—rejected this central feature of the world from which he had come and embraced instead, with passion and supreme resolution, Lincoln's vision for a new world in which all people could be free.

On April 14, 1865, John Wilkes Booth murdered Abraham Lincoln. Just hours later, Andrew Johnson became president of the United States, whose victory in its brutal civil war was by then virtually assured. As judge advocate general, Joseph Holt now moved from doing whatever he could do to support Lincoln and his wartime policies to prosecuting those who had been involved in Booth's conspiracy not only to kill the president but to throw the entire federal government into chaos in order to extend the life of the failing Confederacy. In the weeks, months, and years ahead, Holt stubbornly strove to avenge Lincoln's death, to punish those who had coerced the Southern people to attempt the violent destruction of the nation, and to ensure that Lincoln's goals for the war were fulfilled and that 360,000 white *and* black Federal soldiers' lives had not been sacrificed in vain. He did so in the face of relentless and seemingly overwhelming opposition and, as *Lincoln's Forgotten Ally* makes clear, sometimes with a fervor that may well have undermined his own aims. And yet he pressed on.

Joseph Holt remained judge advocate general—and head of the War Department's Bureau of Military Justice—until his retirement in 1875, near the end of Ulysses S. Grant's second term as president. For close to twenty more years the twice-widowed Holt continued to live in the lovely New Jersey Avenue home he and his second wife had purchased when they first moved to Washington. Although he had been immensely famous and profoundly influential during his lifetime, Holt now emerged into public view only occasionally, as a lingering symbol and reminder of the war and its bitterly contested aftermath and meaning. Eventually he faded almost entirely from popular historical memory, for reasons that have everything to do with how most Americans in the decades after Appomattox came to understand the war as a struggle between brave white brothers on opposite sides of Mason and Dixon's Line, whose causes were equally valid and who, once the war was over, wisely strove to put the whole painful state's rights contest behind them. As readers of *Lincoln's Forgotten Ally* will surely learn, Holt would have found it impossible to stomach such a distortion of what the war was about or for, and of what Reconstruction should have accomplished (or did). But he certainly would have recognized the narrative, which he spent most of his postwar life trying to rewrite.

1

LAYING THE FOUNDATION, 1807–1835

I want you to be good and great.
—*Grandfather Richard Stephens to Joseph Holt, November 27, 1826*

*I hope you will cultivate every talent you possess that will advance
your prospects or promote your fame and rapid march to high political
distinction. I want you to be restless and ambitious of political
preferment.*—*Uncle Daniel Stephens to Joseph Holt, September 1833*

In the early years of the nineteenth century, Kentucky—
more famously the birthplace of Abraham Lincoln (1809) and Jefferson
Davis (1808) than of Joseph Holt—was a new, largely unsettled but rapidly
developing state. Earnest white pioneers had first explored the region
around 1750; George Washington may have visited as a surveyor in 1771.
Then, the year the original thirteen colonies declared their independence
from Great Britain, Virginia declared Kentucky one of its western counties
and named Harrodsburg the county seat. Seven years later, Virginia legislators redefined what had been "Kentucky County" as a "district" now in-
corporating three counties—Fayette, Jefferson, and Lincoln—each named
after a Revolutionary War hero (the Marquis de Lafayette, Thomas Jefferson, and General Benjamin Lincoln). At that time, the district's political
center was removed about ten miles south of Harrodsburg to Danville,
where there was a meetinghouse large enough to accommodate the district court. Soon after, Kentuckians began to organize a series of conventions to express their desire for independence from Virginia, prompted at
least in part, no doubt, by the more than five hundred miles that lay between Danville and the state capital at Richmond. During the mid- to late-
1780s, struggles back east over the merits and durability of the Articles
of Confederation, followed by wrangling over the new U.S. Constitution,
overshadowed the Virginia legislature's concerns about Kentucky. But in
December 1789, the Old Dominion's legislators finally laid out the terms by

which the district of Kentucky could become a state, and in February 1792, Kentucky was admitted to the Union, just the second state after Vermont to be added since the Revolution.[1]

At the time Kentucky became a state (just a decade and a half before Joseph Holt was born), residents had only recently begun to develop independent homesteads and communities, which they hoped to keep safe from attack by the Native people who still used the region as a hunting ground. The first homes white Kentuckians built were one-story log cabins, typically no more than twenty feet square, their chimneys often constructed of clay and twigs, their floors either of dirt or rough wooden boards. In this period, according to historian Lucius Little, "the males of the household improved and cultivated the land, hunted, fished, helped the neighbors, attended musters, or joined occasional expeditions against the Indians," while white women and children "remained at home, engaged in household affairs, spinning, weaving, sewing, and making the plain and simple wearing apparel of the family."[2]

To assist them in the labor of domesticating the land and building families and communities, white Kentuckians at the turn of the nineteenth century held people of African descent in bondage. From early on, notes historian E. Merton Coulter, slavery in the state of Kentucky was diffuse, with very few slaveholders owning a large number of humans as property, but many—perhaps most—white households owning a few. At the same time, slavery was firmly rooted in early Kentucky: although a number of local institutions spoke out against human bondage on a regular basis, Coulter explains, "the most the state ever did toward checking the institution was to pass laws preventing the importation of slaves for sale," laws which were clearly "so difficult to enforce as to become soon obsolete." Fewer than a quarter of a million residents (whites as well as blacks, most of whom—some 40,000—were enslaved) were counted in Kentucky for congressional apportionment purposes in 1800; roughly 400,000 (including more than 80,000 slaves) were counted in 1810, making Kentucky the new nation's ninth most populous state.[3]

Like Kentucky itself, Joseph Holt's maternal grandfather, Richard Stephens, came from Virginia, having served as a private in the Continental Army for three years during the American Revolution. In February 1784, in lieu of payment for his service as a soldier on the Virginia line, twenty-nine-year-old Stephens accepted a hundred-acre land grant on the Ohio River in Kentucky, whose newness offered hope and possibility. Over time, Stephens's business acumen and Kentucky's relative underpopulation enabled him to make a series of additional land acquisitions, in turn allowing him to overcome the constraints that would have held him back in Virginia. By 1799, with over 100,000 acres (about 150 square miles) and at least a dozen slaves,[4] Stephens was the wealthiest landowner in Breckinridge County. Predictably, his prosperity earned Stephens a substantial measure of local respect, social status, and influence.[5]

Richard Stephens did well indeed in Breckinridge County, expanding not only his rich land and slave holdings but also his family. Back in Virginia in September 1780 Stephens had married Elizabeth Jennings, four years his junior and a native of Fairfax County.[6] Together Elizabeth and Richard produced nine children: Ann (also known as Nancy) in 1781, Eleanor (1783), Robert (1786), Richard (1788), Elizabeth (1791), Sarah (1794), Daniel (1795), Mary Ann (1797), and Jemima (1801). It was Richard and Elizabeth's second child, Eleanor Jennings Stephens, who became Joseph Holt's mother four years after she married John W. Holt, who was eleven years her senior and whose ancestral roots can be traced to a seventeenth-century property holding known as Aston Hall in Birmingham, county of Warwickshire, in central England. John Holt's father, like Eleanor's, had fought in the American Revolution.[7]

Soon after their marriage, the couple settled on the fertile, 500-acre portion of the Stephens family land abutting the Ohio River that came to be known as "Holt's Bottom." In the years ahead, John bought additional land and, like his father-in-law, continued to expand his holdings, which eventually encompassed not only the acreage that the family itself occupied and tilled, but also a railroad station and a post office. John Holt also purchased several humans of African descent to work his land; by 1810, he owned eight slaves. Meanwhile, almost exactly nine months after she and John wed, in April 1804 Eleanor gave birth to her first child, Richard, named after her father. Twenty-one months later, on January 6, 1807, she delivered Joseph, whom the couple named after John's father. Joseph was followed by James (October 1810), Thomas (April 1812), Robert (April 1815), and Elizabeth (November 1817). Twenty-four years old when Joseph Holt was born, his mother remained comparatively healthy throughout her childbearing years, and all six of the children she bore lived to adulthood. Growing up, Joseph Holt must have felt a strong sense of entitlement in relation to the world that surrounded him: "Holt's Bottom" took its name from his father; the nearby town of Stephensport, which was officially incorporated in 1825 with a population of 160, was named after his land-rich and widely respected maternal grandfather.[8]

As the first decades of the new century passed, with the help of their human property and their children, John and Eleanor Holt managed their large working farm, where they grew tobacco, wheat, and oats and also raised pigs. John had not always been a farmer: in fact, at the time he married Eleanor he was a highly accomplished lawyer who just two years earlier had been appointed neighboring Hardin County's commonwealth's attorney—the county's chief prosecutor and its highest law enforcement official. Subsequently, John had established a practice in Elizabethtown, the Hardin County seat, about sixty miles southeast of Stephensport. There he had worked with a number of important local figures to organize the first circuit court of Kentucky. John Holt was also instrumental in the construction of the town's first brick courthouse in 1804. While in Elizabethtown, his legal work included a case involving Isaac Bush, whose sister, Sarah, later became Abraham Lincoln's stepmother.[9]

The author of a history of Elizabethtown describes Joseph Holt's father as "a quiet, unobtrusive gentleman" who, although talented as a lawyer, nevertheless found that the profession did not entirely suit him, so he took up farming. Even after he moved to Breckinridge County, however, John Holt did not give up his legal practice entirely. Rather, he continued to put his training and credentials to use, accepting the appointment as Breckinridge County's commonwealth's attorney and later serving as a justice of the peace as well. John Holt also took work as a local surveyor, an overseer of roads, and, eventually, a tobacco inspector. These posts no doubt both reflected and further enhanced his stature and the prominence in the area enjoyed by the growing Holt/Stephens clan. In keeping with their own backgrounds and their growing distinction in the community, John and Eleanor Holt saw to it that all of their children received some education, initially in the form of tutoring within the family and perhaps also at a neighborhood school. Later, with strong support from Eleanor's father and her two most ambitious and politically active brothers, Daniel Jennings Stephens and Robert "Bob" Stephens—both of whom spent time serving in the state legislature—the Holts sought higher education for at least some of their offspring. By age twenty, firstborn son Richard was busy studying medicine with a Dr. Young in John Holt's old stomping grounds, Elizabethtown.[10]

Richard's career path surely pleased his parents and his closely knit extended family. Still, from early on it is apparent that, whether he liked it or not, second-born son Joseph was the repository of their greatest hopes, in large part because he was strikingly bright, bookish, and unusually serious. And so it was *Joseph's* education and *Joseph's* professional, political, and financial future that became the focus of their rapt attention and ambition. The anticipated accomplishments of his siblings and his cousins simply paled in comparison. "Jo," his uncle Daniel Stephens once wrote, "you have but a small idea of the hopes that I have in you & the wishes that I have for your wellfare. . . . [M]arch readily and firmly to that greatness which we hope ere long to environ your every action. . . . [Y]ou are destined to move in a superior circle but your standing in that circle is only to be measured by your mind your eloquence & information." For his part, Grandfather Richard Stephens put great faith in Joseph as the one not only to enhance the family's name in the larger world, but also to protect the family's wealth. "I pray you, my dear grandson," he wrote. "Should I die be carefull that what I have made is g[u]arded by your good sense."[11]

And so, when he was only fifteen years old, Joseph Holt left home with the dreams and expectations of his large family borne upon his shoulders—burned into his psyche, even—to pursue his college education in bustling Bardstown, the political heart of Nelson County and, in many ways at that time, the state's social and cultural center. Bardstown's inhabitants, wrote Lucius Little, were "refined, intelligent, wealthy, and hospitable," and its fine schools drew individuals from all over who were "seeking the advantages afforded by its learned faculties." Only five years before Holt moved there, the construction of the first Catholic cathedral west of the Allegheny Mountains had also declared Bardstown's importance as a new center for Catholicism in the American West. Indeed, St. Joseph's College, where Holt enrolled, was a Catholic school, founded in 1820 by the Reverend Benedict Joseph Flaget, Bardstown's first bishop, "with a view of giving to Catholics a thorough literary education."[12]

Fortunately for Joseph, however, students at the college were not required to be members of the church (the Holts were Protestants); they simply needed to be able to pay the school's fees. In Holt's case, his grandfather provided most of the necessary financial support, although Richard Stephens made it clear that he expected Joseph to pay him back in full eventually, exhorting his cherished grandson to keep in mind at all times that "a provident upright young man makes a wise and happy old man." From May 1822 until November 1823 Joseph Holt remained at St. Joseph's College, where he performed extremely well academically, excelling particularly in his courses on composition and public speaking, both of which would prove extremely important for his future career as a lawyer.[13]

In November 1823, however, Holt unexpectedly came into direct conflict with the president of the college, Father George Elder, a "zealous and efficient" ordained Jesuit priest "of strong mind and unconquerable energy," who was just thirty years old. At issue was an essay Holt had written for a class at the college. When he read the essay, Father Elder became concerned about its unusually high quality and decided to speak about it with others on the college faculty, in the process letting on that he had some suspicions about Holt's academic integrity. Although Elder soon overcame his doubts, word that he was talking about Holt behind the teenager's back leaked out and Holt grew worried that the college president had started spreading rumors that he was a cheater, an insult made even more infuriating by the fact that Elder had not spoken with him directly first. In a fashion that would be characteristic throughout his life, Holt became enraged at the thought of Elder speaking openly about what he considered a supremely private matter having to do with his honesty and his reputation, and when Elder finally apologized for airing his doubts so indiscreetly, the proud young man from Breckinridge County proved inconsolable. Refusing to accept Elder's explanation or apology, Holt stormed away from the college, reportedly walking the entire eighty-five miles home to Stephensport.[14]

The matter did not end there, either. Several weeks later, Father Elder tried to make amends. Elder knew that he had insulted the young man's honor, though he believed that Holt had misunderstood his intentions entirely. Now the priest hoped to achieve a reconciliation, for Holt was a brilliant student of unusual promise whose family—though not Catholic—was large and influential in this region of Kentucky. In the end, however, he could not resist mixing his apology with an attempt to make his own position clear and justify his actions. "I ask your pardon," Father Elder wrote earnestly, maintaining nevertheless that his heart had been in the right place at all times. "I did, it is true," he explained, "suspect that [Mr.] Hays had a hand in the piece, & I told you so." But, he insisted, once Holt informed him that the sparkling essay was entirely original, he had taken the young man at his word. Moreover, by discussing the essay with others at the school he had only meant to demonstrate how impressed he had been with its quality. "It was intended for a compliment," Elder claimed. "I was talking of your composition . . . in terms of commendation," not to evoke others' contempt. "I am sincerely sorry," Elder continued. "It was an error of judgment, not of heart."[15]

Nevertheless, seventeen-year-old Holt still refused to offer the Reverend Elder much in the way of clemency. Having read the priest's January 8 letter "with due diligence & attention," on January 18 he penned his reply, pointing out that by impugning his character publicly, Elder had "violated a principle which every gentleman would hold sacred," and he made clear that time had done nothing to dull his experience of the original insult. Rejecting any pretense that an older man in Elder's exalted professional position should have the edge on offering moral guidance, Holt boldly urged the priest to avoid committing similar errors of judgment in the future and advised him to demonstrate greater sensitivity and compassion toward others than he had demonstrated in Holt's own case. In particular, Holt counseled Elder to guard other men's reputations with care and not to assume that younger men like himself—admittedly, a "boy of half understanding"—were less concerned than older ones about defending their good names. As for the question of whether Holt would be returning to St. Joseph's, the answer was a stern, resounding "no." Elder did not appeal Holt's decision.[16]

In his exchange of letters with George Elder, young Joseph Holt revealed core components of his personality that would remain essentially intact, for better or worse, throughout his long, dynamic life. On the one hand, Holt's encounter with George Elder demonstrated his extraordinarily keen intellect, his strong sense of self-respect and personal honor, and his eloquence, fearlessness, and independence. On the other hand, it exposed his profound sensitivity to real or perceived slights, along with the limitations of his ability to forgive when he believed that an injustice had been committed. In short, the dispute between Holt and Elder, and its failed resolution, provide clear insights into Holt's developing temperament.

At the same time, amplified by the enormous pressure he was under from those in his family who were eager for him to achieve great things and to enhance the family's honor, the incident at St. Joseph's also helped to shape the man Joseph Holt became. Copies of the letters he exchanged with Elder are, in fact, among the very first documents that Holt saved when he began to accumulate the many thousands of items that would ultimately constitute his personal and professional archive. On the bottom of Elder's January 8 missive Holt wrote that he was keeping the letter "as an evidence," and for his records he carefully wrote out and kept a copy of the letter he sent in reply. For Holt, the dispute with Father Elder was rich in important life lessons, not the least of which, as he noted, was that the "blackcoated priesthood are ever base enough to inflict injury, but too dastardly to vindicate themselves when confronted." Such a remark is hardly surprising, given the generalized anti-Catholic sentiments of the era among American Protestants. Holt was hardly immune to his culture's widespread distrust of the Catholic Church. It is also true, however, that Holt's Protestant family had felt entirely comfortable sending him to a Catholic institution, and he himself had thrived there, without complaint, for more than a year. What really aroused Holt's fury, then, was not Elder's Catholicism but the fact that his clerical robes did not prevent his public assault on Holt's character. By saving the evidence of Elder's perfidy and his own bold response to it, the young Holt took a key step toward shaping the contours of his self-understanding and his self-projection into the larger world, identifying and defining the sort of treatment he would tolerate from others along the way, regardless of their status.[17]

The incident with George Elder brought Holt's time at St. Joseph's to an abrupt close, but it did not mark the end of his formal education. Instead, Holt transferred to the equally well-respected Centre College in Danville, roughly forty-five miles east of Bardstown. Founded by Presbyterians but—like St. Joseph's—nondenominational in its admissions and educational policies, Centre College was chartered by the Kentucky state legislature in 1819. There, Holt came under the watchful eye of yet another clergyman, Reverend Barnabas Hughes, who boarded him, maintained communication with his uncles and grandfather back home, and assumed responsibility for keeping young Joseph's tuition and board accounts in order. Soon after he arrived in Danville, Holt wrote to his grandfather and uncles to say that he was much happier at Centre College than he had been at St. Joseph's. "I hope you will proffit abundantly by your present opportunity," Uncle Bob replied soberly. Holt remained in Danville for about a year, studying—among other things—Latin, Greek, rhetoric, and logic and continuing to develop his skills as a writer, speaker, and debater, all of which were designed to lay the foundation for his future in the law and, presumably, in politics.[18]

As he had been at St. Joseph's, Holt was a highly diligent and impressive student across the board at Centre College. Indeed, he spent so much time studying that members of his family became anxious about his health. "I am afraid you do not take exercise enough with your studies," cautioned physician-in-training Richard, who encouraged his brother to walk or go horseback riding or do *something* physical for at least two hours a day. "There is nothing which destroys health sooner," Richard declared, "than an intense application of the mind without exercise of the body." Though he frequently wrote letters urging Holt to remain focused academically and to keep his eyes on the prize of future glory—"let study be your chief employ," he counseled—Uncle Bob was worried, too. "Don't impair your health by to[o] assiduous application," he wrote. "Take exercise enough." For his part, Grandfather Richard Stephens worried not only about Holt's health but also about his ability to stay attentive to his studies over the long term, given his youth and the inevitable temptations of town life. You are, Grandfather Stephens wrote, "the pride of my life in my old age," and, thus, he cautioned, "let sobriety and modesty be your creed."[19]

Although they regularly expressed concern about his health and his mental and moral welfare, however, family members back home refrained as best they could from interfering with the progress of Holt's education. Even at times when an extra hand was needed on the home front for one reason or another they invariably turned to his older brother, whose medical studies, one can only conclude, they deemed less important. "I am now living at Uncle Bob's and will live there until the legislature shall adjourn," wrote Richard to Joseph in November 1824, "as his family could not do well without some person there while he is gone." Richard occasionally grumbled about these interruptions in his training, but he does not seem to have resented his younger brother's preeminence in the family. Indeed, perhaps at some level he was happy not to bear the burden of expectation that Joseph carried. Moreover, the two young men had the sort of affectionate sibling relationship that could easily withstand a degree of good-natured competitive jousting. "I think the country will shortly have more Lawyers & Doctors than of any other profession," Richard wrote to Joseph in February 1825, "but I console myself with the knowing that . . . a physician can make a living where a lawyer may starve." Still, he teased, "I don't want to discourage you."[20]

Holt's education at Danville extended beyond the classroom to include his growing awareness of the relationship between a man's physical appearance—including his clothing—and the impression he made on others, as well as the respect they accorded him. "Jo," wrote Uncle Daniel in July 1824, "be plain & common in your dress. . . . [C]lothes that are clean and warm is [sic] all that nature requires and a great mind is not to look upon them as an ornament but only as necessary." Just a few months after he received this advice, Holt expressed similar sentiments in a letter he wrote to accompany some clothing he was sending to his younger brother James, then fourteen and in school in Elizabethtown: "two pair of good strong country Breeches & a waistcoat of corresponding strength & durability." Of these simple but useful and even symbolic items Holt remarked that, "although they are not so elegant in their texture & making as the cravings of Dandyism might require, yet they seem gifted with the qualities which have long characterized the noble independence of our family—simplicity frowning upon ostentation, and an antiquity of fashion past finding out." As Daniel had advised him, so Joseph now advised his brother. "Strong old fashioned clothes," he declared proudly, are "the Heraldic badge of our family. . . . I wear exactly such and although they do not attract the attention of the 'Bonnie lassies' yet they are highly comfortable & shield me from many a keen little wind." Moreover, he added, "an independent man can never be in fashion, for to be in fashion is to step to and ape the stupidities of other men, to copy after all their follies, which a man of spirit is little disposed to do." In writing this way to James, Holt enthusiastically aligned himself with a kind of heroic rural simplicity that he associated with dignity, self-respect, and honor. Still, there were times when he wished for at least one suit of clothes that was not quite so plain. Having learned that Holt had felt unable to participate in a recent debate because of the state of his wardrobe, in February 1825 Uncle Bob sent him ten dollars. "Make the best use of it you can," Bob wrote. "Your Grandfather is sorry that your shabbyness prevented you from speaking."[21]

Holt's intellectual gifts and his unwavering dedication to his studies garnered him great admiration among the Centre College faculty and administrators, so much so that the college president, Reverend Jeremiah Chamberlin, eventually decided to offer him a full scholarship. Holt did not accept the scholarship, however, nor did he even graduate from the college. In the summer of 1824, Uncle Daniel had already cautioned him that the family's financial ability to underwrite his education would probably limit Holt to one term there; in October, his uncle wrote again to explain that numerous unidentified "misfortunes"—likely associated with the economic crisis then gripping the state—had left the land-rich family embarrassingly cash-strapped. Rather than return to the family homestead, however, in early 1825 Holt worked out an arrangement with Robert Wickliffe of Lexington, an extremely prominent and well-respected lawyer and friend of his Grandfather Stephens, to do some tutoring of Wickliffe's children in exchange for the opportunity to become the older man's protégé. One of the most successful and wealthy lawyers of his day, Wickliffe also had an active political life, serving in the state legislature in 1819 and 1823 and the state senate from 1825 until 1833. Now the man known as "Old Duke" was pleased to employ young Joseph Holt on Holt's terms, and he promised that his children would not require much tending.[22]

And so, in the summer of 1825, Holt moved to Lexington, then one of the largest, most prosperous towns outside of the original thirteen states and, since 1797, the home of Henry Clay. With a total population of about 6,000 when Holt arrived, Lexington was nicknamed "Athens of the West" because of its reputation for thriving intellectual and political activity and cosmopolitan culture. It was, wrote one early historian of Kentucky, "the Jamestown of the West; the advance-guard of civilization; the center from which went forth the conquerors of a savage empire." Lexington was also the home of highly regarded Transylvania University, founded in 1780 as the first college west of the Allegheny Mountains, which Jefferson Davis

Henry Clay. Courtesy of the Library of Congress.

attended from 1821 to 1824 and where Henry Clay taught law. In addition, within the state of Kentucky the town had one of the highest proportions of enslaved people relative to its total population, approaching 50 percent.[23]

Holt trained with Robert Wickliffe for the next two years in the heart of this lively community, where many of the key issues of his day were both confronted and debated. "I can not but congratulate you," wrote his cousin Jefferson Dorsey, "for having obtained a situation . . . where you can have an opportunity of cultivating your mind so as to prepare yourself to act on the theatre of life with that honor to yourself that results from persevering industry and . . . the principles of morality and virtue. Should you persevere in the course you seem to have adopted, to say nothing of natural endowments," he added, echoing the aspirations that Uncles Bob and Daniel, Grandfather Stephens, and others in Holt's extended family had also repeatedly projected onto him, "I have a hope that . . . there will be one of the family whose brow will be enwreathed with the imperishable laurels of renown." "I know of no man in Kentucky whose friendship I would sooner share than his," added family friend James Dozier from Hopkinsville in recognition of Holt's wise choice of mentors, "none with whom I would so soon have my own son, to learn whatever was necessary to qualify him for a lawyer or statesman." Like so many others in Holt's circle of relatives and friends, Dozier recalled the early indications of what he anticipated would be Holt's future prominence. "You were about the smartest little boy I ever saw, with whom I had anything to do," he wrote; "I regarded affectionately your boyhood. I am sure I should sincerely esteem your maturer years."[24]

Conscientious and ambitious student that he was, Holt spent the bulk of his time in Lexington making his way through Wickliffe's vast supply of books: the elder man's private library numbered in the thousands of volumes. Wickliffe also had a rich collection of books that did not pertain to the law, as well as many globes and maps, all of which he welcomed Holt to examine and enjoy, along with providing the young man with room and board, a horse for his use, and any other help he could offer. "I am reading as much as I can," Holt wrote home in June 1826. Holt sat for occasional examinations by Wickliffe on what he had learned from his hours in the library. More than once, he confidently reassured his attentive uncles and grandfather that he considered himself "perhaps as well or better situated than I could be anywhere else upon the same terms," and back home, word of his progress brought cheers of encouragement. When he wrote again in December 1826, cousin Jefferson Dorsey declared himself "very much pleased to see that the obscurity that seems to exist in the law was vanishing and the beauties of the science were discovering themselves to you."[25]

Holt's earnestness, however, was not without cost. For one thing, as the weeks in Lexington passed he simply did not seem to have as much time to stay in touch as he used to, and family members and friends routinely scolded him for burying himself so deeply in his studies, and life in Lexington, that he no longer had time to write. "You appear to have forgotten us in Breckinridge," complained Uncle Daniel in June 1827. "You scarc[e]ly ever write and when you do you do not tell us how you progress." On this occasion, Daniel seemed particularly annoyed that, having received so much financial help from his grandfather, Holt had not demonstrated commensurate gratitude by writing home on a more regular basis. At the same time, Daniel stressed that Holt should continue with Wickliffe no matter what. "Jo," he wrote, "stick with Wickliffe until you are fully qualified to practice. . . . [D]o not fail to lay in a good store of general knowledge as well as law. . . . [D]on't idle away a moment[. Y]ou have now to stand or fall by your own exertions."[26]

As they had done when he was at Centre College, some family members continued to worry that Holt's latest intellectual exertions were affecting his health and threatening his overall wellbeing. "Pray my dear grandson," wrote Grandfather Stephens, "take exercise and ride about or walk . . . [Do] something to amuse you[rself] and strengthen your constitution for I fear your . . . attention to your work will kill you." Folks back home also feared that Holt's diligence would exacerbate his tendency toward isolation, his natural inclination to distance himself from society, which his earlier experiences with Father Elder both reflected and probably amplified. What seems to be the only letter from his father that Joseph Holt decided to preserve (or perhaps the only one he ever received) resonates with this concern: "My Dear Son," John Holt wrote in October 1826, "although you may possess all the learning and good sense possible, yet without friends you cannot pass through life with much satisfaction to yourself." Holt's father urged him to "cultivate the friendship of all good men and lay aside that distant and forbidding turn which you appear to possess." As a lawyer himself, John Holt no doubt felt competent to explain to this son, who was both the most accomplished and the most emotionally reserved of his six children, that learning to interact comfortably with other people was essential to success. "The profession by which you expect to get your living . . . will require," he explained, "that you should be at least sociable with all ranks of people." Among other things, John Holt sought to help his son see that lawyers must make connections to thrive, and that "men who appear to be hard to approach" were less likely than those who were more outgoing to be able to forge those connections effectively. "When you speak to a man," he advised, "look him in the face." Grandfather Stephens, too, encouraged Holt to "be cheerful and act freely," to "ride about and see things," to "learn to play," and to "take more time to become acquainted with your fellow man." And he cautioned, "if you keep [to] yourself . . . no one will ever find out your worth." Holt's uncles added their voices to the chorus of concern about his reticence, Uncle Bob encouraging him to join a debating society and Uncle Daniel counseling him to "lay aside your diffidence." Daniel should, perhaps, have demonstrated a bit more diffidence himself; doing so might have prevented him from engaging in an August 1827 duel that almost cost him his life.[27]

As his time with Robert Wickliffe passed, Holt continued to weigh the advice he was getting from deeply interested family members and friends back home against the expectations of the professional world upon whose threshold he now stood. Just as he had begun to do earlier, Holt tried to balance different features of the man he recognized himself to be—his sharp mind, his ambition, and his wariness about people, for example— with the clear demands of a future life in the law and, perhaps, in politics. He also measured the values gleaned from his early childhood in Stephensport against the realities of his emerging professional life within Lexington's comparatively cosmopolitan and highly competitive setting, where it must have seemed like every man with whom he came into contact was on the move and on the make. As before, Holt's grappling with the issues of professionalism and the implications of a man's presentation of himself to others was occasionally reflected in his thoughts about which clothes to wear and when. "I very much need a pair of Sunday summer . . . pantaloons," he wrote home in June 1826. "My breeches are very good for Breckinridge commonality & even decent among its dandies, but they are not so here" in Lexington, where folks tended to "cast a disrespectful glance at the homespun of our land" and would never be caught wearing "a thread of it" themselves. Holt clearly yearned to avoid embarrassment; at the same time, he remained critical of the world he now found himself inhabiting. "Wickliffe lives well & in splendid style," he wrote to his uncles, "but has an exceedingly extravagant family and he is very indulgent."[28]

By early 1828, twenty-one-year-old Joseph Holt was ready to launch his own career. However much he may have hoped to keep his bright young protégé as his assistant for years to come, Robert Wickliffe did not stand in Holt's way, instead assuring Holt that he would always be his "friend and well wisher," and that no one could possibly feel more pleased with the younger man's successes than he did. As Holt prepared to set out on his own, friends and family members continued to express their lofty expectations for his success, moderated by their concerns about how such a reticent, reflective, scholarly young man would handle both his personal and his professional interactions as the sphere in which he lived and labored grew larger and more complex. His cousin Jefferson Dorsey, for one, acknowledged that difficulties lay ahead, not least in connection with the "frailties & deformities of human nature" that Holt was bound to encounter. "You will see human nature in every shape," Dorsey (himself a lawyer) warned, "and ultimately discover that the professions of friendship and confidence are often made for the purpose of entrapping . . . young men who possess . . . an enterprising spirit." Dorsey counseled Holt not to let down his guard or assume that others would treat him fairly, and pleaded with him to balance trust with skepticism as he moved out into society. "You must not be too distant with the world nor yet so familiar," Dorsey wrote, "as to cause people to take liberties." Given his nature, Holt hardly needed this advice.[29]

For his part, Grandfather Stephens hoped that his grandson would now return to Stephensport, at least for a few months, to share some of his knowledge and experience with his three younger brothers—eighteen-year-old James, sixteen-year-old Thomas, and thirteen-year-old Robert—whose futures remained uncertain. But Holt, determined to set his career in motion, moved instead to his father's old bailiwick, Elizabethtown. Much smaller and much less cosmopolitan than Lexington, Elizabethtown's population in 1830 was only about 600, of whom about 20 percent were enslaved. Still, the town offered Holt a valuable opportunity: the chance to establish a professional association with Robert Wickliffe's first cousin, the famous Benjamin Hardin, an impressively accomplished lawyer who was two decades Holt's senior. "I am pleased to learn that you have associated yourself with a man of Hardin's eminence," cheered one of Holt's old school chums in November 1828. "It will introduce you to suits of magnitude & give you an opportunity of displaying the Herculean powers of your intellect." Although he was initially elected to public office as a Democratic-Republican, from 1824 onward Hardin became, like Henry Clay, a National Republican and, later still, a "faithful Whig."[30]

Hardin's broad range of legal and political knowledge, experience, and influence drew ambitious young lawyers to him like a magnet, as did his reputation for being a splendid orator and debater whose style, "peculiar, pungent, sarcastic, pointed, and energetic," made him "an antagonist to be feared." It was rumored that John Randolph of Virginia, who served for a number of years with Hardin in the U.S. Congress, called him "the Kitchen Knife," by which Randolph meant to indicate that Hardin was "rough and homely, but keen and trenchant." At the same time, according to one biographer, whereas other senior lawyers commonly mistreated the younger attorneys with whom they worked, "appropriat[ing] to themselves all the credit of success," Hardin was generous and attentive, and "his relations with his colleagues were always of the kindest character." Certainly he left a lasting positive impression on Holt, who worked with him in Elizabethtown from 1828 to 1832 and recalled many years later that Hardin had been "uniformly kind" to him, "both personally and professionally." As such, Holt remarked, "with a glowing admiration of his wonderful intellectual gifts, the recollection of him that I cherish is at once grateful and affectionate."[31]

Not everyone felt so favorable toward Ben Hardin, however, especially those whose political beliefs and commitments aligned them not with Clay and the National Republicans but with Clay's nemesis, the rugged former U.S. senator, congressman, military governor of Florida, and War of 1812 hero from Tennessee, Andrew Jackson. At the time Holt moved to Elizabethtown, Jackson was on the verge of being elected president of the United States under the guise of being the spokesman for, and a representative of, the "common man." As it turns out, virtually all of Holt's many politically engaged family members as well as the bulk of his friends and associates were Jackson supporters. Certainly his grandfather and his uncles were, which made them somewhat leery about Holt's partnership with Hardin, although they recognized the professional benefits such a relationship would yield. Still, not long after he settled into practice in Elizabethtown, Holt received a letter from Grandfather Stephens, now in his seventies, indicating some concern that Holt seemed to have hitched his wagon—temporarily at least—to a National Republican. Richard Stephens hoped that Holt would learn what he could from Hardin about the law but would resist becoming the more prominent man's flunky. "Don't look up to no one for advice," he cautioned sternly, "but make all look to you."[32]

As a young and ambitious lawyer in a young and ambitious state, Holt could not have avoided politics even if he had wanted to. But he did not want to. "Give a Kentuckian a plug of tobacco and a political antagonist, and he will spend a comfortable day wherever he is," declared one local journalist in the late 1880s. And indeed, Holt's letters from as far back as his late teens contain a great deal of lively material pertaining to the state's political affairs, which at that time were tightly intertwined with the local effects of the national Panic of 1819, the same post–War of 1812 economic crisis that had limited his grandfather's ability to pay in cash for Holt's education at Centre College. Moreover, by the time Holt moved to Eliza-

bethtown in 1828, he, too, was on his way to becoming a determined, dedicated, and active Jacksonian who believed—like most of his family members—that Clay and the National Republicans (later the Whigs) sought to
enhance the power of the federal government and of the wealthy at the expense of the states and the common folk. As they gathered strength, Jacksonians in Kentucky and elsewhere took particular aim at a centerpiece
of the National Republicans' program: support for Clay's so-called American System, whereby the federal government, with or without a state's express permission, would subsidize the building of roads, bridges, canals,
and other projects associated with developing a national infrastructure
in order to facilitate both commerce and defense. Jacksonians generally,
and young Holt specifically, opposed such a policy, declaring that "internal improvements" did little that was useful for the "people"—who would
be taxed to pay for them—or for the states, whose authority over their own
affairs would be compromised. Internal improvements, Holt insisted on
one occasion, invariably served as the rallying cry of "office seekers who
want to make the Federal Government the great reservoir [of power], till
it be felt in every state, city, or neighborhood, upon our farms and at our
firesides." As it turns out, although Ben Hardin taught Holt many things in
their years together, he did not succeed in diminishing Holt's allegiance to
Andrew Jackson once it became firmly established.[33]

Holt arrived in Elizabethtown just months before Jackson's election to
the presidency, which thrilled him. Not long after, Congress's passage of
an unprecedentedly high tariff on imported manufactured goods provoked
the so-called Nullification Crisis, as many Southerners decried the negative effect they rightly feared the "tariff of abominations" would have on
their ability to purchase inexpensive manufactured goods and to export
agricultural products—especially cotton—to Europe. In response to the
offending tariff, John C. Calhoun of South Carolina, who had been John
Quincy Adams's vice president and became Andrew Jackson's as well, composed his semi-anonymous pamphlet, *The South Carolina Exposition and
Protest*, in which he articulated the principle that states had the right to
"nullify" (or veto) laws they independently determined to be unconstitutional. In Calhoun's view, the 1828 tariff's unconstitutionality lay in the fact
that it favored the economy of one section of the nation over the others.[34]

Nullification was by no means a new idea in 1828, nor was it a South
Carolinian invention. Indeed, the very first state legislature to pass a resolution "nullifying" a federal law was Kentucky's when, in November 1798,
it challenged the controversial Alien and Sedition Acts that John Quincy
Adams's father, President John Adams, had recently signed into law. Sub-

sequently, New England, too, had contemplated nullification in connection with President James Madison's war policy during the War of 1812. In 1828, John Calhoun simply restated and elaborated an earlier American—Kentuckian—principle. But Calhoun's restatement of the principle of nullification was strikingly persuasive and vehement, and over the next four years, like the whole concept of federally subsidized internal improvements, the ideas expressed in *Exposition and Protest* generated heated debates over the power of the federal government versus the power of the individual states, raising important questions about the long term stability of the national Union as a whole.

Although as president Andrew Jackson sometimes sided with the states in the struggle between state and federal authority (as he did in the case of the Cherokee in Georgia), in confronting the Nullification Crisis he played the part of an uncompromising nationalist. Even as South Carolinians were threatening in the late 1820s and early 1830s to secede from the Union and take up arms to defend their rights to oppose the tariff, Jackson boldly proclaimed the principle of nullification incompatible with the Union's preservation, eventually signing the so-called Force Bill, which compelled South Carolina to adhere to the tariff. In response, South Carolina "nullified" the Force Bill, but not before Henry Clay—now a U.S. senator and also a staunch nationalist—helped to negotiate the replacement of the "tariff of abominations" with a lower one. In the end, although Calhoun resigned from the vice presidency in protest, the crisis passed. Still, the struggle offered both participants and observers clear evidence that the Union might actually be more fragile than they had previously realized.

Along with the rest of his politically focused family members, young Holt was an attentive observer of the Nullification Crisis, and like them, he stood against the principle of nullification from the start as a threat to national unity. As they discussed the crisis, Holt and his correspondents remained unwavering in their support for both Andrew Jackson and the Union; when it came to the question of the nation's future, Holt already stood firmly on the side of the Union's perpetuity and its preeminence over the states. At the same time, however, although the Nullification Crisis erupted over a tariff on imported goods, at its core, the dispute had a great deal to do with rising tensions over the future of slavery in the United States, which Nat Turner's August 1831 slave rebellion in Virginia exacerbated. Of key concern to the nullifiers was not just the regionally repugnant tariff but also the very idea that the federal government should have the capacity and right to interfere in any significant way with the internal affairs of its twenty-four (as of 1821) constituent states. For many in the twelve slaveholding states, federal intervention of any sort in state business necessarily implied that the all-important institution of slavery was at risk, especially as new and threatening forms of antislavery activism took shape in the hands of radicals such as William Lloyd Garrison and the abolitionists.[35]

As he pondered nullification and its implications for the Union, therefore, Holt had to ponder slavery: its meaning, its merits, its horrors, its future. Having spent his whole life as a member of a slaveholding family, surrounded by other slaveholding families, in a slaveholding state where, in 1830, roughly a quarter of the population was held in perpetual bondage, Holt's musings were anything but purely theoretical.[36] He surely knew many of his extended family's dozens of slaves well, not just their names and what they looked like, but also the work they spent their days performing for his parents, his aunts and uncles, himself, and his siblings and cousins. Holt surely also knew the families these enslaved individuals struggled to create and protect, as well as the punishments they suffered when they failed to meet the expectations of those who dictated their responsibilities as producers and reproducers and who determined the limits of their mobility. Most likely Holt knew, as well, the physical details of the cabins these slaves retired to when—and if—their work was done. Indeed, as a newborn back in Stephensport, Holt may well have drawn his earliest nourishment from a black wet nurse; as a child, he may have had slave children to play with and a "mammy" to tend to his bodily and emotional needs; as an adolescent he may well have been encouraged— as the white sons of slaveholding families so often were in the pre–Civil War South—to undertake his first sexual experimentation with one of the black women his family members claimed as their chattel property. Certainly Holt had enjoyed many advantages as a result of the presence in his household and community of unfree black people whose job it was to labor in every conceivable way for their owners' diverse profits. And so it comes as no surprise that during these early years of his career, when he handled legal cases that involved slavery, Holt did not oppose the institution in any obvious, public way. How accurately his legal opinions reflected the complexity of Holt's private and developing feelings about slavery is not clear, but there is no denying that beginning in the late 1820s, the young lawyer demonstrated a firm allegiance to the Democratic Party, which in turn was closely identified with the strong defense of slavery.

In any case, as Holt settled into life and work in Elizabethtown his relatives and friends repeatedly expressed their pleasure as they witnessed their professional ambitions for him becoming realized, although his uncles continued to push him relentlessly, as if concerned that he might pull up lame in the race to statewide and then national prominence. In June 1829, both Bob and Daniel vigorously encouraged Holt to join a "Philosophical Society," which, they believed, could provide him with the sort of additional guidance and experience necessary to perfect his political ideas and transform them into action. It was not enough, his uncles agreed, for young "Jo" to become a good and successful lawyer who thought and talked about politics in private; he must set his sights on a life in the public eye, on the largest possible political stage. To achieve this goal, they urged Holt to continue honing his public-speaking skills and learn how to convey information to others in the most compelling manner possible. To be a great man, wrote Uncle Bob, one must learn to "think earnestly and speak well at once," and the time to learn these skills was *now*. For his part, Daniel exhorted Holt to "study incessantly," learn "everything necessary," and "show the world that the Ohio bottom can produce a[s] great men as other parts." "Push," he commanded, "and never look back."[37]

Driven by family expectations such as these, Holt simultaneously dedicated himself to developing his law practice and became an increasingly active participant in Kentucky's dynamic political scene. When he was not busy preparing or arguing legal cases, he attended lectures and other political events in Elizabethtown and the surrounding area and gave speeches, engaged in debates, and lobbied for candidates whose views he shared. Unlike many of his young male peers, however, Holt demonstrated no interest whatsoever in seeking elective office for himself, even at the local level. Indeed, given his particular combination of fundamental personal reserve and sensitivity in the face of both real and perceived slights to his honor, it is difficult to imagine that Holt could have endured even a single electoral campaign at this point in his life, although he was fully aware (as his uncles regularly reminded him) that public office could provide a path to glory. One suspects that as he moved through his early twenties, Holt felt mightily torn between the terrific rewards his talents, his legal work, his political commitments, and his expanding sphere of activity could provide to him on the one hand, and the terrible risks they potentially entailed to his self-respect, his honor, his dignity, and his character on the other. One of Holt's closest friends in this period, Albert Gallatin Hawes, shared this dilemma. Elected as a Jacksonian representative to the Twenty-second U.S. Congress, Hawes wrote from Washington in late 1830 to describe the distance he had uncovered between his ideals and the business of politics in the nation's capital. "Man is the same all over the world," Hawes wrote with some disappointment. "My youthful imagination had painted Congress as a body consisting of dignity talents &c, but there is about as much dignity" among the politicians in Washington, he declared, "as at a Ky log rolling." And "as to talents," he added, "they are few and far between." Hawes's words confirmed suspicions the wary Holt already held about the political realm. Certainly such words did not inspire him to run for political office now, or at any time in the foreseeable future.[38]

Indeed, the hypersensitivity about both his privacy and his good name that Holt had revealed in his conflict with Father Elder reappeared more than once during these early years of his career. In the spring of 1831, for example, he came into painful conflict with one William Davis over a misunderstanding that arose in connection with a political appointee by the name of Charles G. Wintersmith whom they both disliked and whose removal from office they sought (Davis even hoped Holt might become Wintersmith's successor). In the course of an exchange of letters, Holt came to believe that Davis had inappropriately shared some of his (Holt's) opinions about Wintersmith with a number of Kentucky Jacksonians in Washington, including Francis Preston Blair Sr., then editor of the *Congressional Globe*. For his part, Davis admitted having spoken out of school, but rejected "any insinuation that would tend to impugn my motives." Instead, he tried to turn Holt's attention toward some other guilty parties, who, he claimed, had "*basely betrayed*" them both by failing to keep Holt's opinions secret once he (Davis) had revealed them. At the same time, as George Elder had done years earlier, Davis assured Holt that he deeply regretted his "imprudence." But his apology could not heal the rupture, and their correspondence came to a close. Clearly Holt's sensitivity regarding his reputation persisted. As he grew older, and as his career advanced and his influence increased, individuals who crossed Holt or principles he believed in deeply would find that the consequences grew more severe.[39]

Because they recognized this tendency in his personality, some of the people to whom Holt was particularly close during this period continued to encourage him to lighten up and develop a thicker skin, for his own sake at least. Addressing Holt affectionately as "Josy," Charles Fenton "Fent" Mercer Noland in 1834 bravely informed his friend that he considered him somewhat "too sensitive" and inclined to "imagine offence where none is intended," a flaw, he feared, that would ultimately inhibit Holt's ability to fully enjoy satisfying interpersonal relationships. Another good friend, George Work of Bowling Green, agreed, urging Holt not to spend so many hours in his office and to "become a man of more affability." "If you had the proper manners with your talents," Work wrote, "you ought to be the first man in Ky in five years." What neither Noland nor Work acknowledged, or perhaps even recognized, was that beneath the surface of Holt's brilliance, diligence, outward restraint, and concern for his dignity and honor was a deep well of warmth—indeed, passion—which, when released fully in either the political or personal realm, was capable of lifting him to powerful heights, or dangerously derailing him.[40]

Holt's uncles, too, remained worried during these years about the implications of his aloof and exceedingly scholarly nature, in their case because they were apprehensive about its potential to circumscribe his professional and political future. Indeed, they feared—and rightly so—that at some fundamental level their nephew considered all political activity, while in some measure necessary, nevertheless a "dirty business." Still, if they could not force him to pursue elective office, Uncles Bob and Daniel were determined to do whatever they could to keep their nephew as engaged as possible in the rough-and-tumble of political life. As such, they made sure to unite their voices with the growing clamor in and around Elizabethtown, pleading with Holt to write papers and give speeches on Jacksonian themes and generally to make himself a focal point of Kentucky Democratic politics. In December 1830, Uncle Bob even sent some money to underscore his demand that Holt prepare not one but *two* speeches for delivery at the upcoming Jacksonian convention in Hardinsburg, both of which should strive to explicate Jacksonian principles clearly and effectively so that common people such as the folks back home in Stephensport could understand them, and should be of sufficiently high quality to merit their subsequent publication and dissemination so that Holt's name, his oratorical skills, and his political views would become more widely known. "Jo," wrote Uncle Bob, "I have no doubt but if you are well prepared you can be considered the best speaker of the J[acksonian] party." Later, Bob wrote again, summoning Holt to compose a pamphlet that would shatter Kentuckians' support for Clay, the National Republicans, and the whole concept of internal improvements. For good measure, Bob also encouraged his nephew to attack the national bank, which Jackson hoped to crush. Writing the proposed pamphlet, Uncle Bob insisted, was a duty Holt must perform for his country. Unable to accept his nephew's determination to avoid elective office, Bob added that a well-written argument against the opposition would also "insure you a seat in Congress whenever you want it."[41]

One of the very few people in his circle of friends and relatives who worried about what all this pressure would yield was his older brother, Richard, who warned Holt that Jacksonian movers and shakers (including Uncles Daniel and Bob) aimed "to use you without a reciprocation of the favor." Holt must have welcomed Richard's rare and kindly concern. Still, it is clear that nothing his older brother said or felt could ultimately shield him from the elevated destiny others—and undoubtedly some inner authority as well—had mapped out for him. And thus, despite Richard's words of caution, Holt dutifully, energetically, and eloquently carved out a space for himself in Kentucky's Democratic political realm by giving the speeches he was urged to give. As a result, as his legal practice gained traction so, too, did his reputation as a local Democratic Party loyalist and brilliant speaker both in the courtroom and on the stump, which in turn generated new connections for him with Jacksonian power brokers across the state. On at least one occasion in the fall of 1831, Holt uncharacteristically even cohosted a massive political barbeque with his friend John R. Stockman. "I have just recd your kind & flattering invitation to a Barbecue," wrote his friend George Work a few weeks before the barbeque was scheduled, "for which I must beg you & the other gentlemen to accept my sincere thanks." Work looked forward, he added, to meeting the "hundred & forty & four thousand of the elect Jackson spirits who . . . will no doubt be at your Barbecue."[42]

Just a couple of months before the barbecue, Holt lost one of his greatest and most ambitious advocates within his family circle, his grandfather Richard Stephens, whose delight at his grandson's achievements thus far was profound. In his final years, Grandfather Stephens had mellowed some: his last letter to Holt simply brimmed with affection and took a tone that was more nostalgic than insistent or moralizing. By then, Stephens surely knew that his own life was coming to a close. Perhaps, too, his perspective had shifted somewhat following the death of his second wife in early 1829: after she died, Holt's brother Richard claimed that it was only "in the bosom" of his children and grandchildren that Stephens found any respite from his grief. In any case, in his last letter to Holt, instead of pressing him on to future glory, Grandfather Stephens mused upon a distant past on the family farm when Joseph was just a small boy. "My dear grandson grandson grandson grandson," he wrote dreamily, "I am yet alive and yet your friend and would be very glad to [k]no[w] how you come on and how my crop looks how much is rising in the tobacco patch how much in the corn[;] spose you go and count." After an extended confinement from an unknown illness, Richard Stephens died on July 2, 1831, at the age of seventy-seven.[43]

Perhaps it was his grandfather's death that caused Holt to begin thinking more seriously about creating a family of his own, even as his responsibilities as an attorney and his expanding political commitments took up more and more of his time and energy. Back in 1826, when he was nineteen and still under the tutelage of Robert Wickliffe, Holt had given the matter some thought, inspired in part by a letter from his friend Will Sterett informing him that while most of their male friends and relatives were "very idle," in the sense that none of them was getting married or even apparently planning to do so, he himself had "some notions of taking a wife" that winter. Still, Sterett observed that doing so might be difficult, especially because he did not as yet "know who she is, or where she resides." As it turns out, however, Sterett moved swiftly once he found the woman he was looking for, marrying Holt's cousin Elizabeth Eleanor Dorsey in February 1827.[44]

As for Holt, his outward reserve surely did not make finding a wife easier, although it is eminently clear from the rich record he left behind that women were centrally important and deeply attractive to him, as he was to them, in ways that he at times found exceedingly difficult to manage. One suspects that in some ways he probably considered marriage a rather threatening step to take. Some of the things he associated with the idea of marriage must have struck him as deeply desirable: marriage, after all, offered love, companionship, the possibility of building a family, and the freedom of having an acceptable, private outlet for his emotional and physical needs. At the same time, however, marriage threatened to alter his life completely, to bring an end to the solitude and studious habits around which he organized so much of his time when he was not required to be in the courtroom or committed to some public, political speaking engagement. Love also brought with it the danger of rejection, a shattered affair representing, in a manner of speaking, the ultimate in failed campaigns for office. There is no question that Holt struggled mightily with the whole concept of binding his life so tightly to that of another human being, fretting that his serious and solitary disposition did not lend itself to making someone else happy. Others strove to reassure him, including his friend George Work, who insisted that Holt could not possibly be either as poor or "as much prone to melancholy as I was" at the time he met the woman who became his wife. "Marriage," Work asserted, "has redeemed me," and he was confident that it would do the same for Holt.[45]

Whatever else he felt or thought of when he considered the prospect of marriage, Holt knew that for a man in his profession, with his aspirations, finding a life partner was a requirement. He also knew that the "right" partner could further his professional prospects even as she enlivened his private life. "Jo," wrote Uncle Daniel, "mar[r]y wealth[. I]t will aid you to get forward." Indeed, marrying "well" was a common goal for young men in his social and professional position. "Seek a woman of amicability," echoed his friend and political ally in Washington, Albert Hawes, but if possible, Hawes continued, seek one who brought with her "a fortune," too. To his credit, Hawes had more to say about love than he did about the benefits of marrying a woman of wealth, and like George Work, he promised Holt that an affectionate wife would improve his life in ways Holt could not possibly anticipate. "Your sorrows &c," Hawes wrote, "will lose half their force from a communication with a female heart. Man was destined by nature for woman, woman for man." Using words like those Uncle Bob had used to describe Holt's political responsibilities, Hawes encouraged his friend to make the effort to fulfill this "destiny," as he considered marriage "the duty every man owes his country."[46]

As he moved through his early twenties, Holt certainly gave a good deal of thought to finding a wife, even as he worried about being able to accumulate enough wealth to support one properly. Among those family members who expressed concern about his lingering bachelor status not the least vocal was his maternal aunt, Mary Ann Stephens, who was only ten years older than Holt and frequently addressed him as "Brother Jo." Although she herself never married, Mary Ann wrote excitedly a few months after Holt's twenty-fifth birthday that she had recently run across a young woman Holt knew from home. As far as Mary Ann was concerned, Sally Maman would make Holt a good partner. "She [does] not lack beauty," Mary Ann insisted, adding that Sally had "improved more than you would suppose" since she was younger, and anyway, she was "friendly." Declaring Sally "the finest girl I ever saw," Aunt Mary Ann urged Holt to call on the young woman the next time he came home for a visit. Although Holt was very fond of Mary Ann, and over the years grew closer to her than he did to many of his other relatives, there is no evidence that he took her advice on this occasion.[47]

Some months later Uncle Daniel added his general encouragement in the clearest of terms: "Make yourself conspicuous and endeavour to overcome all opposition," he wrote. "Be social, get married, and you will be a real man." But Holt still did not marry. Nevertheless, by late 1831 he did conclude that the time had come for a major change, namely, to bring an amicable end to his association with Ben Hardin and strike out on his own in the newly incorporated city of Louisville. Although it was not the state capital (which was Frankfort), Louisville was booming, its rapid growth attributable, in large part, to its vigorous slave trade and the significance for shipping of its location on the Ohio River. At around 12,000 at the onset of the 1830s, Louisville's population—a quarter of which was enslaved—

was twenty times larger than Elizabethtown's. On the down side, Louisville was known for its dangerous seasonal cholera outbreaks and occasional devastating floods. Still, it was, as the British traveler Frances Trollope described it, "a considerable town" where an up-and-coming young lawyer could hope to make a good living and a name for himself. For these reasons, in January 1832 Holt moved there, rented an upscale office space on Jefferson Street between 5th and 6th Streets in the heart of Louisville's civic center and not far from the Jefferson County courthouse, and set about building on his accumulated professional successes and his reputation as a skilled orator and dedicated Jacksonian political activist.[48]

Most in Holt's circle of important friends and relatives were delighted with his decision to relocate. "You speak of moving to Louisville," wrote his brother Richard, who optimistically declared the plan "advisable." From what Richard had heard, there were as yet few if any really competent lawyers in the city, which meant that Holt should be able to carve out a good living both easily and quickly. Still, as he had done in the past, Richard expressed more concern for Holt's overall happiness than for his professional success. Most important to Richard was that his talented younger brother's earnings in Louisville should provide him with more personal satisfaction than they would elsewhere, or else the move would have been in vain. On this score, however, Richard offered a hopeful forecast: "a gentle support in Louisville," he wrote, "will be worth 4 times as much enjoyment as it would be in E[lizabeth]town."[49]

Unaccustomed as he was to taking advantage of the simple "enjoyments" his earnings could purchase for him, Holt nevertheless surely appreciated, as always, Richard's concern for his happiness. He also appreciated the encouragement of friends such as Albert Hawes, who wrote, "I am glad you are going to Louisville," and who predicted, "you will triumph." Indeed, from Hawes's perspective, Holt's move from tiny Elizabethtown was long overdue: "Should he who is destined to harpoon the whale be angling for trout in a brook?" he asked. Of course not. "Take your stand among the first of the land," he urged, though he offered Holt some cautionary practical advice, too: not to lend money to people he did not know well; to accept business even from individuals who could not pay his full fee, on the principle that "much business draws more" (and anyway, he pointed out, "when you get a fair start you can raise in price"); to take every opportunity to practice his skills in oratory, knowing that the practice would serve him well in the courtroom and that his clients would appreciate the effort; and, finally, to treat people with civility at all times.

These, Hawes explained, "were suggestions which were often urged by my father on me, and he was a man well acquainted with all the workings of the human heart." [50]

Now twenty-five years old, Holt found that his practice in Louisville thrived from the start, somewhat to his Uncle Daniel's surprise. "It scarcely ever happens," Daniel wrote just a year and a half later, "that one of your age belonging to your profession is much pressed with business and I am truly gratified that you are . . . and furthermore that you have the energy and ability and integrity to discharge your duty with honor to yourself and credit to all your relations and friends." As always, however, the ever-ambitious Daniel continued to push his nephew, not just to build his law business but also to resume his ascent to statewide and then national prominence. "I fear you are too retiring," he wrote, challenging Holt to "embrace every opportunity that you decently could to attract publick attention." Daniel worried that his nephew might fail to claim the professional and political limelight that he was due. "You are yet young," he wrote, "and if you can not get to the top rung in the ladder get as high as you can." Under no circumstances, he insisted, should Holt "let sloth enter [his] door." [51]

Holt, of course, knew nothing of sloth. Whatever hours he could spare from his law practice he devoted to political work for the Democratic Party, some of which he performed behind the scenes. Not long after he moved to Louisville, for example, he responded to a request from Hawes, who was now seated in the Twenty-second Congress and pondering how to address and help resolve the protracted Nullification Crisis, which he feared could result in a "national calamity." "I wish it were possible that J Holt could address the house on this subject," Hawes wrote to Holt's Uncle Bob, "and at least make the friends of monopoly tremble at their own error, or that his head could be put on my shoulders for one session; or that I had some of his ideas committed to paper as a text, from which to thunder in their ears." At Bob's urging, Holt immediately devised some language for Hawes's use, for which his friend was deeply grateful, though he predicted that compromise over the tariff between the rival factions would prove impossible, especially because Clay, the nationalist, and Calhoun, the nullifier, were behaving "like two bulls, who pull the same yoke, put on them by enmity to another, but no sooner is it removed from their necks than they gore and harm each other with all the venom of born devils." As for the sixty-five-year-old Jackson, however, Hawes marveled that "his fire is not yet gone," and that at times the former president showed flashes of "the brilliancy of youthful years." Jackson, Hawes informed the admiring Holt, "is a noble old man, and when he departs none such will remain." Holt could not have said it better or more convincingly himself.[52]

As he labored in public ways to advance the Jacksonian cause, Holt simultaneously promoted his own growing eminence within Kentucky's Democratic Party, giving frequent speeches in support of the party's agenda and against that of the National Republicans/Whigs whose leading light, Henry Clay, he on one occasion (and perhaps several) described as a "cold, calculating, political hypocrite." As always, when his Uncle Bob implored him to deliver (and subsequently publish) an "address to the people of Kentucky" in connection with the state's upcoming 1832 Democratic Party convention, where party principles would be vigorously debated, Holt accepted the challenge. That fall, his friend George Work wrote to congratulate him, declaring the speech "a splendid success." "You are spoken of in all the counties of the state," Work proclaimed, "as one of the most astonishing orators of your age," and he predicted that Holt would one day be known as one of the nineteenth century's "great men," unless he undermined his own prospects by not "plac[ing] value enough upon yourself." Meanwhile, Holt also expanded his public presence by serving for a time as an editor of Louisville's radically Jacksonian organ, the *Public Advertiser*, which, along with its rival, George Prentice's Whiggish *Louisville Journal*, was one of the city's two most influential newspapers. "If I was not afraid to subscribe for your paper," wrote Holt's politically ambitious friend Will Sterett, "I would take it, but it would ruin me."[53]

Sometime in the fall of 1832, Holt briefly managed to set aside his longstanding resistance to seeking political office and made known his interest in being appointed as commonwealth's attorney for Jefferson County, of which Louisville was the county seat. Not unlike elective office, such appointments required a considerable amount of what is today called "networking," as well as a willingness to engage in vigorous self-promotion, both of which Holt found so discomfiting that while he waited to learn of the outcome of his efforts he pessimistically considered leaving Kentucky all together. By way of encouragement, his friend Hawes advised him in October to go to the state capital at Frankfort and meet with John Breathitt, a staunch Jacksonian and the first Democrat ever to hold the office of governor in Kentucky. "Make your application boldly," Hawes urged, assuring his tentative friend that success would result and promising that the advice he offered was nothing less than that "of one who will be with you in 6 troubles and not forsake you in the seventh." Holt's uncles Daniel and Bob, predictably, were even more insistent, Uncle Daniel announcing that he was simply "astonished" to discover that there was even the slightest possibility that Holt might *not* apply for the position. Unwilling to accept Holt's hesitation, Daniel declared simply: "You must do it." Somewhat less shrilly, Uncle Bob encouraged Holt to "apply with confidence" and the faith that he was of the intellectual caliber to become not just commonwealth's attorney but "dictator" of the Jacksonian party, should he so desire. Leaders of the party, Uncle Bob insisted, "will crouch if you demand distinction"; given this, he explained, the only option was to demand it. While Uncles Daniel and Bob applied the usual pressure and Albert Hawes offered friendly encouragement, some with valuable connections to Governor Breathitt offered practical support. "I saw the Gov. & spoke in your favor to him with all my soul," wrote George Work in late October. "His opinions of your talents & virtues are as high as they can be." In the end, Holt's bid was successful: in early 1833 he was commissioned Jefferson County's commonwealth's attorney, the same position his father had held in Hardin and later in Breckinridge County, and the equivalent of a state's attorney elsewhere.[54]

For the next two years, Holt "made an enviable record for himself" as a prosecutor on the Jefferson County circuit, and as his reputation grew, he increasingly found that others—aspiring lawyers and office seekers, relatives desiring assistance, Jacksonian political enthusiasts—sought him out for favors. In addition, Holt discovered that he was being welcomed into the social lives of prominent figures in Louisville and beyond, and he began receiving unsolicited memberships in various societies and associations. In July 1834 the "Enodelphian Society" of Miami University in Oxford, Ohio, for example, informed him that he had been "unanimously elected . . . an honorary member," an honor the letter's author, R. W. Snowden, explained was reserved for only "the most Literary and Scientific men of the age; and men most distinguished for their Patriotism and Eloquence." Clearly the stature of the young man from "Holt's Bottom" was rising and his professional and political influence was expanding. By no means were all aspects of these developments unequivocally pleasing, however, as the reserved and sensitive Holt himself had unhappily anticipated. For as his star rose, he also became a more appealing target for those who envied his success, and for political activists who opposed the Jacksonian ideals he so enthusiastically espoused. Following one such attack in late 1833 in the *Louisville Journal*, his friend John Stockman of Hardinsburg attempted to brace Holt's spirits. "Your friends here have seen with feelings of indignation the scandalous & base assault which has been made on your feelings & character," Stockman wrote, assuring Holt that the attack—whose details are unclear—would have no lasting impact and urging him to avoid any sort of retaliation, especially if it took the form of a duel. "I hope you will not be induced," Stockman warned, "to resort to any measure to obtain satisfaction while under the influence of excited feelings, and without cool deliberation." This, Stockman insisted, was exactly the sort of "rash or desperate" response that Holt's opponents aimed to provoke, because it would destroy his career. "You stand much in the way of some aspiring attorneys," Stockman remarked, "& it would rejoice them if you could be gotten rid of in some way or other."[55]

As he had always done, Holt despised these sorts of conflicts, which he experienced as challenges to his honor and integrity, not unlike the sort that Father George Elder had inflicted on him back in his teens. Now that his growing prominence made the avoidance of such conflicts impossible, however, Holt was compelled to consider his options: he could retreat from public view altogether and bury himself in his legal work, where he engaged in argumentation on behalf of others, not himself; he could fight back in private as he had done in past; or he could commit to waging public battles and enduring their costs. For their part, his relentless uncles made clear that they expected him to face his critics boldly and refuse to be cowed. Uncle Daniel in particular insisted that Holt must always stand firm, not just for the sake of his own reputation and his future but also for his family. Daniel rejected the notion "that you our only hope possessing superior talents should suffer your mind to be the least ruffled by any thing that could be said in a newspaper," and that "you should be afraid to make a speech for fear of its attacks. If you lack the firmness to best opposition," he scolded, "you should look out [for] a more retired situation." Letting opponents know that their attacks had hit home was the worst possible response, Daniel insisted, and could only lead to enemies attempting to use additional criticism "to control your actions and behaviour." On this occasion, setting a precedent for the future, Holt decided to fight back publicly through the vehicle of the *Public Advertiser*. Unfortunately, however, the record of his response to his attacker is also lost.[56]

Even as they persisted in pressuring him to continue his ascent to power and glory, Holt's uncles were still moved from time to time by concern for his health, on one occasion urging him to take part of a summer off and spend the time at a hot-spring resort not far from Stephensport. Indeed, by the time he reached his mid-twenties, Holt had begun to display one of a number of symptoms of overwork and exhaustion that would recur periodically throughout his life, including a skin ailment on his face that was probably a form of eczema. "It is a disease," wrote his cousin, Dr. Washington Dorsey, "not uncommon to those persons who have sedentary and studious occupations, and are of weak constitution." (Today Dorsey surely would have added to his diagnosis that unrelieved stress was a contributing cause.) For treatment, Dorsey advised Holt to adopt a regimen that included "gentle exercise," a bland diet, and an elixir made of "equal parts of the flowers of sulphur & cream of tartar (say an ounce of each)," which he recommended that Holt ingest daily mixed with sweetened water. Dorsey also recommended an ointment to be applied to the shoulders and back, and he urged Holt to wash his face at least once a day in "rose water," which he described as "a very cooling application" that would "be of service not only in preventing the return of the pustules but also in removing the blotches which are on it."[57]

That Holt's dermatological problems were related to his overwork seems utterly reasonable: with his hectic schedule he almost certainly ate irregularly and poorly, rarely enjoying the benefits of sunshine or even moderate exercise. Moreover, there are also clear indications that the already serious and solitary Holt was developing an inclination toward dark moods, from which it could be difficult to extract himself. "Do not give way to melancholy feelings," Fent Noland wrote in June 1834 from Jefferson Barracks, Missouri. The cheerful Noland reminded Holt that he had "much to attach you to this earth," and that "your political friends dote upon you, your private friends love you devotedly," and "your enemies dread your talents." Some time later, Holt's younger brother Robert expressed similar concerns. "I am sorry to see the despondency which pervades your letters and colors your thoughts," Robert wrote. "My dear brother you should cheer up. If a cloud hangs over your future see it not, or turn from it and think only of the brightness which may dawn when that cloud has passed away. There is no philosophy in despair, in hope there dwells a far deeper wisdom."[58]

Holt struggled with despondency in 1834, and indeed it was a difficult year for him both professionally and personally. Following the unexpected death of the Democrat John Breathitt in February, the Whigs came to power in the governor's mansion. Not surprisingly, the new governor, James Turner Morehead, did not renew Holt's appointment as commonwealth's attorney for Jefferson County, which triggered feelings of failure. "I must confess," his brother Robert commiserated, "that your termination cast rather a cloud of melancholy over my feelings." But, Robert went on, his own sadness arose not so much from Holt's loss of influence as from his admission that this blow to his fortunes had left him wishing "from the core of your heart that you was once more a plough boy." Far worse, however, that summer Holt learned of the death of his kindly older brother, Richard, in Mississippi, where he had been practicing medicine. Richard had been "carryed off," an angry Robert later reported, "after a few days illness with some of the diseases prevalent in that wretched climate," and "without even a physician to relieve his wants." Robert informed Holt that their parents had borne the news of Richard's death "as well as could be expected," but that "a settled gloom" had fallen on the old homestead. Uncle Bob agreed, recalling with great sadness Richard's goodness of heart and "the gentleness of his disposition." "I could have spared him better," Bob wrote, "if he had been a worse man." Richard's death deprived Holt of one of his dearest and most dependable friends and allies.[59]

2

THE LONG JOURNEY FROM LOUISVILLE TO WASHINGTON, 1835–1857

I have not been an uninterested observer of your rapid strides to fame and fortune. I say it without flattery, that you occupy an elevated position in this state [Mississippi], and I hope to live to see the day when your talent will be put in requisition by your country, and you become distinguished in her service.—*John R. Stockman to Joseph Holt, August 1835*

Although Uncles Daniel and Bob were also deeply saddened by Richard's death, they insisted that Holt—upon whose shoulders the added burdens of being the eldest of his parents' children now fell—continue moving forward on the path to political and professional prominence they had mapped out for him. To this end, they demanded that he overcome as quickly as possible both his frustration over his removal from the position of commonwealth's attorney and his sorrow over Richard's demise and refuse to diminish the pace of either his legal work or his political activities. In early 1835, Uncle Bob urged his nephew to throw off despair and instead declare himself a candidate for a seat in the U.S. Congress. Some weeks later he accused Holt of letting his gloomy mood "subdue" his "manliness" and deprive him of self-confidence. Cheer up, Bob insisted, and get on with it. "I always have de[a]lt freely with you," he added, "and I intend to do so until you get into so high office that freedom becomes presumptuous, which time will come if you shall ever consider yourself man enough to set it for yourself." In response to his uncles' incessant demands, and perhaps also as a means of getting some distance from them, that spring Holt decided to take a trip east, first to New York State, and then to Maryland.[1]

Meanwhile, back in Stephensport—thanks in part to Holt's financial contributions—his family members were just getting comfortable in their spacious, newly built home, an elegant, three-story brick mansion that his seventeen-year-old sister, Elizabeth, described as "much more comfortable than the old one." Like the rich and productive farmland that surrounded it, and the slave quarters that extended back from it toward the Ohio River—Kentucky's boundary with free Indiana—such a residence amply demonstrated the Holt/Stephens clan's prosperity and their elevated stature within their community. True, some locals branded the home "pretentious," situated as it was in the middle of hundreds of acres of farmland with no structure for many miles around reflecting a similar degree of opulence. Others, however, considered the mansion an ornament for the community, destined to become a "favorite gathering spot" where guests could marvel at its high ceilings, fabulously large windows, impressively solid staircases, and massive fireplaces. Visitors also took pleasure in the surrounding scenery, which included "a broad lowland that gently sloped to the river nearby, and gradually lifted to the high precipice hills of Indiana," as well as a verdant and meticulously landscaped lawn that was enhanced by an abundance of trees and bushes. The garden alone was spectacular, filled as it was with unusual flowers, which were attended by a full-time gardener.[2]

There is little doubt that Holt had contributed some of the earnings from his thriving Louisville law practice to the construction of the expensive new family home. The cost of building such an extravagant mansion must have been more than his aging father's income or savings could have supplied (John W. Holt was now sixty-three), and Holt was the only one of John and Eleanor's children capable at this point of providing additional financial support. An avid reader who routinely begged her eldest brother to send her books, Elizabeth was in school at the Loretto Young Ladies Academy, a Catholic boarding school located about ninety miles east of Stephensport. Robert, too, was in school, having left home at age nineteen (in 1833) to begin his formal education at St. Mary's College, not far from Loretto. As it turns out, Uncles Daniel and Bob considered Robert the next most promising of Holt's male siblings—a potential understudy, as it were, should Holt himself fail to achieve all that they hoped—and in 1834 they transferred him to the much more prestigious new Miami University, nicknamed the "Yale of the West" and situated some 200 miles away in Oxford, Ohio. As a student Robert did quite well, but he never seemed to have any money, and, indeed, quickly developed a lasting habit of depending on his accomplished older brother for additional cash to meet his expenses. Meanwhile, Holt's middle brothers, Thomas and James (ages twenty-two and twenty-four, respectively), were struggling toward independence in their own ways. As far back as December 1831, Robert, then

The Holt family mansion in Stephensport, Kentucky, 2009.
Courtesy of Norvelle Wathen, Louisville, Kentucky.

sixteen, had written to Holt regarding Thomas's decision to take up some former, unidentified "perilous and uncertain business," which Robert believed had "already greatly injured [his] constitution" and would, he was certain, "soon wholly destroy it." As for James, he had left Kentucky for what he described as "the wil[d]s of Illinois," hoping to make his fortune by means of what turned out to be a risky and ultimately not very lucrative mercantile and land speculation enterprise. For a time, Thomas considered joining James in Illinois, but in the end he settled down on the family farm while James continued to travel widely for several years, eventually landing in Port Lavaca, Texas, where he studied law and then became a well-respected local lawyer and a judge.[3]

In the spring of 1835, however, only the oldest of the Holt siblings had the resources to extend the family's financial prosperity, material comfort, and social prestige. To be able to do so, after all, was at least a part of the burden that his uncles and grandfather had laid upon Holt's shoulders so many years earlier, even before Richard's death made him the eldest. For his part, Robert deeply admired his brother Joseph, eight years his senior, and he strove, in some measure at least, to emulate his accomplishments, making arrangements during his last term at Miami to take up the private study of law with an attorney in Bardstown, as Holt had done with Robert Wickliffe in Lexington a decade earlier. Even at this early date, however, Robert seems to have known that for all his intellectual promise, he had neither the energy nor the interest to pursue a lifelong professional and political course with the relentless effort and ambition his brother had demonstrated, having taken to heart the toll that both his older brothers' exertions had exacted: Richard was dead, and Holt was exhausted. "You advise me very strenuously to relax in my studies," Robert wrote to Holt in October 1834, but no such advice was necessary. "I never wish to and never will study so hard as you have done," he declared, insisting that he would "rather live in poverty in good health than have wealth to mock me in misery." Perhaps Robert also secretly suspected that he could never match Holt's impressive intellectual abilities.[4]

In any case, as his family moved in to their lovely new Stephensport home in the spring of 1835, Holt—now twenty-eight—headed east, eager, no doubt for a break from his usual routines and for the opportunity to see and experience new places. But the primary purpose of Holt's trip was not recreation; it was to serve, in May, as a Kentucky delegate to the second national convention of the Democratic Party in Baltimore. As he traveled the 600 miles from Louisville to the Atlantic coast, Holt carried heavily with him Uncle Daniel's admonition that he must participate effectively in the convention and thereby burnish his already excellent local reputation in order to further strengthen his position within the party and in national politics generally. "You must prepare yourself well," Daniel had written, laying out an agenda that included examining the party's principles, studying the U.S. Constitution in careful detail, determining which policies the federal government should adopt on various matters and which it should reject, and—perhaps most important—formulating and then delivering "such a speech as will be looked to as the text book for the party," which he was certain would draw his nephew "in to the notice of the general government" and introduce him to other leading politicians from around the country. Should he prepare himself properly and acquit himself skillfully, Daniel insisted, Holt could expect to earn "substantial fame over one fourth of the globe" and take his place as one of the nation's, perhaps the world's, greatest "champions of liberty and good government." Given his fundamental nature, it is hardly likely that Holt expected such spectacular results from his appearance at the Baltimore convention. Nevertheless, he gathered the requisite letters of introduction, including one that described him as "unquestionably the most talented and accomplished orator and writer of his age in the United States," and headed first to Albany, where the

Democratic Party had recently claimed a majority in the state legislature, to meet with local party leaders. From Albany he traveled to Baltimore, to the Fourth Presbyterian Church on Lafayette Street, where the convention was to be held. There, by all accounts, Holt passed a crucial milestone in his long professional and political career.[5]

The delegates to the Baltimore convention completed the first major piece of their scheduled business without controversy, easily selecting Andrew Jackson's vice president, Martin Van Buren, to become the party's nominee for president in the following year's election. But then the delegates found themselves divided: who should the party's nominee for vice president be? It came down to a choice between William Cabell Rives — formerly a member of Congress from Virginia (1823–29), the United States' minister to France (1829–32), and a U.S. senator (1832–34) — and Richard Mentor Johnson of Kentucky, an accomplished lawyer and a venerated veteran of the War of 1812 who had been a representative in the U.S. Congress from 1807 to 1819 and a U.S. senator from 1819 to 1829 and had been serving as a congressional representative again since leaving the Senate. Although many delegates deemed the man commonly referred to as "Colonel Johnson" likely to appeal broadly to potential voters, a significant number were deeply troubled by their knowledge of his intimate relationship with a slave named Julia, with whom he had produced two daughters, whom he later freed (Julia herself died in 1833).[6]

As one observer described the scene, it was just as the Virginia delegates were declaring their opposition to Johnson most vociferously that Holt suddenly rose from his seat and, by way of laying out the case for Johnson's candidacy, made "one of the most eloquent and thrilling speeches that it has ever been my pleasure and privilege to listen to." Holt's "coal-black hair, flashing eye, olive complexion, graceful figure, and thrilling voice electrified the convention," recalled another observer. "Never," he declared, "was there a more dramatic scene." Still another witness characterized Holt's speech as "a stream of eloquence and eulogy in behalf of the old war-worn soldier and patriot" that left him utterly awestruck, "even as a political opponent of the eulogist." Wrote a fourth, "I have never seen in all my life such a powerful effect produced upon a deliberative body. During its delivery almost every member of the body rose to his feet — some clapped, some stamped, others hallooed bravo at the top of their voice, and some mounted the benches. The galleries were crowded with spectators . . . all of whom rose to their feet to catch a glimpse of the orator."[7]

It is interesting to note that when he rose to speak for Johnson, Holt did not take it upon himself either to confirm or to deny the details of Johnson's private life. Rather, he shifted the audience's attention in another direction, eloquently portraying the old war hero in true Jacksonian style as, most compellingly, a common man, "a personage whose plain & simple gaze, whose frank & cordial & unostentatious bearing" clearly identified him as having "sprung from the people." Johnson, Holt continued, was *still* one of the people, an old soldier—a national hero—whose "heart in all its recollections, its hopes, & its sympathies, was blended with the fortunes of the toiling millions." One look at Johnson's "scarred & shattered frame" and his "limping gait," Holt declared, revealed that his life had been one of extraordinary courage under fire and of "unfaltering, unswerving devotion to freedom." Holt urged the delegates to set aside their prejudices and rally together, not just because Johnson was the right candidate but also because only unity would enable the Democrats to achieve victory in the next presidential election. With words that echoed his stance on the Nullification Crisis just a few years earlier, and that also foreshadowed his stern response to secession a quarter of a century later, Holt closed by declaring that "vigilance, action, *Union*, firm & unshaken can alone guard the [Democratic] party from the insidious approaches of their discomfited [Whig] adversaries."[8]

Holt's speech at the Baltimore convention in 1835 was a success on every level. Most immediately, the speech earned him dinner invitations during his Baltimore sojourn from both Andrew Jackson and Martin Van Buren. Of greater long-term importance, the speech ensured Richard Johnson's nomination and guaranteed his lasting gratitude. About a year after Van Buren's inauguration, now Vice President Johnson wrote to Holt, addressing him as "My Worthy Dear Friend" and assuring him that he would "always feel alive to your prosperity, success & happiness." Johnson added, "I hope that if you have a wish as to public life that I can in any way gratify, you will write me confidentially." Some time later, Johnson reiterated his offer: "Shall I ever have the honor to reward you for that one effort which has done more to elevate me [than] all I have ever done[?]" he wrote. "I long for the opportunity." One thing is certain: Holt never intended his speech on Johnson's behalf to serve as a launching pad for himself into electoral politics. "I shrink from the politician's hollow and profligate existence with a loathing," he wrote to one correspondent not long after the convention, and he never did take Johnson up on his offer.[9]

Although he did not seek elective office in his own right, however, Holt's speech at Baltimore, as a *New York Times* article sixty years later recalled, brought him to national attention in the Democratic Party, laying precisely the sort of foundation Uncle Daniel had hoped it would for the growth of his reputation as one of the national party's emerging leaders and a superb orator. Unfortunately, however, the speech also transformed Holt into a larger target than ever before for critics of all stripes, not just from Kentucky. Increasingly, Whigs, anti-Jackson Democrats, and others around the country who simply resented Holt's growing prominence took aim, reinforcing his awareness that he did not need to seek elective office in order to suffer the adversity associated with political activism. According to his attentive brother Robert, now twenty, after Baltimore the opposition Whig press seemed "to have opened a new battery for your especial benefit, from whence they are making . . . wanton and profligate attacks for the edification of their readers." But he noted as well the abundant praise the speech had garnered in Jacksonian circles. As for Holt's critics, well, in Robert's opinion "they could not have devised a scheme more advantageous to your popularity" than to have gone so vigorously on the attack against him.[10]

Following the convention in Baltimore, Holt briefly left both his fans and his detractors behind and returned to New York State where, at the invitation of Andrew Jackson's acting secretary of war, Carey A. Harris, he served as a member of the board of visitors responsible for overseeing the annual examinations in June at the United States Military Academy at West Point. An invitation to serve on the board both acknowledged an individual's stature and conferred additional honor upon him (all visitors were men). Participation in the examination process also gave visitors, who annually included prominent civilians and retired military men from across the country, a greater feeling of intimacy with the academy itself. For two weeks, Holt and the other distinguished members of that year's board observed the academy's 240 cadets as they underwent the grueling process of being tested by their professors in all of their subjects, mostly by recitation. There is little doubt that a quarter century later, when his life and work became inseparably intertwined with the U.S. Army, Holt recalled with pride his introduction to the academy's, and the army's, inner workings. Among those whose examinations he observed in the summer of 1835 were men whose names would later become very familiar: Lewis A. Armistead, P. G. T. Beauregard, Braxton Bragg, Jubal A. Early, Joseph Hooker, Irvin McDowell, George Gordon Meade, and George H. Thomas.[11]

From West Point, Holt headed back to Louisville, but he remained there only briefly, by the end of the year picking up stakes and moving several hundred miles south to Mississippi. Ironically, when he first began contemplating a move away from Louisville, Holt considered heading north to the free state of Illinois, specifically to the town of Springfield, where he almost certainly would have soon met Abraham Lincoln, who moved there in 1837. Instead, however, Holt gathered the customary letters of introduction and headed southward to Mississippi, which had become a state just a year before Illinois, in 1817. This time, Holt's letters included one from William M. Gwin of Louisville to the eminent lawyer and former Jacksonian U.S. senator from Mississippi, Powhatan Ellis. Gwin described Holt as "a distinguished member of the Bar" at Louisville, who "aside from his professional reputation, is admitted to be one of the most eloquent men of his age in this or any country and is withal a genuine and unwavering Democrat."[12]

Holt's motivations for making the move to Mississippi were complex. For one thing, although his practice in Louisville was thriving, Kentucky's economy in the mid-1830s was already experiencing the early warnings of what later came to be known as the Panic of 1837, and Holt may well have anticipated the crisis that was coming. In addition, Holt must have longed to put some distance between himself and Kentucky's Whigs—the Henry Clay faithful—who had already seen to his removal from his post as Jefferson County's commonwealth's attorney and who were numerous and vocal among those who aimed their political barbs at him. Holt may have been concerned, too, that some older leaders within Kentucky's Democratic Party had been trying to exert too much control over his actions and his opinions, not unlike his uncles Daniel and Bob, whose relentless pressure and forceful "guidance" he had endured his entire life. Perhaps Holt hoped that Mississippi would offer terrain where he could breathe and move more freely. It also seems to have offered the possibility of more rapid wealth accumulation than either Louisville or Springfield. According to his friend John R. Stockman, now in Natchez, "almost all lawyers manage[d] to become wealthy in a few years" in Mississippi, and Stockman knew that Holt had more than just ordinary talents. Holt's brother Robert, too, trumpeted the possibilities for becoming rich—and perhaps also even more famous—in Mississippi. "You will quickly amass a fortune," Robert predicted, "and in a few years rise to a height of distinction which you could not reach during half a lifetime in Kentuck." Indeed, it would not be long before Robert himself contemplated a move to the Magnolia State.[13]

Certainly most of the people whom Holt consulted on the question were supportive and encouraging about his proposed relocation, although in light of what had happened to his brother Richard, some family members expressed grave concern about the "almost universal fatality" of Mississippi's climate for "northern emigrants." "Father and mother feel so much solicitude in your behalf and so magnify the dangers to which you are exposed in a southern climate," wrote Robert in January 1836, after Holt had already left Louisville, "that they are in continual misery, unless they hear from you frequently." That same month, Holt's mother, Eleanor, wrote too, complaining that her eldest son had failed to keep the family sufficiently well informed of his specific plans or where he was going to live, and had thus left them to wonder whether or not he was even still alive. Eleanor urged Holt to come north to Stephensport during the summer, not only to spend time with his family but also to keep potentially fatal sicknesses at bay. "I cannot describe to you my feelings," his always-affectionate sister, Elizabeth, wrote in March, "to see you passing to that sickly country, where no more than a year before we lost one of our Dear Brothers."[14]

Settling in Vicksburg, Holt quickly came to be recognized, in the words of one biographer, as "a man of extraordinary work" and "a painstaking scholar" who readily exchanged the benefits and pleasures of an active social life for those he could derive from doing research, preparing his cases, scripting the arguments he planned to use in court, and developing his reputation as one well suited to the "legal Utopia" of the Cotton South and the expanding Southwest. Holt's law practice grew rapidly, making it necessary from early on to engage a partner to help with the load. He selected the accomplished James O. Harrison of Lexington, Kentucky, who remained a friend for many years. Like Holt, James Harrison was well known for having "excellent habits of industry, sobriety, and research," as well as a "clear, steady, ready and strong intellect," traits that in Holt's mind apparently superseded in importance the fact that he was also a close friend of Henry Clay. As their business increased, the quality of their adversaries did, too. Before long, Holt found himself pitted against other brilliant legal minds in the region, including the renowned Vicksburg lawyer, Whig, and U.S. congressman, Sargeant Smith Prentiss, who was famous for his oratorical skills. Holt, who had spent much of his life honing his skills as a thinker, debater, and orator, held his own. According to one source, whereas "Prentiss kept the courtroom amused and fascinated by his humor and his boldness, causing his hearers to forget his argument in the glamour of his personality," Holt, in contrast, "spellbound the jury by the crushing weight of the evidence he could bring to bear on the case."[15]

From Stephensport, Uncle Daniel could not help expressing his delight as he observed Holt's flourishing career. "I am prowed [sic]," he wrote, just months after Holt moved south, "of the fame you have acquired," though he worried that his nephew's focus on his law business might dull his taste for Democratic Party politics. "I hope you have not suffered your desire for wealth to cool your ambition for political distinction," Daniel wrote in June 1836, and as always he urged Holt to "get into Politicks whenever you see an opening." But Holt resisted putting himself forward for elective office in Mississippi as vigorously as he had done in Kentucky, even when it did not involve subjecting himself to a campaign. In 1838, when Governor Alexander G. McNutt (a Democrat) offered him the opportunity to fill the U.S. Senate seat of John Black (a Whig), who had just resigned, Holt declined. Still, his stature in the Democratic Party continued to increase, as is demonstrated by the many invitations he received during this period to speak at one party event or another all across the region.[16]

Also indicative of Holt's growing fame was a letter from a farmer who lived 1,200 miles from Vicksburg in what he himself described as "an obscure part of western N York"—the town of Pike, in Allegany County. Although he and Holt had never met, Jacob Fox knew Holt's name well, having followed the Kentuckian's career as best he could since the 1835 Baltimore convention. Now, Fox wrote that his wife had recently given birth to a son and that, "in looking around among the great names of which our country boasts," it had occurred to him that "no one stood so high in my estimation" as Holt did, with the possible exception of Andrew Jackson and Richard M. Johnson. But Jackson's and Johnson's names had already been "freely used," Fox pointed out, so he had taken the liberty to give his "fine boy" the name Joseph Holt Fox. "I hope," the farmer added, "the boy will prove himself worthy of it."[17]

Letters such as this surely gave Holt an exquisite sense of satisfaction and accomplishment. At the same time, they reminded him that he himself was without a life partner with whom his satisfactions and accomplishments might be happily shared and with whom he, too, might produce an heir who bore his name. Private and self-contained as he certainly was, Holt was also lonely and concerned that he might never find a suitable woman whom he could happily marry and appropriately support. "I have often thought," he had written to George Work back in March 1833, "that if I had one dearer than myself to whom I could tell the story of my triumphs, who would be gladdened . . . in my honors, whose smiles would cheer me," and "whose accents would sprinkle freshness upon the parched striving wearied spirit of ambition, that I would go forth among men and fling the gauntlet to [face] the toils, trials & persecutions of earth in the fierce grapple for fame and power." Sadly, Holt had concluded then, "I have none. I am alone."[18]

George Work was hardly unmoved by Holt's yearnings. Fully a year before Holt moved to Mississippi, Work had tried to set his friend up with his wife's sister, Lucy Morehead, who was also the sister of then acting governor of Kentucky, James T. Morehead, and who was fixed to receive a sizable inheritance, including between fifty and sixty slaves and about $10,000 worth of other property. In the spring of 1836, however, Holt embarked instead on a courtship with the daughter of a prominent Bardstown physician, Burr Harrison, who was an acquaintance of his Uncle Daniel and also of Ben Hardin, with whom Holt had worked in Elizabethtown. For the next three years, Holt and Mary Louisa Harrison exchanged a great many lively letters in addition to enjoying occasional face-to-face encounters whenever Holt was able to break away from the demands and pressures of his work in Vicksburg and travel north. Still, their courtship was hardly smooth: for one thing, Holt fretted openly and constantly about being able to make Mary happy, which in his mind meant, in large part, being able to earn enough money so that they could live as well as her own prosperous family had raised her to expect. "Had I the treasures of the universe I would throw them & myself at your feet," Holt swore. But he insisted, "I will allow you to make for me no sacrifice." As was customary for Victorian couples, Holt offered Mary regular opportunities to opt out of their relationship in favor of a husband who would, presumably, be a better provider. For her part, Mary found such suggestions absurd, even insulting. "I care not for wealth," she wrote, assuring him that "a home, a competency, is all I ask." Mary accused Holt of thinking her "fickle indeed" if he imagined that she could possibly choose another suitor over him. "Oh, how I wish you were here," she wrote lovingly on one occasion. "I have [sat] alone at my window and thought of you until I feel as though I would almost give my existence just for one sound of your dear dear voice. I had not the least idea I should feel so lost, so desolate, without you. You are indeed the very life spring of my heart!!"[19]

At times Holt's hesitation caused Mary to fear his "indifference," but his behavior more likely reflected not only his genuine anxiety about being able to support Mary in the manner to which she was accustomed but also his awareness of the tension between his fundamentally solitary nature and his yearning for the intimacy and joys of marriage. Regardless, the bond between the two was very strong and both, indeed, were deeply smitten. In January 1838, one of Holt's cousins, John B. Lapsley, wrote from Bardstown that he had recently met "Miss H." When they were introduced, Lapsley reported, Mary had looked at him quite closely, "as if endeavoring to trace a resemblance" of Holt in his features. Not finding what she was looking for, Mary had turned away and not paid Lapsley an additional moment's attention. Still, he wrote, she had left an impression. "She looks well," he informed Holt, "and her quiet smile touched (tho but gently) with sadness is sweet & winning." As for any rumors Holt might have heard in recent weeks about Mary growing weary of waiting for him, Lapsley assured him that they were unfounded. "I heard such a report a short time [ago]," he wrote, but "it has given way to one which says that Miss H is to become the future Mrs. Holt, of the truth of which I suppose you are prepared to speak."[20]

On September 11, 1838, John W. Holt died. Perhaps his father's death was just the prodding Holt needed to take the next step forward in his own personal life, for on April 24, 1839, at her family home in Bardstown, twenty-eight-year-old "Miss H" finally did become "Mrs. Joseph Holt." Although he had wed at last, however, Holt had by no means completely overcome his anxiety about providing a proper home for his bride. Indeed, it is not clear whether they ever planned to make a permanent home together in Vicksburg, where for the next three years he continued to develop his law practice while Mary for the most part remained with her family in Bardstown. Happily, Holt was not entirely alone in Mississippi: in 1838, his brother Robert had moved to Benton, about sixty miles northeast of Vicksburg, to open his own law practice, and, he hoped, to amass a fortune, as Holt was in the process of doing.[21]

As Robert struggled to establish his business in Benton, Holt and Mary made do with a life dominated by their physical separation and their shared less-than-vigorous health. For her part, although she visited occasionally, Mary found the southern climate enervating and intolerable. As for Holt, his practice in Vicksburg was thriving, but his earlier complaints about rashes and rheumatism were soon augmented by other discomforts as well. At one point Mary's physician father expressed concern upon learning that during one of Mary's visits to Vicksburg, both she and Holt had begun experiencing respiratory problems. "My anxiety for your return home has increased very much," Burr Harrison wrote, and he encouraged the couple to make Kentucky their residence once and for all. Mary's aunt, Sarah Harrison, similarly urged the Holts to settle together in Kentucky. "My dear Mr. Holt," she wrote after one of Mary's trips south, "our joy at Mary's return to her old home was not so full, as if you had accompanied her, for while you are exposed to any danger, I know that she will not be easy, or happy. Do Mr Holt leave Mississippi the very first hour that you can do so, we shall all feel uneasy about you while you remain there."[22]

Despite the many challenges the couple faced, their correspondence during this period brimmed with words of mutual affection, reassurance, and longing. "I have made many attempts to write," Mary declared soon after one of their partings, "but every sheet has been so flooded with tears that I could not." Mary frequently begged Holt to come and see her in

Bardstown. Then, in the spring of 1842, Holt finally decided that three years of this sort of marriage was enough, especially as he had not been particularly happy in Mississippi to begin with. Financially, the years there had been good to him; they had also advanced his reputation as an excellent attorney, a brilliant thinker and public speaker, and a figure of note in the Democratic Party. But even these advantages did not stack up against the state's hot, humid, and uncongenial climate, the loneliness of being away from the landscape and connections of his youth, and his desire to be close to Mary. And so, having become wealthy and made a number of important new friends along the way, Holt returned to Louisville, now the twelfth-largest city in the United States. There, he and Mary took ownership of a large house at 574 Walnut Street, within walking distance of his old office on Jefferson Street.[23]

Holt and Mary immediately set about elegantly redecorating and re-furbishing in grand style their newly acquired home, attending with similar earnestness to the care of the property that surrounded it. As with his family's Stephensport home, the garden they designed was particularly lovely: a friend described it as "the most beautiful and most admired" garden in Louisville, "indeed a Paradise." The house itself was also magnificent; in the words of Holt's Vicksburg law partner, James O. Harrison—who had recently returned to Kentucky, too—it was an "aristocratic mansion" filled with "gorgeous furniture." Should the Holts come to visit him and his family in Lexington, Harrison warned, "we can only promise an old fashioned, hearty welcome," nothing like the opulence Holt and his wife now enjoyed on a regular basis. Robert, too, was impressed, humbled, and probably jealous, though he expressed it obliquely. "I anticipate much pleasure in enjoying your hospitality during the summer, in a 'corner of your mansion,'" he wrote in May 1842. "We are three of us quiet people as ever won the smiles of Tacitus, and could no doubt share with the rats and mice a much smaller house."[24]

In addition to the impressive house and the elegant garden, the Holts also owned a dog named "Bull," some horses, and at least one cherished pony. Far more significant: they owned humans. Both Holt and Mary, of course, had grown up in slaveholding families, and although Holt does not seem to have owned slaves himself in the early days of his independence, back at the family seat in Stephensport they remained a constant. Then, about eighteen months after he moved to Vicksburg, Holt finally purchased some human beings of his own, although he bought them at his brother Thomas's request and at least primarily for Thomas's use at the Stephensport homestead. "I perceive by your last letter to Uncle Daniel,"

Thomas had written in July 1837, "that you anticipate with confidence that negroes will be sold in your state during the ensuing fall at a very low price." On that occasion, Thomas asked Holt to buy either two adult males or one adult male and a fifteen- or sixteen-year-old boy, for which he promised reimbursement "at some future day." Thomas's request did not fall on deaf ears: Holt bought not two but *thirteen* slaves and sent them north to Stephensport.[25]

As it turns out, within a couple of years, problems had arisen: Holt's ownership of thirteen human beings purchased in Mississippi butted up against Kentucky's 1833 nonimportation law, which forbade, with a few exceptions, the importation to the state of slaves who had been bought elsewhere. For a time it seemed that Holt would be required to pay a fine of $600 per person. In the end, however, he avoided the penalty: from Mississippi, brother Robert arranged for a formal agreement between Holt and Thomas in which they declared themselves partners in the cultivation of the Stephensport farm, and made the claim that Holt's responsibility in connection with the partnership was to provide thirteen "hands" for the work, in return for which he would receive four-fifths of the farm's yield of tobacco. This arrangement circumvented the nonimportation law nicely, and Thomas was able to continue making use of his brother's slaves in the family's tobacco fields and in a host of other ways, too.[26]

Clearly, at least as early as 1837, Holt had become more than just the son of a slaveholding family; he was a slave owner in his own right. And, although for the time being he did not require the human beings he had purchased to labor for him directly, there is simply no getting around the fact that Holt now not only legally defended but was also personally complicit in the slave system. Nor is it likely that the institution's horrors escaped him. In 1887, looking back on the state's slavery days, Kentucky historian Lucius Little insisted that "there was nothing connected with the institution as it existed in Kentucky [that was] repugnant to justice or morality, or incompatible with refinement or humanity." But Joseph Holt knew better. He knew, for example, of the terrible drowning of Betsey, one of his slaves in Stephensport, who fell to her death while trying to get water from a well (Thomas considered Betsey's drowning "rather an unfortunate accident"). Holt knew, too, of his family's carriage driver, William, who, having been deployed to chop wood, hurt himself so badly that he was incapacitated for more than a month. Holt knew that Thomas's house slave Araminta, who Thomas grumbled was "sick half of the time," faced constant suspicion that her frailty was feigned, and constant criticism that her domestic skills, particularly in the kitchen, were inadequate. And he knew that his brother had decided that Araminta—who Thomas believed was also stirring up trouble among the other slaves by claiming to be a "congerer or witch"—must be kept away from her lover, Anthony. Anthony, it seems, had attempted several times to visit Araminta, but Thomas was determined, for whatever reason, to keep them apart and had taken to lying in wait with a "good whip" to catch Anthony should he try again.[27]

Holt knew that in Thomas the slaves he owned in Stephensport had a master who could be harsh.[28] Still, he left his slaves in Thomas's hands until just a few months before he and Mary moved together to Louisville, when he decided to sell them. Even then, his decision was almost certainly based at least in part on business considerations: in a few months the agreement that Robert had worked out with respect to these "imported" slaves would expire, and the fines Holt had so far avoided would come due. Holt may also have been concerned by the news that his slaves had become more and more troublesome, perhaps in response to Thomas's hard treatment. "I have [seen] enough of your negroes," Uncle Daniel wrote in September 1841, "to convince me that they are making preparation at no very distant day to be off." He encouraged Holt to consider selling at least "the most dangerous" of them. "I can see no use in your risking your property after making it," Daniel wrote, and he noted that within about two weeks the tobacco crop would be in and the slaves could more easily be spared. On October 20, Uncle Daniel reported that he and Will Sterett had sold Holt's Stephensport human property for $7,000.[29]

Holt sold his Stephensport slaves, but when he and Mary took up residence in Louisville, they still owned at least three other black people: Dick, Celia, and Lemuel. How they acquired these slaves is unclear, but there is some evidence that Celia, at least, was a gift from Holt to Mary at the time of their marriage. In September 1839, Mary wrote to her new husband from Bardstown to say that she was delighted with Celia, whom she declared "one of the most attentive servants I have ever met with," and who, Mary reported, "can sew beautifully." As for Dick, it is uncertain what his responsibilities were, but Lemuel occupied the comparatively elevated position of being head of the "servant" staff at the Louisville house and was largely responsible—albeit, under the watchful eye of a white caretaker—for making sure that the house, the other slaves, any additional hired servants, and the Holts' animals were all kept in good repair whenever Holt and Mary were out of town. Lemuel, apparently, could always be counted on to follow orders immediately, conscientiously, and without complaint.[30]

Celia, Dick, and Lemuel provided a host of essential services to the

Holts in their Louisville home, making possible many of the comforts they enjoyed as their reward for their economic and racial status. At some point the Holts also acquired his sister Elizabeth's slave, Ellen, along with Ellen's husband, Joshua, and their children. But Ellen did not last long in Louisville: early in 1844, caretaker George Robards informed Holt that she had died. Ellen's death, Robards wrote on February 2, "was not looked for by any person not eaven [*sic*] her husband." In fact, however, just prior to her passing Ellen had given birth to another child, and she had been complaining for a few days about not feeling well. Robards had called in a doctor, who concluded that she was not, in fact, very sick. But Ellen's discomfort (which likely included a postpartum fever) persisted, and by the time her husband Joshua returned from summoning the doctor for a second time, she was dead. It is hard to avoid the suspicion that if Ellen had been white, Robards might have taken her complaints more seriously, though it is also true that even a white woman with a serious postpartum illness was not likely, in the 1840s, to survive.[31]

When Ellen died she left behind several children, including the infant, who was eventually sent to Stephensport, where Thomas and his wife, Rosina Board Holt—whom he had married in 1838—had offered to raise the child. Had she been able to see through the veil of death, perhaps Ellen would have been pleased to know that Celia and Dick were now also living at the Stephensport home. As it turned out, the Holts traveled frequently, which made retaining too many "servants" in Louisville unnecessary. In April 1844, Thomas wrote that Dick had done "verry well" since his arrival in Stephensport, and was behaving himself and performing his tasks acceptably. Celia, in contrast, was proving to be, in his opinion, "verry trifling," complaining of rheumatism and generally acting "sickly." Thomas did not put much stock in Celia's discomfort, although he admitted that she had fainted a number of times while working. Still, by way of "correcting" her, Thomas had taken to "tying her." But he recommended that his brother sell her, especially because he thought that Celia, like Araminta before her, might be stirring up trouble with the other bondspeople. When Thomas wrote again a year later, he continued to praise Dick but no longer mentioned Celia's name. Whether she had been sold, or perhaps had died from whatever was causing her to faint on the job, is unknown.[32]

Even as he consigned his human property to a life of labor (not to mention physical and emotional neglect and abuse), upon returning to Kentucky in 1842, Holt decided to set a substantial portion of his own professional labor aside. In anticipation of his departure from Mississippi, a number of people had expressed the hope that he would invite them as partners into his law practice. Among these was his brother Robert, who was not doing as well as he had expected in Benton. Robert was confident he could enjoy a quiet life there, perhaps even achieving a level of "neighborhood distinction" someday. But, he insisted, "such a life is not to my taste. I desire a more exciting theater of action," and he hoped that working with his accomplished brother in bustling Louisville would provide him with that chance.[33]

Because he had already accumulated so much wealth in Mississippi, however, when he returned to Louisville in 1842 Holt was able, temporarily at least, to cease practicing law and focus instead on promoting Democratic Party politics. Over the years Holt had continued to receive numerous invitations to attend and speak at political meetings across the region.[34] Meanwhile, he had maintained an indirect influence on party affairs by writing letters of recommendation for individuals seeking political appointments of various sorts. Back in Kentucky and removed from the daily work of running a law practice, he now continued to make good on his long-term commitment to the party. But there is no question that Holt also sought rest. Now in his late thirties, he suffered from the effects of having overexerted himself both mentally and physically for more than two decades, and he even exhibited some signs of developing lung disease in addition to persistent rheumatism and eczema.[35]

Even more worrisome than Holt's own health during this period, however, was Mary's. "I regret to learn that cousin Mary is indisposed," wrote Holt's cousin, Washington Dorsey, in January 1842, and he recommended that Holt "have her kept warm & quiet." Still, as the months passed Mary's health remained delicate, and news that cholera was preparing to invade the city in the late winter of 1843 led the couple to embark upon a two-month-long trip to Cuba, where they hoped to find a more benevolent climate. The Holts enjoyed their trip to Cuba: his intense curiosity generated a multivolume diary in which he meticulously recorded their daily activities, the sights he and Mary visited, the fauna and flora they encountered, the foods they ate, and the people they met. Unfortunately, despite the climate, Mary's health did not improve. The following winter the Holts took another trip, this time only as far as New Orleans, again, to little effect. Then, in the summer of 1844, Mary traveled to her father's home in Bardstown—whose climate was better than Louisville's, where cholera remained a threat—with Lemuel and Dick to tend to her needs, but without Holt. In Bardstown, where she found her aging father also ailing, Mary missed her husband terribly, but she also chided him for grumbling about her absence. "My dearest Joseph," she wrote, "I could enjoy my visit more if I did not think so much about your loneliness." Mary stayed in Bardstown for several months, during which Holt's brother Robert provided some of the only uplifting news Holt received in this period: Ann Holt, whom Robert had married in March 1843, had just given birth to their first child, Sarah Ellen Holt, who, he claimed adoringly, "surpasses in beauty and sprightliness any lady of her age in all the country." [36]

Holt visited Mary occasionally, but he did not spend any length of time in Bardstown. For one thing, he felt uncomfortable repeatedly leaving the Louisville house and property in the care of his "servants." Perhaps, too, his solitary nature shrank from the prospect of being surrounded constantly by Mary's family and friends. One wonders whether Holt was not also concerned that too much togetherness might result in Mary becoming pregnant, a development that would surely send her already delicate health spiraling down. That said, in spring 1845 Holt and Mary did take another trip together, this time to Charleston, South Carolina, to visit a longtime friend of her family, the eminent Catholic priest Reverend Ignatius A. Reynolds, who had first known Mary when she was a child and who now feared that she, like her mother and siblings, was "sinking into an early grave." Reynolds's fears were well founded: just a year later, thirty-five-year-old Mary Harrison Holt was dead, the victim of a profoundly debilitating respiratory illness, probably tuberculosis. As it turns out, despite their abundant time apart, Mary may also have been pregnant after all. Just nine months before she died, one doctor theorized that a recent downturn in Mary's condition probably resulted from "a functional disorder," a phrase that commonly referred to an interruption in a woman's menstrual cycle, itself an obvious result of pregnancy. Even more suggestive is the letter from a friend in Lexington, Margaret C. Kavanaugh, written shortly after Mary's death, in which Kavanaugh remarked (not very consolingly) that she had "always feared" that Mary, "on account of her extreme debility and her general poor health, never would be able to get through her confinement," virtually a code word in this period for the end stage of pregnancy. If indeed Mary was pregnant when she died, the loss to her husband must have been doubly painful. Losing an anticipated child in addition to a beloved wife would surely have had lasting implications for the thirty-nine-year-old Holt's sense of his future and his legacy (especially in light of his siblings' growing families) and also for his subsequent relationships with women. Back in Stephensport, Thomas and his wife had just welcomed their *third* child, a healthy boy they named Washington Dorsey, after their much-loved physician cousin, who himself had recently died entirely unexpectedly. In Mississippi, Robert and Ann were also expecting again, and

Holt's sister, Elizabeth, had given birth to her first child, Margaret, in early 1845.[37]

Holt's profound grief made it difficult to dwell on such happy matters, and in the end he seems to have derived very little comfort from any religious faith, either, although over the course of this sad, anxious period of Mary's increasing infirmity he had showed some signs of embracing religion—or at least some kind of intensified spirituality—in a way that he never had before. His mother, Eleanor, for one, was pleased, writing that she "rejoist" to learn that her eldest son now found himself impressed with "the necessity of religion." Eleanor hoped that "god ha[d] begun a good work" with Holt, and she prayed that he might eventually experience a full and complete conversion. Not long after Mary's death, Margaret Kavanaugh's husband, the Methodist Episcopal bishop H. H. Kavanaugh, wrote, "I regard this as a crisis in your history . . . and I rejoice from the expressions of your letter and the previous exercises of your mind to believe that you will improve it to the glory of God and the salvation of your soul."[38]

Most correspondents, however, focused more directly on Holt's anguish than on the state of his soul. "I have just heard of your dramatic affliction," wrote his old friend and former colleague James O. Harrison, calling Mary's death "the most grievous" loss that Holt would probably ever have to endure. "The intelligence contained in your letter is mournful indeed," agreed brother Robert, who went on to describe Mary as the exemplar of "all that angelic purity and gentleness and exalted devotion can make her sex." With great tenderness and compassion, Robert reminded his brother that Mary's love for him had been vast, and he recalled a particular moment, years earlier, when Mary declared "that when she died she wished to go to the same place with yourself whenever & whatever that might be, whether the abode of happiness or of misery."[39]

In the wake of Mary's death, Holt found some measure of comfort in the beautiful garden he and Mary had enjoyed so thoroughly together. Indeed, during Mary's illness, Holt's passion for trees, plants, and flowers seems to have deepened considerably, along with his desire to share them generously with others. In November 1845, for example, Holt had sent his mother a shipment of carefully chosen shrubs and trees to be planted by his brother Thomas around the Stephensport property, and in future years he made many similar gifts of interesting and beautiful flora to family members and cherished friends. "I have rece'd the roses &c sent to me by Wilson," the local florist, "& yourself, all in good order," wrote James O. Harrison on one occasion. "I have given a conspicuous place to the Gingko & hope that you & I & ours may in our old age sit beneath its shade."[40]

Holt surely spent many hours walking quietly among the flowers and shrubs and trees that surrounded the Louisville home that he and Mary had shared so briefly.[41] As he walked, one imagines that he looked back with some wonder over the decade since he and Mary had first begun courting: years of intense labor, great love, wrenching adjustment, painful conflict, wearying anxiety, and, finally, agonizing loss. The nation, too, had witnessed a host of dramatic developments in the years since 1836: five different presidents had occupied the Executive Mansion, and the national population now numbered around 20 million. Americans had also spread out, white pioneers beginning to follow the 2,000-mile-long Oregon Trail westward to rich farmlands, mines, and opportunity, many of them driven by the consequences of the Panic of 1837. Meanwhile, a series of conflicts had erupted between land-hungry whites and the remaining Native people in Alabama, Florida, and Georgia, leading to the latter's subordination and forced removal to regions of the country where their own hopes for survival could be successfully squelched. White settlers across a huge area of Mexican land had declared themselves citizens of the independent Republic of Texas, to which the United States offered diplomatic recognition in 1837, and which it then welcomed into the Union as a state in 1845, provoking a war that broke out the same month Mary died.[42]

During this period, three new states had joined the Union: Arkansas in 1836, Michigan in 1837, and Florida in 1845, raising the total number to twenty-eight (fifteen slave and thirteen free); Iowa's admission as a free state at the end of 1846 brought the total to twenty-nine. In addition, the number of enslaved black persons in the United States had swelled to over 2.5 million, further enhancing tensions between slaveholders and their supporters, on the one hand, and free labor and antislavery activists, on the other. These tensions became manifest in the imposition of a "gag rule" on antislavery petitions in Congress; the 1837 murder of the abolitionist newspaper editor Elijah P. Lovejoy in Alton, Illinois; the schisms that split the national denominations of the Methodist Episcopal and Baptist churches in 1844 and 1845, respectively; and the expanded publication and dissemination of literature either condemning slavery and its horrors, as did Frederick Douglass's stirring 1845 autobiography, or promoting its virtues, like *DeBow's Review*. When Holt looked back, he must have marveled at the twists and turns his own life, and the nation's, had taken. He surely noted, too, the ominous indications that, just as his beloved wife's illness had ultimately taken her life, the stresses that were building along sectional lines in America might ultimately destroy the Union he loved.

In the late spring of 1846, however, the bulk of Holt's attention was focused on his great personal loss. Family members in Stephensport struggled to cheer him up, urging him to come for a visit as soon as he could. Robert also stayed in touch from Mississippi, even trying to arrange a reunion of the Holt siblings at the old homestead, though he was pretty sure that James, who was now living in Texas and may also have joined the U.S. army for its fight with Mexico, would not be able to attend. Close friends, too, invited Holt to come and stay, including James O. Harrison. Lest Holt be deterred by the thought of being in the happily chaotic home of a growing family, Harrison promised his grieving friend, "my noisy children will be on their best behavior when you come."[43]

Others simply acknowledged his grief, offered help, or expressed thanks for the thoughtful keepsakes he had sent to sustain their memories of Mary. Margaret Kavanaugh, whose husband had conducted the funeral, was particularly grateful for a lock of Mary's hair. At the same time, she offered a practical suggestion: should Holt be planning to "break up house-keeping" and dispose of some of his slaves now that Mary was gone, she would be happy to consider taking "Joanah." As had always been the case for bondspeople, Mary's death presented an occasion for dramatic disruption in the lives of those human beings whom she and her husband had claimed as their property while she was living. Even Dick, whom the Holts had owned for several years, faced the possibility of being sold, in lieu of which he made a case for having his labor rented out instead. "Your boy Richard," wrote T. Rucker on June 22, "proposes his services as a dining room servant and says your price is ten dollars per month[.] Mrs Rucker is in want of one and requests me to say to you she will be pleased to have him." Holt's decision with regard to Dick's suggestion is not known.[44]

Two months after Mary died, Robert and Ann sent another rare piece of good news in this grim time, reporting the arrival, at the end of July, of their second child, a "fine little boy" whom they had decided to name after Holt. "I assure you," Robert wrote, "he is a youth of great promise, and I intend that in his prime he shall much more than realize the promise of his infancy." While Holt undoubtedly rejoiced at the news of yet another namesake's birth, he must also have experienced a fresh wave of sadness that this latest child to bear his name was not his own. In addition, it would have been difficult for him to miss the considerable irony in the fact that although he and Mary had produced no living children, he now found himself financially responsible for two adolescents: Cuthbert H. Bain, Mary's nephew by her sister Elizabeth and her husband, William P. Bain, both of whom were dead; and eighteen-year-old Elizabeth "Lizzie" Hynes, who was Burr Harrison's niece by marriage and, therefore, Mary's cousin.[45]

Sadly, neither of these young people did much to brighten Holt's life either now or in the years to come. Over time Cuthbert became something of a ne'er-do-well, squandering the small inheritance he had received from his paternal grandfather, Patterson Bain, as well as whatever bequest he had received from Burr Harrison's estate and the resources Holt regularly contributed for his education, board, clothes, shoes, and other miscellaneous needs. By 1853, Cuthbert disappeared from the historical record, leaving in his place the question of what became of him as an adult, or whether he even survived his troubled youth. Early on, Lizzie Hynes—who lived with her sister, Laura, and Laura's husband, Robert McChord, in Springfield, Kentucky—demonstrated a similar tendency toward extravagance; the problem, Mary's aunt Sarah Harrison wrote, was that Lizzie "knows not what economy is." Even worse, she added, "I fear nothing will ever teach her the lesson." Nevertheless, Holt continued to send Lizzie money. Like Cuthbert Bain, Lizzie always responded to these infusions of cash with warm expressions of gratitude. "You have been more than a friend to me," she declared on one occasion. "If it had not been for you I would have been left in this cold friendless world without a friend." Unlike Cuthbert, however, Lizzie's dependence on Holt's benevolence persisted for more than a half-century.[46]

The deep and essentially solitary depression into which Holt tumbled after Mary's death lasted for almost two years. Worried about his long-term well being, in January 1848, Holt's Aunt Mary Ann somewhat tentatively suggested that he should consider marrying again. As the months passed, Robert, too, worried that Holt might retreat so far into his unhappiness that he would never reemerge. "I was much gratified to hear from you at all," Robert wrote in February 1848, "but think I have much cause of complaint against you, not only for your silence of over six months, but for your failure to say one word about yourself, your health, plans, &c." As it turns out, however, by the time Robert was giving vent to these concerns, Holt was finding his own way out of his self-imposed isolation: he had decided to take an extended trip, not back to Stephensport but to Europe and the Middle East, something he and Mary had once considered doing together. After finding a dependable renter for his Louisville mansion, Holt made the trip alone. His journey would have lasting consequences for both his politics and his worldview.[47]

Setting sail in May 1848 from New Orleans, Holt carried letters of introduction to various U.S. diplomats, as well as secular and religious foreign leaders, a number of whom he expected to encounter in his travels. It is noteworthy that on this occasion, Holt's recommenders included seventy-one-year-old Henry Clay, with whom, after years of political quarrelling, Holt had finally established cordial relations, perhaps through James O. Harrison's efforts. Holt's recommenders also included the eminent Catholic bishop Ignatius Reynolds, whom he had come to know through Mary. Former vice president Richard M. Johnson, too, contributed a letter, in which he described Holt as his "personal friend" and a "distinguished fellow citizen." No man in Kentucky, wrote Johnson, "is more worthy of confidence & your kindness" than Holt, who, he declared, was "held in general, & I might say, universal esteem & respect" in America.[48]

Holt traveled first to London. Then, over the course of the next year and a half, he explored England, Scotland, Ireland, France, Egypt and northern Africa—where he rented and rode on a camel—Palestine, Damascus, Constantinople, and Greece. During his journey, Holt maintained a steady correspondence with his family and friends back home, in which he shared his observations and experiences. James O. Harrison thanked Holt in particular for the letter he wrote from "the top of the big Pyramid" in Egypt. "It is something, you know, even to be thought of by our friends when far away," Harrison mused, "but to be thought of upon the summit of that huge pile to which the wise & the curious have, through so many ages, turned their eyes and their feet, is a circumstance to be remembered with peculiar pleasure." For his part, Holt's brother Robert was grateful for news about the revolutions sweeping across Europe, including the bloody democratic rebellion in Paris in June against the conservative government of the Second Republic. To remain abreast of developments in Stephensport, Holt turned to the letters he received from his Aunt Mary Ann, who described such things as the seasonal onset of cholera in communities along the Ohio River and reported on the birth of his sister Elizabeth's second daughter, named Mary in honor of Holt's late wife. Like his other correspondents, Mary Ann encouraged Holt to keep his family and friends apprised of his adventures, and she begged him to bring her some pebbles from the banks of the Jordan River and, if possible, "a piece of the tree where our saviour spent his agony in the garden." More than anything else, however, Mary Ann was anxious for Holt to return home unharmed. "If you were to get killed or put in prison," she wrote fondly, "I know it would be the end of me. I could not live."[49]

Unfortunately, although he carefully preserved the letters he received on this amazing and ambitious trip, most of the letters Holt wrote to his friends and family are no longer extant. One lengthy letter remains, however, addressed to his brother Thomas's wife, Rosina. In this June 4, 1849, missive—which he surely anticipated would be shared with the rest of his family in Stephensport—Holt discussed his deeply inspiring visit to the Holy Land, where he spent time sitting by Jacob's Well in Samaria reading the biblical story of Jesus' conversation there with the Samaritan woman, attended a worship service, and spoke with local Christians about their longstanding conflict with the Jews. From there Holt moved on to Nazareth, where he viewed a number of other sites "of high biblical interest" and drank from a local spring known as the "Virgin's Fountain" (where Jesus had also supposedly quenched his thirst). At Nazareth, Holt also witnessed, thrillingly, "one of the most gorgeous rainbows which I have ever beheld," and which seemed to "span the Heavens directly over Nazareth & stretched in unbroken splendor from horizon to horizon," while "spreading its glittering folds over the city of the Prince of Peace." Here, as Aunt Mary Ann had requested, Holt gathered some pebbles to bring home.[50]

After Nazareth, Holt traveled on to Tiberias and the Sea of Galilee, and then to Damascus, Lebanon, and Constantinople, all of which he described in glowing terms, though he expressed frustration over having been quarantined at several different locations for a total of twenty-six days, a standard practice designed to forestall the spread of the plague. When he finally reached Greece, Holt was stunned to find it "the most impoverished, worn out looking country in the world," whose inhabitants were "very nearly as poor as their soil," thanks to "nearly four centuries of the most grinding & barbarous despotism of the Turks." Greece, Holt declared, was a place where even his brother Thomas, a fine farmer, "would scarce be able to raise peas on the best land I have seen." Still, he considered the country's cultural attractions unparalleled in their beauty: Athens alone, he wrote, housed the remains of "the most magnificent temples, & works of art, which human genius & power have ever produced."[51]

As he had loved his earlier trip to Cuba with Mary, Holt profoundly enjoyed his great adventure across the sea, during which he came to know more than he could ever have imagined about the larger world and, at the same time, gained an even greater and more enduring appreciation for American democracy, Jeffersonian and Jacksonian ideals, and the Constitution and the Bill of Rights. In addition, despite the persistent threat of plague, Holt enjoyed a notable improvement in his overall physical and mental health. He also made some new friends, including newlyweds Howard and Margaret Crosby. Reverend Crosby was a Presbyterian minister, a professor of Greek at New York University (later at Rutgers), and a Whig. Meeting first in London in July 1848, the three quickly became close. "I assure you," Crosby later wrote, "that the brightest remembrance of my European tour will be ever the fact that it was made in your company. Not

Charles Anderson Wickliffe.
Courtesy of the Kentucky Historical Society, Frankfort, Kentucky.

only has your uniform kindness and courtesy impressed my heart but I have experienced a rare delight in companionship with your *mind*." And he added, "the possession of your friendship is the source of one of the first joys of my life." The Crosbys and Holt remained friends for many years.[52]

With his spirits lifted and his resources depleted, by October 1849 Holt was back in Kentucky. "[I] do thank a kindly superintending Providence," wrote Sarah Harrison, with whom he had remained in contact regarding young Cuthbert Bain and Lizzie Hynes, "that has protected you through all your journeyings, and brought you safely home." Although the adjustment to life back in Louisville cannot have been easy following his extended and fascinating tour overseas, the process was surely sweetened by the advent of a new love: twenty-eight-year-old Margaret Wickliffe (Holt was now forty-two). Margaret's father was the eminent Bardstown lawyer and politician, Charles Anderson Wickliffe; her uncle (her father's eldest brother) was Robert Wickliffe, with whom Holt had studied law in Lexington in the late 1820s, when she was a young child. Charles Wickliffe had been a member of the Kentucky House of Representatives and the U.S. House of Representatives, had served as governor of Kentucky from 1839 to 1840, and had held the position of postmaster general of the United States during the presidency of John Tyler (1841–45). In politics, Wickliffe was no purist: some sources identify him as a Whig, while others say he was a Democrat. What seems to be most true is that he was a dedicated Unionist who considered most issues on their own merits, leading some to call him "inconsistent" and others to praise him for his independence and pragmatism. That said, not all of Wickliffe's positions on political matters were entirely savory: in 1849 he endorsed the passage of laws in Kentucky to punish free blacks for various offenses, either by banishment or sale into slavery. Wickliffe, who owned many slaves himself, believed that "such laws would have a tendency to rid the State of that undesirable class of people," for whose disposal he also suggested that "the State might somewhere procure territory for a penal colony."[53]

It is unclear exactly when or how Holt and Margaret Wickliffe met and became acquainted. Given the professional and political prominence Holt and her father shared, however, the broad terrain over which both men had traveled in their professional capacities, and the connections they had through Robert Wickliffe and even Ben Hardin, they must have had a number of different opportunities. Perhaps Holt first caught a glimpse of Margaret while passing near her family's elegant Bardstown mansion, Wickland, which stood within walking distance of both St. Joseph's College (she was a toddler when he was a student there) and the family home of Holt's first wife, Mary Harrison (Margaret was eighteen when Holt and Mary married in 1839). Bardstown's population was small, not even 1,500 in 1840, and the Harrisons and Wickliffes were almost certainly well acquainted; indeed, they may even have been related. In her letters, Lizzie Hynes, in fact, frequently referred to Margaret as "Cousin Mag," and years earlier, Robert McChord—who later became Hynes's brother-in-law—had been placed under Charles Wickliffe's guardianship following the death of his parents.[54]

In any case, by late 1849, Holt had not only met Margaret Wickliffe but had also fallen in love with her. "Though your ears may weary in hearing," he wrote effusively at the end of that year, "my tongue can never weary in repeating, that I love you fervently, unch[an]geably, & that this sentiment is every hour colouring yet more deeply & clothing with yet brighter hues of beauty every thought & hope & prayer of my existence." Never an overly confident suitor, and now perhaps even less so because his feelings were so strong and because of the terrible loss he had already suffered, Holt worried that his courtship with Margaret might turn out to be illusory. "I may be likened to a miser," he explained, "who dazzled by some priceless jewel, of which he finds himself suddenly possessed, dreads . . . lest his senses should deceive him, & all should prove but a mocking vision." Holt's courtship of Margaret was utterly real, however, and on April 2, 1850, they were married at Wickland.[55]

Aunt Mary Ann, for one, was delighted to know that Holt was no longer alone. "I sincerely congratulate both you & Margaret on the occasion of your marriage," she wrote. "My joy on the occasion is so great that it certainly is inexpressible on paper." For her part, Lizzie Hynes called "Cousin Mag" "one of the loveliest beings I ever kn[e]w" and offered fond, if somewhat awkward, wishes for their future together: "May she be a dear companion to you in all seasons of life," she wrote, "and sympathize with you in the loneliness of declining years. . . . May your future paths," Hynes added, "be watered with the gentle showers of affection." As it turns out, Margaret was not the only one of Charles Wickliffe's daughters to marry a man of both accomplishment and promise: in 1846, the oldest, Nannie, married David Levy Yulee of Florida, who in 1845 had been elected Florida's first U.S. senator (and the nation's first Jewish one). In 1849, Mary, the second oldest, married William Matthews Merrick of Maryland, who became a deputy attorney general for his state, a U.S. circuit court judge in Washington, D.C., and, some years later, a professor of law at George Washington University. In 1855, Margaret's younger sister, Julia, married Kentucky legislator William Netherton Beckham; their son, John Crepps Wickliffe Beckham, would serve as governor of Kentucky from 1900 to 1907. Charles Wickliffe's son, Robert C. Wickliffe, too, made his way to distinction. Like Holt, he attended both St. Joseph's and Centre Colleges (he graduated in 1840). Later, he became a lawyer, eventually moving to Louisiana, where he was elected governor in 1856. Another Wickliffe son, Charlie, proved less successful: having served in the U.S. Army during the war with Mexico, Charlie went on to live an unexceptional postwar life before he died following a fall he took while horseback riding.[56]

Shortly after their wedding, the Holts embarked on an international honeymoon of more than a year's duration, replicating to a great extent the trip Holt had taken by himself in 1848–49. "We were all rejoiced to hear of the happy circumstances which have prompted your new tour abroad and sincerely wish you all the wishes of friendly hearts," wrote Holt's friend from that earlier journey, Howard Crosby. Once again, Holt carried letters of introduction from important people, this time including one from his distinguished new father-in-law. While abroad, the Holts occupied their time with sightseeing and shopping for beautiful furnishings for what was now *their* Louisville home. As he had done on his earlier trip, Holt made a point of keeping in touch with friends and family back home, to whom he described adventures that he was enjoying with his new wife by his side. Aunt Mary Ann seemed to think that Margaret was particularly well suited to the task of enhancing Holt's engagement with the larger world. "You will find," she commented, that "Margaret will notice things you would never think" to consider.[57]

Margaret, too, maintained a correspondence with her family, who missed her sorely but who rejoiced in her excellent choice of spouses. "Indeed, dear Mag," wrote Margaret's sister-in-law, Anne Dawson Wickliffe (Robert C. Wickliffe's wife and the daughter of Louisiana congressman John Bennett Dawson), "the thoughts of your bright future ever spread over my heart a glow of pleasure," and she referred to Holt as Margaret's "estimable husband." Meanwhile, Holt's brother Robert wrote letters filled with news about local, regional, and national politics. These days, Robert was especially eager to keep his brother up to date on the nation's increasing sectionalism. In the time that had passed since Mary's May 1846 death, the U.S. had fought and won its war with Mexico (1846–48), adding to the national domain some 500,000 square miles of new territory, whose status in relation to chattel slavery remained to be determined. Since 1846, too, Wisconsin had entered the Union, temporarily restoring the balance between the slave and the free states. But thanks in large part to the gold rush that had begun when traces of the precious metal were discovered in January 1848 at a place called Sutter's Mill, California was now on the verge of entering the Union and giving the free states an edge. Meanwhile, Mexican war hero and Virginia slaveholder Zachary Taylor, an ardent nationalist, had been elected president in 1848. When he died unexpectedly in July 1850, Taylor was replaced by New Yorker Millard Fillmore, who was fresh from presiding, as Taylor's vice president, over the vigorous debates in Congress concerning the measures that came to be known as the Compromise of 1850.[58]

Initially proposed by the elderly and declining Henry Clay, the Compromise of 1850 was ultimately shepherded to passage in the fall of that year by Illinois's Democratic senator, Stephen Douglas. The compromise was designed to ease growing tensions between the slave and free states by offering complex concessions to both, the most important and controversial being a newly strengthened fugitive slave law that instituted stern fines for law enforcement officials—including U.S. marshals, state militia members, and federal troops—who did not arrest suspected runaways. The compromise also established fines for individuals who aided the runaways in any way, as well as rewards for those who helped to effect captures. Certainly no aspect of the Compromise of 1850 produced more heated discussion both within Congress and beyond its walls. Antislavery activists demanded the passage, at the state level, of "personal liberty laws" that would essentially nullify the Fugitive Slave Act, and slavery supporters angrily revisited the possibility of withdrawal from the Union if the Fugitive Slave Act, and what they insisted were their constitutional rights to own other human beings, were not protected.

In the fall of 1850, from his vantage point in central Mississippi, thirty-five-year-old Robert Holt concluded that those Southern slaveholders who were once again threatening secession from the United States constituted "a treasonable movement" that must be taken seriously. Describing the "revolutionary condition" he saw developing across the South, Robert pointed to the large number of people in the region whose loyalty to the Union and the Constitution had begun to give way to grave discontent and, in some cases, "fierce and defiant hostility." These fanatics, among whom Robert included Uncles Bob and Daniel Stephens, actively pondered not only secession and disunion but also the possibility of armed resistance to the federal government. Some, he reported, had already moved beyond just talking about their plans and were now organizing themselves for action through conventions, committees of correspondence, and other channels. Indeed, the Compromise of 1850 had failed completely to ease the tensions between the slave and free states. Rather, Robert wrote, it had "heated the furnace of Southern Passion several times hotter than before." At the same time, although people in the northern states seemed calm, he suspected that they had a deeper, hidden purpose to carry "to yet greater extremes the policy by which the South has become so incensed," namely, abolitionism. Robert predicted that the national political parties would soon collapse, and that this would be followed by the collapse of the Union in three years or less. Where in the world, he wondered, would the developing crisis lead? "Whether southern chivalry will hereafter condescend to cool its mint juleps with northern ice," he mused, "has not been settled." For his part, Robert—like Holt—remained pledged to the Union, so much so, in fact, that he decided to pull up stakes in May 1851 and move his family from slaveholding Mississippi to free Cincinnati, just across the Ohio River from Covington, Kentucky, and about a hundred miles from Louisville. Falling back on a habit of many years' duration, Robert asked his brother for a loan to help him get his new residence in order, his twenty-seven acres of land under cultivation, and his legal practice up and running. Holt sent him $600.[59]

Although his move to Ohio was prompted at least in part by his anxiety about the growth of "treasonable" secessionist sentiments across the South, however, before long Robert found that he did not much like Ohioans, either. Indeed, he blamed his slow start professionally in Cincinnati on the "character of the people" he had encountered north of the Mason-Dixon Line. "They are," he wrote, in words that anticipated his eventual development into a fire-eating Southern nationalist, "pre-eminently inhospitable, unsocial, avaricious, & selfish." Robert felt that it was "almost impossible to approach" such people: "nothing but a prospect of cheating or robbing you," he wrote, "seems to awaken in them the slightest interest in your existence." It was, in fact, Robert's growing disdain for the people he met in Cincinnati, and the free-labor economy he found there, that opened an irrevocable gap between the once-affectionate brothers, which only grew wider in the years ahead. For although both he and Robert had grown up in a slaveholding family, and both had eventually become slaveholders in their own right, Holt, it seems, had never been a dyed-in-the-wool proslavery man. Instead, although he had long supported the proslavery Democratic Party and had argued the cases of slave owners in court, Holt had in fact harbored at least some ambivalence about the institution as far back as his college days.[60]

Indeed, among the many topics of debate Holt had tackled while a student at Centre College was slavery, which had already become a matter of increasing political interest around the country as a result of the debates in 1819 and 1820 leading up to the Missouri Compromise. At that time, as would also be true in later years, essentially all of Holt's extended family was committed to the institution of slavery, both in theory and in practice. Slavery, after all, had benefited them greatly in material ways and in terms of their social status and political influence, and its abolition was unthinkable. Nevertheless, as a seventeen-year-old in 1825, Holt had spoken out boldly against it. "While we tolerate slavery" as a nation, Holt declared in a speech at the school, "we are only feeding and nourishing our own destroyer, like the hen [roosting] on the serpent's eggs." The system of forced labor, he insisted, "affords a continual source of contention between the states in favor of slavery and those opposed to it," generating a degree of "animosity" that over time, he predicted, would have a "mighty tendency to sever the union." Even more important, however, slavery was "contrary to every principle of justice, every precept of morality, every feeling of humanity, every sentiment of honor." [61]

Years later, as Holt's ideas about slavery continued to develop and even as he himself became a slave owner, members of his family became concerned about the direction his thoughts might ultimately take. In a letter written during the national debate over the future of Texas, Uncle Bob, for one, had indicated that what appeared to be his nephew's growing distaste for slavery had become a matter of common knowledge. "It is said," wrote Bob in October 1845, "that you sometimes speak of the *South* with almost abhorance [*sic*]." Bob urged his nephew to resist criticizing the place of his birth, where he had also "rec'd some favors," and he denied Holt's assertions about the evils of the slave institution, which he had included in an earlier (but unfortunately no longer extant) letter. "That the present system of slavery is either a social political or moral evil (as you say)," Bob wrote, "I deny in toto." Still, Bob unhappily predicted that Holt's views would someday lead him to "settle in a free state," though he hoped that his nephew would never go so far as to become an abolitionist. In the early 1850s, as his brother Robert was beginning to reconsider his move to free Ohio, Holt continued to weigh seriously slavery's advantages for some people (like himself) against its cruel inhumanity to others. In the years to come, and especially when he found himself forced to choose between slavery and the Union, Holt's decision became virtually unconflicted: slavery must go, not just because the Union could not endure with both the free- and slave-labor systems intact, but also because slavery was morally wrong. [62]

It is hardly insignificant that as Holt's ideas about slavery developed, so, too, did his distrust of extremism in any form—including abolitionism. Political extremism of any sort, he believed, led inexorably to revolution, potentially against a legitimate, constitutional, republican government such as the United States enjoyed. Indeed, just as he had done in relation to slavery, as a student at Centre College Holt had begun to articulate his ideas about government, political opposition, and revolution. In a letter to an unknown correspondent, then-nineteen-year-old Holt had shared some particularly thoughtful reflections on the "bold, daring, and enterprising" Napoleon Bonaparte, who, he argued, deserved to be executed for having "violated all the most sacred laws of nations" when he set about destroying the government of France, a republic based, like the United States, on Enlightenment principles and the rejection of monarchy, aristocracy, and religious privilege. (Here, Holt skirted the issue of the French Republic's—and the United States'—birth in revolution.) Decades later, Holt studied the situation developing in the United States and found his opinion unchanged. Political extremism, especially of the sort that could lead to revolution and the collapse of the Union—the American Republic—was treason, pure and simple.[63]

When the Holts returned to Kentucky in September 1851, however, their immediate focus was not on political but on private affairs, which for Holt entailed completing an extensive list of renovations at the Louisville house before he would even consider allowing Margaret to move in. As a result, for the next several months, the two spent most of their time—as he and Mary had also done—living apart, Holt in Louisville supervising the renovations and Margaret lodging with her family in Bardstown, where she looked forward to occasional visits from her husband and awaited word that the house in Louisville was finally ready. As had been true for Holt and Mary during their numerous separations, during this period the couple's correspondence was extremely affectionate. But it also offered indications of their individual frustrations, Holt struggling to understand Margaret's impatience to join him in Louisville and Margaret struggling to understand why Holt did not come to visit her more often in Bardstown in the interim. And the fact of the matter is that Holt was slow to close the physical distance between them, offering one explanation after another as to why he could not travel to Bardstown on a particular occasion, and detailing what remained of the work being done on the Louisville house that made Margaret's presence problematic.[64]

Throughout this period, Holt reassured Margaret repeatedly that he was not simply enjoying the freedoms that their separation offered. "I have called on nobody since I came down," he insisted; "I am practicing the utmost self denial, reserving all my capabilities of happiness for that which you have in store." Holt also wrote effusively of his devotion: "if it were not for the light of your bright eyes which shine even unto here gilding the gloom of my solitude," he declared, his lonely evenings "would be insupportable." Meanwhile, Margaret strove to stifle her disappointment while offering useful advice, not least concerning the work Holt was assigning to their slaves. Margaret, too, of course, had grown up surrounded by human property, and she, for one, had no reservations whatsoever about getting good use out of it. In the end, one has to wonder why the two, so recently married, tolerated such extended separation and why, indeed, Holt himself seems to have been inclined to stretch it beyond all reasonable limits. Most likely, the couple's marital arrangements reflected in part the fact that he remained unable to find a satisfying and graceful balance between his competing needs for companionship and deep relationship on the one hand, and solitude and privacy on the other. In addition, although there is abundant evidence to indicate that Holt truly loved his new wife, and not one letter from a member of her family ever even vaguely questioned his affection for her, nevertheless there are also clear indications that during this period Holt was at least emotionally committed not only to Margaret but also to another woman who wrote frequently and fondly between 1851 and 1853, in French, signing her letters "Anastasie." As it turns out, this was the first such extramarital bond Holt formed; it was not, however, the last.[65]

Beginning sometime in 1852, Margaret finally moved into the Louisville house and the Holts at last began living together. But even then, the pressing political developments that were underway across America at midcentury diminished the amount of time the two were able to share, even as they set the stage for the fierce ideological conflicts in which the Holts, like so many American families—especially on the border between slavery and freedom—could not avoid becoming engaged. Holt, who had been such a rising star in the Democratic Party in the 1830s, and who had not completely withdrawn from party affairs in the 1840s even when he stepped away from his law practice, was incapable of ignoring the antebellum period's burning questions. And as the bond tying the Union together began to disintegrate more rapidly, he began to devote increasing amounts of time and energy to political activity. For her part, Margaret was not opposed to her husband's activism in any fundamental way—she came, after all, from an extremely prominent political family. But she was understandably resistant to the idea of surrendering her husband entirely to the great debates that were raging across the country and cut deeply into her share of his attention. But Holt, whose lengthy travels outside the United States had taught him a great deal about the alternatives to American republicanism and to national union, found himself irresistibly drawn to the work, as he understood it, of sustaining the American experiment as a whole against any and all radical efforts to destroy it. As he later declared in a speech in Boston, "all that we are and all that we have are the fruit of these institutions; and all that we may now generously devote to back their safety . . . they will give back to us and to our children's children, increased a hundred, nay, a thousand fold."[66]

As Holt moved more energetically into the political arena, one of the first speeches he gave was on behalf of the highly acclaimed, exiled Hungarian journalist-turned-politician, Louis Kossuth, who in 1852 was on an extended tour of the United States. To many Americans, Kossuth symbolized the bitter struggle then taking place in Europe between republican ideals and entrenched monarchies. He was also a compelling speaker. Holt's brother Robert, who had heard Kossuth in Cincinnati, found the Hungarian "in manner simple as in matter he is elegant," and "beyond all question . . . the first of living orators," although he predicted that Kossuth's unfailing support for republican ideals and democracy was bound to land him in "a martyr's grave." After Cincinnati, Kossuth traveled to Louisville, where Holt, as one of the city's most eminent and well-traveled citizens, was invited to introduce him. Afterward, a correspondent from the *New Albany (Ind.) Weekly Register* commented that the "Magyar Chief's" speech had been interesting but that Holt had been positively brilliant, proving himself "emphatically the ablest and most finished orator that I have listened to in many a day." Delighted to learn that his brother had stepped onto the public stage again, Robert encouraged Holt to use more of his leisure time doing so. "Your mind," he wrote, "was never made to corrode & waste away amid the monotony of idleness." Just over a month after Holt delivered the speech, the New York editor of *Livingston's Law Register* and the *U.S. Monthly Law Magazine*, John Livingston, requested that Holt send him a biographical sketch to be included in an upcoming issue. At the end of June, Holt was tapped again to give a major speech, this time on the occasion of the death of Henry Clay.[67]

In addition, Holt found himself once again, and almost immediately, fielding requests that he put his name forward as a candidate for elective office. Late that summer, an old friend, Robert Ward Johnson (Richard M. Johnson's nephew), encouraged Holt to make himself available as a possible replacement for Kentucky representative Humphrey Marshall, a Whig who had just resigned from the U.S. Congress. "There is but one opinion throughout the [seventh] district," Ward wrote; "you are the man for his successor." Johnson urged Holt to commence immediately giving a series of speeches, which, he was certain, would yield votes from Whigs as well as Democrats. As others had done before him, Johnson cast Holt's willingness to stand for election as a patriotic duty. "You owe it to your country not to refuse the nomination," he wrote. "Providence has not endowed you with so much genius without intending it should be exerted in behalf of your country. You must not, you cannot refuse." Johnson, moreover, envisioned Holt's candidacy as one step on his way to a higher destiny. "You will at once take the highest position in the house," he predicted, and once that happened, "what rival can you have for the presidency itself[?]"[68]

As he had done so often in the past, Holt ignored this most recent demand that he put his name on a ballot, but he did agree to give a number of speeches for "the Democracy" in the months ahead, and with the 1852 presidential campaign getting underway and the national political parties beginning to fracture, he was in regular demand. Among Holt's most important speeches in this period was the lengthy one he gave from the steps of the Jefferson County courthouse, just a few blocks from his Louisville home. In it he compared the two "antagonistic" national political parties, describing the Whigs as "devoted to power" and "based upon a distrust of the popular intelligence and integrity," and the Democrats as "devoted to the people" and characterized by "an abiding faith in the head and heart of the laboring masses of mankind, whose toil and spirit make up the world's wealth and glory." Holt went on to criticize three key programs the Whigs (and their National Republican predecessors) had supported: the establishment of the National Bank, the extension of an elaborate system of internal improvements, and the imposition of a high tariff, supposedly to protect domestic manufacturing. All such policies, Holt insisted, were in fact primarily designed to strengthen the central government at the expense of state and local authority.[69]

In contrast, Holt lifted up what he called "the Democratic doctrine" of "protection alike to every class, guarding if possible with anxious care, the *independence of all*" (though his "all," for now, did not include black people). Holt recalled with appreciation the Democratic Party's endorsement of the recent war with Mexico, as a result of which, he declared, "the national honor was vindicated; another proof was given of the capability of our institutions to abide the shock of arms; another refutation was afforded of that stale calumny of kings, that great standing armies are alike indispensable for purposes of national defense, and for the successful prosecution of foreign wars; an empire, in point of territory, was added to the Republic; the inexhaustible mines of California have been opened to American enterprise; and the foundations laid of a commerce, destined to gather into its lap, the gorgeous treasures of the Oriental world."

More generally, recalling his much-earlier castigation of Napoleon Bonaparte, Holt also used this speech as an opportunity to rail against tyranny, this time focusing specifically on the Russian czar as the "purest and most intense illustration of an Asiatic Despot to be found on this side of the Bosphorus." Holt further commended the "electric spark" of the popular counterrevolution on behalf of republican ideals that had been ignited in Paris in 1848 and had since "sped in lightning currents throughout the greater part of Europe." Robert Ward Johnson, who still hoped to persuade Holt to run for political office, was thrilled. "I have been all the morning on the street and I am glad to tell you there is but one opinion of your speech. All concur that it was the most statesmanlike & eloquent speech ever delivered in this city."[70]

In the weeks ahead, Holt's "courthouse steps" speech was published in pamphlet form and disseminated widely among his political allies and the Democratic Party's luminaries. Upon receiving his copy, circuit judge E. F. Nuttall gushed that Holt's words offered nothing less than a "beacon light, which makes plain and visible the landmarks which separate the two great political parties of this country," and he too now urged Holt to run for Congress. From New Orleans, John M. Chilton also acknowledged receipt of a copy of Holt's October speech, which he praised heartily for its "execrations of despotism" and it generous display of sympathy with "the oppressed people of Europe." Echoing Holt's own sentiments, which might also be read as opposition to the growing strength of both Southern nationalism *and* abolitionism, Chilton declared that "all must condemn" the "unlicensed use of the sword as a means of attaining power," and he pointed out that even now in America some people were "too prone to look at the government as like one of their log cabins, which they have a right to destroy at will because they aided in establishing it." Even Uncle Bob was pleased: "Your speech is thought by democrats to be the greatest one that was ever given," he wrote, adding, "if you could get into the senate soon, you would be next president or ought to be and I think will be."[71]

Surely none of the responses Holt received to his "courthouse steps" speech interested him more, however, or caused him to think more deeply, than the one his friend and former traveling companion, Howard Crosby, sent from New York. Like others, Crosby offered praise in abundance, to be sure. But he also added some challenges that arose from his political perspective as a committed Whig. Specifically, Crosby criticized Holt's characterization of the Democratic Party as the "party of the *people*" versus the Whigs as the "party of *power*." Both parties sought power, Crosby pointed out, not least the generally expansionist Democrats, many of whom had recently set their sights on the annexation of Cuba and, after that, Central America. "If Cuba is to be taken," Crosby reminded Holt, "it must be by *Power*." Crosby also questioned Holt's assumption that of the two parties, the Democrats were the one whose constituents detested tyranny more. Rather, he insisted, "are we not all alike, as children of a revolutionary ancestry, the born enemies of despotism? Would not you & I go shoulder to shoulder, to battle with fiendish oppression?" The key, in Crosby's view, was to resist the tendency of *all* political parties—or factions—to be either too conservative, and therefore stagnant, or too progressive, and therefore unrestrained and, potentially, explosive. Forced to choose between the two options, however, Crosby declared himself on the side of "palsy" rather than "gunpowder." But either tendency, he insisted, would be destructive to the Union if allowed to run its course.[72]

In the weeks and months ahead, Holt's resurgent party activism, combined with his regular interactions (and correspondence) with careful political thinkers such as Crosby, continued to broaden his perspective on issues ranging from slavery to republicanism to revolution. At the same time, however, his increasingly active engagement in the political sphere collided with a profoundly distressing development in his personal life: namely, the first signs of a decline in his wife Margaret's overall health, which inevitably recalled all the anguish of his first wife's slow collapse and premature death. To put it simply, Holt was emotionally ill prepared to deal with another severely ailing spouse. As a result, not long after the two had finally been united in their Louisville home, he dispatched a reluctant Margaret once again to her family in Bardstown, where he hoped that she would receive the sort of care and attention she needed and that he himself could not provide. And so, another long period of separation began during which Margaret routinely expressed her longing to be with her husband, and Holt responded with a combination of genuine love and anxiety for her well-being and a kind of guilty crankiness that arose from his awareness that the inevitable demands associated with attending to her illness (which seems, like Mary Harrison Holt's, to have been primarily pulmonary) conflicted with both his growing public responsibilities and his incapacity for enduring another crushing personal loss. "There are things in progress here which require my attention so that it would be quite inconvenient for me to go to Bardstown," Holt wrote rather testily in late April 1853. "I am so grieved," Margaret wrote to her still-absent husband in July, "to know you are still in Louisville. Why do you stay?"[73]

Although, as always, it is difficult to understand all the factors that contributed to Holt's readiness to keep the ailing Margaret at bay, it would be wrong to assume that he was simply callous and unconcerned about her condition. Indeed, as the months passed, Holt regularly shared his apprehensions about the future in dark letters to his family members. Aunt

Mary Ann in particular expressed alarm, not least because she knew how deeply Mary's death had affected him, and she feared the emotional consequences for her cherished nephew if Margaret should die, too. Holt, moreover, was hardly unmovable when it came to considering the conditions under which Margaret's health might take a turn for the better. In mid-July 1853, for example, he once again began to explore the possibility of leaving fever-plagued Louisville—and perhaps also Kentucky—altogether, in part because he suspected that Margaret would benefit from a different climate. Perhaps, he thought, they could even take up residence abroad. Family members on both sides opposed such a plan, however; Robert, for one, warned his brother to resist the temptation to pull up stakes and embark upon a nomadic life. Speaking from his own disappointing experience, Robert predicted that "if you carry out your plans, you [will] become a wanderer among strangers, an alien from country, kindred, and friends, and in age will not be able perhaps to find on the earth a spot which you can call home, or a circle to which you will be reunited by the ties of long association, of friendly offices, or early attachment."[74]

Indeed, having made very little progress professionally in Cincinnati and having failed to develop an appreciation for the people in Ohio generally, Robert had decided to move back to the South. "Social life here," he wrote, has "extremely little to commend it." Initially, Robert revisited the idea that the two brothers might open a law practice together—this time in Nashville—where he believed he would be able to raise his now five children "with industriousness, and country habits" and still be reasonably close to the extended Holt/Stephens clan. But Holt did not give the Nashville plan any serious consideration, turning his gaze instead toward bustling Washington, D.C., whose points of attraction no doubt included its absolute centrality to the political debates that he found so consuming. Additionally, although Washington was 600 miles from Bardstown, it was less than 50 miles from Frederick, Maryland, where Margaret's sister, Mary Wickliffe Merrick, and her family had their home. In order to explore what life and work in the nation's capital might be like, in the spring of 1854 Holt escorted Margaret to Frederick and then went on alone to Washington. "I arrived here safely on Saturday night," he wrote to Margaret on May 23, "& have since been occupied in visiting a few friends, & looking at the 'lions' of the city." As Holt well knew, Margaret had been to Washington before in conjunction with her father's long political career (she had been in her early twenties during Charles Wickliffe's stint as postmaster general). "You are so familiar with everything & every body here," Holt joked in one of his letters, "that I can say nothing in regard to them which would interest you."[75]

Although Holt probably anticipated that Margaret would join him in Washington eventually, for now he settled into a single room in a Pennsylvania Avenue boarding house whose other residents included eight congressmen: three from Missouri, two from Pennsylvania, two from Massachusetts, and one from Illinois. To his delight, Holt found his interactions with this assortment of men "most harmonious & agreeable," their varied backgrounds making for "quite a mélange in political sentiment," especially given the lively debates then taking place in Congress over Stephen Douglas's proposed Kansas-Nebraska Bill. Holt found Washington wonderfully stimulating, but he worried deeply about sectionalism's growing intensity, which was exacerbated further by such recent publications as Harriet Beecher Stowe's *Uncle Tom's Cabin* (1852) on the one hand, and George Fitzhugh's proslavery *Sociology for the South* (1854) on the other.[76]

For all the excitement it provided, Holt's visit to the capital did not convince him to move there permanently. Moreover, even as he explored Washington, Holt had begun to contemplate a different move all together: across country to California, whose overall climate was known to be mild, and where a man of skill seemed likely to be able to make a fortune. He was becoming concerned about their financial situation: for a decade, first Holt and Mary, then Holt alone, and now Holt and Margaret had essentially been living off of his once-abundant savings and investments. These days, however, the expenses associated with the demands of his and Margaret's social and political position, keeping up the Louisville mansion and its slave staff, and responding to Margaret's health and other needs, not to mention regular travel back and forth between Louisville and Bardstown, were putting serious pressure on their budget. As such, Holt found the whole idea of a move to the promising West Coast appealing, but he knew that Margaret would be hard pressed to agree to it, especially once she learned that he was thinking of heading west first *without* her. "I am satisfied," he wrote as persuasively as he could, "that if you would allow me to carry out this scheme, I could return to you in two years with an income which would relieve us from all anxiety for the future." As it turns out, Margaret was horrified by Holt's proposition, and she told him in no uncertain terms that she was deeply hurt to learn that he would even entertain the thought of being separated from her for two whole years, and by such a distance, especially when her physical condition could worsen significantly at any moment. Margaret was troubled, too, that Holt considered their current income, derived from a combination of sources that no doubt included Wickliffe family money too, insufficient to support their small household. For this, however, she blamed herself, and she promised that she would learn to live within their means. "Just try me dear husband, once more," she implored.[77]

Holt certainly regretted having sprung the California idea on Margaret so suddenly, though he was also disappointed that she had felt bound to reprimand him so severely, and he did not give up on the idea easily. By mid-August 1854, he was back in Louisville alone, trying to sell their elegant home. No doubt Margaret's limited stays at the house and his own increasingly peripatetic schedule had sharply diminished his interest in maintaining the place, with all of its associated expenses. Selling the beautiful mansion with its magnificently landscaped property was not that easy, however, and in early September, Holt decided to rent it out instead. "This is the worst arrangement that could be made," he complained to Margaret unhappily, "except that of letting the place remain unsold & unoccupied." Meanwhile, Margaret stayed with her sister Mary's family in Frederick, leaving Holt to figure out what to do about their furnishings as well as the enslaved human beings they still owned. Holt briefly contemplated purchasing a new home in the Kentucky countryside, which he thought Margaret might find more restful and beneficial to her health than Louisville had been. But Margaret showed little interest in this idea, either, and it faded away.[78]

At least once during this period, Holt traveled from Louisville to Wickland to consult with his father-in-law on matters both political and personal. He also made a trip to see his own family in Stephensport. There, in the lovely home that he had helped to build for them, and to the extent that his reticent personality permitted, Holt gloomily shared with his mother, Eleanor (now in her early seventies), his uncles Bob and Daniel, his beloved Aunt Mary Ann, and his brother Thomas his concerns about Margaret's progressing illness, their household finances, his own and others' expectations for his professional and political future, and the nation's growing political crisis. Seeing him again, Aunt Mary Ann in particular worried about her nephew's low spirits. "He appears so very lonely without you," she wrote anxiously to Margaret, describing how she often caught him sitting quietly "with his head down for one half an hour at a time," biting his nails and looking utterly miserable. According to Mary Ann, Holt only perked up when he talked about Margaret. And indeed, having learned that simply talking about Margaret improved his mood, Mary Ann now made a point of steering her conversations with him in that direction. "Since I found out what strings to touch," she noted, "I only have to mention you & that keeps him smiling & cheerfull," for "he likes to talk all the time of you."[79]

Even as he sought refuge at the family homestead from his concerns about Margaret's health and about how (or whether) to resume a cash-producing professional life for himself (and where?), public demand for Holt's input on national political affairs persisted, not least in the form of countless invitations to speak to the Democratic Party faithful. In early September 1855, Holt gave one of his most important speeches to date, at a dinner in Louisville in honor of Kentucky's former governor, Democrat Lazarus W. Powell. Holt's speech came on the heels of a local riot that had taken place a month earlier, in which twenty-two people were killed, many more were injured, more than twenty houses were burned, and a great deal of other property was destroyed. "The riot," the historian W. H. Perrin observed, "was precipitated by the rough element of the Know-nothing party," an explicitly anti-immigrant, anti-Catholic political organization, some of whose members, "occasioned by distorted reports that the Catholic people meditated serious disturbances" during the state's August elections, had gone on the attack. The riot continued for several hours, leading not a few citizens—Holt among them—to fear that the entire city would be destroyed. Fortunately, in the end, the concerted efforts of local law enforcement and government officials as well as influential citizens such as Holt had prevented a complete catastrophe.[80]

The 1855 Louisville riot greatly discredited the Know-Nothings in Kentucky, in no small part thanks to outspoken critics such as Holt, who, not surprisingly, found the radical organization's recent electoral successes unnerving. In his September speech, Holt vigorously endorsed the principle of religious liberty, which he considered a fundamental American ideal, one of the most precious legacies of the Revolutionary era, and one of the centerpieces of American republican freedom. On the point of religious tolerance Holt declared himself as uncompromising as he was on the point of national union. "I yield to no man," he thundered, "in horror of that remorseless crusade against all political and religious freedom." The Know-Nothings, he insisted, were dangerous fanatics whose goal, like that of religious bigots throughout history, was the "most treasonable attempt to break down the right of every man to worship as he pleases." In Holt's mind, the Know-Nothings and their counterparts elsewhere had "already convulsed society to its foundations," sowing seed "fruitful of a crop of hissing serpent tongues." Now they threatened to turn "this beautiful earth" into a "smoking hell." Holt scorned the Know-Nothings' secretiveness (the source of their nickname), which he called their "badge of fraud and crime." And he urged recent and would-be immigrants to America not to be discouraged. "This is still the asylum of the oppressed," Holt proclaimed, "and its doors cannot be closed by those who walk with postern lights," for "that glorious tree of liberty, planted in this broad western world, still flourishes, its leaves for the healing of nations, its shade for the weary, its golden fruit for the famishing of all climes and races." No one, Holt declared, should be permitted to "obscure the radiance from our free institutions," which provided so much "cheer and comfort to those in the dark homes of oppression and misrule abroad."[81]

In the months after Holt gave his compelling and well-received speech in Louisville, Democratic activists gearing up for the 1856 presidential campaign called upon him to do more. In addition, about a month before the Democratic National Convention was scheduled to take place in Cincinnati, at least one friend tried secretly to draft Holt as a presidential candidate without consulting him first. Wrote W. M. Corry on May 1, 1856, "here is my letter to Mr. [Pierre] Soulé," the former Democratic U.S. senator from Louisiana and a delegate to the convention, "proposing you for the Presidency." Warning Holt not to interfere in the draft effort, Corry requested copies of his most powerful speeches over the years. He also encouraged Holt to come to Cincinnati in advance of the convention to consult, noting, somewhat paradoxically given what was to come, that he had been "trying for some time to induce Edwin M. Stanton of Pittsburg[h], another great friend of mine, and lawyer, to run for the Presidency with you for Vice P." Stanton, however, had declined, and now Corry was counting on Holt. "I believe you could do it," he wrote, "unless you have said or done something both violent and notorious *pro-Nebraska*," by which he referred to the notorious 1854 Kansas-Nebraska Act endorsing "popular sovereignty" in the territories, and the bloody guerrilla war it had produced. Aware of Holt's longstanding refusal to pursue elective office, Corry anticipated that his friend might be "disturbed, and perhaps indignant" with him for having suggested the idea. He was right to worry: Holt would have none of it, and by the time the party's convention was winding down, Corry was reduced to accepting the nomination of James Buchanan of Pennsylvania instead, although he was pessimistic about Buchanan's chances, both as a candidate and as president. Buchanan, Corry wrote prophetically, "is a gentleman and a statesman, but 'he is old and weak.' . . . What hands he may fall into, I don't know."[82]

By fall 1856, the presidential campaign was well underway, as was the collapse of the flash-in-the-pan Know-Nothings, along with the sudden and impressive debut of the new, explicitly antislavery Republican Party, a conglomeration of defectors from the Know-Nothings, the now-defunct Whigs, the Free Soilers, and even some former Democrats. Proslavery advocates were stunned by what they perceived to be, as one of Holt's correspondents put it in September, the "Black Republican horde who, like Goths & Vandals, are threatening the overthrow of the constitution & the Union." This correspondent urged Holt to go to Pennsylvania, where the Republicans planned to hold their first national convention, and deploy his "great talents and incomparable eloquence" against them. To do so, he insisted, would "give you an immortality of fame," especially in the eyes of the defenders of slavery.[83]

Holt did not travel to Pennsylvania, but he did give pro-Buchanan speeches across Kentucky and in Chicago, Milwaukee, and even, to an audience of about 15,000, in Frederick, Maryland, where Margaret, to all intents and purposes, had taken up permanent residence with her sister's family, the Merricks. In his speech at Frederick, Holt once again roundly criticized the nativist, anti-Catholic Know-Nothings for their radical intolerance. "Discussion, excitement, agitation," Holt declared, "these are a part of the price you pay, and which all must pay for liberty." But extremism such as that promoted by the Know-Nothings constituted a threat to liberty—and the Union—that must be overcome in order for the republic to survive. On this occasion Holt also spoke out harshly against the strident foes of slavery, like others, conflating Garrison's abolitionists with the new Republican Party as the "Black Republicans." For all of his long-standing and growing ambivalence about slavery, Holt still perceived the ardent promotion of immediate emancipation—which many assumed to be the centerpiece of the Republicans' agenda—as just one more version of something even worse than the "peculiar institution" itself: namely, the sort of political extremism that would ultimately destroy the republic. The "Black Republicans," he thundered, seemed to consider the emancipation of a "handful of slaves" more important than the long-term survival of the nation, and as such, not unlike the Know-Nothings (or, for that matter, the increasingly aggressive Southern nationalists), they needed to be stopped. Only then could the nation itself be spared the violence that extremists of every sort were striving to provoke. Holt's speech at Frederick quickly became widely available in pamphlet form, and among those who expressed their gratitude was the future governor of Kentucky, Beriah Magoffin, who predicted that Holt's labors would surely produce nothing less than "the happiest results" for the country.[84]

Fully aware of the momentousness of the times, in early October 1856,

Holt gave another major speech in Louisville, which, he later informed Margaret, lasted two and a half hours, "much longer," he quipped, "than was prudent or kind to the audience." All of this speech making caused Margaret to worry that Holt was putting his own health in danger. "I pray you my beloved husband," she wrote, "not to speak again this fall! How can you think of it when you already feel its consequences? These speeches are too long & too exciting. I believe a gentle effort now & then might be beneficial, but speeches of two & three hours must be *exceedingly* injurious." But the stubborn Holt did not yield. In mid-October he informed her that he had not only given another speech in Louisville a few nights earlier, but that he had also agreed to give one in Elizabethtown on October 27 in conjunction with a "FREE Democratic Barbecue!" Holt offered his anxious wife only the most half-hearted of reassurances, which he then undermined by telling her that his most recent speech had in fact been so vigorous that "I found my clothes almost as wet as if I had been plunged in the river," and that he had contracted a cold as a result.[85]

James Buchanan's election to the presidency in November pleased Holt and also brought him a new measure of resolve: he would collect his delicate wife from Frederick and together they would move to Washington after all. Then, should the offer come, he would accept an appointment in the new president's administration. "I should have much preferred seeing you locate in the southwest," wrote his disappointed brother Robert in December, from his own new home in Yazoo City, Mississippi. At the same time, Robert encouraged Holt — now forty-nine — not to wait too long before resuming his private legal practice, even if he had to do so in the nation's capital. To remain in "retirement," Robert believed, even in the nation's capital, simply was not healthy. "Open an office at once and publish your card in the papers of Louisville, New Orleans, Jackson, Vicksburg, and Natchez," he wrote, "and you will very soon get a good business in the Supreme Court and in the Court of Claims." Back in Kentucky, still others were hardly keen on the Holts moving east permanently. "I regret," wrote his first wife's aunt, Sarah Harrison, "that Kentucky is to be no longer your home." Still, she hoped that Holt and Margaret would "find the change a pleasant one," and she gratefully accepted his offer to send her a picture of her late niece that Holt had uncovered while packing his and Margaret's belongings in preparation for their departure.[86]

3

SERVING BUCHANAN,
SERVING THE NATION,
1857–1860

Amid the harsh & discordant cries with which at times the country has been pained, the music of the Union in any of its variations, like those songs which come to us burdened with the memories of youth & hope, falls meltingly & with the spell & force of love upon our ears.
—Joseph Holt, June 1860

Although he had contemplated a move for some time, in early 1857 Holt was hardly without ambivalence about leaving Kentucky behind, most likely for good. In April, he wrote to Margaret, who had felt strong enough in recent weeks to make a visit to her family in Wickland, of his own recent trip to Stephensport. There, he remarked, the old homestead, the place he claimed to have loved "above all others upon the earth," had "never seemed so beautiful." Indeed, it was not just the land or the magnificent house that tugged at his heartstrings, either; Holt found himself reluctant, too, to part with the various members of his birth family who remained there, and even the slaves, some of whom had been in his family's possession for many years. It was in saying goodbye to them, Holt confessed, that he realized for the very first time that the last link connecting him to his birthplace had finally been broken, and that, "henceforth, I shall be but a stranger there."[1]

Margaret, too, had serious doubts about the move, and she clung to the idea that someday she and Holt would return to Kentucky to live. After three years spent mostly with her sister Mary's family in Maryland, she was homesick. Still, she looked forward to being situated permanently near sisters Nannie and Mary, both of whom now maintained residences in the nation's capital in connection with their husbands' professional responsibilities, David Yulee as a senator from Florida and William Merrick as a district court judge. Margaret looked forward, too, to spending more time with her husband, who by the late spring had selected for their residence a large house at 236 New Jersey Avenue, near Capitol Hill. Margaret followed Holt in the fall, no doubt making good use in the interim of the money he had forwarded to enable her to make a number of purchases on her way east. "Enjoy yourself as much as you can," he wrote from Washington. "There is no occasion for hurry in your return as I believe everything is going on smoothly here."[2]

Ironically, the $200 that Holt had sent Margaret in advance of her journey east proved to be the last draft on his bank that Holt was able to make for some time. Although the nation had been experiencing an economic downturn for several months, the August collapse of the New York branch of the Ohio Life Insurance and Trust Company, which was followed by the failure of a great number of other banks across the country, sent the economy tumbling into what came to be known as the Panic of 1857. "Within an hour after I drew the money from the Bank of Washington," Holt wrote to Margaret, "it suspended [operations], as I presume all the banks in the Union will do." Holt was pessimistic about what lay ahead for the couple financially; indeed, he expected nothing less than "a great calamity" for the country as a whole, and anticipated that he and Margaret would have to suffer right along with everyone else. Still, he was thankful to have been able to lay his hands on any cash at all before the Bank of Washington suspended business. "The providence of life," he wrote, "is truly mysterious."[3]

Margaret was not the only person with whom Holt shared his financial concerns; he also discussed them with his old friend and colleague James O. Harrison, who urged his proud friend to be prepared to accept help should he find he needed it. "I hope," Harrison wrote, that "you will without the slightest reserve call upon me." Generous words like these surely brought some relief. Additionally, by the time Margaret arrived, Holt had a further source of consolation: he had recently accepted a paid position in the Buchanan administration—as commissioner of patents—which, although not a position he had originally sought, might now, as he put it to Margaret, "prove the only plank left to us in the wreck." Holt hoped that his salary, along with the rent they were receiving on the mansion in Louisville and their other miscellaneous income, would prove sufficient until the economy, and their fortunes, rebounded. "Let us not be discouraged," he wrote. Perhaps, he speculated, after he spent a short time in the Patent Office they would have enough money to enable them to move again, either to the South or the West where, as a lawyer, he was certain that he could make a good enough living "for us & our little household." For the time being, however, the two would just have to live within a tighter budget, and with luck and "rigid economy in our living," they would

James Buchanan. Courtesy of the Library of Congress.

weather the crisis. Apologizing to Margaret for what he termed "this most embarrassing predicament," Holt nevertheless reminded her, "it is the fate of uncounted thousands around us."[4]

As head of the U. S. Patent Office, which was created in 1802, Holt came under the supervision of the secretary of the interior, then Jacob Thompson of Mississippi, with whom he had become acquainted during his years in Vicksburg when Thompson was serving as one of Mississippi's representatives in the U.S. Congress. According to historian Kenneth W. Dobyns, the very idea of granting patents in the first place arose from Congress's desire to give "encouragement to the introduction of new and useful inventions . . . as well as the exertion of skill and genius in producing them." Its significance for the government's promotion of citizens' enterprise and innovation, and for the fair and judicious protection of their intellectual property (and the nation's), cannot be overstated. The job of the commissioner was to oversee the issuing of patents and the registration of trademarks, and in the first hundred years, the Patent Office approved approximately 450,000 applications. Holt's immediate predecessor in the post was Charles Mason, who had graduated from West Point in 1829, the same year as Robert E. Lee. Considered one of the office's most effective commissioners, Mason was also noted for having hired Clara Barton in 1854 as his "confidential clerk," and for paying her $1,400 per year, thus making her "the first woman ever to be hired to a regular position in the U.S. government with work and wages equal to that of a man."[5]

When he accepted his first political appointment since being named commonwealth's attorney for Kentucky's Jefferson County two decades earlier, Holt was hardly certain that he would enjoy any professional satisfaction from the job. Others, however, were simply delighted with the news. The Patent Office, declared the *Charleston Mercury* enthusiastically on September 11, 1857, was positively "rejoiced" by the appointment of Holt, whom it described as "a man of great energy and ability." Similarly, the *New Albany (Ind.) Daily Ledger* of September 23 commented that Holt, who had "long enjoyed the reputation of being one of the most earnest, efficient, and eloquent supporters of the Democratic Party," was a superb choice for the post, to which he would bring abundant energy, brains, and talent. The *New York Times* was equally upbeat, insisting that the Patent Office position "demanded perfect integrity of character, added to practical sense and a good knowledge of the law." The *Times* predicted that "whatever may be the future developments of the administration of the Patent Office, it may be set down as a fixed truth that no public or private wrong was ever perpetrated with the knowledge of the Commissioner, while Mr. Holt was at the head of its management."[6]

For his part, Uncle Bob considered the post of Patent Office commissioner less appropriate for his accomplished nephew than the position of secretary of state or some other diplomatic assignment abroad would have been. Still, he offered his congratulations, as did various members of Margaret's extended family including Judge Merrick, who received the news while he and Mary were visiting Wickland. "All of the household were rejoiced," Merrick reported, and he expressed every confidence in Holt's ability to fill the commissioner's post effectively. "It seems fitting," he wrote, "that the man of genius should place the authoritative seal of approbation upon the fruits of the genius of his countrymen." Like Uncle Bob, Margaret's father experienced some initial reservations about the appointment, having "looked upon the patent office," as he explained to his son-in-law, "as it was when I was in congress once, not as it is now grown into importance." Charles Wickliffe quickly set his reservations aside, however, when it became clear that Holt's new job was "one of labour and demanding intellect."[7]

Thanks to his conscientiousness, efficiency, diligence, and intelligence, Holt excelled in his new work. He spent a portion of his time communicating with inventors from all over the country, including individuals such as Thomas Prosser of New York, who invented the "surface condenser," a device of great value to the navy because it made possible, while at sea, the high pressure—but safe—condensation of steam into distilled water for subsequent use in a ship's engines (Holt approved Prosser's application). Among the most important cases Holt dealt with as commissioner, and one that had a substantial and long-term impact on the future of American industrialization, was that of Charles Goodyear. In the spring of 1858, Goodyear had initiated a correspondence with Holt regarding his patent for vulcanized rubber, whose extension was being challenged in a British court by an English inventor who claimed to have discovered the process first. Holt carefully examined all of the documents Goodyear sent him, and in the end he sided with the American inventor and extended his patent for another seven years, insisting that "no inventor probably has ever been so harassed, so trampled upon, so plundered by that sordid and licentious class of infringers known in the parlance of the world . . . as 'pirates.'" In January 1859, Goodyear thanked Holt for his support, noting that in the outcome of his case, "I had great cause of gratitude both to God" and to Holt, who had made it clear that he "could not be swerved by any other influence than that of a sense of justice."[8]

Holt oversaw the processing of an immense number of patent applications, and in doing so was responsible each year for thousands of decisions that had lasting implications for the nation's scientific and creative progress. Indeed, upon receiving his copy of the Patent Office's 1857 annual report, which Holt, as commissioner, composed, Uncle Daniel reiterated the old family concern that the heavy burdens of the job would lead Holt to neglect his health, as his tendency to overwork had done in the past. In 1857 alone Holt's office received almost 4,800 patent applications, of which it approved over 2,900, some 400 more than the office had approved the previous year. Most of the patents went to American citizens (855 of them to New Yorkers), but about 40 went to foreign nationals. "Jo," wrote Daniel, "I never had any idea of the office you fill untill a few days ago. . . . How do you stand the labour and mental fatigue?"[9]

Even more striking than the sheer number of applications Holt's office handled, however, was the deep appreciation that he routinely conveyed for what he considered a uniquely American kind of ingenuity and its fruits. For his part, Holt associated the nation's "inventive genius" with no single group of citizens; rather, he gave credit broadly to what one might call the American "democracy of the mind," a sort of generalized creativity he was certain would never become manifest in the more tradition-bound parts of the world he had encountered in his travels. In America, however, Holt believed that what he called "the national intellect" was free, having been "emancipated from the shackles of the past." Holt was particularly impressed by the innovative spirit and accomplishments of individuals who focused their attention on the modernization of agriculture, which he considered essential to America's future welfare, security, and greatness. In this as in other areas, he favored those practical inventions that were designed to yield "the largest amount of the elements of human comfort, with the least possible expenditure of human labor." Such inventions, he insisted, moved civilization forward, decreasing the "pressure of that ceaseless toil" that historically had burdened most human beings. Only by diminishing the amount of physical labor humans were required to expend for their survival, he was certain, could civilization hope to advance toward the "noonday splendors" of cultural attainment. "We have scarcely crossed the threshold of the temple of human knowledge," Holt wrote in his 1857 report; "we have gathered as yet but a few pebbles and shells on the shore of that ocean of truth, whose depths still lie unexplored before us." It is unclear just how slavery as an institution fit into the model of advanced civilization Holt envisioned at this point in time, but it is noteworthy that he accepted and approved patent applications not just from free persons but also from slaves.[10]

In addition to the hours he spent corresponding with inventors and overseeing patent applications, Holt occasionally answered questions from individuals who had an interest, for one reason or another, in patent law. By necessity, he also devoted considerable energy to dealing with eager lobbyists, many of whom hoped to cash in on the potential profitability of the nation's intellectual property, over which Holt and his office now had so much influence. As tiresome as Holt found these petitioners, he quickly developed a reputation for handling them with fairness and discernment, as he did the many requests he received from individuals seeking his help in getting government appointments. As Patent Office commissioner, Holt did not have a vast amount of patronage power, but what he had he exercised as judiciously and incorruptibly as the power he exerted over the patent system itself. When he felt it was appropriate to help, he did so. When he felt he could not support a request in good conscience—even if the request came from a family member—he turned it down, as he did soon after accepting the post when he informed Margaret that her brother-in-law, Elias Yulee (Senator Yulee's brother), was not eligible for the Patent Office clerkship he had requested as long as his son also held a clerkship in the same department. "The President," Holt explained, "has declared war against nepotism," and as commissioner, Holt was determined to enforce the ban even—or perhaps especially—if it meant turning down a request from someone to whom he himself was related by blood or marriage.[11]

Of course, many of the requests Holt received for jobs were legitimate, including those that came from self-supporting women who were aware that Clara Barton had broken new ground for them when Commissioner Mason hired her in 1854. Holt was pleased to employ a number of these women, primarily as copyists. "I cannot sufficiently thank you," wrote Katie Eldred in August 1858, after learning that Holt had found her some work to do, "for your noble and generous kindness." Holt hired Lucy West, too, who in October 1858 thanked him, and then asked for as much more copy work as he could possibly find for her to do. A widowed mother, West promised not to nag Holt relentlessly, but she urged him to heed how quickly she had completed her first assignment, believing as she did that "promptness in execution tells most earnestly of my need for the means to provide for *my Fatherless Boys*."[12]

Demanding and time consuming as it was, Holt's post as commissioner of patents was hardly without its worldly rewards. For one thing, as much as her delicate health and his reserved and private nature permitted, Holt and Margaret now moved in more elevated social circles than they ever had before as a couple, including being invited on occasion to dine with the president himself, with whom Holt now consulted directly on a regular basis. Other prominent residents of the capital also regularly sought the Holts' company, including Margaret's sisters' families, the Yulees and the Merricks. On April 21, 1858, the *New York Herald* described a recent soirée at the Merricks' as nothing less than "the most *recherché* and brilliant of the season" which, in the end, drew "the *crème de la crème* of the society of Washington." On this particular occasion, Margaret and her sisters clearly

made a powerfully favorable impression: the *Herald*'s correspondent described them as "certainly the most peerless women for beauty, elegance,
and every accomplishment, including that of household affairs (so rare to
be found these days), that grace our republic."[13]

Holt's expanding correspondence from this period also reflected how
high his star had risen: in addition to memos beckoning him to the president's office and to his dinner table, Holt's mail now included letters from
an increasing number of other famous Americans, both within and outside
the political realm. Predictably, too, Holt's growing prominence brought
strangers out of the woodwork who sought to link themselves to him by
blood. Such was the case with one E. A. Holt of Montgomery, Alabama,
who in January 1858 claimed that his father and Holt's father were cousins,
although there is no other evidence to support this assertion. Holt's fame
also brought numerous requests for his autograph, such as the one he received in May 1858 from fourteen-year-old Joel B. Wilson, who promised to
repay the favor "with tenfold interest" should he ever have the opportunity
to do so.[14]

Meanwhile, despite his growing fame, his extremely busy professional
and social life, and the hundreds of miles that separated them, Holt maintained his affectionate bond with his family members back home. Having
lived long enough to witness his nephew's ascent to one of the lesser
halls of federal power, Uncle Bob died in the summer of 1858 at the age of
seventy-two, but Uncle Daniel lived on, writing letters that expressed his
political sentiments, most pressingly on the question of how to resolve
the growing differences between slavery's advocates and its critics. For his
part, by early 1858 Daniel anticipated the complete disintegration of the
Democratic Party along sectional lines, and he criticized longtime party
favorite Stephen Douglas of Illinois for giving the appearance of having
become a dread "Black Republican." In contrast, Holt's sister, Elizabeth,
kept the attention in her letters on family affairs, on the love she hoped
would always endure between Holt and herself, and on her desire that her
brother and his wife would come to Kentucky soon for a visit.[15]

Although Holt did his best to correspond regularly with his distant
family and friends, however, his work at the Patent Office was consuming
and stressful, and visits to Kentucky were out of the question for the time
being. Indeed, the extreme seriousness, conscientiousness, and competence with which Holt approached his responsibilities as commissioner
seem to have created some friction between him and Secretary of the Interior Thompson, who by the end of 1858 had apparently begun to feel
somewhat overshadowed by Holt and eager to bring the dedicated com-

Jacob Thompson. Courtesy of the Library of Congress.

missioner more decisively under his own political control. "We were justly indignant at the proposition of the Sec of Interior," wrote Nannie Yulee to Margaret in late December, "that the Commissioner should report to him instead of Congress." Poor Thompson, joked Nannie, "wasn't he small enough before, that he must seek to bring himself in such unenviable contrast with a man of Mr. Holt's talents[?]"[16] For the duration of Holt's time in the Patent Office, despite the additional wedge between them of Thompson's growing commitment to radical Southern nationalism, he and the secretary of the interior managed to keep their differences from erupting into full-scale conflict. But the strains that became evident between the two of them in this period were never completely relieved, and they grew dramatically worse in the years to come.

Holt received high marks for his service to the federal government and the nation during his time at the Patent Office, a period that coincided with a number of important transformations in his own life. Holt's acceptance of the commissionership, after all, had brought him back from retirement as a lawyer and had thrust him into an extremely demanding public-service role during a profoundly, and increasingly, disorderly time in the nation's history. The Patent Office post and Holt's residence in the nation's capital also enhanced the connection in his mind (and in others' as well) between his own values and interests and those of the federal government, the nation, and the Union. Additionally, Holt's accomplishments as commissioner generated a much wider recognition than he had ever before experienced of his immense intellectual and legal talents, his apparently unshakable professional integrity, and his commitment to fairness and justice, even if they came at the expense of pleasing those to whom he was personally close. Holt's time in the Patent Office further guaranteed that for many years to come his name would be included on almost any short list for important federal government appointments, at least so long as Democrats were controlling the selection process.

It must also be noted that, although he had gone on record at least once condemning abolitionists and "Black Republicans" as vigorously as he did any political extremists who threatened the nation or its fundamental principles, Holt's first two years in Washington only intensified his long-standing ambivalence about slavery as an institution. While the Holts were still in Kentucky, Margaret's frequent absences, Holt's own wanderings in connection with both her illness and his resurgent political activism, and ultimately their decision to rent out their Louisville mansion, had meant that they regularly dispatched at least some of their human property to Wickland or Stephensport, where the slaves presumably could be of greater use. Still, the Holts had not emancipated their slaves, and indeed, as late as the end of 1853 Holt himself was sufficiently committed to protecting the capital he and Margaret had wrapped up in human beings to take out insurance on a slave named Sandy, then in his early twenties.[17]

Nevertheless, by the time the couple relocated to the nation's capital, where slavery remained legal until 1862, Holt's ambivalence about the institution had grown considerably stronger, and he now sought to convince Margaret of the benefits of hiring rather than owning servants. When their slave John made it clear that he was not happy about the prospect of moving to Washington, most likely because he had family of his own back in Kentucky, Holt suggested that attempting to force him to move with them to Washington would be counterproductive, "rendering him discontented & useless." Why not just employ someone, perhaps for as little as twelve dollars a month, who could fulfill John's traditional responsibilities in the dining room? In a separate letter, Holt recommended, too, that the slave Annie and her son William be allowed to remain together at Wickland, which had been their home since 1854 anyway, although Charles Wickliffe had wanted his daughter to have Annie with her in Washington. Similarly, once Holt learned that the slave named Jane had expressed resistance to being separated from her young son if she traveled with the Holts to Washington and her son stayed behind in Kentucky, Holt urged Margaret to honor Jane's wishes and keep mother and son together while sparing them the disruption of a move. Unfortunately, subsequent letters indicate that Margaret refused Jane's request to remain in Kentucky, though it is not clear whether Jane's son came with her to Washington or stayed behind.[18]

Holt's steps toward divesting himself of his and Margaret's slaves were slow, clumsy, and by no means always high-minded. Nevertheless, they stand in sharp contrast to Margaret's apparent disinterest in the question, and to his brother Robert's movements in the opposite direction entirely. As the 1850s waned, Robert had abandoned any respect for free labor that he had ever held and, like most other white Southern slaveholders, was becoming ever more passionately committed to slavery as a "way of life" for his family and for the South generally. By March 1858 he was even recommending that Holt and Margaret leave Washington, move south, and buy themselves a cotton plantation as he and his family had done. In Robert's mind, the Southern planter class increasingly represented not only wealth but also "the finest specimens of the true American type of gentleman and ladies to be found in the Union," and he insisted that as a planter his brother would become wildly rich and would soon come to "enjoy the life which you would lead as much as you now think you would dislike it." Of course, being a planter, especially a small-scale one, did not actually guarantee prosperity. As always, even as a slaveholder Robert himself continued to find it difficult to pay his bills, and he leaned on Holt to make up the difference, at one point asking for a loan of $6,000 to help him consolidate his credit.[19]

Robert Holt was hardly the only person facing gloomy prospects as the 1850s stumbled to a close; the nation as a whole was, too, and not just because of the enduring effects of the Panic of 1857. Since the Holts had moved to Washington, the Supreme Court had handed down its immensely controversial decision in the *Dred Scott* case, overturning the Missouri Compromise—which had stood, since 1820, as a protection against slavery's expansion north of the Mason-Dixon Line—and declaring persons of African descent in America ineligible for citizenship. In addition, the situation in Kansas, which had suffered through two years of brutal guerrilla warfare over the question of its future as a slave or a free state, remained unresolved, President Buchanan having endorsed the deeply contested proslavery Lecompton Constitution for the territory, which pleased slaveholding Democrats like Uncle Daniel but infuriated just about everyone else. In Congress, the seat belonging to the abolitionist Massachusetts senator, Charles Sumner, stood vacant, a silent witness to his being beaten almost to death by an enraged, cane-wielding congressman from South Carolina named Preston Brooks, who resented Sumner's vigorous attacks on slavery. Minnesota had entered the Union, tipping the balance even further in Congress (now seventeen to fifteen) in favor of the free states, and strengthening some Southerners' calls for the formation of an independent nation. And a formerly little-known antislavery Republican by the name of Abraham Lincoln had dared to challenge the powerful Stephen Douglas (known by many as the "Little Giant") for his seat in the U.S. Senate. Lincoln lost the 1858 Senate race, but he won wide public attention, both favorable and hostile, as a result of his willingness to take a bold stand against slavery's further expansion in the two candidates' widely publicized debates that year.[20]

Like so many other Americans, as the year 1859 dawned, fifty-two-year-old Holt feared for the nation's future. The times, wrote his old friend James O. Harrison in January, "are sadly out of joint," and extremists in all forms were to blame. For Harrison as for Holt, the nation's survival now depended on the emergence of people of honesty and integrity to save it, though he could not imagine where such people could possibly be found in sufficient number. "Honesty now," Harrison wrote, "seems rather to be a relic—a sort of topic of a past age—than an active element in the present," and "a general wreck" of the nation was certain "unless Providence shall interpose to prevent it." But, Harrison asked, "what claim have we as a People on his protection? We have trampled on his best blessing & put in danger the fairest heritage the sun ever shone on."[21]

In Holt's mind, many of the nation's problems could be traced to the chaos that seemed to have overtaken the federal legislature, not least its members from the slaveholding South. "I regret the non-organization of Congress," Harrison agreed, "& the bravado & spirit which Southern members so often display." Such behavior, he insisted, "does harm [in] every way. It makes the member ridiculous, offends the North unnecessarily & weakens the moral force of the South." Harrison, for his part, was certain that the American people were "out of patience with all these wranglers," who "scout the idea that any two or three hundred men can break up the union." In the face of such a threat, however, he predicted that Kentucky would remain fast for the Union, seceding only if and when "she sees & feels that there is no safety in it." Indeed, he refused to accept that even the possible election of a "Black Republican" to the presidency the following year (he was probably thinking of the fiercely antislavery Republican from New York, William H. Seward) could be considered a good reason to dissolve the Union. "If the Devil himself" were to be elected president, Harrison declared, "I would stand by the union until he should begin to play the *Devil*." In the meantime, he took consolation from the fact that a man such as Holt could still be found, calmly and honorably attending to the nation's business amidst the growing storm. "It is something," Harrison wrote, "in a corrupt age to keep one's self right &, if ruin must come, to be able to shew that we did what we could to prevent it. You have done that wisely & firmly."[22]

As anxious as he was about national affairs and the long-term survival of the Union, Holt was also deeply worried about Margaret, who was once again staying with her sister Mary in Frederick and whose overall health continued to decline. Holt visited Margaret as often as he felt he could, given his hectic schedule at the Patent Office. Still, as had been true throughout their marriage and in his earlier marriage to Mary, too, Holt struggled to find a good balance between his own needs for work and solitude and his desire to demonstrate his sincere devotion to Margaret and to care for her adequately. At the same time, as busy as he was in the capital, and as much as he genuinely loved Margaret, there is also evidence to suggest that once again during this difficult period, Holt was finding himself drawn in by another woman's claims on his attention. As had been the case with Anastasie several years earlier, this unidentified but obviously important woman friend—who signed her letters "Amalie"—wrote to Holt frequently, and again, always in French. Amalie, who seems to have been considerably younger than Holt, may well have originally been one of the many women he hired to do clerical labor at the Patent Office. But by the time they were corresponding regularly, she wrote from New York, her letters expressing her deep dependence on his emotional support as well as his material assistance and help finding work. Holt and Amalie corresponded for several months; they may also have met occasionally, either in New York or Washington. Although it does not seem that their relationship included any physical intimacy, there was for a time a powerful emotional bond between them that cannot be denied.[23]

By early 1859, Margaret's condition had worsened considerably, prompting Holt to consult a physician in Frederick and to divulge his unease in letters to family and friends, including Rev. H. H. Kavanaugh, who thirteen years earlier had performed Mary Harrison Holt's funeral. Meanwhile, their extended separation, their shared fear that she would never be well again, and perhaps also Margaret's suspicions that Holt was turning elsewhere for emotional intimacy continued to wear on them both. Over and over Holt tried to reassure Margaret of his love and constancy: "There is no interest or duty or association here that can for one moment direct my love & sympathies & solicitude from your dear self," he wrote on one occasion. But he still found it difficult to make time to be with her in person, and one can certainly understand Margaret's loneliness and frustration as she battled a consuming illness without the comfort of his presence or the security of knowing that she alone had a claim on his heart. Things were about to get worse, too, for the professional demands that had been devouring so much of Holt's time, attention, and energy were about to multiply. On March 8, 1859, Buchanan's postmaster general, Aaron V. Brown, died unexpectedly. Within the week, the president, who had been so pleased with Holt's excellent management of the Patent Office, officially appointed him to serve as Brown's replacement.[24]

In accepting this new position—a cabinet-level appointment whose first occupant, in 1775, was Benjamin Franklin—Holt took over a job that his father-in-law, Charles Wickliffe, had held under President John Tyler from 1841 to 1845. Now reporting directly to the president, Holt was expected to oversee the appointment, effectiveness, and, if necessary, dismissal of the department's almost 40,000 employees, including "postmasters, clerks, route agents, messengers, and outside contractors" who were engaged in various ways in transporting letters, newspapers, periodicals, and even government documents from place to place across the nation. As the *Washington Constitution* explained, the U.S. postal system, which had once been such a small concern, had "grown with the growth of the country" until it was now "a machine of vast magnitude, which, like the intricate meshes of the spider's web, covers the entire Union with its complicated network, and, by its arrangements with foreign governments, gives facilities for regular correspondence all over the world." Most Americans, the *Constitution* noted, had more direct contact with representatives of the Post Office than they had with those of any other governmental department. As a result, "all that relates to its efficiency and management is a constant and endless subject of discussion and comment." The *Constitution* went on to point out that every manner of "locomotion" was involved in the "ceaseless business of transporting and handling the mails," including "railroads, steamboats, ships, stages, and wagons of all kinds and description." As such, the details of the department's operations were uniquely complex, and the postmaster general himself must be "a man of the very highest order of intellect" with "an aptitude for untiring devotion to the consideration of the public interests [e]ntrusted to his charge." Joseph Holt, the *Constitution* declared, was just such a man.[25]

Good thing, too, because unlike when he took the Patent Office job, Holt now gained enormous power, at least potentially, as a dispenser (or withholder) of political patronage. According to historian Don E. Fehrenbacher, in the middle of the nineteenth century "there were more appointments and contracts to be obtained in the Post Office than from all other departments of the federal government combined." Moreover, "to an extent now difficult to comprehend," postmasters of the period commonly operated as "active agents of party enterprise" to the extent they desired, not least through the supervisory powers they exerted over the franking privileges accorded to congressional representatives and U.S. senators. For this reason, Holt's longstanding reputation for judiciousness and incorruptibility produced a round of popular applause as word of his appointment became public.[26]

Indeed, confidence in Holt's commitment to fairness tempered the concerns of many who contemplated the role—for good or ill—that the Post Office Department might play in the context of the country's developing sectional crisis: well-maintained postal routes and honest postal carriers, after all, helped to tie the nation together; partisanship (or partisan wrangling) at the department's upper echelons could, in turn, contribute to the nation's disintegration. "The appointment," declared the *Amherst (N.H.) Farmer's Cabinet* on March 16, 1859, "is considered one of the best

Mr. Buchanan has yet made," and it quoted the *Boston Courier*'s description of Holt as "a man of very quiet habits and remarkably unassuming character" known for his "excellent good sense and sound judgment" and his "superior administrative capacities." One of Holt's most appealing qualities, the paper noted, was his now widely familiar disinterest in standing for elective office, although he was known to be a loyal Democrat and a leader in the party. The *Daily Ohio Statesman*, too, cheered Holt's appointment, which, it observed, "appears to afford very general satisfaction." Possessed as he was of "both the talent and the industry" necessary for the job, and "an integrity which no one questions," Holt, the *Statesman* insisted, was simply "the right man for the place," and "what can be done, Mr. Holt will do, ably and honestly." For its part, *Scientific American* expressed regret about Holt's new appointment, but only because the Patent Office was losing his services. Still, the journal conceded, "if, as Postmaster General, Mr. Holt is as diligent and single minded, and exercises his judgment with the same fidelity, as in his former position, he will prove a most valuable member of the Cabinet."[27]

Upon learning the news, James O. Harrison conveyed his personal approval and wished his friend success "equal to your highest hopes." At the same time, he warned Holt prophetically "that the Public will look to *you* & hold *you* responsible" for everything that happened from here on out relative to the Post Office Department and advised him to "get all the information you can," and then, "when it becomes necessary to act, poise yourself on your own judgment & your own sense of duty to the country & go where they point." Other friends and relatives, too, offered their congratulations and expressed their trust. From his old traveling companion, Howard Crosby of New York—who had been a Whig and was now a Republican—came both words of support and a prayer. "The announcement of your appointment," Crosby wrote, "was received this morning in our little family circle with most sincere and earnest expressions of joy. . . . May God long spare you for our country's good."[28]

Delighted to see his nephew continuing up the ladder of professional success and public acclaim, Uncle Daniel, too, responded with enthusiasm. "You appear to have the entire confidence of the people," he wrote. "I know you will do what is right, regardless of the consequences." Similarly, Holt's mother, Eleanor, now seventy-six, had faith in her son's abilities, but she was more worried about the new burdens Holt was about to take on than she was pleased with his promotion to a cabinet post. Always affectionate, Aunt Mary Ann shared her sister's anxiety, though she acknowledged being rather envious of Holt's growing prominence. "If I was a man," Mary Ann wrote boldly, "I never would stop until I was president of these United States." The one close relative who failed to express any support was Robert, and indeed, for some time now the brothers' always-regular correspondence had lagged. Certainly Holt was busy. Perhaps, too, he was growing tired of Robert's perennial financial struggles (he and Ann now had seven children), in which he could not seem to avoid getting entangled. In addition, their steady divergence on political matters had adversely affected their ability to communicate. Robert continued to hope that Holt would leave the federal government sooner rather than later and return to the South, and when he found out that that the Holts had finally managed to sell their Louisville mansion, he was not pleased. To him, the sale of the Louisville house meant that Holt probably had no intention of ever returning to Kentucky. Robert did his best to persuade his brother to change his mind: "By putting yourself in a proper position," he insisted, "you can command any position which K'y can give you and secure all that you can court in political distinction." When he learned that Holt had assumed the postmaster generalship, Robert had no cause for celebration, though he was as yet unwilling to abandon their relationship altogether. Some months later, he visited Holt briefly in Washington when he and his eldest child, Sarah Ellen ("Sallie"), were en route to Maryland to get her settled at the elegant Patapsco Female Institute in Ellicott City.[29]

When one considers the political crisis and dislocation that lay not too far in the future, it is indeed ironic that in June 1859, the *Washington Constitution* described Buchanan's cabinet as filled with "men who possess the wisdom and the patriotism" to manage their individual departments "in the way best calculated to secure the safety and happiness of the citizens of this great country." Secretary of State Lewis Cass's foreign policy, the paper declared, was "characterized by a prudence and energy which elicits the admiration of the world." Secretary of the Treasury Howell Cobb's financial ability, in turn, had "carried our country safely through a monetary crisis which brought ruin to many communities and private individuals," while Secretary of War John B. Floyd's talents had "rendered our little army a match for hosts of enemies scattered over a vast amount of territory." Secretary of the Navy Isaac Toucey's abilities had brought the U.S. Navy "to a state of efficiency never before equaled," and Secretary of the Interior Thompson's wisdom had enabled him to "guide the multifarious duties of the Interior Department with a skill that leaves no room for reproach or censure." Finally, Attorney General Jeremiah Black's "genius and learning" had "won encomiums from political friends and foes," and Postmaster General Holt had immediately "displayed ability and energy of such a high order as to place him in the front rank of American statesmen." Holt, the paper noted, had already "commenced and carried out important retrenchments and reforms" intended to streamline and purify the entire post office system. "Superfluous agents have been discontinued," the paper reported cheerfully, "useless or unnecessary offices suppressed; and postmasters taught that appeals made to him for acts of wrong and oppression will not be made in vain."[30]

Holt took to his new assignment with his usual dedication and seriousness, deploying his considerable administrative skills and his experience in the Patent Office to reorganize the department—and the nation's postal system as a whole—in such a way as "to promote economy and to stamp out fraud." In particular, he took sharp aim at the problem of abuse of the congressional franking privilege. "It may be safely stated," he declared in November 1859, "that no amount of vigilance exercised by the Government, and no regulation of this Department, however stringent, can arrest this widespread and humiliating abuse so long as public officers dread the displeasure of systematic peculators more than they love the law, of which they are the appointed guardians." Still, Holt was determined to do what he could. "Should it come to my knowledge," he warned, "that any employee in the postal service had become a party to such an abuse, by borrowing and using for private purposes the frank of a Government official, I should regard him as meriting dismissal, as certainly as for any other gross legal or moral delinquency." The greater fault, however, lay with the elected politician who permitted the abuse in the first place. "The process of purification, to be effective," Holt explained, "must be applied rather to the fountain than to the stream."[31]

As postmaster general, Holt also worked to ensure that the transportation and delivery of the nation's mail was accomplished safely and efficiently, which he believed to be the Post Office Department's basic function. At the same time, he sought to wipe out fraud at the local level by dismissing postal officials whose practices were suspect. In June, the *Philadelphia Argus* praised Holt for his "energy and spirit" on this particular front, pointing specifically to his firing of Gideon G. Westcott, the city's postmaster, who had garnished a large number of his employees' wages, supposedly to cover a $1,500 theft from the office's accounts for which he claimed he could not identify the specific perpetrator, and subsequently pocketed the difference between what he had collected and what had purportedly been stolen. "It is the mission of the Post Office Department, above all others," Holt wrote, "to inspire and to deserve the complete confidence of the public, which it can only accomplish by discarding from its service those whose lives and characters are not above all reproach and all suspicion." News of Westcott's removal reached as far west as Stephensport, prompting Uncle Daniel to express his "great gratification" that Holt was performing his duties so well. At the Post Office Department Holt was also characteristically resistant to the pressures of favoritism, an approach to leadership that elicited praise from many, but also hostility from those who became the targets of his housecleaning goals or who believed he should be using his powers primarily to enhance the Democratic Party's influence in Washington and across the country. Uncle Daniel attributed any "prejudicial comments" against Holt that he read in the press to some people's unhappiness with his nephew's popularity, reputation, and fame. "Don't let it disturb you, or cause you to hesitate one moment," Daniel counseled, "in discharge of what you consider your official duties. . . . Jo, I never was so proud of you in my life."[32]

Holt's effective leadership of the Post Office Department angered some, but it only fueled others' recurring dreams that he might someday become president of the United States. Indeed, in September 1859, Democrat James M. Nelson of New York, a native of Kentucky, suggested that Holt consider running for the nation's premier elective office in 1860. "The sober, and reflecting, and hence, the controlling portion of the democracy of this City and State," Nelson explained, recognized that Holt had all of the qualities and much of the "absolute good fortune" that a candidate must now possess if he meant to "effectually subvert the treason and conspiracy which are so obviously being prepared for him in the democratic camp." By this Nelson meant the violent feud now brewing between the Northern and Southern wings of the Democratic Party, which he predicted would erupt in a "fierce contest of factions and sections for *supremacy*" at the Democratic National Convention in Charleston, South Carolina, the following April. Any Democratic candidate who hoped to emerge from the coming turmoil intact, Nelson insisted, must be someone "wholly unconnected" with the public debates over the slavery issue, "yet possessed of such an accredited national reputation as to render him universally available." In trying to identify who among the party's luminaries could meet those standards, Nelson declared, the "prominent managing men in this city and elsewhere" had begun "directing their thoughts towards you." Should he be willing to consider a run for the presidency, Nelson advised Holt to remain silent and allow his supporters to put his name forward themselves. "If your friends generally desire to benefit you," he wrote, "let them continue to give public expression to the admirable and well directed efforts to cheapen postage and to introduce efficiency and economy in postal matters generally, which are reaping such a harvest of golden opinions throughout the northern states."[33]

Some three weeks after Nelson sent this letter events in Virginia sharply exacerbated the sectional tensions that were already gripping the nation. In mid-October, the Connecticut-born abolitionist John Brown, who had been active earlier in the decade in the Kansas guerrilla war, set in motion his latest plan for destroying slavery by capturing the federal arsenal at Harpers Ferry, arming slaves in the surrounding area with the stolen weapons, and inspiring them to mass insurrection. With about two dozen recruits, most of them white, Brown attacked and occupied the arsenal on the night of October 16. But his poorly devised plan stumbled badly at that point, and within thirty-six hours it collapsed when Colonel Robert E. Lee, Lieutenant J. E. B. Stuart, and a detachment of U.S. soldiers reclaimed the arsenal and took a wounded Brown and six of his collaborators prisoner (several of Brown's men were killed, including two of his own sons; others escaped). Observers in both the North and the South initially expressed a common horror upon learning of the bungled raid, which so acutely rattled the nation's already-fragile equilibrium. During his subsequent brief trial, however, Brown made clear his willingness, and perhaps even his original intention, to become a martyr for the abolitionists' cause. His calm acceptance of his fate earned him warm praise among those who despised slavery. But the antislavery tributes to Brown's courage and determination that followed only stoked proslavery Southerners' rage and their conviction that the Republican Party, and perhaps even the entire North, had committed itself not just to slavery's containment but also to its destruction by means of brutal violence if necessary. To counter this threat, proslavery Southerners dramatically stepped up their talk of secession.[34]

On December 2, John Brown was hanged. Two weeks later, Howard Crosby expressed the deepening anxiety that increasing numbers of Americans shared about the nation's future now that emotions on both sides of the slavery question seemed to have reached white heat. "Now, if ever," the Republican Crosby wrote in words that echoed Holt's own sentiments, "it behooves conservative men to be stirring to put an end to radicalism everywhere." Crosby called for both North and South to step back from extremism and make concessions. The North, he argued, should commit to returning fugitive slaves and halting the dissemination of "incendiary publications," and the South should discontinue its internal slave trade and, presumably, the ongoing smuggling of slaves from Africa in violation of the ban on slave importation that had been in place since 1808. Hardly least important, white Southerners should stop threatening disunion. Addressing Holt as "a Southerner whom I know and respect," Crosby insisted that being a Republican did not make him an enemy of the South. Rather, he declared, "I love the South as much as I do the North. The whole is my country." [35]

Holt's feelings about the national crisis mirrored Crosby's, and in the wake of Harpers Ferry he made use of his position in the Post Office Department to try and limit sectionalism's advance by obstructing the circulation of written materials that he believed promoted extremist positions, not least those that had a tendency "to excite the slave population to insurrection." Although his personal feelings about slavery were still very much in flux, Holt, like Crosby, was committed first and foremost to defending the Constitution that permitted it, and to preserving the Union and the federal government that the Constitution had created. In general, it seemed absolutely clear to him that fanaticism on either side of the slavery question should be discouraged. In immediate terms, the state of Virginia offered a case in point. Virginia law provided that if a postal official became aware that abolitionist literature in any form had arrived in his local office via the mail, he must "give notice thereof to some Justice, who shall inquire into the circumstances, and have each book or writing burned in his presence." Moreover, the intended recipient of the item, if known to have solicited it knowledgeably, could be imprisoned, and postmasters or deputy postmasters violating the law were subject to a fine of up to $200.[36]

In the Virginia case, the state law was clear. But in late 1859, some local postmasters remained uncertain about its relationship to federal laws pertaining to mail delivery. Indeed, on December 2, the very day John Brown was executed, Holt received an inquiry from the postmaster of Falls Church asking whether the Virginia law was constitutional, as Virginia's attorney general, John Randolph Tucker, had insisted it was. Postmaster Charles A. Orton's concern was that a recent act of the U.S. Congress had established fines (up to $500) and possible terms of imprisonment (up to six months) for any postmaster who "shall unlawfully detain in his office any letter, package, pamphlet or newspaper, with the intent to prevent the arrival and delivery of the same to the person or persons to whom such letter, package, pamphlet or newspaper may be addressed or directed, in the usual course of the transportation of the mail along the route." According to this law, postmasters convicted of withholding the mails could also lose their jobs, permanently. Orton wondered how the federal law squared with Virginia's attempt to prevent the circulation of abolitionist literature.[37]

On December 5, Holt issued his response to Postmaster Orton, to the effect that the attorney general of Virginia, following the example of the attorney general of Mississippi in an earlier case, was correct: federal law must yield to state law in this situation. By way of explanation, Holt cited not the sanctity of slavery, which he privately questioned, but the "right of self preservation which belongs to every government and people." In short, abolitionism, like any other form of extremist political sentiment (including fire-eating Southern nationalism), threatened slaveholding Virginia's stability and thus must be stifled. As Holt explained to Postmaster Orton, "You must, under the responsibilities resting upon you as an officer and as a citizen, determine whether the books, pamphlets, newspapers, &c., received by you for distribution, are of the incendiary character described . . . and if you believe they are, then you are not only not obliged to deliver them to those to whom they are addressed, but you are empowered and required, by your duty to the State of which you are a citizen, to dispose of them in strict conformity to the provisions of the law referred to." Virginians, Holt concluded, "have the same right to extinguish fire-brands, thus impiously hurled into the midst of their homes and altars, that a man has to pluck the burning fuse from a bomb shell which is about to explode at his feet."[38]

Even as Holt struggled to negotiate his increasingly complicated and delicate professional responsibilities, to stem the tide of national disunion as best he could, and to sort through his own feelings about the explosive issues now facing the nation, more and more of his emotional energy was being diverted to his own immediate personal crisis, namely, how to manage and cope with Margaret's now critically declining health. Back in May 1859, Margaret's sister Nannie had reported that one doctor seemed to think that "with care and attention to herself," and an unswerving commitment to an individualized, detailed, and rigorous treatment plan, Margaret could "be fat and on the road to perfect health" within half a year. By summer, however, hope was fading: Margaret was just getting worse. And so, on the assumption that the milder climate and familiar setting of Bardstown would suit her better, and because he remained unable, both emotionally and practically, to attend to her needs himself, Holt escorted her to Wickland, where he felt certain that the care and company of her family, especially her father and her sister Julia, would prove restorative. It did not. In July, Holt's friend W. M. Corry expressed his "sorrow and alarm" at learning that Margaret's doctor now felt that he had done all he could to help her. Corry urged Holt to have Margaret give "Mr. Guilford's medicine" a try. "If the medicine does no more than make Mrs. H comfortable," he wrote, "it will have accomplished a great deal for her." Holt ordered the medicine immediately.[39]

As he had done during their many previous separations, and regardless of all other distractions—professional, political, practical, or personal—Holt wrote to Margaret every few days while she was in Bardstown. He wrote of missing her, and of how much he appreciated her efforts to leave their Washington home in order before her departure. He declared the capital "unspeakably dull" without her and promised to try and make a quick visit to Kentucky sometime in the early fall. By late summer, however, Margaret's failure to improve in Bardstown had convinced the couple that she should head still farther south to a sanitarium where she might benefit from full-time professional care and warmer temperatures. Holt went to fetch her, bringing her back to Washington, where they spent about a month considering just which sanitarium would be best for dealing with her pulmonary problems and making the arrangements. Then, in early November—amidst the loud buzzing of the hornet's nest John Brown had stirred up at Harpers Ferry—they traveled 500 miles south to Summerville, South Carolina, a popular resort town near Charleston favored for its climate, fresh breezes, and generally healthful conditions. Margaret remained at Summerville for several months, during which she missed her husband terribly but was no doubt grateful for the many letters she received from him and from concerned friends and relatives who conveyed their warm wishes for her rapid improvement.[40]

Holt visited Margaret at least once during her stay in South Carolina. Then, as the holidays drew near, they decided to move her to another sanitarium for the winter, this time in Florida, where her sister Nannie Yulee and her family had a residence. Just after New Year's, Holt was back in Washington, his professional responsibilities—and probably also his emotional limitations—having precluded him from escorting Margaret personally the 250 miles further that were required to reach the sanitarium in Magnolia, not far from Jacksonville on Florida's east coast. Whatever he was truly feeling, Holt committed himself once again to writing affectionate letters full of reassurance. "My eyes & my heart followed the steamer that bore you away from me until it disappeared in the distance," he wrote of their farewell in Charleston, "& nothing could have reconciled me to the sadness of this separation but a conviction that our highest earthly intent—your health—required it." A few days after writing this letter, Holt learned from his aunt Mary Ann in Stephensport that his Uncle Daniel had died.[41]

Margaret's confidence in Holt's devotion and in their ultimate reunion under happier circumstances understandably grew dim as her illness continue to prove unresponsive to treatment and as their time apart, like the physical distance between them, grew longer. On February 8, 1860, Holt responded to a "sad, sad letter" whose "strange & desponding tone" had made him "very wretched." Holt urged his wife to set aside her fears about her health and his fidelity, but one wonders how he possibly could have expected her to do so at this point, given his intense dedication to his work, to the nation, and perhaps to some other woman. For her part, Margaret apologized for being such a worrier and chalked her anxiety up to her debilitated state. Then, as winter gave way to spring and Margaret's physical condition failed to improve, Holt decided to bring her home. Wrote Holt's first assistant postmaster general, Horatio King—a native of Paris, Maine, who came to know Holt at the department and remained a good friend for the rest of their lives—"I need not assure you that everything in my power will be done most cheerfully to render your absence as little embarrassing to the public interests as possible." At the end of April, even as Democratic Party delegates from around the country were reeling from their explosive national convention in Charleston, the Holts arrived in Washington. There they were greeted by Margaret's sisters Nannie and Mary, their families, a small circle of solicitous friends, and a host of welcoming, supportive letters, including ones from Margaret's sister Julia, in Bardstown, and Holt's mother, Eleanor, in Stephensport.[42]

Six weeks after the now terribly frail Margaret returned to Washington, the Democrats met again in Baltimore, where the party faithful hoped that the more than fifty enraged proslavery representatives associated with the increasingly radical Southern wing of the party who had bolted the April convention in Charleston would rejoin them in order to complete the business of nominating a single Democratic candidate for president and a single one for vice president. In the end, these hopes were dashed. This time, over a hundred Southern delegates bolted, the majority of them ardent Southern nationalists whose ranks were now swelled by committed Southern Unionists (Kentuckians among them) who nevertheless could not bring themselves to accept the Illinois Democrat, Stephen Douglas, as their candidate. Those Democrats who remained at the Front Street Theater in Baltimore went ahead and nominated Douglas, while the latest set of bolters regrouped at the Maryland Institute (also in Baltimore) to nominate Kentucky's John C. Breckinridge—Buchanan's vice president—for president, and Oregon's Joseph Lane for vice president. Just over a month earlier, in early May, the so-called Constitutional Union Party had chosen a former Whig from Tennessee, John Bell, as their presidential candidate. On May 18, the Republicans nominated Abraham Lincoln.[43]

Although he was a loyal Democrat, it is highly doubtful that Holt, as a cabinet member and a man whose wife was gravely ill, attended either gathering in Baltimore. Nevertheless, sometime during that summer he drafted a lengthy speech that the delegates who met at the Maryland Institute would have been pleased to hear. In it, Holt staked out an unequivocal position in favor of the Union, first and foremost, and those candidates he then considered most likely to be able preserve it: Breckinridge and Lane. "As a southern man," Holt wrote, "I can see no sufficient ground for all this excitement & apprehension, still less for that unholy desire manifested by many for the overthrow of the government." However irritating, he continued, Northern antislavery agitation should not be considered a cause for rending the precious national fabric. Rather, "the late popular movements in Philadelphia, New York, Boston, & elsewhere prove that the masses in the free states are faithful to their constitutional obligations," and even if the nation were to elect an abolitionist president in November—William H. Seward, for example—were that new president "to lift a finger aggressively towards the South," Holt was certain that "the people of the North would be the first to strike him down."[44]

As for how the nation should proceed to handle its current crisis, Holt emphasized that the worst approach possible would be to counsel the dismemberment of the Union, whose establishment had been so hard won, and whose life had thus far been a blessing to its citizens. "Were I a physician & summoned to prescribe for my nearest & dearest friend," he declared, "I would not discuss at his bedside the question of administering to him a deadly poison," and "neither will I debate . . . the question of dissolving the union." Instead, Holt suggested discussing "the means of preserving it, of resisting aggressions upon it, of healing all the disease & sorrows to which it is a prey." In Holt's mind, white Southerners who expected the North, and especially Northern commercial interests, to acquiesce in disunion were sorely mistaken. "There are millions of men as brave as they are free," he declared, "who would dye the waters" of the nation's rivers "with their blood every day in the year rather than submit to such an embargo on their commerce." Disunion, moreover, would do nothing to extend the life of the institution of slavery, if in fact that was what its supporters were hoping for; it would only obliterate any protections—however flawed— the institution still enjoyed. "After dismemberment," Holt insisted, "the South would have more than a thousand miles of frontier, adjoining free states" who no longer felt bound by the Fugitive Slave Law and who now, like Canada, "would stand with outstretched arms inviting her slaves to escape" and "would refuse to surrender the fugitives at the point of the bayonet." Regardless of what the fire-eaters claimed, then, the Union—the nation—must be preserved.[45]

Even if he had been able to deliver a speech as bold as this one to an attentive and responsive audience, by mid-summer 1860 Holt surely recognized that the Democratic Party he had loved and served for so long was in tatters and the nation's very life was imperiled. Sadly, so, too, was Margaret's. On August 7, Aunt Mary Ann encouraged Margaret to be of good cheer. "Do you not know," Mary Ann asked, "that you are more precious" to Holt "than all else in this world?" Margaret probably never read Mary Ann's last fond and reassuring letter to her, for within a few days of its posting, she was dead. Condolences began arriving immediately, including one from Howard Crosby, who had experienced the loss of loved ones more times than he liked to count. "No word of mine," Crosby wrote, "can lighten the burden your afflicted heart sustains." Still, Crosby sought to convey his sadness as one "whose beloved brother, mother and child have in succession left his side to sleep in the grave" and whose "sympathies," he continued, "thus opened by repeated strokes, naturally flow in the channel which friendship and profound esteem have formed." As others had done when Holt lost his first wife, Crosby, a Presbyterian minister, encouraged his friend to find solace in religion. "In such a calamity," he advised, "you & I alike know that our help must be more than human, that He who is the Resurrection & the Life can alone apply balm to our bleeding wounds." James O. Harrison agreed, sadly recalling his son Richard's death by yellow fever just a year earlier. "I know from sad experience," Harrison wrote, "what these domestic afflictions are & how vain are all attempts at condolence. I have none to offer, I have found none for myself."[46]

Holt's in-laws also offered words of consolation and loving support; clearly, for all the time he and Margaret had spent apart over the years, and for all the various strains on their marriage, her family did not consider him in the least a neglectful husband. To the contrary: worried that Holt would not take very good care of himself now that her sister Margaret was gone, Nannie tucked an affectionate letter of encouragement in with a pair of new slippers. Far more important, she gave Holt the precious gift of reminding him how much her sister had loved him. "Sister Mag once said," Nannie recalled, that "if it was the will of God, she would like to live just long enough to perform the last sad duties of affection to you, to enshroud you and then lay down and die. She wanted to live every day by you, to think for your comfort, and to let only loving hands administer to you." Like Howard Crosby, Nannie urged Holt to find his consolation in faith, as the pious Margaret would have wished him to do. Nannie begged him, too, to stay in contact with her and her family and to visit the Yulee home as often as he was able, although she admitted that they might all want to steer clear of discussing national affairs now that her husband's political stance (and perhaps hers as well) inclined increasingly toward Southern nationalism and secession. "If you will come and see me," Nannie vowed, "I promise not to say a word of politics, if I can possibly hold my tongue."[47]

Throughout the fall of 1860, Holt continued to receive many warm letters of condolence. In contrast, however, his brother Robert—whose letters after Mary's death in 1846 had been so consoling—now offered only a few words of sympathy and then turned his attention directly to politics, a subject on which he seems to have felt it necessary, even at this sad time, to offer advice. "I fear you do not read the Southern papers sufficiently," Robert wrote in late September, "to understand the condition of the popular mind in the South. If Lincoln is elected, rely on it, that there will not be a single Gulf or Atlantic coast statesman presented in the next Congress." Lest Holt misunderstand the implications of these words, Robert added, "My fortunes & those of my household are wholly identified with those of the South, nor would I have it otherwise."[48]

Arguably, Robert's decision to focus on his own political musings rather than his brother's great loss reveals something unsavory about his character. It also reflects the fundamental truth, however, that Margaret's death coincided with what must have seemed like the imminent death of the nation itself. And even if Holt had yearned in the fall of 1860 to isolate himself in mourning for an extended period of time, as he had done before, he simply could not have done so without immediately and entirely abdicating his professional—and, indeed, his patriotic—responsibilities. Instead, determined to stay the course, Holt proceeded to fulfill the expectations of the many who believed that he was a more decisive, stable, and reliable Union man than Buchanan himself. Wrote James O. Harrison, who had recently relocated from Lexington, Kentucky, to New Orleans: "permit no outside pressure under any circumstances to swerve you a hair's breadth" from the right. "They never die," he added, "who fall in a great cause.'" Harrison questioned what Buchanan meant to do about the disintegrating national situation and how he might choose to reshape his administration in the weeks ahead. But he declared confidently, "the President may decapitate, but he can't degrade the man who civilly but firmly maintains the right, and though my present anxiety may seem to manifest a fear that you may give way when you should not, yet allow me to say that in truth I have no such fear."[49]

On November 6, 1860, Abraham Lincoln was elected to the presidency. In response, and with the mingled dismay and delight of a Cotton States fire-eater, Holt's brother Robert declared that Lincoln's election amounted to nothing less than "a declaration by [the] northern people individually & collectively through the ballot box of a purpose to emancipate the slaves of the South, and to involve the Southern states in all the horrors which that event would plainly entail." Robert predicted than neither Congress nor the Supreme Court could obstruct the Republicans' plan to abolish slavery, and he wondered what stance border states such as Kentucky would adopt once Mississippi and the other Deep South states made clear their determination to thwart the Republican agenda, by violence if necessary. Indeed, Robert believed that Lincoln and his allies were already stirring up trouble among the slaves, encouraging them to rise in rebellion against their white owners and providing them with the tools—guns, knives, poison, and more—to do so. For this reason, he explained, the Lower South had already reached the point of being "almost unanimously in favor of an immediate withdrawal from the Union," along with the establishment of a separate government and a military force to defend it. "In this feeling," Robert declared, "I concur fully," and he warned Holt that the wisest course for the federal government now was to stand aside and permit secession to occur, if it did not want to "precipitate the bloodyest [*sic*] conflict in modern annals."[50]

Robert further expressed concern about rumors that his high-profile brother had already been heard using language that was "rather condemnatory of Southern resistance," and that Holt's basic aversion to extremism and revolution, along with his longstanding love for the Union as the expression of the republic's highest ideals, would make it impossible to support his native South in the conflict that was now bound to come. Still, he wrote hopefully, "I know your heart is altogether Southern and that you cannot but abhor the fanatics and assassins by whom our rights & firesides are invaded." Robert begged his brother "not to give hasty utterance to any word, thought, or sentiment against the justice of our cause or the wisdom of our course," reminding him that, because of his position of power in the nation's capital, "your voice against us would strike your Southern friends like a cold dagger in their bosoms." Robert closed his letter with an appeal: "I would like to hear from you the assurance that you are with us."[51]

Although Holt's response to this letter is no longer extant, when Robert wrote again on November 20 it is clear that he was disappointed, either because Holt's letter brought unmistakable affirmations of his commitment to the Union, or because it ridiculed Robert's predictions about a rapid and successful secession of the Lower South—or both. "I am sorry to differ with you in relation to a dissolution of the Union," Robert replied coolly. "That it will occur & that speedily is, I think, inevitable." Once again, he affirmed that he was in full sympathy with those who endorsed immediate secession, sharing as he did their conviction "that submission by the south is now death." Echoing what now amounted to the standard language of those who shared his political beliefs, Robert depicted Northerners generally as "marked by dishonesty, injustice, rapacity, and infernal greed of gain & power impelling them to perpetual predatory encroachments upon their neighbors." As such, he concluded, the North and the South could no longer exist peacefully under a common government. Still, he insisted, war could be avoided: once secession was complete, the new Southern nation could simply refuse to trade with the North, which would cause Northern industry to collapse, after which Northerners would surely "become as meek as whipped spaniels," begging for reconciliation. Once again, Robert reiterated his support for immediate secession. Once again, he closed his letter with a plea: "when the separation shall occur," he wrote, "I hope to see you in our midst." [52]

Robert's frustration with Holt's intransigent Unionism only grew stronger as the weeks passed. "In your efforts to save the Union," he sighed in early December, "I know you are animated only by the highest and most patriotic motives, by an imperious sense of duty." But he sorely regretted that "the positions which you conscientiously take are sure to subject you to misconstruction by the southern people, to put you in a false position, and bring upon you a doubt of your loyalty to the south and her rights." Try as he might, however, Robert failed entirely to persuade Holt to abandon either his post in the federal government or his deep-seated loyalty to the Union. Robert's letters did serve an important purpose, however: they provided Holt with regular, firsthand exposure to the passions engulfing the South in the fall of 1860, and a highly personal example of an extreme Southern nationalist, proslavery perspective, with all of its bloodthirsty, destructive implications. They also afforded him an immediate and bitter experience of what thousands of other politically divided families all along the border between slavery and freedom were now enduring.[53]

Others among Holt's correspondents in this period supplied additional information and perspective regarding the shape, development, and variability of public sentiment around the nation in the wake of Lincoln's election. Horatio King reported that in Maine most Republicans seemed "fixed in the belief that the South are only blustering and that everything will soon settle down quietly," while Democrats (as well as "a few of the more intelligent" Republicans) expressed real concern about what they considered the likelihood of imminent disunion. From Louisiana, James O. Harrison informed him that President Buchanan had completely "lost the confidence of the conservative men," such as himself, while secessionists seemed to think of the president as their ally. Harrison was certain the nation was about to break in two, and he suggested that the best possible course now would be for the federal government to avoid trying to force those states that seceded to return to the Union. "The South," Harrison wrote, "is strong in the number of its conservative men, but I believe an attempt at coercion . . . would rally 8/10 of the South against the Federal forces." As such, he recommended that the administration adopt a policy of "calm & 'masterly inactivity.'" From South Carolina, too, Holt learned from the longtime postmaster of Charleston, Alfred Huger, that secessionism increasingly appeared unstoppable. "*This* revolution," Huger wrote, "is beyond the reach of human power. The people seem prepared for any consequences, or they *think* themselves so, and I really believe they would rather die than recede one step!" For his part, Huger swore that he would continue to serve the federal government as long as South Carolina remained in the Union. Should the state secede, however, he would secede with it, though he found the prospect of doing so deeply troubling. "I, born in the Union, but before the Constitution," the elderly postmaster wrote sadly, "am fated to outlive these noble institutions!"[54]

As the debate over secession grew more and more heated across the Lower South, still more stunning developments in Washington inevitably captured Holt's attention just a month after Lincoln's election. On December 8, Secretary of the Treasury Howell Cobb of Georgia resigned from his cabinet post. From Cobb's perspective, Lincoln's election justified secession, and Buchanan's December 3 message to Congress—although it offered a veritable bouquet of olive branches to the slaveholding South—had done nothing to persuade him otherwise. Secretary of State Lewis Cass of Michigan was the next to go, on December 13. Having served the country for so long, explained the *New York Times*, the seventy-eight-year-old Cass had declared himself simply "unwilling to be present" at the nation's dissolution, though the article acknowledged rumors to the effect that unlike Cobb, Cass resented Buchanan's failure to take a sufficiently strong position against secession. For his part, Horatio King predicted that Cass's resignation would do more good for the secessionists than for the friends of the Union. "Why?" he asked. "Because, I suppose, it will be taken as evidence that the administration is in favor of secession!" King prayed that Buchanan would recognize that the time had come to let the South know his administration was "squarely and unequivocally on the side of Union."[55]

When it announced Cass's resignation on December 15, the *New York Times* predicted that other cabinet members would resign soon, too, and that Buchanan himself might "abdicate." Perhaps when Cass requested a meeting with Holt a few days later, he planned to discuss similar concerns. Meanwhile, leaning heavily, no doubt, on the advice of those such as Holt who remained in place, the president scrambled to reorganize his crumbling administration. On December 12, he appointed the Marylander Philip Francis Thomas to replace Cobb (Thomas resigned a month later and was replaced by the New Yorker John Adams Dix). On December 16, Buchanan shifted Jeremiah Black of Pennsylvania, then the attorney general, into Cass's spot, and on December 20, the very day South Carolina declared its independence from the United States, he appointed Ohio Democrat Edwin M. Stanton to become the new attorney general. Back in the spring of 1856, it will be recalled, one of Holt's avid supporters had suggested running Stanton and him together as the Democratic Party's candidates that year for president and vice president. Now Stanton and Holt found themselves becoming a team of a very different sort indeed.[56]

In the final weeks of 1860, it surprised few observers that Joseph Holt stayed put in Buchanan's cabinet. Those who equated the administration's disintegration with that of the nation, and the nation's with disaster, greeted his steadiness with great sighs of relief. "We find that you are a firm friend to our glorious Union," wrote an old friend from Louisville on December 29, "and I tell you, Sir, that Kentucky, your native state, will sustain you, with zeal, honor, & pride. She is intensely zealous that our union should be perpetuated." Also eager to express his support was Howard Crosby, now a professor at Rutgers University in New Jersey. "Of S. Carolina I have no hope," Crosby wrote. "She wants the slave trade & she has the silly pride of a turkey-cock. She must suffer & she will suffer." In the meantime, however, Crosby was grateful to Holt for his constancy to the Union. "God bless Mr. Holt!" he exclaimed, encouraging Holt to position himself as "a thorn in the side of this accursed administration till its exit." Wrote M. W. Jacobus of Newark, New Jersey, "God grant that the firmness of the Govt. may not be compromised. I beg that you may not be outvoted in your noble efforts to assert the majesty of law and order." Still another admirer exclaimed that he wished Holt were president, adding: "it is not an impossibility that you will be, if you will only startle the world with your views & boldly take command. Do this I pray you."[57]

Then, on December 31, 1860, just two days after the Virginian John B. Floyd became the third member of Buchanan's cabinet to resign, the floundering chief executive appointed Holt to fill the vacancy, making him secretary of war.

STANDING FOR THE UNION, 1861–1862

I heard from the bottom yesterday they & your Mother was all well.
The army worms is destroyed all there meadows & some of there corn.
I sent them word that it was a plague sent on them because they were
secessionist. —Aunt Mary Ann Stephens to Joseph Holt, June 1861

As Lincoln's personal secretaries John G. Nicolay and John Hay later recalled, it was Attorney General Edwin M. Stanton who went to Holt's New Jersey Avenue home near midnight on December 31, 1860, to urge him to accept the position of secretary of war, at least on an interim basis, and to "impress upon him the grave nature of the exigency, and the need of a man in that place" whose Unionism was beyond question. Whatever others may have hoped or expected him to do, when Stanton came by that night, Holt immediately determined to make his stance on the integrity and indivisibility of the United States utterly clear. Certainly he cherished his roots and family in Kentucky, as well as the many years of life and the multitude of positive experiences he had enjoyed in the South. He was hardly dismissive, either, of the benefits he had accrued in his home state and region, both personally and professionally, thanks at least in part to slavery. Indeed, it was for these reasons, among others, that Holt had supported the candidacy of the proslavery southern Democrat, John C. Breckinridge, for president in the November election. By accepting the War Department post, however, Holt now boldly, courageously, and with unshakable commitment chose the Union over Kentucky, over the states, over the South, and—potentially—over slavery. To Holt, the importance of the Union's survival superseded all these things, for without it, the great and unique republican experiment in representative government that had been forged by the American Revolution would have failed.[1]

In some ways, of course, this was not such a difficult choice for him to make. Holt's devotion to the Union, his disdain for revolution—unless,

Edwin M. Stanton.
Courtesy of the
Library of Congress.

like Kossuth's or America's founders, it was in the cause of republican ideals—and even his deep-seated ambivalence about slavery dated back many years. Still, Holt surely knew that positioning himself in this particular way on the side of the Union and the federal government would exact a steep and quite likely permanent toll on his relations with many of those individuals and communities he knew best and loved most. Second only to the commander in chief himself, as secretary of war Holt would now have control over the nation's war-making matériel and its military personnel who numbered, at the moment, about 16,000 soldiers. As secretary of war, he would become one of a handful of key government officials responsible, should the time come, for actively prosecuting a war against the rebel South. "I deeply regret," wrote his brother Robert in dismay, "that a sense of propriety or duty induces you still to remain among the advisers of the President." Robert predicted that the vacillating Buchanan would soon adopt a policy of coercion, in which Holt would then become complicit. To Robert, coercion meant "war upon the south, upon your country, your friends, your kindred," war that would, indeed, "probably find its way with fire & sword to the very hearthstone of our childhood."[2]

How, Robert wondered, had his brother failed so completely to understand the Southern people, or "their feelings, opinions or purposes"? How could Holt, who had lived most of his life in the region, not recognize that the principal secessionists were more than just a "village mob"? To the contrary, Robert insisted, these men were heroes, leaders of a great and now-unstoppable "popular revolution." "I am in the midst of these people," Robert wrote, "and I assure you in all soberness and truth that the restoration of the Union is impossible." Slavery, he declared, must be preserved, for "Providence" had joined white slaveholders and their black slaves forever. How, then, could slaveholders be expected to abandon "the social and political institutions by which both are to be governed and beneath which each race is to work out its proper destiny"? Northerners should simply leave the South alone, for "slavery rescued from the power of its enemies in the old Union is now in the hands of its friends," who were both "able to appreciate & defend it, and too wise ever to imperil it by a new political partnership with its sworn & faithless foes."[3]

In the weeks ahead, Robert repeatedly and earnestly begged Holt to reconsider his allegiance, as did a number of his closest friends. "We are truly in evil times," James O. Harrison now wrote sadly from New Orleans. "The glorious old union under which we have lived so long & become so great will soon live only in History—what a History & what an end!" Having reached the conclusion that calm discussion between the sections was no longer possible, however, Harrison stood adamantly against the principle that the federal government, and the new secretary of war, should deploy force against South Carolina or any states that followed its lead. "What is a union worth that is held together only by force?" he asked. "You might as well tie a dead body to a live one and expect them to unite by a healthy growth as to expect a healthy or desirable union when the spirit of union has gone." Although he could understand that as a member of the president's cabinet Holt felt "a strong desire that this vast temple of liberty should not be destroyed during your connection with the administration of it," Harrison nevertheless counseled his old friend and colleague not to join Buchanan in adopting a policy of coercion. "You are a Southern man," he wrote, echoing Robert's sentiments; "your sympathies & all your memories cling to the South as a child clings to its mother." Instead, Harrison encouraged Holt to recognize secession for what it was: a manifestation of the South's determination to be independent, against which force could only fail, but not before it inflicted terrible consequences. "If war is to be made," Harrison pleaded, "if the fanatics of the North are to be armed by the Government & let loose upon us, let me entertain the hope that no Southern man & least of all that you will . . . countenance a movement that is to fill the land with wailing." With all the persuasive strength he could muster, Harrison asked, "How would it look to History *that Kentucky was subjugated by Northern troops aided by her own son?*"[4]

Holt found entreaties such as Harrison's—and Robert's—difficult to dismiss out of hand, as were the violently threatening responses from some ardent secessionists that his decision to accept the War Department post evoked. On January 5, one angry correspondent, who predicted that Holt was preparing to "play false to the South," warned ominously, "My eye is upon you." Like Robert and James O. Harrison, this writer reminded Holt of his Southern roots and of the abundant benefits he had derived from his early life below the Mason-Dixon Line, and he cautioned that, should Holt demonstrate a willingness to adopt a coercive stance rather than accepting the South's peaceful secession, he would be sorry. For although the South's smaller population might prevent it beating the North on the battlefield, there was nevertheless "a secret band of avengers" who were willing to risk their lives to kill every one of secession's key opponents, including Holt. In the years to come, Holt never forgot this early threat.[5]

Even in Washington Holt confronted a string of intensely hostile reactions to his appointment, such as that of the Texas fire-eater, Louis T. Wigfall, a U.S. senator, who on January 2 wrote to South Carolina congressman Milledge L. Bonham in Charleston: "Holt succeeds Floyd. It means war." Happily, not all responses to his appointment were so bitterly negative; many in Washington and around the country were positively thrilled to hear that the War Department was now in his capable, dutiful, Union-loving hands. Wrote Silas Reede from St. Louis: "The Honl. Mr. Holt and Mr. Stanton have the warmest thanks of tens of thousands in the North West for the bold & patriotic stand they have taken in their official positions, to uphold the honor of the Govt. against the conspirators in S. Carolina and elsewhere." Similarly, S. H. Wales of New York thanked Holt for his "noble devotion to our country's flag, and our country's honor in these trying times," and reassured him that New Yorkers had the utmost confidence in his integrity and patriotism and could be relied upon to assist in whatever way he required. Few if any letters can have been more satisfying than that of Holt's friend Dr. T. S. Bell of Louisville, who had known him for thirty years and who remained a close and loyal friend for life. Bell struggled to convey how profoundly Holt's decision to stand by the Union had "stirred the pulses of Kentucky's heart," and he added, "We always feel that a Kentuckian may be trusted anywhere in matters of integrity and the simple fact that you are a Kentuckian in the War Department of the Union has roused the drooping energies of the people." Upon learning of Holt's appointment, Bell noted, "I told every one that I conversed with, that it would be as easy to make the sun swerve from his orbit as to get you to fail in duty or to swerve from the line of integrity. No friend of yours here expected anything else of you than the faithful journey you have made in the path of duty."[6]

Although his official confirmation as secretary of war did not come from the Senate until January 18, Holt began immediately to shape and implement the federal government's response to the military threat posed by the secession of South Carolina. As the *New York Times* declared several months later, Holt quickly became "the animating spirit" of the Buchanan administration. At this point, Holt's goal, like Buchanan's, was to prevent war if at all possible, while at the same time denying the rebellious states' right of secession; years later, Lincoln's personal secretaries Nicolay and Hay recalled that Holt "had not been in the War Department five minutes" when he sent for seventy-four-year-old Winfield Scott, the army's increasingly decrepit commanding general, to enlist his aid. Meanwhile, Holt received numerous letters of advice. "Nothing can be accomplished by force," his old friend Robert Ward Johnson declared, "and surely it is contrary to the theory of our Government to subjugate a people who are unanimously opposed" to remaining united. Like James O. Harrison, Johnson yearned to spare the nation a civil war, and his friend the shame of complicity in a federal attack on his native South. "Would not death," Johnson wrote, "be a thousand times preferable to being the instrument through whom innocent men women & children are slaughtered in their own homes?" Others disagreed, urging Holt to press the administration to show some muscle. "Indeed, the suspicion is currently expressed," Charles Ellet Jr. of Georgetown remarked, "that there is a willingness to allow the forts and arms of the country to fall into the hands of the disunionists, and that no efficient measures will be taken to prevent the seizure of the public buildings in Washington." Ellet did not doubt that Buchanan meant well, but he considered the president utterly ineffective, and as such, he urged Holt to commence immediately reinforcing the nation's military installations, especially those located in Washington and the South. To do so, Ellet wrote, "would do immense good in restoring confidence *in the North*, and perhaps in strengthening the courage of the overawed union men in the South."[7]

As Holt sorted through all of the advice that was flooding his new office, his own instincts inclined him toward trying to demonstrate federal military strength clearly to those gathering in rebellion while resisting overtly aggressive action as much and as long as possible. How exactly to do this, however, was a vexed question, and thanks to the troubling developments underway in South Carolina's Charleston Harbor, there seemed to be very little time to deliberate. Federal concern about the safety of the national troops in Charleston was certainly justified: two days after Lincoln's election the *Charleston Mercury* had proclaimed that "the tea has been thrown overboard," and that "the revolution of 1860 has been initiated." Five days later, and more than a month before the state even declared its independence, South Carolina's legislature resolved to raise and arm 10,000 volunteers to defend against anticipated aggression from the North. By early December, the state's congressmen had begun pressuring President Buchanan to turn all federal properties there over to state control. At the same time, they warned him not to send the military reinforcements that Holt's fellow Kentuckian, Major Robert Anderson, who had been in command of the government's installations in Charleston since mid-November, had made clear would soon be needed.[8]

Less than a week after South Carolina seceded, Major Anderson transferred the Federal army garrison of roughly eighty soldiers from Fort Moultrie—which had been left in a state of "general stagnation" for so long that the surrounding sand dunes had built up enough to allow cows to wander in—to Fort Sumter, which he considered safer. At that time, Holt's predecessor at the War Department, John B. Floyd, had ordered Anderson to remain purely on the defensive. Soon, however, South Carolina troops had occupied Fort Moultrie and nearby Castle Pinckney. Then, the day before Holt agreed to replace Floyd, state troops had taken over the federal arsenal located in Charleston. Word came, too, that Georgia and Alabama had recently offered to assist should the Palmetto State find itself under attack. That same day, General Scott requested Buchanan's permission to send, in secret, "two hundred & fifty recruits, from New York Harbor, to reinforce Fort Sumter, together with some extra muskets or rifles, ammunition, & subsistence stores." Within hours, Buchanan issued the necessary orders, designating the *USS Brooklyn*, a "powerful war steamer," to stand in readiness.[9]

As it turns out, the temporary vacancy in the secretary of war's position briefly delayed putting this first attempt to relieve Fort Sumter into action. But on January 2, Buchanan summoned the just-appointed Holt, Secretary of the Navy Toucey, and General Scott to discuss the situation, and they agreed that the time had come to move forward, especially now that a trio of commissioners sent from South Carolina to present the state's latest demands to the administration had revealed their complete unwillingness to negotiate a compromise. At this point, Buchanan, Holt, Toucey, and Scott agreed to replace the *Brooklyn* with the faster but smaller *Star of the West*—a "side wheel mercantile steamer"—for the mission, on the assumption that it would seem less threatening. Three days later, on Saturday, Janu-

Major Robert Anderson. Courtesy of the Library of Congress.

"Firing on the 'Star of the West' from the South Carolina battery on Morris Island, January 10, 1861." From Harper's Weekly, *January 26, 1861.*

ary 5, the *Star of the West* departed from Governor's Island in New York under the command of Captain John McGowan, carrying supplies and 250 troops, whose commander was Lieutenant Charles R. Woods. No sooner had the *Star of the West* sailed, however, but Major Anderson, as yet unaware of the ship's mission, telegraphed the president to inform him that he was not yet desperate, and that he hoped no ships would be sent for the time being as the appearance of federal supply ships in the harbor would surely incite South Carolinians to violence. Anderson also sent a telegram to Holt restating his message to Buchanan and promising to meet him in Washington in a couple of days to discuss the developing situation.[10]

For better or worse, Anderson's communications came too late for the mission to be cancelled, although the attempt was certainly made to do so. Instead, at daylight on January 9 the *Star of the West* arrived on the outskirts of the harbor. Federal soldiers garrisoned at Fort Sumter raised the Stars and Stripes in greeting and prepared for action, and almost immediately local militia troops began firing from batteries located on Morris Island, less than two miles away. Lacking orders permitting him to abandon the fort's defensive stance, Anderson refused to allow his troops to fire back, and before long, although few of the shots from the batteries actually hit their floating target, McGowan and Woods concluded that the attack was sufficiently intense to prevent them completing their assignment. Instead, McGowan turned the *Star of the West* around and headed back to New York. The following day, relieved that the ship had escaped safely but frustrated by the confusion and the mission's ultimate failure, Holt praised Major Anderson for the "forbearance, discretion, and firmness" he had displayed "amid the perplexing and difficult circumstances in which you have been placed." In addition, he ordered Anderson to remain on the defensive and "to avoid, by all means compatible with the safety of your command, a collision with the hostile forces by which you are surrounded."[11]

In the days and weeks ahead, neither Holt nor the rest of Buchanan's administration, nor General Scott, gave up entirely on finding a way to strengthen Anderson's increasingly fragile position. On January 12, Buchanan summoned Holt, Toucey, and Scott to meet with him again to consider their options. Meanwhile, Holt continued to sift through all the advice he was receiving for clues as to how to proceed. On January 25, W. R. Palmer of the Coast Survey Office sent a map of Charleston Harbor and its surroundings to help with his planning. A few days later, an increasingly nervous Buchanan suggested that perhaps it was time to decide "whether it is practicable, with the means in our power, considering the obstacles interposed in the harbor of Charleston," to try again. For the time being, however, no new attempt was made, and Anderson was cautioned to remain patient.[12]

The situation in Charleston Harbor was by no means the only problem demanding Secretary Holt's close attention at this time. Since South Carolina's declaration of independence on December 20, events threatening a complete and potentially bloody rupture of the Union had followed one upon the other at what must have seemed a dizzying and constantly accelerating rate, even as they required decisions that were both carefully thought through and also capable of being implemented quickly. On January 8 came the resignation of yet another of Buchanan's cabinet members, Secretary of the Interior Jacob Thompson of Mississippi, with whom Holt had previously come into some conflict when he was serving as Patent Office commissioner. As Thompson explained to former secretary of the treasury Howell Cobb, he was angry about the staunch Unionist Holt's appointment to the War Department, which he considered a clear indication that Buchanan was preparing to adopt a policy of coercion toward the rebels. Thompson was angrier still about the *Star of the West*'s expedition, which he had vehemently opposed and the details of which he had actually telegraphed to contacts in South Carolina before he quit. When Thompson resigned, Buchanan replaced him with Caleb B. Smith of Indiana.[13]

Even more important than Thompson's resignation, by February 1, six more states had followed South Carolina out of the Union: Mississippi (January 9), Florida (January 10), Alabama (January 11), Georgia (January 19), Louisiana (January 26), and Texas (February 1). Moreover, in each of these states armed locals had proceeded to take control of Federal properties even before the votes for secession were counted. Georgia troops seized Fort Pulaski near the mouth of the Savannah River on January 3, the same day Holt's War Department cancelled orders—issued by his turncoat predecessor, Floyd—to transfer 124 Federal guns housed at the Allegheny Arsenal in Pittsburgh to various forts in the South. On January 4, Alabama troops commandeered the federal arsenal at Mt. Vernon, and the next day they took possession of Forts Morgan and Gaines in Mobile Bay. On January 6, Florida troops took over the U.S. arsenal at Apalachicola, after which they went on to seize Fort Marion, located in St. Augustine, not far from where Margaret Holt had been a patient in the months before her death. On January 10, armed Louisianans took control of the federal arsenal at Baton Rouge, as well as Forts Jackson and St. Philip in the Gulf of Mexico; later that month they seized the U.S. Mint and the Customs House in New Orleans. Around this time, too, Governor John W. Ellis of North Carolina inquired anxiously about the federal government's plans for his state's forts. "I am directed to say," Secretary of War Holt wrote sternly, "that they, in common with the other forts, arsenals, and public property of the United States, are in the charge of the President, and that if assailed, no matter from what quarter, or under what pretext, it is his duty to protect them by all the means which the law has placed at his disposal."[14]

Meanwhile, U.S. senators and representatives from the seceding states had begun withdrawing from Congress. On January 21, five senators from Florida, Alabama, and Mississippi departed, but not before they had given dramatic speeches in which they expressed their "reluctance, determination, sorrow, and disappointment" at having to bid the Union farewell. These senators included the future president of the Confederacy, Jefferson Davis, as well as the future secretary of the Confederate navy, Stephen Mallory. They also included Holt's former brother-in-law, David Levy Yulee, who a full month earlier (and three weeks before Florida's vote to secede) had initiated a correspondence with then Secretary of War Floyd regarding Floridians' representation in the U.S. Army. "You will oblige me," Yulee had written on December 21, "by a statement of the officers connected with

David Yulee. Courtesy of the Library of Congress.

the Army of the United States who were appointed from Florida, their rank, and pay."[15]

Within days, the sympathetic Floyd provided Yulee with all the information he had solicited. But when Yulee and Mallory followed up in early January with a second request for details about the government's troops in Florida and the types and quantities of guns and ammunition then available in the state's various forts and arsenals, Holt was not so obliging. Although Yulee and Mallory addressed their second request to the "Secretary of War" (now Holt), they delivered their letter directly to the Ordnance Bureau, perhaps because Holt's appointment was not yet confirmed by Congress, and perhaps because they were hoping to bypass his authority. Now, however, to their consternation, after Captain of Ordnance William Maynadier had dutifully gathered the information Yulee and Mallory had requested, he sent it to Holt instead of to them. Holt, in turn, denied the Floridians' bold request, declaring in no uncertain terms that "the interests of the service forbid that the information which you ask should at this moment be made public."[16]

David Yulee's turn toward secession, like Holt's own brother Robert's, came as no surprise to Holt. In one of her letters urging Holt to come for a visit after Margaret's death, Nannie Yulee, after all, had referred specifically to their political differences. Still, it must have been unsettling to witness one after another of his friends and family members abandoning the Union. Unsettling and, at least in the case of Yulee, infuriating. For in Holt's mind, there was no getting around the fact that, like himself, Yulee had been a sworn officer of the federal government when he made the decision to abandon it, and now he was actively engaged in trying to destroy the government and the Union he had pledged to uphold. On a more practical level, Yulee's betrayal exacerbated the problem of Fort Pickens in Pensacola Harbor, which housed a Federal army garrison under the command of Lieutenant Adam J. Slemmer. Like the U.S. troops in Charleston Harbor, those at Fort Pickens were few in number and without sufficient supplies to hang on for very long. Their situation grew graver still when an estimated 1,700 rowdy Florida secessionists surrounded the fort, apparently in preparation for an attack. Fortunately, although the initial effort to resupply Fort Sumter had been a failure, a similar mission to Fort Pickens later in January was a success, and soon Holt felt confident that the installation was secure.[17]

Some weeks after Holt had moved over to the War Department, the staff of the Post Office Department gathered to express their appreciation for his service as postmaster general and for all he had done thus far to stem the tide of disunion. "You came to preside over this Department," declared Thomas P. Trott, the department's chief clerk, "at a season of gloom." And whereas "almost any intelligent landsman could, with a little experience, guide a stanch well-rigged ship over smooth seas," only a highly skilled professional sailor could have been able to stabilize a ship that had recently been "laid over on her boom-ends" by a dreadful storm. Holt had done this for the Post Office and now he was expected to do the same for the nation, for which Trott predicted confidently that Holt's name would be engraved deeply "on the tablets of imperishable history." Dr. H. Wigand of Springfield, Ohio, too, praised Holt for his efforts to preserve the Union, for which, he declared, "you deserve the gratitude the love and respect of every patriot of this nation." Like Trott, Wigand predicted that Holt's name would never be forgotten. "Whatever may be the result of this mad Disunion scheme," he wrote, "the future historian will record your name as the only clear headed noble and honest member of the former cabinet of Mr. Buchanan." For his part, Wigand hoped that following his inauguration, Abraham Lincoln would see fit to give Holt a spot in his cabinet. So did Holt's friend in Louisville, T. S. Bell, who believed that "the friends of the Union were more indebted to Mr. Holt" than to anyone else. For Holt's "fidelity to a public trust amidst almost universal faithlessness and stark, staring, assassin-like treason," Bell hoped that Lincoln would reappoint him secretary of war, a position, he added, that Holt had singlehandedly "redeemed from utter disgrace."[18]

Unfortunately, Holt had little if any time to acknowledge such expressions of glowing praise as he raced to respond quickly and appropriately to developments across the South. Nor could he pay much attention to the violent criticisms that continued to be circulated against him by a host of secessionists and their allies. "This distinguished man, who now so ably fills the important position of Secretary of War," observed the pro-Union *Confederation* in early February, "is having emptied on his devoted head the vials of wrath of the ultra-Union-haters of the South, simply because in the conscientious discharge of his duty, he exhibits a disposition to preserve law and order, and protect public property from the reckless, ruthless hands of those who would destroy it, or appropriate it to their own use." Interestingly, among Holt's most vigorous opponents was California senator William M. Gwin, who around this time confessed to his state's district attorney, Calhoun Benham, that he harbored "such a horror of Holt I cannot hope for his doing what he ought." Such attacks stung, but Holt could not allow them to distract him. For one thing, the Fort Sumter problem was still far from being solved, leading him to caution South Carolinians in a February 6 letter to the state's attorney general, Isaac W. Hayne, that they should heed "all the multiplied proofs" of the Buchanan administration's "anxiety for peace" and resist initiating an assault on the fort that would "peril the lives of the handful of brave and loyal men shut up within its walls and thus plunge our common country into the horrors of civil war." In addition, the unauthorized transfers of federal property into Confederate hands continued, the most dramatic of which was Brevet Major General David E. Twiggs's mid-February surrender of his command of the Department of Texas, in its entirety, which he accomplished while still dressed in his U.S. Army uniform. Two weeks later, Secretary of War Holt ordered Twiggs summarily dismissed from the U.S. Army on account of "his treachery to the flag of his country."[19]

Also of serious ongoing concern was the question of how to protect the federal capital against possible attack by its enemies. Indeed, virtually from the moment he became secretary of war Holt began meeting with the Washington, D.C., militia's Brigadier General William Hickey and others to discuss the district's security, at the same time issuing orders to the loyal states to organize some of their own militia units for deployment to the capital's defenses. General Scott was worried, too. "I must beg the Secretary of War to call to Washington at once the light battery of artillery from West Point," he had written on January 24, requesting that other troops be summoned as well. Although neither of the two states that surrounded the District of Columbia—Maryland and Virginia—had seceded yet, there was certainly no guarantee that either would remain loyal, and even if they did, one or both might prove unwilling to obstruct invaders from the seceded states as they passed through on their way to Washington to assert their independence. Certainly Holt was encouraged by letters such as the one he received from an anonymous Kentuckian who insisted that 5,000 men from Holt's home state would readily volunteer if called to serve as guards over the capital; all Holt needed to do was ask. As it turns out, by mid-February he had managed to gather so many soldiers in Washington that some members of Congress even complained of the city's overly aggressive martial appearance vis-à-vis the seceding states. On February 11—the very day Abraham Lincoln began his twelve-day journey to Washington from Springfield, Illinois, and only a week since the rebel states had convened in Montgomery, Alabama, declared themselves a nation, adopted a constitution, and elected a president and vice president—the U.S. House of Representatives asked Buchanan to explain "the reasons that had induced him to assemble so large a number of troops" in the city. Buchanan forwarded the inquiry directly to Holt for his response.[20]

Holt began by explaining that the number of soldiers now present in the city was in fact not so large and that they were only there to preserve the public peace. Their presence, he went on, was essential thanks to "the secessionist revolution," which had already produced a series of "treacheries and ruthless spoliations," including the capturing of Federal arms and properties and the hoisting of "hostile flags . . . upon their ramparts." No doubt with his former brother-in-law Yulee and others in mind, Holt went on to point out that many of those now engaged in active betrayal of the nation were men who, despite "occupying the highest positions in the public service" and having "the responsibilities of an oath to support the Constitution still resting upon their consciences, did not hesitate secretly to plan and openly to labor for the dismemberment of the Republic whose honors they enjoyed and upon whose Treasury they were living." Moreover, there was simply no doubt that the rebels had as a future goal the capture of the nation's capital, which would strike a fatal blow to the federal government. Indeed, Holt explained, specific plans for such a move on the capital, as well as for disrupting Lincoln's inauguration, had already been discovered, and the best way to undermine those plans was to fortify Washington with loyal defenders. President Buchanan, the rest of his cabinet, and General Scott had approved his actions, Holt reiterated, and the results spoke for themselves. Already, "public confidence" had been strengthened, and the "machinations of deluded, lawless men" had been "suspended, if not altogether abandoned." The Buchanan administration had made clear its determination to protect the capital, and "to transfer in peace to the President-elect the authority that under the Constitution belongs to him." The troops now on garrison duty in Washington were simply ensuring that these goals would be met.[21]

The same day Holt wrote this letter, February 18, the newly formed Confederate States of America inaugurated Jefferson Davis as its president. Four days later, the federal capital joined other cities across the country in celebrating George Washington's birthday. In conjunction with this celebration, and in keeping with his belief that public displays of the nation's military strength could serve as an ongoing deterrent to those who might be plotting against it, Holt permitted Federal troops to join members of the local militia in a peaceful parade. On February 23, in anticipation of his March 4 inauguration and after some careful navigating of threats against his life that were already circulating, Abraham Lincoln arrived safely in Washington. "Mr. Lincoln reached Washington early on Saturday morning," reported one newspaper on March 1, "having left Harrisburg, at an hour's warning, at 9 o'clock the previous evening, in a special train, unknown to but few even of those who composed his party." Lincoln's "speedy flight from Harrisburg," the newspaper noted, was prompted by word he had received from General Scott, William H. Seward—the president-elect's choice for the post of secretary of state—and Holt, that a credible plot had been discovered to assassinate him in Baltimore. In light of this, Scott, Seward, and Holt had urged Lincoln "to come on at once, aside from his party," which Lincoln had agreed to do. "There is no doubt," the paper declared, "that there was wisdom in the course pursued."[22]

Shortly after arriving in Washington, Lincoln met with Buchanan and the members of his cabinet, almost certainly the first time Holt and the incoming president had ever met face to face. A few days later, Holt gave the president-elect's seventeen-year-old son, Robert Todd Lincoln, a tour of the War Department. Meanwhile, although by now he was preparing to hand over the reins of the department to Lincoln's appointee, Simon Cameron of Pennsylvania, Holt remained vigilant and alert to developments in the continuing national crisis, which included the Confederate government's decision to put Pierre Gustave Toussaint Beauregard in charge of military affairs in South Carolina. A West Point graduate (class of 1838), Beauregard had been a student of Robert Anderson's at the academy and one of the cadets whose annual examination Holt had observed when he served on the academy's board of visitors a quarter of a century earlier. Now, Beauregard faced off against his old professor, who informed Holt that events at Fort Sumter were rapidly "arriving at a point where further delay on the decision to evacuate or reinforce would be impossible." For his part, Anderson recommended sending 20,000 reinforcements along with supplies sufficient to sustain them.[23]

On March 2, 1861, following a visit to the Executive Mansion to bid farewell to President Buchanan, General Scott and a group of army officers in full uniform came to see Holt to express their thanks and say goodbye. Two days later, on the morning of March 4, Holt met with Buchanan to update him on Anderson's situation. Then, in one of his last acts as secretary of war, Holt observed the smooth and uneventful inauguration of Abraham Lincoln to the presidency, knowing that he had done his part to make the event—which was attended by at least 20,000 spectators—both possible and safe. It was thanks in large part to Holt, the *New York Herald* declared two days later, that "a new administration is born. Brutus did not appear, and Abraham Lincoln lives in the White House." The *New York Times*, too, gave Holt great credit for the undisrupted transfer of power from Buchanan to Lincoln. "To the bold patriotism of Mr. Holt," the *Times* insisted, "is the country indebted for the avoidance of the first bloody scene in the drama of the Secession rebellion—the assassination, or expulsion of President Lincoln from Washington, and the inauguration of a Southern military dictator in his place." The *Times* praised Holt's loyalty, wisdom, and courage, to which, it claimed, a tremendous debt was due from the nation. For the next two days, while Cameron prepared to assume his new and burdensome responsibilities, Holt remained the secretary of war, meeting with Lincoln and Seward and also composing a statement providing the new president with all the information he had to offer, as well as the recommendation "that Fort Sumter must, in the lapse of a few weeks at most, be strongly reinforced or summarily abandoned." Holt also met with Lincoln's secretary of the navy, Gideon Welles, to discuss the crisis. And then, on March 6, he finally stepped down.[24]

In the aftermath of Holt's sixty-four-day term as Buchanan's secretary of war, a number of individuals criticized him more vociferously than ever. On the question of whether or not someone might try to assassinate him now that he had returned to civilian life, the *Charleston Mercury* declared harshly that Holt did not "deserve the honor of an assassination." Still, the pro-secession paper warned that Holt was "a marked man," and that "if ever he ventures within the confines of the Confederate States, he will never return to practice coercion again." Others, of course, took the opposite position, emphasizing their profound gratitude for all that Holt had done to save the nation, or at least to delay its disintegration. "A purer patriot, sounder Democrat, or better man never occupied a position in the Cabinet of any President," declared the pro-Union *Confederation*. No one, the paper insisted, had been "more conscientious in the performance of his arduous duties," no one had loved the Union more. In the same generous tone, another newspaper described Holt as entitled to the gratitude of all Americans for having "firmly withstood all temptations and maintained to the last . . . the integrity and honor of the government." On a much more personal note, James Buchanan's niece, Annie, wrote to thank Holt for standing by her uncle "through all his vexations, at a time when so many of his old friends have left him." Buchanan, too, conveyed his deep appreciation for Holt's loyalty to the nation, and to him. "From our first acquaintance," the former president wrote on March 11, "I have had the most implicit confidence in your integrity, ability & friendship & this remains unchanged."[25]

Old friends wrote, too, including one who informed him that back home, "it is the wish of many that you had been elected to occupy the *White House* instead of Lincoln." Similarly, a large group of appreciative Democrats from Pennsylvania praised Holt for being "a true man," whom they hoped some day to have the privilege of electing "*President of the whole Union*." "You are worthy," T. S. Bell assured him, "of every word of commendation I have seen bestowed upon you. It makes my heart leap to hear how you are spoken of in Louisville. Kentucky has enlarged her treasures of noble names in adding those of Holt & Anderson to her glorious register." Holt's devoted Aunt Mary Ann also sent warm congratulations and thanks; sadly, she was the only member of his Stephensport family to do so. "You have done all things well," she wrote, adding that she hoped her nephew would now return to his native state. Should he do so, however, Mary Ann jokingly suggested that he would be wise to travel incognito, as Lincoln had supposedly done when he slipped into Washington prior to his inauguration, lest his Kentucky fans (outside the family, anyway) overwhelm him with their enthusiastic welcomes. "I think," she chuckled, "it would be a good plan for you to borrow Linco[l]n's plaid & all his disguise to come home; if the people discovers you are Mr. Holt some of them will eat you up out of pure love." Thanking him for the "political papers" he had sent her, Aunt Mary Ann fondly remarked, "I will be so thankfull to the good almighty if I am permitted to see you once more alive & well."[26]

Even if he had hoped after leaving the War Department to retreat from the public eye once and for all, Holt could not do so. Indeed, no sooner had he turned over the reins to Simon Cameron than he came into sharp and public conflict with his former colleague in the Buchanan cabinet, Jacob Thompson. This time the dispute centered on the details surrounding Thompson's decision, back in January, to inform the authorities in Charleston that the *Star of the West* was on its way to Anderson's relief. Having quit Washington for the Confederacy, Thompson gave a speech sometime in late February in his home state of Mississippi, in which he mentioned that he had been in the midst of writing his resignation to Buchanan when he first learned about the resupply mission. Even before he completed his letter, Thompson boasted, he had telegraphed Judge Augustus Baldwin Longstreet, the future Confederate general James Longstreet's uncle and the president of South Carolina College, to let him know. As a result, Thompson informed his eager Mississippi audience, the batteries in Charleston were "put on their guard, and when the *Star of the West* arrived she received a warm welcome from booming cannon, and soon beat a retreat." Although Thompson claimed that he was glad the ship had not sunk, he admitted that he was "still more rejoiced" that "the concealed trick, first conceived by General Scott, and adopted by Secretary Holt, but countermanded by the President when too late," had failed.[27]

Upon reading word of Thompson's speech in the press, Holt was out-

raged. Two points were especially galling: first, Thompson's revelation that he had *not yet* filed his resignation, and had thus—like David Yulee—still been officially in the federal government's service when he violated his oath of office by contacting Judge Longstreet; second, his suggestion that Holt had acted arbitrarily by sending the *Star of the West* forward, and that Buchanan had been forced to countermand Holt's order after Major Anderson discouraged the sending of any ships to Sumter at that particular time. As attentive as he had ever been to the preservation of his reputation when he felt he had been unduly assailed, Holt felt bound to respond publicly to both of these points. At the same time, he was determined to condemn in no uncertain terms Thompson's arrogance in making the speech in the first place, which treated so lightly issues such as national security and sworn loyalty to the Union.[28]

On March 6, the very day he turned the War Department over to Simon Cameron, Holt's rebuke appeared in the *Philadelphia Inquirer*. In it, he characterized Thompson's communication with Judge Longstreet as a complete betrayal of his official position as secretary of the interior, which, Holt pointed out, "he held under the seals of a confidence that, from the beginning of our history as a nation, had never been violated." Holt then called Thompson's decision to alert the secessionists in Charleston an act that, by "endanger[ing] the highest public interests" and jeopardizing the lives of the 250 soldiers on board, "could not be less than offensive to the heart and to the intelligence of the American people." At the same time, he vigorously denied Thompson's accusation that in sending the *Star of the*

West south, he (Holt) had acted against the president's orders. It is true, he acknowledged, that once the *Star of the West* sailed Buchanan had tried to call the ship back, but he had done so only because Anderson's reassurances about his supply situation and his warning that Charlestonians were preparing for a counterattack had arrived too late to call off the mission sooner. Moreover, Holt made clear that Thompson was already fully aware of these details, and that his Mississippi speech could therefore only be construed as one more contribution to the "persistent falsification" of the "conduct of the late Administration, in its relations to the South" by means of which secessionists were "inflaming the popular mind of that distracted portion of our country, and thus giving an increasing impetus to the revolution."[29]

Holt may well have hoped that his detailed, stern, and logical response would resolve once and for all the issues raised by Thompson's infuriating claims. Thompson, however, was unwilling to allow Holt the final word. A few days later, he extended their public dispute in an article that sought to clarify (or perhaps recast) what he had said in his Mississippi speech. Although he had indeed contacted Judge Longstreet prior to completing his letter of resignation, Thompson now claimed, news of the *Star of the West*'s mission had already been published in the Washington papers, and as such, he had not betrayed a state secret or in any way violated his official position or his oath of office. Rather, he had simply done what "honor, truth, justice to myself and Judge Longstreet required of me," and confirmed what the judge probably already knew. Regarding Buchanan's attempt to halt the resupply mission, Thompson now insisted that the president had indeed issued his countermanding order *after* the *Star of the West* had sailed, as Holt claimed. But, he added, it was up to Holt as secretary of war to see to it that the president's orders were carried out, regardless of the timing or the circumstances. Had Holt done his job properly, and had he not been determined to place his own will above Buchanan's, the mission could have been aborted. Thompson then proceeded to attack Holt personally, insisting that any future attempts on his part to curry favor with southern Unionists were doomed to fail. Holt, Thompson declared, "has forfeited all claim to their consideration, and they will not extend to him their confidence. He has waxed fat on their kindness and patronage it is true, but they will reject his approaches with disdain," for "they hold this is a Government of consent, and cannot be kept together by his sovereign remedy of powder and ball." White Southerners, Thompson added, were committed to the enslavement of black people, but they were even more committed to preserving their own freedom, and would never be coerced back into the shattered Union.[30]

In the wake of Thompson's savage charges, Holt decided not to continue the argument in public, although there is no question that his former colleague's accusations (not to mention his brash arrogance) festered in his mind, never to be forgiven. Still, there were other graver national problems that demanded his immediate attention, and so, for now, Holt concentrated his energy on advising and assisting the new Lincoln administration however he could. As in the past, he also continued to field requests for help in getting government jobs and answered numerous requests to give speeches. At the same time, he eagerly gathered news from his contacts across the country. In late March he heard from T. H. Duval, an old friend from Kentucky who was now the U.S. district judge for Texas's Western District and who informed him that the governor, Sam Houston, had recently been "deposed, for refusing to take the [Confederate] test oath, an oath which no one could take, without virtually abjuring his allegiance to the Constitution of the U. States." Duval, who expected that soon all lawyers in Texas would be required to take the oath, planned to refuse. "I will not take it in any capacity," he insisted. Nor would he agree to step down from the bench. "Should the request be made," Duval declared, "I shall decline, upon the ground that if Texas is placed out of the Union by the ordinance of secession . . . then I have no office to resign."[31]

Following a series of tense and ultimately unsuccessful negotiations, on April 12 Fort Sumter became the site of the first clash between the military forces of the United States and the Confederacy under Lincoln's administration. To Holt, this clearly meant war, a war that the United States should not and *must* not be afraid to fight. "Now that the South has begun an unprovoked and malignant war upon the U.S.," he wrote to James Buchanan a few days later, "I am decidedly in favor of prosecuting the struggle until the citizens of the seceded States shall be made to obey the laws as we obey them." Holt was certain that the United States could win the war, which, even if it ended up costing billions of dollars, would be "well worth the expenditures" if the government and the Union were saved.[32] Lincoln agreed, and on April 15, the day after Robert Anderson and his small, exhausted garrison evacuated the fort and Charleston broke out in holiday-like celebration, he issued a proclamation declaring that a domestic insurrection was underway and calling out 75,000 troops from the loyal states to defeat it. Many states across the North responded so enthusiastically that the number of volunteers far exceeded their state governments' ability to handle them. Other states responded differently: in the weeks ahead, Virginia (April 17), Arkansas (May 6), North Carolina (May 20), and Tennessee (June 8) voted to abandon the Union and join the Confederacy, increasing the number of the latter's constituent states to eleven.

Although more than twice that many states (twenty-three) remained loyal—including Oregon and Kansas, which had joined the Union in 1859 and January 1861, respectively—the states that now made up the Confederacy covered about 750,000 square miles of territory, represented a third of the nation's overall population (including millions of enslaved people who could be forced into laboring on its behalf), and claimed a substantial proportion of the country's overall agricultural wealth. Moreover, in the late spring of 1861 it seemed entirely possible that still more states would join those that had already seceded, especially the states located on the border between slavery and freedom, including Delaware, Missouri, and Maryland, where antigovernment riots had already erupted on April 19 when troops en route to defend the federal capital had passed through Baltimore. Also a threat to secede was all-important Kentucky. "I do believe," Holt's friend T. S. Bell had written him optimistically back in January, "that Kentucky will not swing loose from her moorings in the Union." Some, however, were not so sure, including native sons Joseph Holt and Abraham Lincoln.[33]

The history of Kentucky's relationship to the rest of the United States was a mixed one. According to historian E. Merton Coulter, prior to Thomas Jefferson's election to the presidency, Kentuckians' fervent independence was to a great extent at odds with their desire for a comfortable place within the Union. (As has already been noted, in 1798 Kentucky became the first state to articulate the principle that a state could nullify a federal law that it deemed unconstitutional.) However, in large part because Jefferson so clearly envisioned the western regions of the country as integral to the nation's identity, survival, and expansion, his election in 1800 altered Kentuckians' orientation, such that by the early years of the nineteenth century, declarations of "patriotic love" for the nation became a dominant theme among the state's orators, and "anyone so rash as to support sentiments to the contrary was ostracized."[34]

When the Nullification Crisis erupted in South Carolina in 1828, Kentucky as a whole—like Holt—remained firmly on the side of the federal government. That year, and again in 1832, the state's governors—first Thomas Metcalf and then John Breathitt—spoke out vigorously on behalf of the Union and against both nullification and secession, and the state legislature repeatedly issued resolutions calling upon South Carolina "to return to a becoming sense of patriotism." It is hardly insignificant, either, that the Great Compromiser of the antebellum period, Henry Clay, was a Kentuckian. Moreover, when Kentucky donated its block for the Washington monument in the middle of the century, the state's devotion to the Union was literally carved in limestone. "Under the auspices of Heaven and the precepts of Washington," the inscription read, "Kentucky will be the last to give up the Union." Still, it would be a mistake to assume that states' rights sentiment in Kentucky had died out completely by the time Lincoln was elected. Although three of the six states with which Kentucky shared a border were free states (Ohio, Indiana, and Illinois), the other three were slave states (Virginia, Tennessee, and Missouri), and slavery had long been a central feature of Kentucky's economic and racial organization. By 1860, some 225,000 black people there were in chains.[35]

Regardless of their overall fondness for the Union, at the time the Civil War broke out most Kentuckians identified themselves as Southerners, to a great extent because of their commitment to slavery, their geographical position south of the Mason-Dixon Line, and the fact that the bulk of the state's residents who were not born in Kentucky had come there from other slaveholding states, especially Virginia and Tennessee. Moreover, the Mississippi River that defined the state's far western border with Illinois and Missouri also forced Kentuckians' gaze southward. By mid-century, however, Kentucky also had extensive social ties with the rest of the Union: many Kentuckians, for example, had emigrated to places such as Missouri, Illinois, and especially Indiana, where at least ten counties bore the names of individuals born in the Bluegrass State. Many of the state's agricultural products, too, were routinely shipped to markets in the East, creating strong economic ties that simply could not be ignored.[36]

Politically, the overwhelming influence of Henry Clay had made Kentucky, for much of its history, a predominantly National Republican and then a Whig state, with Democrats such as Joseph Holt generally representing the minority voice. The death of Clay in 1852 and the subsequent decline of the Whigs nationally had driven some former Clay supporters briefly into the Know-Nothing Party, in part because they wrongly expected that the Democrats were inclined toward disunionism. In 1855 the state had even elected a governor from the Know-Nothing Party, Charles S. Morehead. But despite the Democratic Party's increasing disarray, in the gubernatorial race of 1859 the Democrats had prevailed, electing Beriah Magoffin on a platform that was proslavery and pro–states' rights but still not explicitly disunionist. That year, the Democrats claimed both branches of the Kentucky state legislature as well.[37]

As the presidential election of 1860 neared, Kentuckians were divided. Now that the Know-Nothings had collapsed, many of their adherents, along with other former Whigs and even some Democrats, aligned themselves with the Constitutional Union Party, whose candidate, John Bell, "put union to the front" but "still desired to be known as favorable to the rights of the states." As for the state's Democratic faithful, after the convention debacle in Baltimore during the summer some chose to support Stephen Douglas. But many more, including Holt, at least temporarily put their faith in the candidate of the party's Southern wing, Kentuckian John C. Breckinridge, who flipped candidate Bell's priorities around and "played states' rights before everything else" but "did not go before the people as opposed to union." Instead, Breckinridge—who down the road would become the last of Jefferson Davis's five secretaries of war—pledged himself to resolving the differences now dividing the North and the South. Few Kentuckians of any party voted for the openly antislavery Lincoln, who received only 1,364 votes across the state (less than 1 percent). In the end, Kentuckians threw their electoral votes to Bell. Lincoln, it is clear, "was no hero in Kentucky."[38]

As was true for the rest of the border states (and indeed, for the nation), the election of Lincoln and the subsequent secession of South Carolina put Kentucky in a profoundly difficult position. According to one contemporary, writing in 1862, "at that period there was not, probably, one person out of a thousand in the State, who did not feel persuaded that the people of the South had received great injury and provocation from the North, and that there was abundant reason for them to apprehend great danger in the future." At the same time, however, "the number was comparatively small, not one in a hundred, perhaps, of the entire population, who were willing to secede from the Federal Union." To many Kentuckians, the prospect of prioritizing the state's allegiance to one part of the country over another seemed impossible, not least because it presented far more dangers than opportunities, economically and otherwise. In order to determine how to respond to the looming crisis, Governor Magoffin called for a special session of the legislature to convene in Frankfort on January 17, 1861. Two weeks before the special session began, the influential Presbyterian minister and former lawyer Reverend Robert J. Breckinridge—presidential candidate John C. Breckinridge's uncle—gave a long and extremely important speech in Lexington.[39]

Born in 1800, Reverend Breckinridge was known for his antislavery (and anti-Catholic) views, and, like Holt, his tenacious Unionism. In his speech, which one source calls "a trumpet call to the faltering, disheartened Unionists of Kentucky and the other Border States," Breckinridge warned fellow Kentuckians in no uncertain terms against exercising "precipitate haste in leaving the Union." "Our duties," he insisted, "can never be made subordinate to our passions without involving us in ruin . . . our rights can never be set above our interests without destroying both." In Breckinridge's mind, as in Holt's, the Constitution, the Union, and the nation were inseparable, and the preservation of all three was of paramount importance for the future of republican ideals in America and, indeed, around the world. To this end, he urged Kentuckians to resist the siren call of fire-eating Southern nationalists who sought to "initiate [a] reign of lawless passion" by calling for rebellion. Such men, he warned, "rarely escape destruction amid the storms they create but are unable to control." Neither Lincoln's election, he continued, nor the wounds that the North and the South had inflicted on each other over the years offered cause for destroying the Union. Moreover, slavery might be widespread in Kentucky, but it was hardly essential to the state's economy, and therefore, to sacrifice the state's loyalty and future welfare in order to preserve it was simply foolish, especially since Kentucky's secession would not preserve slavery but rather serve as "the most effectual means of extinguishing it." "You never committed a greater folly," he thundered, "than you will commit if . . . you allow this single consideration . . . [to] control your whole action in this great crisis." Breckinridge counseled his listeners to think long and hard about taking any action destined "to tear down the most venerable institutions, to insult the proudest emblems of your country's glory, and to treat constitutions and laws as if they were play-things for children." Rather than being party to the destruction of the nation, Breckinridge called on Kentuckians to defend the Constitution and the Union "to the last extremity." Holt, whose views were so similar, could not have said it better.[40]

In the weeks that followed, Robert Breckinridge's speech was reprinted in many newspapers and a copy was placed on the desk of every state legislator who gathered in Frankfort on January 17th. Although it cannot be known how much this particular speech influenced the men who participated in that special legislative session, like their counterparts elsewhere along the border, Kentucky's legislators chose for the time being to reject secession. Instead, they adopted a wait-and-see approach, which persisted through the late winter and early spring as Abraham Lincoln assumed the presidency and began shaping his administration's response to the crisis. Meanwhile, as Holt completed his term as secretary of war and looked ahead for ways to support the Union, still another Kentucky native, Congressman John J. Crittenden—with whom Holt met on several occasions during this period—desperately struggled with others to craft a compromise that would bring the alienated sections back together peacefully. Crittenden did not succeed. Instead, Fort Sumter was attacked and surrendered, and Lincoln issued his call for troops to put down the rebellion. That Lincoln's call included a request for four regiments from Kentucky presented the state with what one historian has called "the greatest and most dangerous problem it had yet been compelled to face," and made its earlier wait-and-see attitude unsustainable. A decision of some sort was now required, either to send troops to defend the nation or to withhold them. In Louisville, John C. Breckinridge denounced Lincoln's call for troops as illegal, and in the end, like Governor Ellis of North Carolina (which would secede a few weeks later), Governor Magoffin declared that Kentucky would "furnish no troops for the wicked purpose of subduing her sister Southern States."[41]

Those who, like Magoffin himself, imagined that this refusal to send troops to Lincoln represented the first clear step along Kentucky's path to secession were destined for disappointment. For one thing, there were many others who considered Magoffin's response the necessary foundation for a policy of "neutrality," which, presumably, might shield the state from taking sides and suffering the consequences of the war that now seemed unavoidable. On April 19, some 5,000 people attending a meeting in Louisville produced a series of resolutions asserting the state's refusal to take sides, and denying troops to both Lincoln *and* the Confederacy. Less than a week later, Governor Magoffin proclaimed Kentucky purely "in a condition of defense." As Coulter explains, the promoters and supporters of Kentucky's neutrality policy understood their efforts as constituting a logical attempt to mediate the national crisis and to make compromise possible. At the same time, they offered neutrality as "a protest against being forced into a war abhorrent and detestable because it seemed to be criminally unnecessary." Clearly, some Kentuckians believed—or at least, earnestly hoped—this stance would save the Union as their own Henry Clay's masterful compromises had done more than once in the past.[42]

Still others, however, and specifically the state's so-called radical Unionists, were determined to do whatever they could not only to prevent Kentucky from seceding but also to persuade its inhabitants that what masqueraded as neutrality was actually tantamount to disloyalty and that active military engagement on behalf of the nation's defense was the only honorable choice. Lincoln certainly hoped that his birth state would adopt a course of military engagement on the Union's behalf, and with good reason. As he so famously put it, "Kentucky gone, we can not hold Missouri, nor, as I think Maryland. These all against us, and the job on our hands is too large for us. We would as well consent to separation at once, including the surrender of this capital." And so, as the smoke from the attack on Fort Sumter cleared, Lincoln called on Holt to embark on an all-out effort to ensure Kentucky's fidelity and, as carefully and smoothly as possible, to transform its supposed neutrality into active military support. Soon Holt became both the symbolic and the practical leader of the state's radical Unionists.[43]

As always, as he pondered the task that lay before him, Holt received many letters advising him how to proceed. Among his most faithful correspondents during this period was his devoted Aunt Mary Ann, who routinely combined family news with details about local political developments, all of which provided him with powerful insights and impressions. On April 22, for example, Aunt Mary Ann declared that the whole family had become "great disunionists," especially his nephew, Thomas's son John, who seemed determined to "sett them all against the goverment." Mary Ann reported that she had recently challenged various members of the family about their political leanings and had cautioned them "to have patience" and realize that "if they did not like Lincon there might be better rulers come along after a while." But young John, she insisted, was intractable: "his heart & hand goes for disunion & he always speaks on that side." For her part, Aunt Mary Ann found John ridiculous. "I never heard such babblin in all my life," she groaned. She noted that she had done her best to dissuade him, reminding him that his own uncle was "doing all he can to save this goverment" while John was doing everything in his power to destroy it. Unfortunately, according to Mary Ann, John's parents, Thomas and Rosina, thought he was brilliant. Changing the subject, Aunt Mary Ann praised Lincoln's call for troops to put down the rebellion, expressing regret that Buchanan had not acted as forcefully when he had the chance. "I think if what Linkon is doing now had have been done at first when Carolina first went from the union when the rebelion was as it were in the bud," she wrote in her charming but wordy way, "that things would have been settled before this." Now, however, there was no choice but to wait and see what happened next, though she worried about rumors that "the police has put arms into the hands of the free negroes to fight the south & that makes the folks here think hard of the people at Cincinatta," where abolitionist sentiment was so strong.[44]

A fervent Unionist within a family of staunch secessionists, Aunt Mary Ann wrote often to her likeminded nephew in Washington. "There is great excitement here," she informed Holt on May 1, and opposition to Lincoln was growing. "Josey," she worried, "every one here will be killed before they will come under or give up to Lincon," a sentiment she was certain was not so much a response to Lincoln's determination to save the Union as a response to the belief that he meant to do more than just contain slavery, he meant to destroy it. "What President Lincon is doing," she wrote, "I believe they would put up with from any other president but they have an idea that he is going to free all the negrows," a prospect she herself, admittedly, did not particularly welcome. Still, Aunt Mary Ann reiterated her support for the Union, and for the new president. "I think what Lincon is doing is wright," she insisted, acknowledging that to say so openly—at least in Stephensport—could "cost me my life." Indeed, Mary Ann was sufficiently anxious about her safety that she wondered whether Holt, or perhaps the president himself, might be willing to provide her with a weapon for self-defense. "Josey," she wrote, "tell Lincon I am a union person & want him to send me a pistol that will shoot 5 or 6 times." Declaring once again that she had always hoped "Ky would stick to the union," Aunt Mary Ann encouraged Holt to take good care of himself in Washington, where she feared that fighting was about to break out. "We expect [in] every mail to hear of a battle at Washington," she wrote, "& if it comes on stay in doors & don't fight unless they attack you."[45]

Two weeks later, Mary Ann reported that from what she could tell from her vantage point in Breckinridge County, Kentucky was "on the eve of withdrawing from the union." In fact, since she last wrote, Governor Magoffin had convened the legislature again, directing it on May 6 to "to take such action as may be necessary for the general welfare." Ten days later, the state's House of Representatives officially endorsed the principle of neutrality, and on May 20 the state Senate followed suit. Soon after, Governor Magoffin issued yet another proclamation, this time forbidding the presence, recruitment, training, or movement on Kentucky soil of troops on either side of the conflict, "for any purpose whatever." At the same time, Magoffin declared that Kentucky would neither "sever her connection with the general government, nor take up arms for either belligerent party," but would instead "arm herself for the protection of peace within her borders, and tender her services as a mediator to effect a just and honorable peace." On May 27, still inspired by Kentucky's tradition of compromise, a border-state convention met in the state capital. As it turns out, apart from Kentucky, only Missouri sent delegates. Nevertheless, the convention—which was presided over by John J. Crittenden and whose members included Holt's former father-in-law, Charles Wickliffe—declared its delegates' loyalty to the Union but also resolved that the United States must develop constitutional guarantees for slavery. In addition, the delegates called for a national convention to settle the dispute between the sections without further military action, but their numbers were so small that their voices could hardly be heard above the sound of the nation thundering to war.[46]

Like so many Kentuckians in the late spring of 1861, Holt's Aunt Mary Ann remained anxious about the state's, and the nation's, future. In late May, after thanking Holt for his "very interesting & explanatory letter" regarding Lincoln's policies, she commented that "if some of the people" she encountered in her daily life "knew as much as I learnt from your letter," they would be "better satisfied with the goverment." Still, she admitted, "there is others that is so prejudiced against President Lincon that if he was to do the best he could they would [still] abuse him." Predictably, and perhaps most poignantly, Mary Ann also feared the immediate implications of disunion for the Holt/Stephens clan. Not content with simply speaking out against the Union, Thomas's son John had recently enlisted in the Confederate army and was on his way to Virginia. "I told John on last Monday," Mary Ann wrote, "that if the goverment took him prisoner they would be bound to hang him," although she confessed, "I only told him so to scear him." Still, she worried that John might be enough of a firebrand that he would consider killing his Uncle Joseph a legitimate act of war should the two meet up at any point, and she warned Holt to stay out of John's way. More generally, she cautioned him about a "secret society" she had observed called the Knights of the Golden Circle, whose members, she reported, planned to "shoot all the influential men in the cabinet" one after another until "they get them all destroyed." Aunt Mary Ann begged her nephew in Washington to be on his guard at all times.[47]

Letters from Holt's brother Robert during this period conveyed their own disturbing insights and impressions. In contrast with Aunt Mary Ann, Robert described the vehement Unionist sentiment he had recently encountered when traveling in Kentucky, which he characterized as "a degree of vindictive hatred of the South and of Southerners more befitting devils than men." Unionists around the state, he insisted, "avow the purpose to exterminate us"—by "us," he meant secessionists—"and seem in their inordinate vanity & egotism to think that they can do it easily & quickly." Robert regretted deeply that Kentucky had not yet cast its lot with the Confederacy, and perhaps even more so that Holt had not yet abandoned the federal capital in disgust. "I have thought much of your position at Washington," he wrote. "It is a false & dangerous one. As a Southerner & democrat you will be the object of Republican vengeance, while your continuance at Washington will be misunderstood at the South, and cause you to be suspected of a connection still with the government, and thus draw upon you the hostility of the South and perhaps the vengeance of the Southern Soldiers when they enter the capital." Apparently blind to Holt's profound and inflexible Unionism, Robert urged his brother to "immediately so act as to place yourself unequivocally with your friends, and avert the total sacrifice of your reputation, and possibly your life." The best way to do this, he advised, was to return to Kentucky right away, and to "stand boldly forth as the champion of her immediate separation from the north." "You have it in your power," he declared, to do both Kentucky and the rest of the South "a vast service." "He who becomes the boldest & strongest champion of [Kentucky's] emancipation and independence now," Robert advised, "will win & wear the civic crown." How alienated Holt felt when he read these words from his brother can only be imagined.[48]

While some in Kentucky were debating the state's future with respect to secession, others had begun preparing in practical ways for armed conflict. Indeed, what might better be called "armed neutrality" quickly became, in Coulter's words, "a game between the two factions" in Kentucky, Unionists and secessionists, "with the state as the stake." For its part, the federal government had no intention of surrendering Kentucky to the Confederacy. On the contrary, "despite dissimulating promises and obscure and ambiguous agreements," Lincoln's administration "seized every opportunity secretly to fasten its hold on the state." To this end, on May 28, it established the Military Department of Kentucky, covering a hundred-mile-wide band of the state reaching from east to west and south of the Ohio River, with its headquarters in Louisville. The department was placed under the command of Kentucky's own hero of Sumter, Robert Anderson, whom Lincoln quietly ordered to begin recruiting troops from Kentucky and western Virginia for defense of the Union. Exhausted from his ordeal in Charleston, the fifty-six-year-old Anderson communicated to Holt his concerns about being able to manage this new responsibility to anyone's satisfaction. But he promised to do all he could, and he closed by invoking divine blessing on Holt for his own efforts to "save our Country and State from the volcano which is now threatening the destruction of all most dear to us."[49]

Both sides of the sectional divide increasingly competed to control Kentucky's military might, not least because of their shared concern that so many of the state's young men, eager for battle, would go elsewhere—as Holt's nephew John had done—to tender their services to the North or the South if they could not be put to good use at home. For his part, for all his vaunted "neutrality," Governor Magoffin decided to permit the Confederacy to solicit enlistments for its army on Kentucky soil. At the same time,

Joshua F. Speed.
Courtesy of the Filson
Historical Society,
Louisville, Kentucky.

he sanctioned the distribution of the state's armaments, which were under his authority, to the overwhelmingly pro-Confederate "State Guards," who were under the command of Simon B. Buckner. Back in early May, Buckner had arranged with the commander of the Federal army's Department of Ohio—then General George B. McClellan—"to respect the neutrality of Kentucky so far as to agree not to occupy any portion of the State except to respond to the call of the governor to assist in expelling the rebels from the State, in case they should attempt to occupy points within its borders." In the meantime, Kentucky Unionists busied themselves with forming groups of "Home Guards" to "prevent the Confederate sympathizers from taking the state out of the Union," and they began trying to arrange for Washington to send arms and other military matériel. On May 3, fourteen companies of eager Kentucky soldiers volunteered for Federal army service.[50]

As the struggle for Kentucky became more heated, the radical Unionists within the state joined Lincoln in turning to Holt, their staunch ally in Washington, for support. On May 24, Joshua F. Speed implored him to do whatever he could to help their cause. Joshua Speed was Lincoln's closest friend, and he and Holt had also known each other at least since the early

1850s, when the two men lived near each other in Louisville. "Kentucky," Speed now declared, "is nervous and excited & the people [are] strug[g]ling between loyalty to the Government and deep seated distrust of the policy of the administration in regard [to] war." Speed was especially concerned about the many Kentuckians who—like Holt's aunt Mary Ann—feared that Lincoln meant to use the war as an opportunity to free the slaves. In light of this, he wrote, it was essential for someone of stature, with the power of persuasion, to act immediately to convince Kentuckians "that this is no war upon individual property and the institution of slavery." After all, Lincoln himself had promised to preserve the institution even though he personally despised it. Speed was certain that if the proper message were conveyed successfully—namely, that the war would be waged for the Union, not for the slaves—"we would be almost a unit for the Government." "For Heaven sake," he pleaded, "aid us if you can"; for as he put it, "the production of no man in the nation would attract more attention."[51]

On May 31, Holt responded to Speed's request with a long open letter, of which 30,000 copies were subsequently printed and distributed across the state and beyond its borders. The refusal of the May 27 border-state convention in Frankfort to endorse secession, Holt declared, had "afforded unspeakable gratification to all true men throughout the country," for it made clear that Kentuckians had been "neither seduced by the arts nor terrified by the menaces of the revolutionists in their midst," and that "it is their fixed purpose to remain faithful to a Government which, for nearly seventy years, has remained faithful to them." Still, Holt continued, "it cannot be denied that there is in the bosom of that State a band of agitators, who, though few in number, are yet powerful from the public confidence they have enjoyed, and who have been, and doubtless will continue to be, unceasing in their endeavors to force Kentucky to unite her fortunes with those of the rebel Confederacy of the South." Never, he insisted, had Kentuckians' "safety and honor" demanded so much vigilance and courage. The problem, he argued, was attributable to a small band of power-hungry conspirators, not the masses of good folk who could be trusted to do what was right. And now, indeed, was the time to do what was right.[52]

From here, Holt launched into a discussion of the whole concept of "neutrality," which he, like Lincoln, found entirely unacceptable: "I would as soon think of being neutral in a contest between an officer of justice and an incendiary arrested in the attempt to fire the dwelling over my head," he declared. To ignore an attack on the Union, he continued, was tantamount to standing by stupidly to watch the destruction of one's own house, but to actually participate in such an attack was unforgivable. Like Robert J.

Breckinridge before him, Holt had stern words of warning for Kentuckians who were considering secession: no possible benefit could be expected from forsaking the Union. Rather, Holt implored the people of his native state to "rouse themselves from their lethargy, and fly to the rescue of their country before it is everlastingly too late." The ship of state was sinking, and he who "in such an hour will not work at the pumps," Holt insisted, "is either a maniac or a monster."[53]

In the weeks that followed, copies of Holt's open letter to Joshua Speed blanketed the state and the entire border region. "I have heard no discordant opinion about the letter," wrote his friend T. S. Bell, who had been instrumental in having the copies produced in Louisville. Rather, "it is looked upon here as the ablest document the crisis has produced, an opinion in which I concur with my whole heart." Bell predicted that Kentuckians would respond favorably to Holt's call to action. Others, too, sent letters of thanks: "magnificent," proclaimed Judge John Speed, whose son Joshua had solicited the letter in the first place, and whose son James also numbered among Holt's Louisville friends and Kentucky's most radical Unionists.[54]

As May gave way to June, the struggle for Kentucky continued; in the weeks and months ahead, Holt's influence was "almost predominant." Indeed, late in June Holt made plans to visit the state personally with an eye toward furthering the nation's cause now that a special state election on June 20 had resulted in an "overwhelming victory" for Unionist candidates—including Charles Wickliffe—to the U.S. Congress. Although the election demonstrated that the Unionists were making real headway, however, it did not manage to defeat the neutrality policy. "There has never been a time when Kentucky could have given you such a welcome as she is ready to extend to you now," wrote T. S. Bell a few days later. Then, as he had done so many times before, Bell praised Holt for his relentless stand against secession. "Through more than half my days upon the earth, I have rejoiced in your friendship," he wrote, "yet, well as I knew your unsullied integrity, I cannot but feel that you are doubly dear to me now, since, in time of need you have proved yourself my country's friend, and the true & trusted champion of law and order."[55]

On July 1, Holt met with Secretary of State Seward, presumably to discuss border state affairs, and a few days later he was on his way west. Once in Kentucky, Holt gave a number of well-attended and widely acclaimed pro-Union speeches, including two that were particularly noteworthy for their eloquence as well as their vehemence. On July 13, he spoke on "the fallacy of neutrality" to a large crowd gathered at the Masonic Temple in

Louisville. Neutrality, Holt insisted once again, was a myth. "Strictly and legally speaking," he explained, "Kentucky must go out of the Union before she can be neutral. Within it she is necessarily either faithful to the government of the United States, or she is disloyal to it." In essence, he continued, so-called neutrality was "but a snake in the grass of the rebellion" that "necessarily implies indifference," a sentiment he was sure Kentuckians did not really feel. "It is her house that is on fire," he pointed out; "has she no interest in extinguishing the conflagration?" [56]

More vividly that he had ever done before, Holt now declared himself an unswerving, unapologetic Unionist who would go to virtually any lengths to save the nation. The federal government, he insisted, had always fulfilled its constitutional obligations toward the South. Moreover, Abraham Lincoln had been duly elected, which meant that there was no legitimate cause for the "revolutionary outbreak" the South had engineered. And although not so long ago he had criticized the "Black Republicans" and abolitionists for stirring up disunionist sentiment across the South, Holt now turned his scornful eye exclusively on the leading slaveholders who, having come to the erroneous conclusion that Lincoln meant to destroy the racial labor system on which they depended for their vast wealth, had set about deceiving the masses into risking their own lives, and the nation's, simply to support their "way of life." Once again, Holt pointed with particular outrage to the leaders of the rebel "conspiracy" who as politicians and military men had once sworn to uphold the Constitution and the general government but had since revealed themselves to be nothing more than "the ungrateful sons of a fond mother." Holt also directly criticized Kentucky's governor, Magoffin, for his "hostile and defiant" refusal to send troops to the Union's aid. In contrast, he praised President Lincoln abundantly for "heroically and patriotically struggling to baffle the machinations of these most wicked men." Lincoln, Holt declared, "has the courage to look traitors in the face"; "in discharging the duties of his great office, he takes no counsel of his fears," said Holt, and as such was "entitled to the zealous support of the whole country." [57]

Just in case his own position on the national crisis was not yet clear, Holt again pronounced himself "for this Union without conditions," and "for its preservation at any and every cost of blood and treasure against all its assailants." Compromise was impossible, he insisted, if it meant negotiating "under the guns of the rebels." The only option was active support, "complete, enduring and overwhelming, to the armies of the republic over all its enemies." Turning to history, Holt observed that free societies had always found it necessary "to fight for their liberties against traitors within their own bosoms." Now was the time for Kentuckians to take up that fight, and if they did not have "the greatness of soul" to do so, they should face the fact that they would soon be forced to surrender their freedom. "If this government is to be destroyed," he concluded, "ask yourselves are you willing it shall be recorded in history that Kentucky stood by in the greatness of her strength and lifted not a hand to stay the catastrophe."[58]

Holt's July 13, 1861, speech was a resounding success. Calling it a "fiery," "energetic," and "sublime vindication of the Union cause," the *New York Times* praised the Kentuckian's "impassioned eloquence," "fervent patriotism," and "burning invective against his country's foes," attributing to him a "vivid portraiture of the causes, the circumstances and consequences of the gigantic treason that menaces the land." The paper further applauded Holt for summoning, with incomparable persuasiveness, "all the noble sentiments and memories of his hearers, to come up to their duty in this dark hour of the nation's danger." The American public, the *Times* added, "never could understand why a man of powers so extraordinary refused to enter an arena where success would so surely have crowned him." But it explained that those who knew Holt understood that he was an entirely honorable man without political ambition, who "valued his self-respect and independence beyond all earthly offices and rewards."[59]

Two weeks later Holt spoke again, this time on the heels of the Federals' stunning and disheartening July 21 rout at the First Battle of Bull Run and in anticipation of the August 5 elections for the state legislature, which would give Kentuckians yet another opportunity to register via the ballot box their feelings about secessionism, "neutrality," and actively engaged Unionism. Holt's July 31 audience was a group of newly enlisted Kentucky troops under the command of General Lovell Rousseau, who had gathered the men for training at a site just across the Ohio River from Louisville—in Jeffersonville, Indiana—in order to avoid accusations that he was violating the state's neutrality policy, and it included a company known as the "Jo Holt Rifles," led by Captain C. L. Thomasson. In honor of the man they considered their state's preeminent Unionist, General Rousseau's men had named their recently established bivouac "Camp Jo Holt," which eventually grew to be a 1,700-man garrison including two army regiments, two companies of cavalry, and one artillery battery. Holt was deeply moved. "I should have felt proud," he informed the soldiers and the many civilians who joined them for the occasion, "to have had my name connected with the humblest trapping of your encampment, but to have it linked with the encampment itself, and thus inscribed, as it were, upon one of the milestones that mark your progress toward those fields of danger and of fame that await you, is at once an honor and a token of your confidence and good will for which I cannot be too profoundly thankful."[60]

Holt was pleased to have an opportunity to speak to Kentuckians who were no longer deliberating their position vis-à-vis secession, and especially to be able to do so just across the river from his father's farm, from which as a child, he noted, he had gazed upon Indiana's "free homes and grand forests." Holt praised the men before him for having the courage to proclaim their loyalty "unchilled by the arctic airs of neutrality" and to put themselves on the line for the nation's salvation, "unawed by traitors." Theirs, he insisted, was a holy cause, second only to the worship of God. Holt warned the soldiers not to be seduced by the many temptations of camp life, and he pleaded with them to resist characterizing the South as a "foreign enemy" deserving of "conquest or spoliation." Their targets, he reminded them, were the leaders of the secessionist conspiracy, not the Southern people generally and certainly not slavery as an institution, regardless of the rumors anti-Lincoln activists were spreading. "Should you occupy the South," Holt commanded, "you will do so as friends and protectors, and your aim will not be to subjugate that betrayed and distracted country, but to deliver it from the remorseless military despotism by which it is trodden down." Holt urged the men to move forward with optimism, and he promised that they would soon have "not only the moral but the material support of Kentucky" they needed to accomplish their task.[61]

As with his speech on July 13, the response to Holt's speech on July 31 was wonderfully favorable, not just in Kentucky but also in far-flung parts of the Union. "You will be surprised and, I know, not displeased to learn," wrote M. T. McMahon of San Francisco some weeks later, that "the words you addressed to your countrymen of Kentucky in your published letter and at Camp Holt, coming over the great plains and snowy mountains to your fellow citizens here, were republished in pamphlet and circular and sent abroad to every town and village and mining camp in the state." Meanwhile, Holt did more than just give speeches; he also energetically supported the recruitment of loyal men in the state for military service and played a key role in arranging, by clandestine means, to get them the arms they needed. On August 1, Kentucky-born William "Bull" Nelson thanked Holt for this crucial assistance. Immediately after the August 5 elections had increased the Unionists' control over the state legislature, Nelson had established Camp Dick Robinson not far from Danville, the first camp set up in Kentucky for training soldiers specifically for Federal army service. Nelson was especially grateful for the muskets his troops had just received, for which he gave Holt credit and without which, he was certain, "Magoffin and the State Guard would have stampeded us out of the Union." Instead, Nelson declared confidently, Kentucky's neutrality policy could now be expected to give way to active defense of the Union. For his part, Governor Magoffin considered Nelson's establishment of Camp Dick Robinson on Kentucky soil (unlike Camp Jo Holt in Indiana) a breach of the state's "neutrality," and he asked Lincoln to shut it down. The president refused, pointing out that Nelson's men were all native Kentuckians and that they had organized to defend the state. At the same time, Lincoln quietly ordered 5,000 guns to be sent to Cincinnati and distributed, with help from the Speed brothers and Charles Wickliffe, to loyal Kentuckians.[62]

Over the course of the summer of 1861, thanks to the efforts of Holt and his allies, Unionist sentiment in Kentucky grew steadily. In early August, a relieved Holt headed back east, where he undertook a brief speaking tour through New York and New England, echoing the themes he had articulated in Kentucky, including the importance of responding to the Confederate rebellion with armed force while rooting out disloyalty at home in any form. "The rush of visitors yesterday . . . to grasp the hand of Joseph Holt," declared the *Boston Post* following one of his speeches, "gave thrilling evidence of the irresistible magic of devoted, unselfish patriotism. Of all the men brought out in bold relief by the nation's startling peril, none has shone more conspicuously than the gallant Kentuckian whose clarion voice and loyal counsel have ever been for his country." The paper concluded, "With a few men like Joseph Holt in administrative power, all doubts as to our country's salvation would be dispelled." During this period, Holt was also invited to write an article for the *Atlantic Monthly* "on some phase of our national troubles," and in recognition of his efforts to save the Union he was awarded an honorary doctorate of laws by Jefferson College (now Washington and Jefferson College) in Pennsylvania. *Harper's Weekly* commented that Holt's "masterly and impassioned" pro-Union speeches in this period gave him a place "among the most illustrious Americans," for "true patriots," the journal insisted, "are those who are faithful to their country when fidelity is dangerous."[63]

As the summer passed, Holt kept his eye on the latest developments in Kentucky, where Unionists had begun to express fresh concerns, this time that the U.S. Congress's August 6 passage of its first confiscation law of the war would undermine all their efforts to date. The confiscation law allowed the federal government to seize any property being used by supporters of the Confederacy to wage their rebellion. And since the law could easily be interpreted to include human property, many slaveholding Unionist Kentuckians feared that their earnest defense of the federal government's authority might now cast them as emancipationists in the eyes of their opposition, regardless of how much they in fact meant only to support the Union *as it was*. If Unionism came to be equated irrevocably in the popular mind with antislavery sentiment, they were certain, any hope of sustaining the state's loyalty was lost. Writing just two days after the Confiscation Act passed, Joshua Speed urged Holt to make it clear to the powers that be in Washington, and especially to Speed's good friend Lincoln, that "our people can stand defeat upon the battle field, for that can be wiped out. They will stand taxation, too, for war." But Kentuckians would not tolerate the confiscation law, which Speed declared "frightful."[64]

Much more "frightful" still was the proclamation issued by General John C. Frémont, who had been in command since late July of the Federal army's Department of the West, headquartered in St. Louis and encompassing "all states and territories west of the Mississippi River to the Rocky Mountains." Following the Confederate victory earlier that month in the Battle of Wilson's Creek—considered the "second significant battle of the Civil War" after Bull Run, and the only major battle to take place in Missouri—Frémont had declared martial law across the state. Then, on August 30, he unilaterally proclaimed that all slaves in the area under his jurisdiction were free, thereby going beyond the already-troubling dictates of the Confiscation Act passed by Congress on August 6, which legalized the federal *seizure* of slaves but did not necessarily *emancipate* them. Frémont had hoped to undermine the Confederacy's cause by depriving slaveholders for good of the labor of their human property. Instead, he sparked a firestorm: Kentucky Unionists were horrified. The *Louisville Journal* pronounced the proclamation "dangerous and odious" and demanded that it be "promptly repudiated by the Government."[65]

As they had done so many times before, Kentucky's radical Unionists once again called on Holt, asking him to use whatever influence he had in Washington to have Frémont's proclamation withdrawn. On September 7, Joshua Speed commented that he had already written to the president detailing his concerns, having conferred with other strong antisecessionists in the state, all of whom were equally convinced that Frémont's proclamation would certainly weaken, and probably completely shatter, Kentucky's support for the federal government. Now Speed turned to Holt. Sudden emancipation, he wrote, would be a disaster for Kentucky, and the man who attempted to enforce such an abrupt change in the state's racial labor system might as well "attempt to ascend the falls of Niagara in a canoe." Speed was confident that Holt, who had grown up in a slaveholding Kentucky family, would understand these concerns viscerally in a way that Lincoln could not, having been raised in free Indiana and Illinois and having never owned another human being himself. He implored Holt to use whatever influence he had with the president to prevent "the foolish act of a military popinjay" from driving Kentucky into the arms of the Confederacy. As it turns out, Holt had written to Lincoln on his own on September 2, warning him that traitors within the state were "preparing to cast her out of the Union by a *coup de main*" and pleading with him to authorize "an *immediate* demonstration of some kind indicating the purpose & present ability of the govt to sustain its friends there." Lincoln, however, had already reached the conclusion that Frémont's order would "alarm our Southern Union friends, and turn them against us," and "perhaps ruin our rather fair prospect for Kentucky." Still, he was not keen to pull rank on one of his generals, and he settled for the time being for asking Frémont to modify his proclamation in such a way as to bring it into conformity with the August 6 legislation.[66]

Even as Lincoln was conveying his subdued request to Frémont, however, the military situation in Kentucky was becoming explosive. Neutrality proved impossible to maintain, and on September 3, Confederate forces under the command of Brigadier General Gideon Pillow, on orders from Major General Leonidas Polk, invaded the extreme southwestern tip of the state, taking a position near Columbus. Polk claimed that he sent the troops to protect Kentucky from an anticipated Federal incursion into the strategically important area that stood at the intersection of the Tennessee and Ohio Rivers and not far from the mouth of the Cumberland. In addition, he insisted that the federal government had already violated Kentucky's neutrality by establishing Camp Dick Robinson within the state's borders, by creating the Military Department of Kentucky, and by building up its forces in Missouri. Now the Confederacy was simply acting on Kentucky's behalf. Four days after the Confederate troops arrived, Federal troops under the command of Ulysses S. Grant followed suit, capturing Paducah, located forty miles from Columbus at the mouth of the Tennessee, and giving Union forces control of that waterway. This was Grant's first major victory in the war, and it was a bloodless one.[67]

As these events were taking place, Holt wrote to Lincoln again, reminding him that Frémont's proclamation had greatly alarmed the Union-loving citizens of Kentucky and urging him to reconsider how important it was to preserve the state's loyalty at all costs. Holt urged the president to take bolder steps than he had done so far to make clear that Frémont's emancipation order did not reflect the administration's views or its future plans: presumably Lincoln could use his powers as commander in chief to revoke the order. Tired of waiting for Frémont to respond to his earlier prodding, Lincoln concurred, and he now dispatched Holt—fresh from giving a rousing progovernment speech in New York—to St. Louis, bearing orders explicitly overturning that portion of Frémont's proclamation pertaining to slave emancipation. On September 20, a grateful James Speed thanked Holt effusively for all that he had done to counteract Frémont's dreadful blunder. "I think," Speed wrote, "that in procuring what you did from the President, you did a great service to Kentucky." From his friend T. S. Bell, Holt also received thanks. "The world has recognized you as the embodiment of the purest patriotism," Bell wrote, and "as one of the clearest, most determined and thorough champions of free institutions, and I cannot but rejoice that one in whom I recognized an unblemished integrity twenty nine years ago, held it pure and unsullied when infidelity seemed the rule, and treason arrayed itself in blandishments that made men quake at times for themselves." [68]

According to Bell, Kentucky had responded as expected to Lincoln's revocation of Frémont's proclamation: neutrality was now officially dead, having collapsed "so suddenly that a coroner would be justified in issuing a writ of inquiry to ascertain whether it was a case of suicide." Kentucky, Bell wrote, and "indeed the whole Union is under a debt of gratitude to you . . . that cannot soon be paid." A September 24 editorial in the *Detroit Tribune*, however, suggested that some people were not so sure. "It appears," the editorial began, "that the Hon. Joseph Holt interceded for the modification of Fremont's Proclamation. If it was to come, we are glad it came on the representations of such a man." Still, the *Tribune* wondered if it might not have been better to let the rebels "feel the crushing weight of this rebellion," which likely would, and probably should, result in the destruction of slavery. "Let those who do not obey" the Constitution and the laws, the paper demanded, "take care of themselves. We can't even stop to convert them; we want them suppressed now and forever." [69]

Looking back after the war, at least one late-nineteenth-century historian of Kentucky argued that "fallacious and almost ridiculous" as the state's initial neutrality policy was, it nevertheless "served its purpose in preventing hostilities within the State, and in securing to the Union men time for organization and preparation to resist secession" in case state elections "should result in seating a majority of 'southern-rights' men in the legislature." In any case, neutrality as an official policy in the state was indeed dead by mid-September, although rich pockets of secessionist sentiment persisted, encouraged by figures such as Simon B. Buckner, who now called upon Kentuckians "to defend their homes against the invasion of the North," and prepared to turn his services over to the Confederacy. For this reason, Holt in Washington and his Unionist allies in Kentucky did not rest in their efforts to ensure that the state's loyal population and the troops they were raising for the Federal army were sufficiently well armed. On September 15, Robert Anderson's brother Larz reported from Cincinnati that Joshua Speed had managed to procure "Four Thousand Belgian rifles & muskets, to be forwarded immediately to Jeffersonville," though they were still waiting for cartridge boxes and ammunition. Anderson noted, too, that Lincoln and Secretary of War Cameron had "promised that the rest of the guns needed should be forwarded as soon as possible," but that a bit of additional prompting and encouragement from Holt might speed the process. T. S. Bell urged Holt to make sure the guns and equipment that had been earmarked for Kentucky were sent quickly. "I have a great deal of hope for our success in your unceasing vigils and indomitable energies," he wrote, adding in a telegram two days later: "Push everything you can in this direction immediately."[70]

The work of arming Kentucky for Federal service continued deep into the fall: on October 18, Joshua Speed wrote that General McClellan, now serving as the army's general-in-chief, had approved another order for almost 2,000 Belgian-made guns, but that, as before, there was some question about the ammunition and "accoutrements" that should accompany them. "The guns will be worth nothing unless we get these," he wrote, requesting that Holt investigate and report back. "Will you be so good as to write fully about the Bayonets only fitting each particular gun," he asked, "& have them so packed as there will be no mistake. Also about the needles & filing the nipples to make the caps fit." The following day, Speed reported from New York that he had just purchased 500 French rifles, "the best gun I have seen." He hoped to be able to get another hundred good muskets in the city, and some Springfield rifles, too. "I find that to do anything here," Speed wrote, "I will have to buy in small lots, which will probably keep me here till the last of next week."[71]

Although both Federal and Confederate forces had been present in Kentucky since early September, their first real clash did not occur until late October at a place called Camp Wildcat, about 120 miles southwest of Louisville. In this fierce fight, General Felix Zolicoffer and about 5,400 Confederate troops confronted some 7,000 Federals led by the Polish-born Brigadier General Albin F. Schoepf. Schoepf, it turns out, had served in the 1840s with the Hungarian revolutionary Louis Kossuth—whom Holt had introduced when he visited Louisville in 1852—and after emigrating to the United States he had worked with Holt in both the Patent Office and

Buchanan's War Department. Following the battle, in which the Confederates were finally forced to withdraw, James Speed was pleased to inform Holt that Schoepf, whom Holt had recommended to Lincoln for an army command, had performed extremely well, making "a most favourable impression upon officers & men." Joked Speed: "As Mr. Lincoln said to us, that you must bear the blame or take the credit of his conduct as the case might be, I am glad to inform you of the first impression made by him." Lincoln himself wrote to Holt on November 12: "You are not mistaken in supposing I am gratified extremely by the excellent conduct of *your* general at Camp Wildcat." Holt remained friends for many years with Schoepf, his wife Julie, and their nine children, one of whom they named after him.[72]

Through the fall of 1861, Holt, T. S. Bell, the Speeds, and other determined Kentucky Unionists continued collaborating to keep the state's progovernment military forces adequately supplied. During this period, Holt learned of the birth of yet another child who would grow up bearing his name: in late October, Colonel William Gates of Brooklyn informed him that he and his wife had just had a son, and they had decided to name him Joseph Holt Gates. There were other honors, too: from David L. Collier of Nebraska, Holt received the news that an entire county had just been named after him in that state. Around this same time, the *Detroit Free Press* also noted that while visiting the city that fall, former president Franklin Pierce, a Unionist Democrat, had declared that "he would rather see Joseph Holt President than any man living."[73]

In late November, Joshua Speed was back in Washington, where he and his wife stayed at Brown's Hotel but gratefully accepted Holt's offer to make his carriage, horses, and driver available to them. "We have made pretty free use of them," wrote Speed, "for which we are thankful," and he added with humor, "I feel that you are my friend, and acting upon the old adage, that a man must learn to use his friends, I have ventured very far in the use of your property." As the two men continued to ensure that the flow of military supplies to Kentucky approached a comfortingly steady and sustainable level, Speed wrote again, this time with relief. "I am getting a pretty fair supply of arms for Ky," he reported, "and as much money as we need." The state, he added, "has now thirty regiments armed and enlisted for three years or the war, and will have ten more so soon as I can get it the guns."[74]

By mid-January 1862 Speed had returned to Louisville, where he maintained regular contact with Holt regarding the military situation in their home state. Then, on January 18, he requested that Holt provide him with a letter of introduction to Edwin Stanton, whom Speed hoped to visit in

Washington within the next few weeks. Speed's request reflected an important change in Lincoln's cabinet: on January 11, Secretary of War Cameron had resigned and Lincoln had replaced him with Stanton, a choice that surprised many, including Speed, who had anticipated that the president would select Holt instead. Back in December, Speed had confided to Holt that the president had indicated in a private conversation that he was preparing to appoint Holt to a position in his administration "commensurate with the service [he had] rendered the country" in its hour of need. At that time, Speed had assumed that Lincoln was considering turning the War Department over to Holt, and he recommended that Holt take the post if Lincoln offered it. "You could render great service to the nation in that position," he wrote, adding that Holt's return to the War Department would also enhance the possibility that he would someday become president. Speed declared Holt's chances for earning the nation's highest office "better than those of any other man." After all, he pointed out, "No man now has so firm a hold upon the popular heart." When Lincoln chose Stanton to head the War Department instead, Speed declared himself "sorely disappointed."[75]

For his part, however, Holt seems to have been quite content with Lincoln's decision, and indeed, it may have been he who recommended Stanton for the War Department slot in the first place, as Stanton had recommended him for the post back in late December 1860. In Stanton, Holt assured Lincoln on January 15, "you will find a friend true as steel, & a support which no pressure from within or from without will ever shake." He added, "With his great talents, he is the soul of honor, of courage, & of loyalty." To Stanton himself, Holt also made clear his satisfaction with Lincoln's choice: on January 25, Stanton thanked Holt for his "generous and cordial support," which, he insisted, "strengthens my heart more than I can tell." Stanton also recalled with pride and appreciation their work together during the secession winter. "We stood together at the beginning of this mighty contest," he wrote, "and by God's blessing we will stand together until the end." Stanton encouraged Holt in the months ahead to speak his mind freely on matters of national defense and to give him the benefit of his own experience in the War Department. "I need your counsel and aid more now than ever," Stanton wrote; "advise and instruct me in all things where you think it may do good." Stanton was rightly convinced that the two still shared "but one feeling and purpose, the same that animated us both when we were in counsel together twelve months ago," namely, "to crush this rebellion and restore the majesty of this Government and the authority of its Constitution and laws."[76]

Within weeks, even skeptical Joshua Speed found himself in agreement with Holt that Stanton was indeed "the man for the place." For one thing, Speed greatly appreciated the new secretary's efforts to impose order on the previously chaotic, fraud-wracked War Department and to fill his requests for guns and other matériel immediately. "Thus I have accomplished in a few days what heretofore it would have taken as many weeks to do," he wrote in early February. "I shall be much mistaken if [Stanton] does not infuse into the whole army an energy and activity which we have not seen heretofore." T. S. Bell, too, declared himself "delighted with Mr. Stanton's appointment," having already known "something of his manliness & ability through your commendations." Bell admitted that there had been "much grumbling" among Holt's supporters when Lincoln did not offer him the War Department post, but he also noted that he was pretty sure Holt had had enough of that experience during the secession winter. Others were pleased, for very different reasons, that Holt had not— at least, not yet—accepted a position in the Lincoln administration. "For God's sake do not accept a seat in the present Cabinet," wrote one Philadelphia correspondent. "If you do, it will destroy the hopes of your friends" and "ruin . . . your career." This correspondent urged Holt to keep a good distance between himself and the president, whose administration, he was certain, was destined to fail. "Keep quiet," he wrote, and "do not identify yourself with things as they are; your time is coming."[77]

Although Lincoln had elected not to appoint him as Simon Cameron's replacement, Holt had plenty to do. In addition to continuing to cement Kentucky's place in the Union and ensuring its military preparedness, Holt also served from late October 1861 to March 1862 with Hugh Campbell and David Davis—an old friend of Lincoln's and a former college classmate of Stanton—as a member of a War Department commission organized to investigate claims against Frémont's Military Department in the West. Holt acknowledged his appointment in a November 12 letter to the president: "Not wishing to occupy any portion of your valuable time with a personal interview," he wrote, "I avail myself of this mode of expressing my thanks for the token of confidence with which you have honored me." Holt promised to leave for St. Louis immediately and to do his best "to execute the trust committed to me in a faithful & satisfactory manner." "You have with you my good friend Judge David Davis," Lincoln replied, "and allow [me] to assure you, you were never associated with a better man." Then, beginning in mid-March, Holt accepted another short-term appointment from the War Department, this time to serve as its commissioner of ordnance claims, which required him "to audit and adjust all contracts, orders, and claims in the files of the Department relating to arms, ammunition, and ordnance." For both commissions, Holt was required to make extensive, detailed, and time-consuming reports for review by the president, the War Department, and Congress.[78]

Late in the summer of 1862, with Kentucky secured to the Union, the war well into its second year, and the surrenders of Forts Henry and Donelson, the Battle of Shiloh, the capture of New Orleans, and the Peninsula and Valley campaigns in Virginia now in the record books, Lincoln found a much bigger job for which he considered Holt the ideal candidate. On September 3, he enthusiastically accepted the unqualified recommendation of Secretary of War Stanton and appointed Holt judge advocate general of the army.[79]

5

LINCOLN'S JUDGE ADVOCATE GENERAL, SEPTEMBER 3, 1862– APRIL 14, 1865

With a formidable foe in arms in his front, and this fire in his rear, I am
fearful he will not be able to save this republic. It is a dark hour for us.
—Jesse Kincheloe to Joseph Holt, on Lincoln, January 1863

Joseph Holt was not the nation's first judge advocate general of the army, but the post that he assumed on September 3, 1862, had changed dramatically since the war began, not unlike the Federal army itself, which had grown from a small force of about 16,000 regular soldiers into a massive conglomerate of regular and volunteer regiments in which more than 2.2 million men served before the war came to a close. Prior to the Civil War, the federal government "agency" assigned to monitor the application of military law had consisted of a single bureaucrat, whose responsibilities had been limited to maintaining the army's court-martial records. On July 17, 1862, however, the U.S. Congress substantially expanded the size and purview of the judge advocate general's office, assigning to its head the rank, pay, and allowance of a colonel of cavalry and authorizing him to appoint a team of assistant judge advocates, each of whom served with the rank and pay of a major. The tasks assigned to the office also multiplied: henceforth they included (but were not limited to) receiving, revising, and recording the proceedings of all courts-martial, courts of inquiry, and military commissions conducted by the army; providing reports to the secretary of war in connection with those cases that required the action of the president; dealing with applications for clemency received either by the president or the secretary of war; overseeing— and in many cases, personally preparing—the charges against individuals being brought to trial; rendering an opinion on any and all questions of military law (or on the internal legal workings of the War Department), as requested by the president, the secretary of war, or the army's commanding general; and assisting in the review of cases brought for appeal. In sum, the army's judge advocate general became the government's premier adjudicator of military law in much the same way that the attorney general was the premier arbiter of the law in the civil realm.[1]

Holt became the nation's first judge advocate general under the July 1862 act, and as had been true with all of his earlier federal appointments, news of his installment in this post of supreme importance spread quickly. Even *Scientific American* took happy note of his latest assignment. Within a week of his appointment, Holt heard from an assistant of Frank Moore, the author and compiler of a number of books about the war, who hoped to include a brief biography of the new judge advocate general in his forthcoming work, *Heroes and Martyrs*. Perhaps even more gratifying (if familiar in its contents) was the letter he received from Owen Hitchens of Frostburg, Maryland, not long after the news of his appointment became public. "I have a little boy that I desire to call after your name," Hitchens wrote, "and having seen it in public prints sometimes Joe and others Joseph—will you be kind enough to inform me which is correct?"[2]

As had been the case before, Holt had little time to savor such accolades. Virtually from the moment he took office he was inundated with the work of organizing, conducting, and reviewing the results of the seemingly endless stream of legal cases that now came under his authority, many of which demanded careful analysis, thorough reconsideration and review, and the production of additional and often lengthy written reports. Holt's duties required him to consult directly and on a regular basis with the president, whose opinion and decision-making power were frequently essential components of the process, especially in cases where a defendant faced dismissal from the army or execution. Investigation into the court-martial files of the judge advocate general's office during this period indicates that Lincoln, Holt, and the president's secretary, John G. Nicolay, typically met in the morning (when the president was available), Holt making the half-block trip to the Executive Mansion from his War Department office on 17th Street NW, near F Street. On some occasions the trio considered more than seventy cases in a single sitting; at least once, they spent six straight hours in consultation.[3]

For each case that he brought to Lincoln's attention, Holt summarized the charges, the evidence, the sentence, the opinions presented by previous reviewers, and his own recommendations. When Holt and the president disagreed on how to handle a particular case, it was typically Holt who took the harder line, though his often extended written opinions also reveal him to be capable of demonstrating "compassionate good sense." Moreover, Holt was disinclined to try to impose his will on the president.

"I certainly have no disposition to oppose the impulses of your kind heart in the matter," he wrote on one occasion, regarding a case where their opinions differed sharply. Holt himself admitted that Lincoln's overarching desire to save a life, if he could do so, tended to make him the more forgiving of the two men. Holt, too, valued life. But as he had made quite clear since South Carolina's attack on Fort Sumter, he was determined to punish rigorously those who strove to destroy the nation, as well as those who were derelict in their duty to save it. Nevertheless, if one detailed analysis of more than 15,000 cases that came under Lincoln's and Holt's review during the war is in fact correct, the president and his judge advocate general agreed more than 90 percent of the time.[4]

When he appointed Holt to the post of judge advocate general, Lincoln was on the verge of issuing two major proclamations, both of which he fully expected Holt to endorse and implement. The first came just days after Federal forces drove Confederate general Robert E. Lee to abandon his invasion of Maryland following the Battle of Antietam, which claimed over 3,600 soldiers' lives. On September 22, Lincoln issued his preliminary Emancipation Proclamation, which built upon the foundation of the Second Confiscation Act that Congress had passed two months earlier (on the same day, in fact, that it created the judge advocate general's office). Even stronger than its August 1861 predecessor, the Second Confiscation Act recalled John C. Frémont's aborted proclamation, which had produced so much anxiety among Kentucky Unionists, by providing that "slaves of all those who supported or aided the rebellion would be free when they came within Union control." In addition, the act empowered the president to employ freed slaves for the purpose of suppressing the Confederate rebellion, even as soldiers. Now, Lincoln's preliminary Emancipation Proclamation broadened the implications of the Second Confiscation Act by putting Americans on notice that as of January 1, 1863, "all persons held as slaves, within any state, or designated part of a state, the people whereof shall then be in rebellion against the United States shall be then, thenceforward, and forever free." Thanks to Congress's action that summer, these former slaves could now be enlisted to serve the federal cause, militarily and otherwise.[5]

Two days after he issued his preliminary Emancipation Proclamation, Lincoln also suspended the writ of habeas corpus, opening the door wide for the military trial not just of enlisted men and their officers but also, by means of military commissions, of "all Rebels and Insurgents, their aiders and abettors within the United States, and all persons discouraging volunteer enlistments, resisting militia drafts, or guilty of any disloyal practice," such as "affording comfort to Rebels against the authority of the United States." As a result, on top of all the strictly military cases for which they were responsible, it now fell to Judge Advocate General Holt and his assistants to evaluate the evidence against civilians accused of disloyalty in any form and to determine whether or not those civilians should be subjected, like soldiers under indictment, to trial in a military court. Clearly, both Holt's workload and his sheer power in connection with the interpretation, application, and enforcement of military law over soldiers as well as civilians were immense. So, too, was his sense of personal and professional accountability for ensuring the nation's safety and survival by maintaining order in the army, keeping Federal soldiers focused on and committed to their goal of destroying the Confederacy, and disarming civilian enemies of the state and its military arm wherever they appeared.[6]

Although each of Lincoln's September 1862 proclamations was distinct in terms of its specific content, the consequences of the two were tightly intertwined. Among other things, both proclamations indicated that eighteen months into the war, Lincoln was prepared to renounce his earlier "soft-war" tactics, by which he had originally sought to train the Federal army's sights as completely as possible on their enemies in Confederate uniform rather than on the rebellion's civilian supporters and their human and other property. (Holt had taken this same "soft-war" approach in his speech to the recruits at Camp Jo Holt in July 1861.) Lincoln's decisive shift in the fall of 1862 toward a "hard-war" approach now identified Confederate civilians and any of their allies located in the border states and across the North as just as responsible for the war as the Confederacy's army and its political leadership. The suppression of civilian support for the Confederate war effort—even, if necessary, their demoralization by means of the loss of their property—had become as much of a federal war aim as victory on the battlefield. Henceforth, civilians on either side of the border between slavery and freedom could much more easily be held legally liable for endangering the nation's and the Federal soldiers' welfare.[7]

Slaveholders, moreover, faced not just the possible loss of their human property but also the specter of men whom they had held in bondage being handed weapons and ammunition to fight them. As such, it is hardly an exaggeration to say that Lincoln's September 1862 proclamations, and his appointment of the stern and resolute Holt to help enforce and implement them, raised the emotional stakes in the war to an unprecedented level. For unwavering Unionists willing to sacrifice some measure of civil liberty in order to win the war, save the nation, and free the slaves, Holt's appointment and Lincoln's proclamations offered cause for celebration.

For those who aimed to preserve slavery by destroying the Union, however, they offered reasons to fight even harder. And for many in the North and on the border who had supported what they understood to be a war for the reestablishment of the Union *as it was*, the combination of the preliminary Emancipation Proclamation, the suspension of the writ of habeas corpus, and the appointment of the uncompromising Holt as judge advocate general served as an incitement to consider joining the opposition. These latter included Holt's former father-in-law, Charles Wickliffe, who had been returned to Congress in late 1861, and who a year later denounced the principle that as a war measure the president, as commander-in-chief, "any of his officers, high or low," or Congress had the right to abrogate state laws and free the slaves. Wickliffe declared himself ready "to make any sacrifice which honor and obedience to the Constitution will allow" in order to save the Union from destruction, but only if that Union left slavery untouched and protected. Wickliffe labeled all other interpretations of the war's meaning tantamount to "a John Brown raid upon a national scale."[8]

Holt fully recognized the many implications for public sentiment, soldier morale, and even the abolitionists' optimism of Lincoln's September 1862 proclamations, and not long after he accepted his new job he took the opportunity to make his own position clear. In an open letter to Hiram Barney, the staunchly pro-Lincoln, antislavery Republican collector of customs for the port of New York, Holt wrote vigorously in favor of the president's recent course of action and the preservation of the Union at all costs. The suspension of habeas corpus, Holt argued, was a necessary act in order to suppress debilitating opposition to the Federal army's heroic efforts. And then, having struggled for years with the concept of human bondage, Holt openly and unequivocally acknowledged that slavery and the Union could no longer both be saved, and that in his mind there was no question of sacrificing the latter for the former. Slavery, Holt insisted, was not only a great pillar of Confederate strength but also a ghastly offense against human rights. "No human institution," he declared, "no earthly interest shall ever by me be weighed in the scales against the life of my country," especially "an institution, the fountain of whose being—the African slave-trade—the laws of my country have for more than forty years denounced as a crime worthy of death." Finally, in the fall of 1862, Holt came down firmly and publicly on the side of slavery's opponents. For the rest of his life, it was a stance he neither varied nor regretted.[9]

In his letter to Hiram Barney, which Barney subsequently had published in the *New York Evening Post*, Holt also made it clear that he saw no other option for defeating the Confederacy than the hard-war approach. At the same time, however, he knew better than to believe that all Unionists in the North and along the border felt the same way. Indeed, he expressed considerable concern about the emergence of what he called a "conspiracy" of troublemakers within the Democratic Party in the North who sought to end the war as quickly as possible and restore the Union with slavery intact. For Holt, these so-called Peace Democrats, or Copperheads, constituted an exceedingly dangerous source of aid and comfort to the rebellion. In his mind, Copperheads were hardly different from the fire-eating Southern nationalists who had started the war in the first place. Reprising his long-standing disdain for extremists of all sorts, Holt insisted that both groups, though few in number, were nevertheless mighty in spirit and corrupting influence. Significantly, both had demonstrated their ability to turn the heads of the otherwise typically moderate and law-abiding masses of their regions and across the nation, making it necessary for the government to fight a war on two fronts against the Confederate South and against the Copperheads. Still, Holt's primary focus was on the battlefield, where he hoped to hear soon that the Federals had made "an immediate, bold and aggressive movement upon the enemy." "If those who are in the front will not go forward," he wrote, "the public safety will demand that they be assigned to positions in the rear." Here there is no doubt that Holt was thinking specifically of General George B. McClellan, whose repeated failures to launch decisive attacks on the Confederate armies he confronted, especially in light of his stunning hubris, had stretched the patience of many in the administration, including Holt, Stanton, and Lincoln himself. As it turns out, just two weeks after Holt wrote to Barney, Lincoln fired "Little Mac" once and for all. "I congratulate you on having reach[ed] the goal, upon which your eyes have long been fixed," wrote T. S. Bell when he heard the news. "If it had been done 8 or 9 months ago, the land would now be rejoicing in the prospect of a thorough settlement of all its troubles."[10]

As his letter to Barney makes clear, from the moment he took office Holt's intention was to support the president and his policies unwaveringly, to put his (and his staff's) muscle firmly behind emancipation, and to make use of all the legal means at his command to move immediately and boldly against the nation's enemies, wherever he found them. Wrote O. M. Dorman of Baltimore with enthusiasm, "when I [say] that there is no voice in the whole land which can touch the patriotic heart of Americans like yours, it is not flattery." Dorman encouraged Holt to use every possible opportunity to reiterate in other public settings the sentiments he had expressed in his letter to Barney; by doing so, Dorman insisted, Holt could do much good for the Union cause and simultaneously earn himself a great deal of praise and fame. "I know well you shrink from such notoriety," Dorman admitted. "But when you have the position & power to speak so potently, do not duty & the country require, if need be, the sacrifice of the finer feelings?"[11]

Not all of Holt's correspondents were so supportive. Hugh Campbell, with whom Holt had served earlier that year on the War Department's commission to examine wartime contract abuses in the West, was certain that Lincoln's decision to suspend habeas corpus would severely damage the ship of state the president was attempting to pilot. Even more troubling to Campbell was Lincoln's apparent eagerness to emancipate the slaves, which he considered tantamount to the president arbitrarily claiming the right to deprive American citizens of "their oxen or sheep." In an earlier letter, written just after Lincoln issued his September proclamations, Campbell had implored Holt to advise the president that a "dignified retreat" from his recent policies, particularly on the point of emancipation, offered the only hope for peace. "Can you not prevail on him," Campbell had groaned on that occasion, "to be entirely silent on 'negro-ology'?" Now, although he admitted that Holt's letter to Barney offered a good example of his felicity of language and his "unconditional patriotism," Campbell's feelings about the dangers of emancipation had only grown stronger.[12]

Substantially more critical still was E. T. Bainbridge, who complained from Louisville that Lincoln and, by association, Holt had gone too far by identifying themselves so indelibly with what he called "the higher law party," namely, individuals who believed that the destruction of slavery as a moral principle superseded the sanctity of the U.S. Constitution. Like Campbell, Bainbridge did not doubt Holt's patriotism. But he did recall a conversation back in June 1861 at the Louisville Hotel in which Bainbridge had forewarned Holt that "every departure from the constitution and the laws" that the government authorized during the war "would necessarily produce or breed a necessity for a dozen more." Now he asked, "*Has not this proved true?*" For his part, Holt was hardly blind to the potential impact of emancipation on the border states' commitment to remaining loyal. "Is it not too much," inquired an old friend from Kentucky, "for the government to ask of its friends, who have put in peril all, even life for its defense, to submit to robbery & outrage from its representatives?" Indeed, one good reason for paying close attention to what his own (and Lincoln's) critics had to say was that those same critics offered information about how wartime public opinion was shaping up on the border. In the fall of 1862, the military situation in Kentucky had once again become perilous. As had been true a year earlier, the cause of trouble was an invasion of the state by Confederate forces, this time under the command of General Braxton Bragg, who threatened to wreak a good deal of havoc and perhaps also drive the state into the Confederacy, especially now that so many local Unionists were feeling vexed by Lincoln's recent proclamations. Meanwhile, Bragg and his troops had actually occupied Bardstown, while Federal forces under General Don Carlos Buell were stationed about twenty-five miles away at Elizabethtown. John Speed, James and Joshua Speed's father, informed Holt that many of the region's women and children had been sent across the Ohio River to Indiana, but that the men who remained were bravely steeling themselves for "a capital Kentucky fight," though Speed himself lacked confidence in Buell's abilities and those of the largely untested Federal soldiers he commanded.[13]

The battle Speed anticipated finally came at Perryville, about thirty miles south of Elizabethtown, on October 7 and 8, just a month after Holt became judge advocate general and three weeks after Robert E. Lee's retreat from Maryland. Some 15,000 Confederate and 23,000 Federal soldiers were engaged, producing more than 7,600 casualties. In the end, as had been true at Antietam, the Confederates' inability to claim the field after the shooting stopped, combined with their failure to find much active sympathy within the invaded state's population, resulted in their retreat to more friendly terrain. But a good deal of damage had already been done. Grumbled T. S. Bell from Louisville on October 12, "the vile treason & piracy of Jeff. Davis's disunion are reveling in the devastation of Kentucky." Bell particularly bemoaned the fact that the Federals—and especially the Kentuckians among them—had not done more to demolish the enemy's forces while they had the chance. A few days later he wrote again, asking Holt to do whatever he could to get more Federal troops into the area. "Whenever Kentucky gets into trouble," Bell remarked, "we naturally turn to you, even when we are feeling that we may be depositing our feather on the back of the fully laden camel."[14]

Somewhat less discouraged than Bell, James Speed reported late in October 1862 that the rebel army's departure had greatly disappointed the Confederate leadership in Richmond, though he, like Holt, remained doubtful that General Buell was up to the task of protecting Kentucky in the future. As it turns out, Lincoln had the same concerns, and on October 24 he relieved Buell of command, replacing him with General William S. Rosecrans. "Whatever a certain clique of men may urge to the contrary," wrote a pleased Holt to Lincoln four days later, "I am satisfied that the heart of Ky will be rejoiced at your recent displacement of Gen Buell, whose gross incapacity & inaction have given up the whole state to the ravages of the rebels." By early November, James Speed's spirits were also rising. For one thing, he was confident that the state's Confederate sympathizers were losing ground. Speed was also happy to report that the Confederate invasion had induced many local men who had previously left, presumably to join the Confederate army, to return to Kentucky in order to defend the state. At the same time, like so many of the state's most ardent Unionists, Speed continued to worry about Kentucky's ability to accept the end of slavery gracefully, though he himself welcomed it. Like Holt, Speed hoped fervently that he would live to see Kentuckians "rise with magnanimity & let the bondsman go free," and he wrote approvingly of a recent order by General Jeremiah Boyle, whom Lincoln had appointed military governor of the state in May, which was designed to protect runaway slaves in Federal army camps from being reenslaved. Holt, too, endorsed Boyle's order.[15]

Speed also worried about the overall effects of the nation's militarization. On the one hand, he was convinced, this produced a form of "military despotism," in which the people turned increasingly to representatives of the armed forces for solutions to their disputes, so that "if a man loses a hog, a horse, a cow, or a chicken, he goes at once to some military commander; the commander hears the story; his sense of justice is shocked & [he] naturally stretches his authority to do what he can." On the other hand, Speed noted the disturbing lack of discipline he had seen among the Federal forces who had stood bravely against Bragg the previous month but who had otherwise proved themselves, in many cases, little more than "mere marauders," and he regretted that ill-behaved soldiers and their equally ill-behaved officers could not just be shot without first obtaining the approval of the president. As the person now most responsible, next to the president, for arbitrating cases involving soldiers' offenses against military law and discipline, as well as civilians' "disloyal practices" of all sorts, Holt shared Speed's concern. His own general inclination was to respond to breaches of law, discipline, and professional responsibility—not to mention loyalty—with severity rather than leniency. Just weeks into his new job, in what became one of the most famous, and controversial, cases of the war and of his entire career, Holt had a dramatic opportunity to demonstrate his firmness on these matters.[16]

The charges were against General Fitz John Porter of Portsmouth, New Hampshire, a West Point graduate (class of 1845), a veteran of the Mexican War, and a dedicated and outspoken supporter of the recently deposed General McClellan. Porter had served with the Army of the Potomac courageously for over a year. Now, however, he was accused of having violated

James Speed. Courtesy of the Library of Congress.

the ninth and the fifty-second articles of war by disobeying the orders of his commanding officer in the newly created Federal Army of Virginia, General John Pope, during the August 1862 Second Battle of Bull Run in Virginia, where the Federals had once again suffered a humiliating defeat. Notably, prior to the battle, Porter had openly criticized Pope for his hard-war, antislavery views and his staunch opposition to McClellan. To disagree with or even to despise one's commander privately was not a crime, of course, but to speak out against him publicly was a serious problem, and to disobey him in battle was a violation of military discipline punishable by death. For his part, Pope blamed the army's embarrassing failure at Second Bull Run on Porter's "shameful" refusal to follow his orders on several occasions, which he in turn traced back to Porter's blind allegiance to McClellan and his consequent unwillingness to obey McClellan's successor.[17]

In early November 1862, having already been relieved of command by Lincoln, Porter appeared before a court-martial organized by the new judge advocate general and presided over by General David Hunter to face the charges against him. Over the course of the next several weeks, witnesses—many of whom were striving to preserve or restore their own reputations in connection with the battle's unsavory outcome—alternately praised Pope for his heroism and condemned Porter for his betrayal, or commended Porter's faithfulness and damned Pope for his incompetence. In the end, although Porter had pleaded not guilty to all of the charges and specifications against him, the court—for which Holt served as both lead prosecutor and recorder—found him guilty and sentenced him to be cashiered from the army and "forever disqualified from holding any office of trust or profit under the Government of the United States." When the documents Holt subsequently prepared in connection with the case reached the president's desk for review in early 1863, Lincoln approved the proceedings, findings, and sentence, and the former rising star of the Federal army was discharged.[18]

Even while it was still underway, the Fitz John Porter case, widely covered in the national press, proved bitterly controversial, taking place as it did in the public arena, where opinions about the war and its progress were diverse, and against the backdrop of sharply conflicting estimates of McClellan's competence as well as his responsibility for the nation's failure to make much headway so far against the rebels in the war's eastern theater. "My first emotion when I heard of Fitz-John Porter's condemnation," wrote New Yorker George Templeton Strong in his diary, "was sorrow for the downfall of an old friend, and regret that he should have put him-

General Fitz John Porter. Courtesy of the Library of Congress.

self in a technically false position. But as I look further into the matter," he continued, "it assumes another aspect, and [his] name now seems to me likely to hold the lowest place in our national gallery but one—that of Benedict Arnold. Holt's review of the evidence for and against him," Strong concluded, "is crushing."[19]

In contrast, McClellan's supporters were convinced that Porter was the victim of a vicious plot led by Pope, Stanton, and Holt to use the defendant to further discredit "Little Mac" even after he had been removed from duty, and to advance Lincoln's hard-war policies—including emancipation—against the sadly misguided South. Porter himself was sure that he had been railroaded, and he and many of his influential allies (his cousins included admirals David G. Farragut and David D. Porter) strove to set the record straight. Several months after the trial was completed, Pope informed Holt that some of the New York newspapers had been publishing intimations that Reverdy Johnson—a prominent Maryland attorney and Democrat who had served as attorney general of the United States from March 1849 to July 1850, had defended John F. A. Sanford in the landmark *Dred Scott* case in 1857, and had been Porter's attorney at the trial—was preparing a pamphlet designed to vindicate his client's reputation.

The rumors were true: in the spring of 1863, Johnson published an attack on the Porter trial whose fundamental premise was that "never in the history of jurisprudence, civil, criminal or military," had a judgment been handed down that "so shocked and startled the sense of public justice." Although he had made no such claims either during or immediately after the trial itself, Johnson now charged that Lincoln had stacked the court against the defendant from the start, had rewarded the members of the court for their guilty verdict with promotions and more favorable assignments, and had wrongly deferred the examination of the evidence in the case to Holt, who, Johnson was certain, had eschewed objectivity in order to do Lincoln's bidding. He further charged that Holt had manipulated, distorted, and concealed portions of the evidence in order to reach the harsh verdict that Lincoln had predetermined. When he finally had the opportunity to read Johnson's pamphlet that summer, John Pope declared it to be "so grossly unfair" and so full of "deliberate misrepresentations" that "it would be idle to answer it in detail."[20]

Still, answer it he did, in the form of an eloquent rebuttal penned by his ally and friend, Andrew Dickson White. In a series of articles in the *Washington Chronicle* that were later compiled as a pamphlet, White vigorously disputed Reverdy Johnson's claims and accused him of trying to embarrass the Lincoln administration and of wrongly striving to protect Porter "from the merited scorn of our people by unblushing falsehood, distortion of evidence, and an appeal to prejudice." Johnson, White declared, seemed content to "trample upon the many distinguished men connected with this trial"—including Holt—"as heedlessly as a maddened bull paws the sands beneath his feet." White defended the court and Holt's performance throughout the proceedings, reminding readers that the charges against Porter could well have yielded a death sentence. "The wonder of military men, who understand the atrocity of Porter's offence in all its bearings," White concluded, "is, not that he was condemned, but that his life was spared."[21]

General Rufus King, who had served as a judge in the case, agreed. "*You* know how utterly false & unjust this charge is," King wrote bracingly to Holt, whose sensitivity to criticism and attacks on his integrity was no secret. After the Porter trial concluded, King recalled that Reverdy Johnson himself had commented on Holt's wise and evenhanded supervision throughout, which had made the trial "the fairest and most impartial he ever saw." T. S. Bell also sent words of support to his beleaguered friend. "With what kind of a face Reverdy Johnson can lend himself to bolstering up such a man as Fitz John Porter," he wrote, "I cannot imagine. He must have cheeks of something harder than brass." Bell summed up his perspective by noting that "the man who can suppose that any power could seduce you into an act inconsistent with professional honor and integrity . . . does not know the first element of your character." In the end, Bell assured Holt, such "surges of personal wrath" were sure to "fall harmlessly at [Holt's] feet."[22]

Holt rose to the position of Lincoln's judge advocate general not because he lacked a temper or was impervious to criticism but because of his widespread reputation for being a brilliant, rational, stunningly articulate, painstakingly careful attorney, and because he was a fearlessly determined supporter of the Union and the Lincoln administration, including Lincoln's policies on civil liberties, slave emancipation, and the need for a hard-war approach to crush the Confederate rebellion. "I believe there is no power on earth [that] could induce you to stop working for Old Abe," wrote one friend in the fall of 1863. For his part, Lincoln was deeply grateful for Holt's fidelity, his talents, his apparent tirelessness, his firm hand, and his adherence above all to the principle that the Union *must* be preserved. Indeed, the nation was immensely fortunate to have Holt on its side.[23]

But it must also be acknowledged that precisely those characteristics that made Holt such a faithful servant of the federal cause, combined with the more prickly and sensitive features of his basic temperament, made him supremely vulnerable as a lightning rod for the antipathies of those who were either outright enemies of the government or whose views about how to preserve it differed from those that Lincoln's policies reflected. And once Holt became Lincoln's judge advocate general, other people's responses to him personally could no longer be separated from the army's fortunes as well as its internal conflicts. From September 1862 forward, Holt's actions as the federal government's lead arbiter of military law were interpreted largely according to whatever stance a particular observer took with regard to the rebellion, Lincoln, the progress the federal government and the army were making, and the observer's own views on how the government and the army should proceed vis-à-vis its enemies.

Predictably, then, just as the dispute between Holt and Jacob Thompson had done in the spring of 1861, the bitterly contentious Fitz John Porter case, taking place virtually at the start of Holt's tenure as judge advocate general, contributed powerfully to the emergence of sharply divergent images of Holt, how he operated in his professional capacity, what he accomplished, and how, ultimately, he should be remembered. To uncompromising, pro-Lincoln Unionists wherever they lived, Holt continued to be seen as a stern but wise, careful, talented, courageous, and evenhanded jurist who sacrificed his time, energy, health, wealth, privacy, and personal and family relationships for the nation's cause. To ardent Confederates and their sympathizers North and South, however, Holt assumed the character of a corrupt, self-interested, shamelessly vindictive autocrat who was determined to suppress the slaveholders' legitimate revolution and crush as brutally as possible anyone he suspected of providing the revolution with either overt or covert support. No doubt Holt's nature—austere and reserved on the one hand, gracious, charming, and refined on the other—lent itself readily to such caricatures, as did his passion and his intense commitment both to the Union and to his privacy. Moreover, over time the public promulgation of sharply delineated caricatures of Holt unavoidably *shaped* his behavior, and his perspective. In particular, attempts to challenge his integrity and undermine his reputation for upstanding professionalism by suggesting that his labor on behalf of the nation's welfare was anything but righteous, just, and honorable—which harkened all the way back to George Elder's questioning of his intellectual integrity when he was a teenager—drove Holt to defend himself, his efforts, and his cause ever more fiercely, not always in ways that were to his best advantage.

Fortunately, most of the cases Holt handled during his years as Lincoln's judge advocate general were both less high profile and less controversial than Fitz John Porter's, even when they shared, on a much smaller scale, some of the same features. For one thing, the majority of purely military cases he dealt with resulted in sentences of neither summary execution nor dismissal from the army but instead a period of imprisonment (often at hard labor), or the loss of some pay, or a demotion in rank, or some combination of the three. Upon review, many cases elicited Holt's forbearance in a way that Porter must have envied, including the case of General Henry Washington Benham, who had been cashiered following his conviction for disobeying orders from General David Hunter (who presided over the Porter court) at the mid-June 1862 Battle of James Island, in which Federal soldiers had attempted to capture Charleston. Reviewing the case at Lincoln's request, Holt concluded in early 1863 that, in contrast with Porter, "the principal ground on which General Benham was dismissed from the volunteer service was a total misapprehension." According to Holt, Benham—an 1837 graduate of West Point who had been a cadet under examination when Holt served on the board of visitors in 1835—had "given some twenty-five years of his life to his country" and had proven himself an able and aggressive officer. Unlike Porter's, "General Benham's record as a soldier," he wrote, "is one of which he may well be proud; it belongs to the country, and should not be hastily darkened by such a condemnation as that which now rests upon him." Holt recommended Benham's restoration to duty.[24]

Holt could be flexible when it came to analyzing the circumstances that lay behind a charge of disobedience of orders. He was also fully capable of grasping the complex reasons why an individual soldier might desert, as Henry Lake of the 107th Pennsylvania had done. Lake was one of five brothers, three of whom had been killed in the war; a fourth was too young and too unhealthy to serve. After learning that his father's health, too, had seriously deteriorated, Lake requested a pass to visit his family home and help his mother. When the pass was denied, he went home anyway. Subsequently, Lake was convicted of desertion and sentenced to serve an extra year in the army and forfeit ten dollars of his thirteen-dollar monthly pay for four months. But when he reviewed the relevant documents, Holt decided that the sentence was unjust. "In view of the patriotism of the prisoner's family, his three brothers having fallen in the military service, and of his own distinguished character for courage and faithfulness as a soldier previous to his offense," Holt wrote, Lake's offense should be downgraded to "absence without leave under strongly extenuating circumstances." Holt recommended that Lake be released from the army and allowed to return home.[25]

Holt had the capacity to take a range of circumstances into account when shaping his recommendations for a given case, but he demonstrated little tolerance for the sort of cruelty displayed by soldiers such as Private William Dormody of the 1st Pennsylvania Light Artillery, who was found guilty and sentenced to hang for participating in the gang stabbing of an elderly citizen at Yorktown, Virginia. Upon reviewing the case, Holt pronounced the sentence entirely appropriate, not least because of the "great brutality" of the murder, which had been committed "in a most cowardly and atrocious manner" by a group of soldiers "on an unarmed senior citizen, who had never wronged them or offered them the slightest offense." Equally unforgivable was Private Richard O'Connor's murder of Private Thomas Gray after the two had fallen to arguing about guard duty. For Holt, what was most important in the O'Connor case was that the defendant, who had walked away from the scene of the argument and then returned with his gun, had clearly "formed a deliberate design and purpose to take the life of the deceased," which revealed his "wicked and depraved heart." Holt recommended that O'Connor be hanged according to the terms of the original sentence.[26]

Holt had no patience for cold-blooded murder, but he could sometimes understand what might drive one man to kill another, especially (and perhaps predictably) when the murderer felt that his honor had been viciously challenged. Such was true in the case of Captain Bernard McMahon of the 71st Pennsylvania Infantry, convicted of killing a fellow officer. In his review, Holt concluded that McMahon, who had proven his courage in both the Mexican and the Civil Wars, was in fact no murderer. Rather, he had simply responded appropriately to the verbal abuse to which the other officer—who routinely called him a "coward" and a "loafer"—had subjected him. In Holt's mind, the dead man had essentially committed suicide by abusing McMahon so bitterly. Indeed, "the outrage which he committed on the sensibilities and character of the accused would scarcely have been more aggravated had he applied a horse whip to his shoulders," Holt wrote, and had McMahon not responded to such taunts, he would only have exposed himself as the coward the other man had made him out to be. Holt strongly recommended a full pardon. Conversely, he declared 2nd Lieutenant Edward Lohmann of the 24th Illinois "unworthy of a commission" in light of his disrespectful, goading treatment of the enlisted men in his regiment and his drunken denunciation of the federal government.[27]

Generally speaking, Holt was a stickler for legal detail, and when he felt that a defendant's legal rights had been violated in any significant way—especially in a capital case—he was inclined to overturn the sentence, as he was in the case of John W. Sailor, who shot and killed two civilians and eight Union soldiers in Page County, Virginia. When Sailor's case came to Holt's attention for review, the judge advocate general urged that the convicted man's death sentence be overturned. The case record, Holt pointed out, was "fatally defective" on technical grounds because the general order convening the court had not been read out loud and Sailor had not had an opportunity to object to the inclusion of particular judges or even to see the charges against him presented in written form or to offer his plea. "In a proceeding involving life," Holt insisted, "such irregularities are wholly inexcusable and make the execution of the death sentence legally impossible."[28]

Holt was concerned with the technical details of nonmurder cases, too, as he demonstrated when he saw to it that Captain Benjamin P. Walker was restored to duty following his dismissal from his post as assistant commissary of subsistence. Walker had been convicted of "habitual absence from his post" and "gross and willful neglect of duty." Examining the original findings in the case, however, Holt determined that the charges could not be proven. "The wastage which is made so conspicuous a feature in the complaint," he declared, "does not appear to have exceeded what the Army Regulations allow." Even more important, he noted that the examination into Walker's competence had been done in a "superficial and unreliable" manner, and, as such, he urged that Walker "be unhesitatingly acquitted of all the charges made against him" and restored to service. However, in the case of Andrew Bartee, convicted in Tennessee for "obtaining money by false pretenses" and sentenced to three years in the penitentiary, Holt displayed a bit more flexibility. Although he acknowledged a number of clear precedents for overturning Bartee's conviction, he nevertheless insisted that the conviction should stand, given the wartime situation on the border between slavery and freedom with which he was so familiar. "In a country," Holt wrote, where "the ordinary civil courts are not open and the conditions of things are unsettled and individuals are left dependent upon military tribunals for protection," their protection trumped any legal technicalities that might be introduced to challenge a criminal's conviction.[29]

Many of the cases that came under Holt's authority involved crimes committed by Confederate soldiers. Holt had only contempt for figures such as Confederate Major Clarence J. Prentice who, while participating in the fall 1862 invasion of Kentucky, had left his command to visit his father in Louisville and was captured by Federal forces and sent to Camp Chase in Columbus, Ohio. Major Prentice's father begged Lincoln to offer his son clemency. Warm as ever on the subject of Kentucky's loyalty, however, Holt insisted that no oath could counteract Prentice's betrayal when he "wantonly banded with traitors for the overthrow of the Government of his country." Holt had no sympathy, either, for Frank Gurley, who faced the death sentence after being convicted of killing a Federal general while the general was lying sick in an ambulance. Gurley, Holt wrote, was nothing more than "a cowardly murderer in the fullest acceptation of the term," and the fact that he was a soldier in the enemy's army when he killed the Federal officer did not diminish the horror of what he had done or his culpability. Holt was no more patient with troublesome Confederate women such as Sallie Pollock, who at age seventeen was arrested and tried for carrying mail and other information to the Confederate lines in Maryland. The court found Pollock guilty and sentenced her to imprisonment at a penitentiary in Pittsburgh for the duration of the war, and although a number of people subsequently wrote appeals on her behalf citing her presumably fragile female health, Holt was unmoved. "Anyone who could repeatedly ford the Potomac River in winter and ride long distances while wet and cold," he pointed out, "was probably not overly delicate"; her sentence should stand.[30]

It is simply impossible to examine in detail the tens of thousands of cases that Holt dealt with during his tenure as Lincoln's judge advocate general. But it would be wrong not to point out that some of the most interesting and important cases he handled, particularly after Lincoln issued his final Emancipation Proclamation on January 1, 1863, involved slaves and former slaves whose legal, civil, and human rights had been violated. In these cases, Holt—the former slaveholder—repeatedly and energetically rose to the blacks' defense even when they initially appeared in the case records as perpetrators of crimes against whites. Such was true for West Bogan of Arkansas, convicted of murdering his white former owner with an axe. When he reviewed Bogan's case, Holt agreed that the defendant should be treated "as a whole man" in terms of his responsibility for having killed another human being. At the same time, however, Holt made clear that he considered Bogan to have been acting in self-defense. West's former owner, Holt explained, was known for being "cruel and exacting," for having forced his slaves, under threat of punishment, to work extraordinarily long hours with few if any breaks, and for whipping at least one slave every day. Following the Emancipation Proclamation, Bogan had briefly remained on his former owner's farm, but then he had begun to move about more freely, laying claim to the proclamation's promises. One day, his former owner threatened to beat or even kill Bogan if he did not stop "running about and going away from home" without permission, and this time the normally quiet and cooperative Bogan lost his temper. The two men fell to fighting, in the midst of which Bogan grabbed an axe and hit the white man twice in the neck, nearly severing his head. In his review of the case, Holt disagreed with the murder conviction, declaring Bogan a free man who had killed only after he had "doubtless borne the oppressions of his taskmaster till endurance seemed to him no longer possible." In Holt's mind, the white man deserved what he got for behaving in a manner that, "under the changed relations of the white and black population of the Southern States, he had no right to do." Bogan, Holt insisted, had acted out of passion in response to a great and inexcusable provocation.[31]

Similarly, in the case of John Glover of Tennessee, a freedman convicted by a military commission of murdering a white man, Holt stepped in to save the black man from hanging. "There can be no doubt," he wrote in his review of the case, "that the prisoner discharged a pistol at [George] Redman, the result of which was his [Redman's] death." From Holt's perspective, however, Glover's violence—like West Bogan's—was justified by the circumstances: Glover and another black man, identified only as "Dave," had crossed the Mississippi River into Arkansas solely in order to rescue Dave's daughters, whom the elderly Redman had been holding in slavery "against their father's will and in violation of the President's emancipation proclamation," promising to kill anyone who tried to free them. Dave and Glover had decided to go and get the girls anyway and had just managed to slip away with one and were going back for the other when Redman came after them with a gun. Initially the black men tried to run back to where their boat was waiting, but Redman kept up the pursuit, and at last Glover, who was also carrying a gun, turned and fired. Redman died a few days later from his wounds.[32]

In reviewing the case, Holt admitted that some might question why, in the first place, Glover had participated in the mission that led to Redman's death. "It is true," Holt wrote, that Glover "had no personal interest in the rescue of the two girls," who were, after all, not his children but Dave's. Still, in light of the Emancipation Proclamation, Holt considered the rescue effort in and of itself "a lawful and justifiable act," making Glover's participation in it "no less justifiable and lawful." Moreover, Glover had not meant to murder Redman but only to help a friend "in the delivery of his children from bondage." But when Redman came after him with a gun, Glover had feared for his own life and had acted in self-defense. That Glover had armed himself before setting out on the rescue mission should not be a cause for criticism, either, Holt argued, given "the extreme severity with which offenders of his race are treated by their white masters." For

Holt, the case was one in which a white man had "rashly thrown away his [own] life in an endeavor to enslave a feeble young woman in defiance of the proclamation of the President which had declared her free."[33]

The case of Fountain Brown—a white, Methodist clergyman from Arkansas convicted by a military commission of selling back into slavery eight individuals whom the Emancipation Proclamation had declared free—offers yet another example of Holt's determination to use his powers as judge advocate general to enforce the former slaves' rights. Brown, it appears, had initially cooperated with the proclamation (at least, once Federal troops arrived to enforce it) and had released all of his slaves from service. Rather than leaving the area, however, the freedpeople had remained nearby, not far from where a white man named McAfee also lived. Over the years, McAfee had "cohabited" with one of the women, Lucy, on a number of occasions, producing two children, although Lucy also had a black husband of her own and McAfee had a white wife. After Lucy and her children became free, McAfee decided to try and spirit them off to Texas, which was still not under Federal control, and he asked their former owner to help. When Brown refused, McAfee offered to buy Lucy and five of Brown's other former slaves for $7,000 (notably, he did not offer to buy Lucy's husband). For this price, Brown agreed to "sell," even though he could no longer legally claim the women and children as his property. McAfee then abandoned his white wife and took off with Lucy, another adult freedwoman, and six children. Struck with remorse—or, more likely, fear of the government's retaliation—Brown subsequently went to the federal authorities and confessed what he had done. To his surprise, he was arraigned, tried, convicted, and sentenced to five years in a military prison.[34]

"In the opinion of this office," Holt wrote when Brown appealed his conviction, "it is recommended that the sentence be confirmed." Although many of Brown's friends and neighbors had signed a petition describing the clergyman as a "good and influential man in the church and the community," Holt pointed out that the petition said nothing about Brown's loyalty to the federal government. Other solicitations on Brown's behalf also failed to provide any persuasive reason why he should be pardoned, especially those claiming that the former slaves had gone willingly, even happily, to Texas. "It is a mockery of truth," Holt insisted,

> as shallow as it is wicked, to attribute consent to the six helpless and mindless children, the oldest of whom was a boy of seven and the youngest a baby but a few months old. It would require a rule of law as repugnant to reason as the extinct slave-code of Arkansas was re-

volting to humanity, to impute the exercise of volition to the unhappy little beings, whom his barbarous avarice, proving stronger than his sense of the obligations of the law, human or divine, impelled a presiding elder of the Methodist Church to sell into a life of hopeless bondage in a distant state.

In sum, Holt declared, "The crime of the prisoner was a deliberate and willful violation of law," which "set at naught the proclamation of emancipation." That the defendant was a man who, by virtue of his clerical profession, claimed to be an "exemplar of public and private morality" only made his crime worse. To Holt, Brown's audacity in requesting a pardon from the federal government, whose edicts he had scorned, was "an instance of effrontery scarcely paralleled even in the annals of the present rebellion." To pardon Brown would make light of the crime he had committed; it would also undoubtedly signal that the federal government did not intend to follow through on the promises of the Emancipation Proclamation. Not to follow through, however, would be immoral. It could also have serious implications for the Federal army's efforts to win the war, not least because black men—most of them former slaves—were now risking their lives as part of that army. To pardon a man such as Brown while black soldiers were courageously serving the Union's cause at great personal peril was to commit a ghastly and dishonorable breach of faith that Holt refused to tolerate. Lincoln concurred, and Brown's request for a pardon was denied.[35]

Holt wrote his opinion in the Fountain Brown case in May 1864, fifteen months after Lincoln issued his final Emancipation Proclamation and almost two years after black men had begun enlisting in the Federal army. Indeed, just a month after the Second Confiscation Act passed in July 1862—a month before Lincoln's *preliminary* Emancipation Proclamation—Secretary of War Stanton had quietly begun to authorize the recruitment of freedmen as Federal soldiers; their numbers would reach almost 200,000 by the time the war was over. From the start, Holt was as supportive of the idea of arming black men in the nation's service as he was of the Emancipation Proclamation itself, which he made clear when he responded that fall to Stanton's request for his opinion. Holt's immediate response was an emphatic endorsement.[36]

A year later, in August 1863, he penned a more extended and thorough statement on the question, in which he reiterated the government's right "to employ for the suppression of the rebellion persons of African descent held to service or labor under the local laws." This right, Holt declared, had two distinct legal foundations. First, the U.S. Constitution recognized slaves as *property*, and the federal government had the authority to seize enemy property and make use of it however the government saw fit, even putting uniforms on "it," giving "it" guns, and sending "it" into battle. Second, the Constitution recognized individuals of African descent as *persons* for the purpose of representation in Congress. They were, therefore, constituents of the government, and since all male constituents were required to bear arms "in defense of the Government under which they live, and by which they are protected" (provided they were physically able to do so), and as it was the duty of the government to call upon its male constituents to bear arms against an enemy "whenever the public safety may demand it," black men could, and should, serve as Federal soldiers.[37]

Moreover, Holt pointed out, the "tenacious and brilliant valor" and the "obstinate courage" black soldiers had already displayed at battles such as Port Hudson, Milliken's Bend, and Fort Wagner demonstrated their potential as effective soldiers, which the nation would be foolish to ignore. "A man precipitated into a struggle for his life on land or sea," Holt wrote, "instinctively and almost necessarily puts forth every energy with which he is endowed, and eagerly seizes upon every source of strength within his grasp." Likewise, "a nation battling for existence, that does not do the same, may well be regarded as neither wise nor obedient to that great law of self preservation, from which are derived our most urgent and solemn duties." On the question of what black soldiers should be led to expect once the war was over, Holt responded that they should expect and be permitted to enjoy all of the rights that the Constitution they had so bravely defended granted to its citizens. Holt's opinion on the place of black men in the Federal armed services heartened the idea's many supporters, not least those who were certain, as Lincoln was, that the war could not be won without black men's help. At the same time, however, Holt's support for black male enlistment only further hardened the sentiments of his opponents, who believed that he, like Lincoln, had once again gone much too far, and that his primary reason for saving the Union was now to transform it into a racially egalitarian state.[38]

Holt's official opinion on the legitimacy of black men's military service offers a good reminder that as judge advocate general, he did more than serve as the War Department's supreme adjudicator of military law; he also profoundly influenced its formulation and development. Some observers recognized his potential to do so right away: just two months after taking office, Holt received a letter from William E. Boulger of Chicago urging him to create a handy book of military rules and regulations to be distributed to every enlisted man to aid him in avoiding prosecution for acts he did not realize were violations. Holt did not end up devising such a manual, but he did contribute materially to the production of probably the most famous set of instructions relating to the behavior of armies in the field during this period: the Lieber Code, which was promulgated in April 1863 as General Orders No. 100 and which remains a keystone in the international rules of war today. Indeed, from the time Holt became judge advocate general, Francis Lieber—a German legal scholar who had immigrated to the United States in the late 1820s and, at the time of the war, was a professor of history and political economics at Columbia University—was one of his regular correspondents. During the period when he was crafting the code, Lieber consulted with Holt several times, including in February 1863, when he asked Holt to have a look at a draft of what he had written and to return it with his suggestions and revisions.[39]

In its final form, the 157 articles of the Lieber Code were comprehensive in their attempt to deal with issues of war that included, among others things, martial law, military jurisdiction, property rights, desertion, espionage, treason, raiding, prisoner exchange, capitulation, and assassinations. Among Lieber's deepest concerns was that a war conducted by an "advanced civilization" such as the United States should reflect values that included the avoidance of cruelty, the extension of humane treatment to the enemy whenever possible, the preservation of works and institutions of religion, art, knowledge, and culture, and the idea that the ultimate goal of any war was not war itself, but peace. Lieber also demonstrated a sharp interest in using America's Civil War as an opportunity to undermine the whole concept of human bondage, and he sought to establish lasting protections for black soldiers, whose potential mistreatment at the hands of their white Confederate enemies was a very real concern. Echoing Holt's feelings and also anticipating the horrors of the Fort Pillow massacre nine months later, Lieber wrote to Holt in June 1863 that "the utter recklessness of our enemies in every respect—in truth, honor, oath, law, duty, language—is, I think, their most prominent feature in this war. They dare to do things which no civilized people, even in periods of the highest passion, have had sufficiently depraved courage to do, for nearly two centuries." Lieber recommended finding ways to force white Southerners to recognize that the federal government was prepared to avenge their many outrages—not least their ill treatment of black soldiers—and he urged Holt to talk with Stanton and others, including Lincoln, about issuing a strongly worded statement on the matter. In July, Lincoln issued his General Orders No. 252, declaring that for every black soldier the Confederates killed in the line of duty, a white rebel soldier would be put to death.[40]

In addition to assisting Lieber in the development of the Lieber Code, Holt later published an extensive, alphabetically organized compilation of his own opinions on a wide range of military legal matters—from his interpretations of the articles of war to his view on what sorts of remuneration a witness in a military trial could properly expect—which appeared in 1865 as the *Digest of Opinions of the Judge Advocate General of the Army* and later in a number of revised editions. Meanwhile, of course, Holt also continued to manage with energy, focus, and dedication the massive responsibilities of his office, to which were soon added the protracted and politically thorny mess brought on by the activities of a particularly ardent "Peace Democrat," U.S. congressman Clement L. Vallandigham of Ohio. On May 1, 1863, Vallandigham had defied General Ambrose E. Burnside's General Order No. 38, published on April 13, warning that public expressions of support for the Confederacy would no longer be tolerated in the Department of the Ohio, where Burnside was in command, and that offenders would be arrested immediately and brought before a military commission for trial. Ignoring Burnside's warning, Vallandigham made a speech at Mount Vernon, Ohio, in which he declared the war a failure, attacked the principle of emancipation, and criticized the suspension of habeas corpus. Four days later, he was arrested, and on May 6, a military commission authorized by Holt convened in Cincinnati to try him for "expressing public sympathy for those in arms against the Government, and declaring disloyal sentiments and opinions, with the object and purpose of weakening the power of the Government in its efforts to suppress an unlawful rebellion." Ten days later, the commission—whose jurisdiction Vallandigham had challenged unsuccessfully—reached the unanimous conclusion that he was guilty as charged. The court sentenced Vallandigham to imprisonment at Fort Warren in Massachusetts for the duration of the war.[41]

This was Holt's and the Lincoln administration's first major case involving a civilian dissident against the administration's civil liberties policies, and like the Fitz John Porter case, whose reverberations remained very much in play at the time Vallandigham's trial was being conducted, it vehemently polarized public opinion. Those who believed that Copperheads such as Vallandigham must be silenced in order for the Union's war effort to succeed were pleased with Holt's management of the trial and its outcome. Those who sympathized with either the Confederacy or the principle of a citizen's freedom to speak freely regardless of the setting and the consequences—or both—were outraged and condemned Holt in particular for what they considered his collusion in Lincoln's repressive, unconstitutional measures. In the end, in any case, Vallandigham did not go to jail.

Clement Vallandigham. Courtesy of the Library of Congress.

Instead, on May 19 Lincoln commuted his sentence to banishment into the Confederacy, at least in part because the president realized that Vallandigham's anti-administration, antiwar, anti-emancipation allies threatened to transform the convicted man into a First Amendment martyr.

Subsequently, Vallandigham slipped away to Canada and from there appealed his conviction (and also ran for governor of Ohio). Holt, in turn, wrote at length to the members of the U.S. Supreme Court providing extensive detail about the case and asking that Vallandigham's appeal be denied. "The Supreme Court," Holt argued boldly, "might with as much propriety be called upon to restrain by injunction the proceedings of Congress" as to "reverse the proceedings of the military authorities in time of war." Handing down its decision in *Ex parte Vallandigham* in February 1864, the Supreme Court ruled against the defendant. Sometime later, Vallandigham brazenly returned to the United States, where he gave a number of powerful speeches and helped write the Democratic platform for the fall 1864 elections, in which George McClellan appeared as the party's presidential candidate. Vallandigham was not arrested again, however, and his power and influence ultimately collapsed.[42]

Even without Vallandigham at full throttle, the Copperheads were managing to stir up a good deal of trouble as the war ground through its third, brutal year, particularly in the Old Northwest—Ohio, Indiana, Illinois—and along the border between slavery and freedom. So much trouble did they generate, in fact, that on July 12, 1864, Secretary of War Stanton ordered Holt to proceed personally and immediately to Kentucky. There he was to meet with the governor, Thomas E. Bramlette, a Federal army veteran who had roundly beaten Charles Wickliffe in the state's 1863 gubernatorial election. (In the campaign that preceded the election, Holt's former father-in-law surrendered his unequivocal Unionism once and for all and ran as the candidate of the state's Peace Democrats.) Now, traveling back to his home state for the first time since the summer of 1861, Holt arranged to meet with Governor Bramlette and Major General Stephen G. Burbridge to discuss military and political affairs in Kentucky and across the region. In addition, he prepared to investigate the operations of any secret organizations that were suspected of giving aid and comfort to the enemy and undermining the federal cause.[43]

When he headed west in the summer of 1864, Holt did so as chief of the War Department's newly created Bureau of Military Justice. Retaining his title of judge advocate general, Holt now held the rank of brigadier general and enjoyed a hike in pay. Holt thanked Stanton warmly for this latest honor, which recognized his faithful and manifold contributions to the nation's welfare, security, and future. When he took the oath on June 29 at age fifty-seven, Holt swore perhaps even more vigorously than he had done on the four previous occasions when he had accepted federal appointments, that he had "never voluntarily borne arms against the United States," that he had "given no aid, countenance, counsel, or encouragement to persons engaged in armed hostility thereto," that he had "neither sought, nor accepted, nor attempted to exercise the functions of any office whatever, under any authority, or pretended authority, in hostility to the United States," and that he had not "yielded any voluntary support to any pretended Government, authority, power, or constitution within the United States, hostile or inimical thereto." Holt swore further that, to the best of his ability, he would continue to support and defend the Constitution of the United States against all of its enemies. It seems safe to suggest that no federal office holder ever took the oath more seriously, or with greater conviction and purpose.[44]

Just over a month after his swearing in, Holt reported to Stanton from St. Louis that the situation in Kentucky was grave. Secret organizations of Confederate sympathizers were only a part of the problem, too. In addition, he explained, guerrilla warfare was tearing the state apart. No one seemed to be able to stand up to the "thieves and murderers" who, moving in parties of between four and twenty, rode the "fleetest and best horses of the country" and were "thoroughly armed with weapons, which they conceal in their boots and under their clothes." Local Unionists were particularly vulnerable: wrote Holt's old friend, T. S. Bell, "I do not know a neighborhood in Kentucky in which an active loyal man has any security for his life," and he added, "public sentiment has been demoralized."[45]

To a great extent, Holt attributed the increase in guerrilla activity across the region to Lincoln's initial Proclamation of Amnesty and Reconstruction, issued in December 1863, in which the president had proposed a reasonably mild process for returning individual states to the Union once they came under the control of the Federal army. Although he recognized the proclamation as a reflection of Lincoln's generosity, forgiveness, and forbearance, Holt was convinced that many rebels saw it simply as an opportunity to be exploited. "So far as Kentucky is concerned," Holt wrote, "the rebels have used this proclamation . . . only as a means for returning to the State, visiting their friends, making observations upon our military affairs, and then arming, mounting, and equipping themselves either for the Confederate service or for the career of robbers and cut-throats." In addition, Holt reported that although the recruitment of regional blacks into the Union army was proceeding at a reasonably good pace, still, many of the runaway slaves who were trying to enlist or simply seeking safety within the Federal lines were instead being "waylaid, beaten, maimed, and often murdered." Holt urged Lincoln to suspend wartime reconstruction, at least in Kentucky.[46]

In a subsequent report, Holt focused on the secret antigovernment organizations he had gone west to investigate, including the Order of the American Knights, the descendant of the Knights of the Golden Circle, about which his observant Aunt Mary Ann in Stephensport had warned him as far back as May 1861. That fall, Brigadier General Henry B. Carrington reported from Indianapolis that he had captured confidential materials—including information about "rituals, signs, passwords, and plans"—from a number of organizations whose purpose was to stir up trouble across the North should Lincoln be reelected in November. More generally, Holt's contacts convinced him that antigovernment organizations such as the Order of the American Knights were more than just a rumor. They were real and extremely effective, and their members were armed, drilling for revolution, and dedicated to the preservation of slavery and the overthrow of the federal government by means of a range of tactics, including harboring and protecting deserters; discouraging Federal army enlistments and encouraging resistance to the draft; circulating disloyal and treasonable publications; communicating with and giving intelligence to the Confederacy; aiding the Confederacy by recruiting for its military forces within Federal army lines; furnishing the rebels with arms, ammunition, and other supplies; cooperating with and sponsoring raids and invasions into Federal territory; destroying government property; persecuting and destroying the private property of people loyal to the government; and engaging in the assassination and murder of loyal civilians and soldiers. To Holt, such organizations represented a radical and influential fraternity and, like the fire-eating Southern nationalists who had produced the war in the first place, or the Know-Nothings even earlier, a manifestation of the power of a few "conspirators" to corrupt the minds of otherwise mild-mannered people, arousing in them a fiercely "parricidal spirit" and driving them into violent action against the benevolent institutions and leadership of the Republic and its loyal citizens. Collectively, and more than ever before, they represented a raging fire at the army's rear.[47]

Upon reading Holt's lengthy report about the "hellish conspiracy" of virulent Copperheads that he had uncovered in the West, Francis Lieber expressed his dismay. "I can hardly command sufficient calmness to write to you," he confessed. The Columbia professor's "horror at the loathsomeness of this huge mass of crime" was mixed with grief regarding the state of affairs Holt had described, and he urged Holt to disseminate his informative report quickly and widely. For her part, Holt's Aunt Mary Ann worried most about how the secret organizations he had set out to expose might ultimately retaliate against him personally. "Josey," she wrote in October, "I know there is a secret conspiracy & I am sorry that you have exposed it for it surrounded you by dangers & assassins. Brother Jo I want you . . . to be more particular of your life than ever, for after this I believe they will send emisarys to Washington City in deguise on purpose to poison or kill you in some other way."[48]

Mary Ann was right: among the many things Holt's report accomplished—which included advancing the administration's hard-war policy—it served to sharpen the antigovernment animus that was directed against him in particular, as at least one anonymous but shrill correspondent from Oswego, New York, made clear. Enclosing a newspaper article about the recent investigation, this writer made light of Holt's Democratic credentials and called him a traitor to his party and his birthplace whose name, henceforth, would evoke only scorn and contempt among those who had witnessed his betrayal. Back in Washington in the fall, Holt dismissed as best he could such hostile reactions to his ongoing attempt to save the Union. Instead, he focused on continuing to identify and crush the fomenters of the madness he had witnessed on the border and in the West. In his view, the Union's very life—not to mention Lincoln's November reelection—depended just as much on suppressing the nation's internal enemies as it did on battlefield victories against the Confederate army. In essence, this is what he had meant to do when he urged the Supreme Court to sustain Clement Vallandigham's conviction in December 1863. In October 1864, he sought to do it again when he oversaw the trial of Lambdin P. Milligan, arrested in Indiana and charged with treason.[49]

By the time he was taken into federal custody, Milligan, an ardent Democrat, lawyer, and politician who years earlier had been a friend of Edwin Stanton, had long been recognized as a purveyor of antigovernment, antiwar sentiment in the Old Northwest. As early as July 1862, Milligan had publicly declared the war a lost cause. In August 1863, despite the encouraging Federal victories at Gettysburg and Vicksburg, Milligan had expressed his conviction that the North could not possibly win the war in the end, and that the western states would do well to tie their fortunes to an independent South instead. That same year, he successfully argued the case of an Indiana legislator who, like Vallandigham, had violated Burnside's General Orders No. 38. Subsequently, Milligan became widely known as a leader in the Indiana branch of the Order of the American Knights, whose stated goal was to instigate an antiwar rebellion across the North by raiding government arsenals, attacking federal prisoner-of-war camps and liberating incarcerated Confederate soldiers, then massing those released soldiers (and their liberators) in Louisville to create a serious distraction for the Federal forces. This, the organization's members believed, would destroy confidence in the Lincoln administration and ensure its demise.[50]

In the end, of course, the plot failed when federal informants infiltrated the order and revealed its plans to the authorities. By early October, Milligan and others were in jail in Indianapolis. Their trial before a military commission on charges of conspiring against the government, giving aid and comfort to the rebels, inciting insurrection, engaging in disloyal practices, and violating the laws of war began on October 21. Prosecuted for the government by Colonel Henry L. Burnett, Holt's trusted judge advocate for the Department of the Ohio, Milligan's was as public and dramatic a case as Porter's and Vallandigham's had been, and key to the government's effort to convict him and the others was the fact that a number of their fellow conspirators turned state's evidence. The trial lasted about six weeks, during which—thanks in large part to General William T. Sherman's stunning occupation of Atlanta—Lincoln was resoundingly reelected. In early December, Milligan and his codefendants were found guilty and sentenced to death by hanging.[51]

As the Vallandigham case had done the previous year, Milligan's case generated a great deal of controversy around the question of what sorts of offenses committed by civilians could be considered sufficiently disloyal and detrimental to the Federal army's efforts to justify imprisonment or execution. The Milligan case also added considerable fuel to the fire being stoked by those who questioned the scope and reach of the War Department's military justice system, and Holt himself, including its— *his*—seemingly boundless jurisdiction over civilian behavior in the form of military commissions. Like Lincoln's suspension of the writ of habeas corpus—which Congress had legitimized with its March 1863 Habeas Corpus Act—and the federal government's restrictions on civil liberties generally, the question of the military's right to try cases involving civilians had already become a thorny topic; it generated even more vexed debate in the wake of the Milligan trial. For his part, it is clear, Holt remained unequivocally committed to limiting civil liberties and extending the legal powers of the military justice system in order to win the war and save the Union. As was true of Lincoln, Holt's understanding of the concept of "constitutionality" was inseparable from his understanding of what it would take to save the Constitution in the first place, which included protecting and defending the president, his administration, and his policies; suppressing the rebellion and its allies with force; delivering the Union from the diabolical enemies who were arrayed against it; and restoring the public peace. Tolerance and magnanimity would simply have to wait until the war was over, the South was punished, treason was crushed, and the freedpeople's future was secure.[52]

In late November 1864, in the wake of the resignation of Attorney General Edward Bates, a newly reelected Lincoln demonstrated his appreciation for Holt's ongoing and dedicated service to the Union, his administration, and his war policies by offering the judge advocate general Bates's post in the cabinet. Deeply honored, Holt nevertheless turned the president down. Holt, recalled Nicolay and Hay, "with that modesty and conscientiousness which formed the most striking trait of his character, believed that the length of time which had elapsed since he had retired from active service at the bar had rendered him unfit for the preparation of cases in an adequate manner before the Supreme Court, and therefore declined the appointment." Indeed, this was precisely the reason Holt gave for saying no. "After the most careful reflection," he explained to the president, "I am satisfied that I can serve you better in the position which I now hold, at your hands, than in the more elevated one to which I have been invited." Holt insisted that his decision had not been an easy one to make, and that he had "reached this conclusion with extreme reluctance & regret." At the same time, he assured Lincoln of his gratitude for the offer, which reflected the president's confidence and also provided him with new energy to pursue the work he had already taken on. In his place Holt recommended that Lincoln appoint their mutual friend, James Speed. "I can recall no public man," Holt wrote, "of *uncompromising loyalty*, who unites in the same degree, the qualifications of professional attainments, fervent devotion to the Union, & to the principles of your administration, & spotless purity of personal character." Moreover, he pointed out, Speed offered "a warm & hearty friendship for yourself, personally & officially," which Holt considered an essential attribute. Lincoln heartily approved Holt's recommendation, and on December 2, James Speed became attorney general.[53]

By the time Speed took his cabinet seat, the war was almost over. General Grant's protracted but eventually successful siege of Petersburg, Virginia, was well underway, as was Sherman's celebrated march from Atlanta to the sea (the Federals occupied Savannah, Georgia, on December 21). After this Sherman would take his army north through the Carolinas with the goal of joining Grant in Virginia for the final destruction of Lee's Army of Northern Virginia. Meanwhile, Confederate general John B. Hood's Tennessee campaign that fall had failed, and he was about to sacrifice the remainder of his forces at Nashville (December 15 and 16). Soon, too, congressional passage of the Thirteenth Amendment to the Constitution (in February 1865) would virtually guarantee the permanent end of slavery in the United States. As he considered all of these encouraging developments, and for all the invective he, the president, and the administration had endured, Holt must have been pleased: the news was good; the Federals were winning the war. Holt was also exhausted. In a March 1865 report to Stanton he indicated that just since November 1863, the Office of the Judge Advocate General had reviewed almost 34,000 records of general courts-martial and military commissions and had made about 9,000 reports "as to the regularity of proceedings on applications for restoration to the service, the pardon of offenders, the remission or commutation of sentences," and other miscellaneous questions.[54]

In the years since Buchanan appointed him secretary of war in late December 1860, by far the great majority of Holt's attention, time, and energy had been devoted to doing whatever he could to help save the Union from destruction. But it would be a mistake to forget that throughout these years Holt had a personal life, too, one that, like any life, offered a rich mix of opportunities for laughter, anxiety, frustration, weariness, self-recrimination, anger, celebration, and grief. Almost certainly the most significant personal loss that Holt experienced over the entire course of the war was the loss of his only sister, Elizabeth Holt Sterett, who died in early 1863. That January, even as Holt was finalizing his report to President Lincoln regarding the Fitz John Porter case, his faithful Aunt Mary Ann had informed him that Elizabeth was severely ill—it is not clear with what disease. "I ought to have writen to you earlier," Mary Ann explained, "only I have been hoping that Elizabeth would get better." Within a couple of weeks, however, Elizabeth's recovery no longer seemed likely. "I have been doing all I could for her both night & day since new years day," Mary Ann insisted, but "instead of mending she is sinking all the time & every moment I think will certainly be her last." Then, in early February 1863, a letter from his brother Thomas brought the grim news of Elizabeth's death. Some months later, Mary Ann sent Holt a lock of Elizabeth's hair, declaring her death "a heavy sorrow to me," but one for which Elizabeth herself had seemed prepared. "She was not affraid to die," Mary Ann recalled, "for her path was clear & bright." In May, Elizabeth's daughter Margaret, now eighteen, thanked her uncle for the letter he sent following her mother's death, and assured him that she still loved him. Margaret also expressed her fervent desire that the war would soon be over, and the family reunited.[55]

The loss of Elizabeth was compounded by Holt's persistent disappointment over the political beliefs of the majority of his family members, most of whom remained, from start to finish, enthusiastic supporters of the rebellion. Holt found it simply impossible during the war to sustain openly affectionate bonds with most of his kin, who seemed committed to undermining everything he himself was struggling to protect. At the same time, however, he was immensely grateful for his spunky Aunt Mary Ann's unshaken fidelity to the Union, to Lincoln, and to him personally. Their correspondence, which remained active and affectionate throughout the war, covered topics ranging from family affairs to the Federal army's fortunes on the battlefield, to the dangers of dissent in Kentucky and elsewhere, to Lincoln's policies on black enlistment. On this score it bears noting that in March 1863, Aunt Mary Ann confessed her concern that her one slave, Wesley, might be recruited. Unmarried and childless, Mary Ann was extremely fond of Wesley and probably also completely dependent on him, and she begged her nephew to see that he was exempted from the service "on the account of me being a lone woman & having but one negrow & that being all the support in a manor that I have."[56]

As was true for divided families across the border states, Holt's relations with the rest of his family were terribly strained. Their refusal to recognize the Confederacy's complete depravity pained him deeply. In turn, his determination to stand firmly by Lincoln and the Union struck them as a cruel betrayal of his roots and his community. In August 1863, Mary Ann informed Holt that his brother Thomas had recently been arrested in connection with some local guerrilla activities, and that the Federals had captured Thomas's son John, a Confederate soldier, and shipped him to "Columbus Ohio Prison No 3" (Camp Douglas), where she feared that his ardent secessionism would result in his execution. Mary Ann implored Holt to convince President Lincoln to spare the young man. According to Will Sterett, Holt's old friend and his late sister Elizabeth's husband, this was John's second imprisonment, his first having occurred about a year earlier, on which occasion Thomas had spent $2,000 to get him released on the promise of his good conduct. Thomas had then brought John back to Stephensport, but John had refused to remain home for long: after three months he rejoined the Confederate forces, leaving Thomas without the money or his son. Will Sterett also wrote that Holt's brother Robert in Mississippi was being ruined financially by the war, and that he and his large family (he and Ann now had *nine* children) were "tented out in the woods with ten days rations." Sterett encouraged Holt to set politics aside and help his needy family members if he possibly could, but there is no evidence that Holt responded to Sterett's request. The gulf between him and Robert had simply grown too wide.[57]

Holt's decade-long friendship with his former brother-in-law, Florida senator David Yulee, was another early casualty of the conflict, as was his equally long friendship with his former brother-in-law William Merrick (Mary Wickliffe's husband). A native of Maryland who had been a federal circuit court judge in Washington since 1855, Merrick came under suspicion of disloyalty at the very beginning of the war when, among other acts of defiance, he refused to administer the oath of office to a Lincoln appointee to the Department of the Treasury. In late October 1861, Lincoln temporarily suspended Merrick and then confined him under guard to house arrest at his F Street home. After he was released Merrick remained on the bench for a time, but Republican opposition to him did not abate, and eventually he decided to sell the house in Washington and move his family back to Frederick, where they remained for the war's duration.[58] Although Holt had visited with the Merricks in Maryland many times in the past, especially during the long periods Margaret had spent there under her sister Mary's care, he did not visit again. Nor did he return to his former father-in-law's elegant home in Bardstown, Wickland. Charles Wickliffe's decisive 1863 turn toward the Peace Democrats made Holt's affection for him unsustainable.

Happily, Holt's connection with a number of his old friends, and particularly T. S. Bell in Louisville, remained as strong as ever. In contrast, although it ultimately endured, his relationship with James O. Harrison—who had exchanged his staunch Unionism for loyalty to Louisiana once the state's secession was effected—took something of a beating. When the Federals reclaimed New Orleans in April 1862, Harrison learned that he could not practice law unless he agreed to take the oath of allegiance to the United States. He refused, on the principle that although he had originally opposed secession, in the end he had cast his fate with rebel Louisiana and could not honorably turn his back now. Within months Harrison found himself on the brink of poverty, clinging to what little property he still had in cotton and humans and hoping that the Federals would not confiscate these for military purposes. In late 1862, a mutual friend asked Holt to write to the military authorities in New Orleans "manifesting your interest in him & your hope that he thus may be protected & respected as far as may be proper." However he felt about the choices Harrison had made, Holt agreed to write on his behalf. Some time later, General Nathaniel P. Banks promised to accede to Holt's wishes by doing anything he could to help Harrison out.[59]

In a more intimate realm, it is noteworthy that Holt did not remarry following Margaret's August 1860 death, which had left him a widower twice over. Although Holt and "Maggie" had spent long stretches of time apart, and although he had developed unusually intimate—if not necessarily physical—relationships with at least a couple of other women over the course of their ten-year marriage, he had surely loved his wife, and her death, perhaps especially because the two had not produced any children together, left him with a deep sense of loss that his alienation from her sisters' husbands and her father only exacerbated. Holt did not remarry after Margaret died, but he did continue to develop deep connections with women for the rest of his life. Most of these relationships did not last very long, nor do they generally seem to have moved much, if at all, beyond the realm of the written page and the participants' romantic imaginations. Nevertheless, Holt had a tendency to bond intensely and meaningfully, and sometimes also explosively, with women. Indeed, his correspondence includes an abundance of letters from doting female admirers—some of them married, some of them single, most of them younger than he and beholden to him in one way or another—whom he came to know in a variety of settings and who, for some period of time, captured his interest, concern, affection, and confidence.[60]

The woman who looms largest in Holt's wartime correspondence of this sort is Mary W. Cash, who was only twenty-one or twenty-two years old and living in Philadelphia with her family when she and Holt first began writing in the summer or fall of 1861. It is not clear precisely when or how Mary and Holt became acquainted, but once their correspondence became frequent, she routinely addressed him as "Cousin," apparently referring to a familial link through his marriage to Margaret. Moreover, in a January 1860 letter to Margaret, who was then convalescing in Florida, Holt mentioned escorting a "Miss Cash" and her mother, then in Washington, to an event hosted by President Buchanan's niece, Harriet Lane. This letter suggests that Margaret knew Mary personally and would not have been troubled at the time by the thought of her husband serving as the younger woman's escort on a formal occasion when she herself could not be on his arm.[61]

In any case, by late into the war's first year, about a year after Margaret's passing, Holt had begun receiving regular letters from Mary Cash, who early on seemed surprised that a man of his stature and eloquence would even bother writing back to her. Soon, however, Mary and Holt grew more comfortable with each other. Both initially assumed that Mary would eventually marry someone else, and indeed, in the spring of 1862, she boldly joked about someday having to surrender her status as the "Virgin Mary" when she and a man whose last name was "Labarre" were finally wed. Then, suddenly, the wedding was off, and Mary turned to Holt—her "one dear true abiding friend"—for all the consolation he was willing to provide. "I know," she wrote, "there is no one so ready to offer me a kind sympathy as yourself." Now the two began corresponding more frequently. Holt also traveled to Philadelphia to visit her, probably more than once, and as the summer passed, they became more and more deeply attached, Mary describing Holt's influence over her as "irresistible." In the case of Mary Cash, it is clear that Holt eventually gave in, at least in some measure, to their mutual physical attraction. In early July 1862, Mary described her longing to "come to your arms and have you bid me a long sweet good night," or, better yet, "keep me there always." At the same time, she and Holt tried to keep their relationship reasonably quiet, not least on account of his eminence and their age difference.[62]

Holt was powerfully drawn to Mary, both emotionally and physically, but as had been the case during both of his marriages, and perhaps even more so now in the context of the country's all-consuming war, he found it difficult to sustain a comfortable balance between his desire to be connected intimately to a woman, on the one hand, and his need to keep his emotional distance, on the other. On a very practical level, he also struggled fiercely with the potential implications of his physical desire, especially the possibility of pregnancy, about which Mary, interestingly, seems to have been considerably less concerned. As a result, Holt soon began to grow more distant physically, though he remained a faithful and loving correspondent. For her part, Mary was unable to understand his profound need for solitude. Nor did she seem to grasp the gravity of the war and the nation's peril: "I believe we women have the worst of it," she once quipped. "We have no excitement to keep us up and not even the privilege of nursing the sick & wounded. I offer my services in vain. Too young and I suppose not good enough." Mary's focus was almost entirely on her relationship with Holt, and she urged him repeatedly to visit her again, promising to make it worth his while. Occasionally she also attempted to provoke him into becoming jealous of another potential suitor, to no avail.[63]

In early October 1863, Mary finally got her wish: Holt came to see her again. "Truly," she wrote a few days later, "it was the pleasantest visit you ever paid me." One reason Mary was so happy was that, for whatever reason, Holt seems to have managed at long last to suppress his apprehensions (or perhaps he had simply lost control), and he had spent the night. Mary was elated about what she imagined was a new development in their love affair, but Holt immediately regretted his momentary lapse. Rather than honoring his concerns, or even trying to understand his withdrawal, Mary chose to punish him for growing distant again, and she let him imagine for a few days that she had become pregnant, although she had not. Then, once she had given him a good scare she apologized, chiding him for not having enough faith in her "good sense & *good management*" to avoid conceiving. "Forgive me," Mary wrote, "if I have scared you almost to death." Still, she insisted that she found the whole situation humorous. "What would not I give to see you read this letter, my poor frightened cousin? I can imagine the relieved happy change of countenance when he reads 'all is well.'" Even as she chuckled over her prank, however, Mary mused about the potential joys of bearing a child they had created together. "I think," she wrote wistfully, "if I had the *prospect* of one of your *boys* to bring up I should feel an approaching amount of responsibility scarcely equaled in this world. . . . I *wonder* what you would have done had it been true." Once again, she cheerfully encouraged Holt to come and visit her soon, noting seductively that even as she wrote her letter she was "all ready for bed, & *right* happy would I be to find you there, my *own dear* cousin."[64]

Mary's sense of humor was entirely lost on the stern and sober Holt who, rather than feeling relief when he learned that she had been teasing him about the pregnancy, became enraged. Although Mary continued to apologize, she still seemed incapable of understanding why Holt was so upset. A letter he received from his Aunt Mary Ann later that month surely only added to his unease. For all their (or at least his) attempts to keep the relationship a secret, rumors of it had spread all the way to Kentucky. Mary Ann informed him that she had recently heard that "you was going to be married to a lady that was a relation of the Wickliffes," whose last name was Cash. Mary Ann was delighted by the prospect, "for I know," she wrote, "if she is a kin to Margaret she is nothing else but the best of women & if she is only half such a woman she will do, for on this earth you will never come across such a pure just good & pious woman as Maggie & you need never expect it."[65]

Holt did not break off his relationship with Mary Cash immediately. After some time they were able to smooth things over and eventually, in early 1864, he even invited her to spend a few days at his Washington home. Her visit, however, only provoked a new and bitter quarrel: shortly after her departure, two of his hired black servants, Ellen and Jane, informed him that Mary had been boasting to them that she was going to become the next mistress of the house and that she had also made a number of disparaging comments about his late wife Margaret and about the quality of his and Margaret's marriage. Once again Holt unleashed his fearsome temper, catching the lighthearted Mary completely off guard. Mary was devastated to discover that Holt had lost faith in her, and she denied his accusations, insisting that Ellen and Jane had meant to cause trouble between them.

How, she openly (and foolishly) wondered, could he possibly place more value on the claims of "two negroes" than on her own? "The injustice you have done me," Mary wrote, "cuts me to the heart," and she urged Holt to punish Ellen and Jane for their wicked scheming. He refused to do so.[66]

In the months ahead, Mary clumsily struggled to set things right, soliciting Holt's forgiveness repeatedly even as she continued to criticize him for failing to recognize black people's flaws generally. "Your faith in the African race is complete," she wrote with disgust. "I think it will bring you but little happiness in this world." Meanwhile, back in Stephensport, Aunt Mary Ann was wondering what had become of Holt's liaison. "Josey," she wrote, "I cannot hear what become of Miss Cash that I heard you was going to be maried to. I was in the hopes there was truth in the report." But Holt had moved on. Indeed, by the end of 1864, he was receiving letters from yet another woman, Mary H. Bowman of Harrodsburg, Kentucky, complaining—as Mary Cash had long done—that he did not answer her letters more promptly, and insisting that he certainly would write more often if only he realized "the *great, big* dark shadow of disappointment that saddens my spirits when I do not hear from [you]."[67]

Mary Bowman was by no means the only voice from Kentucky Holt entertained in his correspondence as the war wound down. In January 1865 he heard again from Will Sterett, who brought news about the family. "Your friends & relations are all well in this section of the country," Sterett wrote. "I was at Tom Holt's a few days ago & your mother"—Eleanor Holt was now in her early eighties—"is in better health than usual, walks about much better than she has," and "seems to be cheerful & keeps her mind well." As for Thomas's second son, Washington Dorsey Holt, Sterett reported that he, too, had joined the Confederate army. Meanwhile, Will and Elizabeth's daughter, Margaret, had recently married a man by the last name of Bowmer, and their teenage son Billy (William Sterett Jr.) was now in school, where his father hoped he would remain. "Boys are very unmanageable these times," Sterett wrote, "tho I don't think he will disobey me." Sterett went on to describe the grim state of affairs in Breckinridge County, where Holt was born almost sixty years earlier: "We are having a hard time in this part of the state," Sterett explained. "The country is at the mercy of the guerrillas, or Southern soldiers as they term themselves. They hesitate at nothing, take homes, kill & steal, and whatever they choose to do. The country is ruined, every man is in fear of his life, & if he saves it he will indeed be lucky. We have no way to defend ourselves & have to submit to every & any thing they choose to inflict without a murmur." Sterett reported that his own slaves were now all gone, but that he was content to have been able to get his children to adulthood and to come through the conflict "in a better condition than many others," despite the death of his beloved wife, Elizabeth.[68]

On April 2, the Federal army captured the Confederate capital at Richmond, putting President Jefferson Davis and the remaining members of his collapsing administration to flight and signaling the imminent end of the war. Two days later, W. G. Snethen described "the enthusiasm that glowed on all sides in the faces" of Baltimore's "Union-loving friends" now that federal victory was at hand. "Baltimore street was red with the Stars and Stripes," Snethen wrote, and "soldiers were marching under arms from point to point to prevent the pent-up anger of loyal men from bursting forth in deeds of violence against the wretched minions of Jeff Davis and slavery." A week later, on April 11, Holt's brother Robert wrote to Thomas in Stephensport, sadly confirming the Confederacy's demise in a letter that Thomas subsequently forwarded to Washington. "It is now manifest," wrote Robert, "that the cause of the south has failed and is rapidly approaching the most disastrous end." Although he had anticipated this conclusion for almost a year, Robert still felt stunned. It was almost impossible, he admitted, to grasp the damages that the South had sustained over the course of four years of bloody conflict. "Fully seven tenths of our able bodied males between the ages of 17 and 50 years have perished," he wrote. "Our fields every where lie untilled, naked chimneys and charred ruins all over the land mark the spots where happy homes, the seats of refinement and elegance, once stood. Their former inhabitants wander in poverty and exile wherever chance or charity affords them shelter or food. Childless old age, widows, and helpless orphans, beggared and hopeless, are every where." Surely, Robert surmised, "our offence must have been great, that God has thus scourged us by the hands of our Demoniac enemies."[69]

Robert struggled to imagine what possible future lay ahead for the South, and the nation, especially now that the vanquished Confederacy was essentially at the mercy of the victorious Union, of which his brother had been such a resolute defender. Having already endured the forced emancipation of his slaves, Robert now anticipated that his land would be confiscated; even if it were not, he noted, it would be of little value without the slaves to tend to it. Robert predicted that his remaining stores of cotton would probably be taken, too. In his letter to Thomas, Robert confided that he believed their brother Joseph had the power to step in on his behalf, but that he probably would refuse to do so, given how bitter the division between them—like that between the North and the South—had become. Still, Robert planned to write to Holt directly on the theory that doing so "cannot make matters worse."[70]

When he did write to Holt, Robert reiterated many of the points he had made in his letter to Thomas, emphasizing those things for which he was thankful—"My life & the lives of my wife & children have all been spared"— but turning quickly to a long list of his losses, including his human property, his entire law library, many of his household possessions, and most of his crops. Plaintively, but also unapologetically, Robert urged Holt to do whatever he could "to shield me in the last extremity" from the federal government's confiscation of his land and cotton and to help him weather whatever punishment Lincoln had in store for the Confederacy, if only so that he might be able to provide his nine children with a proper education. "Does it not seem a little strange and hard," Robert asked, "that I, who have nearly all the children in the family, should be the only member of the family impoverished by the war? Yet it is so, and if I cannot educate my children I fear that they will be poorly prepared to represent the family in the next generation."[71]

Just a few days before Robert wrote, Mary Goldsborough of Frederick, Maryland, tucked "some dear little violets" into a letter in which she invited Holt to come and spend the Easter holiday at her home. Holt, however, had other obligations. Indeed, Good Friday, April 14, 1865, found him in Charleston, South Carolina, participating in the ceremonies surrounding the raising of the U.S. flag over Fort Sumter in the wake of Lee's April 9 surrender to General Grant at Appomattox. There, Holt attended a dinner at the Charleston House, where he also gave a speech entitled "Treason and its Treatment" to a rapt audience. "From the first moment" the rebel conspiracy "disclosed its cloven feet in the Capital until now," Holt thundered, "I never doubted of my own duty, and had the entire race of man confronted me on the question, my convictions in regard to that duty would not have been the less complete." As Holt understood it, his duty had been, simply, to do whatever he could to ensure federal victory. And in that victory, which Americans across the North, and even some in the South, were now celebrating, lay the proof "that the republic which was born on the 4th day of July 1776, was born not for death, but for immortality, and that though its bosom may be scarred by the poignards of conspirators, and though its blood may be required to flow on many fields," still "neither the swords nor the bayonets of traitors can ever reach the seat of its great and exhaustless life."[72]

But what next? Victory itself brought new dangers, Holt pointed out, dangers that were "quite as great as those that marked the battle, though of a totally different character." Above all, Holt hoped and prayed that in the weeks and months ahead, "the fruits of this prolonged and sanguinary conflict," especially universal liberty, might endure. This, however, meant that the remnants of treason, in all of its forms, must be obliterated and that every single "root of that cancer of slavery which has been eating into the national vitals" must be destroyed. Otherwise, the "thousands of millions of treasure" the nation had expended, and the sacrifice of the bravest of its sons "on the red altars of war," would have been in vain. "Let it then be our fond and solemn trust," Holt implored his audience, "that the Government will maintain to the end the position which it has occupied from the beginning—that this is, in very deed, a war upon crime and criminals—criminals with whom we cannot fraternize, with whom we can make no compromises, without, in the judgment of mankind, and at the bar of history, becoming criminals ourselves." As Stanton had also done in a cabinet meeting on April 11, Holt recommended that the states of the former Confederacy now be placed under military rule, at least for a time, until they completely and irrevocably renounced their wicked ways and accepted emancipation and federal supremacy. "While the ballot box is the rightful source of authority over loyal men," Holt explained as forcefully as he could, "the legitimate and reliable foundation for the authority of the Government over traitors, is the sword."[73]

Even as Holt spoke these stern words, back in Washington his beloved and deeply respected commander in chief, Abraham Lincoln, lay mortally wounded on the floor of the presidential box at Ford's Theater.

ASSASSINATION AND ITS AFTERMATH, APRIL 14, 1865– APRIL 3, 1866

I feel overwhelmed with grief at the awful deeds of Friday night that have shrouded our land in gloom, & fear your life too was included in the plot; but in the midst of it all, we feel deeply grateful to divine Providence for placing you beyond the reach of the assassin's hand.
—Mary Goldsborough to Joseph Holt, April 17, 1865

Word of the events at Ford's Theater reached Holt quickly, almost certainly by telegraph directly from Stanton, who single-handedly kept the War Department's telegraph office operating at break-neck speed through the night of April 14–15 while also interviewing witnesses and gathering information about possible suspects.[1] Five hundred miles lay between Charleston and Washington, however, and by the time Holt was able to reach the capital the president was already dead, having expired at 7:22 A.M. on April 15 at the Petersen House, directly across the street from the theater. "I never saw anything like the horror that pervaded this community when the dreadful tidings were announced," wrote Holt's friend, Mary Goldsborough, of Frederick, Maryland, a couple of days later. (It was Goldsborough's Easter invitation that Holt had turned down because of his obligations in Charleston.) "I think the first feeling of the rebels was merely astonishment, & not grief, but a few moments' reflection convinced them, that they too had lost a friend." Lincoln, after all, had seemed to promise that Reconstruction would be gentle; now that he was gone, there was no clear indication of how the postwar "peace" would shape up. Describing the reaction to the assassination in New York City, Frank W. Ballard remarked, "We are bound down with the great sorrow and our city is broken hearted over the murder of Mr. Lincoln." Ballard, however, was certain that the hand of God was at work: the assassination was clearly a warning to Unionists not to forgive the rebels too readily, as Lincoln had seemed prepared to do. "He who said 'Vengeance is mine,

I will repay,'" Ballard wrote sternly, "has no further use for men who assume the divine prerogatives and who speak peace to devils whom God has no intention of pardoning." Ballard also urged Holt to publish his recent speech at Charleston so that its themes could be widely disseminated among the public. "Its doctrines," he was certain, "are the kind of meat upon which the people need to feed just at this moment."[2]

People everywhere were in shock, but none more so than Holt, who had been instrumental in guaranteeing President-elect Lincoln's physical safety back in the spring of 1861, and whose forceful efforts on behalf of the nation's survival over the past four years had also, if indirectly, encompassed safeguarding the president's life. In his speech at Charleston on Good Friday, Holt had warned the country of new dangers now that the shooting war was drawing to a close, but he had not anticipated that those new dangers would reveal themselves so soon, or converge so completely and violently on Lincoln as their target. It is true that others had also been selected for attack on the night the president was shot, including Secretary of State Seward, who was brutally slashed on the face and throat while lying in bed at his Lafayette Square home, and whose recovery, for many weeks, seemed unlikely. Also marked for murder was Lincoln's vice president, Andrew Johnson, whose assassin seemed to have lost his nerve, and probably also General Grant, who had been expected to join the Lincolns at Ford's Theater with his wife but had not done so. Holt's shock, grief, and fury were easily broad and deep enough to embrace all of these victims and potential victims of the plot that had left Lincoln dead and the secretary of state grievously wounded. But for the moment his anguish was concentrated most vividly on the president, to whom he had pledged his loyalty and devotion, whom he had served so faithfully, and whose remains he now offered to accompany on their journey back to Illinois. Stanton, however, had other plans. "The Secretary of War," Assistant Adjutant General Edward D. Townsend informed Holt on April 20, the day after Lincoln's memorial service in the capital, "deems your services here as indispensable and has desired me to substitute another officer in your place to accompany the remains of the late President to Springfield."[3]

Although it was Stanton who got the federal government's assassination investigation underway, he now delegated to Holt and the Bureau of Military Justice the responsibility for continuing to collect and evaluate the evidence, which a number of other agencies—including the Washington, D.C., metropolitan police, the Provost Marshal General's Bureau, and the Secret Service—had been assembling as well. Stanton also assigned Holt the responsibility of determining the form that any trial (or trials) should take, and of conducting the trial(s) when the time came. Much of the "evidence" Holt and his assistants ultimately accumulated was useful, but much of it was, in the generous words of historian William Hanchett, "earnest but mistaken." Some of it was simply false, such as the forged letter supposedly written by the Maryland-born actor John Wilkes Booth to Jefferson Davis on May 1, in which "Booth" claimed to have received $20,000 from Davis to commit the terrible deed. Still, from within the hearty mix of good, bad, helpful, and purely misleading material Holt and his investigators had to sort through, some key details became entirely clear almost immediately. First and foremost among these was that the president's killer was indeed Booth, a passionate supporter of the Confederacy whose face many in the theater audience had recognized right away and who, despite having broken his leg when he leaped dramatically but awkwardly from the president's box to the stage, had escaped the theater and the district and vanished. Also clear was the fact that Booth had not acted alone: someone else entirely had attacked Secretary Seward at almost exactly the same time Booth shot the president, and the attacks had obviously been carefully coordinated. Moreover, it was apparent that Booth and Seward's assailant must have conspired with a number of additional accomplices in order to realize their violent plans. With this particular detail in mind, Holt cast a wide net across Washington, Maryland, and Virginia, seeing to it that hundreds of suspects were detained for questioning.[4]

Even as they continued working to identify the individuals who had been most central to Booth's planning on the local level—a number of whom had already been arrested—Holt and his assistants at the bureau reached a profoundly important conclusion about the assassination conspiracy itself, which Stanton made public on April 24: namely, that the chain of events leading to Lincoln's murder had been set in motion by a group of Confederate activists located in Canada—known as Jefferson Davis's "Canadian Cabinet"—and that Davis himself had approved the original plan. Two days later, Booth himself was discovered by a detachment of the 16th New York Cavalry hiding in a barn in northern Virginia with another young man, David Herold. There, a soldier named Boston Corbett unexpectedly shot Lincoln's killer dead, without orders and to the great consternation of those who had hoped to hear what Booth might reveal under close examination about the overall plot.[5]

After Booth was killed, Herold was arrested and returned to Washington—along with Booth's dead body—aboard the steamer *John S. Ide*. This brought to nine the number of local individuals upon whom Holt's wide-

John Wilkes Booth. Courtesy of the Library of Congress.

ranging investigation increasingly focused, thanks to the intimate nature of their associations with Booth over the past several months. In addition to Herold, the alleged conspirators included Booth's longtime friends Samuel Arnold and Michael O'Laughlen; George Atzerodt, who was believed to have been assigned to kill the vice president; Samuel Mudd, a Maryland physician who had not only seen Booth and Herold after the murder but had also set Booth's broken leg; Lewis Thornton Powell, identified by a number of people as Secretary Seward's attacker; Edman Spangler, an employee at Ford's Theater who was suspected of having assisted Booth in his escape; Mary Surratt, the widowed owner of a Washington, D.C., boardinghouse located on H Street, just blocks from Ford's Theater, where it was believed that the conspirators had hatched their plans; and Mary Surratt's son, John Surratt, who had introduced the other men, including Booth, to the H Street boardinghouse. Except for John Surratt, who had disappeared, and Herold, who had spent two weeks in hiding with Booth, all of these suspects were brought into custody within three or four days of the assassination. On April 29, they were moved with Herold to cells at the Old Arsenal Penitentiary, situated about a mile south and slightly west of the Capitol on Greenleaf's Point.

Early on, Holt and his investigators became convinced that these eight individuals and John Surratt had served, in various capacities, as Booth's main "action team." But they continued to believe strongly in a "grand conspiracy": that key figures in the Confederate leadership in Richmond and Canada had set the conspiracy in motion and had supported it from start to finish. When President Johnson—who had been sworn into office by Chief Justice Salmon P. Chase on April 15—inquired on May 2 about the investigation's results thus far, Holt decided to name names. He specifically identified as coconspirators with Booth and his local accomplices six influential Confederate leaders, most (if not all) of whom he knew personally, starting with Jefferson Davis who, as a U.S. senator from Mississippi when Holt was serving as Buchanan's secretary of war, resigned with great fanfare the same day as Holt's brother-in-law, Florida senator David Yulee. Along with Davis, Holt also named Jacob Thompson of Mississippi, the former U.S. secretary of the interior who had been Holt's boss when he was head of the Patent Office, and with whom he had clashed so bitterly in the wake of the *Star of the West*'s mission to Charleston in January 1861. After resigning from Buchanan's cabinet, Thompson had gone on to serve as the Confederate army's inspector general before heading to Canada in late 1864 to serve as one of Davis's agents there.[6]

Also on Holt's list was Clement C. Clay, a former U.S. senator from Alabama who withdrew from Congress following Alabama's secession and then spent time as a senator in the Confederate congress before joining Jacob Thompson in Canada. The Holts and the Clays had once been good friends and had remained cordial before the war despite the disintegrating national political situation. Holt also named Beverly Tucker of Virginia, once a U.S. consul in England, who had been sent to Canada by Davis in the spring of 1864 to organize shipments of matériel to the South; and George Sanders of Kentucky, yet another of Davis's Canadian agents, whom Holt must have known in the 1850s when Sanders was working as a political activist on behalf of the Southern wing of the Democratic Party. Finally, Holt identified William C. Cleary, who had apparently served as an administrative assistant to both Thompson and Clay in their Canadian operations. Upon receiving Holt's list of high-ranking suspects, Andrew Johnson immediately issued a proclamation offering rewards for their capture: $100,000 for Davis; $25,000 each for Clay, Thompson, Sanders, and Tucker; and $10,000 for Cleary. Posters with the men's names, pictures, and reward figures appeared all over the Washington area as well as in the popular press, provoking Tucker and Sanders, who were then in Montreal, to issue a public denial of their involvement. "Your proclamation," the two fugitives wrote to the *New York Times* on May 7, addressing the new president, "is a living, burning lie, known to be such by yourself and all your surroundings." That same day the *Times* also published William C. Cleary's refutation of the charges against him. For his part, Thompson had left Canada on a ship bound for England and was incommunicado.[7]

When he presented Johnson with his list of top Confederate suspects on May 2, Holt had in mind that Booth probably had Copperhead support, too, a presumption—true or not—that his detailed examination of secret antigovernment organizations in the West the previous fall probably made unavoidable. Holt's suspicions on this front were both evinced and enhanced by his decision, just two days after taking over the investigation from Stanton, to have Colonel Henry L. Burnett detailed to Washington to work with him. As Holt's judge advocate for the Department of the Ohio, Burnett had successfully prosecuted Lambdin Milligan and the Order of the American Knights, and once he arrived in Washington he focused much of his attention on finding links between such organizations and the events of April 14. As a result, on the same day Holt produced his list of leading Confederate suspects, Burnett reported that his study of the evidence had revealed conclusively the involvement of the "fiend-like" Order of the American Knights. For Holt and Burnett, the assassination conspiracy's web had Booth and his Washington, D.C., action team at the center, but it also stretched north to Davis's Canadian Cabinet, south to Richmond, and west to the heartland of the country's most determined anti-Lincoln, antiwar, anti-emancipation subversives.[8]

Holt and Burnett were hardly alone in their conceptualization of the conspiracy's makeup. An anonymous correspondent from New York City offered a similar analysis: "There was a plot on the part of numerous conspirators to kill the chief officers of our Government," wrote the man who identified himself only as "Loyalty." Like Holt and Burnett, "Loyalty" was certain that the plot "embraced the rebels in the south, the rebels in Canada, the rebels secreted in the north and the members of the Knights of the Golden Circle and other secret societies." Holt's Aunt Mary Ann envisioned the conspiracy in exactly the same way, insisting just days after the attacks that Booth had been in the employ of the Knights of the Golden Circle, who had hired him to kill the president.[9]

For now, however, for practical reasons much of Holt's immediate attention remained focused on the eight individuals who were already in prison at the Old Arsenal and whose involvement with Booth seemed incontrovertible. What was the best way to expose their guilt and ensure their proper punishment? Now that the war on the battlefield was virtually over, and the civil courts were fully operational in Washington, D.C., some observers quite reasonably argued that the civil courts were the only appropriate, legal venue for trying civilians, even civilians who had been charged with the horrendous and unprecedented crime of murdering the nation's chief magistrate. (Even treason, after all, was defined in federal law as a civil offense to be tried in civil court.) Predictably, however, given his understanding of the scope of his responsibility as the judge advocate general, combined with his intense determination to punish whoever had inflicted this most recent and heinous injury on the nation, Holt strongly favored trying all of the leading local suspects at once in a military setting under the War Department's—and his—authority and control.

In the weeks following the assassination, Holt built his case for convening a military commission to assess the suspects' guilt, arguing—among other things—that as of April 14 peace had in fact not yet been declared: at the time Lincoln was murdered the Confederate president and most of his cabinet, after all, remained at large; General Joseph E. Johnston had not yet surrendered his Army of Tennessee to General Sherman (he did so on April 26); and a number of smaller Confederate forces remained in the field (the last of which only surrendered on May 26). In addition, Holt pointed out that killing the Federal army's commander in chief was not treason per se but rather a war crime that should be prosecuted in a military court. To many observers, both within and outside the federal government, these arguments made perfect sense. Still, just to be sure, Holt submitted the issue of jurisdiction to the attorney general, James Speed, for consideration. Speed agreed with Holt. "If the persons who are charged with assassination of the President committed the deed as public enemies, as I believe they did," he declared, "they not only can, but ought to be, tried before a military tribunal." And he added, "If the persons charged have offended against the laws of war, it would be palpably wrong for the military to hand them over to the civil courts, as it would be wrong in a civil court to convict a man of murder who had in time of war killed another in battle."[10]

In the wake of Speed's ruling on the question President Johnson ordered the assistant adjutant general and Holt to select nine military officers to serve on the commission, and he directed Holt to draft the charges against the accused, inform them of those charges, and choose assistant judge advocates to work with him at the trial. On May 6, the names of the commissioners appeared in Special Orders No. 211, including, as president of the commission, Major General David Hunter, who had also presided over Holt's controversial court-martial of Fitz John Porter back in the fall of 1862 and who had recently returned from escorting Lincoln's remains to Springfield, as Holt himself had hoped to do. As his assistant judge advocates Holt designated Colonel Burnett and the Honorable John A. Bingham, a staunch Republican representative to the U.S. Congress from Ohio and an experienced lawyer who had also spent time during the war as a judge advocate in the West. Special Orders No. 211 further announced the names of the accused and directed the commission to commence its business on or as soon after May 8 as possible. On May 9, Holt, his assistant judge advocates, and the nine commissioners—all dressed in their full uniforms, as they would be for the duration of the trial—met for the first time in a specially arranged courtroom on the third floor of the Old Arsenal Penitentiary. That same day, Arnold, Atzerodt, Herold, Mudd, O'Laughlen, Powell, Spangler, and Mary Surratt were arraigned, and their requests for legal counsel were approved. In addition, Holt, the commissioners, the assistant judge advocates, and a staff of court stenographers led by Benn Pitman, who had been the recorder at the fall 1864 Milligan trial as well, were sworn in.[11]

Over the next couple of days Holt and the court struggled to resolve a series of controversial issues, including whether or not the trial should be held behind closed doors or kept open to the public and the press. On May 10—the same day Jefferson Davis was captured by a detachment of the 4th Michigan Cavalry near Irwinville, Georgia, and taken (along with

John A. Bingham, Joseph Holt, and Henry L. Burnett.
Courtesy of the Library of Congress.

Clement Clay, who had surrendered) to Fortress Monroe, Virginia, for imprisonment—the *New York Times* grumbled about the judge advocate general's decision to keep the doors shut in order to control the press's access
to what the witnesses revealed. "The testimony, when written out in full, is
to be placed in the hands of Judge-Advocate Holt," noted the *Times*, "who
will designate such portions of it as may be proper for publication." By way
of explanation, the *Times* grudgingly informed its readers that Holt and
the bureau feared that some testimony might implicate individuals who
were not yet under arrest and who might then take their cues from what
they read in the trial record to make an escape. As it turns out, the hue and
cry over his original closed-door policy soon persuaded Holt to change his
mind. On May 13, the doors of the courtroom were reopened (though Holt
reserved the right to close them occasionally, as necessary, to prevent the

exposure of particularly sensitive information), and the press and the public were invited back in.[12]

Even more prickly than the issue of public access to the trial was the lingering question of the military commission's jurisdiction, which many had considered settled but which the defendants' lawyers revived immediately. The key individual to raise the point was none other than the politically complex Maryland senator Reverdy Johnson, who had defended Fitz John Porter at his 1862 court-martial before General Hunter and then, following Porter's conviction, had vigorously attacked Holt's handling of the trial. More recently, and somewhat ironically, given that he had supported George B. McClellan in the election of 1864, Senator Johnson had served as a pallbearer at Lincoln's funeral. Now, in the first phase of the assassination conspiracy trial, Johnson assumed the role of Mary Surratt's lead attorney, though he soon handed her case over to two junior associates, Frederick Aiken and John W. Clampitt. Before doing so, however, Johnson sternly and at considerable length challenged the commission's jurisdiction, to no avail: the nine commissioners unanimously (and predictably) agreed that they had the right to try the case. For its part, the *New York Times* reminded readers that not just Judge Advocate General Holt and Attorney General Speed but also the president and every member of his cabinet had approved the commission's legitimacy. The *Times* further expressed the opinion that those who sought to deny the commission's jurisdiction on the basis of the defendants' civilian status simply missed the point. "It is the nature of the crime, and not the dress of the criminal," the *Times* declared, "that determines the tribunal by which he may be tried." And given that "the Commander-in-Chief of the Army of the United States was assassinated by tools of a conspiracy, within the lines of the army, in a fortified city, patrolled day and night by a mounted guard, from which no man could go South without a pass, and while the laws and regulations of a state of war were in full force," it was clear that "the perpetrators of that crime must be tried and punished by military law, no matter who they were."[13]

On May 12, one day before Holt reopened the courtroom doors to the public and the press, the witnesses began to appear. Soon the court settled into a regular routine, meeting generally, as Commissioner August V. Kautz later recalled, at 10 A.M. each day (except Sunday) and remaining in session until after 6 P.M., with a break for lunch around 1 P.M. This routine was interrupted on May 16, when the court held its morning session at Ford's Theater in order to familiarize the various members with the crime scene. The daily routine was interrupted again for the Grand Review of the Armies on May 23 and 24, as well as on June 1, a day that President Johnson had set aside for "humiliation and prayer." Dozens of spectators visited the courtroom each day, many of them bearing passes solicited from the judge advocate general himself. "Are ladies admitted daily?" asked one woman friend. "If so, can I be permitted to be present some day?" "I was very much pleased with my visit to the Arsenal on Monday," wrote another. "If you don't object to my troubling you again, to send to you for admittance, I will come again with Lily on Saturday." Indeed, a *New York Times* reporter noted that "the ladies" in their elaborate dress frequently packed the courtroom "most suffocatingly"; and according to the *Philadelphia Inquirer*, so many spectators crowded the courtroom from day to day that they occasionally prompted the defendants' lawyers to appeal for a limit to their numbers.[14]

The "trial of the assassins," as it quickly came to be known, lasted from May 9 until the end of June, during which time military protection was provided for each of the commissioners, who were picked up at their residences, escorted to the courtroom, guarded there throughout the day, and escorted back home in the evening. Soldiers also watched over Holt, who had in fact been under military protection since April 28, when Major General Winfield Scott Hancock, in command of the Federal forces in the capital, had ordered guards to surround Holt's New Jersey Avenue home. Still, some friends continued to worry about his safety. Wrote one, "I have desired to see you to beg you to use every precaution necessary for personal protection in this fearful time. It does seem to me that it's hardly safe for you to go back & forth & to remain at night in your house without a *strong guard*. Do think of it. Your life is of the greatest importance to [the] community now & ever of importance to your immediate friends." Meanwhile, some thirty soldiers reported daily to General John F. Hartranft, the officer in charge of the Old Arsenal Penitentiary, on orders to be "prepared for any emergency" involving the prisoners. Still others patrolled the streets between the Old Arsenal and the Executive Mansion, or stood vigilant in the courtroom itself.[15]

Over the course of the several weeks the court was in session almost 300 witnesses testified, some behind closed doors but most with the eyes of the nation upon them. All testified in an atmosphere charged with a general and profound war weariness as well as the desire of some for vengeance against the Confederacy and its allies in the North, the anxious anticipation of others about possible federal government retribution for the rebellion, and the yearning of many to return as quickly as possible to a state of peace and national unity. As numerous studies over the years have ably demonstrated, the case against each of the defendants had its own points of keen interest. Among the many questions the court explored were how much had individuals such as Arnold and O'Laughlen, who had clearly been in on Booth's original kidnap plot, known about Booth's revised plans? Why had Atzerodt failed to assassinate Andrew Johnson after agreeing to do so and after taking a room in the same hotel, the Kirkwood House, where Johnson was staying? What role, if any, had Spangler played in enabling Booth to make his well-planned escape from Ford's Theater? Had he also, in advance, drilled the hole in the door of the president's box, through which Booth had aimed his gun? And what about Mudd? Was it true, as he said, that he had not recognized the injured murderer when Booth and Herold had arrived at his Maryland home, or even after the two fugitives spent an entire day there, during which Mudd got close enough to Booth to examine his leg, provide him with a splint and crutches, and then escort the men on their way further south?

Holt and his assistant judge advocates worked assiduously to determine the answers to these and other important questions, some of the most intriguing and ultimately provocative of which revolved around the lone woman among the eight defendants, Mary Surratt. Certainly the circumstantial evidence against her was suspicious: her son John was known to be both a Confederate activist and a close friend of Booth's, and it was he who had invited Booth to the boardinghouse several times in the winter of 1864–65. Atzerodt and Powell had also visited the boardinghouse on one or more occasions, consulting with John Surratt and perhaps also with his mother. Even more damning, the first place Booth and Herold stopped after fleeing Washington on the night of the 14th was a house that Mary Surratt owned in Maryland, less than twenty miles from the capital. Moreover, the evidence was clear that Surratt herself had visited the Maryland house twice in the days before the murder, once on April 11, when Booth lent her the money to hire a horse and buggy for the trip, and again on the 14th, when—at Booth's request—she delivered a small, mysterious, paper-wrapped parcel to her tenant and property manager there, John M. Lloyd. When Booth and Herold arrived at Surratt's Maryland house later that night, they picked up some guns that had been stashed there, presumably for their use, as well as a set of field glasses that were roughly the size of the package Surratt had delivered earlier in the day and two bottles of whiskey. Also important in the case against Mary Surratt was the fact that late on the night of April 17, Lewis Powell, the man identified as Secretary Seward's attacker, had turned up at her H Street boardinghouse just as law enforcement officials were interrogating its occupants about the events at

Ford's Theater and the whereabouts of Surratt's son. Neither Mary Surratt nor Lewis Powell had been able to explain his sudden appearance satisfactorily.

To prove the defendants' guilt—and especially Mary Surratt's—Holt and his assistant prosecutors adopted a modified version of the tactic that Henry Burnett had used successfully against Lambdin Milligan and the others in Indiana the previous fall: making skilled use of witnesses close to the events in question who were willing to go on the attack against the accused in order to save their own lives. In the trial of the assassins, Holt and his assistants relied heavily on one of Mary Surratt's boarders, twenty-two-year-old Louis J. Weichmann, a War Department clerk who had been sufficiently intimate with John Surratt and several of the other prisoners at the bar in the months before the assassination to be considered a suspect in his own right. Weichmann made his first appearance for the prosecution on May 13. As it turns out, however, he had been working behind the scenes in crucial ways as far back as the morning after the assassination, when he voluntarily went to the local police to tell them what he knew about the recent goings-on at the boardinghouse and offered to help them locate the fugitive Booth. Once he began to testify in court, Weichmann wove a persuasive tale in which his own shining innocence contrasted sharply with the others' evident guilt. In the end, the apparently upstanding and respectable Weichmann succeeded in constructing a solid foundation upon which the rest of the testimony against the prisoners at the bar could be erected.[16]

Holt's primary goal during the trial was to establish the guilt of the eight defendants he had on hand. At the same time, however, he and Burnett and Bingham made a concerted effort to provide evidence in support of the theory he had first floated on April 24: namely, that the local conspirators had received their original orders from Jefferson Davis and that members of Davis's Canadian Cabinet—Thompson, Sanders, Clay, Tucker, Cleary—had helped to develop, fund, and execute the plans. Even more broadly, Holt and his assistants strove to impress upon the court and the attentive public that the events of April 14 were of a piece with all of the other horrifying deeds the Confederacy's diabolical leadership had sponsored (or intended to sponsor) over the years, starting with bringing on the immensely bloody and destructive war in the first place. Holt was certainly aware that he would ultimately have to prove the case against Davis and the others in a courtroom; still, there was no harm in laying the groundwork early. With this in mind, he brought in witnesses such as Richard Montgomery, who declared under oath that he had been in Canada in the summer of 1864 and again in January 1865, and that while there he had discussed with Thompson, Clay, Sanders, Tucker, Cleary, and others their willingness "to go to any lengths to serve the cause of the South," including killing Lincoln. Davis's Canadian agents, Montgomery reported, had also discussed the possibility of attacking cities and towns along the northern frontier such as St. Albans, Vermont, where a raid in October 1864 had in fact resulted in considerable mayhem and one civilian death.[17]

James B. Merritt similarly testified that he had met a number of Confederates in Canada in the late winter of 1864–65 who had openly discussed assassinating Lincoln and that Jefferson Davis had authorized them to do so. John Deveny testified that he had seen Booth and Sanders in secret consultation in Montreal, and Rev. W. H. Ryder stated that he had found, among the scattered papers of the Davis administration in Richmond, a February 1865 letter to the Confederate president regarding plans for "harassing the enemy by means of burning their shipping, towns, etc." In addition, Edward Frazier testified that in 1864 he had met several Confederate loyalists in St. Louis who boasted of having engineered the burning of steamboats being used to transport federal supplies. Frazier also claimed to have discussed with Jefferson Davis the possibility of burning the Long Bridge between Nashville and Chattanooga. Godfrey Joseph Hyams recalled being offered no less than $100,000 by a Confederate operative in Canada to distribute clothing infected with yellow fever and smallpox to places where the Federal army was stationed, and some to Lincoln himself.[18]

Three weeks into the trial, T. S. Bell described how grateful he was to know that his old friend Holt was in charge of the assassination conspiracy case. Thanks to Holt, Bell declared, "the investigation has been conducted with great impartiality and in strict conformity to the reason of the law." So pleased was another of Holt's correspondents with his handling of the trial that he echoed a familiar refrain: "I would like to see you President, & if all hands felt towards you as I do, you would be the next President without any trouble." There is simply no escaping the conclusion, however, that in the end, Holt's conduct of this crucial trial did not entirely live up to his longstanding and well-deserved reputation for being meticulously evenhanded and careful when it came to the law and his professional responsibilities. Although Holt undoubtedly did the best he could under horrible circumstances to maintain the highest possible standards of justice and impartiality, it is absolutely clear that some of his decisions were governed unduly by how powerfully he had been affected by the war, the weight of his profound grief over Lincoln's death, and his towering rage toward those who, as he understood it, had so boldly and shamelessly tried to destroy the nation in order to enhance their own power and preserve the immoral institution of slavery. Never one to forgive lightly, by the spring of 1865 Holt was overwhelmed—some would say justifiably—with a desire to make the nation's (and Lincoln's) enemies pay dearly for their crimes, if only to ensure that Lincoln's great sacrifice and the Federals' victory, with all of their implications for the nation's future, would not be squandered. As a result, Holt found it difficult to adhere to his own basic principle that his efforts to develop any case must be ethically beyond reproach. Rather, his driving impulse to avenge Lincoln's death and defend the nation against its debased and criminal enemies caused him, with almost breathtaking blindness, to make some very bad judgment calls indeed. Almost certainly the worst of these was his willingness to engage as a witness a good-looking, thirty-three-year-old man from New York who identified himself as Sanford Conover.[19]

Like Louis Weichmann, Sanford Conover had contacted the authorities even before the trial began, apparently approaching Holt immediately after the May 2 announcement linking Jefferson Davis and various members of his Canadian Cabinet to the April 14 events, and perhaps even earlier. Having persuaded Holt that he could provide a range of evidence in support of the grand conspiracy theory, Conover then appeared as a trial witness on May 20 and 22. In his testimony, Conover claimed to have worked as a clerk in the Confederate War Department and then to have spent the past several months in Canada as a correspondent for the *New York Tribune* under the alias "James Watson Wallace." During these months, Conover continued, he had become familiar with Sanders, Thompson, Clay, Tucker, Cleary, and others, including Booth and John Surratt. He further claimed that he had heard Surratt discussing with Thompson some encoded dispatches from Richmond, and that Thompson and others had invited him to participate in a plot to kidnap Lincoln. Conover discussed being informed, too, of the plans to assassinate the president and his vice president, as well as Stanton, Seward, Grant, and even Chief Justice Chase, and he described being clued in by Davis's Canadian agents about plans for the raid on St. Albans and another on Ogdensburg, New York, as well as others to destroy New York's Croton Dam, set fire to the city, and poison its water supply. He further recalled meeting Dr. Luke Blackburn, who had organized the distribution of pestilence-infected clothing that Godfrey Hyams described in his testimony. Indeed, in the late winter of 1864–65, Conover insisted, Davis's agents in Canada had discussed the assassination conspiracy and other dastardly plans "about as commonly as one would speak of the weather."[20]

Holt intended the man who testified as Sanford Conover to do for his case for a grand conspiracy what Weichmann had done so effectively for the case against Booth's local accomplices. But whereas Weichmann, for better or worse, proved utterly believable to the members of the court and to many beyond its walls as well, Conover did not, and for good reason. Even before the trial was over Holt found himself confronting a series of vigorous and irrefutable challenges to the reliability of Conover's testimony. These included a letter from General John A. Dix, dated June 24, in which Dix reported that his own investigation into the witness's background and credibility had revealed that "Conover" was actually only one of a number of aliases being used by a corrupt New York journalist and confidence man whose real name was Charles A. Dunham and whose testimony should not be taken seriously. When someone claiming to be the real James Watson Wallace subsequently wrote a newspaper article denying all of the claims Conover had made at the trial relating to his purported work as a correspondent, more than one observer suggested that the witness's testimony was "from beginning to end, a tissue of falsehoods" that should be summarily dismissed.[21]

Continuing revelations about Conover's duplicity—and concerns that Holt may have even encouraged it—seriously undermined the judge advocate general's ability to use the trial of the assassins as a venue for fleshing out his case against Davis and the rest of the Confederate leadership. For the time being, however, these revelations did not have any substantial effect on the cases against the eight defendants who were actually on trial, or even against John Surratt, who had yet to be brought into custody. Indeed, by the time General Hunter and the other military commissioners began their deliberations on June 29, the defendants' convictions were virtually certain. On June 30, the commissioners reported their conclusions to Holt, declaring all of the prisoners at the bar guilty as charged. They sentenced Atzerodt, Herold, Powell, and Mary Surratt to death by hanging, Spangler to six years in prison, and Arnold, Mudd, and O'Laughlen to prison for the rest of their lives.[22]

In his memoir of the trial, August Kautz commented that upon learning of the commissioners' rulings, Holt and his assistants, Burnett and Bingham, openly conveyed their disappointment that four of the defendants had escaped the noose. "In these early days after the assassination," Kautz wrote, "the country seemed to require victims to pay for the great crime." In his memory, Holt was at least as distressed to learn that five of the nine commissioners, including Kautz and General Hunter, had expressly requested that President Johnson commute Mary Surratt's sentence—which they themselves had devised to reflect the seriousness of her crime—from hanging to life imprisonment. Although the commissioners' petition for Surratt offered her sex and age as reasons why they felt she should be spared (Surratt was in her mid-forties), Kautz recalled anticipating that if Surratt were hanged—making her the first woman to be executed by the federal government in the nation's history—there would be a backlash, and that those who had authorized her execution would regret having done so. How much this particular consideration factored into the commissioners' decision to present their petition on her behalf is impossible to know.[23]

One suspects that what Kautz later claimed to recall about Holt's explicit reaction to the commissioners' rulings and their petition for Mary Surratt probably reflects more about developments between the time of the events Kautz was describing and the time he was writing about them years later than it does about what really happened. Considering the level of his rage over the rebellion and the president's murder, as well as his absolute certainty that all of the defendants (as well as the absent John Surratt) were entirely guilty, it is certainly easy to imagine that Holt was disappointed that four of them were to be imprisoned rather than executed. It is safe to assume, too, that he *personally* objected to the petition for Mary Surratt. At least as far back as his spring 1863 discussions with Francis Lieber regarding the rules of war Holt had rejected the idea that female enemies of the nation should be handled more gently than male ones. Still, it seems highly unlikely that he would have openly revealed his personal disagreement with the commissioners' decisions, given how inappropriate it would have been for him to do so, and given his great respect for military authority and procedure. In any case, it was not Holt's job to challenge them; his job was to present the record of the trial, the commissioners' verdicts, their recommended sentences, and all other pertinent materials—including the petition for Mary Surratt—to the president for review, as he had done so many times before when Abraham Lincoln was alive.[24]

Holt probably hoped to fulfill this summary responsibility immediately on June 30. Instead, he was compelled to wait: Johnson, it appears, had fallen ill and was not available for several days. Then, on July 5, Holt and the president finally met, in private, the judge advocate general presenting his report of the trial along with all of the relevant documents from the commissioners. Holt assured Johnson that the evidence was sufficient and that the rights of the accused had been ensured by their lawyers, and he recommended that all eight of the sentences the commissioners had devised be carried out. Johnson agreed, signed the report, and ordered the four executions for two days hence. When the commissioners' findings and the president's decision were made public, few in Washington or across the nation were surprised. Most people, the *Philadelphia Inquirer* observed, had anticipated these results from the closely watched trial, although some had expected that all of the defendants would be condemned to die.[25]

While few were surprised by the verdicts or the sentences, and despite the fact that public outcry against Surratt had been vigorous before and during the trial and that some observers had even gone so far as to declare her the ringleader of the assassination plot, in the brief time that remained before the actual executions were scheduled to take place, several attempts were made to save Mary Surratt's life. Now that she faced execution, the *Philadelphia Inquirer* commented, "a mawkish sort of sympathy" for Surratt had become tangible, not least among individuals who considered it unseemly for the federal government to execute a woman at all, no matter what crime she had committed, and who now hoped that Johnson would pardon her or at least reduce her sentence as the five commissioners had requested (word of the commissioners' petition had quickly made it into the press). In contrast, the *Inquirer* grumbled that those same people who now advocated Surratt's pardon were exactly the same kinds of people who "would sympathize with Satan himself, if there was any possibility of bringing him to justice."[26]

As part of the effort to keep Mary Surratt from the gallows, on the morning she was scheduled to die her lawyers filed a habeas corpus petition with the Supreme Court of the District of Columbia in which they charged that she had been wrongly arrested, confined, and then tried by a military commission that was acting outside the constraints of its jurisdiction. Johnson, intransigent, denied the petition. Johnson also dismissed an urgent letter he had received from the principal of a Catholic boys' school in Washington, John Brophy, assailing Louis Weichmann's reliability as a witness. In addition, he refused to meet with Mary Surratt's daughter, Anna, who went directly to the Executive Mansion hoping to persuade the president to relent. Instead, Johnson referred her to Holt, who informed the despondent young woman, as he now informed all other callers, that there was no turning back. Still expecting that Johnson would ultimately agree to a pardon, General Hancock posted soldiers along the streets extending from Pennsylvania Avenue to Greenleaf's Point to relay Surratt's anticipated stay of execution, which never came.[27]

George Atzerodt, David Herold, Lewis Powell, and Mary Surratt were hanged early on the afternoon of July 7, 1865, in the Old Arsenal Penitentiary courtyard, with throngs of observers watching. Later that month, Samuel Arnold, Samuel Mudd, Michael O'Laughlen, and Edman Spangler — who had been kept in the dark for some time about their own fates — were shipped off to far-distant Fort Jefferson, located in Florida's Dry Tortugas, to serve out their terms of imprisonment. "Permit a stranger," wrote one grateful correspondent from Iowa around this time, "to express to you his thanks for the results reached by the Court which you have so ably & honorably represented." V. O. Taylor, too, gave Holt credit for seeing that justice was done, and encouraged him to continue his noble work of bringing Davis and the rest of the Confederate leadership to justice. So did a correspondent from St. Louis, who described himself as "a radical Union man, a lover of my country, and a sincere hater of treason in all its forms." Calling Davis "the arch traitor," Harvey Yeaman demanded that the Confederacy's former president be executed, though he felt that even hanging "would be no compensation for his crimes." T. S. Bell commended Holt for a job well done, congratulating him as fondly and as admiringly as ever "upon the great vindication of the laws in the conviction & punishment of the rebel tools, the Conspirators."[28]

As he looked back over the weeks since Lincoln's death, Holt undoubtedly shared a measure of Bell's satisfaction, at least with respect to the outcome of the recent trial. At the same time, he was sorely frustrated by his failure to make headway against Davis and the others, in part because Conover, whom he had considered a star witness on this front, had turned out to be so problematic. Holt's frustration was amplified considerably in the days ahead as he contemplated the disturbing claims of some of his correspondents from the West and the South regarding the refusal of the former rebels in their areas to submit quietly and cooperatively to their undeniable defeat. Holt learned from T. S. Bell that the influx of paroled Confederate soldiers into Kentucky was causing all sorts of problems across the state. Meanwhile, a South Carolina correspondent wrote that he had heard a number of "gentlemen" in Charleston openly declaring that they had "erred, not as to the right of secession, but as to the time of [its] execution" and denying that the former slaves were really free. Such boldness, Tal P. Shaffner insisted, demonstrated how premature it was even to consider reestablishing civil government in South Carolina, where influential men had shown themselves to be "as hostile at heart to the supremacy of

Nationality over *State Sovereignty* as before the war," and had made it clear that they intended to reassert their authority as quickly as possible.[29]

At least as troubling to Holt as reports such as these were the implications of the two proclamations Andrew Johnson had issued at the end of May, only six weeks after his predecessor's death and while the trial of the conspirators was still in progress. At his second inaugural, Lincoln, of course, had famously summed up with the phrase, "with malice toward none," words that, in conjunction with his mild December 1863 Proclamation of Amnesty and Reconstruction, seemed to suggest that he intended to bring the North and the South back together as quickly and gently as possible once the fighting was over. In contrast, upon assuming the presidency in mid-April, Andrew Johnson had suggested that he would take a stern and punitive approach toward the Confederate political, social, and military leadership. Johnson's willingness in early May to endorse the theory that Davis and some of his key subordinates had authorized Lincoln's assassination, followed by his willingness at the beginning of July to execute four of Booth's coconspirators (including a woman) and send four others off to oblivion in far western Florida, enhanced some people's expectations that he would follow through on his original promises.

On May 29, however, only three days after Edmund Kirby Smith surrendered the last significant Confederate army in the field, Johnson issued his own proclamations pertaining to amnesty and reconstruction. Like Lincoln's proclamation of December 1863, Johnson's laid out simple and generous protocols over which the president—not Congress, which was then out of session and not scheduled to return until December 4—had complete authority, and by which the states that had been in rebellion could return to the Union quickly and those individuals who had supported the rebellion, with limited exceptions, could regain their full rights as U.S. citizens. Around this time Johnson also began issuing pardons, which he continued to grant at an ever-accelerating rate to those who fell outside the proclamations' general guidelines. Hardly less alarming was the president's May 30 order converting convicted antigovernment operative Lambdin Milligan's sentence from death by hanging to imprisonment at hard labor for life.[30]

Holt sharply disagreed with both the president's proclamations and his decision about Milligan. So did the delegation of Republican congressmen who made a special visit to Washington in early June to ask Johnson to call Congress into session so that the legislators could weigh in on how best to move the nation from a state of war toward a lasting peace, in which the freedpeople's rights could also be protected. Johnson refused the delegation's request, and as a result, like the Charleston "gentlemen" Tal P. Shaffner had described to Holt, many white Southerners who had watched in terror to see how the victorious federal government would treat its vanquished foe began to feel encouraged. Perhaps the potentially transformative consequences of the Federals' hard-won victory on the battlefield would be minimized after all, not least with regard to the former slaves. By early July—just three months after Lee surrendered to Grant at Appomattox—it was impossible to miss the fissure developing between the president and those who endorsed his rapidly emerging, magnanimous approach toward the former rebels, on the one hand, and Holt and others who remained determined, on the other hand, to call the Confederacy and its supporters to account for all of the war's bloody consequences. These latter also aimed to do whatever they could to ensure the rights and future welfare of those whom Holt characterized, in a May 1865 opinion in a case involving the murder of a freedman in Alabama, as "this long downtrodden, but now emancipated, race," who, thanks to black men's courageous and costly military service to the Union during the war, "have the strongest claims upon the national gratitude."[31]

In Washington, additional signs of the developing breach between Johnson and his opponents appeared almost immediately following the executions of Booth's coconspirators. As early as July 8 the *Philadelphia Inquirer* observed that although the "general sentiment" in the capital stood strongly behind the hangings, some people had begun to express consternation over what they considered the exceedingly short amount of time (two days) that had been allowed for the prisoners to prepare themselves spiritually for their deaths or to organize legal appeals. Similarly, the *New York Times* remarked that now that she was safely dead, Mary Surratt seemed to have found a number of supporters who had taken to criticizing the government openly for having hanged her on the basis of inconclusive evidence, although the *Times* itself insisted that Holt, in fact, had conducted the trial with "extraordinary patience" and had decisively demonstrated the guilt of all eight defendants. Still, the critics continued to multiply. As Louis Weichmann later recalled, Mary Surratt's lifeless body was yet warm when claims about her innocence began to circulate as they had not done when she was still living. Most upsetting to Weichmann was the fact that he, Holt, and virtually anyone else who was associated with Surratt's execution were suddenly being subjected to public attack, "denounced in the most violent language" and "characterized as perjurers, murderers, and executioners."[32]

The most vigorous attacks by Mary Surratt's newfound supporters appeared overwhelmingly in the Democratic press. In mid-July, Weichmann responded to one article that targeted him specifically for having turned against his kindly former landlady after she had treated him like a son. In an open letter to the *Philadelphia Inquirer*, Weichmann argued that both during and immediately after the trial he had in fact done all he could to generate sympathy for Surratt. "No person throughout the whole trial," insisted the wounded, hypersensitive, and, as it turns out, utterly self-centered and self-righteous young man, had done so much, and no one else had had his "good character so fully vouched . . . as regards loyalty, veracity, or morality." When he wrote this response Weichmann was surely aware that whereas just weeks earlier Holt's endorsement had counted strongly in his favor, now, among those who questioned Holt's judgment and conduct of the trial, especially in relation to Mary Surratt, Weich-mann's credibility, too, came into serious doubt.[33]

Commissioner Kautz was right when he anticipated that regardless of the degree of her guilt, the execution of Mary Surratt would elicit a torrent of recrimination against those who had approved it, although even he probably did not expect the torrent to burst forth quite so soon. But the emerging conflicts over how to reunite the country's warring sections, how much the Confederate South should be punished for its armed rebellion against the federal government, and how the nation could adapt and respond most fruitfully to the former slaves' new freedoms and expectations provided a richly fertile — or perhaps toxic — context. For all his many flaws, Weichmann was by no means entirely wrong when he attributed the backlash against Surratt's execution to angry Catholics who felt that the harshness of her sentence only further demonstrated Americans' virulent anti-Catholic tendencies. (Paradoxically, these angry Catholics often failed to acknowledge that Weichmann was Catholic, too, and that Samuel Mudd, though Catholic, had been spared the noose.) Even more persuasive still is Weichmann's observation that those who now voiced their opposition to the trial as a whole were, for the most part, diehard Confederates, along with disgruntled Northerners who had either supported the Confederacy all along or, for one reason or another, had become sympathetic toward the South now that the war was over and the rebellion had been crushed. In the weeks after the trial, among people who saw the Confederacy and the greatly romanticized "Old South" as victims of the North's cold, brute, industrial power who were now destined to face the federal government's stern and unforgiving wrath, the executed Mary Surratt came to stand in for the thwarted rebellion itself.

At the same time, to those who now endorsed Johnson's emerging vision for Reconstruction, Joseph Holt came to seem like the embodiment of Northern cruelty, vindictiveness, and willingness to subordinate white people's rights and needs to advance those of black people, although he had once been widely perceived across the North as an exemplar of Unionist courage, steadfastness, and righteousness—one of a few key men, such as Edwin Stanton, to whom the nation's welfare and security could be absolutely and unreservedly entrusted. Secessionists, of course, had adopted a strongly negative view of Holt ever since he seemed to turn his back on his Kentucky roots at the end of 1860. Copperheads had come to see him in a similar light by 1863, when he endorsed emancipation; so, too, had many Southern Unionists who resented Holt's enthusiastic support for Lincoln's shift toward hard-war tactics. Now others, too, espoused a similar perspective, in which Holt appeared no different from the "butcher" general who had won the war by exploiting the North's industrial advantages and by wantonly expending tens of thousands of young men's lives; or the general who had torn through Georgia and the Carolinas leaving only destruction and the memory of his brutality behind him; or Lincoln's callous, unfeeling secretary of war, who had implemented Lincoln's hard-war policies with delight, erasing the line between civilian and military targets and violating long-standing traditions about the sanctity of private property (human and otherwise), and enlisting black men as soldiers to do so. In this view, Holt was also indistinguishable from the ambitious and "radical" Republicans in Congress who had consistently shown that they meant to punish the former Confederacy with vigor and to lift up black Southerners to rule over whites. In sum, to those who hoped for an easy peace in which the formerly rebellious South could rejoin the United States without having to endure even a hint of the social, economic, and political transformation that emancipation and federal victory had portended, Holt—like Stanton, the Radical Republicans in Congress, and the soldiers and officers who represented the Union's victory and Reconstruction's enforcement— stood in stark contrast with the vaunted compassion of Andrew Johnson and his far more generous—and malleable—reconciliationist allies, who claimed to be Lincoln's true heirs.

Perhaps because he anticipated the bitterness of the long national struggle that lay beyond Appomattox, in the spring of 1865 Holt, now fifty-eight, had briefly considered resigning his post when the trial of the assassins was over. Learning of his weary friend's plans, T. S. Bell strove energetically to dissuade him. "No one who comprehends fully all of the past of this rebellion, & the immensity of the issues yet involved, as you do," Bell wrote, "should think of retiring and of passing the scepter of patriotism over to incompetent hands." Bell urged Holt to consider carefully the negative implications of his stepping down, and he noted that no dedicated public servant could hope to avoid all criticism. Insisting that Holt's resignation would be a victory for those who resented the Confederacy's defeat as well as those who supported the idea of a swift and undemanding reunion of the sections, Bell added reassuringly, "let your heart be comforted with the knowledge that every loyal heart in the land loves you with deep devotion."[34]

Holt chose to stay on after the trial, pursuing his goal of tracking down and bringing to justice as many of the leading rebels as he possibly could. At the same time he confronted what must have seemed like a mountain of distractions, including not just the increasingly voluble criticism of the trial in pro-South circles but also—as always—an abundance of requests for his help. Among those who were particularly eager for Holt's assistance was Samuel Mudd's wife, who wrote several times from Rock Hill, Maryland, imploring him to release her husband from prison. "I do not believe there ever has been on record," she declared, a trial in which "so much false testimony has been taken against any one man." Sarah Mudd went on to detail her intense suffering as the mother of four young children with no one to help her with her farming, and she promised that if Holt agreed to have her husband released, "I will teach my little babys to offer daily prayers for you from their innocent little hearts."[35]

Also demanding of Holt's attention were the many individuals who felt they deserved some portion of the rewards that had been offered in connection with the assassination investigation and the pursuit of John Wilkes Booth. Others who had worked with Holt during the trial sought formal recognition that they had accomplished the duties he had assigned to them. Even as Holt tended to these and other details—not to mention the ongoing regular work of the Bureau of Military Justice—a significant proportion of his attention remained focused on the question of what to do about Jefferson Davis, who, along with Clement Clay, was still in prison at Fortress Monroe. Andrew Johnson, too, was thinking about Davis, whose fate he raised for consideration at a cabinet meeting on July 18 and again on July 21. As it turns out, due at least in part to Holt's failure thus far to develop an ironclad case for Davis's complicity with Booth, most of the cabinet—including Attorney General Speed and perhaps even Stanton—had already begun to lean toward the conclusion that the former Confederate president should be tried for treason instead of for having been involved in Lincoln's murder. The issue, however, was a tricky one: if tried for treason, Davis would have to appear before a civil court in the state where he had committed his crime(s), namely, in Mississippi or, more likely, Virginia. But the civil courts were not yet operating in either place and would not be for the foreseeable future. Even more problematic, it was highly unlikely that a jury in either Mississippi or Virginia would convict Davis, given that both had been Confederate states. For these reasons, and no doubt because he still hoped to oversee Davis's trial himself, Holt continued to recommend trying the former Confederate president and his leading henchmen for a series of war crimes before a military commission. Such a tribunal, Holt explained, offered a venue "unencumbered by the technicalities and inevitable embarrassments attending the administration of justice" in a civil court. Only in a military context, he went on, could the government make effective use of its full power to see that the proper conclusion was reached and the "inner and real life, alike treacherous and barbaric" of the rebellion could be fully revealed.[36]

As the weeks passed and the fates of Davis and his top subordinates remained in limbo, Holt continued to feel certain that he could achieve a conviction against them. Unfortunately, Holt's confidence derived at least in part from his ongoing communication with the murky character who had disappointed him during the trial of the assassins, Charles Dunham, alias Sanford Conover. Following the trial, and unpunished for his earlier deceit (for which he had deployed an elaborate and confusing set of explanations), Dunham had returned to New York. Since then, and still using the "Conover" alias, he had written repeatedly to Holt promising to obtain the evidence he had failed to gather previously and bring it to Washington. Although he was fully aware of the many problems that had cropped up with Conover's testimony in May, Holt's desire to bring Jefferson Davis to justice overrode his caution, and he allowed himself to believe that the bold, colorful, and wily perjurer would eventually come through for him. And thus, in the weeks ahead, Holt let himself be hoodwinked again as he eagerly received Conover's numerous letters from Richmond, Charleston, New Orleans, and other locations, in which the con man reported that he had found one or more pieces of the puzzle or gave the names of others whom he hoped to persuade to testify, and frequently requested money to fund his complicated and difficult but, he insisted, worthwhile efforts.[37]

Meanwhile, no thanks to Conover, news of John Surratt's whereabouts reached Holt at the end of September when Vice Consul Henry Wilding wrote to Secretary of State Seward alerting him that Surratt was in Liverpool, staying in a Catholic mission run by Father Charles Jolivet. Wilding's information came from a Canadian doctor, Lewis McMillan, who had recently crossed the Atlantic on the same ship as Surratt, both of them having boarded the British *RMS Peruvian* at Quebec on September 16. As it turned out, Surratt had spent most of his time since the assassination moving from place to place in Canada under the protection of a series of Catholic priests. By early September, however, he had decided to go to Europe under the alias "John McCarty" (or "Macarthy"), probably with the goal of putting more distance between himself and his pursuers. Nevertheless, while at sea he inexplicably decided to open up to Dr. McMillan about his life and his pro-Confederate wartime activities, even going so far as to reveal his true name and to confess—apparently without a hint of remorse—that he had been one of the original planners of a scheme to kidnap Lincoln, and that he had prior knowledge of Booth's murder plans, too, though he claimed not to have been in Washington on the night of April 14. Upon reaching England, McMillan brought this information directly to Vice Consul Wilding, who notified Seward, expressing his eagerness that "such a wretch ought not to escape." Seward in turn apprised Holt and Stanton of the information he was receiving (Wilding sent additional reports as he tracked Surratt's movements). But in early October the three men concluded that Surratt should be left alone for the time being.[38]

Although their decision comes as something of a surprise—one might have expected any one of the three to jump at the opportunity to lay his hands on the last of the nine individuals associated with Booth's local "action team"—it can be explained by the fact that initially they were understandably concerned that the man who claimed to be Surratt might actually be someone else who was simply looking for trouble or adventure, or to create a distraction. McMillan, after all, had never met Surratt before, and all he knew was that the roughly five-foot-eight, twenty-five to thirty-year-old man with dyed black hair who had been his companion aboard the *Peruvian* and had *claimed* to be Surratt basically matched the young man's description on the "wanted" posters. Moreover, there was the whole problem of arranging for an extradition. Holt, Stanton, and Seward were simply not certain at first how to proceed. Late in October, however, when word arrived from the U.S. consul general in Montreal, John F. Potter, that the man known as Surratt was apparently planning to leave England for Rome once he received some money from unnamed individuals in Canada, Seward, Holt, and Stanton agreed to take action. They requested that Attorney General Speed "procure an indictment against the said John H. Surratt as soon as convenient, with the view to demanding his surrender." Unfortunately, they had waited too long: Surratt had slipped away again.[39]

Even as he pondered what to do next with regard to John Surratt, Holt was mired in the work of exposing the crimes of yet another Confederate villain who was then in custody at the Old Capitol Prison and against whom he had already assembled the necessary evidence. The accused was Henry Wirz, the former commandant of Andersonville Prison, where 13,000 Federal soldiers had died in just over a year under horrifying conditions. Like Davis, Wirz had been arrested in May. When his trial began in August, Holt and others were just digesting the news of Andrew Johnson's latest concession to the former rebels: ordering Commissioner Oliver Otis Howard of the Bureau of Refugees, Freedmen, and Abandoned Lands to restore to its original owners all of the confiscated land that the Federal army had handed over to the freedpeople earlier to smooth their path to economic self-sufficiency. Around this time Holt also heard from a Vicksburg correspondent informing him that Johnson's willingness to pardon just about everyone who had supported the rebellion was having a terrible effect on former Confederates in Mississippi, who were now engaged in a variety of efforts to undermine any and all Unionist sentiment in the state. Because Johnson's policies were already making it possible for former military leaders to assume political office, wrote A. Burwell, white Mississippians "naturally conclude that rebellion is not so bad after all, and that loyalty is not a virtue, at least not one to be rewarded." In Vicksburg, Burwell went on, "we have daily proofs that we have been in too much hurry to have restoration of what is called civil rule," and that "this people needs to be told plainly & at the point of the bayonet, that for the present Military Law & rule prevail." Like Holt, Burwell expressed particular concern about the need for the federal government to protect the freedpeople from the many injustices to which their former owners were preparing to subject them.[40]

Holt carried his own and others' growing concerns about the postwar situation, and the president's policies toward the former Confederacy, into the Wirz trial, which got underway on August 23 before an eight-man military commission presided over by General Lew Wallace, who just a few weeks earlier had been a member of the commission that tried Booth's co-conspirators. Over the course of the next two months, approximately 150 witnesses presented evidence, much of which was familiar from the trial of the assassins. In the end, and probably inevitably, Wallace and the other commissioners found the Swiss-born Wirz guilty on all counts and sentenced him to hang. "Language," declared Holt in his report on the case, "fails in an attempt to denounce even in faint terms the diabolical combination for the destruction and death, by cruel and fiendishly ingenious processes, of helpless prisoners of war who might fall into their hands, which this record shows was plotted and deliberately entered upon . . . by the rebel authorities and their brutal underlings at Andersonville Prison. Criminal history presents no parallel to this monstrous conspiracy." As commandant of Andersonville, Holt concluded, Wirz had openly "claimed to be doing the work of the rebellion," and "in all his murderous cruelty and baseness" he did most faithfully "represent its spirit."[41]

At Wirz's trial and in his report to Stanton afterward, Holt strove once more to demonstrate, as he had at the trial of the assassins, that the crimes under immediate examination must be understood as of a piece with all of the other similarly heinous misdeeds committed (or planned) by those who had led the rebellion. Wirz and Booth's coconspirators, Holt explained, were not just guilty as charged; as Jefferson Davis's "hirelings and accomplices," their ultimate goal was nothing less than the destruction of the nation for the sake of the preservation of slavery. It was simply not enough, therefore, to convict only the prisoners at the bar; Davis and his cabal must be brought to justice, too. If they were not, then the victory the U.S. Army had achieved so masterfully and at such great sacrifice on the battlefield could not possibly endure, and the war could have no lasting significance. Although President Johnson had long since begun laying the foundation for an entirely different vision of the country's transition from civil war to peace and reunion, and in early October had paroled from prison all of Davis's cabinet members as well as the former Confederate vice president, Alexander Stephens, he approved the record of Wirz's trial and the convicted man's sentence. On November 10, Wirz was hanged, and his body was buried at the Old Arsenal Penitentiary alongside those of Atzerodt, Herold, Powell, and Mary Surratt.[42]

Surely Holt was pleased with the outcome of the Wirz trial and the president's endorsement of the sentence. More generally, he was pleased with the work he and the Bureau of Military Justice had accomplished over the last several months. As he reported to Stanton on November 13, since April 1865 the bureau had seen to it that eight conspirators in the Lincoln assassination had been captured, tried, and punished, either by execution or imprisonment. It had also dispatched one of the Confederacy's most heinous criminals, Henry Wirz, and had made substantial progress toward bringing a number of other leading Confederates to justice, including the arch-traitor himself, Jefferson Davis. In addition, the bureau had "received, reviewed, and filed" over 16,000 records of general courts-martial and military commissions, and had made over 6,000 other special reports.[43]

Holt was immensely proud of the recent work of the bureau, but beyond its walls other developments in this same period troubled him deeply. On a very personal level he was stunned by the unexpected and vicious attack

Lincoln's former postmaster general, Kentucky-born Montgomery Blair, had launched on him just three days into Henry Wirz's trial. In fact, Blair's younger brother had fired the first salvo in mid-July. On that occasion, Frank Blair—who had played a key role in preserving Missouri's loyalty at the start of the war and had served as one of General Sherman's corps commanders toward the war's end, but whose sympathies were quickly tending toward a rapid reconciliation of the sections—made a speech in Lexington, Kentucky, in which he raised startling and unprecedented questions about the quality of Holt's loyalty to the Union during the final days of the Buchanan administration. After hearing the younger Blair's outlandish speech, Holt's friends had urged him to respond. "The prestige of your good name, your talents, and your position," wrote C. B. New, "all demand that you should not be pushed aside by such men as Blair but that you should lead, and give direction to public opinion." New called upon Holt to abandon his traditional reserve in order to "crush such reptiles" as Frank Blair summarily.[44]

In July, Holt had demurred. Then, on August 26, Montgomery Blair—who shared his brother's reconciliationist attitude—upped the ante. Somewhat incomprehensibly, he declared before a Clarksville, Maryland, audience that as Buchanan's last secretary of war Holt had actually done everything he could to *prevent* the reinforcement of Fort Sumter and to obstruct Southern Unionists' plans to defend themselves militarily against the rebels in their states. Upon learning of this latest bizarre attack on his loyalty, Holt confessed to a correspondent his "unqualified astonishment," especially in light of Jacob Thompson's March 1861 accusation that his loyalty and desire to protect Fort Sumter had been so fervent that he had unilaterally authorized the *Star of the West*'s mission. Holt noted, too, how odd the Blairs' criticisms seemed, considering how many secessionists had relentlessly attacked him as a traitor to the South for having endorsed (perhaps even engineered) Buchanan's turn toward coercion in his final months as president. "My recollection is distinct," Holt wrote, "that during that dark and eventful period of our history, I advocated . . . every measure calculated in any way to strengthen the hands of the government and the country against the impending rebellion." How was it possible that he was now being accused of having done too little when others previously had accused him of doing too much?[45]

For his part, Secretary of the Navy Gideon Welles considered Montgomery Blair's attack on Holt (and his simultaneous attacks on Seward and Stanton) an attempt simply to advance his own political career by denigrating the accomplishments of others and thereby pushing potential opponents—especially those whose wartime contributions to the nation's survival had been great—out of the way. The Blairs, it turns out, had been Jacksonian Democrats like Holt and Andrew Johnson but had become Republicans in the late 1850s. Now that the war was over, they hoped to rebuild their relationships with their old party while still trumpeting their own wartime contributions, a maneuver—not unlike Johnson's—that required creating distance between themselves as loyal patriots and those who had fought to save the Union and now sided with the Radical Republicans on the question of what the federal victory's long-term impact should be. "It is painful," Welles remarked in his diary, "to have a man like Holt denounced." Himself a former Democrat, Welles considered Holt "a stern, stubborn, relentless man," but one who had proven himself a faithful Unionist and a fine statesman, the most capable member of Buchanan's cabinet, and probably the one most responsible for having enabled the nation to avoid war in the early months of 1861. Welles even went so far as to recall his regret that Holt had not become secretary of war instead of Stanton, although his diary from that earlier time does not entirely substantiate this claim.[46]

In the wake of Montgomery Blair's speech, Holt's friend Frank Ballard in New York urged him to stand up to such insults. "I feel indignant," Ballard wrote, "that such men as he should be permitted to cut right and left at *our best men* without being answered and squelched." Ballard promised to see to it that any response Holt provided to the Blairs' attacks would be published and widely disseminated, and this time, despite the burdens of managing Wirz's trial, Holt decided to fight back. His statement appeared in the *Washington Chronicle* on September 13, and in other national papers after that. "I assert, most positively," Holt wrote, "that there never was a day, during the period referred to, when the President [Buchanan] was not perfectly free to perform his duty, and his whole duty, in defense of the forts and other property of the United States, and to open fire from these forts whenever, in his judgment, their safety demanded it." Never, Holt went on, had he himself expressed even "the slightest trace of sympathy with the rebellion, or its guilty authors," nor had he given any hint of a foundation for the charge that, "in the event of a conflict of arms, I would not stand by the flag everywhere and under all circumstances, and to the end." Rather, he had struggled fervently in the early months of 1861 to "strengthen the hands of the Government to meet the impending rebellion," and "to unmask and baffle the machinations of those conspirators, who, with perjury on their souls, were daily and nightly plotting the ruin of the Government and country in whose services they were." As he had done privately when he first got wind of the Blairs' claims, Holt now publicly pointed out that back in the spring of 1861 Jacob Thompson had accused him of precisely the opposite offense: trying to reinforce Fort Sumter on his own against Buchanan's will. Both accusations, Holt insisted, were absurd, and they would never stick. "The opinion is confidently entertained," Holt declared with conviction, "that I shall suffer no more damage from this last denunciation than I did from the first."[47]

In the aftermath of his public reply to the Blairs, Holt received many enthusiastic letters of support. "You have [Blair] on the hip," wrote Frank Ballard on September 15, "and I should think he would have to *limp* through the rest of his useless life." W. G. Snethen noted that many Marylanders were convinced that Blair and Andrew Johnson were of one mind about the rebellion, Reconstruction, the future prospects of the Democratic Party, and—necessarily—Holt. "I predict to you," Snethen added presciently, "that if Andy Johnson has it in his head to turn against the radical portion of the party that elected him"—Lincoln's Republicans—"we shall see a conflict in the next Congress such as we have never seen in the halls of legislation in this country."[48]

Even as Holt was managing the Wirz trial and fending off the Blairs' attacks, he continued to perform the less high-profile but nevertheless fundamental work of the judge advocate general's office, managing and reviewing cases involving offenses against military law. Among the most interesting of these was the case of Edward W. Andrews of South Carolina, convicted of murdering a black man for no apparent reason. In his review of the case Holt insisted that crimes such as Andrews's, which reflected the "brutal contempt for the lives and rights of the negro race so commonly prevailing with certain classes of the south," must be punished as harshly as possible for as long as necessary by those charged with "the protection of the negro from tyranny at the hands of his former master." Should they abdicate their responsibilities, Holt observed with vigor, "it is to be feared that the consequences of the war for freedom, so lately brought to a successful issue, will be only misery, and a servitude worse than slavery, to that oppressed and unhappy race."[49]

Meanwhile, throughout the late summer and fall of 1865 Holt remained in steady contact with Charles Dunham who, still as "Conover," continued to offer tempting tidbits regarding the evidence and the witnesses he claimed to be gathering against Davis, while also plying Holt regularly with requests for additional funds for travel and expenses and for use in persuading reluctant potential witnesses to reveal their secrets. Holt also stayed in touch with Louis Weichmann, who, since leaving Washington after the trial of the assassins, had written numerous times from his home in Philadelphia. Weichmann hoped to impress upon Holt how much he had endured as a consequence of his testimony on the government's behalf and how much he and other members of his Catholic family were feeling the sting of their local church's wrath in response. Weichmann urged Holt to compensate him by procuring him a government job, on one occasion informing the judge advocate general that he was hoping for a clerical appointment at the federal customs house in Boston. "You know best where to place me," Weichmann remarked cloyingly, however; and he promised, "I will be content in any place." Finally, by December, Holt was able to secure for his former star witness an appointment at the customs house in Philadelphia. "Permit me to return you my sincere thanks for the untiring interest that you have personally taken in me," Weichmann gushed. "My own father, had he been in your place, could not have done more."[50]

As he had done all along, Holt kept his eye on Andrew Johnson's developing relationship with the former Confederacy, which seemed to be growing fonder by the day, thanks in large part to the president's generous pardoning practices. Indeed, on September 11 white representatives from nine Southern states came to Washington to express their appreciation personally: by now Johnson was issuing as many as a hundred pardons a day. "I fear the haste of the government in bringing back the rebellious states," Holt's old friend Jesse Kincheloe cautioned from Hardinsburg, Kentucky. "It strikes me, the rebels have been simply overpowered, not subdued, and that we may look for future conflicts, upon new fields." According to Kincheloe, former rebels in Kentucky, at least, now felt free to infer from the president's actions "that the rebellion was only a mistake," that treason was not a crime, and that even former traitors were once again "worthy of trust."[51]

Similarly, T. H. Duval in Texas was concerned about rumors that Johnson was eager to see the representatives from all of the former Confederate states returned to Congress immediately. Duval indicated that he, too, welcomed national reconciliation in principle, but only if the rebel states' reentry into the Union could be effected without hazard to the nation's future safety. As far as he could tell, however, not one of the conventions organized to devise the former rebel states' new state constitutions had as yet demonstrated a willingness to adjust the states' prewar and wartime laws, particularly in relation to slavery and secession, to bring them into alignment with federal law. "They repeal the ordinances of secession," Duval wrote, "but leave the *right of secession* still an open question." Similarly, "while abolishing slavery, they *dodge* the ratification of the proposed [Thirteenth] amendment to the Constitution," and "at the same time fail to make any provision to secure the freedmen in their rights of life, liberty, & property." As Duval explained, "all these failures & evasions evince anything but a sincere and *bona fide* disposition to do what their duty requires, & what the Nation expects." News like this only enhanced Holt's resolve to see that the long, hard war had not been fought in vain.[52]

On November 30, Holt took the oath of office for the sixth time, having recently been promoted by Stanton to the rank of brevet major general in recognition of his wartime service. When he took the oath this time Holt did so with the knowledge that less than a week earlier, on the president's orders, the secretary of war had revoked the government's offers of reward money for the capture of Jacob Thompson, Beverly Tucker, George Sanders, and William Cleary, purportedly because the men were presumed to have gone abroad and beyond the reach of the government anyway. But considering Johnson's parole of Davis's cabinet members and vice president in October, the implication was clear: Holt's opportunity for bringing even Jefferson Davis to justice was rapidly slipping away. Still, he remained determined. That same month, he took lengthy and intriguing depositions from a number of individuals Charles Dunham had finally rounded up and brought to Washington as potential witnesses, including men who introduced themselves as William Campbell, Joseph Snevel, and Farnum B. Wright.[53]

Subsequently, Dunham and his witnesses dispersed pending the as-yet-unscheduled trial, where Holt expected them eventually to seal the case against the Confederacy's former president. Perhaps not surprisingly, from their various locations these individuals, too, now began trying to wring money from Holt for their efforts. Wrote Snevel on November 14, "I have been looking for more than a week for the $500 draft promised me." And he added later, "Mr. Conover told me when I engaged in this business that I would be compensated for my time and that my expenses should be fully defrayed." Similarly, William Campbell wrote from Vermont asking for $200, supposedly to cover the expenses of an information-gathering trip to Canada. With what can only be characterized as a remarkable, willful lack of caution about throwing more good money after bad, Holt honored many if not all of these requests. At the same time, he urged Conover to finish the work he had set out to perform, warning him to "do your work thoroughly, & do not lose sight of any witnesses you may deem important."[54]

On December 4 the Thirty-ninth Congress—whose members had been elected in November 1864, and whose Republican members now outnumbered Democrats by a margin of three to one—finally convened in Washington for its first session. By then, without the slightest input from Congress, Andrew Johnson had gone ahead and declared all of the states of the former Confederacy (except Texas) fully reconstructed. Holt was dismayed. Among the most disturbing features of Johnson's claim that Reconstruction was a fait accompli was the fact that three of the supposedly reconstructed states—Georgia, Florida, and Mississippi—had, like unreconstructed Texas, still not met the minimum standard for reentry into the United States of ratifying the Thirteenth Amendment. Perhaps even worse, most if not all had been active throughout the summer and fall creating postwar "black codes" to circumvent the implications of emancipation for blacks' advancement socially, politically, and economically, and organizing armed state militias, purportedly for self-defense. Clearly, although Johnson and his allies considered the work of restoring the Union virtually complete, many former Confederates actually remained utterly unrepentant and essentially unsubmissive to the federal victory. For these and other reasons, when the loyal representatives of the Thirty-ninth Congress came together on December 4, they voted resoundingly not to seat the former rebel states' recently elected representatives. They also immediately established the fifteen-member Joint Committee on Reconstruction, made up of nine representatives and six senators, including John A. Bingham and Reverdy Johnson, who had played important—if opposing—roles in the trial of the assassins. Presided over by the moderate Republican Senator William P. Fessenden of Maine, the Joint Committee's task was to investigate the progress President Johnson had made thus far on his own toward bringing the nation back together permanently and fulfilling the promises inherent in the Union's victory, not least for the freedpeople.

Relieved that Congress had reconvened and seemed determined to intercede in the Reconstruction process whether Johnson liked it or not, Holt wrote to Stanton in the days ahead to update him on the latest information he had acquired in connection with the case against Davis. Among other things, Holt now presented evidence against Burton N. Harrison, Davis's private secretary, who was currently in federal custody and who, Holt was convinced, had also been intimately involved in the plot to kill Lincoln. Among other things, Holt pointed out that none other than Frank Blair, who was still trying to gain favor with the Democrats by siding with Johnson and the former Confederates against Holt (and Stanton and the Radical Republicans), was one of Harrison's strongest supporters. According to Blair, Harrison had been "merely an amanuensis to Davis" and had never taken up arms against the government himself, and therefore he should be released. To the contrary, Holt argued, Davis's secretary offered a key link to the actions of his boss and must not be paroled under any circumstances. Holt was infuriated, too, that Blair's appeal on Harrison's behalf had a strong personal component: Harrison was engaged to one of Blair's wife's relatives who, Blair explained, was hoping that her betrothed might be released from prison in time for a Christmas wedding. Holt urged Stanton in no uncertain terms to reject Blair's appeal, and for now, Harrison remained in custody.[55]

As 1865 gave way to 1866, Holt continued to gather disturbing information from his correspondents regarding the consequences of Andrew Johnson's Reconstruction policies. In January, however, he did receive some uplifting news from his friend Jesse Kincheloe, who expressed surprise that in and of itself, emancipation had not been a catastrophe in Kentucky. "I feared mischief & suffering would follow the sudden change of the labor system of our country," Kincheloe wrote, "but have been very agreeably disappointed. The change has been generally acquiesced in, and has gone off quietly." As far as he could tell, the former slaves were not reluctant to work now that their chains had been removed. Rather, they persistently sought jobs at reasonable wages, and Kincheloe was optimistic about the future. "I believe the Negroes, generally, will comply with their contracts," he wrote hopefully, "if the whites act fairly & justly toward them." And he concluded, "I take it for granted, that a trifling vicious slave will not make a very good freeman, and that a faithful slave will make an honest and respectable freeman. In short, I am of opinion there is a good deal of *human nature* in a negro." In January 1866 Holt also received the uplifting news that yet another set of new parents—this time in Springfield, Iowa—had been so impressed by his commitment to the Union during the war and since that they had named their son after him.[56]

On January 18, in connection with the Joint Committee on Reconstruction's investigations, Holt responded to a request for an official explanation as to why Jefferson Davis and Clement Clay remained in prison despite the fact that they had not yet been formally charged with specific crimes. Davis, Holt replied, was still under investigation for his involvement in the Lincoln assassination and probably also for treason, and Clay had been one of his key associates. Moreover, he added, "my conviction is complete that the punishment of the wretched hirelings of Davis, some of whom have been sent to the gallows and others to the penitentiary, has made no sufficient atonement" either for the war or for Lincoln's murder, both of which had "covered our land with mourning." From beyond the grave, he insisted, Lincoln was still demanding a proper response to the

South's crimes: not vengeance, of which Lincoln was incapable, but justice, "that justice without which no nation can long live in honor or peace or happiness."[57]

Holt also took the opportunity to reiterate that during the trial of the assassins, and subsequently in a series of depositions, Clement Clay had undeniably been implicated in Lincoln's murder as well as numerous other "treasonable enterprises, in violation of the laws and usages of civilized war." He then moved on to the recent appeal of William Marvin, whom Andrew Johnson had appointed provisional governor of Florida back in July. Marvin requested a pardon for two of his constituents who were also still in federal custody, one of whom was Holt's former brother-in-law, David Yulee, who had spent much of the war living on his Florida sugar plantation, Homosassa, with his wife, his children, and his English sheep dog, "Secesh." Around the time Jefferson Davis was captured in Georgia, Yulee had been captured in Gainesville, and since then he had been held without charge at Fort Pulaski, near Savannah.[58]

Years earlier, when he was serving as James Buchanan's commissioner of patents, Holt had shown that he had no patience whatsoever for requests for special favors from the government or its officials, even—and perhaps especially—when the potential beneficiaries of those favors were family members. Later, when he became Buchanan's secretary of war, Holt had made it clear that he would not show mercy, or even offer the benefit of the doubt, to anyone whom he considered a traitor to the nation, no matter how close a friend or how intimate a relation. When David Yulee, as a U.S. senator, had tried to commandeer valuable information about U.S. military installations and troops in Florida, and then when he had followed the state out of the Union, Holt had displayed unswerving firmness, choosing to defend the nation at the expense of his relationship with his former brother-in-law. Now that the war was over and Yulee's friends were agitating for his release and pardon, Holt remained utterly unmoved. Indeed, he may well have been even more determined than before to resist all such special pleading in light of the many favors he had already witnessed President Johnson handing out so generously. In Yulee's case, there is no doubt that Holt felt an enhanced degree of resistance, knowing what he did about his former brother-in-law's actions in the early days and weeks of 1861 while he was still under oath to support the U.S. Constitution.[59]

It comes as no surprise, then, that Holt responded with icy disdain to Governor Marvin's request for a pardon for Yulee and for former U.S. senator Stephen Mallory, Davis's secretary of the navy, who had walked out of Congress with Yulee and Davis in January 1861. Marvin's appeal on their behalf, Holt insisted, ignored the men's crimes and spoke only of the petitioner's desire that the prisoners' "personal interests and comfort" be considered. But both Yulee and Mallory had betrayed their positions of trust and their sworn oaths when they endorsed secession. They were traitors then, and they were traitors now. Mallory, moreover, had amplified his original guilt by accepting the appointment as Davis's secretary of the navy. And although Yulee's wartime activities were less well known, his application for a pardon was no less absurd, claiming as it did that he had not withdrawn from Congress for the purpose of aiding the rebellion and that he had done nothing to help create the Confederacy or to shape its conduct. In addition, Yulee's claims that he essentially had no choice but to follow Florida into the Confederacy and that he had consistently supported a solution to the nation's rupture were outright lies. Neither Yulee nor Mallory was to be trusted, and both should be tried for treason. Thanks to Holt's stern letter to Congress, Yulee's and Mallory's status remained, for the time being, unchanged.[60]

So did that of Jefferson Davis and Clement Clay, although the likelihood of being able to bring either of them before a military commission *or* a civil court grew increasingly remote as the months since Lee's surrender ticked by. Moreover, the longer Davis, Clay, and other leading Confederate political figures remained in prison without being either charged or brought to trial somewhere, the more they came, like Mary Surratt, to represent—to the advocates of a rapid, relatively painless peace—symbols of Northern justice gone awry and Northern malice in a situation where forgiveness was in order. This became even truer as the rift widened in the new year between Johnson and those in Congress and outside of it who opposed his Reconstruction policies. For his part, Johnson had become convinced that in order to pursue his Reconstruction agenda successfully he would need to stand firm against Congress *and* against Holt. Although years earlier Johnson had saluted Holt as "a noble son of Kentucky," now he was determined to limit the judge advocate general's power vis-à-vis the former Confederates as much as possible. As Secretary of the Navy Welles noted in his diary in early February, the president had recently informed his cabinet members (with the possible exception of Holt's close ally, Stanton) that he "wished to put no more in Holt's control than was absolutely necessary." In Johnson's view, Holt had proved himself to be "cruel and remorseless," a man whose inclinations with regard to the defeated South "were very bloody." And as it turns out, Welles himself was beginning to agree with Johnson that Holt was "severe and unrelenting," and that, although he undoubtedly possessed "a good deal of mental vigor and strength," he was nevertheless guilty of becoming "the dupe of his own imaginings." Holt, Welles now felt, had become much too inclined to condemn those he disagreed with "on shadowy suspicions," without giving them the benefit of a fair and unbiased trial.[61]

In the early months of 1866, the tension between Johnson and Congress, like the tension between Johnson and Holt, continued to build. When Congress attempted to extend the life and authority of the all-important Freedmen's Bureau, established in March 1865 to ease the former slaves' transition to freedom, Johnson vetoed the bill. Less than a month later, on March 13, Congress also passed a Civil Rights Bill, which for the first time defined the rights of the freedpeople and gave federal courts the power to enforce those rights. Johnson vetoed this bill, too. Keenly conscious of the implications of such actions for any future attempt to call the Confederacy to account, Holt pressed on in his attempt to get Conover to deliver the goods on Davis and Clay. In addition, on March 20 he sent Stanton another update, alerting the secretary of war that he had deposed a number of new witnesses, whose statements he enclosed and whose testimony in a courtroom, he was certain, would demonstrate beyond a reasonable doubt Davis's (and Clay's) connection to the assassination. "With these depositions," Holt declared, "the preparation of the cases by this Bureau is properly terminated." All that remained was to arrange for the military tribunal he had been urging all along, so that Davis and Clay could be arraigned, tried, convicted, and punished. Holt emphasized to Stanton (probably unnecessarily) that the window of opportunity for convening military commissions generally was closing. Indeed, rumor had it that the president was preparing to issue a proclamation officially declaring the nation at peace. Should this come to pass, military tribunals would cease to have any jurisdiction whatsoever, and in that case—given the difficulties still associated with trying Davis and Clay in civil court—it seemed likely that "their crime, certainly one of the most atrocious and appalling of the nineteenth century," would go unpunished.[62]

On balance, in the spring of 1866, given time to ponder the events of the past year, Holt must have experienced only limited satisfaction. True, the Federal army had won the war, but it had done so at an unthinkably, unbearably high cost in every way that cost might be tallied. Moreover, although the shooting war had been over for months, the ultimate implications of the federal victory remained obscure, not just for the reunion of the sections but also for the nation's enduring stability. Also painfully uncertain was the future of the 4 million former slaves who, with the help of their allies and against enormous resistance, now struggled to make good on the promises of emancipation. The war, the federal victory, and Johnson's quest for a rapid reconciliation of the sections had been immensely costly for Holt personally, too. Though there were many who still venerated him as an exemplar of courageous, dedicated, unwavering, and untiring Unionism, there were growing numbers who attacked him as a symbol (and tool) of Northern vengeance against white Southerners who had fought so valiantly for their region's independence from federal domination and for the right to protect their time-honored "domestic institutions," especially slavery.

Almost a year after Appomattox, Holt's reputation in the public eye was badly battered. So, too, were many of his most important personal relationships. Sadly, the one family connection that had remained sturdy and dependable throughout the war gave way within months of its end: following the trial of the assassins, Holt's Aunt Mary Ann, who had recently moved to Indiana, had congratulated him on its outcome and complained that the former rebels who were returning to Kentucky showed not the least bit of remorse for their attempt to destroy the nation. "Josey," she begged, "tell the President not to be too lentient on the rebels," but rather to confiscate their land and deprive them of the vote for a decade or two, "for as certain as he lets them vote they will destroy the goverment at the ballot box." As she had done all along, Mary Ann shared Holt's views on how the federal government should manage the postwar peace, and she encouraged him enthusiastically to stay the course against every obstacle that Lincoln's successor and others threw in his path. At the same time, Mary Ann continued to express her concerns about her nephew's safety, advising him regularly and affectionately to be on his guard against those who were determined to harm him, particularly individuals associated with the Knights of the Golden Circle.[63]

Meanwhile, however, sixty-eight-year-old Mary Ann was ill, and in early August 1865 she begged Holt to "take all my things & do not let any of my relations have one cent," as she was convinced that others in the family would only use what remained of her limited resources to foment a new rebellion against the government, having failed during the war to destroy it. Just over a month later, her sister Eleanor—Holt's mother—informed him of Mary Ann's death on September 12. "I feel her loss very much," Eleanor wrote. The following day, W. S. Lamb acknowledged the very special bond that Holt and Mary Ann had enjoyed: "No doubt you have many warm friends," wrote Lamb, "but you can't have any in this world" who were "more devoted to you than your departed aunt." In her will, written in 1857, Mary Ann left Holt her land, $5,500, and her slave Wesley, with the request that Holt "treat him kindly in the way I have always treated said servant." Of course, thanks to the Federals' victory and the Thirteenth Amendment—not to mention Holt's own repudiation of slavery—Wesley was now free.[64]

Despite her sense that Holt had picked the wrong side in the nation's great war, his mother did not wait until Mary Ann died before trying to mend fences with him herself. Although she does not seem to have written to him at all during the war, Eleanor picked up her pen as soon as the fighting was over, in part because she genuinely hoped to rebuild their relationship and in part because she hoped that he would use his power and influence to shield other family members—especially his brother Robert in Mississippi—from whatever retribution the federal government was planning to inflict. In late April 1865 Eleanor thanked Holt for his recent letter, which she claimed had "cheered me greatly in my troubles." She thanked him, too, for the money he had sent, some of which she had given, as directed, to the family's former slaves. Eleanor admitted that she was glad the war was over. "It has been a savage, barbarous war," she wrote, and she was weary of all the bloodshed. Eleanor further noted that the family was sorry to learn of Lincoln's death. Although she felt that he had allowed himself to be controlled "by bad ambitious men" (her own son, no doubt, excepted), Eleanor admitted that Lincoln had always given the impression of being kindhearted. Of Johnson she was not so sure: she worried what he might do to those who had actively supported the Confederacy. Eleanor urged Holt to intervene if necessary on Robert's behalf. Robert, she explained, was "entirely broken down in spirits" since the rebellion had been crushed, his slaves had been freed, and his future seemed hopeless. "It is only the thoughts of his wife and nine children being left almost in the depths of bitter poverty," she went on, "that prevents him from wishing it would be God's will to remove him to a peaceful rest." Eleanor begged her oldest son to see to it, if possible, that Robert's remaining property was not confiscated.[65]

Over the next many months Holt held up his end of their renewed correspondence, often sending money, of which he always earmarked some for the family's former slaves. Eleanor had feared that all of the family's newly freed black laborers would take off as soon as they could. Instead, however, Holt's brother Thomas, who had been running the family farm since their father's death in 1838, had decided to hire them. As a result, Eleanor noted with relief, "things go on much in their usual way"; and, indeed, she found coming to terms with the whole concept of emancipation easier than she had expected. "Since the freedom of the negro has been forced upon us," she wrote, "I accept it as one of the results of the re-bellion, and have ceased to trouble myself about public matters." Eleanor was much more concerned, she confessed, about Robert and about Holt's brother James, in Lavaca, Texas, who by early 1866 had fallen into a "very desponding" mood as a consequence of the presence in his area of black Federal soldiers—occupation forces from the U.S. Colored Troops—who, James claimed, seemed to be "arresting everybody in that section."[66]

As for Robert, he continued to write over the months following the end of the war, typically mixing claims about the urgency of his own family's situation with expressions of deep distress about the Confederacy's de-feat. Holt responded neither as quickly nor as often as Robert wished to his brother's pleading and only semi-conciliatory letters. "I am only de-sirous, in peace and kindness," Robert reminded Holt rather plaintively after not hearing back, "to live out the [balance] of my days in the labori-ous discharge of those duties which I owe to my family." In the aftermath of Johnson's May 1865 proclamations, Holt did request some information from his brother to assist him in evaluating the merits of Robert's applica-tion for amnesty. By the end of the summer, however, Robert's application had still not been approved, and he wrote again with some frustration ask-ing Holt to check on its progress. "I do not ask you to assist me in the mat-ter," he snapped, "otherwise than by giving me the information for which I ask." It is unlikely that Robert improved his chances for Holt's assistance when he noted that all his efforts to make a living were currently being obstructed by the federal government's oppressive military domination of Mississippi.[67]

Holt's correspondence after the war with his late sister Elizabeth's daughter, Margaret "Maggie" Sterett Bowmer, was considerably warmer and less burdened with the weight of the war than his correspondence with Robert. "Why do you not come to see us?" wrote Maggie encouragingly in December 1865, noting that the entire family had hoped he would come during the previous summer, and that "Grandma" (Eleanor) had instructed her to "tell you how anxious she is for you to come to see her once more." Like Holt, Maggie sorely missed Aunt Mary Ann, whose watch—which may have originally belonged to his grandfather, Richard Stephens—she even-tually sent to him. On a happier note, Maggie reported that her father, Holt's old friend Will Sterett, was getting married again. In addition, Maggie happily informed her uncle that she had recently given birth to a daughter, whom she named after her mother. "She is so pretty and smart," Maggie wrote, "that I think if you were to make a special visit to Ky to see her, you would feel yourself well paid." More somberly, Maggie pleaded with Holt not to think that his stance on behalf of the Union had diminished her own or her brother Billy's affection for him. Her mother, she explained, "taught us to reverence and love you always as her dear brother and to know you were so much entitled to your opinions as we were."[68]

As Holt—like millions of other Americans—began the slow and difficult emotional work of trying to restore relationships with his family that the war had derailed, he did so in the midst of the ongoing and potentially explosive national dispute over what shape the postwar "peace" should assume. Surely he was greatly, if only fleetingly, buoyed by such letters as the one he received in early February 1866, signed by the three young children of his erstwhile protégé and good friend General Albin Schoepf and his wife, Julia. "You made us little ones very happy yesterday," Julia wrote kindly, as if she were taking dictation from the boys. "It made us wonder if the Judge was not a little fellow once just like us and like us capered and jumped at the arrival of cakes and candies." Having declared through their maternal amanuensis that "we all mean when we grow up to be men to do like you, make the little ones happy and jump for joy," the Schoepf boys signed their own names: Frank, Will, and—notably—Holt. Unfortunately, only a tiny portion of Holt's correspondence with his friends in this period offered this sort of lighthearted distraction from the burdens at hand. In contrast, from his old law colleague, James O. Harrison, in New Orleans, Holt learned of Harrison's continuing struggle to regain control of his property, despite the fact that he had taken the required oath of allegiance to the United States. Harrison wrote gloomily, too, of his confusion about whether he should apply for a presidential pardon or not. "For the life of me," he groaned, "I can not see that I have violated the law & therefore can not feel a consciousness of guilt & of course do not see the necessity for a pardon."[69]

During this period Holt also continued to receive letters from a number of different women with whom he had developed powerful connections in recent years, including his former lover, Mary Cash. Over time, Mary and Holt seem to have reached a degree of equilibrium, or at least she thought so. "My sister Beckie has urged me to write," she explained in a spring 1865 letter, "and ask you if it would be possible for her to see the President or General Grant should she come to Washington for the purpose." But if Holt and Mary Cash had come to a reasonably peaceful understanding, the same was not true of his relationship with Mary Bowman of Kentucky, whom he had first met in the fall of 1864 when he was investigating secret antigovernment societies in the West. In January 1866 Bowman wrote to complain about Holt's "long silence & indifference," and to accuse him of having captured and then broken her heart. "I had thought when I saw & knew you at the 'Louisville Hotel,'" Bowman wrote, in terms that suggested they had become physically intimate (at least to some degree), "that I had found one that could be relied on . . . whose sentiments echoed my own, whose softness & gentleness of manner wooed & won the heart, whilst his talents & acquirements surprised & controlled the *mind*." At some point since their Louisville meeting, however, Bowman's frustration over Holt's reserve and distance had led her to try and provoke a jealous response from him by claiming that she had accepted another man's marriage proposal. Her ruse was as unsuccessful and infuriating to him as Mary Cash's "joke" about being pregnant had been. Like Cash, Bowman subsequently expressed her desire to make amends and her hope that he might someday feel for her as he once had, and "*pet* me as you did" on that earlier occasion in Louisville. Holt, however, remained silent. Bowman tried well into 1866 to persuade him to change his mind, but, as in previous cases, Holt had closed the door on their relationship for good.[70]

How much the weight of his professional responsibilities factored into his decision to break off his relationship with Mary Bowman, and how much his retreat reflected his familiar struggle to find a tolerable balance in his intimate relations with women, is not clear. What is clear is that during this same time period, Holt had begun to develop a growing attachment to yet another woman, this time the wife of his old friend Howard Crosby. Sometime in the spring of 1865, Holt had enjoyed a visit from the Crosbys, who had traveled to the capital from New York. After their visit Holt began to receive regular letters from Margaret. "Your visit did me so much good," Margaret wrote in June 1865, even as the trial of the assassins was winding down, "that I *must* write to tell you so, although I have nothing else to say." On this occasion, Margaret fondly recalled Holt's graciousness as well as his "mingling of sadness and drollery" and his "expressions of true patriotic feeling," all of which had suddenly deepened her appreciation for him after so many years of friendship. A couple of weeks later she wrote again, recalling his solo trip to Europe and the Middle East in 1848–49, when they had all first met. "I have always had pleasant remembrances of our foreign trip," Margaret wrote, and "a vivid consciousness of the kind toleration you showed for my childish foibles" (Margaret was about twenty years Holt's junior). Later, when the war began, she noted, she had followed the news about Holt "with peculiar interest," and was pleased to discover that he "did in *everything* . . . *just* what I thought right," and "without flinching." What impressed her most, Margaret explained, was that Holt had acted courageously on the nation's behalf no matter how hard the task and despite "every natural tie binding you to the other side." Now, she rightly anticipated that as a Southerner by birth Holt was destined to face tremendous criticism for his unyielding defense of the Union. Still, she insisted encouragingly, "I believe the Southerners, even, in after times, will be proud of you."[71]

In the months ahead, Margaret Crosby continued to write Holt regularly, congratulating him on the outcome of the trial of the assassins, sending him handmade gifts, and conveying her affection time and again. In addition to her warmth and attention, surely one of the things that Holt found attractive about Margaret was her political perspective, which seems to have mirrored his own. In the early spring of 1866, in fact, Margaret grumbled that she and her husband Howard simply did not see eye to eye on the country's ongoing political crisis. For whereas "Mr C" was "conservative," she, "so far as a woman can understand matters," considered herself "very radical." Like Holt, Margaret worried that President Johnson had already extended far too much forgiveness to the former Confederates, producing a resurgence of just the sort of behavior that had led to the war in the first place. Like Holt, she was convinced that the strong Southern impulses that provoked secession and civil war needed to be rooted out once and for all, and that if they were not, the nation's "troubles" would only increase and multiply.[72]

In the spring of 1866, however, when Margaret sent this particular letter, it was unmistakably clear that Johnson had no intention of voluntarily altering the model for Reconstruction that he had pursued for the last eleven months. Indeed, he was more determined than ever to resist any effort by Congress to force him to revise his policies, despite all the accumulating evidence that those policies had managed to reinvigorate precisely the sort of rebellious attitude toward the government that the Federals' victory on the battlefield had meant to subdue. "If the President intends to make treason infamous," Holt's friend Jesse Kincheloe wrote in March, "he has no time to lose." Treason, Kincheloe declared, was already "rampant and triumphant in Kentucky," where "men who have opposed the war for the preservation of the Union, and whose sympathies have been with the rebellion, are now holding conventions through the country to nominate candidates for county office &c." Even more disturbing was the fact that men who had returned after leaving loyal Kentucky in order to fight for the Confederacy now seemed more likely to win their electoral races than candidates who had pledged themselves to saving the Union. Soon, Kincheloe unhappily predicted, "loyal men will have to ask an amnesty from the rebels." He added that he was "exceedingly sorry to see a split between the President & Congress," particularly on the Freedmen's Bureau and Civil Rights bills, as all hands were needed to put the pieces of the country back together and protect the former slaves' freedom and future welfare.[73]

Like his friends Jesse Kincheloe and Margaret Crosby, Holt was certain that Johnson's policies toward the former Confederacy were on a trajectory to undermine completely every important potential consequence of the victory that more than 2 million U.S. soldiers—almost 200,000 of them black—had won against the white South's bloody, destructive armed rebellion. He was deeply disappointed, too, when Johnson decided, in late March, to free former senator David Yulee after having released Stephen Mallory a couple of weeks earlier. Then, as many had anticipated that he would do, on April 2 Johnson officially proclaimed the rebellion and the war at an end in every state except Texas, which had yet to form a new state government. The following day the U.S. Supreme Court handed down its five-to-four ruling in the case known as *Ex parte Milligan*. Now an associate justice, David Davis—whom Lincoln had appointed to the court in late 1862 after Davis served with Holt on the War Department's commission to investigate claims against the Military Department in the West— wrote the opinion. In it, Lincoln's old friend denied the jurisdiction of the military commission that Holt and Burnett had used to convict Milligan and the others in fall 1864, on the principle that the civil courts in Indiana had been fully operational and the state itself had not been under martial law. Although not explicitly, by implication the court's opinion also revived questions about the jurisdiction of other military commissions that had been conducted between the start of the war in April 1861 and Johnson's declaration of peace on April 2, 1866, notably, some would go on to argue, the trial of the assassins. Nine days after the court issued its ruling, Lambdin Milligan walked out of prison, taking with him any hope Holt had sustained of eventually being able to convene a military tribunal for the purpose of bringing to justice the last two Confederate leaders still being held in federal custody, Jefferson Davis and Clement Clay.[74]

FIGHTING THE TIDE,
APRIL 1866–DECEMBER 1868

*It is a political mystery if not iniquity, that a triumphant
government should exalt its enemies . . . above its friends. . . .
This is a strange conclusion to a triumphant war!*
—*Jesse Kincheloe to Joseph Holt, September 1866*

On April 9, 1866, the first anniversary of Robert E. Lee's
surrender of the Army of Northern Virginia at Appomattox and just days
after the Supreme Court's ruling in *Ex parte Milligan*, the heavily Republican Thirty-ninth Congress voted to override Andrew Johnson's veto of the
Civil Rights Bill. In doing so, the legislators signaled their growing determination to resist Johnson's efforts to forge a rapid reunion with the
former Confederacy in which the rights of the freedpeople would remain
unprotected. Joseph Holt was pleased.

Also on April 9, in light of Johnson's April 2 declaration that the war was
over, the Judiciary Committee of the House of Representatives took up the
question of whether any of the individuals named in the president's May 2,
1865, proclamation linking Jefferson Davis and various members of his
Canadian Cabinet to the Lincoln assassination conspiracy should, or even
could, still be brought to trial. In conjunction with its examination of this
question, the committee, chaired by Republican James F. Wilson of Iowa,
requested that Holt appear before them, bringing with him copies of all
the relevant papers and documents held by the Bureau of Military Justice.
When Holt met with the committee on April 13 and 14—now a full year
since Lincoln's murder and the attack on Secretary Seward—he discussed
the evidence he had collected so far, including depositions from several
of the potential witnesses Charles Dunham, as "Conover," had identified.
As before, Holt displayed his firm confidence in the strength of the case
against Davis and his subordinates. In addition, he expressed his faith in
the Conover witnesses' veracity, boldly offering to arrange for the most

important of them, including Conover himself, to meet with the committee directly. Clearly, any doubts Holt may have experienced about Charles Dunham's behavior at the trial of the assassins had given way before his determination to prosecute Davis.[1]

Meanwhile, however, Andrew Johnson was continuing to move in a very different direction indeed with regard to those he had implicated in the May 2 proclamation. In keeping with the logical progression of his Reconstruction policies, Johnson's interest in prosecuting Davis or any other leading Confederates was waning: just days after the Judiciary Committee interviewed Holt, Johnson ordered Clement Clay's release from Fortress Monroe, where Clay had been in prison for almost a year. As he later did for David Yulee, back in November General Grant had written to the president on Clay's behalf, in this case noting that the accused man's willingness to turn himself in constituted an implied guarantee that he would not flee should Johnson parole him. Johnson considered Grant's recommendation for four solid months. Clay, after all, was second only to Davis among the federal government's remaining high-profile captives, and paroling him could have serious political implications. Once he declared the nation at peace on April 2, however, Johnson felt emboldened to lay down yet another important marker of his vision for Reconstruction. Two weeks later, he ordered Clay released, giving him permission to return to Alabama and to move freely about the country "as his personal business may render absolutely necessary," on the sole condition that he take the oath of allegiance to the United States and swear to "conduct himself as a loyal citizen of the same." Holt's reaction to the news of Clay's discharge from prison must have been grim indeed.[2]

For the time being, however, Holt's attention was largely absorbed by the investigation still underway in the House Judiciary Committee, which he hoped would yield congressional support for pursuing the case against Davis and his leading associates, including the newly freed Clay. As it turns out, committee members had decided to take Holt up on his offer to summon Conover and a number of his witnesses to Washington to meet with them in person. To this end, on April 26 Holt dispatched one of his trusted judge advocates, Colonel Levi C. Turner, to New York. Turner's charge was to meet with Conover and the others and arrange the logistics for bringing them back to Washington. Holt also wrote to Conover expressing his enduring confidence in the latter's willingness and ability to do what was best "in the interests of truth & public justice," and to expedite matters, he indicated that Turner was on his way. It was probably for this very reason that upon arriving in New York, Colonel Turner found the job of locating

Conover and his associates considerably more difficult than he or Holt had expected. Far worse, when Turner finally met with the witness known as William Campbell, Campbell confessed that he and several others had, in fact, been engaged all along in an elaborate deception of which Charles Dunham was the ringleader.[3]

Over the next few weeks, the intricate web of lies Dunham had woven and used so successfully to recapture Holt's trust steadily but irrevocably began to unravel. On May 8, Campbell—whose real name turned out to be Joseph Hoare—came before Holt and the Judiciary Committee to detail Dunham's scheme. Among other things, Hoare explained how Dunham had persuaded him and the others to participate in the deception by promising them large sums of money, only a small portion of which had ever actually materialized. Not surprisingly, when the committee subsequently interviewed Dunham, he immediately began to concoct yet another grand deceit, to the effect that Hoare and some of the others whom Holt had previously deposed were no longer to be trusted, for they had decided that they were more likely to profit from an alliance with Jefferson Davis's friends than from one with his enemies. According to Dunham, Hoare, Joseph Snevel, and a number of others had switched sides and were now perpetrating a new scheme designed to utterly discredit him as well as Holt and the Bureau of Military Justice. Dunham insisted that in contrast with his own entirely pure motives, the turncoats' ultimate goal was to engineer Davis's release from prison on the premise that there was no longer a shred of credible evidence against him.[4]

In the wake of Hoare's and Dunham's stunning—and thoroughly contradictory—testimony before the committee, Holt was understandably confused and at a loss for how to proceed. For lack of a better plan, he and the committee decided to dispatch Dunham back to New York—now in the company of a security officer—under orders to track down the remaining witnesses whose testimony against Davis he (Dunham) still considered trustworthy. Upon reaching New York, the con man promptly (and predictably) evaded the security officer's grasp and disappeared, leaving one to wonder, a century and a half later, how the otherwise brilliant Holt could have been duped again so easily. It would be months before Dunham resurfaced. In the meantime, as Holt struggled to locate his troublesome collaborator, the now even more confused and frustrated members of the Judiciary Committee pressed on with their investigation, at one point interviewing "Joseph Snevel," whose real name turned out to be William Roberts and who confirmed and then elaborated on what Hoare had confessed about Dunham's subterfuge. The committee also continued to review the documentary materials Holt had been presenting to them: the record of the testimony from the original trial of the assassins, the various depositions Holt had taken at the Bureau of Military Justice over the past many months, and a mountain of other items Holt and the bureau had collected both before the trial and since. Notably, these now included an abundance of materials taken from the Confederate archives in Richmond after Davis and his government had escaped, which Holt's old friend from Columbia University, Francis Lieber, was in the process of organizing and examining.[5]

As the spring progressed, Holt's distress over what soon came to be known as the "Conover scandal" was surely mitigated, at least in part, by some good news out of Norfolk, Virginia. There on May 11 a grand jury had finally indicted Jefferson Davis for treason. Prior to their deliberations, jury members had listened to an emotional charge from Judge John C. Underwood in which he urged them, in the sort of tone that Holt himself might have employed, to consider broadly the issues that were at stake in bringing Davis to trial. Underwood observed that many Northerners had complained about the delay in prosecuting Davis and other leading former Confederates who were likely to be charged with treason. But, he explained, "this great question of the punishment of the authors of the terrible and unprovoked rebellion" deserved the sort of slow and careful consideration that Lincoln would have given it, if only "so that no unnecessary blood shall be added to the torrents that have already soaked the soil of our devoted State." Underwood went on to explain that the process of restoring the machinery of civil justice in Virginia had been slow, largely because when the state's secessionist leadership had been toppled from power, the dependent and education-deprived masses—white and black—had been in no condition to take the reins of power immediately or to restore order on their own. Underwood strove to impress upon the jury the opportunity they now had before them, to transform Virginia (and, presumably, the South as a whole) by calling to account those who had mired the state in ignorance and slavery. Only after justice was properly meted out could the current chaos—including growing violence against the freedpeople and their white allies—be relieved; only then would Virginia become something other than an object of scorn. "Yours," Judge Underwood emphasized, "is the rough pioneer work of removing the great obstruction of crime and violence from our midst, so that education . . . different in kind and degree from the past, may come to cure the evils under which we suffer."[6]

On May 11, the grand jury to which Underwood had addressed these strong words indicted Davis for treason. Once they had done so, most observers expected that the trial would take place sometime in June at the U.S. District Court in Richmond (where martial law would be terminated), with Chief Justice Salmon P. Chase presiding. On June 3, however, the *New York Times* reported that Davis's case seemed likely to be postponed until fall, and that his lawyers—James T. Brady, Charles O'Connor, William B. Reed, and ex-governor of Maryland Thomas Pratt—were expected in the interim to make a motion for their client's release on bail. How exactly such a release could be effected remained unclear. For one thing, Davis was still in military custody and would have to be transferred to civil custody before bail could be considered. For another, treason itself was technically "not a bailable offence." In any case, as predicted, on June 4, the judge in Richmond postponed the case and denied Davis's release on bail, consigning him to his second long, hot summer at Fortress Monroe.[7]

Eager as he was that Davis should be brought to trial one way or another, Holt was pleased with the indictment and the news that the nation's arch traitor had been compelled to remain in a military prison. At the same time, however, he remained deeply troubled and embarrassed by the Conover scandal, which had further blistered his professional reputation. The scandal also added new fuel to questions Holt's detractors had begun to raise shortly after the trial of the assassins regarding his judgment, his motivations, and what they considered his outright malice toward the former Confederates, whose blunders, they felt, deserved to be forgiven. On June 13, Congress passed the Fourteenth Amendment, drafted principally by one of Holt's assistants at the trial of the assassins, John A. Bingham, and designed to guarantee the rights of the freedpeople permanently. Five days later, Holt met with the Judiciary Committee again, this time to discuss his complicated, year-long relationship with the now utterly discredited (and fugitive) Charles Dunham. In response to the committee's questions, Holt did not attempt to deny that Dunham's credibility had been challenged as far back as the summer of 1865. But he reiterated with sincere (if mystifying) conviction that until Joseph Hoare had exposed the con man's latest scam, he (Holt) had felt that Conover's experience and intelligence, along with his history of interactions with various Confederate sympathizers in Canada, had offered exceptional possibilities for gathering information about Davis's designs, and these considerations had trumped any other concerns. Holt also pointed out that the claims Conover and his witnesses had made in their depositions were not only convincing but also completely in line with other evidence the Bureau of Military Justice had gathered from more reliable sources. Holt realized and freely admitted that he had been tricked and that Conover was a fraud and a criminal. But he reminded the committee that it was he who had suggested originally that they should interview Charles Dunham and his associates in person, which he certainly would not have done if he had been in on the scheme.[8]

In the weeks ahead as he waited for the Judiciary Committee to conclude its investigation, Holt submitted a lengthy report to Secretary of War Stanton essentially restating the testimony he had given before the committee. Then, to his horror, reports began appearing toward the end of July in the traditionally staunchly Democratic *New York Herald*—even as Johnson was striving to minimize the Radical Republicans' influence over his cabinet by replacing Attorney General James Speed and Postmaster General William Dennison—indicating that wherever he was hiding, Dunham had decided to extend his latest set of lies. Now he was claiming that Holt had hired him, not to gather *genuine* evidence linking Davis to the assassination conspiracy but rather explicitly to destroy Davis by carefully and purposefully manufacturing a credible evidentiary trail leading from the Confederate president's office to John Wilkes Booth's smoking gun.[9]

In support of Dunham's claim the *Herald* published a series of new "depositions" as well as letters purportedly written by Dunham's associates corroborating his latest assertions. One letter was dated April 27, 1866 (when Colonel Turner was in New York looking for Dunham), and was addressed to Conover from "William Carter," whose real name was John Martin. In the letter, Carter warned Conover that Campbell (Hoare) had decided to expose Dunham's plot to the Judiciary Committee (which was true), for which he had received a substantial payment from a group of Jefferson Davis's supporters (which was probably a lie). Carter, moreover, claimed that Holt was already aware of Campbell's decision to switch sides and that he had sent Turner to New York specifically to press Conover to "get the scamp in the traces again or keep him away & let only such come before the committee as can be relied on" (this was certainly a lie). Carter's letter, along with other items that appeared in the *Herald* over the next few weeks, presented Holt as anything but a victim of Dunham's elaborate shell game. Rather, they depicted him as the scheme's cruel, single-minded instigator and sponsor. In addition, the *Herald* articles curiously and provocatively portrayed Andrew Johnson as the wise individual whose "penetrating eye" had exposed Holt's plot, complete with all of its faked evidence and false witnesses.[10]

The *Herald*'s purported "revelations" significantly complicated Holt's attempt to defuse the Conover scandal, which he and others quite logically attributed to the pro-Johnson forces' efforts to push back against the Radical Republicans and their allies, including Holt. On July 28, however, he enjoyed a moment of relief when the Judiciary Committee finally issued its report. Written by George S. Boutwell of Massachusetts, a founder of the Republican Party who had previously served as Lincoln's commissioner of internal revenue, the report affirmed that even excluding the useless material Dunham and his accomplices had produced (and that the committee members had now discarded), the evidence from other sources still offered "probable cause" to believe that Jefferson Davis was implicated in Lincoln's assassination, and perhaps others named in Johnson's May 2 proclamation were, too. The committee's report also sustained Holt's claim that he had acted in good faith when he accepted the depositions of Dunham and the others. Holt had admitted to being duped, and the committee believed him. The report further agreed with Holt that the discredited "evidence" Dunham and his associates had provided in fact "harmonized in every important particular with facts derived from documents and other trustworthy sources," including the material gleaned from the Richmond archives. The committee therefore recommended that the investigation of Davis's link to the assassination go forward. Should the former Confederate president and his leading subordinates prove innocent, the report pointed out, "it is due to them that a thorough investigation should be made, that they may be relieved from the suspicion that now rests upon them." Should they prove guilty, "it is due to justice, to the country and to the memory of him who was the victim of a foul conspiracy, that the originators should suffer the just penalties of the law."[11]

The Judiciary Committee's report lifted Holt's flagging spirits, as did Congress's passage, on the same day the report was published, of the Army Reorganization Act, which restructured and streamlined the regular army for its postwar responsibilities on occupation duty in the South and against the Native Americans in the West. Among the questions Congress had considered in connection with the bill was the future of the Bureau of Military Justice. Probably the most vehement opponent of extending the bureau's life—and, by default, Holt's position—was Democratic senator Willard Saulsbury Sr. of Delaware who argued, among other things, that Holt's practice of convening military commissions to try civilians in wartime was an intolerable violation of Americans' civil liberties. In contrast, Senator James H. Lane of Indiana, a Republican and former general in the Federal army during the war, ardently defended both the bureau and its chief officer, not least because he considered it improper to shut down the bureau when it still had so much war-related business to complete.

More broadly, Lane insisted that the bureau's record was not one of denying innocent individual Americans their rights. To the contrary, only "the rebel traitor and the rebel sympathizer, the assassins of the President of the United States, and their co-conspirators North and South" had reason to fear the bureau's procedures and judgments. Lane went on to describe Holt as one of the rare "faithful among the faithless in the Cabinet of that weak and wicked old man Mr. Buchanan," and a man who had bravely set his Democratic Party loyalties aside when others in his party had risen up to destroy the Union. In Lane's mind, no words could accurately describe all that Holt had done for the nation. In the end, in this initial effort to reorganize the army for postwar duty, the voices of Lane and other Holt supporters prevailed: the Army Reorganization Act of 1866 preserved the bureau, along with positions for ten judge advocates and, of course, the judge advocate general himself.[12]

Unfortunately, reassuring developments such as these competed for Holt's attention with the *New York Herald*'s ongoing "revelations" in connection with the Conover scandal. Also distressing was the sharply worded, ferociously oppositional "minority report" submitted by the Judiciary Committee's sole Democratic member, Representative Andrew J. Rogers of New Jersey. In his lengthy addendum to the official report of July 28, Rogers charged that Boutwell and the other Republican committee members had made it virtually impossible for him to examine the relevant documents pertaining to the Davis case, presumably because they knew of his support for Johnson's Reconstruction policies and aimed to control the results of the committee's investigation so that they could bolster their own ruthless agenda for the vanquished South and its leaders instead. Unwilling to yield to such an insidious plot, however, Rogers had managed to get his hands on the documents anyway, and he was now prepared to criticize virtually every feature of the case Holt had built against Davis, beginning with the jurisdiction of what he called the "mock trial" that had convicted Booth's local accomplices and continuing through Holt's extended suborning of Dunham's (and his accomplices') perjury over the last several months. Not least outrageous, Rogers declared, was Holt's infuriating and entirely inappropriate attempt to influence the Judiciary Committee: during one of his recent interviews, Rogers claimed, Holt had bluntly "offered" his opinion about how committee members might interpret the evidence he had set before them, rather than allowing them to reach their own conclusions. This, Rogers insisted, was proof of Holt's intention to exploit Lincoln's murder "as a pretext to hatch charges against a number of historical personages"—Davis, Clay, Thompson, and others—"to blacken their pri-

Hon. Andrew J. Rogers. Courtesy of the Library of Congress.

vate character, and afford excuse for their trial through the useless form of a military commission." Pointing out that Holt and the Bureau of Military Justice had been struggling in vain for more than a year to prove Davis's guilt, Rogers concluded emphatically that there was, in fact, not one iota of convincing evidence *yet* to implicate the former Confederate president, or any of the other men named in Johnson's May 2 proclamation, and he urged the committee to locate, arrest, and interrogate Dunham in order to further flesh out the details of Holt's dastardly scheme.[13]

Holt was enraged by Rogers's "minority report," whose purpose, it was clear, was to bolster the president at Holt's expense and at the expense of those who increasingly shared Holt's vehement opposition to the president's Reconstruction policies. As far as Holt could tell, those policies had produced nothing but trouble, especially for the freedpeople. In late May, a horrendous race riot in Memphis had resulted in the deaths of almost fifty blacks; this was followed by an equally horrible riot in New Orleans in July that killed over thirty more. Many observers, including Holt, were certain that these riots and other eruptions of violence against the former slaves and their allies were nothing more than the inevitable fruits of Andrew Johnson's excessive generosity toward those white Southerners who had so recently tried to destroy the nation in order to keep blacks in chains. On August 2, a New York friend of Holt's expressed his concern that chaos would soon follow the Memphis and New Orleans riots and that eventually, unless the president took decisive action to the contrary, there would be "little left for the loyal Union people of the South to do but to escape for their lives." For his part, Holt was determined to stay the course in order to prevent such a future, though his commitment—like his commitment to Lincoln and the Union during the war—took a great personal, emotional, and professional toll.[14]

Among those who sought late in the summer to offer Holt advice about how to handle his most recent struggles was his brother Robert. Sadly, Robert's own diehard, proslavery Southern nationalism made it impossible for him to express sympathy for his brother without seasoning it with reproach. "I deeply regret to perceive the attacks now being made upon you," he wrote on August 21. But he went on to insist that schemers such as Charles Dunham were "born of the corruption of the times," and that Holt's position in the federal government, of which Robert had so long disapproved, had actually made Holt's becoming this sort of target unavoidable. Still, Robert urged his brother to fight back against his enemies, not just for his own sake but also—and perhaps even more importantly—for the sake of his friends and family members, who had a right to expect him to defend his honor, which reflected directly on theirs.[15]

Even if Holt was disinclined to accept any advice from Robert, there were certainly others who believed that he should opt for a public defense of his reputation against Rogers, Dunham, the *New York Herald*, and the former Confederacy's (and Johnson's) increasingly vocal supporters. But there were still others who suggested that his time and energy might be better spent simply tracking down the fugitive Dunham, who seemed to be at the center of so much of the trouble. "Conover ought to be exposed and if possible arrested," wrote Frederick Aiken, who had, ironically, been one of Mary Surratt's junior defense lawyers two years earlier. Aiken pointed out in late August that arresting Conover would put a stop to the perjurer's shenanigans, limit his future "power of mischief," and simultaneously demonstrate to the public that Holt was neither his sponsor nor his fool. In contrast, not to arrest Conover meant permitting his "unmerited abuse & detraction" to continue to the point that "the public mind" would be poisoned permanently by his lies.[16]

Others argued that there was nothing to be gained for Holt, the bureau, or the investigation against Davis from Holt's issuing a lengthy, public refutation. Particularly skeptical was James Speed's replacement as attorney general, Henry Stanbery, who felt strongly that a focused attempt by Holt to prove his uprightness would ultimately prove embarrassing, drawing more attention than before to the fact that he had been taken in and manipulated more than once by the same sly con man. Moreover, a vigorous public reply might just encourage Holt's enemies to attack him again, perhaps even more viciously than before. Stanton, who remained one of Holt's closest allies, agreed. And whereas Stanbery may have had an ulterior motive in suggesting that Holt hold his fire—he was, after all, Andrew Johnson's handpicked attorney general and may well have been trying to protect his boss by stifling Holt's rage—the same charge could not possibly have been leveled at Stanton, at least not at this point.[17]

Having considered all of this advice, in the late summer of 1866 Holt followed his familiar and, in many ways, classically white, Southern male pattern of striking back fiercely and eloquently against individuals who wounded him personally or insulted his honor. At his request, on September 3, the Republican *Washington Daily Chronicle* published his detailed response to the charges Rogers, Dunham, and others had issued against him. Subsequently, the *Chronicle* piece also appeared in pamphlet form (with some additions) as the *Vindication of Judge Advocate General Holt*

President Andrew Johnson. Courtesy of the Library of Congress.

from the Foul Slanders of Traitors, their Aiders, Abettors, and Sympathizers, Acting in the Interest of Jefferson Davis. Holt's self-defense included excerpts from his testimony before the Judiciary Committee in April and June and a summary of the history of his involvement with Dunham, including pertinent letters he had received from the con man before Joseph Hoare exposed him in early May, and examples of letters Dunham had fabricated since then trying to blame Holt for his own crimes. The *Vindication* also included a severe castigation of Congressman Rogers for his "shameless

. . . perversions and falsehoods" and offered the *Chronicle*'s own commentary to the effect that a conspiracy involving Dunham, Rogers, and other supporters of Andrew Johnson's Reconstruction policies had been formed to humiliate Holt and the Bureau of Military Justice and provoke such an abundance of popular contempt for both that bringing Davis to justice would become impossible and Davis would be released. The pamphlet was widely disseminated, not least by Holt himself.[18]

As had always been the case in the past, after reading his *Vindication* Holt's friends and allies showered him with praise and encouragement. "You certainly have made yourself master of the situation," wrote Frank Ballard from New York. Similarly, D. H. Hoopes of Baltimore declared Holt's self-defense "complete" and reminded him that his reputation stood simply "too high to be injured by any such malicious assaults." From Kentucky, Jesse Kincheloe declared Holt's *Vindication* nothing short of "perfect," although he worried that many Kentuckians' strong support for Johnson's policies might preclude its contents' ready acceptance there. Although Holt's native state had rejected secession in 1861, Kincheloe noted, now more than ever since the war's end Unionists were being persecuted and former rebels were rapidly gaining influence. Some Kentuckians, he added sadly, were simply "resolved to hate you," though he insisted that among Kentucky's Unionists, Holt needed no justification.[19]

T. S. Bell, too, applauded Holt's response to his critics, which corresponded with Bell's own mounting disdain for Lincoln's bumbling, dangerous successor, though he clung to the hope that Johnson would lose in the end. "The triumphs secured by loyal arms will be maintained," Bell declared with conviction, "even if we have to take them up and try them over again." Holt's former associate, Henry L. Burnett, insisted that "when the patriotic people of this country cease to remember, that you and [Stanton] in the beginning grappled almost single handed with the leaders of the rebellion and hurled them from their high places, and tore loose the fangs they had fastened on the very life arteries of the Government . . . they will cease to love liberty or their native land." Holt also received congratulations on his *Vindication* from Massachusetts representative George Boutwell, author of the Judiciary Committee's original July 28 report and himself a target of Andrew Rogers's invective. As a member of the Judiciary Committee, Boutwell assured Holt that he could personally vouch for the judge advocate general's integrity, and he added, "your enemies will fail." Similarly, Congressman James Wilson, who had chaired the committee, declared himself not the least bit surprised by "the attack made on you by the friends of Jefferson Davis." Wilson insisted that Davis's supporters—

among whom he now unequivocally numbered Andrew Johnson—"will spare no pains to shield him from the penalty of his great crime." Like Boutwell, Wilson reaffirmed that Holt's conduct of the Davis investigation to date had been entirely upright and that, although they had turned out so badly, his dealings with Dunham had nevertheless been well intended and honest. Around this same time, the Union League of Philadelphia offered its own ringing endorsement by awarding Holt its Silver Medal "as a mark of their respect and a testimonial of their appreciation of your gallantry and distinguished services to our Country in the most perilous days of her history."[20]

On September 11, Holt took a further dramatic step in his counteroffensive against his critics by asking Stanton to bring him and his entire professional record before a court of inquiry to determine the merits of the questions the Conover scandal had raised about his honesty and his handling of the Davis investigation. Stanton forwarded Holt's request to Johnson, who had recently returned from his notorious eighteen-day "Swing around the Circle" campaign trip across the North, during which he had repeatedly denounced the Fourteenth Amendment, encouraging states not to ratify it, and had so brashly confronted opponents at his rallies that even his supporters became embarrassed. Back in Washington, the unrepentant president discussed Holt's request with his cabinet, which now also included a new secretary of the interior, Johnson having replaced James Harlan with the more moderate Republican Orville Hickman Browning at the end of August. "Judge Holt asks a court of inquiry," noted Secretary of the Navy Gideon Welles in his diary, adding that he considered it unnecessary but that Stanton seemed inclined to grant the request. In the end, however, Johnson turned Holt down, likely fearing that a verdict in the judge advocate general's favor would work to his own disadvantage. When Stanton informed Holt of the president's decision, he added his own strong words of support, namely, that all of the accusations that had been lodged against Holt were "entirely groundless," and that as judge advocate general he had in all cases performed his duties "fairly, justly and with distinguished ability, integrity and patriotism, and in strict conformity with the requirements of your high office and the obligations of an officer and a gentleman."[21]

In late September, as Holt gratefully collected his friends' and allies' expressions of confidence and encouragement, he and the nation prepared for the anticipated trial of Jefferson Davis for treason. On September 25, however, the *New York Times* reported from Richmond that new rumors had begun to circulate to the effect that the trial would be delayed again indefinitely and might not even occur. Two weeks later, the *Times* reported that there was still no sign of the trial getting underway, though no one seemed to understand why. A few days later, however, the mystery of the latest postponement was explained: according to Attorney General Stanbery, Virginia's civil courts were now open, which meant that it was possible to conduct a treason trial in the state. The problem was Congress, which on July 23 had passed a law redrawing the lines of some of the federal judicial circuits, including the Fourth Circuit, to which Chief Justice Chase, who was to try Davis's case, had originally been assigned. Subsequently, questions about the constitutionality of the July 23 law had provoked other questions about which justices would now be assigned to which circuits. None of these questions had as yet been resolved either by Congress or by the Supreme Court, and until they were, the necessary mechanisms for transferring Davis from military to civil custody and then bringing him to trial could not be activated. Just as well, Stanbery added generously: Davis was both more comfortable and more secure at Fortress Monroe—where the conditions of his incarceration had improved steadily since his May 1865 capture—than he could be anywhere under civil authority.[22]

Holt's frustration over the lack of progress in Davis's treason case was hardly relieved by the ongoing reverberations of the Conover scandal. On a positive note, in late October Holt sent his assistant Levi Turner back to New York to locate and actually arrest Charles Dunham, and this time Turner succeeded. Back in Washington, Dunham was indicted for having committed perjury before the House Judiciary Committee and for having caused his accomplices to do so as well; subsequently, he was brought to trial, convicted, and sentenced to ten years in prison at the New York State Penitentiary at Albany. Meanwhile, Holt continued to attend to his responsibilities at the bureau, where a much smaller "peacetime" regular army (whose size was fixed by the 1866 Reorganization Act at 54,000) yielded far less legal wrangling than had the vast wartime force. When he filed his annual report that fall, Holt observed that the bureau had overseen slightly more than 8,000 courts-martial and military commissions over the past year, less than a quarter the number they had handled in 1865. In addition, Holt indicated that the bureau had produced approximately 4,000 "special reports," only about a third as many as the previous year. "The number of records of military courts received at this Bureau," Holt noted, "reached a minimum soon after the passage of the late army bill," but he anticipated that the bureau's business would increase substantially as the new regular army filled its ranks.[23]

Also on Holt's mind throughout the fall of 1866 was the future of Louis Weichmann, who had grown increasingly concerned about the implications of the shifting political sands for the security of his patronage job at the Customs House in Philadelphia. Weichmann's concerns had merit: in recent months, Johnson and his allies had removed hundreds—perhaps even thousands—of federal bureaucrats from office, replacing them with individuals presumed or known to be more favorable to the president's policies. That fall, Weichmann wrote frequently to ask for Holt's advice, using a tone that can only be described as perpetually ingratiating. "I was pained to find that you were deceived in the villain Connover [*sic*]," Weichmann wrote in October, "and that you were grossly slandered by the traitorous Rogers in the interest of Jeff. Davis." But he reassured Holt, "on the part of the loyal people with whom I have intercourse, that your character and reputation are too firm to be assailed." In his letters Weichmann also routinely revisited the trial of the assassins and its aftermath, highlighting as obsequiously as possible the indestructible bond he believed that he and Holt had forged during their work together in the spring and summer of 1865, which he somehow felt put Holt permanently in his debt. For this reason, as it became clear in the late fall that the new customs collector in Philadelphia was planning to surround himself with individuals whose politics were more in line with his own—which in turn were in line with the president's—Weichmann once again resorted to begging for help finding a different position.[24]

Perhaps somewhat grandiosely, Weichmann also worried about his physical safety. In particular, he was anxious about the possibility that John Surratt had returned to the United States and was plotting to harm him. He did not seem to know that in late April former Union general Rufus King, now the U.S. minister to the Vatican, had informed Secretary of State Seward that an old friend of Surratt's had positively identified as the fugitive John Surratt a man who was currently serving with the Vatican Guard at a post in Sezze, Italy. Moreover, once identified, Surratt had once again boldly acknowledged his participation in the conspiracy that led to Lincoln's murder, as he had done when he spoke to the Canadian doctor, Lewis McMillan, on his transatlantic voyage in the fall of 1865. According to Rufus King, Surratt had also confirmed Jefferson Davis's knowledge of the assassination plot, if not his direct involvement in it. In May, King had forwarded to Seward two detailed depositions from his informant, who turned out to be a young Canadian, Henri Beaumont de Sainte Marie, who had met Surratt years earlier in Maryland. Seward showed the material to Stanton, who then shared it with Holt. Subsequently, Holt recommended that King obtain a sworn deposition from Sainte Marie detailing Surratt's confession.[25]

Around this same time, Seward informed the Judiciary Committee— then still thick into its investigation of the case against Davis—that Surratt had been located, and that plans were underway to arrest him and return him to the United States for trial, although the absence of an extradition treaty between the United States and the Vatican posed a potential obstacle. So did the thousands of miles that lay between Washington and Rome, making communication back and forth laborious, even with the availability of translators and the telegraph. Nevertheless, over the next few weeks Rufus King secured the statement from Sainte Marie that Holt had requested and sent it on to Washington. King also informed Seward that Cardinal Giacomo Antonelli had promised that the Vatican would not stand in the way of Surratt being handed over to the U.S. authorities, even without an extradition treaty. Still, many more weeks followed of slow, careful negotiation over how to arrest and transport Surratt back to Washington. Weichmann may have been looking over his shoulder regularly in the fall of 1866 to see if Surratt was lurking there, but in fact his former friend was still on the other side of the Atlantic, apparently unaware of the efforts underway to effect his capture.[26]

The November 1866 election brought some encouragement to Holt and others who continued to hope that President Johnson's rush to redeem the former Confederacy could still be stalled or, even better, completely derailed. Described by historian Eric Foner as a "referendum on the Fourteenth Amendment," the election represented a sharp if temporary defeat for Johnson and his allies, although virtually all of the former Confederate states later went on to repudiate the amendment. Still, thwarting tradition, in this midterm canvass Republicans were elected or returned to office in huge numbers, ensuring that the Fortieth Congress, scheduled to convene for its first session in December 1867, would have the same two-thirds-plus Republican majority that the Thirty-ninth had enjoyed and that was necessary to override a Johnson veto. "Was not the result of our elections invigorating?" asked one of Holt's close friends. "I could not feel thankful enough." Indeed, from the moment the incumbent Thirty-ninth Congress came together for its second and final session (scheduled to end in early March 1867), there were signs that the Radicals within the Republican Party were now preparing for all-out battle with the president, not least because their supporters had been increased by migrating moderates, whose patience with the president was growing thin. As they had done a year earlier, when the legislators convened in December 1866 they refused to seat the representatives from the "redeemed" South, although they made exceptions for Senators Joseph S. Fowler and David T. Patterson and eight congressmen from Johnson's home state of Tennessee, whose Reconstruction—alone among the former Confederate states—they had, ironically, deemed successful back in July.[27]

Members of the Thirty-ninth Congress immediately began to discuss the possibility of implementing new and much more rigorous requirements for the erstwhile rebel states before they could be readmitted to the Union. Early in January the legislators took another bold step: overriding Johnson's veto of a bill that extended suffrage to Washington, D.C.'s black male residents. Even more revealing of their new purpose was Ohio congressman James M. Ashley's resolution, presented on January 7, calling for the president's impeachment on the basis of his wanton "usurpation of power and violation of law" during his less than two years in office, including corruption in his use of the power of appointment as well as in his powers to pardon individual Southerners and to veto legislation. Ashley asserted that Johnson's misuse of his powers amounted to the sort of high crimes and misdemeanors for which he deserved to be thrown out of office. Ashley's resolution was immediately referred for consideration to the House Judiciary Committee, which began a wide-ranging investigation into its merits that continued well into the summer.[28]

Holt surveyed these developments in the struggle between Congress and the president with great interest and a measure of optimism. Ideally, the Judiciary Committee's hearings would result in Johnson being compelled to submit to the Radicals' will for Reconstruction, if he was not forced to resign. Holt also hoped that the hearings—which were certain to touch on the president's apparent unwillingness, since the trial of Henry Wirz, to punish any of the Confederacy's leading figures—would breathe new life into the case against Jefferson Davis, either for treason or for complicity with Booth, or both. Perhaps the hearings would also lay to rest lingering criticisms of the trial of the assassins as nothing more than an exercise in Northern vengeance. With these things in mind, on February 7 and 11 Holt appeared before the committee once again, comfortable in the knowledge that its members had not changed since his appearance there the previous April, although he was surely not eager to have to deal with Rogers again. This time, the committee took its conversation with Holt in a new direction: what, they wanted to know, could he tell them about the "diary"—actually more of a memo book—that John Wilkes Booth had apparently kept in the weeks surrounding Lincoln's murder?[29]

The "diary," it seems, had been found on Booth's body when he was killed by Sergeant Corbett on April 26, 1865. Subsequently, it was examined briefly by secret service agent Lafayette C. Baker, who had been responsible for securing Booth's corpse once it reached Washington. It was then handed over to Stanton, who looked it over, and, ultimately, to Holt and the Bureau of Military Justice. Committee members asked Holt whether the memo book, which he brought in at their request, had been mutilated all along (it was missing more than a dozen pages) or had been tampered with since its original discovery. Holt responded, and Stanton later confirmed, that the diary was in the form in which it had been received. Questioners also asked Holt whether, shortly after the assassination, he had obtained from Lafayette Baker an eight-to-ten-page "abstract of letters" supposedly written by Davis and other Confederate leaders to their agents in Canada, which was rumored to indicate incontrovertibly the authors' complicity with Booth. Holt answered that he had in fact received the abstract, but that it had since disappeared from his bureau files. Nor had he been able, since first viewing the abstract, to track down the original letters from which it was drawn, despite having sent Baker back to Canada to find them.[30]

In their conversations with Holt in the late winter of 1866–67, the members of the Judiciary Committee strove once again to evaluate his handling of the trial of the assassins and its aftermath. They did so, of course, against the backdrop of the escalating conflict between Congress as a whole and the president over Reconstruction's shape and ultimate significance. Clearly, almost two years after Appomattox the trial of the assassins remained a powerful touchstone for both sides of the debate over Reconstruction. Johnson's allies and supporters considered Holt and the Bureau of Military Justice, like the Radical Republicans, exemplars of the worst kind of reckless, corrupt vindictiveness toward the white South that the North could produce. In contrast, many of the president's detractors saw in Holt a rare representative of the kind of courage and determination required to do the work of giving the war meaning, not to mention lasting relevance, by bringing to justice not only all of Lincoln's killers but also all remaining unrepentant traitors, and thereby securing the peace and ensuring the former slaves' future welfare.[31] In the late winter of 1866–67, most of the Judiciary Committee's members took Holt's side. After meeting with him, they went on to interview dozens of other witnesses on topics ranging far from their original focus on the assassination, as their primary goal now was to determine whether, as Congressman Ashley had suggested, Andrew Johnson had criminally misused his powers as president by displaying too much generosity much too quickly toward the former rebels and undermining all that the war had been fought for: the nation's survival, and, ultimately, the freedom and human rights of 4 million former slaves.

On February 18, even as the Judiciary Committee debated the merits of Ashley's resolution, the nation's attention was diverted to the arrival at the Washington Navy Yard of the USS *Swatara*. On board was John Surratt, who, it turns out, had been captured three months earlier. On November 10, Rufus King had informed Seward that on Cardinal Antonelli's orders, Surratt had been arrested about sixty miles from Rome at his latest Vatican Guard post in Veroli. But King's letter brought bad news, too: shortly after his arrest, and before he could be transferred to the authorities in Rome, Surratt had managed to free himself, apparently by jumping into a hundred-foot-deep ravine, despite supposedly being guarded by six armed men. "As Surratt was in his Zouave dress when he effected his escape," King had added hopefully, "I think the chance a fair one that he will be retaken." [32]

In fact, Surratt remained beyond the law's grasp for another full month. Then, on December 2, just as the Thirty-ninth Congress was gathering in Washington for its confrontational second session, the U.S. consul general in Alexandria, Egypt—nearly a hundred miles from Veroli—telegraphed news of the fugitive's recapture. Two days later, Seward informed the consul general, Charles Hale, that a "proper national armed vessel" would promptly be sent to Alexandria to collect the prisoner and transport him directly back to Washington. On December 5, a newly brave Louis Weichmann—who had kept abreast of these developments as the press reported them—offered to go to Egypt as the Bureau of Military Justice's personal emissary to identify his former friend and housemate who, he whined, had "destroyed my prospects in life, and rendered me an object of mean hatred and suspicion to the copperheads and rebels, and especially to the people of my own church." Weichmann's services, however, were no longer needed. Nor were those of one Lawrence A. Hudson of St. Louis who, in early January 1867, offered to assist Holt with any effort he might now mount to "elicit all the facts that *Surratt* may possess concerning the assassination conspiracy." Hudson seemed eager to take a page from the notebook of the now-exposed con man, Charles Dunham. "The accomplishment of my designs," Hudson wrote, "will involve much risk, in various ways, and I shall require liberal remuneration for my services." Holt did not take Hudson up on his offer. [33]

John Surratt's arrival in Washington caught the nation's attention; it certainly caught Holt's, although thanks to Johnson's April 1866 declaration of peace between the sections, Surratt's future trial would by necessity take place in a courtroom over which Holt and the Bureau of Military Justice had no official authority. This fact was signified vividly by Surratt's transfer directly from military custody aboard the *Swatara* to the custody of David Gooding, the marshal serving the Supreme Court of the District of Columbia, which was, paradoxically, the same court in which Charles Dunham's trial for perjury was then winding down. Still, if his own power to exact retribution against the nation's leading enemies had diminished sharply in the last eighteen months, Holt nevertheless held out hope that Congress would find a way to wrest control of Reconstruction from the president's hands and prevent a complete return to power of the former Confederates. So did many of his correspondents. "We are looking with great interest and anxiety for some definite and final action by Congress in reference to the reconstruction of the states South," Holt's friend T. H. Duval had written from Texas just weeks earlier. "If they are to be permitted to stand as the President has fixed them up, with all their powers wielded by rebellious hands, as they now are, the result of the war will not prove a Union triumph."[34]

Holt and his allies had reason for optimism: even as the Judiciary Committee's investigation into the merits of Congressman Ashley's impeachment resolution continued, Congress as a whole moved forward in other ways to assert its authority over the complicated and deeply emotional process of national reconciliation. On March 2, the legislators forwarded their first Reconstruction bill to Johnson, in which they pointed out that despite the president's efforts since May 1865, all but one of the former rebel states still remained without a legitimate state government or "adequate protection for life or property" for the citizens—white and black—living within their borders. This situation, they declared, must not continue. Rather, "peace and good order should be enforced in said States until loyal republican State governments can be legally established." To this end, Congress had determined to divide the region encompassing the former Confederacy (with the exception of successfully reconstructed Tennessee) into five military districts under the authority of military governors, each of whom was to be supplied with adequate armed support to ensure his ability "to protect all persons in their rights of person and property, to suppress insurrection, disorder, and violence, and to punish, or cause to be punished, all disturbers of the public peace and criminals." Congress's March 2 Reconstruction bill further established new guidelines for the former rebel states' readmission to the Union and the readmission of their representatives to Congress: namely, the creation of new state constitutions that conformed to the contours of the U.S. Constitution, including the Thirteenth and Fourteenth Amendments. Perhaps even more provocatively, these new state constitutions were to be devised by special conventions whose delegates had been elected by a fair proportion of the state's resident male population aged twenty-one and older regardless of "race, color, or previous condition," with the exception of felons and those who had lost their right to vote as a result of their participation in the rebellion.[35]

It comes as no surprise that Johnson promptly vetoed the March 2 Reconstruction bill; equally unsurprising was Congress's swift action to override his veto. Then, on March 3, the last day of its second session, the Thirty-ninth Congress took two more crucial steps toward consolidating its control over Reconstruction and over the president, who had begun to demonstrate a desire to exert more direct influence over the Federal soldiers then stationed in the South, many of whom, along with their officers, seemed disinclined to tolerate the former Confederates' (re)assertions of power within their communities and over their former slaves. In response, by means of a rider attached to an army appropriations bill (the so-called Command of the Army Act), the legislators approved a requirement that all orders from the president to the army be channeled through the general of the army, still General Grant, whom Secretary of the Navy Gideon Welles now grumbled had been spending too much time consulting with Stanton and Holt.[36]

In addition, the retiring Congress passed the Tenure of Office Act in recognition of the fact that, since launching his program for Reconstruction, Johnson had replaced a number of the cabinet officers he had inherited from Lincoln with men who were more supportive of his own magnanimous plans for the white South. Many Republicans believed with good reason that Holt's ally, the stubborn and oppositional Stanton—who, like Holt, had supported the idea of a militarized Reconstruction even while Lincoln was still alive—would be Johnson's next target. Now supporters of the Tenure of Office Act aimed to make it illegal for the president, without Senate approval, to remove any government officer who had been appointed during the previous presidential term. Once again, Johnson exercised his veto power, but to no effect. For now, Stanton's job—and, indirectly, Holt's—was secure. Once they had accomplished these things, the Thirty-ninth Congress gave way to the newly elected Fortieth, whose members they had summoned into special session immediately on March 4 in order to maintain the legislative branch's momentum against the president and prevent him from operating unilaterally during the recess that customarily lasted until December.

As if to confirm the justice of Congress's recent actions, in the weeks ahead Holt received numerous letters from his friends across the South describing the dismal conditions that Johnson's policies continued to yield in their regions, especially for the freedpeople. On March 14, A. H. Arthur wrote from Vicksburg that while the city's older former rebels seemed inclined to accept defeat as well as emancipation and its implications for black uplift, "a set of young hotspurs" had begun "endeavoring to play the demagogue by operating upon the prejudices of the people against negro suffrage." Two weeks later T. H. Duval predicted that efforts to carry out the March 2 Reconstruction Act's stipulations, particularly those pertaining to black male suffrage, would face stiff opposition in Texas. "It is absolutely disgusting, sickening to witness the state of affairs here," wrote Jesse Kincheloe from Kentucky some weeks later. "Loyalty is a crime, and treason a virtue. Our representation in Congress, and our probable representatives in the state offices, are a reproach to the state & I think it almost impossible the present generation can wash out the stain upon them."[37]

Needless to say, the constant strain that he had been under for the last several years was wearing on Holt, who was now sixty years old. By early April 1867, he was not feeling very well. Precisely what his complaint was is unclear, but Dr. John F. Gray of New York—who sent some "powders" to provide relief—diagnosed the ailment as "decidedly rheumatic in its character." Such things, Dr. Gray warned ominously, "can produce disturbance of the brain, or terminate in paralysis." Some time later, Dr. Gray sent out another set of "powders"; he also invited Holt to come to New York for a week, "that I may apply the needle capping to the legs in addition to the internal remedies." Later still, Dr. Gray recommended the use of quinine to "modify the noises in your head," which he suggested might be the result of a "malarious influenza." Holt was suffering.[38]

Despite his unremitting physical discomfort, however, Holt did not go to New York for treatment, or even for rest. Rather, when the House Judiciary Committee summoned him again in April, he returned to answer still more questions. Once again, the committee focused primarily on Booth's "diary," which Holt presented for the second time for their consideration and whose contents were published in the New York Times several weeks later. Holt's questioners quite reasonably wondered why he had not introduced the memo book at the trial of the assassins, especially since its contents made clear that Booth's original plan had been to kidnap Lincoln, which had been a point of some controversy. In essence, Holt responded that he had not considered the "diary" or the evidence it offered particularly valuable in the grand scheme of what the government was trying to prove. Presumably, the issue of whether or not Booth and his accomplices had been planning to abduct Lincoln before they decided to murder him had no bearing on the larger matter of their overall conspiracy to do him serious harm. Holt also reaffirmed that the mutilated "diary" was in precisely the same condition it had been in when he first received it, and he noted that since it came into his hands he had kept the memo book safely locked up, almost always at his home, probably because he believed it was less likely to be stolen from there than from storage in a government building, as the abstract of letters from leading Confederates may well have been.[39]

Being called before the nevertheless overwhelmingly friendly committee yet again to explain his actions in the spring of 1865 must have been frustrating for Holt. Surely much more distressing, however, were the indications that after almost two years in federal custody Jefferson Davis was about to be released. Holt was painfully aware that his opportunity to try Davis in a military court had receded virtually to the vanishing point since Johnson's proclamation declaring the war at an end, which was followed by the president's paroling of Clement Clay and David Yulee, the Supreme Court's decision in *Ex parte Milligan*, and the eruption of the Conover scandal. Johnson himself had obviously pulled back dramatically from the effort to bring Davis to justice, and now it was evident that popular interest in trying the former Confederate president for treason was also evaporating, in part because of the sheer complexity of the issue of jurisdiction, and in part because for many Americans on all sides of the debate, finding a resolution to the competing visions for Reconstruction increasingly seemed much more pressing than the fate of this one man.

As Holt feared, on May 8—a year to the day since the Conover scandal erupted—Andrew Johnson ordered Davis paroled from Fortress Monroe. Three days later, the former Confederate president's case was transferred to the U.S. District Court in Richmond, and on May 13—the same day Holt made his second appearance before the Judiciary Committee in connection with the Booth "diary"—Judge Underwood called Davis's case. "The expected trial of Jefferson Davis has caused an unusual excitement among the citizens of Richmond," the *New York Times* reported, describing the huge crowds surrounded by armed guards who waited outside Judge Underwood's courtroom to see what would happen. Around 11:30 A.M. Davis himself came through the door and took a seat next to his lawyers. Shortly thereafter the commander at Fortress Monroe, General H. S. Burton, presented the judge with the writ of habeas corpus that had been withheld from Davis for two full years. District Attorney L. H. Chandler then announced that the government was seeking a continuance in the case at least until the court's fall term. Promising that Davis would return to court whenever he was summoned to do so, defense lawyer Charles O'Connor requested that his client be released on $100,000 bail, which more than a dozen individuals who were already present in the courtroom were prepared to fund. With little further ado, Underwood agreed to the arrangement, bail was posted, and Davis was discharged. "Then the feeling broke forth," the *Times*'s correspondent remarked. "There was a loud exultant cry and a clapping of hands. The Marshal stilled the tumult, and announced the Court adjourned." Within minutes, Davis left the courtroom in the company of a friend. Within days, he and his wife Varina were on their way to Canada.[40]

Although the crowds gathered outside Judge Underwood's Richmond courtroom were thrilled when Davis was released, by no means all Americans were elated by the news. "What more could the Government have done to encourage another treasonable outbreak?" demanded long-time abolitionist Wendell Phillips in the *Anti-Slavery Standard*, expressing sentiments Holt certainly shared. "What more to bring law itself into disgrace — to bring, indeed, republican government into disgrace? For if this be all republics can do to punish treason, on how insecure a tenure we hold peace! If such be the easy path of traitors, why should not any disappointed and baffled party-chief thus achieve world-wide notoriety? Surely, as they say in England, 'High treason is one of the cheapest amusements one can now indulge in.'" Some, Phillips continued, might think that "the lesson the people will learn from this disgraceful exhibition, will be one of forgiveness." But the contrary was true: "the fawning spaniel is no emblem or teacher of forgiveness." In Phillips's mind, the two worst things about the whole Davis affair were its demonstration that the nation had been so corrupted by slavery that it was no longer capable of distinguishing between right and wrong, and the evidence it seemed to offer that the deaths of hundreds of thousands of Union soldiers during the last war had been in vain. Holt could not have said it better.[41]

Still more disheartening news was on its way, too, this time of a much more personal sort: just over two weeks after Davis was released on bail, Holt learned that his thoroughly "unreconstructed" and bitter brother Robert, to whom he had been so close before the war, had died in Mississippi at the age of fifty-two. Among Robert's last letters to Holt was one he had written the previous September in which he included pictures of his sons Joseph and John, both dressed in the uniform of a military institute they were then attending. Robert sent the pictures, he explained, on the assumption that Holt might "feel some interest in them, as among the future representatives of our name and family." On that occasion, Robert had proudly described his sons as "very ambitious of distinction, hard students, and without a single objectionable habit," though he unrepentantly recalled that both boys had taken up arms against the government during the war. Still, they had done so, he explained, only to defend their state and their home, and when the boys surrendered with their regiments at the war's end they had done so in "good faith." When he died, Robert Holt left behind his wife, Ann, and their nine children, ranging in age from four to twenty-three. One of Robert and Ann's children would die the following year, and two more—including the son they had named after Holt—within three days of each other in August 1882, probably from a disease.[42]

Even as Holt struggled to digest the hard news of Davis's release and his brother Robert's death, the long-awaited trial of John Surratt began on June 10 at the Supreme Court of the District of Columbia. Presiding over the court was Republican judge George P. Fisher, a native of Delaware who had been that state's attorney general from 1855 to 1860 and a congressman from March 1861 to March 1863. Prosecuting the government's case against Surratt were Edward C. Carrington, U.S. Attorney for the District of Columbia and a former general in the Federal army during the war; Carrington's assistant, Nathaniel Wilson; J. Edwards Pierrepont, who in 1875 became the attorney general; and Albert G. Riddle of Ohio, who had served with Judge Fisher in the Thirty-seventh Congress. Not surprisingly, Surratt's defense attorneys were all prominent Democratic lawyers in Washington who apparently took the case on a pro bono basis. They included Joseph H. Bradley Sr.; his son, Joseph H. Bradley Jr.; and Richard T. Merrick who, it turns out, was also the half-brother of William M. Merrick, Holt's former brother-in-law.[43]

Although the case opened as an examination of Surratt's guilt in connection with the assassination of Abraham Lincoln, by the time it was over it had reached far beyond its original bounds to revisit in detail, and with great heat, the original trial of the assassins, focusing especially on the details associated with (and arising from) the conviction and execution of the defendant's mother. Holt hardly needed to be physically in attendance for his presence to be strongly felt. By extension, Judge Fisher's courtroom became yet another battlefield upon which the former Confederacy's allies and its most passionate opponents continued their postwar conflict. Moreover, although it would seem that a conviction should have been inevitable given how fully John Surratt's involvement with John Wilkes Booth and the rest of Booth's local accomplices had already been spelled out—not least by Surratt's own confessions—when Nathaniel Wilson opened the case for the prosecution on June 14, his bold and confident promise that the government intended to prove Surratt's guilt to the jury's "entire satisfaction" belied the difficulty of the task at hand. Among other things, the four charges contained in the indictment were problematic, overlapping, and confusing: they accused Surratt of pulling the trigger on Lincoln himself; of "aiding, helping, and abetting, comforting, assisting and maintaining" Booth in *his* commission of the murder; of doing the same for George Atzerodt, David Herold, Lewis Powell, Mary Surratt, and unnamed "others" as they, too, supported Booth in the crime; and, finally, of participating in a conspiracy with all of the above to kill the president. In addition, a much heavier burden of proof now fell on the prosecution's shoulders than had been the case with the military commission in 1865.[44]

For these reasons and more, Surratt's conviction was hardly a foregone conclusion, however much Holt and others may have wished it would be so. Over the course of the next two months, close to 300 witnesses testified before the court, a jury made up of twelve civilians from New York, Virginia, Maryland, and the District of Columbia, and a large, revolving set of observers. Many of the witnesses who appeared at this trial had also appeared at the trial of the assassins two years earlier, and much of the evidence they presented was also familiar. But a number of new witnesses made important new contributions, too, including Lewis McMillan, who elaborated on his conversations with Surratt during their September 1865 voyage from Canada to England. Also new to the courtroom was Henri B. de Sainte Marie, the young Canadian whose identification of Surratt in Italy had ultimately resulted in the fugitive's arrest. Some of the issues raised at the trial were new as well. Among the most provocative of these were the defense attorneys' revelations about the Booth "diary" and their suggestions about the potential impact of its very existence—and Holt's failure to produce it as evidence in 1865—on popular understanding of the assassination conspiracy and the participants' motivations.[45]

Testimony began on June 17, with Holt and others who had worked with him on the earlier trial looking on attentively from a distance while offering to help the prosecution if they were able. (How much help they actually provided is unclear.) As Andrew Jampoler points out, the prosecution's case fell into three parts, the first being a "flashback to the president's assassination," in which the lawyers and their witnesses laid out the events of April 14 and the days preceding it. Next, the prosecution reconsidered in detail the evidence that had been presented at the 1865 trial, in conjunction with which they brought Louis Weichmann back to Washington and questioned him at great length. Finally, the prosecutors sought to trace virtually every step Surratt had taken during the week extending from April 12 to April 18 in an effort to prove that, in addition to being in Canada and Elmira, New York, that week, Surratt had also managed to make it down to Washington in time to be an active participant in the attacks on Lincoln and Seward. This particular effort was aided by a number of witnesses who testified that they had seen Surratt in Washington on April 14, including one who claimed to have recognized him outside of Ford's Theater shortly before the murder, calling out the time to Booth, presumably to assist him in coordinating his attack on Lincoln with Powell's attack on Seward.[46]

For their part, Surratt's defense lawyers had two primary goals when they opened their portion of the proceedings on July 5. First, they aimed to raise as many doubts as possible about key prosecution witnesses such as Weichmann, Sainte Marie, and McMillan, in order to call into question the theory that Surratt had participated in any conspiracy whatsoever against the federal government. (At the same time, just to be sure, they strove to shift the jury's attention *away* from the broad conspiracy charge and *toward* the charge that Surratt had murdered Lincoln himself, which could not possibly stand up in light of how many people at Ford's Theater had recognized John Wilkes Booth right away.) The defense team's second overarching goal was to prove—by means of a thorough presentation of the relevant railroad maps and train schedules, along with the testimony of various witnesses who claimed to have seen him elsewhere—that Surratt could not possibly even have been in the city of Washington on the day Lincoln was killed, making it impossible for him to have offered much if any practical assistance to Booth or any of the members of his "action team."[47]

Among the most striking features of the John Surratt trial as a whole was the colorful, even unprofessional behavior of the lawyers on both sides, not least in their shameless attempts to discredit each other's witnesses, behavior that drew Judge Fisher's ire more than once. "I have never, in all my judicial experience," he declared on July 2, "seen a case in which there has been so much trouble with regard to the examination of witnesses, and so much bitterness of feeling displayed. . . . I have never seen witnesses cross-examined with so much asperity." Some observers then and later argued that Fisher, a Republican, was unduly hard on the defense lawyers. In particular, critics noted the persistent friction between the judge and Joseph Bradley Sr., whom Fisher ended up disbarring on the last day of the trial. Still, it must be acknowledged that Fisher's was by no means the only temper that flared that summer: at one point, Bradley Sr. purportedly

Richard T. Merrick. Courtesy of the Library of Congress.

challenged the judge to a duel. Admittedly, it hardly seems surprising that the emotions of the various participants were so close to the surface, given how much was at stake in terms not only of Surratt's own future but also the future of Reconstruction and of the nation.[48]

Closing arguments began on July 27, with the prosecution first offering a thorough summary of its case and attempting to refresh the jury's impression of Surratt as one of Booth's key (and self-confessed) coconspirators. The prosecution's argument, though long, was basically simple: the other members of Booth's "action team" had been convicted and punished in 1865, and now John Surratt should be, too. Beginning on August 31, Richard Merrick then summed up the case for the defense. In the course of trying to persuade the jury that Surratt was not guilty of the murder of

Lincoln or of participating in the conspiracy that had produced it, however, Merrick did much more than just review the pertinent evidence. In addition, he strove to portray the defendant as a poor, penniless victim of the federal government, and specifically of Holt who, as judge advocate general, had unscrupulously deployed the government's abundant resources—including its treasury and its "swarm of spies and detectives"—to hunt John Surratt down. Then, throughout the current trial, Merrick asserted, Holt had done everything in his power to pursue the hapless Surratt "to the gibbet," not least by tampering materially with the witnesses and the evidence. Was this not essentially the same tactic Holt had adopted two years earlier in order to achieve a conviction against the defendant's poor, martyred mother? Had Holt not manipulated the witnesses and the evidence in her case, too? Following her conviction, had he not stood firmly and heartlessly "between her and the seat of mercy" by obstructing all of the attempts between July 5 and July 7, 1865, to save her life? Indeed, Merrick declared, Holt had even gone so far as to withhold from the merciful Andrew Johnson the commissioners' petition recommending that Mary Surratt's sentence be converted to life in prison. Now he wanted to kill her son. What would it take to satisfy Holt's craving for the blood of the innocent? Even the Supreme Court had acknowledged and condemned Holt's bloodlust, Merrick claimed, when it ruled in *Ex parte Milligan* that the trial of the assassins was nothing more than "an illegal, unconstitutional tribunal, without authority."[49]

Merrick's vituperative closing argument must have struck Holt like a swift kick from a strong horse, even without Holt's being there to hear it firsthand. Others inside the courtroom were similarly stunned, the prosecution immediately attempting to turn Merrick's virulent attack on Holt back on its source. On August 3, lawyer J. Edwards Pierrepont rose to refute Merrick's mischaracterization of the Supreme Court's ruling in *Ex parte Milligan* as a judgment on the trial of the assassins. Pierrepont then attempted to refocus the jury's attention away from Merrick's outburst and back to the current trial's central question, namely, how strong were the many threads of evidence that tied John Surratt to Booth and to Lincoln's murder? Next, Pierrepont expanded his own argument dramatically, reminding jurors of the trial's significance for the dispute raging over Reconstruction between those who believed that forgiving the former Confederate leadership was an essential first step toward bringing the sections back together quickly and those who aimed to punish the leading rebels for their crimes while simultaneously ensuring the rights of the people whom they had once held in cruel bondage. "Gentlemen," Pierrepont asked, "we have passed through a great struggle, during which rivers of blood have been shed. . . . Is it all for nothing?"[50]

In his August 7 charge to the jury, Judge Fisher further expanded on Pierrepont's efforts, forcefully refuting Merrick's claim that the 1865 trial of the assassins had been a sham managed by the murderous, vindictive Holt and brought to its corrupt conclusion by his handpicked, villainous judges. To the contrary, Fisher insisted, under the careful and wise guidance of Holt and the Bureau of Military Justice all members of the court had functioned precisely as honorable seekers after justice do, and their efforts at that critical juncture in the nation's history should not be condemned, but praised. Like Pierrepont, Fisher also denied that the Supreme Court's ruling in *Ex parte Milligan* reflected in any way on the legality of the trial of the assassins or on Holt's conduct of it. He further reminded the jury that their charge was simply to decide, based on the evidence that had been presented over the last several weeks, whether or not John Surratt was guilty of having participated in Lincoln's murder. Fisher urged the twelve members of the jury to disregard Merrick's histrionics, and then he reviewed the legal principles specific to the case and released the jury to commence their deliberations. The jury met for three straight days before returning to Fisher's courtroom at about 1 P.M. on August 10 to announce that they had been unable to reach a verdict and that regardless of how much time they spent in additional debate, they were sure that they would be unable to come to a unanimous conclusion. As such, they requested that Judge Fisher dismiss them and allow them to go home. Having no good alternative, Fisher did as the jury asked, remanding Surratt to the custody of the marshal, who in turn escorted the defendant back to his cell.[51]

By the time the John Surratt trial sputtered to an inconclusive close, Holt was five days into a thirty-day leave of absence he had requested on August 3, just after Merrick completed his vicious attack on him before the court, the jury, and the public. It is not clear how long Holt had been planning this respite from Washington: it is entirely possible that he had been thinking about it for some time, in part because his health was still not strong and in part because he had hoped to attend the September wedding of his former colleague, Henry L. Burnett, in Cincinnati. Under the current circumstances Holt was grateful to have some time away from the capital: while on leave he hoped to get a little rest and also to ponder the broad implications of the recent trial's outcome, which served the purposes of Andrew Johnson and his reconciliationist allies so richly. As it turns out, Merrick's accusations had elicited a dramatic and startling statement from Johnson himself, to the effect that he had in fact not seen the commissioners' petition for Mary Surratt back in July 1865, presumably because Holt had failed to present it when he brought the trial record and the commissioners' verdicts to the Executive Mansion for Johnson's approval. Now Johnson clearly meant to imply that if he had only seen the petition, he would have granted it, although his actions during the days prior to the execution of Booth's coconspirators strongly suggest otherwise.[52]

Declaring Johnson a notorious "friend of rebels and conspirators," at least one newspaper now commented, with perhaps undue confidence, that the president's claim about the petition could never stand up against the public's faith in Holt's integrity. "Mr. Johnson's reputation is so bad," the *Cincinnati Gazette* insisted, "that without additional evidence the case will inevitably be decided against him. His word will not stand a moment against that of any respectable citizen," let alone Holt. After everything he had been through in the last several years, Holt himself was not so sure. Before he could decide what to do, however, Holt received another blast of bad news: on August 12, with Congress now out of session and in spite of the Tenure of Office Act, the president had finally taken the long-anticipated step of suspending Secretary of War Stanton. Johnson had actually considered suspending (or firing) Holt, too: on August 9, Secretary of the Navy Welles had noted in his diary that he had advised Johnson personally to dismiss the two men together. Like others among the president's allies, Welles, who had previously defended Holt, had come to see Holt and Stanton as the two individuals in the administration who were causing Johnson the most trouble by virtue of their avid support for the Radical Republicans' program for Reconstruction. Cynically, Welles suspected that Holt and Stanton also harbored fears that a rapid restoration of the Union would limit the power each had been accumulating since their days in the Buchanan administration.[53]

If Secretary Welles was delighted by Johnson's decision to suspend Stanton, at least, many others around the country were horrified, even if they were not terribly surprised. "We all feel outraged here," wrote Holt's friend Frank Ballard from New York, adding that he had seen a newspaper article that morning predicting that Johnson would soon remove Holt from office, too. "The Gods evidently wish to destroy the President," Ballard wrote, "if they have maddened him to this extent." Another friend in North Carolina begged Holt not to resign now under any circumstances, though he understood the temptation, especially if Holt's great ally, friend, and boss, Stanton, was on the way out. Wrote William Doherty bracingly, "you have the *full approbation*, the *esteem & love of all the honest, & true hearted Union men.*" And he promised that "the sterling integrity, devoted & self-sacrificing patriotism—& disinterested love of justice & truth, which have in all cases been pre-eminent in your [deeds] will secure the gratitude of posterity, and redeem the honor of your name, from the miserable calumnies with which vanquished & malignant Rebels have tried to surround it." Wrote still another of Holt's friends, "I wish you could know how I feel for you when I see the continual wounds you receive from our wretched enemies."[54]

Traveling in upstate New York when he heard about Stanton's suspension, Holt immediately considered returning to Washington. For the moment, however, one of his assistants at the Bureau of Military Justice, William Winthrop, urged patience, promising to telegraph if anything should change. At the same time, Winthrop informed Holt that Johnson was now using Benn Pitman's official trial record—in which the petition for Mary Surratt did not appear—to "prove" that he had never seen the commissioners' request on her behalf. Still, Winthrop assured Holt that the president would ultimately fail in his latest attempt to enhance his own standing among the former Confederates at the expense of Holt's reputation for loyalty to the Union, devotion to justice, and honest dealings. "Among those who know you, as you are," Winthrop insisted, "I have not heard the slightest expression of doubt as to the question of veracity between you & the President. They *know* that you *must* be right—that it is *impossible* that it can be otherwise."[55]

Following his suspension of Stanton, Johnson persuaded Ulysses Grant, still the nation's top military officer, to serve as secretary of war ad interim, too. Confident that Grant would never betray the cause for which he had already fought so hard, Holt was content with the arrangement for the time being. "God bless him!" Frank Ballard exclaimed after learning Holt's opinion on the question. "If he fails us now all is lost till Congress meets," but "if he holds his own . . . Johnson's gun is spiked and the miserable mule will bite and kick and balk without doing further damage." Meanwhile, others continued to worry that Holt would be the next to go as Johnson continued trying to outmaneuver those who aimed to punish the former rebels and their leadership. And as it turns out, although William Winthrop had initially intended to let Holt complete his leave of absence in relative peace, he was unable to follow through. Just a day after Stanton's official suspension, after meeting with the secretary of war's son (who had, in turn, just spoken with his father), Winthrop telegraphed Holt advising him to return to the capital.[56]

Back in Washington and uncertain what the president's next move would be, Holt took seriously the advice he received from one friend to make copies of all of the bureau's most valuable documents and store them somewhere secure. Wrote W. C. Dodge: "It is obvious that the wicked man now acting as president, and his associates, desire to get you out of the way, as well as Stanton; and in their madness, they will stop at nothing. With you out of the way, and those records & documents once in their hands, they would be suppressed or destroyed, wherever and whenever it would suit their purpose. There is nothing at which they will hesitate in their madness." Meanwhile, the news Holt was continuing to receive on the progress of Reconstruction across the South was hardly encouraging. Writing from Atlanta, General John Pope described a situation in which "nothing but violence and brutality remain," where "justice is unknown," and where "personal rights are as little regarded as oaths." In Pope's opinion, most Southern whites were still unfit to rejoin the Union or regain their civil and political rights, and he was doubtful that they ever would be, not least because their interest in education was minimal. In contrast, black Southerners seemed eager to learn and advance, although Pope worried that the former slaves would not be able "to hold their own against the Southern whites without powerful aid from the Federal government for a long time to come."[57]

As summer gave way to fall, Holt once again began to gather letters and documents to be used in defending his reputation, this time specifically against Johnson's (and Merrick's) damaging assertions that he had deliberately and maliciously withheld the commissioners' petition for Mary Surratt simply in order to ensure the convicted woman's execution. As had been true in the past, news of Holt's determination to fight back— yet again—filled many of his friends with cheer. "I hasten to express my satisfaction," wrote Frank Ballard, "at learning that you are as plucky as ever in fighting rebels, traitors, and conspirators." Recalling Holt's famous May 1861 letter calling on Kentucky to join the Union cause, Holt's longtime friend and ally in Louisville, Joshua F. Speed, declared that "whatever traitors and their sympathizing friends may say of you now, I *know* that in times past when it required some pluck to speak out on the side of the Government, that you did speak and write in such language and gave utterance to such thoughts as had their effect upon the popular heart of the country." And he added, "my valued friend Mr. Lincoln frequently spoke of it to me." Speed went on to note that Confederates and their supporters had been "watching every opportunity to poison the public mind against you" ever since the war began, and he urged Holt to take heart in the knowledge that "the loyal masses have confidence in you." From Texas, T. H. Duval, too, encouraged Holt to continue doing whatever he could "to warn the people of the danger that threatens them" now that Johnson seemed to be on a rampage. Duval hoped that Holt would throw his weight behind the impeachment effort, for in his mind, Johnson's betrayal of the Union was no different from Jefferson Davis's.[58]

Holt had other work to do besides preparing yet again to defend his name and reputation. As judge advocate general, the majority of his time was still occupied in overseeing the work of the Bureau of Military Justice, and when he filed his annual report in October, Holt noted that the bureau had remained busy, managing more than 11,000 records of military courts and composing over 2,000 other special reports over the past year. Holt also noted that five members of the bureau's staff had now been reassigned so that each of the military districts created by the March 2, 1867, Reconstruction Act had its own judge advocate on duty at the district's headquarters, a policy he considered wise. Among the most interesting cases Holt had to review during this particular year was that of Albert M. D. C. Lusk, a white civilian in New Orleans who was accused of having murdered a young freedman, Wilson Calcoat, "without cause or provocation." In April, the military commission had found Lusk guilty and sentenced him to death by hanging. When he reviewed the case in September, Holt concluded that Lusk had committed a "frightful and causeless murder . . . in pure wantonness, upon the body of an unoffending colored boy whom he had never seen till the moment of the homicide, and whom he shot down in cold blood, with a malignity truly fiendish." Holt recommended that Lusk's death sentence be carried out, and the case then went to the president for his consideration, where it sat for an unknown period of time without Johnson taking any action. This same year Holt also reviewed the cases of Corporal Charles Wood and other troopers in Company E of the Ninth Cavalry (one of the new black regiments in the regular army created by the Army Reorganization Act of July 1866), who had been convicted in June 1867 of mutiny against their white commanding officer, Lieutenant Edward M. Heyl, while in camp near San Antonio, Texas. The black mutineers had been sentenced to death, but when he reviewed the testimony concerning the events that led up to the men's rebellion, Holt concluded unambiguously that Heyl—who was well known for violently abusing the men on a regular basis—was responsible. "The sense of cruel wrong which must have governed these men after the acts of Lieut. Heyl's brutal tyranny . . . would go far to mitigate punishment for any offences committed while they were so influenced," Holt declared. He recommended that the sentence be remitted and the soldiers returned to duty, which they were.[59]

The Fortieth Congress convened for its second session in December

1867, just weeks after the November elections, which had yielded a series of encouraging Republican victories in the South. Across the North, however, Democrats made significant gains. "I am glad in my heart, that you remain in your important official position in this government," wrote one of Holt's friends reflecting on the election results. "There is some hope to our hearts, amid all the treachery, when we know *you* are there." To Holt's certain satisfaction, despite the Democrats' advances—or perhaps because of them—almost as soon as the legislators came together in the capital, the House of Representatives picked up where the Judiciary Committee had left off in terms of its evaluation of Congressman Ashley's impeachment resolution. Although in his December annual message to Congress Johnson was moved to assert that blacks, in his mind, had less "capacity for government than any other race of people"—a remark that Eric Foner calls "probably the most blatantly racist pronouncement ever to appear in the official state paper of an American president"—racism, however, did not amount to a high crime or misdemeanor. Later that month, the impeachment resolution was defeated, with many Republicans and all of the Democrats voting to bring it down. Ironically, however, congressional defeat of Ashley's resolution emboldened Johnson to go just one step too far in terms of provoking his opponents on Capitol Hill, for just a few weeks later, toward the end of February 1868, the president decided to remove Stanton from office permanently, without the Senate approval required by the Tenure of Office Act. House Republicans responded by voting on February 24 to impeach Johnson after all. The following day Holt's former associate at the 1865 trial of the conspirators, Congressman John A. Bingham, went with Pennsylvania congressman Thaddeus Stevens to inform the Senate of the House's decision.[60]

Now that Congress seemed poised to cut Johnson's presidential term essentially in half, Holt was encouraged. But a letter from his brother Thomas struck a harsh blow to his improved spirits. "Brother James died on the 31st of last month," wrote Thomas, now Holt's sole remaining sibling. Happily, although he had never married, the fifty-seven-year-old James was not alone when he died after a short but severe illness. At his side had been Thomas's son, Washington Dorsey Holt, as well as the son of Holt's late sister, Elizabeth, Billy Sterett, both of whom had gone to Texas to study law with their uncle. Holt had not seen his brother James for many years, and the two had never enjoyed more than intermittent written communication. The war had only widened the gap between them as James—like most of the Holt/Stephens clan—chose to support the Confederacy. Still, it was James to whom Holt, so many years earlier, had sent those sturdy Kentucky breeches that symbolized to him the family's plain, yeoman heritage, and he no doubt had fond memories of their childhood together in Stephensport. Certainly James's death highlighted for him, at sixty-one—as it did for Thomas, at fifty-five—that the members of their birth family were passing away quickly. In 1868, Thomas still lived on the family farm—and in the beautiful family mansion—with his wife, Rosina, and his and Holt's eighty-two-year-old mother, and he continued to employ a number of the family's former slaves. In his letter announcing their brother James's passing, Thomas noted that he had recently heard from Robert Holt's widow, Ann, in Mississippi, who had expressed an interest in returning to Kentucky now that Robert was gone, though she did not seem to have the financial resources to actually make the move, let alone pursue her husband's dream of being able to provide a proper education for their many children.[61]

Although Holt was surely saddened by the news of James's death, the bulk of his attention understandably remained focused on the events getting underway in the U.S. Senate. Presided over by Chief Justice Salmon Chase, Andrew Johnson's trial began on March 5. Named to "manage" the case against Johnson were Congressmen Stevens and Bingham, along with Congressmen Benjamin Butler, George S. Boutwell, James F. Wilson, Thomas Williams, and John A. Logan. Defending the president against the eleven articles of impeachment Congress had drafted were Attorney General Henry Stanbery, William M. Evarts (who went on to replace Stanbery as attorney general in July), and Benjamin R. Curtis, a former Supreme Court justice who was famous for having written the dissenting opinion in the court's 1857 ruling in the *Dred Scott* case.[62]

Of the eleven impeachment articles, the first eight were centered on the question of whether Johnson had violated the Tenure of Office Act when he attempted to remove Stanton from office; the ninth charged him with violating the Command of the Army Act by trying to get the army's commander in Washington, William H. Emory, to accept his direct orders. But only the tenth charge got to the real heart of Congress's complaint: it accused Johnson of trying to thwart Congress's plans for Reconstruction by "excit[ing] the odium and resentment of all the good people of the United States" against those who opposed him. The eleventh article, in turn, essentially reiterated all of the others in a single, summary charge. Clearly the impeachers (and their allies, such as Holt) had had their fill of Johnson's obstructionist tactics and had determined, finally, to move their vision of Reconstruction forward by getting him out of the way. "The loyal men of this state are watching with deep interest the progress of the impeachment measure," wrote T. H. Duval from Texas on March 8, "and hoping that it may be successfully carried out." Were Johnson to be acquitted, Duval was convinced, "the war for the Union will have been fought for nothing, the freedmen will again be slaves in fact, loyalty at the South will be crushed out, and treason and traitors will be every where triumphant."[63]

The various preliminaries for Johnson's trial lasted more than three weeks; Benjamin Butler did not present his opening argument assailing the president until March 30. After that, the trial continued steadily until May 16, just five days before the Republican Party's national convention in Chicago nominated Ulysses S. Grant to be its presidential candidate in the fall and Speaker of the House Schuyler Colfax of Indiana to be Grant's running mate. In response to the charges, Johnson's defense attorneys offered three basic arguments: that "a government official can be impeached only for criminal offenses that would be indictable in ordinary courts"; that in attempting to fire Stanton, Johnson had only meant to "test the constitutionality of the Tenure of Office Act," which was different from violating it outright; and that the Tenure of Office Act in fact only applied to cabinet officers who had been appointed during a previous presidential *term* (which in this case would be Buchanan's), not those who had been appointed by a president whose vice president, for one reason or another, had been elevated to fill out the balance of his *unfinished* term. On their side, the House "managers" (the prosecutors) replied that Johnson's interpretation of the Tenure of Office Act was wrong; that a president should not disobey a law in order to test its constitutionality; and that, in any case, what really mattered was that by abusing his powers over the past two years Johnson had committed a series of offenses that undermined federal government principles and the public interest.[64]

In the end, the spring 1868 impeachment trial of Andrew Johnson failed to bring about his removal from office. Rather, despite an extremely lengthy and impassioned summation by Congressman Bingham—who had been so successful in presenting the government's case against the Lincoln assassins two years earlier—the Senate vote fell just short of the two-thirds necessary for a conviction. According to historian James McPherson, in addition to tempers generally having cooled over the weeks between February and May, a number of moderate Republicans feared "the creation of a precedent by which a two-thirds majority of Congress could remove any president who happened to disagree with them." Such a development, they worried, could permanently damage the political system, with its emphasis on the balance of power among the different branches. Moreover, some moderate Republicans who might otherwise have voted against Johnson were unwilling to hand the presidency over to Benjamin Wade, the president pro tempore of the Senate, who endorsed the legislature's most socially, politically, and economically transformative ideas for Reconstruction, not least for the freedpeople. Johnson had no vice president, and Wade, therefore, stood next in line in the order of succession. It also appears to be the case that throughout the trial moderates had been in contact with the president himself, in an attempt to extract from him a promise to abandon his oppositional stance in exchange for their support. "For the first time," writes McPherson, "Johnson responded to such overtures. He conducted himself with dignity and restraint during the trial. He gave no more speeches or interviews denouncing Congress, and he promised to enforce the Reconstruction Acts." Ten days after the Senate voted not to convict the president, the beleaguered and worn-out secretary of war, Edwin Stanton, resigned. On June 1, Andrew Johnson replaced him with General John M. Schofield, a Republican and highly considered veteran who had served most recently as the military governor of Virginia, where his performance had earned him generally favorable marks. At the Bureau of Military Justice, Holt remained in place.[65]

Less than three weeks after the close of Johnson's impeachment trial, John Surratt reappeared in court. Back in late January the Supreme Court of the District of Columbia had scheduled Surratt's retrial to begin on February 24, but a series of delays—including those imposed by the impeachment trial—had followed. On June 22, however, Surratt's second trial finally convened in a Washington courtroom presided over by Judge Andrew Wylie. Almost immediately an argument ensued between the returning lawyers—Richard Merrick for the defense and Edward Carrington for the prosecution—over the nature of the current charges against the defendant. Losing patience, Judge Wylie silenced them and then ordered Surratt discharged on $20,000 bail pending his trial on an indictment for murder. A week later Richard Merrick requested that the case be continued, and Judge Wylie agreed to a new court date, September 21. When he appeared in court on that day, however, prosecutor Carrington informed Wylie that he no longer intended to pursue the murder indictment against Surratt. He entered a declaration in the court's record—a *nolle prosequi*—to that effect and indicated that he would attempt to convict the accused by some other means at some other time. Over the next couple of days Surratt's lawyers presented arguments in support of the theory that their client should be exempted from future prosecution because the statute of limitations had expired and it was just too late for Carrington to file a new indictment of any sort. In the end, Wylie was persuaded. He ordered Surratt released, "and with that," writes Andrew Jampoler, "the trial of John Harrison Surratt vaporized."[66]

For Holt, the fact that Surratt had finally managed to successfully evade conviction and punishment for his certain participation in the assassination conspiracy was bad enough news. In addition, throughout the summer and fall—as senators and representatives from the states of Alabama, Arkansas, Louisiana, North Carolina, South Carolina, and Florida were readmitted to Congress under the new terms for Reconstruction—he continued to receive letters indicating that, in fact, the progress of *true* Reconstruction across the South, in the sense of bringing security to the freedpeople and suppressing the former Confederates' attempts to reassert their authority, remained terribly slow. "You ask me," wrote T. H. Duval, "if there is any chance of completing the work of reconstruction in Texas, before the Presidential election. I think none whatever." According to Duval, the former rebels in Texas had actually been greatly encouraged by the Democratic Party's July nomination of Horatio Seymour for president and Holt's old nemesis, Frank Blair, for vice president. Both men's fierce and explicitly racist opposition to the Radicals' goals for Reconstruction—including the extension of civil and political rights to black men—were well known. "If Seymour can be elected over Grant," Duval warned, "the loyal men of the State, black & white, will be at once the victims of the most intolerable tyranny and persecution." In Duval's opinion, the only way to move Texas forward, or at least control its rebels until after the November elections, was to impose martial law and send in more troops to enforce it.[67]

Still, as always during this turbulent period, there was some cause for optimism. On July 28 the Fourteenth Amendment to the Constitution was ratified, guaranteeing—on paper at least—the civil rights of all American (male) citizens. Meanwhile, the work of the postwar Bureau of Military Justice continued to go reasonably smoothly. In October, Holt filed his annual report for 1868, noting that the bureau had overseen more than 15,000 military court records during the past twelve months and had produced almost 1,500 special reports. Throughout, Holt insisted, the bureau's staff members had "performed their duties with fidelity," whether they were stationed in Washington or elsewhere. Holt pointed out, however, that although the Army Reorganization Act of 1866 had authorized places for ten judge advocates in the army, in fact only eight of those positions had been filled, and as a result the bureau remained severely short staffed. For Holt, such a situation represented "an embarrassment in the administration of this branch of the service which, it is hoped, may not long be suffered to continue."[68]

On November 3 Ulysses S. Grant was elected to the presidency. Upon hearing the news, Margaret Crosby wrote to acknowledge her relief, which she was sure Holt shared. "I know," Margaret declared fondly, "your unselfish heart is full of thanks." At the same time, she jokingly described herself as "a miserable inhabitant of New York State," the home of Horatio Seymour, and she playfully begged Holt not to condemn her on account of her geographical location. Margaret insisted that she had done all she could to bring about a Republican victory in New York, and she added, "don't we feel as if we should have smooth sailing now?" Holt, too, hoped for smooth sailing now that Grant was moving into the Executive Mansion. Still, there were four more months of Johnson's presidency to endure, during which the chief executive determined that the time had come to extend universal amnesty to all former insurgents against the United States. On December 25, Johnson did precisely that in his famous "Christmas Pardon," which effectively did away with the possibility that Jefferson Davis or any of his leading subordinates would ever be brought to trial on any charge relating to the war or the assassination of Lincoln.[69]

THE GRANT YEARS,
RETIREMENT, AND BEYOND,
JANUARY 1869–AUGUST 1894

Among those great men who in those trying days gave themselves,
with entire devotion, to the service of their country, one who brought
to that service the ripest learning, the most fervid eloquence, the most
varied attainments, who labored with modesty and shunned applause,
who in the day of triumph sat reserved and silent and grateful, . . .
was Joseph Holt, of Kentucky. —James G. Blaine, September 1881

As the year 1869 dawned, Holt eagerly anticipated
Andrew Johnson's departure from the Executive Mansion. He hoped, too,
that, as president, Ulysses Grant might once again prove "strong enough
to pull us through and save the Country," as he had done during the war.
"The abject Man of Iniquity has but a few days yet to occupy and disgrace
the exalted position which a conspiracy and an assassin helped him to
occupy," wrote Holt's friend Thomas Shankland in mid-February. Among
Johnson's final acts, which only intensified Holt's impatience to see him
go, was his decision to issue a full and unconditional pardon to convicted
Booth coconspirators Samuel Mudd, Samuel Arnold, and Edman Spangler,
who were promptly released from prison in the Dry Tortugas and allowed
to return to their homes (Michael O'Laughlen had died of yellow fever
during an outbreak at the prison in September 1867). Somewhat less troubling, one suspects, was the outgoing president's willingness to permit the
exhumation and reburial, in locations more congenial than the Old Arsenal Penitentiary grounds, of the remains of Booth, his four coconspirators
who had been hanged in July 1865, and Henry Wirz.[1]

Holt must have had mixed feelings indeed about yet another development in the final weeks of Johnson's presidency: on February 9, the president pardoned convicted perjurer and master manipulator Charles A.
Dunham. Even after Dunham's April 1867 conviction and imprisonment
witnesses had continued to come forward confirming and elaborating on

the con man's plan to provoke as much trouble as possible for Holt now that he had lost the judge advocate general's confidence. Even so, when Dunham applied for a pardon just weeks into his confinement, he had nevertheless boldly sought Holt's support, which he promised to repay by providing the prosecution team in the John Surratt trial—then just getting underway—with witnesses who would strengthen their case. Although it is doubtful that Holt or the government prosecutors put much stock in Dunham's promises at that point, by late July it appears that the perjurer had managed, from within his prison cell, to supply what A. G. Riddle subsequently described as "much valuable information both as to facts and witnesses" for Surratt's prosecutors.[2]

In the end, Dunham's contributions did not result in Surratt's conviction, but they did elicit from Holt a restrained endorsement of his pardon request. In it, Holt acknowledged that Dunham had been of some service to the government's lawyers, and he went on to invoke the "principle of public policy," which, as he put it, "leads Governments to encourage by all honorable means, those charged with crimes to make disclosures which may, and often do, result in unmasking even greater offenders." Whenever valuable informers such as Dunham voluntarily and in good faith provided assistance in the prosecution of a suspect, Holt explained, they deserved some reward, even if they had committed crimes of their own. Then, with uncommon deference, Holt concluded that it was now up to the president to decide how useful Dunham's service had been in connection with the Surratt case, and how far it should go toward being considered evidence of his remorse and atonement for his crime. Although he did not explicitly object to granting Dunham a pardon, Holt's support for the idea was merely tepid.[3]

Even as he sought support from Holt, Dunham amazingly but also characteristically courted a number of anti-Holt congressional Democrats to endorse his pardon application, including Congressman Andrew Rogers, who, as the only Democrat on the House Judiciary Committee, had issued the angry "minority report" back in July 1866. Exercising all his options simultaneously, Dunham also seems to have appealed directly to President Johnson, promising that in return for a pardon he would be willing to publicly accuse certain Radical Republicans (especially Johnson's archopponents, Benjamin Butler and James Ashley) of trying to manipulate him (Dunham) into giving false testimony before the Judiciary Committee and at the Surratt trial. As it turns out, between the time of his incarceration in the spring of 1867 and the first weeks of 1869, every one of Dunham's efforts to solicit support for a pardon was overshadowed or derailed by other more important political events and concerns. Then, with less than a month to go before leaving office, Johnson finally reviewed the pardon appeal and approved it. As Carman Cumming notes, when the president granted Dunham's controversial pardon, he publicly cited Holt's "recommendation" on Dunham's behalf as having favorably influenced his decision. "Holt must have choked at this," Cumming remarks, "but he kept silent."[4]

Holt had other things to occupy his attention during the final weeks of Johnson's presidency, including the pardon application of Thomas Jenkins of Mississippi, convicted of shooting a freedman, Jefferson Banks, after accusing the former slave of collaborating with Republican radicals to inflict some sort of harm on local white Democrats. "The record of Jenkins' trial," wrote Holt in his review, "affords . . . a striking instance of the injustice and inhumanity of the treatment accorded to the colored people" in the South "by their late masters, and the slight importance attached by the civil authorities to any outrage committed upon them." In this case, Holt urged the president in no uncertain terms to deny Jenkins's request for a pardon (his sentence was three years in the state penitentiary). Instead, Johnson saw to it that Jenkins was released.[5]

In the eyes of many Americans, Ulysses S. Grant's March 4, 1869, inauguration brought a welcome end to Johnson's deeply troubling presidency. Now, perhaps, the ongoing conflict between the sections could finally be resolved by the man who in the spring of 1865 had brought its battlefield phase to a close. Predictably, in contemplating the men Grant might appoint to serve in his administration, some observers hoped the new president would reassign Holt to the last position he had held under James Buchanan: secretary of war. Others thought that perhaps leadership of the Treasury Department would be more fitting. For his part, Thomas Shankland hoped that Grant would keep Holt on as judge advocate general, in which position he had already demonstrated so much courage and had done so much good for the country. "Your name," Shankland declared, "is a tower of strength throughout the land, and among all good men and true, it is spoken with the greatest respect and reverence." Grant agreed with Shankland, and for the next nearly seven years Holt remained faithfully at the post to which Lincoln had appointed him in September 1862, bringing his total number of years as judge advocate general to just over thirteen.[6]

Over the course of Ulysses Grant's presidency the nation's "peacetime" army stayed busy with its work of policing Reconstruction in the South and fighting, conquering, relocating, and containing the Native Americans in the West. In conjunction with the ongoing operations of the army, which

Congress downsized from 54,000 to 45,000 soldiers just as Grant came to office, Holt's Bureau of Military Justice, too, remained busy, reviewing and managing the paperwork from an annual average of about 14,000 military court cases, by far the majority of which were handled at the garrison and regimental levels. In addition, Holt and his small staff of assistant judge advocates and clerks produced an average of about 960 special reports yearly.[7]

During these years Holt and the bureau also completed a variety of other tasks, among the most important of which was organizing and indexing the massive and important papers associated with the work of Judge Advocate Levi C. Turner, who had died in March 1867, and Provost Marshal and Brigadier General Lafayette C. Baker, who had died in July 1868. Both of these men had direct links to Holt's investigation of the Lincoln assassination and Davis's possible complicity in Booth's conspiracy, but their official papers encompassed thousands of other investigations of civilian disloyalty that the men had undertaken since 1861. It took until the end of 1871 before Holt could report that Turner's files were finally in order, no thanks, apparently, to the failure of Congress that year to appropriate sufficient funds for him to hire the number of copyists the work required. It took two more years before Holt's staff completed processing Baker's materials. Today, the Turner and Baker papers fill more than 130 rolls of microfilm at the National Archives and Records Administration in Washington, D.C.[8]

Throughout the Grant years Holt had cause more than once to defend the bureau's very existence, in spite of the fact that his staff of clerks was already far too thin to perform properly the vast amount of work it was regularly assigned. To Holt's evident dismay, in April 1869 Congress reduced the bureau's total number of judge advocates from ten to eight, six of whom were subsequently posted to different military departments, where they served directly under the authority of the department commanders (the other two remained with Holt in the Washington office). Having enjoyed the support of four times as many judge advocates in the Washington office alone during the war, Holt found the change barely tolerable. A total of eight widely dispersed legal assistants was insufficient, he complained, "to enable me to supply all the requisitions received from military commanders for skilled officers in this branch of the service." Holt's complaints went unheeded, however, leaving him to concede his "satisfaction" that the bureau and its staff had not been eliminated entirely.[9]

As Congress continued to seek ways to shrink the national army and its attendant bureaucracy—including the Bureau of Military Justice—Holt determinedly held his ground, arguing that persistent understaffing led to inefficiencies, delays, misunderstandings, and friction in the attempt to dispense and oversee military justice, which in turn reinforced some politicians' (and army officers') calls for the bureau's closure. According to Holt, however, maintaining the bureau was not only practical, it was essential. "Some such an establishment," he declared, "is certainly necessary in every civilized country that proposes to submit its military administration to the guidance and limitations of law." And while it was true that the bureau imposed "a strict and judicious discipline" on the army, it was also true that its overarching purpose was to protect officers and their enlisted men from mistreatment and to guard their civil rights, "thus counteracting that tendency to arbitrary action which, as its history shows, has characterized the profession of arms, in varying degrees, under all forms of government."[10]

Holt was determined to protect the bureau and its staff, as well as his own official position. At the same time, he strove to utilize his influence to bring about improvements in military judicial procedures. Of particular concern to him in the early 1870s was what he perceived to be a serious inconsistency in the sentencing practices of the different military departments. Holt worried, too, about the custom, in areas where proper military prisons did not exist, of confining soldiers convicted of purely military offenses in state penitentiaries. Holt considered the practice "pregnant with deplorable results," as he was certain that in state institutions soldiers who might otherwise be returned to duty after completing their sentences instead found themselves associating with hardened criminals and enduring the sorts of harsh disciplinary procedures state institutions were known to impose. As a result, otherwise decent soldiers were permanently corrupted rather than being saved for the service. To correct this problem, and also as a cost-saving measure, Holt recommended the building of a series of small military prisons at various points across the vast area in which the army continued to operate. There, convicted offenders in uniform could be confined under military control and then returned to their posts chastened but not ruined.[11]

As Holt grappled with the myriad tasks that were directly related to his position as judge advocate general, he also remained keenly alert to what was happening beyond the walls of the Bureau of Military Justice. After Grant assumed the presidency, Democrats and Republicans initially asserted their willingness to seek common ground and strive to reduce the racial tensions that had been building during the Johnson years. In practice, however, numerous events and developments from March 1869 on revealed how far apart the two parties really were and how determined the Democrats were to resist the changes congressional Reconstruction aimed to impose on the South. Indeed, to frustrated observers such as Holt, each step forward toward a true sectional reconciliation—in which federal authority was acknowledged unequivocally and blacks' civil, political, and, indeed, human rights were ensured—seemed to be countered with at least one step back, and more often several. Just months after Grant's inauguration, a friend in Jackson, Mississippi, described to Holt the grim situation there, where the murder of freed blacks and their white Republican allies had become commonplace. Just recently, Judge A. Alderson reported, a white man who had killed a black woman for no apparent reason had discussed his crime openly "with as much indifference as if he had killed a dog." Moreover, Alderson warned, the state's levers of power seemed likely in the next election "to fall into the hands of those *very* rebels who first plunged her into the sin of rebellion," which would be nothing short of a disaster. As it turns out, Mississippi did not elect a Democratic governor or legislature for several years to come, and in February 1870 the state became the first to send a black man to Washington to serve in the U.S. Senate: Hiram Revels, a veteran of the U.S. Colored Troops and now a member of the delegation whose arrival in the federal capital signaled Mississippi's formal readmission to the Union. (That same year South Carolinians elected Joseph Hayne Rainey as the nation's first black congressman.) But Judge Alderson's premonition, if hasty, was nevertheless accurate in its essence.[12]

By 1870 the representatives from Virginia and Texas had also been readmitted to the U.S. Congress, and those from Georgia—the last of the unreconstructed former rebel states—followed suit a year later. However, the seating of the representatives—even black ones—from the states of the former Confederacy by no means signified Reconstruction's unambiguous and permanent success. For one thing, the question of black male suffrage, which the Fifteenth Amendment (first proposed in late February 1869) had aimed to ensure, was nevertheless still very much in dispute. Holt and others had celebrated the amendment's March 1870 ratification, but to most former Confederates the Fifteenth Amendment represented nothing less than "'the most revolutionary measure' ever to receive Congressional sanction, the 'crowning' act of [a] Radical conspiracy to promote black equality and transform America from a confederation of states into a centralized nation." It was, in short, a law that must be overturned or thwarted in one way or another.[13]

And so, in the months and years ahead, the amendment's opponents developed a series of means by which black men's voting rights could be obstructed, probably the most effective of which was also, in some sense, the simplest: raw violence. Indeed, as the 1866 race riots in Memphis and New Orleans had prefigured, white supremacist organizations such as the Ku Klux Klan, the Knights of the White Camelia, and the White Brotherhood had begun to make their presence felt across the South—where well over 90 percent of black Americans continued to live long after the war—even before the Fifteenth Amendment became part of the U.S. Constitution. In the wake of its ratification, these organizations expanded their efforts to intimidate the freedpeople into submission, to undermine Reconstruction, and to destroy the Republican Party. To their credit, the Forty-first and Forty-second Congresses passed a series of increasingly forceful bills in response, culminating in the Ku Klux Klan Act of April 1871. Still, if Congress's passage of the KKK Act evinced the federal government's intention to guarantee the safety and rights of blacks and their white allies, its decision to shut down almost all of the operations of the Freedmen's Bureau the following year suggested otherwise. So did its passage of the 1872 Amnesty Act, which removed virtually all of the voting restrictions and office-holding disqualifications that the Fourteenth Amendment had imposed on the former rebels, leaving only about 500 former Confederate officers and leading political figures without the right to vote. It is hardly surprising, then, that violence against blacks and their white supporters persisted, assuming a particularly horrifying form in the spring of 1873 in Colfax, Louisiana. There, a contested gubernatorial election produced a racial clash that left at least 50—and perhaps as many as 150—blacks dead, many of whom had previously surrendered (only two or three whites were killed).[14]

Holt observed with distress and bitter disappointment each unmistakable indication that Reconstruction would, in the end, fail to make good on the promises of the Emancipation Proclamation and the Federal army's victory on the battlefield. He of all people understood how much Andrew Johnson's early and enthusiastic concessions to the defeated white South had contributed to the country's ongoing struggle to establish a lasting peace and to ensure the freedpeople's future welfare. Moreover, as his years as Grant's judge advocate general wound down, Holt found himself with other, highly personal reasons to remain resentful of Lincoln's successor. For although Johnson's departure from the Executive Mansion had brought a measure of relief from the two men's direct conflict, that relief had been only temporary. In the fall of 1872, in the context of an attempt to revive his political career by means of a run for one of eastern Tennessee's seats in the U.S. House of Representatives, Johnson injected new venom into their old and painful dispute. When his Democratic opponent, former Confederate general Benjamin Cheatham, criticized Johnson for having executed Mary Surratt back in 1865, Johnson sought to shift the blame onto Holt. To this end, as he had done at the end of John Surratt's trial back in August 1867, the former president publicly stated that Holt had failed to show him the military commissioners' petition on the convicted woman's behalf. Johnson's former private secretary, General R. D. Mussey, immediately stepped forward to counter this claim, declaring emphatically that Johnson "did know of the recommendation for mercy, as it was a prominent fact of the court's record." But although Johnson went down to defeat at the polls in November, his earlier accusation against Holt had been given new life, prompting Holt once again to attempt to defend his own record, reputation, and honor by demonstrating that his adversary was lying.[15]

In the time he could spare from his abundant responsibilities at the bureau, over the next several months Holt contacted as many people as he could think of who were still living and could testify directly to his handling of the trial of the assassins and particularly the Mary Surratt petition. Gathering the evidence he sought was hardly easy: when Holt brought the trial record and the commissioners' verdicts, sentences, and petition to Johnson for his review and approval on July 5, 1865, the two men had met alone. Now, because no other individual had been in the room to hear their conversation or to see precisely how Holt presented the various documents to the president for his consideration, Holt was compelled to rely on the recollections of those who, like R. D. Mussey, had discussed with Johnson soon afterward what transpired when he and Holt were alone together. These indirect witnesses included Holt's assistant at the trial, John A. Bingham, who was still serving as a representative to Congress from Ohio.

In a February 11, 1873, letter Holt questioned whether Bingham had heard anything about a possible discussion between Johnson and the members of his cabinet concerning the Surratt petition, rumors of which Holt himself had encountered. Yes, Bingham replied. Sometime after the execution (and clearly after Johnson first suggested that Holt had purposely withheld the petition), he (Bingham) had met with Secretaries Seward and Stanton, both of whom had insisted that they knew Holt had presented the petition to the president because Johnson had reviewed the petition specifically with his cabinet, whose members had been united in declaring it unworthy of his approval. At this same time, however—probably in the late summer of 1867—Stanton had expressed considerable reluctance to push back too hard against the president's misrepresentation of the event in question. Perhaps he was more concerned for the moment about Johnson's plan to remove him from the War Department than he was about Holt's reputation. In any case, Stanton had urged Bingham not to make a public statement defending Holt against Johnson's charge but to "rely upon the final judgment of the people" instead to sort through the dispute in a judicious manner.[16]

Holt was shocked by Bingham's revelation: that his longtime friend and ally, first against the secessionists and then against Johnson, had refused to come to his defense publicly and had discouraged Bingham from doing so, too, was a crushing blow. To his former assistant judge advocate he now observed, in words that revealed his painful disillusionment, that he wished Bingham had not followed Stanton's "extraordinary" recommendation, as the results had been so damaging to him back in 1867, and had now become so again. Stanton's recommendation that Bingham remain silent on the question of the Surratt petition, Holt wrote, "was neither more nor less, than urging a suppression of the truth at the very time when, alike the interests of public justice, the honor of the military administration, & the calumniated reputation of one of its officers—who was also his personal friend—required that truth to be made public." Moreover, having died in December 1869, Stanton was no longer available to correct his earlier error.[17]

Also gone was former secretary of state Seward, who had died in October 1872. In response to Holt's inquiry, Seward's son Frederick—who had been badly injured by Lewis Powell on the night of Lincoln's murder—wrote to say that, regrettably, his father had not kept a diary or journal during his years in the cabinet, a record, his son admitted, that "would now be of great value." Nevertheless, the younger Seward assured Holt that all of his father's "allusions to the events of that period were such as would be entirely consistent with the accuracy of your own statement and that of Judge Bingham." Frederick Seward also observed that five of the members of Johnson's cabinet were still living: his secretary of the treasury, Hugh McCulloch; his secretary of the navy, Gideon Welles; his first postmaster general, William Dennison; his first attorney general, Holt's old friend, James Speed; and his last secretary of the interior, Orville Browning. "Might not the fact you wish in regard to the petition," Seward asked, "be definitely ascertained from one or more of them?" As it turns out, Holt had already contacted Speed. Believing that the conversations that took place during cabinet meetings were entirely confidential, however, Speed had refused to divulge the details of any of Johnson's discussions with his chief advisers in the course of their official business. But he tried to answer

Holt's question indirectly by informing him explicitly that "after the finding of the Military Commission that tried the assassins of Mr. Lincoln, and before their execution" he himself had seen "the record of the case in the President's office, and attached to it was a paper, signed by some of the members of the Commission, recommending that the sentence against Mrs. Surratt be commuted to imprisonment for life."[18]

That summer Holt also wrote to R. D. Mussey, who had been the first person to put himself on record refuting Johnson's latest claim about the petition, asking him to provide whatever information he could. In this letter Holt noted that other old accusations had now begun to circulate again, too, including that it was Holt—not Johnson—who had prevented Mary Surratt's daughter Anna from visiting her mother on the day of the execution. To the contrary, Holt recalled, on the night before the execution, Anna and two friends had come to his New Jersey Avenue home bearing numerous documents and requesting to be allowed to see Mary Surratt. On that occasion, Holt explained, "I listened patiently to all they had to say, received the papers from their hands, and promised to deliver them to the President the following morning," a promise, he pointed out, that he "faithfully kept." In the end, however, the decision about Anna's right to see her mother "belonged to the President," whose answer was no. Holt now solicited confirmation from Mussey that Johnson had been responsible for keeping Anna Surratt away from her mother's cell in those final hours, and that the former president had seen the commissioners' petition prior to Mary Surratt's execution. On both counts, Mussey readily obliged.[19]

As he had already informed the *Boston Globe*, Mussey explained that after the president's meeting with Holt on July 5—which had lasted for two or three hours—Johnson had informed him (Mussey) that he had looked over the trial record and had approved in full the findings and sentences of the court. Although Mussey admitted that he could not be absolutely certain that Johnson had mentioned the petition in their conversation *immediately* after Holt departed—possibly, he conceded, it had been later that day or the following one—nevertheless, he was sure that Johnson had discussed it with him prior to the execution and that the former president had insisted that the commissioners' reasons for suggesting the conversion of Surratt's sentence were "insufficient." Johnson, Mussey recalled, had declared that if Mary Surratt was guilty, then her sex should not make any difference in her punishment, and that anyway, thanks to the illogical custom of allowing women to avoid the penalty for any crime no matter how heinous, there had not been "women enough hanged in this war."

Subsequent to their conversation, Mussey continued, Johnson had given him permission to relay the results of his meeting with Holt to the press, and soon after, word of the president's actions in connection with the final phase of the trial of the assassins had become public. As for Anna Surratt's attempt to visit her mother shortly before the execution, Mussey recalled clearly that when he and Holt had discussed the young woman's request early on July 7, Holt had mentioned meeting with the poor girl the night before at his home. "I shall never lose the impression then made upon me," he wrote, "of your deep pity for her, and of the pain which her distress caused you," which contrasted so sharply with Johnson's cold indifference. Summing up, Mussey condemned his former boss's recent efforts to transform Holt into a villain, an act, he declared, that constituted a disgrace to the office of the president and to the nation. Mussey encouraged Holt to remain confident in the knowledge that he had behaved throughout the trial and afterward "as a patriot and a gentleman." Perhaps, Mussey suggested, Holt should consider suing Johnson for libel or demanding a court of inquiry, or both.[20]

During this period Holt corresponded with a number of other individuals, too, including Secretary of War William Worth Belknap, to whom he observed that Johnson's tired old charges against him were being "industriously circulated" by individuals who had performed their share of the Confederacy's "bloody work" of trying to destroy the nation and who now, out of mourning for the rebellion's demise, had decided to express their political preferences and perhaps advance their reconciliationist, antiemancipation agenda by reviving earlier criticisms of the trial and execution of the Lincoln assassins and of any and all who had been associated with them. Then, in late August, Holt gathered up portions of his recent correspondence for publication in the *Washington Daily Chronicle*, which soon reprinted the material in pamphlet form under the title *Vindication of Hon. Joseph Holt, Judge Advocate General of the United States Army*.[21]

As always, following the publication of this latest "vindication," Holt received an outpouring of letters of congratulation and encouragement. From Louisville he heard from his old friend, T. S. Bell, who was now on the faculty of the University of Louisville's medical department. Mary Surratt's execution was entirely just, Bell declared, as she had served as nothing less than the heart and soul of Booth's conspiracy. From New York, Holt's former assistant in the post office department, Horatio King, expressed his outrage that Stanton had not provided the conclusive evidence "which it was his duty to have promptly furnished when he saw you so unjustly misrepresented and assailed." In addition, King described his amazement that Johnson could be so corrupt as to continue circulating a false charge against Holt in order to advance his own career. James A. Ekin, who had been a member of the military commission that convicted Mary Surratt, sent a simple telegram: "The vindication is full and complete. It confirms what was known to your friends, it pulverizes your enemies." John Bingham wrote fondly, "You were an Atticus to me." Even Lincoln's former secretary, John Hay, assured Holt that henceforth there could not be "the shadow of a doubt in any candid mind about the preposterous charges you have so ably refuted."[22]

But Holt's fight with Johnson was not yet over. On October 13, the former president gave an interview to a reporter from the *Washington Evening Star* in which he rather bizarrely accused Holt of being the one to revive the Surratt petition controversy in order to draw attention to himself in the hope that President Grant would take notice and appoint him to the U.S. Supreme Court (there is no evidence in either the Grant or the Holt Papers to support this theory). Then, in November, Johnson issued a lengthy formal reply to Holt's *Vindication*, which appeared in the *Chronicle* and elsewhere. In it, Johnson questioned why, among other things, Holt had not made an effort to defend himself more vigorously and sooner. After all, he argued, several years had already passed since he had first announced that Holt had withheld the petition for Mary Surratt. Furthermore, James Speed's recollection that he had seen the trial record and the petition at the Executive Mansion shortly after Holt had originally brought them there for Johnson's review and approval could not possibly be accurate because, after their meeting, Holt had taken all of the documents back to the Bureau of Military Justice with him. Johnson pointed out that even court stenographer Benn Pitman's published record of the trial did not make reference to the Surratt petition, and he discussed at length his certainty that it was actually *Holt*, not he, who had most vehemently insisted that Mary Surratt's sex should not preclude her being punished severely for her deeds. It was Holt, Johnson claimed to recall, who "with peculiar force and solemnity" had insisted that Surratt's sex "was in itself no excuse or palliation," that "when a woman unsexed herself and entered the arena of crime it was rather an aggravation than a mitigation of the offense," and that "he thought the time had come when it was absolutely necessary in a case so clearly and conclusively established, to set an example which would have a salutary influence." Although a discussion of the sort Johnson described in his reply probably could not have occurred without the petition also being explicitly considered, this detail does not seem to have troubled the former president in 1873.[23]

A couple of weeks after Johnson's response to Holt appeared, Holt issued yet another lengthy statement in his own defense: a public rejoinder in the *Chronicle* that was also published later in pamphlet form and in which Holt strove—carefully, methodically, and with barely contained fury—to counter what he called the "fallacies and perversions" that pervaded Johnson's argument and marked the former president's overall behavior. Holt reminded readers that a number of people besides himself (not least, the nine military commissioners) had known of the existence of the petition for Mary Surratt for almost a week before the execution, and numerous members of the press had been informed of it by the morning of July 7, 1865. As such, it was simply inconceivable that the president himself could have been unaware, even if Holt had elected not to draw his attention to the petition personally (which, he reiterated, he had). Regarding Johnson's observation about Benn Pitman's failure to mention the petition in his published record of the trial, Holt—who had corresponded with Pitman since reading Johnson's response to his *Vindication*—explained that the petition was not in fact part of the official trial record, inasmuch as it was drawn up after the trial was over and represented a personal appeal to the president from the military commissioners. As such, it had no place in Pitman's volume.[24]

Holt argued further that even if he had purposely kept Johnson in the dark about the petition in order to ensure Mary Surratt's execution, nevertheless, once Johnson and the larger public had become aware of his (Holt's) perfidy, the president would have been bound to punish Holt severely, most likely with a trial and removal from his powerful government post. Holt, after all, would have been guilty of failing to fulfill his official responsibilities and, worse still, of committing an "outrage on humanity," which, "in the sight of God and men and of my own conscience, would have made me a moral murderer." Instead, however, even after he first accused Holt of withholding the petition, Johnson had retained his services as judge advocate general for as long as he himself remained in office, almost two more years. It was only now that Stanton and Seward were both dead and James Speed had made clear he would not reveal any details from Johnson's discussions with his cabinet about Mary Surratt's fate that the former president had dared to resuscitate the controversy. Holt further disputed Johnson's claim that it was he who was most determined to have Mary Surratt hang as an example to other women rebels. "The same sentiments expressed by Mr. Johnson himself," Holt insisted, "he now seeks to put into my own mouth." As for Johnson's possible motive for making such vicious claims, Holt explained that the former president's political ambitions were to blame: his desire to reclaim his position as a leader in the Democratic Party required him to appeal to the constituents of the powerful Catholic Church—which had essentially declared Mary Surratt a martyr—and to the former rebels, who resented any attempts to punish them for anything they or any of their deceased comrades had done during the war or since. In contrast, Holt himself could have had no possible motive for concealing the Surratt petition back in July 1865. Indeed, to do so would have undermined all of his efforts to conduct the trial of the assassins "calmly, justly, without bitterness or reproach, and in a spirit" of "complete impartiality," as even one of Mary Surratt's own defense lawyers had acknowledged he had done. At the same time, tampering with the trial record or the petition for any reason would have imperiled his reputation, his high government post, and his own conscience, in all of which he placed enormous value.[25]

Fortunately for Holt, by early 1874, and following Johnson's election defeat, the latest flames from the controversy over the Surratt petition had begun to die down. "Thank God," wrote Louis Weichmann from Philadelphia, where he was working once more as a customs house clerk, "you have been able yourself to disprove this atrocious slander, and not left it for others to do when you are dead and gone." Weichmann decried Johnson's "unparalleled treachery" and expressed his hope that Holt's most recent self-defense would settle the dispute once and for all. "I trust, dear sir," he wrote, "that your last reply may be a final one, and that now the hounds who have been snarling at you for the last eight years will cease their dirty work." Weichmann certainly wished this for Holt's sake. He wished it for his own sake, too, having felt all along, as he explained, that "every attack made upon you [was] an attack on me." Late that summer, Holt was once again able to relax a bit during his customary leave of absence, and the year ahead brought no further assaults on his reputation. When Andrew Johnson died on July 31, 1875, his passing must have inspired in the nearly seventy-year-old Holt a welcome sense of relief.[26]

The same month Johnson died, Holt once again requested his annual summertime leave of absence. Quite likely it was during this brief respite from his responsibilities at the Bureau of Military Justice that he resolved, finally, to retire. In considering the possibility of leaving the federal government's service, Holt surely took the time to look back over the eighteen years since he had first arrived in Washington. Among the questions he must have pondered most seriously was how much the war had really accomplished, in terms not only of defeating the Confederate rebellion on the battlefield but also of suppressing, for good, white Southern arrogance toward the federal government. How much had the war and its after-math actually achieved toward ensuring the freedpeople's future welfare? To be sure, regardless of just how Holt answered these difficult questions, he could be certain of some things: namely, that he had done the best he could since the winter of 1860–61 to restrain and then vanquish those who had tried to destroy the nation in order to preserve slavery. Then, once the guns fell silent, he had labored with equal vigor, using all of the power at his command, to punish those who had instigated and prosecuted the rebellion and to give lasting meaning to the national dominance the federal government had earned over four years of armed conflict, and by means of the sacrifice of almost 400,000 of its bravest soldiers. In the fall of 1875, as he wrote to Secretary of War Belknap requesting that he be relieved from active duty, Holt considered all of these matters carefully. On December 1, his retirement was approved, and Holt was replaced as judge advocate general and head of the Bureau of Military Justice by his immediate subordinate, Colonel William McKee Dunn. Dunn, a Republican, was a native of Indiana who had served in the U.S. House of Representatives from March 1859 to March 1863, been appointed judge advocate general in the Department of the Missouri on March 13, 1863, and been promoted to assistant judge advocate general of the U.S. Army in June 1864.[27]

Not surprisingly, news of Holt's retirement spread quickly. Among those who immediately offered their praise and thanks for a job well done was the abolitionist newspaper editor Theodore Tilton. "I want to say frankly," Tilton wrote, "that I have known personally, and with more or less intimacy, many of the large-minded public men of my day, but never have I met— no, not among them all—a nobler spirit than your own." Countless other friends and former colleagues also expressed their appreciation for all that Holt had done for the country, and in January 1876, *Harper's Weekly* published a long article describing the scope and quality of Holt's service in a thoroughly glowing light. "When the treasonable conspiracy of 1860 began its work," the paper declared, "it encountered no more heroic, unquailing, and efficient opponent than the Kentucky statesman" who had gone on, brilliantly and over thirteen years, to bring "the weight and authority" of his "great legal learning and his judicial mind" to bear on his post as judge advocate general. And although Holt's abilities and experience had qualified him for just about any position in the government—perhaps, the paper seemed to suggest, even for the presidency—nevertheless, his sense of duty, his lack of personal ambition, and his devotion to the nation had prevailed to keep him at the Bureau of Military Justice. There, Holt had fulfilled his responsibilities well and with absolute, unshake-

Judge Advocate General Joseph Holt. Courtesy of the Library of Congress.

able integrity. "Among the prominent public men of the last fifteen years," *Harper's Weekly* predicted, "none will be more honorably remembered, nor for purer and nobler service, than Joseph Holt."[28]

As he moved into retirement, accolades such as these must have provided soothing balm to Holt's weary and battered spirits. Once widely extolled as a model of national honor, courage, tenacity, and dignity, Holt's years of service to the government had coincided with its most dramatic and consequential crisis, throughout which he had found himself squarely in the line of fire. Especially since the spring of 1865, the very nature of his work, combined with his own inflexible determination to make the Confederate South pay steeply for its crimes against the nation, had generated enough animosity toward him to crush an individual of feebler convictions. To many though certainly not to all Americans in the postwar years, Holt became perhaps *the* supreme exemplar of perversely "Negrophilic" Northerners' cold, vindictive plot to destroy whatever remained of the militarily vanquished but nevertheless proud and still heroic (white) Old South, a caricature made even uglier when enhanced with the detail that Holt was a son of the Old South himself. It is no wonder, then, that once he retired from public service, although he remained in Washington, D.C., for the rest of his life, Holt to a great extent retreated from the public eye. For the next two decades—with a few notable exceptions—he led a quiet, overwhelmingly private life, enjoying the comfort and security of the New Jersey Avenue home he and Margaret had purchased back in 1857. Holt entertained only occasionally, preferring to spend most of his time reading, chatting with his neighbors and their children, and taking long daily walks along the paths of what one girl who grew up nearby later recalled as his "carefully tended fruit and flower gardens."[29]

During these years, Holt devoted a measure of his remaining goodwill and energy to restoring relationships with his extended family back in Stephensport. Tentative steps toward reconciliation with his relatives had begun as soon as the war ended, when Holt's brother Robert reached out in his clumsy, critical, and unrepentant way, predictably without much success. Holt's mother, Eleanor, accomplished more in the way of mending fences by writing warm, loving letters that primarily provided information about various family members' comings and goings and conveyed her appreciation for the money Holt always sent, a substantial portion of which he continued to ask her to divide among those former family slaves who had remained on the property. On this front, Eleanor clearly thought her son was being too generous: "I think you are doing yourself injustice," she wrote in May 1870, "by sending so much money to the servants, for they are all doing well, and are able to support themselves." Still, Eleanor did not criticize with any vigor, and she even admitted that some of the black laborers to whom the family was now paying wages could use a little help. Eleanor also repeatedly urged Holt to come home for a visit, and sometime in 1870—probably during his usual summer leave—Holt finally gave in and made the trip. He would do so several times more in the years ahead.[30]

On October 31, 1871, four years before Holt retired, Eleanor Stephens Holt died at almost ninety years of age. "The event," Holt wrote to one family member upon hearing the news, "was not wholly unexpected, though, great as was her age, I had hoped that her precious but weary life would have been spared to us for some years to come." Eleanor, Holt insisted, had been a good mother, full of virtue, who had set a valuable example for her children. Following her death, Holt stayed in touch with his last surviving sibling, Thomas, to whom Eleanor had willed the beautiful family home and property. He also kept in touch with Thomas's wife, Rosina, their son, Washington Dorsey Holt, and their daughter-in-law, Vanda Vineyard Holt, whom Washington had married just a year before Eleanor's death. Then, in September 1876, almost a year after Holt retired, Thomas died. The elegant Stephensport mansion and the surrounding property now went to Thomas's son, Washington, who was the last in the family line to occupy it.[31]

Thomas's death seems to have stirred in Holt an even greater desire to put the war's damage to his family relationships behind him, and in the years ahead he made a concerted effort to stay connected, not just to his remaining Kentucky kin but also to the land on which he had been raised. In his will, Thomas Holt had provided for the permanent upkeep (and permanent family ownership) of a fifty-foot-square family graveyard adjacent to the mansion, where both Eleanor and John Holt had been buried, and where Thomas, too, was laid to rest. Toward the end of the 1870s, Holt decided to add to this perpetual mark of his family's claim on their corner of Breckinridge County by building a small chapel on the family land, to be dedicated to Eleanor Holt's memory. In conjunction with the chapel project, Holt corresponded regularly with his nephew, Washington, whom he charged with getting the project done right, and to whom he regularly sent money for the project's expenses. Constructed with only the finest materials and completed in the fall of 1882, the 200-seat chapel sat on a half-acre of land, which, thanks to Holt's longstanding love of plants, was carefully landscaped with trees, shrubs, and flowers.[32]

Around the time that Holt and his nephew were first working out their plans for the chapel, Washington's wife Vanda became ill. Although it is unclear precisely what afflicted her, Vanda's condition was sufficiently worrisome to convince Holt—who had grown deeply fond of her since she joined the family—that Vanda should come east to take advantage of the medical care available in the national capital. Washington agreed, and by the spring of 1879 Vanda was staying in the New Jersey Avenue house and undergoing treatment. For all his fundamental love of solitude, Holt—who had always enjoyed the company of younger women—thoroughly enjoyed having Vanda around. Hardly least among the benefits associated with her presence was the fact that she brought her daughters Mary (who was about seven) and Rose (who was four) with her. It is probably a good indication of how happy Holt would have been to have children and grandchildren of his own that he took such pleasure these girls. "Mary," Holt wrote to Washington on one occasion, "is the light & joy of the whole house. She is as bright as a butterfly, & as restless in her playful spirit as its wings." In the same letter Holt cheerfully declared little Rose "as playful & contented as a kitten." While Vanda and the girls were staying with him Holt saw to it that Mary and Rose occasionally played with a little girl from across the street whom they knew as "Topsy" (or "Toppie"). Topsy—whose real name was May Meigs—was the granddaughter of Return Jonathan Meigs III, chief clerk of the Supreme Court of the District of Columbia during the Lincoln administration, a friend of Andrew Johnson's from Johnson's days in Tennessee, and a distant cousin of Lincoln's quartermaster general, Montgomery Meigs.[33]

Vanda remained with Holt through the winter of 1879–80. At some point while she was there, her husband came for a visit and took Mary back with him to Kentucky so she could start school, and perhaps also because he thought that having two young children plus their ailing mother in the house was more than Holt, now seventy-three, could be expected to handle, even with his servants to help. Once she was gone, it is clear that Holt missed the company of little Mary. In addition, he routinely praised the quality of her letters, encouraged her in her studies, and eventually went on to contribute financially to her education, as his grandfather had done for him. "What you say of the progress you are making in your studies at school," he wrote on one occasion, "delights me. I am sure that you will continue to be diligent & to do as well as you have been doing. I hope to hear by & bye that you are at the head of all your classes. That would make me very happy indeed." Later that year, Vanda and Rose, too, returned to Stephensport, where Vanda's health continued to improve. Perhaps reflecting on the ways in which his own wives' deaths had shaped and darkened his personal life over the years, Holt counseled his nephew to keep in mind "how much of the future is bound up with that life"—Vanda's—"which is so unspeakably precious to your family & home."[34]

Although he unfortunately did not leave a record of exactly where he went or what he saw, late in 1880 Holt seems to have taken one more trip abroad. It is possible that he traveled to Europe but more likely that he went to Cuba or the Caribbean, which would have been much more accessible and considerably less draining for a man of his age. This time Holt took as his guest his brother Thomas's widow, Rosina, who was now in her late sixties and whose apparent reliance on various opiates during the trip troubled him deeply, perhaps also contributing to her death in the spring of 1881. After Rosina died, Holt clung even more tightly to his bond with Washington, Vanda, and their children; his connection with them went a long way toward healing the painful disruptions the Civil War had inflicted on his family as it had on millions of others around the country. Moreover, Holt's affection for his nephew's family and the "Old Home" itself lured him back to Kentucky a few more times in his declining years, and sometimes when he came he brought saplings, shrubs, and other growing things to be planted around the family property, the mansion, and the chapel. In anticipation of one such visit in the spring of 1882, and for perhaps the first time since the war, Holt was able to make a joke in which the war itself played a central role: in a letter to Vanda he quipped that while he did not find the name of her "intelligent & kind" horse "especially endearing," he promised nevertheless to "give him my heart unreservedly." Vanda's horse was named Stonewall.[35]

In the summer of 1882, Holt's overall health deteriorated noticeably. In August he wrote to Vanda of having been "under electrical treatment" three times a week for the past three weeks for rheumatism and numbness in his extremities. "The electricity," Holt wrote cheeringly, "is given very gently & without the slightest shock & so far from being unpleasant, is slightly exhilarating." Holt wrote to his nephew, too, expressing his appreciation of Vanda's offer to come to Washington to care for him but insisting that he did not want her to make such a sacrifice on his account, especially now that his symptoms, "so decided at the beginning," had "very much abated under treatment, & may pass entirely away."[36]

As he struggled to regain his strength, Holt continued to correspond with Washington and Vanda, and also with Mary and Rose, whom he frequently praised for their good handwriting and for other signs of their educational advances while simultaneously offering them advice on matters that arose in their letters. "I was very much interested in what you said about your little pet deer," Holt wrote in August 1883. "I told your Ma I feared they would suffer from the heat, if kept in the house lot. They love the woods & the cooling shade." Holt, it turns out, was a great lover of animals, and he commended the girls for their gentleness and respect toward their nonhuman friends who, he predicted, would "reward with a full measure of love all the caresses and kindnesses bestowed upon them." Perhaps rather wistfully, Holt explained to the girls that "birds, fowls, & animals are quick to find out people who have tender warm hearts, and they rarely make a mistake in choosing their friends." As for himself, Holt reported that he had recently developed a hearty appreciation for dogs, whose basic intelligence and whose "faithful, true hearts" he found deeply compelling. Holt described his two current dogs as bright and playful, utterly devoted to both him and his servants, and always thrilled to take a carriage ride into town, the larger of the two typically sitting up front with George, his driver. "They watch everything very closely," Holt noted, "& become at times so excited by the sights of the city, as to express themselves in a bark not easily repressed." Years later the *Washington Evening Star* commented on Holt's great fondness for animals, remarking that "it was one of the peculiarities of Judge Holt's nature that while he was rigid in the belief that reasoning beings should be held to strict accountability for their actions, he could not bear the idea of seeing a bird or an animal injured. On the old place in Kentucky he would never allow a quail or any other bird or harmless animal to be killed, and his intimate friends have heard him express wonder many times at the predilection of men for the sport that is afforded in the hunting field. He could never understand how a man could shoot birds."[37]

Holt's correspondence with Vanda gave him particular pleasure during these years: on one occasion he described her letters as "the manna of my weary life, compared with which the manna of the Israelites, though fallen from the skies, was but as dust & ashes," and he expressed his confidence that she, among all people, had a unique understanding of his nature. Holt, of course, had experienced a profound emotional closeness with a number of women over the years. Throughout his later life, Holt maintained similarly significant connections with at least a couple of women outside of his family circle, especially Margaret Crosby. Sometimes their correspondence reflected nothing more than the mutual regard of good friends; sometimes, however, it took a turn that seemed at odds with Margaret's status as someone else's wife. "Your kind letter came last night," she wrote not long before Grant's first inauguration, around the time of her own fortieth birthday. "I have read it over and over with great pleasure and great pain; 'pleasure' at your deeply prized friendship for me; 'pain' that your life must be so lonely, and that the most heart-felt sympathy and affection, can do so little to make you happy. . . . I wish I could express my yearning to give you comfort, in words." Some months later, while traveling with her children in North Conway, New Hampshire, Margaret begged Holt to open his heart up to her even more than he had done so far. "Let me know *you*—your thoughts and feelings," she wrote, reassuring him, "I am *very* careful," by which she presumably meant "careful" about keeping her separate friendship with Holt, and the correspondence between them, a secret from her husband. Later still, Margaret teased Holt for finding some fault with one of her earlier, particularly lighthearted letters. "Now dear Mr. Holt, what *is* it you desire different in my letters?" she asked. "I am sure I do not know how I dare to write to you, or why I take so much pleasure in doing so. . . . I suppose it is magnetism—it's a real force whatever it is, and I'll not try to resist it any more than gravitation." Indeed, evidence suggests that the two eventually went beyond corresponding on paper to actually finding a way to meet alone during one of his leaves of absence from the bureau. In a February 1870 letter, Margaret jokingly accused Holt of having been disappointed with her when they met the summer before. "Didn't I always warn you it would be so?" she asked.[38]

Perhaps inevitably, however, given his fundamental nature, the geographic distance between them (the Crosbys continued to live in New York), and the fact that she was married in the first place, Holt's relationship with Margaret suffered over time. In May 1873, he received an apologetic letter, apparently in response to his expression of concern about the degree to which he had come to depend on her emotionally, and about the possibility that her husband would find out about their special bond. "I received your kind note last week," Margaret wrote. "I cannot tell you how grieved I have felt for the pain I know I have inflicted upon your true kind heart." In this letter Margaret assured Holt that "Mr. C never sees or cares to see the letters I receive." At the same time, however, she admitted having thought for some time that her husband would find Holt's letters to her objectionable if he read them. Now she blamed herself for eliciting from Holt expressions of affection that exceeded the limits she claimed rather disingenuously to have tried to maintain between them. "Please forgive me," Margaret begged, "and do not allow your friendship to be chilled."[39]

Holt and Margaret Crosby continued to correspond intermittently well into the 1880s, but in the year he turned eighty (she was approaching sixty) their relationship finally collapsed, provoking an angry December 1887 letter from her in which she described her amazement that, after more than thirty years of friendship, Holt had seen fit for some reason to accuse her of behaving in a "contemptuous" manner toward him. It is unclear what provoked Margaret's fury or what she might possibly have done to trigger Holt's. What is clear is that although Margaret later relented and made several unsuccessful attempts to repair their relationship—"I would not like to die, or to have you die," she wrote in May 1888, "without a reconciliation with a friend to whom I have for so many years looked up with respect and genuine affection"—Holt had withdrawn for good. That November, Margaret wrote again asking Holt's forgiveness, but there is no evidence that Holt ever gave in to her pleas.[40]

Perhaps it was easier for Holt to turn a deaf ear to Margaret Crosby because by the end of the 1880s, despite his advanced age, he could claim the attention of other devoted female correspondents, including his niece Vanda and also one who never gave her name but who regularly addressed him as "my dearest, truest, kindest Friend" and signed her letters with such loving phrases as "forever and only Thine." In December 1887, just as Holt's friendship with Margaret Crosby was falling apart, this correspondent wrote effusively of the joy she had felt when she received one of his letters, upon which she had "imprinted many kisses before removing the cover." In November 1890, when Holt was almost eighty-four, he received an equally affectionate letter addressed to "My precious cousin," which may have been from Mary Cash, who years ago had been accustomed to using similar salutations and who would now have been fifty-one. "I know you must be so lonely without some congenial friend around you," she observed, bemoaning the fact that "cruel fate" had denied her the opportunity to spend her life with him. Even now, she wrote, "my impatient heart grows sick and weary to be with you. Oh darling, you can never know the pure undivided love my heart has always treasured up for you and every day I live I feel that love growing fresher and more lasting."[41]

Over the course of his retirement, Holt's correspondents included devoted female admirers like these as well as good friends such as T. S. Bell and Horatio King. Louis Weichmann, too, continued to write, routinely discussing various details associated with the Lincoln assassination and the trial of the assassins, about which he eventually decided to write a book (which was finally published in the 1970s). Weichmann also kept Holt informed of the ups and downs of his professional life, and in the spring of 1887, he thanked Holt effusively for having been his "friend and protector for 24 years." Without Holt's consistent kindness and generosity—which, perhaps not surprisingly, seems to have included occasional infusions of cash—Weichmann insisted, "I could not have stood alone."[42]

Holt may have hoped during his retirement years to distance himself once and for all from the painful controversies in which the war, Lincoln's assassination, and the bitter disputes over Reconstruction had embroiled him, but he was unable to do so. At the very least, his correspondence with Weichmann and others from that period made it impossible to let the past go entirely. Even more important, Holt's very nature, his upbringing, his sense of honor, and his political perspective virtually required him to engage others who purposely tried to bring the painful (and vital) postwar debates in which he had been so intimately involved roaring back to life. Aging, the passage of time, and the opportunity to take refuge away from the front lines of public service may have slowed Holt down, but they did not, in the end, undermine his inclination or his determination to defend himself or his role in the federal government's response to the rebellion and its treacherous leaders.

In keeping with these impulses, beginning in early 1883 Holt set about trying yet again to ensure the accuracy of the historical record in relation to Mary Surratt's execution. Holt wanted to make it clear once and for all that Surratt was no martyr to Northern vindictiveness but rather an eager rebel who had been duly convicted of conspiring in Lincoln's murder, and that her execution was the logical consequence of meticulously applied federal legal procedures that the president himself had approved. To this end, Holt undertook an exchange of letters with his old friend and colleague James Speed, who, following his departure from Johnson's cabinet in 1866, had returned to private practice in Louisville, becoming a professor of law at the University of Louisville Law School in 1872. Now that Andrew Johnson had been dead for eight years, Seward for eleven, and Stanton for fourteen, Holt hoped that Speed would be willing to lift his self-imposed ban on discussing the contents of cabinet meetings and would declare publicly and unequivocally that at some point between his lengthy discussion with Holt on July 5 and the hangings on July 7, the former president had informed the members of his cabinet about the Surratt petition. Were Speed to do this, Holt was convinced, it would put to rest forever the question of who was telling the truth and would relieve him of the burden of having to defend himself on this score ever again, or others of having to defend him after he was dead.[43]

Holt and Speed corresponded steadily from April 1883 to the end of the year. To Holt's obvious chagrin, however, Speed resolutely (and rather mysteriously) refused to acquiesce, and Holt finally gave up on nagging him. Then, in May 1887, just a month before he died, Speed gave a speech in Cincinnati in which, although he did not specifically address the question of Johnson's conversations with his cabinet members, he stated in no uncertain terms that Holt's behavior in conjunction with the trial, conviction, sentencing, and execution of the assassins—including Mary Surratt—had been entirely and indisputably honest, upstanding, and proper. "Judge Holt," Speed declared before his Cincinnati audience, "needs no vindication from me or any one else." Still, aware that Holt had come under considerable criticism over the years, Speed now insisted that his own position as Johnson's attorney general had enabled him to "know the facts." And the facts were that Holt's conduct both during and after the trial had been characterized by nothing less than "perfect purity and uprightness." As judge advocate general, trial manager, and chief prosecutor, Holt had "performed his duty kindly and considerately," and "in every particular, he was just and fair."[44]

James Speed died on June 25, 1887. Several months later, Holt wrote Allen Thorndike Rice, editor of the widely read *North American Review*, asking him to publish their 1883 letters. As yet unaware that Speed had publicly exonerated him, Holt could not forgive yet another old friend's unwillingness to rise to his defense, and he was determined to have the last word. More broadly, Holt remained troubled by the principle that a member of the president's cabinet could withhold information pertaining to the innocence of another government officer just because the president told him to do so. Also disturbing was what he termed the "astounding wickedness" of a president who would defame a subordinate "in order to avoid the responsibility of his own act." Crimes such as those Andrew Johnson had perpetrated against him, Holt insisted with tangible bitterness, concerned not just his own but also the nation's honor and must not be forgotten.[45]

The *North American Review* published Holt's correspondence with Speed in July 1888, first in the journal and then separately in pamphlet form. Later that month, R. C. McChord reported reading the pamphlet along with Holt's original 1873 *Vindication* and his rejoinder to Johnson's subsequent reply. "It seems to me," McChord observed,

> the conclusion is irresistible, that at the time the petition was presented by you to Prest Johnson, he was laboring under the impression that the people of the United States (particularly in the North where he desired plaudit) demanded the execution of the Judgment of the court, condemning the assassins of President Lincoln. . . . Doubtless President Johnson believed if he would disregard the appeal for mercy the people would en mass[e] recognize him as a man who "*would not shrink from any responsibility in connection with the execution of President Lincoln's assassins or . . . the faithful discharge of any other duty imposed by the constitution and laws of the country*.". . . But when the excitement incident to the assassination and trial of the assassins had subsided, and the natural sympathy for a *woman* in the heart of us all, had assumed its sway, President Johnson saw he had not "reckoned well." He saw that he had misunderstood the clamor of an excited nation, and like Pilot [*sic*] he sought to wash his hands . . . and . . . devise some means of appeasing the wrath of the storm that was about to break upon him.

From McChord's perspective, the means Johnson had deployed for "appeasing the wrath of the storm" was to lay the blame on Holt. Unfortunately for Johnson, however, Holt's *Vindication* and subsequent rejoinder had undermined his plan, dooming the former president to "political death." Now, with the publicity gained by the *North American Review* article, Holt could rest assured that "the judgment of coming generations, unbiased by present considerations, will denounce the action of President Johnson as a crime as great as that of Benedict Arnold and a disgrace unparalleled by the act of any rule of a nation." John Bingham agreed. "The verdict of History," he wrote after reading the Holt-Speed letters, "is and will be that this accusation against you was false."[46]

Several months after Holt's correspondence with Speed appeared in the *North American Review*, his former colleague Henry L. Burnett gave a speech to the Military Order of the Loyal Legion of the State of New York in which he, too, defended Holt's conduct of the trial of the assassins (where Burnett, admittedly, had played a major role as one of Holt's assistants). Addressing Johnson's accusation about the Surratt petition, Burnett insisted that the only possible conclusion was that Johnson was lying. Holt would never have been "so malicious and murderous in purpose," or "so reckless and foolish in execution of such purpose" as Johnson had claimed. Moreover, one need only consider the disparate characters of the two men to know which one was telling the truth. On the one hand, Johnson was "a man of controlling prejudices and strong personality . . . ambitious, bold, hot-tempered, obstinate," and not infrequently "unscrupulous." Holt, on the other hand, was "refined and sensitive in his nature, gentle and kindly in his intercourse and in all relations with those about him, pure in his private life, exalted in his ideas and ideals, dignified, and courtly in his bearing, yet always thoughtful, considerate, and courteous." Burnett's glowing depiction of Holt elevated him somewhat beyond the human realm. Still, his continuing faith in his former boss was noteworthy. "I can now as little associate him in my mind with the commission of a dishonorable action," Burnett concluded, "as any man I have ever known."[47]

Sometime in the spring of 1889, Holt must have begun to hear rumors about Speed's speech two years earlier in Cincinnati. On April 22 he wrote to John Mason Brown, a former colleague of Speed's in Louisville, asking for information. Brown—who was probably surprised that Holt had been unaware of the speech—was happy to oblige, replying that he had spoken with Speed regarding the Surratt petition controversy at least a dozen years earlier. At the time, Brown recalled, he had encouraged Speed to reveal what he knew, but Speed had refused to do so, this time on the premise that he was unwilling to speak out against Johnson, who was now dead and could not defend himself. At the same time, however, Speed had confessed that if Johnson were alive he would certainly have contradicted any statement Speed might make in connection with the controversy. Brown took this to mean that in his own mind, Speed had "perfectly absolved" Holt of all of Johnson's public accusations against him.[48]

Brown then described Speed's Cincinnati speech, in preparation for which, he recalled, Speed had told him that the time had come to "vindicate Judge Holt" once and for all. It was for this reason, he believed, that Speed had used words in the speech that he "certainly intended as his testimony that the charge made by Andrew Johnson was baseless" and that, Speed hoped, would finally prove satisfactory to Holt. Moreover, Brown added, "I believe he died in that conviction." Six weeks later a correspondent from Elizabethtown sent Holt a copy of the Cincinnati speech that was given to him by James Speed's nephew, Thomas Speed of Louisville. It is hard to imagine the powerful mix of feelings the eighty-two-year-old Holt must have experienced upon reading Speed's speech for himself, now almost a quarter of a century since the events in question took place.[49]

In the course of his retirement Holt revisited more than just his battles with Andrew Johnson. In 1883 he also came to blows yet again with Jacob Thompson, with whom he had clashed in the spring of 1861 over the details of the *Star of the West*'s expedition to Fort Sumter. Later, as a leading figure in Jefferson Davis's "Canadian Cabinet," Thompson had become one of Holt's prime targets as he sought to determine the extent of John Wilkes Booth's conspiracy. In mid-September 1883, the same year that he resumed his efforts to persuade James Speed to unseal his lips, Holt learned that Thompson had given an interview to the press in which he made a number of stinging claims to which Holt now felt he must respond. Among other things, Thompson boasted that Holt owed to *him* both his first and second appointments in the Buchanan administration (as commissioner of patents and as postmaster general). Moreover, Thompson even went so far as to joke that Buchanan's call for suggestions for a less kindhearted successor to postmaster general Aaron Brown had motivated Thompson to recommend Holt, whom he deemed friendless, heartless, and soulless. Worst of all, perhaps, Thompson attempted in the interview to breathe new life into the old Conover scandal by once again accusing Holt of having bribed witnesses during the trial of the assassins, not least so that he could lay a portion of the blame for Lincoln's murder on Thompson's own innocent shoulders.[50]

On October 8, 1883, in the midst of his frustrating back-and-forth with James Speed, Holt responded at length to Thompson's assorted claims in an open letter to the editor of the *Chronicle*, which was later published as the *Reply of J. Holt to Certain Calumnies of Jacob Thompson*. In it, Holt angrily contended that Thompson had used his recent interview as an opportunity for "vomiting forth upon me fetid calumnies, long since buried out of the sight," and for releasing rage that had been "pent up for some twenty-two years." Thompson, Holt observed, seemed "almost insanely joyful" to have been given a chance to attack him again. Now Holt methodically challenged his accuser's claims one by one: Thompson's shameless mischaracterization of every single detail he had presumed to give about Holt's appointments under Buchanan; his attempt at wit in his comment about Holt's qualifications to replace Postmaster General Brown; and his implication that Buchanan had been unhappy with Holt's work when in fact the president had displayed "constant proofs of his confidence and good will," even at the very end declaring simply, "Holt, you have been true."[51]

Turning to Thompson's attempt to revive the Conover controversy, Holt called it "the resurrected cry of a rebel pack that was at my heels seventeen years ago. Furiously and fast they pursued," he recalled, "but their cry proved harmless then, and it will prove harmless now." For what must have seemed like the millionth time, Holt laid out the details of his interactions with Charles Dunham, reminding readers that as soon as Dunham's duplicity became clear it was he, Holt, who had made sure the perjurer was prosecuted and sent to jail and that the false depositions he and his associates had produced were removed from the record. "What more could have been done?" he asked. With evident frustration, Holt pointed out that the Conover scandal had, in fact, already been resolved and that Thompson was wrong to believe that the judgments of the past could be "reversed or modified by the invectives of to-day, however audacious and vindictive they may be." As for Thompson's motives for going on the attack again, Holt did not offer any suggestion, but he did remind readers that Thompson's animus towards him had its roots in their dispute over the *Star of the West*'s mission and even more deeply in their very different responses to the crisis of the Union, which Thompson had worked to destroy and Holt had risen to defend.[52]

A few weeks after Holt's reply to Jacob Thompson appeared, *Harper's Weekly* published an article on the Thompson-Holt conflict that came down firmly on Holt's side. "The prominent actors in a great civil war will always be the victims of bitter calumny and malignant falsehood," the article observed, "and the leaders of the American contest of twenty years ago do not escape the common fate." Summarizing the argument between the two men, the article noted that in recent weeks, Burton N. Harrison—

Jefferson Davis's private secretary, whom Holt had hoped to try for complicity with Booth as well—had also tried to cover his own crimes against the nation by accusing Holt (and Stanton) of fabricating damning information against Davis and himself. According to Harrison, Stanton and Holt were well aware that Davis "could never be convicted upon an indictment for treason, but were determined to hang him anyhow, and were in search of a pretext for doing so." To this the paper responded that such claims were in fact the result of Harrison's own "most devilish malignity" and were "wholly unsustained by evidence." Indeed, the evidence proved that in the course of their official duties, both Stanton and Holt had been exemplars "of honesty, of humanity, of justice, and of legality." Using a term that would eventually come to symbolize a host of energetic efforts by white Southerners after the war to rewrite the war's history, the journal confidently predicted that "the lost cause will certainly not gain by re-opening controversy, nor by assailing honorable and patriotic men." How accurate *Harper's Weekly*'s prediction was in the end is open for debate. In any case, Jacob Thompson died in 1885, bringing the direct dispute between the two men to a close.[53]

Having outlived all of his siblings and many of his wartime colleagues and critics, in June 1892, the increasingly infirm, eighty-five-year-old Holt—who was suffering from rheumatism, painful eczema, and probably also cataracts—wrote to Vanda back in Stephensport about having visited a doctor in Philadelphia. "He seems to think that his course of treatment will finally relieve me," Holt wrote, "but he is not earnest or emphatic in the expression of his opinion, so that I doubt whether he has more faith in the ultimate result than I have myself." Holt informed Vanda that he expected to take the train back to Philadelphia in a few days for additional treatment, and that he would continue to do so periodically as long as it seemed to be helping. In the meantime, Holt begged Vanda to keep up her end of their correspondence despite his own inability to write as often as in the past. "Your letters," he explained, "are almost the only fountain left me in the desert of my closing life out of which I can drink and be glad."[54]

That fall Holt also wrote to his nephew, Washington, who had recently suffered an attack of sunstroke while working in the family fields. On this occasion Holt advised the weakened Washington not to pursue an unidentified legal dispute that he predicted would end up bearing "thorns and thorns only, that would fall not only under your own feet, but also under the more tender and shrinking feet of Vanda and the children." No doubt with an acute awareness of the price he himself had paid over the years for fighting back, repeatedly and fiercely, against his opponents, Holt now cautioned Washington to avoid conflict if at all possible. "Between the two evils before you," he wrote, "I am sure, that in forbearing you will select the best." Holt closed by saying that he would like to make another trip to Stephensport but did not expect to be able to do so any time soon. Several weeks later, he informed Vanda that his overall health had declined to the point where he could no longer write using his own hand but depended on his servant, Fannie Wickliffe, to help him. Holt also noted that he had recently abandoned his experiment with electroshock therapy, switched doctors, and was now consulting with a homeopath.[55]

Holt never did make it back to Kentucky during his lifetime, but a piece of Kentucky came to him in the form of visits from his great niece, Mary, who was now a young woman and had come to Washington to spend the winter of 1892–93 with the family of the head of the Interstate Commerce Commission, Judge Judson C. Clements, a Confederate veteran. While she was in Washington Mary ate lunch every other day with her great uncle, "prattling on," as she recalled more than thirty years later, about cheerful topics "instead of learning many things that none of us now know." Looking back, Mary described Holt in this period as "ill and very pathetic in his heroic loneliness." From Holt's perspective, Mary's visits were like "sunbursts for my darkened room and yet more darkened life." Then, the following April after Mary had returned to Kentucky, Holt wrote to Vanda of his yearning to visit the old homestead just one more time. "If ever I am able to make so long a journey," Holt sighed, "I will certainly go west & have the unspeakable happiness of once more clasping you all heart and hand."[56]

In January 1894 Holt thanked Vanda—then on a visit to faraway California with Mary—for her unwavering faithfulness as a correspondent, tucking in a check for $500. By this point, he was frequently bedridden, spending most of his time secluded in his room under the watchful eyes of his servants, taking slow walks around the house and in his garden, or, when the weather was warm, sitting among his trees to read the morning paper. Half a year later, still terribly feeble, Holt stumbled while coming down some steps in the house. In his hard fall he acquired some bruises. More important, he broke a femur, which laid him up completely and precipitated a sharp decline in his condition. In the days that followed, he was visited frequently by his late sister's son, Billy Sterett, and his wife, Elizabeth. After studying law with Holt's brother James in Texas, Sterett had become a newspaper editor in Dallas, and since 1885 he had been working in Washington, D.C., as a correspondent for the *Dallas Evening Times*. While in the capital, the Steretts and their two daughters had visited Holt regularly, and when Holt's condition became grave they tended to him as best they could, with the servants' help. For a time Holt's spirits remained upbeat and he seemed to be "in possession of as clear and vigorous an intellect as he had half a century ago." But he abruptly grew worse, and, at 2 A.M. on August 1, he died, apparently from complications from his fall, probably pneumonia.[57]

Upon learning of the former judge advocate general's death, then-Secretary of War Daniel S. Lamont immediately announced the news to the army. The following day, the *New York Times* noted Holt's demise with a strong dose of nostalgia. "The death of Joseph Holt," the *Times* remarked, "severs one more of the ties that link the present generation to those who fought the war for the Union." As so many other newspapers would do in the days ahead, the *Times* recapped the highlights of Holt's professional career, emphasizing his years in the administrations of James Buchanan, Abraham Lincoln, Andrew Johnson, and Ulysses S. Grant. To an earlier generation, the *Times* observed, Holt's patriotism and his accomplishments had been common knowledge, his "eloquent and stirring voice" resounding across the land in whose "hour of trial" he had proved "courageous and faithful." Now, however, less than three decades after Appomattox, less than twenty years since Holt had retired from public life, and in contrast with all earlier predictions that his fame and contributions would never fade, "the exact nature of the service [Holt] then rendered is not generally known and its value is not fully appreciated."[58]

A few days later, Kentucky's *Breckinridge News* also reported Holt's death. Although the paper described Holt as a "wonderful man, with a splendid intellect and a mighty genius as an orator," its correspondent could not help alluding to the trial of the assassins and offering an opinion that reflected Kentucky's sharp swing toward the Confederacy after the war's end. "Even if he only did his duty as a public official," the paper noted, "that trial was an irreparable misfortune to him and an everlasting regret to the country." The *Nelson County (Ky.) Record* adopted a somewhat different tone, recalling Holt as a tall, "very distinguished looking man" with abundant gray hair and a face "strongly marked with indications of great force of character." In his later years, the *Record* commented, Holt had fiercely guarded his privacy, "his only companion being his books and a few intimate friends who used occasionally [to] drop in upon him." Asked repeatedly to resume his life in the public sphere, Holt had always refused, "saying that he had had all that sort of thing he desired, and did not care to get again into the whirlpool of political life."[59]

Holt seems to have made only two things clear before his death with

Joseph Holt's gravestone in Stephensport, Kentucky.
Courtesy of Norvelle Wathen, Louisville, Kentucky.

regard to his burial wishes: he requested that his body be wrapped in an old battle flag he had kept since the war and that his remains be returned to Stephensport to be interred in the small family graveyard next to what was now Washington and Vanda's home. Both requests were granted. On August 3 Adjutant General George Ruggles transmitted orders from the commander of the army, now General John Schofield, to the commanding officer at nearby Fort Myer summoning at least one and preferably all available cavalry troops stationed there to Holt's home to escort his body to the fort, where a proper military service would be held in his honor. Later, with the War Department flag flying at half staff as a tribute to his contributions to the nation's life and survival, Holt's nephews Billy Sterett and Washington Dorsey Holt, who had joined Sterett in the capital immediately upon learning of their uncle's death, escorted Holt's remains home to Kentucky. There, on August 5, 1894, funeral services were conducted in the chapel Holt had built to honor his mother. According to his request, Joseph Holt's remains were then buried in the Holt family cemetery, where they were later marked by a massive, elegant memorial stone topped with a magnificent bronze eagle.[60]

EPILOGUE

Nothing is known of the condition in which Judge Holt left his worldly
affairs. While he was probably well off at the time of his death, he had
given away large amounts of property during his lifetime, for beneath
what was regarded by many as a severe and austere exterior was the
heart of a philanthropist who was ever doing good. —Washington
Evening Star, *August 2, 1894*

In the days after his death and before they escorted his
remains back to Stephensport, Billy Sterett and Washington Dorsey Holt
searched Joseph Holt's New Jersey Avenue home for a will. To their surprise and disappointment, none turned up, leaving them with no alternative but to formally declare their customarily meticulous uncle intestate.
Then, on August 26, 1895—just over a year after his death—a sealed en-
velope containing a small document that purported to be Holt's missing
will arrived in the mail from an unidentified source at the office of the District of Columbia's Registrar of Wills. This "will," which appeared to have
been witnessed by General William T. Sherman, Sherman's wife, Ellen, and
General Ulysses S. Grant (all of whom were now dead) named two women
as Holt's beneficiaries: Miss Josephine Holt Throckmorton of New York,
Holt's goddaughter and the daughter of Charles B. Throckmorton and
Fannie Hill Wickliffe, who was Margaret Wickliffe Holt's cousin; and Miss
Elizabeth (Lizzie) Hynes of Kentucky, now around sixty, who almost fifty
years earlier had become Holt's ward following the death of his first wife,
Mary Harrison Holt. Each woman was to receive fifty percent of his estate.[1]

Holt's nephews were stunned by this unexpected development and
immediately decided to contest the document's authenticity. On May 19,
1896, the Circuit Court of the District of Columbia began its examination
of the case. The trial lasted about three weeks, and news of the proceedings
was published widely in the press. Ultimately, the court declared the "will"
a forgery. And although representatives for Josephine Holt Throckmorton
later won on appeal (Hynes chose not to contest the district court's original
ruling), Holt's nephews took the case to the U.S. Supreme Court, which in
1901 reversed the appeals court's ruling and upheld the original one. The
case was then closed, and the controversy faded into oblivion.[2]

Many years later, Topsy Olds—who had played with little Mary and Rose
Holt when they and their parents visited the capital—recalled the will dispute. "It seemed such a pity," she wrote, "that one of his generous and

just nature and thorough knowledge of law should have left his affairs in a tangle that was the cause of so much controversy." Olds's point is well taken. Perhaps even more remarkable, however, especially given how little Holt is remembered today, is how much attention the sudden and mysterious appearance of the forged will attracted. It is clear that after nearly two decades of relatively quiet and reclusive retirement and then his death, Holt's name and memory elicited a considerable amount of interest, both positive and negative.[3]

Indeed, it is hardly an exaggeration to say that right into the twentieth century Holt remained a lightning rod for conflict, in connection not just with the events of the sectional contest and its aftermath but also with the way Americans would "remember" the war and Reconstruction over time. As is now well known, as the nineteenth century waned and white Americans came together around a new, imperialistic national agenda, a majority of them—northerners as well as southerners—yearned to put the Civil War and its bitter repercussions behind them. In order to do so, they rallied to a great extent around a narrative that obliterated the war's most morally challenging aspects: that it was fought over slavery, for example; that the ultimate goal of the Confederate rebellion was, in fact, the destruction of the United States; that Robert E. Lee had proved himself as much a "butcher" of his men as Ulysses Grant had appeared to be in the spring and summer of 1864; that in his invasion of Pennsylvania, Lee had sanctioned the wholesale kidnapping of free blacks, who were then sent south into bondage. Inspired in particular by resurgent former Confederates, many white Americans opted instead to focus on the common courage white soldiers on both sides of the struggle had displayed ("forgetting," in the process, that 10 percent of the Union army, at least, was black). Similarly, they drained most of the real substance from the question of why the war was fought in the first place, so that each side's cause seemed equally valid and no substantial difference remained between the South's "quest for independence" and the North's struggle to preserve the Union. In addition, with regard to Reconstruction, Andrew Johnson came to be understood by many as the true and worthy heir of the martyred Lincoln, in contrast with the vengeful, punitive, "negrophilic" Radical Republicans who had done their best to permanently crush the already vanquished South and to subordinate white Americans to politically and intellectually unprepared black ones. In the end, this narrative explained with relief, the Radicals had been overcome, whites (and especially white veterans) across the country had forgiven one another, blacks had been put back in their "proper place," and the reunited nation could move forward in "peace."[4]

On the day Joseph Holt died, the *Washington Post* remarked on his willingness to allow himself in the final years of his life to slip into obscurity. In fact, true obscurity for Holt would come, but only after these late nineteenth-century disputes over the memory of the Civil War and Reconstruction had played themselves out. Once the "reconciliationists" had achieved virtual dominance, however, there was basically no meaningful, respectable space left in the story for a Kentucky-born former slaveholder and leading light in the Southern Democratic Party who, in the context of the nation's greatest crisis, had turned bravely and with uncommon conviction away from his family, his section, and his party to embrace Lincoln, the Union, Emancipation, and Radical Reconstruction.

Initially, it is true, Holt's fans and his enemies competed vigorously over the memory of who he had been and what he had done for the nation. By the end of the first decade of the twentieth century, however—and in keeping with the perspective of the reconciliationists—Holt's enemies and their descendants (both figuratively and literally) had gained the advantage. Determined to preserve only those features of his story that comported well with the emerging narrative of the war and Reconstruction, they distilled Holt's eighty-seven years of life and his nearly twenty years of service to the federal government down to his supposedly essential malice toward his native South and its earnest defenders. Certainly one of the most vivid examples of this sort of distortion appears in a 1909 article by C. Wickliffe Yulee, the son of David Yulee, who had died in 1886. In it, Yulee made a point of discussing his father's wartime imprisonment primarily in the context of the former senator's previous friendship—and extended family relationship—with Holt, noting that any reasonable person would have expected Holt to speak up on David Yulee's behalf after the war rather than trying to have him convicted of treason. After all, Yulee insisted, prior to Holt's second wife's death the Yulee family had shown him many years of the sort of "affectionate hospitality which Southerners extend to all those who are of their family, by blood or marriage." And yet, instead of doing what he could to help his sister-in-law's husband—who had, after all, only followed Florida out of the Union because his faithfulness to his state required him to do so—Holt had been relentlessly cruel, keeping his former brother-in-law in prison as long as he possibly could and even threatening to have him put "to an ignominious death" as a traitor. To Yulee, as to so many other Americans in the early twentieth century, Holt's ferocious "nature" and his vindictiveness contrasted sharply with the gentle and wise benevolence of both Abraham Lincoln and Andrew Johnson, who were—like so many among the heroic leadership of the former Confederacy—"notable men, of a notable era . . . atoms of the upper or nether millstones, with which the Gods are slowly grinding out the destinies of the human race."[5]

As C. Wickliffe Yulee's article suggests, in the years after his death Holt's memory fell victim first to the efforts of reconciliationists who ably, and with reductionist precision, condemned him as a traitor both to the noble South and to Lincoln and Johnson, whose generous but judicious efforts to repair the national fabric he had supposedly viciously obstructed. Then, as the century progressed and the war and Reconstruction receded from view, Holt faded from historical memory almost entirely, leaving only a lingering caricature that was preserved by students of the Lincoln assassination: Holt as the bitter, self-interested former slaveholder who oversaw the brutal "judicial murder" of Mary Surratt. There were, of course, some who strove all along to preserve his complex memory whole and intact, including the descendants of Vanda and Washington Dorsey Holt, to whom Holt left his enormous archive of personal and professional papers. After Washington himself died in May 1906, his daughter Mary and her husband, attorney Walter Malins Rose, deposited more than eighty cartons of Holt's papers at the Library of Congress in Washington, D.C. Additions to this collection were made by their son, Joseph Holt Rose Sr., in the 1950s, bringing the number of containers up to 117, filling thirty-one linear feet of shelf space. In the 1970s, Joseph Holt Rose Sr. gave eight additional boxes of papers to the Huntington Library in San Marino, California. But he held on to some particularly precious items, including a number of artifacts that he later entrusted to the care of his children.[6]

Meanwhile, in November 1910 Vanda Vineyard Holt—who had done so much to restore Holt's relations with at least one branch of his once pro-slavery, pro-Confederate Kentucky family—sold the Stephensport mansion and about 500 acres of the surrounding farmland for $25,000, her daughter Mary Holt Rose having settled in California, and her other daughter, Rose (who became Rose Holt Luckett), having moved to New York. "She hated to part with it, but there was nothing else to do," recalled Joseph Holt Rose Sr. in 1956. For many years the house belonged to a family with the last name of Dutschke, who seemed, Joseph Holt Rose Sr. noted in the mid-1950s, "to take considerable pride in its traditions." By the late 1960s, however, the house had been resold again and then finally vacated, though it still stands, unlike the chapel Holt built in his mother's memory, which was torn down in 1987. In contrast is the family graveyard on the property; lovingly preserved by Thomas Holt's California descendants, it remains in excellent condition. In order that a more accurate version of Joseph Holt's life story might be similarly preserved, I have written this book.[7]

NOTES

Abbreviations

The following abbreviations are used throughout the notes.

HFPC	Holt Family Private Collection, held by Dr. Joseph Holt Rose, Pasadena, California
Holt Papers, Huntington	Joseph Holt Papers, Huntington Library, San Marino, California
Holt Papers, LC	Joseph Holt Papers, Library of Congress, Washington, D.C.
JHRS	Joseph Holt Rose Scrapbook, held by Dr. Joseph Holt Rose, Pasadena, California
Lincoln Papers, LC	Abraham Lincoln Papers, Library of Congress, Washington, D.C. (http://memory.loc.gov/ammem/ alhtml/malhome.html [accessed December 7, 2009])
OR	*War of the Rebellion: A Compilation of the Official Records of the Union and Confederate Armies* (Washington, D.C.: Government Printing Office, 1880–1901)

Preface

1. See Leonard, *Yankee Women*. Walker's medal—along with those of several hundred soldiers—was revoked in 1917 when Congress revised the award's definition to include combat experience, but Walker herself never acknowledged Congress's decision. She died in 1919. Her medal was reinstated in the 1970s.

2. See Leonard, *Lincoln's Avengers*. See also Mary E. Walker to Joseph Holt, August 16, 1890; August 20, 1890; August 27, 1890; September 28, 1890; and December 29, 1890, container 88; and December 1, 1893, container 92, Holt Papers, LC.

3. Thomas and Rosina's son was Washington Dorsey Holt. Washington and his wife, Vanda Vineyard Holt, had two daughters, Mary and Rose. Mary Holt married Walter Malins Rose, and their son, Joseph Holt Sr., was the father of Cathy and her siblings. See Cathy Rose to Elizabeth D. Leonard, March 4, 2006, author's private collection.

4. See Leonard, "One Kentuckian's Hard Choice," 373–407.

Chapter One

1. Levin, *Lawyers and Lawmakers of Kentucky*, 7–14, 22.

2. Ibid., 8; Little, *Ben Hardin*, 17–18.

3. Coulter, *The Civil War and Readjustment*, 5–8; Perrin, Battle, and Kniffin, *Kentucky*, 1:286. In 1810, the total population of Breckinridge County, white and black, was 3,430. (Collins, *History of Kentucky*, 2:258, 260.)

4. This is an estimate, as I have been unable to find conclusive census material on Stephens's slaveholdings. But his son-in-law, John W. Holt, who had far less

land, is shown in 1810 to have owned eight slaves. Surely Richard Stephens owned at least half again as many, and quite possibly many more than that.

5. See document headed "An Explanation," prepared by Margaret Bowmer Minary of Benton Harbor, Mich., in 1939, HFPC. See also the document headed "Richard Stephens," and Joseph Holt Rose to Alice Thomas, May 27, 1982, HFPC; and Daniel Stephens to Joseph Holt, March 29, 1834, container 3, Holt Papers, LC. Little is known about Stephens's early life beyond that he was a descendant of English colonists and was born in Loudon County on September 7, 1855, to Richard Stephens Sr. and Eleanor King Stephens, the daughter of John and Mary Osborne King. While a number of people have claimed (and Holt family lore agrees) that Stephens became the "youngest captain in George Washington's army," the historical record does not support the claim. See James Holt to Joseph Holt, December 23, 1832, container 3, Holt Papers, LC; *Hardinsburg County (Ky.) Frontier News*, April 15, 1987; Little, *Ben Hardin*, 7; James Dozier to Joseph Holt, September 1, 1826, container 1, Holt Papers, LC; *Breckinridge County (Ky.) Herald-News*, March 23, 1988; and http://apps .sos.ky.gov/land/military/revwar/Revdetail.asp?Type=v&warrant=2413.0 (accessed September 2, 2009).

6. Elizabeth Jennings was born on July 9, 1759, to Daniel Jennings and Ann Williams Jennings. See "Richard Stephens," HFPC. The Jennings (alternatively, Jenings) family also traced its roots back to England. See J. Jenings to Joseph Holt, May 15, 1850; brochure about the "Jennings Estate"; Mary Ann Stephens to Joseph Holt, May 1850, container 13, Holt Papers, LC.

7. Eleanor Stephens married John W. Holt on July 5, 1803. See various documents in HFPC; the undated article produced by the Hardin County Historical Society, entitled "Who Was Who in Hardin County," JHRS; *Breckinridge County (Ky.) Herald-News*, April 6, 1988. A typed document in the HFPC, entitled "Holt Family History," lists a Joseph Holt of Albemarle County, Virginia—probably John Holt's father—as the first American member of the family. On the Holt side of the family and its involvement in the Revolution, see James Holt to Joseph Holt, December 23, 1832, container 3, Holt Papers, LC.

8. Various documents in HFPC; *Breckinridge County (Ky.) Herald-News*, March 16, 1988, and March 23, 1988; Breckinridge County Census for 1810; undated, unidentified article from the private collection of Norvelle Wathen of Louisville, Kentucky; Johnson, *History of Kentucky and Kentuckians* 3:1381.

9. Bartman, "The Contribution of Joseph Holt," 6; Haycraft, *History of Elizabethtown*, 81; Little, *Ben Hardin*, 168; *Breckinridge County (Ky.) Herald-News*, March 16, 1988; undated article produced by the Hardin County Historical Society entitled "Who Was Who in Hardin County," JHRS; Collins, *History of Kentucky*, 2:376.

10. *Breckinridge County (Ky.) Herald-News*, March 23, 1988; document labeled "Copied from the Old Stephens Bible," HFPC; Allen, "Joseph Holt," 47; Richard Holt to Joseph Holt, June 6, 1824; J. Jenings to Joseph Holt, July 20, 1826; Richard Holt to Joseph Holt, November 15, 1824, container 1, Holt Papers, LC; Collins, *History of Kentucky*, 2:772; and Haycraft, *History of Elizabethtown*, 154.

11. Daniel Stephens, insert, in Robert Stephens to Joseph Holt, July 20, 1824;

Richard Stephens to Joseph Holt, undated but probably summer 1824, container 1, Holt Papers, LC.

12. Little, *Ben Hardin*, 27, 161; Herbermann et al., *The Catholic Encyclopedia* 5:372; Perrin, Battle, and Kniffin, *Kentucky*, 2:991.

13. A document in container 1 of the Holt Papers, LC, dated April 18, 1826, provides a record of Joseph Holt's ongoing account with his grandfather and includes expenses for tuition, room and board, and travel while he was in school. See also the August 29, 1823, document beginning, "Received of Richard Stephens"; Richard Stephens to Joseph Holt, undated but probably late summer 1824; Robert Stephens to Joseph Holt, February 15, 1824, container 1, Holt Papers, LC. See also Bartman, "The Contribution of Joseph Holt," 8.

14. Collins, *History of Kentucky*, 1:489; Ranck, *History of Lexington*, 191; *Breckinridge County (Ky.) Herald-News*, April 6, 1988.

15. George Elder to Joseph Holt, January 8, 1824, container 1, Holt Papers, LC.

16. Joseph Holt to George Elder, January 18, 1824, container 1, Holt Papers, LC.

17. Note by Joseph Holt appended to George Elder to Joseph Holt, January 2, 1824, container 1, Holt Papers, LC. On anti-Catholicism in mid-nineteenth-century America, see Knobel, *Paddy and the Republic*.

18. http://www.centre.edu/web/library/sc/history.html (accessed May 29, 2008); Robert Stephens to Joseph Holt, July 20, 1824; Richard S. Holt to Joseph Holt, November 15, 1824; Barnabas Hughes to Joseph Holt, August 19, 1825; Robert Stephens to Joseph Holt, May 20, 1824, container 1, Holt Papers, LC. See also Bartman, "The Contribution of Joseph Holt," 12; Little, *Ben Hardin*, 18. In the "heroic age" of Kentucky history, writes Lucius Little, "one of the gifts of leadership . . . was persuasive speech."

19. Richard S. Holt to Joseph Holt, August 23, 1826; Robert Stephens to Joseph Holt, July 20, 1824; Richard Stephens to Joseph Holt, undated but probably fall 1824, container 1, Holt Papers, LC.

20. Richard Holt to Joseph Holt, November 15, 1824; Richard Holt to Joseph Holt, February 1, 1825; and Richard Holt to Joseph Holt, June 18, 1826, container 1, Holt Papers, LC.

21. Daniel Stephens to Joseph Holt, July 20, 1824; Joseph Holt to James Holt, December 9, 1824; James Holt to Joseph Holt, May 14, 1827; Robert Stephens to Joseph Holt, February 15, 1824, container 1, Holt Papers, LC.

22. Barnabas Hughes to Joseph Holt, August 19, 1825; Daniel Stephens, insert in Robert Stephens to Joseph Holt, July 20, 1824; Daniel Stephens to Joseph Holt, October 20, 1824; Robert Wickliffe to Joseph Holt, January 22, 1825, container 1, Holt Papers, LC. See also Ranck, *History of Lexington*, 43; Johnson, *History of Kentucky and Kentuckians*, 2:170–71, 200; Collins, *History of Kentucky*, 5:200; and Levin, *Lawyers and Lawmakers of Kentucky*, 627.

23. Ranck, *History of Lexington*, i, 40, 56, 57, 205; Perrin, Battle, and Kniffin, *Kentucky*, 1:287–88; Collins, *History of Kentucky*, 2:258, 260, 263.

24. Jefferson Dorsey to Joseph Holt, December 23, 1826; James Dozier to Joseph Holt, September 1, 1826, container 1, Holt Papers, LC.

25. Little, *Ben Hardin*, 23; Robert Wickliffe to Joseph Holt, January 22, 1825; Jefferson Dorsey to Joseph Holt, December 23, 1826, container 1, Holt Papers, LC. See also Joseph Holt to Daniel or Robert Stephens, June 11, 1826, Holt Papers, Huntington.

26. J. Jenings to Joseph Holt, July 30, 1826; Daniel Stephens to Joseph Holt, June 2, 1827, container 1, Holt Papers, LC.

27. Richard Stephens to Joseph Holt, undated but probably fall 1826; Richard Stephens to Joseph Holt, November 27, 1826; Richard Stephens to Joseph Holt, September 9, 1826; John W. Holt to Joseph Holt, October 31, 1826; Robert Stephens to Joseph Holt, March 20, 1827; Daniel Stephens to Joseph Holt, June 2, 1827; William Sterett to Joseph Holt, August 17, 1827; Richard Holt to Joseph Holt, August 17, 1827; Richard Holt to Joseph Holt, April 2, 1827, container 1, Holt Papers, LC. See also Collins, *History of Kentucky*, 2:772.

28. Joseph Holt to Daniel or Robert Stephens, June 11, 1826, Holt Papers, Huntington.

29. Robert Wickliffe to Joseph Holt, August 9, 1834, container 4; Jefferson Dorsey to Joseph Holt, January 3, 1829, June 10, 1830, and March 21, 1828, container 1, Holt Papers, LC.

30. See Richard S. Holt to Joseph Holt, February 1, 1825; J. B. Warren to Joseph Holt, November 20, 1828; Richard Stephens to Joseph Holt, November 27, 1826, container 1, Holt Papers, LC. See also Collins, *History of Kentucky*, 1:352 and 2:258, 260, 263, 645–47; Johnson, *History of Kentucky and Kentuckians*, 3:1180; Little, *Ben Hardin*, 14, 27, 31, 37, 38, 49, 150; Thomas, *Abraham Lincoln*, 5. See also the biographical sketch of Holt in container 117, Holt Papers, LC.

31. Collins, *History of Kentucky*, 2:647; Little, *Ben Hardin*, 578.

32. Hardin, wrote Lucius Little, not only "never came to respect General Jackson," but he also "ridiculed and denounced him quite sincerely." See Little, *Ben Hardin*, 150. See also Richard Stephens to Joseph Holt, 1829 (precise date unknown), container 1, Holt Papers, LC.

33. Quoted in Bartman, "The Contribution of Joseph Holt," 28–29. See also Perrin, Battle, and Kniffin, *Kentucky*, 311–20; Levin, *Lawyers and Lawmakers in Kentucky*, 29; Little, *Ben Hardin*, 105, 109, 149. See also William Sterett to Joseph Holt, June 19, 1824; Robert Stephens to Joseph Holt, November 26, 1824; Jefferson Dorsey to Joseph Holt, March 21, 1828, container 1; Robert Stephens to Joseph Holt, January 16, 1831, container 2, Holt Papers, LC; Egnal, *Clash of Extremes*, 35; Remini, *Henry Clay*, 281; Baxter, *Henry Clay and the American System*; Remini, *Andrew Jackson*.

34. On nullification, see Freehling, *Prelude to Civil War*.

35. On Garrison, see Mayer, *All on Fire*. On Nat Turner's Rebellion, see Oates, *The Fires of Jubilee*.

36. Collins, *History of Kentucky*, 2:259.

37. Bartman, "The Contribution of Joseph Holt," 64–73; Daniel Stephens in Robert Stephens to Joseph Holt, June 24, 1829, container 1, Holt Papers, LC.

38. Albert G. Hawes to Joseph Holt, December 5, 1830, container 2, Holt Papers,

LC. Hawes was re-elected twice thereafter before he returned to Kentucky and re-sumed life as a farmer in 1837. (Collins, *History of Kentucky*, 1:351.)

39. William Davis to Joseph Holt, April 12, 1831, and July 7, 1831, container 2, Holt Papers, LC. Wintersmith went on to serve in the state legislature in 1838 and 1847, and from 1851 to 1855. (Collins, *History of Kentucky*, 2:307) About a year after his tussle with Davis, Holt also had a conflict with one L. Singleton. See L. Single-ton to Joseph Holt, February 13, 1832, container 2, Holt Papers, LC.

40. C. F. M. Noland to Joseph Holt, January 9, 1834, container 3; C. F. M. Noland to Joseph Holt, April 7, 1834, container 4; C. F. M. Noland to Joseph Holt, Octo-ber 29, 1836, container 6, Holt Papers, LC. It is unclear how Noland and Holt met (Noland's home was in Arkansas), but they wrote frequently in the early years of Holt's career, and Noland remained a correspondent even as he himself went on to become a soldier, adventurer, and the author of stories such as "Pete Whetstone's Last Frolic." See also George Work to Joseph Holt, October 12, 1834, container 4, Holt Papers, LC.

41. Robert Stephens to Joseph Holt, undated but probably early 1832; document that begins, "The undersigned members of the Delegation from Lincoln," Septem-ber 11, 1832; Robert Stephens to Joseph Holt, undated but probably December 1830; Francis Peyton to Joseph Holt, January 26, 1831, container 2, Holt Papers, LC. It is unclear whether Holt chose to attack the national bank at this point, but he did in 1834, giving a speech at a state convention in which he celebrated the impending collapse of "the mammoth Bank and the British Lords and the American aristo-crats that sustained it." See Bartman, "The Contribution of Joseph Holt," 39–40. On Jackson and the bank, see Remini, *Andrew Jackson and the Bank War*.

42. Richard Holt to Joseph Holt, October 16, 1832, container 2; Thomas Chilton to Joseph Holt, January 18, 1830; Samuel S. English to Joseph Holt, December 16, 1829, container 1; John R. Stockman to Joseph Holt, July 15, 1831, and Septem-ber 11, 1831; George Work to Joseph Holt, September 9, 1831, container 2, Holt Papers, LC.

43. Richard Holt to Joseph Holt, April 18, 1829; Richard Stephens to Joseph Holt, undated, container 1; Robert Stephens to Joseph Holt, July 5, 1831, container 2, Holt Papers, LC.

44. William Sterett to Joseph Holt, October 26, 1826, and J. Jenings to Joseph Holt, February 5, 1827, container 1; John W. Tyler to Joseph Holt, June 30, 1834, con-tainer 5, Holt Papers, LC. See also Johnson, *History of Kentucky and Kentuckians*, 3:1381.

45. George Work to Joseph Holt, March 18, 1833, container 3; Addison Young to Joseph Holt, February 7, 1831, container 2; Addison Young to Joseph Holt, March 10, 1834, container 3, Holt Papers, LC.

46. Daniel Stephens to Joseph Holt, September 6, 1833, container 3; Albert G. Hawes to Joseph Holt, December 10, 1831, and Albert G. Hawes to Joseph Holt, January 2, 1832, container 2, Holt Papers, LC.

47. Mary Ann Stephens to Joseph Holt, June 8, 1832, container 2, Holt Papers, LC. Mary Ann's brother, Uncle Bob, worried about Holt's bachelorhood, too, in part

because he feared that if Holt failed to find a wife he might turn to prostitutes, if he had not done so already. See Robert Stephens to Joseph Holt, September 1833 (exact date unknown), container 3, Holt Papers, LC.

48. Daniel Stephens to Joseph Holt, March 29, 1834; Richard Holt to Joseph Holt, March 16, 1834, container 3; Daniel Stephens to Joseph Holt, October 16, 1832; Richard Holt to Joseph Holt, October 16, 1832, container 2, Holt Papers, LC. See also Collins, *History of Kentucky*, 2:355, 364; Trollope, *Domestic Manners of the Americans*, 47; *Breckinridge County (Ky.) Herald-News*, April 6, 1988; and Bartman, "The Contribution of Joseph Holt," 31.

49. Richard Holt to Joseph Holt, May 8, 1831; J. Jennings to Joseph Holt, June 3, 1831, container 2, Holt Papers, LC.

50. Albert G. Hawes to Joseph Holt, December 10, 1831, and January 15, 1832, container 2, Holt Papers, LC.

51. Daniel Stephens to Joseph Holt, September 6, 1833, June 25, 1833, and September 9, 1833, container 3, Holt Papers, LC.

52. Albert G. Hawes to Joseph Holt, January 2, 1832; Robert Stephens to Joseph Holt, February 14, 1832; Albert G. Hawes to Joseph Holt, February 19, 1832, and March 8, 1832, container 2, Holt Papers, LC. See also Robert Stephens to Joseph Holt, November 29, 1832, and Samuel Haycraft to Joseph Holt, January 2, 1833, container 3, Holt Papers, LC.

53. Bartman, "The Contribution of Joseph Holt," 39–41; Robert Stephens to Joseph Holt, undated, but evidence suggests early 1832, and George Work to Joseph Holt, October 22, 1832, container 2; and J. M. McCalen to Joseph Holt, March 12, 1833, container 3, Holt Papers, LC. See also the letter to Holt of September 11, 1832, container 2, signed by fourteen Democrats from Lincoln County, testifying to the brilliance of a speech he gave the previous day; Kleber, *The Encyclopedia of Louisville*, 655; Collins, *History of Kentucky*, 2:363.

54. James Holt to Joseph Holt, December 24, 1832, container 3; Albert G. Hawes to Joseph Holt, October 16, 1832; Daniel Stephens to Joseph Holt, October 16, 1832; Robert Stephens to Joseph Holt, October 16, 1832; George Work to Joseph Holt, October 22, 1832, container 2, Holt Papers, LC. Holt's cousin, Jefferson Jennings, recently elected to the state legislature from Breckinridge County (Collins, *History of Kentucky*, 2:772), also offered his help. See J. Jennings to Joseph Holt, December 13, 1832, and January 5, 1833; L. Landers to Joseph Holt, February 3, 1833, container 3, Holt Papers, LC. And see the *New York Times*, August 2, 1893; Bartman, "The Contribution of Joseph Holt," 33.

55. Bartman, "The Contribution of Joseph Holt," 34; Daniel Stephens to Joseph Holt, September 6, 1833; Lewis Helm to Joseph Holt, July 17, 1833, container 3; R. W. Snowden to Joseph Holt, July 26, 1834, container 4; Robert Holt to Joseph Holt, February 23, 1835, container 5, Holt Papers, LC. Robert, then a student at the university, informed his brother that a literary club to which he belonged had also decided to invite Holt to give a speech at an upcoming event. The last person to address the club, Robert noted, was South Carolina's John Faucheraud Grimké, a wealthy plantation owner and lawyer whose daughters Sarah and Angelina went on to become leaders in the abolitionist movement. See also L. H. Woodson to Joseph

Holt, December 12, 1834, container 4; John R. Stockman to Joseph Holt, January 24, 1834, container 3; Robert Holt to Joseph Holt, March 7, 1834, container 5, Holt Papers, LC.

56. Daniel Stephens to Joseph Holt, April 21, 1834, container 4, Holt Papers, LC.

57. Robert Stephens to Joseph Holt, July 17, 1832, container 2; Washington Dorsey to Joseph Holt, February 10, 1833, container 3, Holt Papers, LC.

58. C. F. M. Noland to Joseph Holt, June 21, 1834, container 4; Robert Holt to Joseph Holt, May 14, 1843, container 10, Holt Papers, LC. The 1832 city directory for Louisville lists only his office, no private address, which suggests that he was either living *in* his office or, more likely, renting a room in a boarding house.

59. Bartman, "The Contribution of Joseph Holt," 42; Robert Holt to Joseph Holt, May 27, 1834; Washington Dorsey to Joseph Holt, June 18, 1834; Robert Holt to Joseph Holt, May 27, 1834; Robert Holt to Joseph Holt, August 10, 1834; Robert Stephens to Joseph Holt, September 4, 1834, container 4, Holt Papers, LC; *Louisville City Directory*, 1832.

Chapter Two

1. Daniel Stephens to Joseph Holt, January 15, 1835, container 4; Robert Stephens to Joseph Holt, February 19, 1835, and March 17, 1835, container 5, Holt Papers, LC; see also the letter of introduction from Holt's cousin, David Holt, to Washington Irving, March 8, 1835, container 5, Holt Papers, LC.

2. Robert Stephens to Joseph Holt, September 4, 1834, container 4; Elizabeth Holt to Joseph Holt, March 11, 1835, container 5, Holt Papers, LC; 1830 Breckinridge County Census; *Breckinridge County (Ky.) Herald-News*, March 16, 1988, and March 23, 1988. The *Hardinsburg (Ky.) Frontier News* of April 15, 1987, indicates that the home John W. Holt built in around 1810 burned down, and this new one was constructed on the same site.

3. Elizabeth Holt to Joseph Holt, July 3, 1834, container 4, Holt Papers, LC; Perrin, Battle, and Kniffin, *Kentucky*, 2:923; Collins, *History of Kentucky*, 1:488. See also Robert Holt to Joseph Holt, October 20, 1836, container 6; Elizabeth Holt to Joseph Holt, March 13, 1836, and May 14, 1836, container 5; Robert Holt to Joseph Holt, September 24, 1833; Daniel Stephens to Joseph Holt, August 19, 1833; Robert Holt to Daniel Stephens, December 15, 1833, container 3, Holt Papers, LC; Kiddle and Schem, *Yearbook of Education for 1878*, 255; Rudolph, *The American College and University*, 113–14; Robert Holt to Joseph Holt, October 11, 1834, and October 26, 1834, container 4; Robert Holt to Joseph Holt, December 6, 1831, container 2; Robert Holt to Joseph Holt, September 24, 1833, container 3; James Holt to Joseph Holt, February 19, 1835, and July 16, 1835; Elizabeth Holt to Joseph Holt, March 11, 1835, container 5, Holt Papers, LC; Webb, *The Handbook of Texas*, 2:668.

4. Robert Holt to Joseph Holt, February 1, 1834, container 3; Robert Holt to Joseph Holt, July 5, 1835, container 5; Robert Holt to Joseph Holt, October 26, 1834, container 4; Daniel Stephens to Joseph Holt, June 11, 1836, container 5, Holt Papers, LC.

5. Daniel Stephens to Joseph Holt, September 6, 1833, container 3; Robert Ward Johnson to Martin Van Buren, May 9, 1835, container 5, Holt Papers, LC. See also

the *Richmond Enquirer*, May 26, 1835; and the *New Albany (Ind.) Ledger*, September 23, 1857. The party's first national convention had also been held in Baltimore in 1832.

6. There is some evidence that Johnson was personally responsible at the Battle of the Thames for the death of the Shawnee leader, Tecumseh. (Levin, *Lawyers and Lawmakers of Kentucky*, 568; Collins, *History of Kentucky*, 2:403–5.)

7. Bartman, "The Contribution of Joseph Holt," 48; handwritten copy of an article in the *Baltimore Republican and Commercial Advertiser* of May 25, 1835, container 5, Holt Papers, LC; *New York Times*, August 2, 1894; *New Albany (Ind.) Daily Ledger*, September 23, 1857.

8. Handwritten copy of an article on the speech, from the *Baltimore Republican and Commercial Advertiser* of May 25, 1835, container 5, Holt Papers, LC.

9. Both invitations are dated May 26, 1835, and are located in container 5, Holt Papers, LC. See also Richard M. Johnson to Joseph Holt, February 23, 1838, container 6; and Richard M. Johnson to Joseph Holt, January 14, 1839, container 7, Holt Papers, LC. In his January 14, 1839, letter, Johnson encouraged Holt to seek political office himself. "Can we not get you to come to Congress[?]" he wrote. As always, Holt's answer was "no." Johnson remained a faithful friend to Holt until his death in 1850. See also Bartman, "The Contribution of Joseph Holt," 63.

10. *New York Times*, August 2, 1894; Bartman, "The Contribution of Joseph Holt," 48; Robert Holt to Joseph Holt, July 5, 1835, container 5, Holt Papers, LC.

11. *St. Louis Daily Commercial Bulletin*, June 12, 1835; C. A. Harris to Joseph Holt, May 21, 1835, container 5, Holt Papers, LC; Ambrose, *Duty, Honor, Country*, 67–68, 80; *Register of the Officers and Cadets of the U. S. Military Academy, 1835*, United States Military Academy Library, Special Collections, West Point, New York.

12. *New York Times*, August 2, 1894; Bartman, "The Contribution of Joseph Holt," 51; John T. Stuart to Joseph Holt, February 28, 1835; William M. Gwin to Powhatan Ellis, October 10, 1835, container 5, Holt Papers, LC.

13. Perrin, Battle, and Kniffin, *Kentucky*, 320–21; T. J. Pew to Joseph Holt, December 11, 1835; John R. Stockman to Joseph Holt, August 21, 1835; Robert Holt to Joseph Holt, July 5, 1835, and December 18, 1835, container 5, Holt Papers, LC.

14. Robert Holt to Joseph Holt, July 5, 1835, container 5; Jefferson Jennings to Joseph Holt, June 25, 1833, container 3; Robert Holt to Joseph Holt, January 18, 1836; Eleanor Holt to Joseph Holt, January 31, 1836, and March 19, 1836; Elizabeth Holt to Joseph Holt, March 13, 1836, container 5, Holt Papers, LC. Some of Holt's family members and friends also worried that his personality and tastes were not well suited to life in the Deep South. For her part, Holt's mother had trouble imagining her son at ease among congenial, sociable Mississippians. (Eleanor Holt to Joseph Holt, January 31, 1836, container 5, Holt Papers, LC.) In contrast, Holt's friend A. E. Addison expected that the refined and intellectual Holt would find Mississippians intolerably coarse. "There is a kind of bullying gasconad[e] of manner en vogue not at all to my taste," Addison wrote, and probably not to Holt's either. "It is not uncommon," he continued, "to see a man traveling about with a pair of pistols and a Bowie knife at a time when he has no idea of an attack." Most men in the state were armed at all times, he added, "with dirks & pistols," and even the law-

yers and other professional men with whom Holt was likely to interact tended to be "uncultivated and rough in their manner & appearance." Still, Addison pointed out, it was precisely these sorts of people who generated the abundant litigation upon which lawyers could grow rich. (A. E. Addison to Joseph Holt, April 21, 1835, and July 12, 1835, container 5, Holt Papers, LC.)

15. Bartman, "The Contribution of Joseph Holt," 53–58; Mary Bernard Allen, "Joseph Holt," 48–49; Levin, *Lawyers and Lawmakers of Kentucky*, 624–25. According to Levin, Clay chose Harrison to be one of the executors of his will (ibid.). See also *Breckinridge News*, August 6, 1894, JHRS.

16. Daniel Stephens to Joseph Holt, March 28, 1836, container 6; Daniel Stephens to Joseph Holt, June 11, 1836, container 5; Richard M. Johnson to Joseph Holt, May 11, 1838, container 7, Holt Papers, LC. See also Allen, "Joseph Holt," 49; and see the invitation from A. T. Moore and others from Canton, Mississippi, representing Madison County, on August 28, 1840, container 8, Holt Papers, LC. Black's seat then passed to another Jacksonian, James F. Trotter.

17. Jacob Fox to Joseph Holt, January 24, 1839, container 7, Holt Papers, LC.

18. Joseph Holt to George Work, March 6, 1833, container 3, Holt Papers, LC.

19. George Work to Joseph Holt, October 12, 1834, and January 19, 1835, container 4; Daniel Stephens to Joseph Holt, March 28, 1836, container 6; Joseph Holt to Mary Harrison, September 24, 1836; November 3, 1836; and November 5, 1836, container 98, Holt Papers, LC; Collins, *History of Kentucky*, 2:645. On nineteenth-century American courtship, see Lystra, *Searching the Heart*.

20. Mary Harrison to Joseph Holt, January 1, 1837, container 98; John B. Lapsley to Joseph Holt, January 17, 1838, container 6; John W. Tyler to Joseph Holt, June 30, 1836, container 5, Holt Papers, LC.

21. Various items in the HFPC document this. See also *Breckinridge County (Ky.) Herald-News*, March 16, 1988; Bartman, "The Contribution of Joseph Holt," 61–62; Engerman and Gallman, *The Long Nineteenth Century*, 157. Despite Bardstown's relative proximity to Stephensport, members of Holt's family were not present at the wedding. Indeed, for reasons that are unclear, they were not even entirely sure the wedding was actually going to take place, though they had heard the rumors. Two months after the ceremony, Holt's brother Thomas commented that he had just got wind of the wedding from their mother, Eleanor, who had only recently learned of it from Holt himself. Thomas did not seem disappointed, however: "The family was all glad to [know] that it was the fact," he wrote, and he reassured his brother that "we all feel proud of our new relative." (See Thomas Holt to Joseph Holt, June 16, 1839, container 7; J. B. Lapsley to Joseph Holt, January 17, 1838, container 6; Robert Holt to Joseph Holt, August 24, 1838, and September 13, 1838, container 7, Holt Papers, LC.) Like her thirty-two-year-old husband, Mary was several years older than most women in this period at the time of first marriage.

Professional success did not come easily to Robert, who also struggled with his health, which he blamed on Mississippi's climate. One wonders how much the mercury-based treatments he occasionally received for his unidentified ailments could possibly have helped. On one occasion Robert explained that the treatment had resulted in a series of energy-draining "salivations," the mercury having "formed so strong a lodgment in my system that my salivation returns with every rain, and the shooting pains which herald the rising of the cloud even before it is seen promise to make me quite a weather oracle." (Robert Holt to Joseph Holt, October 16, 1840, container 8, Holt Papers, LC.)

22. George Work to Joseph Holt, October 27, 1838; William P. Duval to Joseph Holt, September 2, 1839, container 7; Burr Harrison to Joseph and Mary Harrison Holt, January 20, 1842, container 9; Sarah Harrison to Joseph Holt, June 13, 1840, container 8, Holt Papers, LC.

23. Mary Harrison, insert in Sarah Harrison to Joseph Holt, June 13, 1840, container 8, Holt Papers, LC; Collins, *History of Kentucky*, 2:264; *Breckinridge County (Ky.) Herald-News*, April 6, 1988; *Louisville City Directory*, 1844–45 and 1845–46. Holt may have received this house in return for some claims he had against one J. W. Tyler. See J. W. Tyler to Joseph Holt, July 14, 1841, container 9, Holt Papers, LC; and (regarding the repairs and remodeling) J. Eliot to Joseph Holt, January 1, 1842, and May 6, 1842, container 9, Holt Papers, LC.

24. Ironically, it was right around this time that the Holt family's elegant mansion in Stephensport was severely damaged by a fire that started in an upstairs room occupied by his unmarried aunt, Mary Ann Stephens. See Daniel Stephens to Joseph Holt, April 18, 1836, and June 11, 1836, container 5; Richard Holt to Joseph Holt, June 6, 1824, and November 11, 1824, container 1, Holt Papers LC. See also Mary Ann Stephens to Joseph Holt, undated but probably spring 1832, container 3; Mary Ann Stephens to Joseph Holt, June 8, 1832, container 2; and Mary Ann Stephens to Joseph Holt, March 28, 1840, container 7; Thomas Holt to Joseph Holt, March 3, 1842 [says 1841], container 8; Robert Holt to Joseph Holt, March 3, 1842, and March 29, 1842, container 9; C. Pirtle to Joseph Holt, June 11, 1849, container 13; Joseph Holt to Eleanor Holt, November 1845 (precise date unknown), container 11; James O. Harrison to Joseph Holt, July 10, 1843, container 10; Robert Holt to Joseph Holt, May 8, 1842, container 9, Holt Papers, LC.

25. C. Pirtle to Joseph Holt, March 11, 1836, container 12, Thomas Holt to Joseph Holt, October 9, 1840, container 9; Thomas Holt to Joseph Holt, April 7, 1841, container 8; George Robards to Joseph Holt, February 2, 1844, February 17, 1844, and February 25, 1844, container 10; Robert Holt to Joseph Holt, April 3, 1836, container 5; and Thomas Holt to Joseph Holt, July 4, 1837, container 6, Holt Papers, LC. The Nelson County Census for 1810 shows Burr Harrison owning six slaves; in 1820, he owned eighteen, ranging in age from under fourteen to over forty-five. The manuscript census pages that contain Harrison's slaveholding figures in 1830 and 1840 are, unfortunately, illegible.

26. Martin, *The Anti-Slavery Movement in Kentucky*, 94; Thomas Holt to Joseph Holt, April 4, 1840; Robert Holt to Joseph Holt, April 12, 1840, and April 6, 1840, container 7; Robert Holt to Joseph Holt, May 13, 1840, container 8, Holt Papers, LC.

27. Little, *Ben Hardin*, 540; Thomas Holt to Joseph Holt, June 4, 1840, and April 7, 1841, container 8, Holt Papers, LC.

28. Even his kindly sister Elizabeth—who had married Holt's old friend Will Sterett in December 1840 following the death of Sterett's first wife, Elizabeth Dorsey—was not so kind when it came to her slaves, especially Ellen, whom she

considered a thief. When Ellen's former owner, J. M. Chilton, informed Holt that Ellen had absconded with some of the family's linen sheets when he sold her, her husband Joshua, and the couple's children (J. M. Chilton to Joseph Holt, September 19, 1840, container 9, Holt Papers, LC), Elizabeth was quick to believe the accusation. Although she described Ellen as "assuredly a most *excellent* servant," whose faults were few, Elizabeth was nevertheless sure she was guilty of taking the Chiltons' sheets. To her credit, Elizabeth also believed that there might be a reasonable explanation for Ellen stealing in the first place, one that had nothing to do with bad character. "I do not think she would practice pilfering," Elizabeth wrote, "and might have done it in that instance, from thinking she had not received her dues." (Elizabeth Holt to Joseph Holt, November 18, 1840, container 8, Holt Papers, LC.)

29. Daniel Stephens to Joseph Holt, September 6, 1841, September 30, 1841, and October 20, 1841; Thomas Holt to Joseph Holt, September 28, 1841, container 9, Holt Papers, LC.

30. Thomas Holt to Joseph Holt, May 16, 1843, container 10; Charlotte E. [illegible] to Joseph Holt, April 28, 1842, container 9; Mary Harrison Holt to Joseph Holt, September 24, 1839, container 98; Samuel Forwood to Joseph Holt, April 10, 1843; George Robards to Joseph Holt, February 2, 1844, February 17, 1844, and February 25, 1844, container 10; Llewellyn Powell to Joseph Holt, February 10, 1845, and August 1, 1845, container 11, Holt Papers, LC.

31. George Robards to Joseph Holt, February 2, 1844, container 10, Holt Papers, LC.

32. George Robards to Joseph Holt, February 2, 1844, and February 25, 1844; Thomas Holt to Joseph Holt, April 2, 1844, and May 16, 1844, container 10; Thomas Holt to Joseph Holt, April 20, 1845, and May 6, 1845; Eleanor Holt to Joseph Holt, February 15, 1845, container 11, Holt Papers, LC.

33. Thomas H. Holt to Joseph Holt, March 6, 1842; James O. Harrison to Joseph Holt, June 17, 1842; Robert Holt to Joseph Holt, May 8, 1842, container 9, Holt Papers, LC.

34. Perhaps he even accepted the invitation that came in the summer of 1844 from "the democracy" of Kentucky's Anderson County, who sought to engage him as an opponent in a debate with none other than his former law partner, the now ardent Whig, Ben Hardin, "on the great questions now dividing the political parties of the country." See George W. Kavanaugh et al. to Joseph Holt, July 2, 1844, container 10, Holt Papers, LC. See also the invitations from the "Democracy of Tennessee" and the "Democracy of Kentucky" to address mass meetings in the summer of 1844, container 10, Holt papers, LC.

35. Thomas H. Holt to Joseph Holt, April 29, 1845, container 11, Holt Papers, LC. In March 1844 a physician friend worried that Holt might be suffering from "either an abscess in the right lung, or a slight affusion of serum (water) in the side," and he recommended that Holt undergo a thorough chest examination "to ascertain certainly the condition of the right lobe of the lung." (E. Pickett to Joseph Holt, March 26, 1844, container 10, Holt Papers, LC.) Some time later, Holt's cousin, Dr. Washington Dorsey, indicated that the earlier doctor's diagnosis had been wrong: "I am much gratified," Dorsey wrote, "to learn that you have no organic dis-

ease of the lungs." But even he noted that Holt's lung tissue exhibited some "adhesions"—possibly a precursor of tuberculosis—that he did not consider necessarily life threatening, but which were undoubtedly a persistent source of discomfort. (Washington Dorsey to Joseph Holt, August 23, 1845, container 11, Holt Papers, LC.)

36. Washington Dorsey to Joseph Holt, January 5, 1842, and January 7, 1842, container 9; Burr Harrison to Joseph and Mary Holt, March 30, 1843, container 10; Burr Harrison to Mary Harrison Holt, February 24, 1843, container 9; Holt diary, folder 1, container 102; Thomas Holt to Joseph Holt, May 16, 1843, container 10; Robert Holt to Joseph Holt, November 29, 1843, Thomas H. Holt to Joseph Holt, January 10, 1844; Mary Harrison Holt to Joseph Holt, August 15, 1844, container 10; Robert Holt to Joseph Holt, March 6, 1843, container 9; Robert Holt to Joseph Holt, November 15, 1844, container 10, Holt Papers, LC.

37. Thomas Read to Joseph Holt, January 18, 1845; Ignatius A. Reynolds to Joseph Holt, May 25, 1845; Eleanor Holt to Joseph Holt, February 15, 1845; Mary Harrison Holt to Joseph Holt, undated but probably summer 1845; Joseph Holt to Eleanor Holt, November 1845 (precise date unknown), container 11; C. Pirtle to Joseph Holt, March 11, 1846, container 12; Washington Dorsey to Joseph Holt, August 23, 1845, container 11; M. C. Kavanaugh to Joseph Holt, May 23, 1846; Eleanor Holt to Joseph Holt, February 23, 1846, container 12; Robert Holt to Joseph Holt, October 6, 1845; and Eleanor Holt to Joseph Holt, February 15, 1845, container 11, Holt Papers, LC. On nineteenth-century women's health, and particularly pregnancy, see Wertz and Wertz, *Lying In*.

38. Eleanor Holt to Joseph Holt, April 30, 1845, container 11; H. H. Kavanaugh to Joseph Holt, June 1, 1846, container 12, Holt Papers, LC.

39. James O. Harrison to Joseph Holt, May 30, 1846, container 12, Holt Papers, LC. Six weeks later, however, Harrison did express delight that Holt was apparently becoming more focused on religious matters. "Even our old nurse Betty," he wrote in early July, "shouted with joy when she heard that you had fixed your affections on a better world." (James O. Harrison to Joseph Holt, July 8, 1846, container 12, Holt Papers, LC. See also Robert Holt to Joseph Holt, June 5, 1846, container 12, Holt Papers, LC.)

40. Joseph Holt to Eleanor Holt, November 1845; Thomas Holt to Joseph Holt, April 20, 1845; James O. Harrison to Joseph Holt, November 11, 1845; M. C. Johnson to Joseph Holt, July 29, 1845, container 11, Holt Papers, LC.

41. After the funeral Holt decided to send his late wife's beloved horses and pony to Stephensport, where Thomas promised to care for them as she would have done. For his part, Bull the dog had already taken off. "I regret to inform you," a friend in Louisville wrote just a couple of months before Mary died, "that your dog Bull could not be prevailed upon to stay at home. When Mr. J. H. Coleman filled your ice house he requested me to have him locked up while they were unloading the ice &c. I did so, and his honor seemed to be unsettled. He took himself off and was gone a week and finally after going and returning for some several different times he left us with chain & block fast to him." This same friend informed Holt that he had not

seen Bull for several weeks, and indeed there is no indication that the dog ever returned. See C. Pirtle to Joseph Holt, March 11, 1846, container 12, Holt Papers, LC.

42. Daniel Stephens to Joseph Holt, June 11, 1836, container 5, Holt Papers, LC. Most Kentuckians had enthusiastically supported America's war with Mexico, some 10,000 more of them volunteering for duty in the army than could be enlisted. (Perrin, Battle, and Kniffin, *Kentucky*, 2:337.)

43. Thomas Holt to Joseph Holt, June 13, 1846, container 12; James Holt to Joseph Holt, July 18, 1843, container 10; Robert Stephens to Joseph Holt, July 22, 1845; Eleanor Holt to Joseph Holt, August 14, 1845, container 11; Robert Holt to Joseph Holt, August 1, 1846, and August 19, 1847, container 12; Robert Holt to Joseph Holt, May 5, 1848, container 13; James O. Harrison to Joseph Holt, July 8, 1846, container 12, Holt Papers, LC.

44. Margaret C. Kavanaugh to Joseph Holt, June 30, 1846; T. Rucker to Joseph Holt, June 22, 1846, container 12, Holt Papers, LC.

45. Robert Holt to Joseph Holt, July 27, 1846, and August 19, 1847, container 12, Holt Papers, LC; McChord, *The McChords of Kentucky*, 23–29; Sarah Harrison to Joseph Holt, June 27, 1846; Elizabeth Hynes to Joseph Holt, undated but probably May or June 1847, container 12; Elizabeth Hynes to Joseph Holt, May 15, 1850, container 13, Holt Papers, LC.

46. Burr Harrison to Joseph and Mary Harrison Holt, January 20, 1842, container 9; J. F. Coons to Joseph Holt, June 16, 1846, and June 20, 1846, container 12; Cuthbert H. Bain to Holt, February 3, 1850, and March 18, 1850, container 13; J. F. Coons to Joseph Holt, November 19, 1849; Cuthbert H. Bain to Joseph Holt, December 11, 1849, and December 24, 1849, container 98; Cuthbert H. Bain to Joseph Holt, February 3, 1850, March 18, 1850, and July 1850 (exact date unknown); Sarah Harrison to Joseph Holt, September 6, 1850, container 13; J. F. Coons to Joseph Holt, March 4, 1852; Sarah Harrison to Joseph Holt, March 12, 1852, and June 23, 1852, container 14; Sarah Harrison to Joseph Holt, January 11, 1853, and September 21, 1853, container 15; Sarah Harrison to Joseph Holt, October 29, 1849, container 98, folder 3; Sarah Harrison to Joseph Holt, June 27, 1846, and May 1847 (exact date unknown); R. C. McChord to Joseph Holt, May 6, 1847, container 12; Sarah Harrison to Joseph Holt, March 1, 1848, container 13; Elizabeth Hynes to Joseph Holt, undated but probably spring 1847; Elizabeth Hynes to Joseph Holt, June 1847 (exact date unknown); Elizabeth Hynes to Joseph Holt, September 25, 1847, container 12; and Elizabeth Hynes to Joseph Holt, November 2, 1849, container 98, folder 3, Holt Papers, LC.

47. "Family Tree," HFPC; Mary Ann Stephens to Joseph Holt, in Thomas Holt to Joseph Holt, January 27, 1848; Robert Holt to Joseph Holt, February 29, 1848, container 12; Thomas H. Holt to Joseph Holt, January 10, 1844, container 10; C. Pirtle to Joseph Holt, June 11, 1849, container 13, Holt Papers, LC.

48. Robert Holt to Joseph Holt, May 5, 1848; Henry Clay to "To Whom It May Concern," April 11, 1848, container 13, Holt Papers, LC. Two years before Clay died, Holt sent him a gift of a cane (*Washington Constitution*, May 1, 1850), which is still part of the collection of Clay's personal effects at his magnificently preserved

home, Ashland, in Lexington, Kentucky. A newspaper clipping in a letter from Margaret Wickliffe Holt's sister Nannie to Margaret (May 28, 1850, container 13, Holt Papers, LC) describes the event as follows: "Joseph Holt Esq., formerly one of the most eminent lawyers and orators of Mississippi, but since retired and living on a large fortune in Louisville, Ky, has presented the Hon. Henry Clay with a beautiful, gold headed, highly ornamental cane, cut at Thermopylae, Greece, near the tumelas, where it is supposed Leonidas and his 300 Spartans are buried. Holt has been the political opponent of Mr. Clay through life." See also Ignatius Reynolds to Joseph Holt, April 18, 1848; Richard M. Johnson to "Gentlemen," April 2, 1848, container 13, Holt Papers, LC.

49. See the Arabic document, dated January 20, 1849, container 13; biographical sketch, container 117, Holt Papers, LC. See also James O. Harrison to Joseph Holt, May 22, 1849; Robert Holt to Joseph Holt, June 3, 1848; Mary Ann Stephens to Joseph Holt, May 15, 1848, July 11, 1848, and July 17, 1848, container 13, Holt Papers, LC.

50. Joseph Holt to Rosina Holt, June 4, 1849, Holt Papers, Huntington.

51. Joseph Holt to Rosina Holt, June 4, 1849, Holt Papers, Huntington.

52. Howard Crosby to Joseph Holt, May 24, 1853, container 15; Howard Crosby to Joseph Holt, December 12, 1848, container 13, Holt Papers, LC. See also Howard Crosby to Joseph Holt, July 24, 1848, container 13, Holt Papers, LC; and Howard Crosby to Joseph Holt, February 4, 1849, container 98, folder 3, Holt Papers, LC.

53. Sarah Harrison to Joseph Holt, October 29, 1849, container 98, folder 3, Holt Papers, LC; Little, *Ben Hardin*, 204–12, 546; Collins, *History of Kentucky*, 1:60; Levin, *Lawyers and Lawmakers of Kentucky*, 332.

54. Elizabeth Hynes to Joseph Holt, May 15, 1850; Sarah Harrison to Joseph Holt, September 6, 1850, container 13; Julia Wickliffe to Margaret Wickliffe Holt, March 6, 1851, container 14, Holt Papers, LC; McChord, *The McChords of Kentucky*, 12.

55. Joseph Holt to Margaret Wickliffe, December 30, 1849, container 98, folder 3; James O. Harrison to Joseph Holt, April 1, 1850; J. F. Coons to Joseph Holt, April 2, 1850; Charles A. Wickliffe to Daniel Webster, April 4, 1850, container 13, Holt Papers, LC.

56. Mary Ann Stephens to Joseph Holt, May 1850 (exact date unknown); Elizabeth Hynes to Joseph Holt, May 15, 1850, container 13, Holt Papers, LC; Guide to the David Levy Yulee Papers at the University of Florida; Kleber, *The Kentucky Encyclopedia*, 65; Bartman, "The Contribution of Joseph Holt," 78. See also Nannie Wickliffe Yulee to Margaret Wickliffe Holt, July 8, 1850, container 13; Julia Wickliffe to Margaret Wickliffe Holt, March 6, 1851, container 14, Holt Papers, LC; Little, *Ben Hardin*, 212.

57. Howard Crosby to Joseph Holt, April 16, 1850; Charles A. Wickliffe to Daniel Webster, April 4, 1850; Henry Clay to William Cabell Rives, April 16, 1850; Henry Clay to Joseph Holt, April 16, 1850; Jefferson Jennings to Joseph Holt, May 15, 1850; printed document labeled "The Jennings Estate"; printed document entitled "Jennings Family Convention, Charlottesville, Virginia, May 15, 1850"; Mary

Ann Stephens to Joseph Holt, undated but probably June 1850, container 13, Holt Papers, LC.

58. Anne Dawson Wickliffe to Margaret Wickliffe Holt, May 28, 1850, and November 2, 1850, container 13, Holt Papers, LC. Charles Wickliffe missed his beloved daughter, too, although he noted that having Anne's child around the house provided some consolation. "Dear sweet Mag," he wrote with wry humor, "looks more like her Aunt Margaret than she does like me. I will not complain of this." (Charles A. Wickliffe to Margaret Wickliffe Holt, June 17, 1850, container 13, Holt Papers, LC.) See also Nannie Wickliffe Yulee to Margaret Wickliffe Holt, July 8, 1850, and December 17, 1850; Julia Wickliffe to Margaret Wickliffe Holt, November 4, 1850, container 13, Holt Papers, LC. Nannie encouraged Margaret to follow her example and have children quickly.

59. Robert Holt to Joseph Holt, October 27, 1850, container 13; Robert Holt to Joseph Holt, March 21, 1851; May 21, 1851; August 9, 1851; October 14, 1851; and October 30, 1851, container 14, Holt Papers, LC. On U.S. politics in the 1850s, see Holt, *The Political Crisis of the 1850s*; Walther, *The Shattering of the Union*.

60. Robert Holt to Joseph Holt, October 14, 1851, container 14, Holt Papers, LC.

61. In Kentucky the Presbyterian Church specifically took up the discussion, with more and more of its clergy in the state agitating for the end of slavery or, at the very least, the establishment of church-run schools for the religious instruction of enslaved people. See Martin, *The Anti-Slavery Movement in Kentucky*, 37. See also the draft of Joseph Holt's prepared remarks for a debate on slavery, 1825, quoted in Bartman, "The Contribution of Joseph Holt," 12–14.

62. Robert Stephens to Joseph Holt, October 6, 1845, container 11, Holt Papers, LC.

63. Joseph Holt to Unknown, October 9, 1825, container 1, Holt Papers, LC.

64. Joseph Holt to Margaret Wickliffe Holt, September 16, 1851, and October 17, 1856, container 14, Holt Papers, LC.

65. Joseph Holt to Margaret Wickliffe Holt, October 31, 1851; Joseph Holt to Margaret Wickliffe Holt, dated only "Wednesday Night" [probably early November 1851]; Joseph Holt to Margaret Wickliffe Holt, November 7, 1851, container 14; Joseph Holt to Margaret Wickliffe Holt, dated only "Friday evening," but probably late November or early December 1851, container 15; Joseph Holt to Margaret Wickliffe Holt, November 18, 1851; Margaret Wickliffe Holt to Joseph Holt, March 20, 1852, container 14, Holt Papers, LC. See also numerous letters from "Anastasie" to Joseph Holt, container 98, folder 4, Holt Papers, LC.

66. *Boston Courier*, August 28, 1861.

67. Robert Holt to Joseph Holt, undated but probably late February 1852, and February 27, 1852; John Livingston to Joseph Holt, April 29, 1852, container 14, Holt Papers, LC. See also the *Galveston Weekly Journal*, April 2, 1852. During this period, Holt was grappling with his deep anxiety about the well-being of his sister Elizabeth, who had recently come to Louisville to find a good doctor to treat her undisclosed illness. See Joseph Holt to Margaret Wickliffe Holt, July 6, 1852, container 15, Holt Papers, LC. Fortunately, by September Elizabeth was back home and, accord-

ing to their brother Thomas, feeling much better. (Thomas Holt to Joseph Holt, September 11, 1852, container 15, Holt Papers, LC.)

68. Robert Ward Johnson to Joseph Holt, August 6, 1852; S. English to Joseph Holt, August 9, 1852; and W. M. Corry, August 16, 1852, container 15, Holt Papers, LC.

69. See the petition, dated August 27, 1852, container 15, Holt Papers, LC; "Speech of Joseph Holt Delivered at a Democratic Meeting Held at the Court House," 1–15, in Holt Papers, Huntington.

70. "Speech of Joseph Holt Delivered at a Democratic Meeting Held at the Court House," 1–15, in Holt Papers, Huntington; Robert Ward Johnson to Joseph Holt, October 19, 1852, container 15, Holt Papers, LC.

71. E. F. Nuttall to Joseph Holt, March 3, 1853; John M. Chilton to Joseph Holt, March 3, 1853; Robert Stephens to Joseph Holt, May 24, 1853, container 15, Holt Papers, LC.

72. Howard Crosby to Joseph Holt, March 8, 1853, container 15, Holt Papers, LC.

73. Joseph Holt to Margaret Wickliffe Holt, April 25, 1853, and April 29, 1853; Margaret Wickliffe Holt to Joseph Holt, July 1853 (exact date unknown), container 15, Holt Papers, LC.

74. Robert Holt to Joseph Holt, October 25, 1853, container 15; Mary Ann Stephens to Margaret Wickliffe Holt, January 23, 1854, container 16; Robert Holt to Joseph Holt, July 7, 1853; Thomas Holt to Joseph Holt, August 6, 1853, container 15, Holt Papers, LC.

75. Robert Holt to Joseph Holt, January 16, 1852, and February 10, 1852, container 14; Robert Holt to Joseph Holt, November 11, 1852; July 7, 1853; and October 25, 1853, container 15; Joseph Holt to Margaret Wickliffe Holt, May 23, 1854, container 16, Holt Papers, LC.

76. Joseph Holt to Margaret Wickliffe Holt, May 29, 1854, container 16, Holt Papers, LC.

77. Joseph Holt to Margaret Wickliffe Holt, May 29, 1854, container 16; Robert Holt to Joseph Holt, July 7, 1853; Thomas Holt to Joseph Holt, August 6, 1853, container 15; Margaret Wickliffe Holt to Joseph Holt, June 1, 1854, container 16, Holt Papers, LC.

78. Joseph Holt to Margaret Wickliffe Holt, June 2, 1854; Thomas H. Holt to Joseph Holt, July 31, 1854, and August 14, 1854, container 16; Thomas H. Holt to Joseph Holt, January 26, 1857, container 17; Joseph Holt to Margaret Wickliffe Holt, August 17, 1854; Charles A. Wickliffe to Joseph Holt, September 11, 1854; Joseph Holt to Margaret Wickliffe Holt, September 8, 1854, and November 3, 1854, container 16, Holt Papers, LC.

79. See Joseph Holt to Margaret Wickliffe Holt, September 18, 1854; Mary Ann Stephens to Margaret Wickliffe Holt, October 26, 1854, container 16, Holt Papers, LC.

80. Perrin, Battle, and Kniffin, *Kentucky*, 329. "In no part of the Union," wrote Perrin, "was the feeling against the Catholics or the foreign element more pronounced than in Kentucky," although he also notes that at this time "the foreign population" of the state was "few in numbers, and the great majority of native

Catholics among the most honorable and respectable citizens of the common-wealth" (328). On the Know-Nothings, see Anbinder, *Nativism and Slavery*.

81. *New Albany (Ind.) Daily Ledger*, September 11, 1855.

82. W. M. Corry to Joseph Holt, May 1, 1856; May 19, 1856; and June 20, 1856, container 17, Holt Papers, LC. On the Kansas-Nebraska crisis, see Etcheson, *Bleeding Kansas*.

83. Thomas H. Holt to Joseph Holt, September 25, 1856, container 17, Holt Papers, LC. On the rise of the Republican Party, see Foner, *Free Soil, Free Labor, Free Men*.

84. Victor B. Bell to Joseph Holt, June 20, 1856; Beriah Magoffin to Joseph Holt, October 5, 1856, container 17, Holt Papers, LC; Bartman, "The Contribution of Joseph Holt," 88; "Speech of Joseph Holt, Esq., of Kentucky, Delivered before the Democratic Association of Frederick, Maryland," in Holt Papers, Huntington.

85. Joseph Holt to Margaret Wickliffe Holt, October 11, 1856; Joseph Holt to Margaret Wickliffe Holt, October 14, 1856; and Margaret Wickliffe Holt to Joseph Holt, October 18, 1856, container 17, Holt Papers, LC. See also the undated broadside announcing his Elizabethtown speech, container 17, Holt Papers, LC.

86. Robert Holt to Joseph Holt, December 29, 1856; Sarah Harrison to Joseph Holt, January 8, 1857, container 17, Holt Papers, LC.

Chapter Three

1. Joseph Holt to Margaret Wickliffe Holt, April 17, 1857, container 17, Holt Papers, LC.

2. Julia Wickliffe to Margaret Wickliffe Holt, August 21, 1857, container 17; biographical sketch of Holt in container 117; Joseph Holt to Margaret Wickliffe Holt, September 27, 1857, container 17, Holt Papers, LC.

3. Joseph Holt to Margaret Wickliffe Holt, September 25, 1857, container 17, Holt Papers, LC. On the Panic of 1857, see Huston, *The Panic of 1857*.

4. James O. Harrison to Joseph Holt, October 28, 1857; Joseph Holt to Margaret Wickliffe Holt, September 25, 1857, and September 27, 1857, container 17, Holt Papers, LC. One source comments that Buchanan appointed Holt to the Patent Office post "in recognition of his great services on the stump in the campaign of 1856," which had persuaded Kentuckians, for the first time ever, to cast their ballots for the Democratic ticket. See *Breckenridge News*, August 6, 1894, JHRS.

5. *New York Times*, August 2, 1894; Bartman, "The Contribution of Joseph Holt," 97–100; Dobyns, *The Patent Office Pony*, 1, 2, 23, 41, 132, 142–44.

6. *Charleston Mercury*, September 11, 1857; *New Albany (Ind.) Daily Ledger*, September 23, 1857; *New York Times*, September 3, 1861.

7. Robert Stephens to Joseph Holt, November 10, 1857; J. M. Chilton to Joseph Holt, October 27, 1857; William M. Merrick to Margaret Wickliffe Holt, September 10, 1857; Nannie Wickliffe Yulee to Margaret Wickliffe Holt, September 25, 1857; Charles A. Wickliffe to Joseph Holt, September 25, 1857, container 17, Holt Papers, LC.

8. Bartman, "The Contribution of Joseph Holt," 101; *Journal of the Franklin Institute* 66 (July 1858): 234; Thomas Prosser to Joseph Holt, December 17, 1857, con-

tainer 18, Holt Papers, LC; "The Sufferings of a Man for Genius," *Daily Ohio States-man*, July 7, 1858; Charles Goodyear to Joseph Holt, June 1, 1858, container 18; Charles Goodyear to Joseph Holt, January 1, 1859, container 19, Holt Papers, LC; Joseph Holt, "Extension of the Goodyear Patents," June 14, 1858, 688–89, Holt Papers, Huntington.

9. *Baltimore Sun*, January 25, 1858; Daniel Stephens to Joseph Holt, November 18, 1857, container 17, Holt Papers, LC.

10. Bartman, "The Contribution of Joseph Holt," 103–4; *Baltimore Sun*, January 25, 1858; Dobyns, *The Patent Office Pony*, 152.

11. George W. Seavy to Joseph Holt, November 27, 1857, container 18, Holt Papers, LC. See also Bartman, "The Contribution of Joseph Holt," 105; Joseph Holt to Margaret Wickliffe Holt, September 27, 1857, and September 30, 1857; George G. Gaither to Joseph Holt, October 16, 1857, and November 2, 1857; Esther W. P. Lowe to Joseph Holt, November 2, 1857, container 17; Robert Holt to Joseph Holt, July 15, 1858, container 18, Holt Papers, LC.

12. Katie Eldred to Joseph Holt, August 5, 1858; Lucy West to Joseph Holt, October 1, 1858, container 18; Emily J. Bowen to Joseph Holt, March 8, 1859, container 19, Holt Papers, LC.

13. James Buchanan to Joseph Holt, October 28, 1857, container 17, Holt Papers, LC. The Holts received their first invitation to an Executive Mansion dinner on October 7, 1857, just weeks after Joseph accepted the Patent Office appointment (the invitation came from Buchanan's niece, Harriet Lane, who filled the role of first lady during her bachelor uncle's presidency). See Harriet Lane to Joseph Holt, October 7, 1857, container 17, Holt Papers, LC; *New York Herald*, April 21, 1858.

14. Ellen Key Blunt to Joseph Holt, June 12, 1858; E. A. Holt to Joseph Holt, January 6, 1858; Joel B. Wilson to Joseph Holt, May 21, 1858, container 18, Holt Papers, LC.

15. Mary Ann Stephens to Joseph Holt, August 21, 1858, container 98, folder 5; Daniel Stephens to Joseph Holt, February 23, 1858, container 18; Elizabeth Holt Sterett to Joseph Holt, December 25, 1858, container 19, Holt Papers, LC.

16. Nannie Wickliffe Yulee to Margaret Wickliffe Holt, December 21, 1858, container 19, Holt Papers, LC.

17. Thomas Holt to Joseph Holt, January 29, 1853, March 27, 1853, and August 6, 1853, container 15, Holt Papers, LC. Sandy had been in Stephensport with Thomas, but now that the tobacco crop was cut Thomas was planning to send Sandy back to Louisville and was concerned about sending him up the Ohio without insurance. "It is common now," Thomas pointed out, "to have Negroes insured when they run on a steamboat and I think it would be a very good plan with Sandy." Thomas worried that Sandy "might fall overboard or something happen," perhaps that Sandy would run away. (Thomas Holt to Joseph Holt, November 13, 1853, container 16, Holt Papers, LC.) In response, Holt purchased a six-month "slave policy" from the Kentucky Mutual Life Insurance Company, which cost $29.75 and guaranteed a benefit of $700, despite the fact that the small print (literally) seemed to absolve the insurance company of responsibility in what seemed like every imaginable situa-

tion. See the "Slave Policy" issued by the Kentucky Mutual Life Insurance Company, container 98, folder 4, Holt Papers, LC.

18. Joseph Holt to Margaret Wickliffe Holt, April 1, 1857, and April 17, 1857, container 17; Joseph Holt to Margaret Wickliffe Holt, November 26, 1858, container 19, Holt Papers, LC. Many years later, Jane Lowery was described in a newspaper article as "an intelligent colored woman" who "was in the Holt household for twenty years," from 1857 to 1876. According to Lowery herself, "I belonged to [Holt's] wife . . . and came up with her from Kentucky after her marriage. . . . I was left free by his wife a short time before the war, when she died, and he gave me the house I live in," which was on First Street between C and D Streets, SE. (See unidentified, undated article from 1896, "Who Had Holt's Will," JHRS.)

19. Robert Holt to Joseph Holt, February 28, 1858, and March 23, 1858, container 18; Robert Holt to Joseph Holt, April 13, 1857, container 17, Holt Papers, LC.

20. On the *Dred Scott* case, see Fehrenbacher, *The Dred Scott Case*. On the caning of Sumner, see Donald, *Charles Sumner*. On the Lincoln-Douglas debates, see Guelzo, *Lincoln and Douglas*. On antebellum Kansas, see Oertel, *Bleeding Borders*.

21. James O. Harrison to Joseph Holt, January 1, 1859, container 19, Holt Papers, LC.

22. James O. Harrison to Joseph Holt, January 1, 1859, container 19, Holt Papers, LC. On Seward, see Van Deusen, *William Henry Seward*.

23. Joseph Holt to Margaret Wickliffe Holt, November 13, 1858; November 26, 1858; and December 1, 1858, container 19, Holt Papers, LC. See also folder 1, container 99, Holt Papers, LC. It is clear that many women in this period found Holt charming, charismatic, generous, and attractive. See, for example, L. M. Ray to Joseph Holt, December 31, 1856; October 15, 1857; and November 21, 1857, container 17; L. M. Ray to Joseph Holt, December 31, 1857; January 19, 1858; and August 28, 1858, container 18, Holt Papers, LC.

24. William Waters to Joseph Holt, February 16, 1859; H. H. Kavanaugh to Joseph Holt, February 28, 1859; Joseph Holt to Margaret Wickliffe Holt, March 13, 1859, container 19; biographical sketch of Joseph Holt, container 117, Holt Papers, LC; *New York Times*, August 2, 1894; Bartman, "The Contribution of Joseph Holt," 111.

25. Holzer, *Lincoln, President Elect*, 235; *Washington Constitution*, June 24, 1859.

26. Fehrenbacher, *Lincoln in Text and Context*, 24, 28. The postmaster general ceased to be a member of the president's cabinet in 1971.

27. *Amherst (N.H.) Farmer's Cabinet*, March 16, 1859; *Daily Ohio Statesman*, March 13, 1859; *Scientific American* 14 (March 19, 1859).

28. James O. Harrison to Joseph Holt, March 10, 1859, container 19; James O. Harrison to Joseph Holt, March 26, container 20; A. Houlden to Joseph Holt, March 11, 1859; Howard Crosby to Joseph Holt, March 10, 1859, container 19; M. W. Jacobus to Joseph Holt, March 19, 1859; Samuel Haycraft to Joseph Holt, March 21, 1859, container 20, Holt Papers, LC.

29. Daniel Stephens to Joseph Holt, March 25, 1859; Eleanor Holt to Joseph Holt, May 2, 1859; Mary Ann Stephens to Margaret Wickliffe Holt, April 14, 1859, container 20; Robert Holt to Joseph Holt, February 3, 1859, and March 6, 1859,

container 19; Robert Holt to Joseph Holt, August 20, 1859; Joseph Holt to Margaret Wickliffe Holt, August 30, 1859, container 21, Holt Papers, LC.

30. *Washington Constitution*, June 21, 1859, and June 24, 1859; Van Holst, *The Constitutional and Political History*, 68. Years later, a source devoted to telling the story of the Francis Preston Blair family—who became bitter opponents of Holt during Reconstruction—accused him of mismanaging the Post Office and allowing its deficit to grow "until it reached $10,652,593 more than receipts in the year 1860," a blunder Montgomery Blair, Lincoln's postmaster general, subsequently was able to correct. See Smith, *The Francis Preston Blair Family*, 2:90. See also William S. Harney, quoted in the *Daily Ohio Statesman*, March 13, 1859.

31. *Washington Constitution*, November 17, 1859.

32. Bartman, "The Contribution of Joseph Holt," 113–14, 156; Joseph Holt to the *Washington Constitution*, May 17, 1859, and June 16, 1859; Howard Crosby to Joseph Holt, June 19, 1859; Daniel Stephens to Joseph Holt, July 11, 1859, and August 25, 1859, container 21, Holt Papers, LC. In addition to dealing with corrupt postmasters and appeals for patronage, one of the most interesting cases that Holt confronted during this period had to do with a husband demanding that letters directed to his estranged wife be delivered to *him* rather than to *her*. Not surprisingly, the wife disagreed, demanding that the local postmaster ensure the safe delivery of her mail without her estranged husband's intervention. To his credit, Holt rejected the husband's notion of what he called "marital power" and agreed with the wife. (*Boston Daily Courier*, December 5, 1859.)

33. James M. Nelson to Joseph Holt, September 26, 1859; Robert Holt to Joseph Holt, October 4, 1859, container 21, Holt Papers, LC. On the collapse of the Democratic Party and other prewar political developments, see Potter, *The Impending Crisis*.

34. McPherson, *Ordeal by Fire*, 125–28. On John Brown, see Reynolds, *John Brown, Abolitionist*; Oates, *To Purge This Land with Blood*.

35. Howard Crosby to Joseph Holt, December 16, 1859, container 22, Holt Papers, LC; *New York Herald*, December 8, 1859.

36. *New York Herald*, December 8, 1859.

37. Ibid.

38. Ibid.

39. Nannie Wickliffe Yulee to Joseph Holt, (date unclear, but internal evidence suggests May 1859), container 13; W. M. Corry to Joseph Holt, July 12, 1859; Joseph Holt to Margaret Wickliffe Holt, July 17, 1859, container 21, Holt Papers, LC.

40. See also Joseph Holt to Margaret Wickliffe Holt, July 16, 1859; July 22, 1859; July 23, 1859; July 27, 1859; August 21, 1859; and September 1, 1859, container 21, Holt Papers, LC; *Washington Constitution*, September 20, 1859, and November 3, 1859; Nannie Wickliffe Yulee to Margaret Wickliffe Holt, November 28, 1859; Charles A. Wickliffe to Margaret Wickliffe Holt, December 4, 1859; James Morrow to Joseph Holt, December 15, 1859, container 22; Mattie Rhodes to Margaret Wickliffe Holt, November 14, 1859, container 21, Holt Papers, LC.

41. Mary Wickliffe Merrick to Margaret Wickliffe Holt, December 2, 1859; Joseph

Holt to Margaret Wickliffe Holt, January 2, 1860, container 22; Joseph Holt to Margaret Wickliffe Holt, January 18, 1860; Elizabeth Hynes to Margaret Wickliffe Holt, January 26, 1860; Mary Ann Stephens to Margaret Wickliffe Holt, February 2, 1860; Joseph Holt to Margaret Wickliffe Holt, January 24, 1860, container 23, Holt Papers, LC.

42. Joseph Holt to Margaret Wickliffe Holt, February 8, 1860, container 23; Margaret Wickliffe Holt to Joseph Holt, March 15, 1860; James Buchanan to Joseph Holt, April 4, 1860; Horatio King to Joseph Holt, April 10, 1860; Julia Wickliffe to Margaret Wickliffe Holt, April 29, 1860; Eleanor Stephens Holt to Joseph Holt, May 13, 1860, container 24, Holt Papers, LC. Eleanor also thanked her son for the money he had been sending her for the past several months. Many additional letters to Margaret wishing her well can be found in container 24.

43. On John C. Breckinridge, see Davis, *Breckinridge*.

44. Container 22 of the Holt Papers, LC, contains a long, handwritten draft of the speech, which, according to a note added later by an archivist, seems to be part "campaign biography of Joseph Lane," part "eulogy of John C. Breckinridge," and part pro-Union proclamation.

45. Handwritten draft of a speech, container 22, Holt Papers, LC.

46. Mary Ann Stephens to Margaret Wickliffe Holt, August 7, 1860; Howard Crosby to Joseph Holt, August 16, 1860, container 25; James O. Harrison to Joseph Holt, September 23, 1859, container 21; James O. Harrison to Joseph Holt, August 20, 1860; Horatio King to Joseph Holt, August 21, 1860, container 25, Holt Papers, LC.

47. Nannie Wickliffe Yulee to Joseph Holt, August 19, 1860, container 25; Nannie Wickliffe Yulee to Joseph Holt, undated but clearly fall 1860, container 26, Holt Papers, LC. See also Nannie Wickliffe Yulee to Margaret Wickliffe Holt, December 10, 1859, container 22, Holt Papers, LC.

48. Julia Wickliffe to Joseph Holt, August 27, 1860; Mary Ann Stephens to Joseph Holt, September 14, 1860; Eleanor Stephens Holt to Joseph Holt, November 2, 1860; Robert Holt to Joseph Holt, September 26, 1860, container 25, Holt Papers, LC.

49. James O. Harrison to Joseph Holt, October 2, 1860, container 25, Holt Papers, LC.

50. Robert Holt to Joseph Holt, November 9, 1860, container 25, Holt Papers, LC. Holt was not able to vote in the election; residents of Washington, D.C., were not legally allowed to vote in a presidential election until 1961. On the election of 1860, see Edgerton, *Year of Meteors*.

51. Robert Holt to Joseph Holt, November 9, 1860, container 25, Holt Papers, LC.

52. Robert Holt to Joseph Holt, November 20, 1860, container 26, Holt Papers, LC.

53. Robert Holt to Joseph Holt, December 8, 1860, container 26, Holt Papers, LC.

54. Horatio King to Joseph Holt, November 13, 1860; James O. Harrison to Joseph Holt, November 16, 1860; Alfred Huger to Joseph Holt, November 27, 1860, and December 4, 1860, container 26, Holt Papers, LC.

55. Buchanan sent Holt a draft of his speech beforehand, for his approval. See

James Buchanan to Joseph Holt, November 30, 1860, in John Bassett Moore, *The Works of James Buchanan*, 11:6. See also *New York Times*, December 15, 1860; Horatio King to Joseph Holt, January 14, 1860, container 26, Holt Papers, LC.

56. *New York Times*, December 15, 1860; Lewis Cass to Joseph Holt, December 18, 1860, container 26, Holt Papers, LC. On Stanton, see Thomas and Hyman, *Stanton*. On the secession of South Carolina, see Sinha, *The Counterrevolution of Slavery*.

57. J. F. Dozier to Joseph Holt, December 29, 1860; Howard Crosby to Joseph Holt, December 31, 1860; M. W. Jacobus to Joseph Holt, December 31, 1860; M. H. Conrad to Joseph Holt, undated but clearly end of 1860, container 26, Holt Papers, LC.

Chapter Four

1. See Nicolay and Hay, *Abraham Lincoln*, 3:89n. See also Burlingame, *Oral History of Abraham Lincoln*, 73; Allen, "Joseph Holt," 56–57.

2. Robert Holt to Joseph Holt, January 10, 1861, container 26, Holt Papers, LC.

3. Robert Holt to Joseph Holt, February 11, 1861, container 27, Holt Papers, LC.

4. James O. Harrison to Joseph Holt, June 15, 1860, container 25; James O. Harrison to Joseph Holt, January 1, 1861, container 22; James O. Harrison to Joseph Holt, January 23, 1861, and January 24, 1861, container 26, Holt Papers, LC.

5. Anonymous to Joseph Holt, January 5, 1861, container 26, Holt Papers, LC.

6. Louis T. Wigfall to Milledge L. Bonham, January 2, 1861, in *OR*, ser. I, 1:252; Silas Reede to Joseph Holt and Edwin M. Stanton, January 4, 1861; S. H. Wales to Joseph Holt, January 8, 1861; T. S. Bell to Joseph Holt, January 8, 1861; Richard McAllister to Joseph Holt, January 15, 1861, container 26, Holt Papers, LC. The first letter I have seen from Bell to Holt was dated October 27, 1836.

7. *New York Times*, January 1, 1861; January 19, 1861; and September 3, 1861; *Vermont Phoenix*, January 24, 1861. In the HFPC, a handwritten document with the simple heading "January 18, 1861," reads: "On the question, Will the Senate advise and consent to the appointment of Joseph Holt? It was determined in the affirmative, Yeas 38, Nays 13." Those who voted "nay" were Senators Bayard, Benjamin, Bragg, Clingman, Green, Hemphill, Hunter, Iverson, Lane, Mason, Polk, Slidell, and Wigfall. See also Nicolay and Hay, *Abraham Lincoln*, 3:109; James Buchanan to Joseph Holt, January 2, 1861, quoted in John Bassett Moore, *The Works of James Buchanan*, 10:372; Robert Ward Johnson to Joseph Holt, January 16, 1861, container 23; John G. Winter to Joseph Holt, January 1, 1861, container 26; Charles Ellet Jr. to Joseph Holt, January 1, 1861, container 22; Howard Crosby to Joseph Holt, January 8, 1861, container 26, Holt Papers, LC.

8. Joseph Holt to Henry J. Hunt, January 16, 1861, *OR*, ser. I, vol. 51, pt. 1, 311; Long, *Civil War Day by Day*, 3. Five days later, Georgia's legislature also voted to arm the state, as did North Carolina's on December 12.

9. John Bassett Moore, *The Works of James Buchanan*, 12:169–70. On the progress of secession, see Freehling, *The Road to Disunion*; Lankford, *Cry Havoc*.

10. John Bassett Moore, *The Works of James Buchanan*, 12: 172–73. See also William McWherter to Joseph Holt, January 13, 1861, container 26, Holt Papers, LC;

Isaac Toucey to W. S. Walker, January 7, 1861, in the *OR*, ser. I, 4:220; St. John B. L. Skinner et al. to Joseph Holt, January 5, 1861; telegram from Robert Anderson to Joseph Holt, January 6, 1861, container 26, Holt Papers, LC.

11. John Bassett Moore, *The Works of James Buchanan*, 12: 173; Joseph Holt to Robert Anderson, January 10, 1861, *OR*, ser. I, 1:137; Joseph Holt to Robert Anderson, January 16, 1861, *OR*, ser. I, 1:140.

12. Robert Anderson to Joseph Holt, January 21, 1861, *OR*, ser. I, 1:143; James Buchanan to Joseph Holt, January 12, 1861; W. R. Palmer to Joseph Holt, January 25, 1861, container 26; James Buchanan to Joseph Holt, January 30, 1861, container 27, Holt Papers, LC.

13. Joseph Holt to Robert Anderson, February 23, 1861, *OR*, ser. I, 1:182–83; Jacob Thompson to Howell Cobb, January 16, 1861, quoted in Bartman, "The Contribution of Joseph Holt," 171.

14. Thomas and Hyman, *Stanton*, 103; *Milwaukee Daily Sentinel*, February 7, 1861; *Philadelphia Inquirer*, January 29, 1861.

15. Long, *Civil War Day by Day*, 28; David L. Yulee to John B. Floyd, December 21, 1860, *OR*, ser. I, 1:348.

16. John B. Floyd to David L. Yulee, December 28, 1860, *OR*, ser. I, 1:348–49; David L. Yulee to "Secretary of War," January 2, 1861, *OR*, ser. I, 1:349; William Maynadier to Joseph Holt, January 3, 1861, *OR*, ser. I, 1:349–50; Joseph Holt to David L. Yulee and Stephen R. Mallory, January 9, 1861, *OR*, ser. I, 1:351.

17. Israel Vodges to Lorenzo Thomas, February 7, 1861, *OR*, ser. I, 1:357–58; Lorenzo Thomas to Israel Vodges, January 21, 1861, *OR*, ser. I, 1:352; Stephen R. Mallory to John Slidell, January 28, 1861, *OR*, ser. I. 1:354; Joseph Holt to Adam J. Slemmer, January 29, 1861, *OR*, ser. I, 1:355; A. J. Slemmer to Joseph Holt, February 1861 (precise date unknown), *OR*, ser. I, 1:358–59.

18. Typed document titled "The Post Office Department," Holt Papers, Huntington; Dr. H. Wigand to Joseph Holt, January 24, 1861; T. S. Bell to Joseph Holt, January 19, 1861, container 26; Benjamin P. Fuller to Joseph Holt, February 17, 1861, container 27, Holt Papers, LC. Right around this time, Lincoln's friend Orville Browning suggested to the president-elect that he reappoint Holt secretary of war. "Would it not take the life out of secession in the border slave states?" he asked. Browning described Holt as having "shown himself a devoted and Union loving patriot possessed of nerve and ability for the crisis which is upon us." See Orville Browning to Abraham Lincoln, January 19, 1861, Lincoln Papers, LC. See also John J. Speed to Joseph Holt, January 28, 1861, container 27, Holt Papers, LC.

19. The *Confederation* article was reprinted in the *Louisville Daily Journal*, February 8, 1861. See also William M. Gwin to Calhoun Benham, February 8, 1861, *OR*, ser. II, 2:1015; *New York Times*, February 9, 1861; General Orders No. 5, March 1, 1861, *OR*, ser. I, 1:597.

20. W. Hickey to Joseph Holt, January 12, 1861, container 26, Holt Papers, LC; Winfield Scott to Joseph Holt, January 24, 1861, *OR*, ser. I, vol. 51, pt. 1, 312; "A Native of Kentucky" to Joseph Holt, February 2, 1861, container 27, Holt Papers, LC.

21. Joseph Holt to James Buchanan, February 18, 1861, *OR*, ser. I, vol. 51, pt. 1, 436–38; Nicolay and Hay, *Abraham Lincoln*, 3:146.

22. James Buchanan to John Tyler, February 22, 1861, container 27, Holt Papers, LC; *Amherst (N.H.) Farmer's Cabinet*, March 1, 1861.

23. Abraham Lincoln had been in touch with Winfield Scott as early as January 11. See Abraham Lincoln to Winfield Scott, January 11, 1861, in Basler, *Collected Works of Abraham Lincoln*, 4:172–73. See also Lyman Trumbull to Joseph Holt, February 28, 1861, container 27, Holt Papers, LC; Joseph Holt to Robert Anderson, February 23, 1861, *OR*, ser. I, 1:182.

24. *Baltimore Sun*, March 4, 1861; Long, *Civil War Day by Day*, 45; *New York Herald*, March 6, 1861; *New York Times*, September 3, 1861; William H. Seward to Joseph Holt, March 6, 1861, container 28, Holt Papers, LC; Nicolay and Hay, *Abraham Lincoln*, 3:376; Joseph Holt to Abraham Lincoln, March 5, 1861, quoted in John Bassett Moore, *The Works of James Buchanan*, 12:191–93; Welles, *Diary of Gideon Welles* 1:3–4. On March 5, 1861, Holt received a one-time payment of $1,422.22 for sixty-four days of service as secretary of war, dating back to December 31, 1860. See the undated note from Joseph Holt to himself regarding this payment, container 28, Holt Papers, LC.

25. The *Mercury* article was in the *San Francisco Bulletin*, March 22, 1861. See also *Confederation*, February 4, 1861; "Be Just," undated newspaper clipping, container 28; Annie Buchanan to Joseph Holt, February 6, 1861, container 27; James Buchanan to Joseph Holt, March 11, 1861; March 16, 1861; and May 21, 1861, container 28, Holt Papers, LC; John Bassett Moore, *The Works of James Buchanan*, 11:168–78.

26. Samuel Haycraft to Joseph Holt, February 9, 1861, container 27; "Many Holt Democrats" to Joseph Holt, March 22, 1861; T. S. Bell to Joseph Holt, March 11, 1861; Mary Ann Stephens to Joseph Holt, March 4, 1861, and April 22, 1861, container 28, Holt Papers, LC.

27. *Philadelphia Inquirer*, March 6, 1861.

28. This was in fact not the first time Holt faced this charge: on January 9, John W. Powell wrote to Holt warning him of a rumor that was circulating to the effect that Holt had ordered the *Star of the West* to South Carolina entirely on his own. Powell feared that the rumor might become "the cause of reflection upon you in the Senate," but he assured Holt that he himself did not "believe or credit the assertion." See J. W. Powell to Joseph Holt, January 9, 1861, container 26, Holt Papers, LC.

29. *Philadelphia Inquirer*, March 6, 1861; "The Letter of Secretary Holt," March 6, 1861, in the Holt Papers, Huntington.

30. *Philadelphia Inquirer*, March 19, 1861.

31. On March 12 Lincoln summoned Holt for a conversation, the contents of which are not known. See Abraham Lincoln to Joseph Holt, March 12, 1861, container 27, Holt Papers, LC. See also Ben Hardin Helm to Joseph Holt, March 14, 1861, container 28; James E. Jouett to Joseph Holt, February 26, 1861, container 27; Joseph Holt to Joseph Holt, December 18, 1860, container 26; Jos. H. Bradley et al. to Joseph Holt, March 20, 1861; Thomas H. Duval to Joseph Holt, March 24, 1861, container 28, Holt Papers, LC.

32. Joseph Holt to James Buchanan, May 24, 1861, quoted in Bartman, "The Contribution of Joseph Holt," 196.

33. McPherson, *Ordeal by Fire*, 204–26; Gienapp, *The Civil War and Reconstruction*, 76–77; T. S. Bell to Joseph Holt, January 19, 1861, container 26, Holt Papers, LC.

34. Coulter, *The Civil War and Readjustment*, 3.

35. Ibid., 3–5.

36. Ibid., 13, 14; Harrison, *Lincoln of Kentucky*, 124.

37. Coulter, *The Civil War and Readjustment*, 18; Robertson, "Sectionalism in Kentucky," 55–56; "The Secession Conspiracy in Kentucky," 113.

38. Robertson, "Sectionalism in Kentucky," 58; Coulter, *The Civil War and Readjustment*, 24, 35.

39. "The Secession Conspiracy in Kentucky," 118; Coulter, *The Civil War and Readjustment*, 10, 26; Townsend, *Lincoln and the Bluegrass*, 256.

40. Ranck, *History of Lexington*, 111–12; Perrin, Battle, and Kniffin, *Kentucky*, 2:799; Collins, *History of Kentucky*, 1:477; Townsend, *Lincoln and the Bluegrass*, 260; Coulter, *The Civil War and Readjustment*, 27; Wakelyn, *Southern Pamphlets on Secession*, 247–61.

41. Townsend, *Lincoln and the Bluegrass*, 260; John J. Crittenden to Joseph Holt, January 7, 1861, container 26; John J. Crittenden to Joseph Holt, February 25, 1861, container 27, Holt Papers, LC; Perrin, Battle, and Kniffin, *Kentucky*, 1:350.

42. Coulter, *The Civil War and Readjustment*, 39, 41. Perrin says the meeting took place on the twentieth. (Ibid., 1:350.) Coulter notes that "under the tutelage of Clay, the state had almost come to believe that devising compromises was one of her chief functions in the Union." (Coulter, *The Civil War and Readjustment*, 30.)

43. Quoted in Donald, *Lincoln*, 317. For a complete discussion of the importance of the border states to the Union, see Freehling, *The South versus the South*. See also Coulter, *The Civil War and Readjustment*, 26; Perrin, Battle, and Kniffin, *Kentucky*, 1:352.

44. John M. Harlan to Joseph Holt, March 11, 1861; Mary Ann Stephens to Joseph Holt, April 22, 1861, container 28, Holt Papers, LC.

45. Mary Ann Stephens to Joseph Holt, May 1, 1861, container 28, Holt Papers, LC.

46. Mary Ann Stephens to Joseph Holt, May 12, 1861, container 28, Holt Papers, LC; Perrin, Battle, and Kniffin, *Kentucky*, 1:350; Coulter, *The Civil War and Readjustment*, 56, 81.

47. Mary Ann Stephens to Joseph Holt, May 28, 1861, and June 9, 1861, container 28, Holt Papers, LC.

48. Robert Holt to Joseph Holt, May 1, 1861, container 28, Holt Papers, LC.

49. Coulter, *The Civil War and Readjustment*, 85–86, 100; Robert Anderson to Joseph Holt, August 4, 1861, container 29, Holt Papers, LC.

50. Perrin, Battle, and Kniffin, *Kentucky*, 1:350–51, 358; Coulter, *The Civil War and Readjustment*, 49, 87–88; Long, *Civil War Day by Day*, 69.

51. Joshua F. Speed to Joseph Holt, May 24, 1861, container 28, Holt Papers, LC.

52. Joseph Holt to Joshua F. Speed, May 31, 1861 (open letter, published in pamphlet form), container 29, Holt Papers, LC.

53. Ibid.

54. T. S. Bell to Joseph Holt, June 10, 1861; John Speed to Joseph Holt, June 10, 1861; Joshua F. Speed to Joseph Holt, June 18, 1861, container 29, Holt Papers, LC. A few years younger than Holt and also an attorney, James Speed had attended St. Joseph's College and then Transylvania University. Now, like his brother Joshua and Holt, he was a passionate Unionist and a Lincoln man of considerable influence. See Levin, *Lawyers and Lawmakers of Kentucky*, 282.

55. Neighboring Missouri, it bears noting, was also struggling. In mid-June, writes E. B. Long, the state's pro-Confederate governor, Claiborne Jackson, had "called for fifty thousand state militia to protect citizens against what he termed Federal efforts to overthrow the state government." See Long, *Civil War Day by Day*, 85; Coulter, *The Civil War and Readjustment*, 95–96; Harrison, *The Civil War in Kentucky*, 10–11; T. S. Bell to Joseph Holt, June 24, 1861, container 29, Holt Papers, LC.

56. William H. Seward to Joseph Holt, July 1, 1861; Thornton F. Marshall to Joseph Holt, July 5, 1861, container 29, Holt Papers, LC; Holt, *The Fallacy of Neutrality*, 1–14; *New York Times*, July 18, 1861.

57. Holt, *The Fallacy of Neutrality*, 1–14.

58. Ibid.

59. *New York Times*, July 20, 1861.

60. Coulter, *The Civil War and Readjustment*, 96; Harrison, *The Civil War in Kentucky*, 11; C. L. Thomasson to Joseph Holt, July 13, 1861, container 29, Holt Papers, LC; *Frank Leslie's Illustrated Newspaper*, October 1861; Moore, *The Rebellion Record*, II: 50.

61. Frank Moore, *The Rebellion Record*, 2:450–54; M. T. McMahon to Joseph Holt, September 5, 1861, container 30, Holt Papers, LC.

62. M. T. McMahon to Joseph Holt, September 5, 1861, container 30, Holt Papers, LC; Harrison, *The Civil War in Kentucky*, 11; William Nelson to Joseph Holt, August 1, 1861, container 29, Holt Papers, LC; Coulter, *The Civil War and Readjustment*, 89, 103. Lincoln, writes Coulter, was "sagacious enough to leave no written record to accuse; he conducted all of these transactions by word of mouth." (Ibid., 90.)

63. Benjamin A. G. Fuller to Andrew Johnson, August 17, 1861, in Graf and Haskins, *The Papers of Andrew Johnson*, 6:683; *Boston Courier*, August 28, 1861; *Boston Post*, August 27, 1861; Ticknor & Fields (publishers of the *Atlantic Monthly*) to Joseph Holt, August 27, 1861; M. W. Jacobus to Joseph Holt, August 7, 1861, container 29, Holt Papers, LC; *Harper's Weekly*, August 3, 1861.

64. Joshua F. Speed to Joseph Holt, August 8, 1861, container 29, Holt Papers, LC.

65. Faust, *Historical Times Illustrated Encyclopedia*, 814; Long, *Civil War Day by Day*, 108. It was, writes Coulter, "the most stupendous blunder any officer connected with the Federal government could have made." (Coulter, *The Civil War and Readjustment*, 111–12.)

66. Joshua F. Speed to Joseph Holt, September 7, 1861; E. T. Bainbridge to Joseph

Holt, September 10, 1861, container 30, Holt Papers, LC; Joseph Holt to Abraham Lincoln, Lincoln Papers, LC; Long, *Civil War Day by Day*, 114; Coulter, *The Civil War and Readjustment*, 107.

67. On September 11, in response to these developments, the now heavily Unionist Kentucky state legislature passed a resolution calling on Governor Magoffin to order the Confederate troops out of the state. When Magoffin vetoed the resolution, the legislature repassed it immediately. (See Coulter, *The Civil War and Readjustment*, 114.) On Grant during the war, see Grant, *Personal Memoirs*.

68. Joseph Holt to Abraham Lincoln, September 12, 1861, *OR*, ser. II, 1:768–69; *Louisville Daily Journal*, September 12, 1861; Long, *Civil War Day by Day*, 118; James Speed to Joseph Holt, September 20, 1861; T. S. Bell to Joseph Holt, September 19, 1861, container 30, Holt Papers, LC.

69. T. S. Bell to Joseph Holt, September 19, 1861, container 30, Holt Papers, LC. On September 24, 1861, the *Greenville (Mich.) Independent* reprinted an editorial from the *Detroit Tribune* regarding Holt's involvement in the Frémont proclamation situation. On September 25, Holt wrote again to Lincoln, urging him not to pardon a known secessionist in Kentucky who had recently been arrested. See Joseph Holt to Abraham Lincoln, September 25, 1861, *OR*, ser. II, 2:808.

70. Perrin, Battle, and Kniffin, *Kentucky*, 1:357; Long, *Civil War Day by Day*, 118; Larz Anderson to Joseph Holt, September 15, 1861; T. S. Bell to Joseph Holt, September 21, 1861, and September 23, 1861 (telegram), container 30, Holt Papers, LC.

71. Joshua F. Speed to Joseph Holt, October 18, 1861, and October 19, 1861, container 30, Holt Papers, LC.

72. James Speed to Joseph Holt, October 29, 1861, container 31, Holt Papers, LC; Abraham Lincoln to Joseph Holt, November 12, 1861, in *Collected Works of Abraham Lincoln*, 5:21–22; Joseph Holt to Abraham Lincoln, November 2, 1861, Lincoln Papers, LC. See also Julie Schoepf to Joseph Holt, January 10, 1861, container 26; Julie Schoepf to Joseph Holt, November 18, 1861, container 31; Julie Schoepf to Joseph Holt, August 17, 1862, container 34, Holt Papers, LC.

73. William Gates to Joseph Holt, October 27, 1861, container 31; David L. Collier to Joseph Holt, January 18, 1862, container 32, Holt Papers, LC; *Detroit Free Press*, December 10, 1861, in *OR*, ser. II, 2:1256.

74. Joshua F. Speed to Joseph Holt, November 28, 1861, container 31, Holt Papers, LC.

75. Joshua F. Speed to Joseph Holt, January 18, 1862, container 32; James or Joshua Speed to Joseph Holt, December 8, 1861, container 31; Joshua F. Speed to Joseph Holt, January 18, 1862, container 32, Holt Papers, LC; Niven, *The Salmon P. Chase Papers*, 1:325.

76. Stanton's biographers do not believe that Stanton would have recommended Holt for the job. (Thomas and Hyman, *Stanton*, 126.) I think they are wrong. See Joseph Holt to Abraham Lincoln, January 15, 1862, in the Lincoln Papers, LC. Thomas and Hyman do agree that "Holt, for his part, quickly subdued any resentment he may have felt and wrote for the press a rhapsodic eulogy on Stanton's virtues, which served to make the appointment acceptable to many moderates of

both parties in the North, and this was a substantial assistance to the new Secretary." (Thomas and Hyman, *Stanton*, 140.) See also the *New York Times*, January 25, 1862; Edwin M. Stanton to Joseph Holt, January 25, 1862, Holt Papers, Huntington.

77. Joshua F. Speed to Joseph Holt, February 4, 1862; T. S. Bell to Joseph Holt, January 29, 1862, container 32; Hugh Campbell to Joseph Holt, January 24, 1862, container 34; Hugh Campbell to Joseph Holt, May 29, 1862, container 33; E. T. Bainbridge to Joseph Holt, January 20, 1862, container 32; E. T. Bainbridge to Joseph Holt, August 19, 1862, container 34, Holt Papers, LC.

78. Edwin Stanton to Joseph Holt, January 25, 1862, in Holt Papers, Huntington. See also Treasury Department document dated April 22, 1862, container 33, Holt Papers, LC, which indicates that he was paid $1,451.60 "for compensation as from November 3d, 1861, to March 10th, 1862, including mileage from Washington to St. Louis and back, two trips." And see Bartman, "The Contribution of Joseph Holt," 237–38; Joseph Holt to Abraham Lincoln, October 29, 1861, Lincoln Papers, LC; Abraham Lincoln to Joseph Holt, November 12, 1861, cited in *Collected Works of Abraham Lincoln*, 5:21–22; Hugh Campbell to Joseph Holt, March 17, 1862, container 32, Holt Papers, LC; David Davis, Joseph Holt, and Hugh Campbell to Edwin Stanton, March 10, 1862, Holt Papers, Huntington; Thomas and Hyman, *Stanton*, 156; biographical sketch of Joseph Holt, container 117; Hugh Campbell to Joseph Holt, March 14, 1862, and March 16, 1862; David Davis to Joseph Holt, March 14, 1862; and J. S. Fullerton to Joseph Holt, March 21, 1862, container 32, Holt Papers, LC. Holt also seems to have been a member of the United States Sanitary Commission during this period. See Alfred J. Bloor to Joseph Holt, February 17, 1862, container 32, Holt Papers, LC.

79. Thomas and Hyman, *Stanton*, 234.

Chapter Five

1. Clous, "Judge Advocate General's Department." See also U.S. House of Representatives, Report No. 74, *Army Staff Reorganization*, 204–7, in which Holt provides an excellent history of the post. And see Bland, "Were the Lincoln Conspirators Dealt Justice?" 38; Allen, "Joseph Holt," 86–87.

2. Clous, "Judge Advocate General's Department"; Allen, "Joseph Holt"; Bartman, "The Contribution of Joseph Holt"; *Scientific American* 7 (September 20, 1862): 181; Charles Weyman to Joseph Holt, September 8, 1862, container 34; Owen Hitchens to Joseph Holt, November 20, 1862, container 35, Holt Papers, LC.

3. Lowry, *Don't Shoot That Boy!* 93. See also Lowry's Index Project, Inc. (www .theindexproject.com). In Basler's, *Collected Works of Abraham Lincoln*, 8:539, it is indicated that Lincoln and Holt reviewed seventy-one cases on April 21, 1864. There were many other days on which they viewed thirty or forty cases. There are also a number of notes in Holt's papers from John Nicolay, summoning him to meet with Lincoln on the business of Holt's office. See, for example, John Nicolay to Joseph Holt, June 1, 1863, container 39; John Nicolay to Joseph Holt, February 13, 1864, container 42; John Nicolay to Joseph Holt, April 13, 1864, container 43, Holt Papers, LC. See also Joseph Holt to John G. Nicolay, February 13, 1864, Lincoln Papers, LC. On top of all of his regular responsibilities as judge advocate general, Holt received

scores of letters from strangers as well as friends, relatives, and acquaintances seeking his assistance with a host of different concerns. See, for example, John B. Bland to Joseph Holt, January 16, 1863, container 36; George P. Finlay to Joseph Holt, February 20, 1863, container 37; Jane P. Holt to Joseph Holt, August 24, 1863, container 39; Nannie W. Dorsey to Joseph Holt, October 3, 1864, container 45; S. E. Moseley to Joseph Holt, December 7, 1864, container 45; Washington Dorsey Gibbs to Joseph Holt, December 14, 1864, container 46, Holt Papers, LC.

4. Lowry, *Don't Shoot That Boy!* ii, 13, 18, 21, 53; Joseph Holt to Abraham Lincoln, February 17, 1865, Lincoln Papers, LC.

5. McPherson, *Ordeal by Fire*, 316–17. On emancipation, see Guelzo, *Lincoln's Emancipation Proclamation*; Vorenberg, *Final Freedom*.

6. McPherson, *Ordeal by Fire*, 317. Lincoln originally suspended the writ of habeas corpus on April 27, 1861; in May, the Supreme Court ruled this suspension unconstitutional, but Lincoln did not bend to the ruling. The September 24, 1862, proclamation was a restatement and expansion of his previous position, grounded on the notion that "the Constitution provided for suspension [of the writ] in cases of rebellion or invasion where public safety required it." (Long, *Civil War Day by Day*, 79.) President Andrew Johnson restored habeas corpus on April 2, 1866.

For a focused examination of Holt's influence on the use and jurisdiction of military commissions, see Allen, "Joseph Holt."

7. For a thorough discussion of the difference between the Union's "soft war" and "hard war" approaches, see Grimsley, *The Hard Hand of War*.

8. "Speech of Hon. C. A. Wickliffe," 7, 15.

9. T. S. Bell to Joseph Holt, March 24, 1863, container 38; Jesse Kincheloe to Joseph Holt, January 18, 1863, container 36, Holt Papers, LC; Joseph Holt to Hiram Barney, October 25, 1862, quoted in the *New York Times*, November 13, 1862.

10. Hiram Barney to Joseph Holt, November 7, 1862, and November 11, 1862, container 35, Holt Papers, LC; Joseph Holt to Hiram Barney, October 25, 1862, quoted in the *New York Times*, November 13, 1862. See also T. S. Bell to Joseph Holt, November 16, 1862, container 35, Holt Papers, LC. For a thorough study of the wartime history of the Copperheads, see Weber, *Copperheads*. On McClellan, see Sears, *George B. McClellan*.

11. O. M. Dorman to Joseph Holt, November 13, 1862, container 35, Holt Papers, LC.

12. Hugh Campbell to Joseph Holt, September 26, 1862, container 34; Hugh Campbell to Joseph Holt, November 15, 1862, container 35, Holt Papers, LC.

13. E. T. Bainbridge to Joseph Holt, December 23, 1862, container 36; E. T. Bainbridge to Joseph Holt, September 12, 1862, container 34; Jesse W. Kincheloe to Joseph Holt, November 26, 1862, container 35; Alice Key Pendleton to Joseph Holt, December 17, 1862, container 36, Holt Papers, LC. Earlier in 1862, John Hunt Morgan's Confederate cavalry had also invaded the state, and he raided Kentucky again later in the war. "Such raids," Harrison writes, "were annoying, sometimes even embarrassing, but they did not pose a serious threat to Union forces in the state." (Harrison, *The Civil War in Kentucky*, 39, 57.) See also John Speed to Joseph Holt, September 23, 1862, container 34, Holt Papers, LC.

14. T. S. Bell to Joseph Holt, October 12, 1862; October 20, 1862; and November 1, 1862, container 35, Holt Papers, LC.

15. Harrison, *The Civil War in Kentucky*, 47; James Speed to Joseph Holt, October 23, 1862; November 8, 1862; and November 25, 1862, container 35; James Speed to Joseph Holt, November 27, 1862, container 41; James Speed to Joseph Holt, December 12, 1861, container 31; Gordon Granger to James F. Robinson, November 22, 1862, container 35, Holt Papers, LC; Joseph Holt to Abraham Lincoln, October 8, 1862, and October 28, 1862, Lincoln Papers, LC. According to Harrison, "The 1862 invasion of Kentucky was the high-water mark of the Confederacy in the West. The state would be the scene of numerous minor actions during the rest of the war; but after Bragg and Kirby Smith led their weary troops into Tennessee, the Confederate threat to seize Kentucky was at an end." (Harrison, *The Civil War in Kentucky*, 57.) In a late November conversation with "unconditional Union Kentuckians," Lincoln announced that "he would rather die" than rescind his emancipation policy. At this meeting, Holt's name was lifted up as one who could be sent through the state at an appropriate time in order to build support for the idea of ending slavery. See *New York Tribune*, November 24, 1862, in Basler, *Collected Works of Abraham Lincoln*, 5:503. See also Joseph Holt to Edwin Stanton, April 9, 1863, *OR*, ser. II, 5:456–57. Kentucky did not ratify the Thirteenth Amendment until 1975.

16. James Speed to Joseph Holt, November 8, 1862, container 35, Holt Papers, LC. Eighteen months later, General William T. Sherman also complained to Holt about this "problem." See William T. Sherman to Joseph Holt, April 6, 1864, *OR*, ser. II, 7:18–19; Joseph Holt to William T. Sherman, April 7, 1864, *OR* ser. II, 7:20.

17. The Articles of War under which the U.S. Army operated during the Civil War were approved in 1806 and not revised again for a century.

18. Special Orders, No. 350, November 17, 1862, *OR*, ser. I, vol. 12, pt. 2, 506. On November 25, Special Orders No. 362 dissolved the commission and organized a court-martial in its place. The court-martial was to begin meeting in Washington on November 27, or as soon after that as possible. (Special Orders, No. 362, November 25, 1862, *OR*, ser. I, vol. 12, pt. 2, 507.) Documents pertaining to the case begin on 505. See also ser. I, vol. 12, pt. 2 (supplement), 821–1134, and Holt's report to Lincoln on the case: Joseph Holt to Abraham Lincoln, January 19, 1863, Holt Papers, Huntington.

In addition to General Hunter, the members of the court were Major General E. A. Hitchcock and Brigadier Generals Rufus King, Benjamin Prentiss, James Rickets, Silas Casey, James Garfield, Napoleon Bonaparte Buford, and John P. Slough.

19. See Abraham Lincoln to Joseph Holt, January 12, 1863, in Basler, *Collected Works of Abraham Lincoln*, 6:54; Nevins and Thomas, *Diary of George Templeton Strong* 3:291.

20. Reverdy Johnson, *Reply to the Review of Judge Advocate General Holt*, 6; John Pope to Joseph Holt, August 25, 1863, container 40, Holt Papers, LC.

21. White, *Reply to the Hon. Reverdy Johnson's Attack*, 3, 6, 8–9, 19. White later went on to become the first president of Cornell University.

22. Rufus King to Joseph Holt, September 5, 1863; T. S. Bell to Joseph Holt, October 16, 1863, container 40, Holt Papers, LC. For a negative view of how the Porter case was handled, see Jermann, *Fitz-John Porter*. The reverberations from the Porter trial went on for many years as his defenders sought to have the results of the case overturned and him restored to the army. President Chester Arthur finally reversed the sentence in May 1882, although Porter's critics remained vocal. Subsequently he was restored to the army and retired as a colonel. President Grover Cleveland pardoned him completely in 1886. See Simon, *Papers of Ulysses S. Grant*, 17:327–40.

23. Mary W. Cash to Joseph Holt, October 14, 1863, container 40, Holt Papers, LC.

24. Abraham Lincoln to Joseph Holt, January 3, 1863, *OR*, ser. I, 14:979. See also Basler, *Collected Works of Abraham Lincoln*, 6:35; Joseph Holt to Abraham Lincoln, January 26, 1863, *OR*, ser. I, 14:979–83. Lincoln approved Holt's recommendation. See H. W. Benham to Joseph Holt, February 27, 1863, container 37, Holt Papers, LC; and the case of Brigadier General Julius White, Special Orders, No. 256, "Proceedings of a Military Commission," September 23, 1862, *OR*, ser. I, vol. 12, pt. 2, 766–805.

25. Lowry, *Don't Shoot That Boy!* 134–35. Lincoln agreed. Holt also recommended overturning the sentence given to deserter Corporal James Benson, of the 8th Infantry, of demotion to the ranks, confinement at hard labor until the end of his enlistment, followed by a dishonorable discharge. Back during the secession winter, when David Twiggs had shamelessly surrendered the Federal installations in Texas to the fledgling Confederacy's control while Holt was secretary of war, Benson, Holt noted, had stood firm, withstanding "all attempts to seduce, persuade, or force" him to abandon the government and its flag. Holt recommended that Benson be pardoned, and Lincoln pardoned him. (Ibid., 127)

26. Ibid., 172–76. In this case, Lincoln disagreed, and he converted the sentence to five years in confinement.

27. Ibid., 33–34, 70. Lincoln agreed in McMahon's case; his opinion on Lohmann's case is unknown.

28. Ibid., 211, 221.

29. Joseph Holt, "On the application of Capt. Benjamin P. Walker," December 1, 1862, *OR*, ser. II, 5:3–5. Lincoln agreed with Holt's assessment. See also Lowry, *Don't Shoot That Boy!* 194–95, 202.

30. Joseph Holt to Edwin M. Stanton, May 16, 1863, *OR*, ser. II, 5:528–29. See a similar comment about a Californian named E. M. Strange, in Joseph Holt to Henry Halleck, April 29, 1863, *OR*, ser. II, 5:536–37. See also Joseph Holt to Abraham Lincoln, March 11, 1864, *OR*, ser. II, 6:1029–33; Lowry, *Don't Shoot That Boy!* 190–91, 210; Lowry, *Confederate Heroines*, 53–55. On this occasion, Lincoln again displayed greater patience, and despite Holt's recommendation, Pollock was released. For more on women spies during the war, North and South, see Leonard, *All the Daring of the Soldier*.

31. For the archival records of the tens of thousands of cases Holt considered during the war, see the vast files of RG 153, Records of the Office of the Judge Advo-

cate General, at the National Archives, Washington, D.C. For Bogan's case, see Joseph Holt, "Opinion in the Case of West Bogan," May 30, 1864, container 38, Holt Papers, LC.

32. Joseph Holt, "Opinion in the Case of John J. Glover," June 6, 1864, container 43, Holt Papers, LC.

33. Ibid. See also Lowry, *Don't Shoot That Boy!* 247, where he discusses the case of Private William Elliott of the 8th U.S. Infantry, who, while his regiment was stationed at Rectortown, Virginia, attempted to rape a black woman, Kate Brooks. Commenting on the case, Holt described Elliott's act as "a brutal attempt at rape on a gray-haired Negro woman between 60 and 70 years of age" and declared him unequivocally guilty. With Lincoln's approval, Elliott was sentenced to spend the rest of his life in prison.

34. Joseph Holt, "Opinion in the Case of Fountain Brown," May 24, 1864, container 43, Holt Papers, LC.

35. Ibid.; *OR*, ser. II, 7:159–62; Joseph Holt to Edwin M. Stanton, November 22, 1864, *OR*, ser. II, 7:1151; Basler, *Collected Works of Abraham Lincoln*, 7:357.

36. McPherson, *Ordeal by Fire*, 379; D. S. Curtiss to Joseph Holt, April 4, 1863, container 38, Holt Papers, LC; Thomas and Hyman, *Stanton*, 234.

37. Joseph Holt to Edwin M. Stanton, August 20, 1863, container 39, Holt Papers, LC.

38. Joseph Holt to Edwin M. Stanton, August 20, 1863, container 39, Holt Papers, LC; Joseph Holt to Edwin M. Stanton, August 17, 1863, *OR*, ser. II, 6:209–11; Joseph Holt to Abraham Lincoln, August 19, 1863, *OR*, ser. II, 6:216–18; Joseph Holt, "The writer of this letter," December 4, 1863, *OR*, ser. II, 6:604. For a thorough discussion of black men's service in the Federal army during the Civil War, see Glatthaar, *Forged in Battle*.

39. William E. Boulger to Joseph Holt, November 18, 1862, container 35; Francis Lieber to Joseph Holt, February 22, 1863, container 37, Holt Papers, LC. For an overview of legal changes during the Civil War, in many of which Holt's hand can be seen, see Samito, *Changes in Law and Society*; Neff, *Justice in Blue and Gray*.

40. In April 1863, Holt called for a stern policy against both men and women who demonstrated themselves to be "incorrigible rebels." (Joseph Holt to Edwin M. Stanton, April 24, 1863, *OR*, ser. II, 5:515.) Lieber built this policy into his code. See Francis Lieber to Joseph Holt, June 11, 1863, and July 17, 1863, container 39, Holt Papers, LC.

41. Joseph Holt, *Digest of the Opinions*; McPherson, *Ordeal by Fire*, 374; Joseph Holt to the U. S. Supreme Court, December 1863, *OR*, ser. II, 6:620–24. For a critical look at the government's handling of the Vallandigham case, see Klement, *The Limits of Dissent*; Neely, *The Fate of Liberty*. See also Lincoln's reply to a series of critical resolutions regarding the case, from a group of citizens in Albany, New York, in Lincoln, *Truth from an Honest Man*.

42. Joseph Holt to the U.S. Supreme Court, December 1863, *OR*, ser. II, 6:620–24; John W. Forney to Joseph Holt, February 16, 1864, container 42, Holt Papers, LC. Holt took a similarly hard line against other political prisoners accused of trying to

undermine the Federal government and its army. See Joseph Holt to J. H. Martindale, June 24, 1863, *OR*, ser. II, 6:38–39.

43. Harrison, *The Civil War in Kentucky*, 83–85; Joseph Holt to Stephen G. Burbridge, May 14, 1864, *OR*, ser. II, 7:144–45; Stephen G. Burbridge to Joseph Holt, May 20, 1864, *OR*, ser. II, 7:155; E. D. Townsend to Joseph Holt, July 12, 1864, *OR*, ser. I, vol. 52, pt. 1, 567–68.

44. Clous, "Judge Advocate General's Department"; *OR*, ser. III, 4:774; Joseph Holt to Edwin M. Stanton, June 29, 1864, and Joseph Holt, Oath of Office, June 29, 1864, H834 CB 1864, in RG 94, Records of the Adjutant General's Office, 1780s–1917, Letters Received by the Commission Branch of the Adjutant General's Office, 1863–1870, Roll 96, 1864, H579–H835, National Archives and Records Administration, Washington, D.C.

45. T. S. Bell to Joseph Holt, June 28, 1864; Mary Ann Stephens to Joseph Holt, July 4, 1864, container 44, Holt Papers, LC.

46. Lincoln's so-called Ten Percent Plan offered full pardons and the restoration of property (except human property) to most rebels who took the oath of allegiance to the United States. It also authorized rebel states to reenter the Union whenever 10 percent of those who had voted in the 1860 election had taken the oath and had adopted a new republican state government that recognized emancipation. See McPherson, *Ordeal by Fire*, 425; Joseph Holt to Edwin M. Stanton, July 22, 1864, *OR*, ser. I, vol. 39, pt. 2, 198; Joseph Holt to Edwin M. Stanton, July 31, 1864, *OR*, ser. I, vol. 39, pt. 2, 212–15.

47. T. S. Bell to Joseph Holt, August 8, 1864, container 44, Holt Papers, LC; Henry B. Carrington to Joseph Holt, November 4, 1864, *OR*, ser. II, 7:1089; *OR*, ser. II, 7:930–53. On antigovernment organizations during the war see Weber, *Copperheads*; Klement, *Dark Lanterns*.

48. Francis Lieber to Joseph Holt, October 16, 1864; Mary Ann Stephens to Joseph Holt, October 31, 1864, container 45, Holt Papers, LC.

49. Anonymous to Joseph Holt, October 15, 1864, container 45; Joshua F. Speed to Joseph Holt, September 8, 1864, container 44; Joshua F. Speed to Joseph Holt, September 30, 1864, container 45, Holt Papers, LC; Bartman, "The Contribution of Joseph Holt," 253–54.

50. See Stampp, "The Milligan Case," 41–48; Towne, "Dissent and Treason"; Pitman, *The Trials for Treason*; and Klement, *Dark Lanterns*. It was, writes Stephen E. Towne simply, "an ambitious plot."

51. The members of the court were Brevet Brigadier General Silas Colgrove and Colonels William E. McLean, John T. Wilder, Thomas I. Lucas, Charles D. Murray, Benjamin Spooner, Richard P. DeHart, Ambrose A. Stephens, Ansel D. Wass, Thomas W. Bennett, Reuben Williams, and Albert Heash.

52. See *OR*, ser. II, 6:620–24, for Holt's justification of the use of military commissions generally, and in the Vallandigham case specifically, and for his explanation of the military commission's jurisdiction. On Lincoln, habeas corpus, and civil liberties, see Farber, *Lincoln's Constitution*; McGinty, *Lincoln and the Court*.

53. In his journal, Secretary of the Navy Gideon Welles speculated that Lincoln

also offered the post to Holt because he deemed it politically wise at this stage in the war to appoint someone from one of the border states. (Welles, *Diary of Gideon Welles*, 2:183.) Welles thought Holt erred in turning the attorney generalship down. "No man," Welles wrote, "should decline a place of such responsibility in times like these, when the country is unanimous in his favor." (Ibid., 187.) See also Nicolay and Hay, *Abraham Lincoln*, 9:346–47; Joseph Holt to Abraham Lincoln, November 1864 (precise date unclear), container 45, Holt Papers, LC; Joseph Holt to Abraham Lincoln, December 1, 1864, Lincoln Papers, LC.

54. Joseph Holt to Edwin M. Stanton, March 2, 1865, *OR*, ser. III, 4:1216.

55. Mary Ann Stephens to Joseph Holt, January 13, 1863; C. C. Green to Joseph Holt, January 19, 1863; Thomas Holt to Joseph Holt, February 3, 1863, container 36; Mary Ann Stephens to Joseph Holt, June 3, 1863, container 39; Margaret Sterett to Joseph Holt, May 7, 1863, container 38, Holt Papers, LC.

56. Mary Ann Stephens to Joseph Holt, March 10, 1863, container 37, Holt Papers, LC.

57. Mary Ann Stephens to Joseph Holt, August 7, 1863, container 39; William Sterett to Joseph Holt, September 15, 1863, container 40; William Sterett to Joseph Holt, July 2, 1864, container 44; C. C. Green to Joseph Holt, January 30, 1864; Mary Ann Stephens to Joseph Holt, February 10, 1864, container 42; John R. Holt to Joseph Holt, October 15, 1864, container 45, Holt Papers, LC.

58. Jonathan W. White, "'Sweltering with Treason,'" 2–3, 5, 9. (Note: my page numbers coincide with the online version of this article at http://www.archives.gov/publications/prologue/2007/summer [accessed October 16, 2009].)

59. F. K. Hunt to Joseph Holt, December 22, 1862, container 36; C. W. Wooley to Joseph Holt, February 23, 1863, container 37; Nathaniel P. Banks to Joseph Holt, May 5, 1863; James O. Harrison to Joseph Holt, May 14, 1863, container 38; James O. Harrison to Joseph Holt, December 26, 1864, container 46, Holt Papers, LC.

60. See the insert in a letter from H. N. Stanard to Joseph Holt, February 1861 (precise date unknown), container 27; Unknown to Joseph Holt, December 20, 1860, container 26; Anna W. Curtis to Joseph Holt, December 29, 1861; Henrietta P. Dunn to Joseph Holt, undated but probably summer/fall 1861; Roberta Rhodes to Joseph Holt, undated but probably summer/fall 1861, container 31; Lydia Secor to Joseph Holt, November 23, 1862, container 35; Lydia Secor to Joseph Holt, March 22, 1864, container 43; Marcellina Adams to Joseph Holt, October 13, 1863, container 40; Marcellina Adams to Joseph Holt, March 19, 1861, container 28; Marcellina Adams to Joseph Holt, March 24, 1865, container 47, Holt Papers, LC.

61. In one of her letters Mary identified her birth date as September 12, 1839. See Mary W. Cash to Joseph Holt, September 10, 1862, container 34, Holt Papers, LC. See also Mary W. Cash to Joseph Holt, March 5, 1862, container 32; Mary W. Cash to Joseph Holt, July 6, 1862, container 34; Mary W. Cash to Joseph Holt, May 15, 1863, container 38, Holt Papers, LC. I have been unable to identify with certainty much about Mary's background or family connections, but I believe she was the daughter of Andrew D. Cash, who appears in the 1850 U.S. Federal Census as a resident of Philadelphia's Lombard Ward, and whose household included, among others,

three girls named Julia Cash (then age fifteen), Rebecca Cash (then age twelve), and Mary Cash (then age ten). See also Joseph Holt to Margaret Wickliffe Holt, January 7, 1860, container 23, Holt Papers, LC.

62. Mary W. Cash to Joseph Holt, undated, but internal evidence suggests summer/fall 1861, container 31; Mary W. Cash to Joseph Holt, November 21, 1861, container 41; Mary W. Cash to Joseph Holt, March 4, 1862, container 36; Mary W. Cash to Joseph Holt, June 3, 1862, container 39; Mary W. Cash to Joseph Holt, July 6, 1862, container 34, Holt Papers, LC.

63. Mary W. Cash to Joseph Holt, November 8, 1863, container 40; Mary W. Cash to Joseph Holt, August 28, 1862; September 1, 1862; and September 10, 1862, container 34; Mary W. Cash to Joseph Holt, December 18, 1862; January 4, 1863; and January 31, 1863, container 36; Mary W. Cash to Joseph Holt, February 9, 1863, container 37; Mary W. Cash to Joseph Holt, May 1, 1863, container 38; Mary W. Cash to Joseph Holt, August 22, 1863, container 39, Holt Papers, LC.

64. Mary W. Cash to Joseph Holt, October 14, 1863, and November 1, 1863, container 40, Holt Papers, LC.

65. Mary W. Cash to Joseph Holt, November 8, 1863, container 40; Mary W. Cash to Joseph Holt, October 19, 1862, and November 12, 1862, container 35; Mary Ann Stephens to Joseph Holt, November 24, 1863, container 41, Holt Papers, LC.

66. I suspect that this Jane was probably the one who came to Washington when Holt and Margaret first moved there. She was probably very loyal to Margaret, though that hardly means that she aimed to, or even did, provoke the dispute with Mary Cash. See Mary W. Cash to Joseph Holt, undated but seems to be the beginning of 1864, container 41; Mary W. Cash to Joseph Holt, undated, container 46, Holt Papers, LC, which seems to be from this same period.

67. Mary W. Cash to Joseph Holt, undated but seems to be from the beginning 1864, container 41; Mary W. Cash to Joseph Holt, undated, container 45; Mary Ann Stephens to Joseph Holt, July 4, 1864, container 44; Mary W. Cash to Joseph Holt, undated, container 46; Mary W. Cash to Joseph Holt, April 2, 1864, container 38; Mary W. Cash to Joseph Holt, December 23, 1864, container 41; Mary H. Bowman to Joseph Holt, November 17, 1864, container 45; Mary H. Bowman to Joseph Holt, February 7, 1865, container 46, Holt Papers, LC.

68. Barely a month into Lincoln's presidency, Holt had attempted to use his influence to have Washington Dorsey Holt reappointed postmaster at Covington, Kentucky. It is not clear whether Holt's request to Lincoln's postmaster general, Montgomery Blair, was satisfied or not. See Abraham Lincoln to Montgomery Blair, April 11, 1861, in Basler, *Collected Works of Abraham Lincoln*, 4:326–27; William Sterett to Joseph Holt, January 13, 1865, container 46, Holt Papers, LC.

69. W. G. Snethen to Joseph Holt, April 4, 1865; Robert Holt to Thomas Holt, April 11, 1865, container 47, Holt Papers, LC. On the condition of the South and the attitudes of Confederates after the war, see Grimsley and Simpson, *The Collapse of the Confederacy*; Phillips, *Diehard Rebels*.

70. Robert Holt to Thomas Holt, April 11, 1865, container 47, Holt Papers, LC.

71. Robert Holt to Joseph Holt, April 12, 1865, container 47, Holt Papers, LC.

72. Mary Goldsborough to Joseph Holt, April 5, 1865, container 47, Holt Papers, LC; Joseph Holt, "Treason and its Treatment," April 14, 1865, Holt Papers, Huntington.

73. Joseph Holt, "Treason and its Treatment," April 14, 1865, Holt Papers, Huntington.

Chapter Six

1. For a complete discussion of the events surrounding the assassination and the trial of John Wilkes Booth's coconspirators, see, among others, Leonard, *Lincoln's Avengers*; Chamlee, *Lincoln's Assassins*; Hanchett, *The Lincoln Murder Conspiracies*; Kauffman, *American Brutus*; Oldroyd, *The Assassination of Abraham Lincoln*; Peterson, *The Trial of the Assassins and Conspirators*; Pitman, *The Assassination of President Lincoln and the Trial of the Conspirators*; Poore, *The Conspiracy Trial for the Murder of the President*; Steers, *Blood on the Moon*; Swanson, *Manhunt*; Weichmann, *A True History*.

2. Mary Goldsborough to Joseph Holt, April 17, 1865; Frank Ballard to Joseph Holt, April 19, 1865, and April 24, 1865; Jesse W. Kincheloe to Joseph Holt, May 1, 1865, container 47, Holt Papers, LC.

3. E. D. Townsend to Joseph Holt, April 20, 1865, Holt Papers, Huntington.

4. Hanchett, *The Lincoln Murder Conspiracies*, 63–65; forged letter, John Wilkes Booth to Jefferson Davis, May 1, 1865, container 47; William W. Murphy to William Hunter, May 17, 1865; Statement of Lewis F. Bates, May 29, 1865; W. H. Emory to [illegible] Morgan, June 4, 1865; Statement of Lou McAleer, June 7, 1865; Statement of Major Myers, June 8, 1865, container 92; Annie Ford to Joseph Holt, May 15, 1865; William Prescott Smith to Joseph Holt, May 18, 1865, container 47, Holt Papers, LC; *New York Times*, May 2, 1865.

The records of the evidence gathered by the bureau in connection with the conspiracy are a part of RG 153, Records of the Office of the Judge Advocate General (Army), National Archives and Records Administration, Washington, D.C. They are also available on microfilm, taking up sixteen reels and denoted (and hereafter cited) as "M-599."

According to Stanton's biographers, "so far as Stanton was concerned the trial of the conspirators was Holt's responsibility from beginning to end. His own official concern with it was finished when the assassins and conspirators were caught, although he continued to play a significant part in collecting evidence and examining witnesses. He did not, however, predetermine the outcome." (Thomas and Hyman, *Stanton*, 424.)

5. Hanchett, *The Lincoln Murder Conspiracies*, 64.

6. Edwin Stanton to Joseph Holt, May 2, 1865, ser. I, reel 14, Andrew Johnson Papers, Library of Congress, Washington, D.C. For a detailed study of Holt's grand conspiracy theory, see Tidwell, Hall, and Gaddy, *Come Retribution*.

7. Clay-Copton, *A Belle of the Fifties*, 148. Clay's wife claimed that Holt had targeted her husband because of his own guilt over siding with the Union for cynical professional reasons when his heart was really with the Confederacy. See also

Turner, *Beware the People Weeping*, 131; Tidwell, Hall, and Gaddy, *Come Retribution*, 20, 175, 189, 192; Hanchett, *The Lincoln Murder Conspiracies*, 64; *New York Times*, May 7, 1865; Cumming, *Devil's Game*, 14.

8. H. L. Burnett to Edwin Stanton, May 2, 1865, in *OR*, ser. II, 8:523.

9. "Loyalty" to Joseph Holt, May 22, 1865; Mary Ann Stephens to Joseph Holt, April 20, 1865, container 47, Holt Papers, LC.

10. Oldroyd, *The Assassination of Abraham Lincoln*, 115. Holt has often been criticized for abusing his right to call for a military tribunal in order to maintain control over cases that should not have fallen under his, or the bureau's, purview. A May 19, 1865, letter from Stanton to General Grant offers a somewhat different perspective. It reads, in part, "it appears that a Provost Court established by Major General Schofield is exercising jurisdiction over civil matters, and other subjects not pertaining to military operations. You are aware that the jurisdiction and authority of such courts have been investigated and reported upon by the Judge Advocate General, and that it has been held that all such jurisdictions are void, unauthorized by any law, and tend greatly to oppression, and the demoralization of the army. You will please issue orders to General Schofield that will put a stop to these abuses of authority by Provost Courts, or any military tribunals." See Edwin M. Stanton to Ulysses S. Grant, May 19, 1865, in Simon, *The Papers of Ulysses S. Grant*, 15:477.

11. Chamlee, *Lincoln's Assassins*, 215–18; Pitman, *The Assassination of Abraham Lincoln*, 17. Assigned to work with Hunter were Generals Lew Wallace, August V. Kautz, Alvin P. Howe, Robert S. Foster, and Thomas M. Harris, along with Lieutenant Colonel David R. Clendenin, Brevet Brigadier General Cyrus B. Comstock, and Brevet Colonel Horace Porter. (For reasons that are not entirely clear, Comstock and Porter were replaced the following day with Brevet Brigadier General James A. Ekin and Brevet Colonel C. H. Tomkins.)

12. See Henry Harnden to Joseph Holt, May 1865, *OR*, ser. I, vol. 49, pt. 1, 520–23; *New York Times*, May 16, 1865. Davis and Clay, and their wives, arrived at Hampton Roads on May 11. They remained on board the ship that had brought them until May 22, when the men were transferred to cells within the fort. See also Virginia Clay to Joseph Holt, May 23, 1865, container 48, Holt Papers, LC; *New York Times*, May 10, 1865, and May 11, 1865.

13. *New York Times*, May 13, 1865, and May 16, 1865. The other lawyers for the defendants were General Thomas Ewing Jr. (Spangler, Mudd, and Arnold); Frederick Stone (Herold); Walter S. Cox (Arnold and O'Laughlen); and William E. Doster (Atzerodt and Powell). Ewing also lodged a strong objection to the commission's legitimacy.

14. Kautz, *Diary*, May 12, 1865; May 16, 1865; and May 31, 1865; and Kautz, *Memoir*, II; John Hitz to Joseph Holt, June 5, 1865, container 92; H. L. C. Pierpont to Joseph Holt, May 21, 1865, container 47; Elise P. [last name unknown] to Joseph Holt, June 7, 1865, container 48, Holt Papers, LC; *New York Times*, May 23, 1865; *Philadelphia Inquirer*, May 20, 1865.

15. Kautz, *Diary*, May 30, 1865; Kautz, *Memoir*, II; A. E. King to G. W. Gile, April 28,

1865, *OR*, ser. I, vol. 46, pt. 3, 1002; H. L. C. Pierpont to Joseph Holt, May 21, 1865, container 47, Holt Papers, LC; Chamlee, *Lincoln's Assassins*, 226–27.

16. Jampoler, *The Last Lincoln Conspirator*.

17. Pitman, *The Assassination of Abraham Lincoln*, 24–25, 35–37, 39, 48–49.

18. Ibid., 54–56.

19. T. S. Bell to Joseph Holt, June 2, 1865, container 48; J. M. McAlpine to Joseph Holt, May 18, 1865, container 47, Holt Papers, LC; Chamlee, *Lincoln's Assassins*, 296–97; Cumming, *Devil's Game*, 6, 9.

20. Pitman, *The Assassination of Abraham Lincoln*, 28–33.

21. John A. Dix to Edwin Stanton, June 24, 1865, Edwin M. Stanton Papers, Library of Congress, Washington, D.C.; Pitman, *The Assassination of Abraham Lincoln*, 34. For a thorough examination of the complicated career of Charles Dunham, see Cumming, *Devil's Game*. Cumming indicates that it was probably Charles Dunham himself who wrote the letter signed by Wallace, in which "Wallace" claimed that "Conover" had been impersonating him. (144–50)

22. Kautz, *Memoir*, II; Documents of the Military Commission pertaining to their Deliberations, Judgments, and Sentences, June 29 and 30, 1865, container 92, Holt Papers, LC.

23. Kautz, *Memoir*, II. The five who signed the petition were Hunter, Kautz, Foster, Ekin, and Tompkins. See the Petition for Clemency in the case of Mary E. Surratt, container 92, Holt Papers, LC.

24. The following day, Holt addressed the request of a Mrs. Broadhead to visit Jefferson Davis in prison at Fortress Monroe. "The number and atrocity of the crimes alleged to have been committed by Davis," he wrote in his response to Mrs. Broadhead, "and the overwhelming proof of his guilt believed to exist, would seem to make it proper, and indeed necessary, that the strictest prison discipline should be enforced in his case." (Opinion of Joseph Holt, June 30, 1865, *OR*, ser. II, 8:690.)

25. Hanchett, *The Lincoln Murder Conspiracies*, 70; *Philadelphia Inquirer*, July 6, 1865, and July 7, 1865.

26. *New York Times*, July 7, 1865; *Philadelphia Inquirer*, July 7, 1865.

27. Habeas Corpus Petition for Mary E. Surratt, July 7, 1865, container 92, Holt Papers, LC.

28. V. O. Taylor to Joseph Holt, July 7, 1865, container 48; Harvey Yeaman Sr. to Joseph Holt, July 16, 1865, container 49; T. S. Bell to Joseph Holt, July 7, 1865, container 48, Holt Papers, LC.

29. T. S. Bell and J. W. Calvert to Joseph Holt, May 8, 1865, container 47; Tal P. Shaffner to Joseph Holt, June 27, 1865, container 48, Holt Papers, LC.

30. Edwin Stanton to Alvin P. Hovey, May 30, 1865, *OR*, ser. II, 8:583–84.

31. Quoted in Graf, Simpson, and Muldowny, *Advice After Appomattox*, 104–5. See also Holt's September 20, 1865, opinion in the case of Samuel Smith, a black sergeant in the 5th Cavalry (USCT) convicted of involuntary manslaughter in the shooting of a white man, discussed in Graf and Haskins, *The Papers of Andrew Johnson*, 9:104.

32. *Philadelphia Inquirer*, July 8, 1865; *New York Times*, July 8, 1865, and July 13, 1865; Weichmann, *A True History*, 284–85.

33. *Philadelphia Inquirer*, July 17, 1865.

34. T. S. Bell to Joseph Holt, June 2, 1865, container 48, Holt Papers, LC.

35. Sarah F. Mudd to Joseph Holt, September 4, 1865, container 49; Sarah F. Mudd to Joseph Holt, November 27, 1865, container 50, Holt Papers, LC.

36. W. B. Evans to Joseph Holt, March 12, 1866, container 51, Holt Papers, LC; *Awards for the Capture of Booth and Others*; H. L. Olcott to Joseph Holt, July 28, 1865, and September 15, 1865, container 49; H. L. Burnett to Joseph Holt, October 18, 1865, container 50, Holt Papers, LC; Hanchett, *The Lincoln Murder Conspiracies*, 75; Welles, *Diary of Gideon Welles*, 2:337–38.

In June, Holt consulted with attorney Benjamin Stanton, a former member of the U.S. House of Representatives who was also a distant cousin of Secretary Stanton, regarding the question of trying Davis for treason. "The trial of Jefferson Davis for treason," wrote Stanton, "will be a marked event in the judicial history of the country. . . . He committed treason enough to hang a legion of men." (Benjamin Stanton to Joseph Holt, June 7, 1865, container 92, Holt Papers, LC.) See also Joseph Holt to Edwin M. Stanton, November 13, 1865, *OR*, ser. III, 5:492–93.

37. Sanford Conover to Joseph Holt, July 26, 1865; August 2, 1865; August 24, 1865; September 1, 1865; and September 4, 1865, container 92, Holt Papers, LC. Writes Thomas R. Turner, "It is true that Judge Advocate Holt and others were at best badly deceived and at worst involved in a plot to suborn perjured testimony," but "there was still a volume of apparently untainted testimony that led to the same conclusion of southern involvement and foreknowledge of the plot." (Turner, *Beware the People Weeping*, 68.) Holt, writes Carman Cumming, "was in some ways Dunham's ideal foil," because Dunham was a trickster and Holt was desperate to have faith in him. (Cumming, *Devil's Game*, 19.) It bears noting that even Cumming, who has little respect for Holt, does not think that Holt instigated Dunham's deceit. (161–62)

38. Henry Wilding to William H. Seward, September 17, 1865; John F. Potter to William H. Seward, October 25, 1865; Deposition of Lewis McMillan, September 26, 1865; Henry Wilding to William H. Seward, September 30, 1865; Henry Wilding to William H. Seward, October 10, 1865; and W. Hunter to Henry Wilding, October 13, 1865; in U.S. House of Representatives, Executive Document No. 9, *John H. Surratt*. See also Jampoler, *The Last Lincoln Conspirator*, 87. According to Jampoler, Beverly Tucker, who had been named as one of the Canadian Cabinet members involved in the assassination, was also on board the Peruvian. (67)

39. John F. Potter to William H. Seward, October 25, 1865; John F. Potter to William H. Seward, October 27, 1865; and William H. Seward to James Speed, November 13, 1865; in U.S. House of Representatives, Executive Document No. 9, *John H. Surratt*.

40. A. Burwell to Joseph Holt, August 18, 1865, container 49, Holt Papers, LC.

41. H. T. Drinkhouse to Joseph Holt, August 28, 1865, container 49, Holt Papers, LC; Joseph Holt to Andrew Johnson, October 31, 1865, *OR*, ser. II, 8:775–81.

42. Joseph Holt to Edwin M. Stanton, November 13, 1865, *OR*, ser. III, 5:492–93.

43. *OR*, ser. III, 5:490.

44. C. B. New to Joseph Holt, July 19, 1865, container 49, Holt Papers, LC. Lincoln replaced Blair with William Dennison in September 1864.

45. Joseph Holt to Preston King, September 1, 1865; Preston King to Joseph Holt, September 4, 1865, container 49, Holt Papers, LC.

46. Welles, *Diary of Gideon Welles*, 2:370.

47. Frank Ballard to Joseph Holt, September 5, 1865, container 49, Holt Papers, LC; "Reply of Hon. J. Holt to Hon. Montgomery Blair, Late Postmaster General," *Washington Chronicle*, September 13, 1865.

48. Frank W. Ballard to Joseph Holt, September 15, 1865; W. G. Snethen to Joseph Holt, September 15, 1865, and September 16, 1865, container 49; Benjamin Stanton to Joseph Holt, September 19, 1865; D. H. Hoopes to Joseph Holt, September 18, 1865; C. D. Drake to Joseph Holt, September 20, 1865, container 50, Holt Papers, LC; Y. L. Smith to Joseph Holt, September 19, 1865, Holt Papers, Huntington.

49. Joseph Holt to Edwin Stanton, September 16, 1865, *OR*, ser. II, 8:750–53; U.S. Senate, Executive Document No. 11, *Letter of the Secretary of War*, 35–36. See also Joseph Holt's letter to Andrew Johnson regarding the case of C. C. Reese, sentenced to death for killing an elderly freedwoman, Nellie West, in which Holt summarily rejected three petitions on Reese's behalf. "The fiendish barbarity of the murder," he wrote, "committed by Reese with his own hand" and "his cruel and unprovoked threats of death to the aged, feeble, and despairing woman on the morning of the homicide" were "circumstances which aggravate immensely his original crime, and should be regarded as justly taking from him every ground on which to base a hope of Executive favor." Still, Johnson suspended Reese's execution and he was eventually released. (Joseph Holt to Andrew Johnson, December 27, 1865, in Graf and Haskins, *The Papers of Andrew Johnson*, 9:541–43.)

50. Sanford Conover to Joseph Holt, September 4, 1865; October 10, 1865; November 1, 1865; and November 15, 1865, container 92; Louis Weichmann to Joseph Holt, October 10, 1865; November 12, 1865; November 23, 1865; November 28, 1865; and December 18, 1865; Louis Weichmann to H. L. Burnett, November 10, 1865, container 50, Holt Papers, LC.

51. Jesse W. Kincheloe to Joseph Holt, September 20, 1865, and October 9, 1865, container 50, Holt Papers, LC.

52. T. H. Duval to Joseph Holt, November 1, 1865, and December 4, 1865, container 50; T. H. Duval to Joseph Holt, January 14, 1866, and February 12, 1866, container 51, Holt Papers, LC.

53. Joseph Holt to the Adjutant General, November 30, 1865, H834 CB 1864, in RG 94, Records of the Adjutant General's Office, 1780s–1917, Letters Received by the Commission Branch of the Adjutant General's Office, 1863–1870, Roll 96, National Archives and Records Administration, Washington, D.C.; Hanchett, *The Lincoln Murder Conspiracies*, 75. All of the depositions are in container 92, Holt Papers, LC, along with that of John McGill, taken on August 17.

54. Joseph Snevel to Sanford Conover, November 14, 1865, container 50, Holt Papers, LC; Joseph Snevel to Joseph Holt, December 23, 1865, Holt Papers, Hunting-

ton; William Campbell to Joseph Holt, November 15, 1865; William Campbell to Sanford Conover, November 19, 1865, container 50, Holt Papers, LC; Joseph Holt to Sanford Conover, December 15, 1865, Holt Papers, Huntington.

55. Joseph Holt to Edwin M. Stanton, December 21, 1865, *OR*, ser. II, 8:838–40.

56. Jesse W. Kincheloe to Joseph Holt, January 17, 1866, container 51, Holt Papers, LC; Unknown to Joseph Holt, January 30, 1866, in Holt Papers, Huntington.

57. Joseph Holt to Edwin M. Stanton, January 18, 1866, *OR*, ser. II, 8:847–67.

58. Joseph Holt to Edwin M. Stanton, January 18, 1866, *OR*, ser. II, 8:847–67. See also Yulee, "Senator David L. Yulee," 3–22.

59. See the many letters from William Merrick to David Yulee during Yulee's imprisonment, which are in the David Levy Yulee Papers, Special and Area Studies Collections, George A. Smathers Libraries, University of Florida, Gainesville, Florida.

60. Joseph Holt to Edwin M. Stanton, January 18, 1866, *OR*, ser. II, 8:847–67.

61. Andrew Johnson, in a speech to a Cincinnati audience on August 31, 1861, in Graf and Haskins, *The Papers of Andrew Johnson*, 4:702; Welles, *Diary of Gideon Welles*, 2:423.

62. McPherson, *Ordeal by Fire*, 556; Joseph Holt to Sanford Conover, March 17, 1866, Holt Papers, Huntington; Joseph Holt to Edwin M. Stanton, March 10, 1866, *OR*, ser. II, 8:890–91.

63. Mary Ann Stephens to Joseph Holt, August 10, 1865, container 49, Holt Papers, LC.

64. Mary Ann Stephens to Joseph Holt, August 10, 1865, and August 21, 1865, container 49, Holt Papers, LC. Mary Ann Stephens was a Unionist, but she was no racial egalitarian. "Brother Jo," she wrote in this letter, "tell Andrew Johnson if congress passes a law for the negrows to vote get him to veto it & not let them vote until they get to [Liberia] & I think they will be sent there in time I think by degrees government will send them back to there [*sic*] own country & they will be the means of civilizing Africa." See also Eleanor Stephens Holt to Joseph Holt, September 14, 1865, container 21; Thomas Holt to Joseph Holt, October 17, 1865, container 50; W. S. Lamb to Joseph Holt, September 15, 1865, container 49; handwritten copy of Mary Ann Stephens's will, dated July 11, 1857, in container 98, folder 4; Mary Ann Stephens to Joseph Holt, November 9, 1862, container 35; Jesse W. Kincheloe to Joseph Holt, October 9, 1865, container 50, Holt Papers, LC.

65. Eleanor Holt to Joseph Holt, April 25, 1865, container 38, Holt Papers, LC.

66. Eleanor Stephens Holt to Joseph Holt, September 14, 1865, container 21, Holt Papers, LC. In an April 20 letter to Holt, Aunt Mary Ann indicated that Holt's brother Thomas had been to Washington, where the two brothers saw each other for the first time since before the war began. Unfortunately, there is no known account offering details of their meeting. See Mary Ann Stephens to Joseph Holt, April 20, 1865, container 47, Holt Papers, LC. See also Eleanor Stephens Holt to Joseph Holt, February 2, 1866, container 23, Holt Papers, LC.

67. Robert Holt to Joseph Holt, May 20, 1865, and June 8, 1865, container 47; Robert Holt to Joseph Holt, August 25, 1865, container 49, Holt Papers, LC.

68. Margaret Sterett Bowmer, December 4, 1865, container 41; Margaret Sterett Bowmer, January 9, 1866, container 51, Holt Papers, LC.

69. Frank, Holt, and Will Schoepf to Joseph Holt, February 7, 1866, container 51; James O. Harrison to Joseph Holt, June 22, 1865, container 48; James O. Harrison to Joseph Holt, July 14, 1865, container 49, Holt Papers, LC.

70. Mary W. Cash to Joseph Holt, undated but clearly spring 1865, container 46; Becky M. Cash to Joseph Holt, June 19, 1865, container 48; Mary H. Bowman to Joseph Holt, January 30, 1866, container 51; Mary H. Bowman to Joseph Holt, June 11, 1866, container 52; and Mary H. Bowman to Joseph Holt, August 29, 1866, container 53, Holt Papers, LC. During this period Holt's friendship with Mary Goldsborough also suffered a serious and perhaps mortal blow, thanks, it seems, to Goldsborough's indiscretion in sharing with some women friends, and in such a manner as to give the appearance that they were on intimate terms, how very fond she was of him. See Mary Goldsborough to Joseph Holt, September 15, 1865, container 49, Holt Papers, LC.

71. Margaret E. Crosby to Joseph Holt, June 2, 1865, and June 19, 1865, container 48, Holt Papers, LC.

72. Margaret E. Crosby to Joseph Holt, July 10, 1865, container 49; Margaret E. Crosby to Joseph Holt, October 10, 1865, and November 28, 1865, container 50; Margaret E. Crosby to Joseph Holt, April 5, 1866, container 51, Holt Papers, LC.

73. Jesse W. Kincheloe to Joseph Holt, March 22, 1866, container 51, Holt Papers, LC.

74. Ulysses S. Grant to Andrew Johnson, March 22, 1866, quoted in Simon, *Papers of Ulysses S. Grant*, 16:127. See also Yulee, "Senator David L. Yulee," 15.

In 1867, a group of congressmen identifying themselves as "The Union Congressional Executive Committee" published a series of articles in the *Washington Chronicle* (later published in pamphlet form), condemning the Supreme Court's ruling and predicting that it threatened to undermine the war's outcome and meaning. (*Review of the Decision of the U. S. Supreme Court*) In 1868, Milligan, free since April 12, 1866, filed suit for $500,000 in damages against the officers who had served on the military commission and against several other people who had been involved in the trial, including court reporter Benn Pitman. The case was finally decided in Milligan's favor in 1871, but only on the level of principle: in practice, he was awarded a token five dollars to cover his suffering. (Towne, "Dissent and Treason," 15.) Johnson declared the rebellion at an end in Texas on August 20, 1866. See also McGinty, *Lincoln and the Court*.

Chapter Seven

1. Hanchett, *The Lincoln Murder Conspiracies*, 78; Turner, *Beware the People Weeping*, 215–17; "Summons to Appear," April 12, 1866, container 52, Holt Papers, LC. The nine members of the House Judiciary Committee in the Thirty-ninth Congress were James Wilson (R-Iowa), George Boutwell (R-Mass.), Francis Thomas (R-Md.), Thomas Williams (R-Pa.), Frederick Woodbridge (R-Vt.), Daniel Morris (R-N.Y.), William Lawrence (R-Ohio), Burton Cook (R-Ill.), and Andrew Rogers (D-N.J.).

2. Ulysses S. Grant to Andrew Johnson, November 26, 1865, in Simon, *Papers of Ulysses S. Grant*, 15:419–20. See also E. D. Townsend to Nelson A. Miles, April 17, 1866, *OR*, ser. II, 8:899.

3. Joseph Holt to Sanford Conover, April 26, 1866, Holt Papers, Huntington; Cumming, *Devil's Game*, 162; Deposition of L. C. Turner to James F. Wilson, June 2, 1866; L. C. Turner to Joseph Holt (telegram), May 18, 1866, container 52; L. C. Turner to Joseph Holt, September 10, 1866, container 53, Holt Papers, LC; *OR*, ser. II, 8:962–64.

4. *Vindication of Judge Advocate General*, 6; Cumming, *Devil's Game*, 180, 183.

5. Joseph Holt, *Vindication of Judge Advocate General Holt*, 6; Cumming, *Devil's Game*, 184–86; U.S. House of Representatives, House Report No. 104, *Assassination of Lincoln*, 1.

6. *New York Times*, May 12, 1866, and May 15, 1866.

7. Ibid., May 12, 1866; May 15, 1866; June 4, 1866; and June 5, 1866; *New York Independent*, May 24, 1866.

8. Joseph Holt, *Vindication of Judge Advocate General Holt*, 5–6.

9. Joseph Holt to Edwin Stanton, July 3, 1866, container 100, Holt Papers, LC. In Speed's place, Johnson installed Henry Stanbery; in Dennison's place, he appointed David Tod.

10. Cumming, *Devil's Game*, 189, 196, 298; William Carter to Sanford Conover, April 27, 1866, container 52, Holt Papers, LC.

11. U.S. House of Representatives, House Report No. 104, *Assassination of Lincoln*, 1, 28–29.

12. For a study of the involvement of black soldiers in particular in the army's postwar activities, see Leonard, *Men of Color to Arms!* When the Army was reorganized again on April 10, 1869, the number of judge advocates was reduced to eight. Clous, "Judge Advocate General's Department."

13. U.S. House of Representatives, House Report No. 104, *Assassination of Lincoln*, 36–37, 39.

14. Thomas Shankland to Joseph Holt, August 2, 1866, container 53, Holt Papers, LC.

15. Robert Holt to Joseph Holt, August 21, 1866, container 53, Holt Papers, LC.

16. Frederick A. Aiken to Joseph Holt, August 29, 1866, container 53, Holt Papers, LC.

17. William W. Winthrop to Joseph Holt, August 6, 1866, container 53, Holt Papers, LC.

18. Joseph Holt, *Vindication of Judge Advocate General Holt*, 3. For a thorough study of the Southern antebellum culture of male honor see, for example, Wyatt-Brown, *Southern Honor*; and Wyatt-Brown, *Honor and Violence in the Old South*.

19. Frank Ballard to Joseph Holt, September 6, 1866; D. H. Hoopes to Joseph Holt, September 10, 1866; Jesse W. Kincheloe to Joseph Holt, September 18, 1866, container 53, Holt Papers, LC.

20. T. S. Bell to Joseph Holt, September 25, 1866; Henry L. Burnett to Joseph Holt, September 13, 1866, container 53; Henry L. Burnett to Joseph Holt, December 20, 1866; C. B. New to Joseph Holt, November 2, 1866; James O. Harrison to Joseph Holt, September 29, 1866, and November 7, 1866, container 54; George S. Boutwell to Joseph Holt, September 13, 1866, container 53; James F. Wilson to Joseph Holt, September 29, 1866; D. Morris to E. W. Dennis, October 15, 1866, container 54; L. C.

Turner to Joseph Holt, September 10, 1866, container 53, Holt Papers, LC; *OR*, ser. II, 8:962–64; Document from the Union League of Philadelphia, September 13, 1866, container 53, Holt Papers, LC. The recipient of the league's gold medal that year was George Gordon Meade. See *Chronicle of the Union League*, 543.

Although Holt gratefully acknowledged the great honor the league had bestowed upon him, in deference to the dangerous political waters he was then trying to navigate he asked that the award and his acceptance of it be kept quiet for the time being. Boker pledged to hold the news of the award in confidence until it could be announced "under skies that will be more open and brighter to men of our way of thinking." George Boker to Joseph Holt, September 27, 1866, container 53; George Boker to Joseph Holt, December 13, 1866, container 54, Holt Papers, LC.

21. Robert Holt to Joseph Holt, September 29, 1866, container 54; Joseph Holt to Edwin M. Stanton, September 11, 1866; Frank Ballard to Joseph Holt, September 6, 1866, container 53, Holt Papers, LC; Foner, *Reconstruction*, 265; D. H. Hoopes to Joseph Holt, September 10, 1866, container 53, Holt Papers, LC; Welles, *Diary of Gideon Welles*, 2:601, 616; Edwin M. Stanton to Joseph Holt, November 14, 1866, container 53, Holt Papers, LC.

22. *New York Times*, September 25, 1866; October 11, 1866; October 14, 1866; October 26, 1866; and October 31, 1866.

23. L. C. Turner to Joseph Holt, November 8, 1866, container 54, Holt Papers, LC; *OR*, ser. II, 8:973–74; *New York Times*, December 1, 1866; *New York Independent*, May 2, 1867; Cumming, *Devil's Game*, 199–209; Joseph Holt to Lorenzo Thomas, October 8, 1866, in the *Annual Report of the Secretary of War*, 1866, 45.

24. Foner, *Reconstruction*, 266; Louis Weichmann to Joseph Holt, August 9, 1866, and September 1, 1866, container 53; Louis Weichmann to Joseph Holt, October 10, 1866; October 19, 1866; October 23, 1866; and November 29, 1866; Louis Weichmann to William F. Johnston, October 15, 1866, container 54, Holt Papers, LC.

25. Louis Weichmann to Joseph Holt, June 21, 1866, container 52, Holt Papers, LC; Rufus King to William H. Seward, April 23, 1866, and May 11, 1866; Joseph Holt to Edwin M. Stanton, May 19, 1866; Joseph Holt to Frederick W. Seward, May 22, 1866, in U.S. House of Representatives, Executive Document No. 9, *John H. Surratt*. In December 1867, Sainte Marie sought compensation for his services to the federal government in identifying John Surratt. See U.S. House of Representatives, Executive Document No. 36, *H. B. Sainte-Marie*. Holt recommended that he be paid $15,000.

26. William H. Seward to James Wilson, May 25, 1866; William H. Seward to Edwin M. Stanton, May 28, 1866; Rufus King to William H. Seward, June 23, 1866; July 14, 1866; August 8, 1866; November 2, 1866; and November 3, 1866; and William H. Seward to Edwin M. Stanton, July 20, 1866; William H. Seward to Rufus King, October 16, 1866, in U.S. House of Representatives, Executive Document No. 9, *John H. Surratt*.

27. Foner, *Reconstruction*, 267–69; Margaret E. Crosby to Joseph Holt, November 30, 1866, container 54, Holt Papers, LC.

28. See *Impeachment Investigation*, 1–2.

29. See Edwin M. Stanton to Andrew Johnson, May 14, 1867, in Graf and Haskins, *The Papers of Andrew Johnson*, 12:268. In this letter Stanton described the "diary" as a "memorandum book found on the person of J. Wilkes Booth at the time of his capture."

30. *Impeachment Investigation*, 28, 32, 281. Holt, it turns out, had elected *not* to introduce Booth's diary at that trial, and by law the defense lawyers could not introduce it, though they certainly knew of its existence. Although Lafayette Baker claimed to believe that there had once been "a great deal more of the original diary than appears here now," he did not necessarily mean to imply that the missing pages had been in place when he first delivered the book to Stanton. Booth may have torn them out himself (32). See also Henry L. Burnett to E. G. Bowdoin, July 10, 1867, container 56, Holt Papers, LC. Bowdoin was the committee's clerk.

31. See U.S. House of Representatives, Executive Document No. 116, *Names of Persons Pardoned by the President*. See also Executive Document No. 32, *Additional List of Pardons*; and Executive Document No. 16, *Pardons of the President*.

32. Jampoler, *The Last Lincoln Conspirator*, 145; Rufus King to William H. Seward, November 10, 1866, in U.S. House of Representatives, Executive Document No. 9, *John H. Surratt*.

33. Charles Hale to William H. Seward, December 2, 1866; William H. Seward to Charles Hale, December 4, 1866; William H. Seward to Gideon Welles, December 4, 1866; William H. Seward to Rufus King, December 4, 1866; William H. Seward to Thomas H. Dudley, December 6, 1866, in U.S. House of Representatives, Executive Document No. 9, *John H. Surratt*; Louis Weichmann to Joseph Holt, December 5, 1866, container 54; Lawrence A. Hudson to Joseph Holt, January 10, 1867, container 55, Holt Papers, LC.

34. Jampoler, *The Last Lincoln Conspirator*, 151. According to Carman Cumming, John Surratt's and Charles Dunham's paths actually crossed at the courthouse on February 23, the day Dunham was supposed to be sentenced and Surratt was to be arraigned. (Cumming, *Devil's Game*, 208). See also T. H. Duval to Joseph Holt, January 23, 1867, container 55, Holt Papers, LC.

35. Foner, *Reconstruction*, 276.

36. Ibid., 276; Welles, *Diary of Gideon Welles*, 3:62. Holt must have been surprised indeed to learn that those voting in favor of the override even included his old nemesis, Reverdy Johnson.

37. A. H. Arthur to Joseph Holt, March 14, 1867; T. H. Duval to Joseph Holt, March 29, 1867, container 55; Jesse W. Kincheloe to Joseph Holt, June 5, 1867, container 56, Holt Papers, LC.

38. John F. Gray to Joseph Holt, April 5, 1867; April 15, 1867; and May 19, 1867, container 56, Holt Papers, LC. See also Charles Sumner to Dr. Brown-Sequard, April 5, 1867, Holt Papers, Huntington.

39. George Boutwell to Joseph Holt, April 1, 1867, container 55, Holt Papers, LC; *New York Times*, May 22, 1867; *Impeachment Investigation*, 285. See also E. J. Conger to Joseph Holt, April 13, 1867, container 56, Holt Papers, LC. Other members of the committee who were holdovers from the Thirty-ninth Congress were George Bout-

well (R-Mass.), Francis Thomas (R-Md.), Thomas Williams (R-Pa.), and Frederick Woodbridge (R-Vt.). New members were William Lawrence (R-Ohio), John Churchill (R-N.Y.), Samuel Marshall (D-Ill.) and Charles Eldredge (D-Wis.).

40. James F. Wilson to Joseph Holt, May 13, 1867, container 56, Holt Papers, LC; *New York Times*, May 14, 1867. Those who posted bail include Horace Greeley (N.Y.), Augustus Schell (N.Y.), Aristides Welsh (Pa.), David K. Jackman (Pa.), W. H. McFarland (Va.), Richard Barton Haxall (Va.), Isaac Davenport, (Va.), Abraham Warwick (Va.), Gustavus A. Myers (Va.), William W. Crump (Va.), John A. Meredith (Va.), William H. Lyons (Va.), John Minor Botts (Va.), Thomas W. Doswell (Va.), and James Thomas (Va.).

41. *New York Times*, May 23, 1867.

42. Joseph H. Holt to Joseph Holt, May 29, 1867, container 59, Holt papers, LC. On March 1, 1867, Holt's old friend C. C. Green of Louisville noted in a letter that he had an eight-year-old grandson "whom I've named after you Jo Holt Green who takes the first Honors at school." See C. C. Green to Joseph Holt, March 1, 1867, container 55, Holt Papers, LC. See also Robert Holt to Joseph Holt, September 29, 1866, container 54, Holt Papers, LC.

Robert's children were Sarah Ellen, b. 1844; Joseph, b. 1846 (d. 1882); John, b. 1848; Lockie, b. 1850; Annie, b. 1853 (d. 1868); Robert, b. 1855; Thomas, b. 1858; Lena, b. 1860 (d. 1882); James, b. 1863.

43. Jampoler, *The Last Lincoln Conspirator*, 172; Noel and Downing, *Court-House of the District of Columbia*, 56. For a complete record of the testimony at the trial, see *The Trial of John H. Surratt in the Criminal Court for the District of Columbia*.

44. *Trial of John H. Surratt*, 1:118; Jampoler, *The Last Lincoln Conspirator*, 156–58.

45. Jampoler, *The Last Lincoln Conspirator*, 163, 216; *Trial of John H. Surratt*, 1:464–82, 492.

46. H. L. Olcott to Joseph Holt, June 27, 1867, container 56, Holt Papers, LC; Jampoler, *The Last Lincoln Conspirator*, 182–83; *Trial of John H. Surratt*, 1:135–37, 158, 164, 197, 207, 369–434, 440–59.

47. *Trial of John H. Surratt*, 1:533, 542, 724, 725; 2:771–72, 853, 865; Jampoler, *The Last Lincoln Conspirator*, 208.

48. *Trial of John H. Surratt*, 1:469–70; Jampoler, *The Last Lincoln Conspirator*, 170, 215.

49. *Trial of John H. Surratt*, 2:1155, 1208, 1209, 1236.

50. Ibid., 2:1249–365.

51. Ibid., 2:1370–71, 1370–79.

52. Official document signed by E. D. Townsend, August 3, 1867; Henry L. Burnett to Joseph Holt, August 9, 1867, container 56, Holt Papers, LC; Hanchett, *The Lincoln Murder Conspiracies*, 87–88.

53. Undated clipping from the *Cincinnati Gazette*, container 53, Holt Papers, LC; Welles, *Diary of Gideon Welles*, 3:163. See also J. Warren Bell to Andrew Johnson, September 6, 1867, quoted in Graf and Haskins, *The Papers of Andrew Johnson*, 13:30.

54. Frank W. Ballard to Joseph Holt, August 13, 1867, container 56; Thomas Shankland to Joseph Holt, August 7, 1867; William H. Doherty to Joseph Holt, Au-

gust 10, 1867, container 57; Margaret E. Crosby to Joseph Holt, August 9, 1867, container 61, Holt Papers, LC.

55. William Winthrop to Joseph Holt, August 12, 1867, container 57, Holt Papers, LC.

56. Frank Ballard to Joseph Holt, August 29, 1867; Thomas Shankland to Joseph Holt, August 13, 1867; William W. Winthrop to Joseph Holt, August 13, 1867, container 57, Holt Papers, LC.

57. W. C. Dodge to Joseph Holt, August 19, 1867; T. H. Duval to Joseph Holt, August 20, 1867; John Pope to Joseph Holt, August 10, 1867, container 57, Holt Papers, LC.

58. James A. Ekin to Joseph Holt, August 26, 1867; Frank Ballard to Joseph Holt, August 29, 1867; Joshua F. Speed to Joseph Holt, August 30, 1867; T. H. Duval to Joseph Holt, October 24, 1867, container 57, Holt Papers, LC.

59. Joseph Holt to Lorenzo Thomas, October 1, 1867, in the *Annual Report of the Secretary of War*, 1867, 523; U.S. House of Representatives, Executive Document No. 47, *Albert M. D. C. Lusk*, 1, 17, 22. For more on Holt's cases during the Grant years, see also Simon, *Papers of Ulysses S. Grant*, 17:325–27, 516–18, 526, 578; 18:309–14; 19:367–69, 370–73, 386–88, 418–19, 446, 465–67, 566, 577–79.

60. Foner, *Reconstruction*, 180, 314–15; D. P. Henderson to Joseph Holt, January 15, 1868; T. S. Bell to Joseph Holt, January 27, 1868, container 58, Holt Papers, LC; U.S. House of Representatives, Judiciary Committee Report No. 7, *Impeachment of the President*; *The Great Impeachment*, 18.

61. Thomas Holt to Joseph Holt, February 16, 1868, container 58, Holt Papers, LC.

62. *The Great Impeachment*, 20; U.S. Senate, Miscellaneous Document No. 42, *Articles of Impeachment*; McPherson, *Ordeal by Fire*, 574.

63. McPherson, *Ordeal by Fire*, 574; T. H. Duval to Joseph Holt, March 8, 1868; Thomas Shankland to Joseph Holt, April 16, 1868, container 58, Holt Papers, LC.

64. McPherson, *Ordeal by Fire*, 574.

65. *The Great Impeachment*, 263–84; McPherson, *Ordeal by Fire*, 575. On the impeachment trial, see Benedict, *Impeachment and Trial of Andrew Johnson*.

66. Jampoler, *The Last Lincoln Conspirator*, 249–60.

67. T. H. Duval to Joseph Holt, July 23, 1868, and August 5, 1868; Samuel Holt to Joseph Holt, October 15, 1868, container 59, Holt Papers, LC.

68. Joseph Holt to E. D. Townsend, October 1, 1868, in the *Annual Report of the Secretary of War*, 1868.

69. Margaret E. Crosby to Joseph Holt, November 4, 1868, container 60; Margaret E. Crosby to Joseph Holt, May 30, 1868, container 59, Holt Papers, LC; Jampoler, *The Last Lincoln Conspirator*, 236.

Chapter Eight

1. Thomas Shankland to Joseph Holt, February 11, 1869, and March 3, 1869, container 60, Holt Papers, LC.

2. See, for example, the depositions of Francis McFall, John Martin, James E. Matterson, and Nathan Auser, May 17, 1867, container 56, Holt Papers, LC. See also

Albert G. Riddle to Andrew Johnson, July 23, 1867, container 57, Holt Papers, LC. This is most likely the source of Richard Merrick's accusation that Holt had manipulated the witnesses at the trial.

3. Joseph Holt to Andrew Johnson, July 23, 1867, container 57, Holt Papers, LC.

4. Cumming, *Devil's Game*, 210, 258; undated article, entitled "The Johnson-Conover Conspiracy," from the *Cincinnati Gazette*; undated article, entitled "The Conover Swindle," from the *Baltimore American*, container 53, Holt Papers, LC.

5. See Joseph Holt to Andrew Johnson, February 26, 1869, in Graf and Haskins, *The Papers of Andrew Johnson*, 15:478–80.

6. D. P. Henderson to Joseph Holt, March 3, 1869; Edmund Flagg to Joseph Holt, February 25, 1869; James O. Harrison to Joseph Holt, February 28, 1869; Thomas Shankland to Joseph Holt, February 11, 1869, and March 3, 1869, container 60, Holt Papers, LC. Grant named John A. Rawlins secretary of war instead. Rawlins died after about six months in office and was replaced by William W. Belknap in October 1869.

7. See Joseph Holt to E. D. Townsend, October 9, 1869, in the *Annual Report of the Secretary of War*, 1869, 181–82; Joseph Holt to W. W. Belknap, October 1, 1870, in the *Annual Report of the Secretary of War*, 1870, 97; Joseph Holt to William W. Belknap, October 1, 1871, in the *Annual Report of the Secretary of War*, 1871, 115; Joseph Holt to William W. Belknap, October 1, 1872, in the *Annual Report of the Secretary of War*, 1872, 129–30; Joseph Holt to William W. Belknap, October 1, 1873, in the *Annual Report of the Secretary of War*, 1873, unnumbered pages following p. 89; Joseph Holt to E. D. Townsend, October 1, 1874, in the *Annual Report of the Secretary of War*, 1874, unnumbered pages following p. 97; Joseph Holt to E. D. Townsend, October 1, 1875, in the *Annual Report of the Secretary of War*, 1875. Beginning in 1874, Holt tabulated the records of general courts-martial and garrison and regimental courts-martial separately "with a view of indicating how vast a proportion of the offenses tried were petty in their character, and therefore the subjects of the most subordinate military jurisdiction." (Joseph Holt to E. D. Townsend, October 1, 1874, in the *Annual Report of the Secretary of War*, 1874.) In his final year at the bureau, Holt did note that the number of military trials generally had declined to around 11,400. He chalked this change up to improved soldier morale, which he believed was a consequence of the army's enlistment of fewer married men than had been the case in the past. (Joseph Holt to E. D. Townsend, October 1, 1875, in the *Annual Report of the Secretary of War*, 1875.) See also U.S. Senate, Executive Document No. 11, *Letter from the Secretary of War*, 18.

8. Joseph Holt to William W. Belknap, October 1, 1871, in the *Annual Report of the Secretary of War*, 1871, 115; Joseph Holt to William W. Belknap, October 1, 1872, in the *Annual Report of the Secretary of War*, 1872, 129–30; Joseph Holt to William W. Belknap, October 1, 1873, in the *Annual Report of the Secretary of War*, 1873. The microfilm, housed at the National Archives in Washington, D.C., is denoted "M797."

9. Joseph Holt to E. D. Townsend, October 9, 1869, in the *Annual Report of the Secretary of War*, 1869, 181–82.

10. U.S. House of Representatives, Report No. 74, *Army Staff Reorganization*, 206–7.

11. Joseph Holt to William W. Belknap, October 1, 1872, in the *Annual Report of the Secretary of War*, 1872, 129–30.

12. Foner, *Reconstruction*, 412; A. Alderson to Joseph Holt, July 18, 1869, container 61, Holt Papers, LC. Revels served until March 1871. Rainey served until March 1879. Ironically, Mississippi did not ratify the Thirteenth Amendment abolishing slavery until 1995, twenty years after Kentucky.

13. Foner, *Reconstruction*, 446–49.

14. Ibid., 342, 422, 426, 455. The "pervasive impact and multiplicity of purposes" of the white supremacists' violence, Foner adds, "lacks a counterpart either in the American experience or in that of the other Western Hemisphere societies that abolished slavery in the nineteenth century" (425). On the post–Civil War KKK, see Chalmers, *Hooded Americanism*. On the Colfax Massacre, see Keith, *The Colfax Massacre*.

15. *New York Times*, August 23, 1872, and September 14, 1872; Trefousse, *Andrew Johnson*, 362; *Boston Globe*, October 1, 1872; Hanchett, *The Lincoln Murder Conspiracies*, 94–95.

16. Joseph Holt to John A. Bingham, February 11, 1873, container 66, Holt Papers, LC; Joseph Holt, *Vindication of Hon. Joseph Holt.*

17. Joseph Holt to John A. Bingham, February 18, 1873, container 66, Holt Papers, LC. At the time Stanton died Holt deeply grieved his loss, as did many others who had known the great war secretary. "I have admired and loved Mr. Stanton, and coveted his good opinion more than that of any other man," wrote General F. E. Spinner. "I have always thought, and often said, that you were much like him, and made of the same stuff." (F. E. Spinner to Joseph Holt, February 26, 1870, Holt Papers, Huntington.) Secretary of the Navy Welles offered a very different opinion of the late secretary of war, however, writing to Johnson: "I would not deny him a good deal of ability . . . [but h]e was a sycophant as well as a tyrant. . . . I know him to have been faithless and treacherous to your administration. . . . The War Department was the hot-bed of radical intrigue, and with him and his associates, the unconstitutional reconstruction measures had their origin." (Gideon Welles to Andrew Johnson, January 14, 1870, in Graf and Haskins, *The Papers of Andrew Johnson*, 16:163–65.)

18. Frederick W. Seward to Joseph Holt, April 13, 1873, and May 24, 1873, container 66, Holt Papers, LC; James Speed to Joseph Holt, March 30, 1873, quoted in Joseph Holt, *Vindication of Hon. Joseph Holt*, 7. See also James Speed to Joseph Holt, November 28, 1873, container 66, Holt Papers, LC.

19. Joseph Holt to R. D. Mussey, July 9, 1873, container 100, Holt Papers, LC.

20. R. D. Mussey to Joseph Holt, undated (but clearly a response to Holt's July 9, 1873, letter), and August 19, 1873, container 66, Holt Papers, LC; Joseph Holt to James May, September 16, 1873, Holt Papers, Huntington.

21. Joseph Holt to William W. Belknap, August (exact date unknown) 1873, in the Holt Papers, Huntington.

22. T. S. Bell to Joseph Holt, August 27, 1873; Horatio King to Joseph Holt, August 28, 1873; James A. Ekin to Joseph Holt (telegram), August 29, 1873; John A. Bingham to Joseph Holt, October 13, 1873, container 66, Holt Papers, LC. See also T. H. Duval to Joseph Holt, September 22, 1873, Holt Papers, Huntington. Duval considered Stanton's decision to remain silent both "strange" and "dishonorable in the extreme." Wrote Duval, "It seems almost incredible that he could have been guilty of such cold blooded meanness towards a friend, but the evidence is absolutely conclusive against him. . . . His conduct towards you, in this matter, has forever stamped a blot upon his name and fame." See also John Hay to Joseph Holt, August 29, 1873; Henry L. Burnett to Joseph Holt, October 20, 1873, Holt Papers, Huntington;

23. See Graf and Haskins, *The Papers of Andrew Johnson*, 16:456–58; *Washington Daily Chronicle*, November 11, 1873; *New York Times*, November 12, 1873. See also Gideon Welles to Andrew Johnson, November 5, 1873, in Graf and Haskins, *The Papers of Andrew Johnson*, 16:471–75.

In the fall of 1873, an additional, curious flap indirectly involving Holt erupted in the *New York Tribune* regarding the question of whether or not Mary Surratt had been manacled while in prison. Holt and John F. Hartranft, who had been in charge of the prisoners at the Old Arsenal Penitentiary and who was now governor of Pennsylvania, both refuted the accusation. See John F. Hartranft to Joseph Holt, September 4, 1873; Joseph Holt to Editor, *New York Tribune*, September 6, 1873, and September 9, 1863, container 66, Holt Papers, LC; Graf and Haskins, *The Papers of Andrew Johnson*, 16:438–42, 458, 471–75, 491–95.

24. Joseph Holt to Benn Pitman, November 20, 1873; Benn Pitman to Joseph Holt, November 22, 1873, container 66, Holt Papers, LC.

25. "Rejoinder of J. Holt, Judge Advocate General, to Ex-President Johnson's reply to his Vindication of 26th August last," container 116, Holt Papers, LC. See also *New York Times*, December 2, 1873; David Hunter to Joseph Holt, November 24, 1873, container 66; August V. Kautz to H. B. Burnham, December 17, 1873, container 68, Holt Papers, LC.

26. Louis J. Weichmann to Joseph Holt, April 6, 1869, container 61; Louis Weichmann to Joseph Holt, February 10, 1874; Joseph Holt to E. D. Townsend, August 14, 1874, container 68, Holt Papers, LC. Most years, Holt took a twenty- to thirty-day leave in the summer. See, for example, the official document signed by E. D. Townsend, August 11, 1869, container 61; and Joseph Holt to E. D. Townsend, September 29, 1873, container 66, Holt Papers, LC.

27. Joseph Holt to the Adjutant General, July 12, 1875; Joseph Holt to William W. Belknap, November 20, 1875; General Orders No. 98, from the Adjutant General's Office, December 1, 1875, H834 CB 1864, in RG 94, Records of the Adjutant General's Office, 1780s–1917, Letters Received by the Commission Branch of the Adjutant General's Office, 1863–1870, Roll 96, National Archives and Records Administration, Washington, D.C.

28. Theodore Tilton to Joseph Holt, December 1, 1875, container 70, Holt Papers, LC; *Harper's Weekly*, January 1, 1876.

29. Olds, "Memories of the Old Meigs Home," 88. The U.S. Census for 1870 shows

Holt living at his New Jersey home with Fannie Wickliffe, who was identified as a twenty-one-year-old black "house servant." Fannie's last name suggests that she came into Holt's employ through his late wife's family, perhaps originally as a slave child.

30. Eleanor K. Holt to Joseph Holt, May 19, 1870; Rosina Holt to Joseph Holt, November 25, 1870, container 63, Holt Papers, LC.

31. Joseph Holt to Vanda Vineyard Holt, November 10, 1871, HFPC; Rosina Holt to Joseph Holt, February 27, 1872, container 65, Holt Papers, LC. In 1880 the Federal Census for Breckinridge County listed the occupants of the Holt house in Stephensport as "Washington D. Holt, age 34; wife Vanda Lee Holt, 29; daughter Mary, 8; daughter Rosie, 5; his mother Rosina, 64; white servant Jenny Ford, 20; black servant Eliza Jones, 13; black servant Alice Robinson, 25; and George Moredock, 28-year-old mulatto boarder on the farm."

32. *Breckinridge County (Ky.) Herald-News*, March 16 and March 23, 1988; Joseph Holt to Washington Dorsey Holt, May 13, 1879, HFPC. See also Joseph Holt to Washington Dorsey Holt, May 20, 1882; and Joseph Holt to Washington Dorsey Holt, May 31, 1882; July 2, 1882; August 11, 1882; October 6, 1882; October 18, 1882; and October 29, 1882, in Holt Papers, Huntington. See also the unidentified, undated newspaper clipping about the chapel in a collection of Holt-related articles given to me by Norvelle Wathen, of Louisville, Kentucky. Unfortunately, the church was torn down in 1987 and no sign of it remains on the property.

33. Joseph Holt to Washington Dorsey Holt, May 13, 1879, HFPC; Joseph Holt to Rosa Holt, January 26, 1880, Holt Papers, Huntington; Joseph Holt to Mary and Rose Holt, August 5, 1883, HFPC; Olds, "Memories of the Old Meigs Home," 81–95.

34. Joseph Holt to Rosa Holt, January 26, 1880, Holt Papers, Huntington; Olds, "Memories of the Old Meigs Home," 88; Joseph Holt to Mary Holt, March 9, 1880, HFPC; Joseph Holt to Washington Dorsey Holt, July 2, 1882, and August 17, 1882; Joseph Holt to Vanda Vineyard Holt, August 17, 1882, Holt Papers, Huntington. The 1880 U. S. Census shows Holt living with Anna Richardson, married white housekeeper, age thirty-nine; George Johnson, single black coachman, age twenty-seven; and Susan Patrick, widowed black cook, age fifty-five.

35. A memo dated September 24, 1880, from the adjutant general's office, reads: "Write Gen. Holt (retired) a letter authorizing him to go abroad for six months or such longer period as he may desire to remain." See Adjutant General's Memo, September 24, 1880, in RG 94, Records of the Adjutant General's Office, 1780s–1917, Letters Received by the Commission Branch of the Adjutant General's Office, 1863–1870, Roll 96, H834 CB 1864, National Archives, Washington, D.C.; Joseph Holt to Vanda Vineyard Holt, April 17, 1881; March 25, 1882; and April 30, 1882; Joseph Holt to Washington Dorsey Holt, February 26, 1882, and March 15, 1882, Holt Papers, Huntington; Joseph Holt to Vanda Vineyard Holt, March 19, 1882, HFPC.

36. Joseph Holt to Vanda Vineyard Holt, August 17, 1882; Joseph Holt to Washington Dorsey Holt, July 2, 1882, Holt Papers, Huntington.

37. Joseph Holt to Mary and Rose Holt, August 5, 1883, HFPC; *Washington Evening Star*, August 2, 1894, JHRS.

38. Joseph Holt to Vanda Vineyard Holt, September 10, 1882, HFPC; Margaret E.

Crosby to Joseph Holt, December 25, 1869; January 12, 1869; January 24, 1869; February 28, 1869, container 60; Margaret E. Crosby to Joseph Holt, July 20, 1869, container 61; Margaret E. Crosby to Joseph Holt, September 10, 1869, and February 11, 1870, container 62, Holt Papers, LC.

39. Margaret E. Crosby to Joseph Holt, May 23, 1873, container 66, Holt Papers, LC.

40. Margaret E. Crosby to Joseph Holt, December 27, 1887, container 81; Margaret E. Crosby to Joseph Holt, May 26, 1888, container 82; Margaret E. Crosby to Joseph Holt, September 21, 1888, container 83,; Margaret E. Crosby to Joseph Holt, November 8, 1889, container 86, Holt Papers, LC.

41. This writer, too, seems to have been younger than Holt, for she worried about him dying first and leaving her behind. "I cannot think of you leaving me in this selfish and friendless world," she wrote. "Should your life be taken from mine the half of my being would have left me and the other could not long survive, nor could it care to remain." Unknown to Joseph Holt, December 7, 1887, container 81; Unknown to Joseph Holt, February 15, 1888, and February 29, 1888, container 82; Unknown to Joseph Holt, October 28, 1890, container 88; E. V. D. Miller to Joseph Holt, June 28, 1890, container 88; Unknown to Joseph Holt, November 4, 1890, container 88, Holt Papers, LC.

42. Louis J. Weichmann to Joseph Holt, December 18, 1883, container 76; Louis J. Weichmann to George C. Gorham, August 13, 1887; Louis J. Weichmann to Joseph Holt, August 30, 1887, container 80; Louis J. Weichmann to Joseph Holt, December 30, 1887, and February 1, 1888, container 81; Louis J. Weichmann to Joseph Holt, February 10, 1888, container 82; Louis J. Weichmann to Joseph Holt, April 5, 1890, container 87; Louis J. Weichmann to Joseph Holt, September 10, 1891, container 89; Louis J. Weichmann to Joseph Holt, May 24, 1893, container 91; John Cadwalader to Louis Weichmann, September 24, 1886, container 79; The Valentine Brothers to Louis J. Weichmann, December 19, 1886; Louis J. Weichmann to Joseph Holt, December 23, 1886, and January 5, 1887; Louis J. Weichmann to Joseph Holt, March 5, 1888, container 82; Louis J. Weichmann to Joseph Holt, November 20, 1888; January 11, 1889; February 18, 1889; March 6, 1889; and March 16, 1889, container 84; Louis J. Weichmann to Joseph Holt, June 8, 1891, container 89; Louis J. Weichmann to Joseph Holt, October 22, 1891, container 90, Holt Papers, LC.

Eventually, Weichmann moved to Indiana, where his brother lived. There he became the principal of the Anderson Institute of Shorthand, Typewriting, Book-Keeping, English Branches and Foreign Languages. See Louis J. Weichmann to Joseph Holt, April 7, 1889, and April 29, 1889, container 84, Holt Papers, LC.

43. Levin, *Lawyers and Lawmakers of Kentucky*, 282.

44. Joseph Holt to James Speed, April 18, 1883; June 21, 1883; October 22, 1883; and December 19, 1883; James Speed to Joseph Holt, April 25, 1883; June 27, 1883; October 25, 1883; and December 26, 1883, in Holt Papers, Huntington; John F. Hartranft to Joseph Holt, August 12, 1885, container 78; R. D. Mussey to Joseph Holt, October 20, 1886, container 79, Holt Papers, LC; *Address of Hon. James Speed*, 7.

45. Joseph Holt to Allen Thorndike Rice, February 27, 1888, container 82; A. M. Brown to Joseph Holt, June 17, 1888, container 83, Holt Papers, LC.

46. John H. Holt to Joseph Holt, July 14, 1888; R. C. McChord to Joseph Holt, July 26, 1888, container 83, Holt Papers, LC. This is the same R. C. McChord with whom Holt's ward, Lizzie Hynes, had gone to live back in 1846. See also John A. Bingham to Joseph Holt, August 1, 1888, container 83; Louis J. Weichmann to Joseph Holt, November 20, 1888, container 84, Holt Papers, LC.

47. Burnett, *Some Incidents*, 38, 42–43, 49.

48. Joseph Holt to John Mason Brown, April 22, 1889, HFPC; John Mason Brown to Joseph Holt, April 29, 1889, container 85, Holt Papers, LC.

49. John Mason Brown to Joseph Holt, April 29, 1889; A. M. Brown to Joseph Holt, June 12, 1889, container 85, Holt Papers, LC; *Address of Hon. James Speed*, 6–7.

50. Joseph Holt, *Reply of J. Holt*, 3–20, in the Holt Papers, Huntington.

51. Ibid.

52. In closing, Holt returned to the general topic of Buchanan's response to the secession crisis, praising the former president for his loyalty to the nation. Buchanan may have "shrunk from the contemplation of civil war and the bloodshed it would involve, and sought to postpone it to the last possible moment," Holt admitted, but nowhere in Buchanan's response to the crisis—or, he implied, his own—was there even the slightest "taint of disloyalty." See also Joseph Holt to James Buchanan Henry, May 26, 1884, Holt Papers, Huntington.

53. *Harper's Weekly*, November 17, 1883.

54. Joseph Holt to Vanda Vineyard Holt, June 26, 1892, Holt Papers, Huntington.

55. Joseph Holt to Washington Dorsey Holt, September 3, 1892; Joseph Holt to Vanda Vineyard Holt, November 25, 1892, Holt Papers, Huntington.

56. Mary Holt's comments appear in a letter she wrote to a cousin named Robert—probably Robert S. Holt, born in 1855 and the son of Holt's brother Robert—in which she also noted that her own son, whom she had named after Holt (Joseph Holt Rose) "looks exactly like the Holt's [*sic*] of your father's time" and "might be taken for one of them." (Mary Holt Rose to "Cousin Robert," April 10, 1928, in HFPC.) See also Joseph Holt Rose to Robert M. Mummey, May 9, 1956, in HFPC; Joseph Holt to Vanda Vineyard Holt, February 4, 1893, and April 16, 1893, Holt Papers, Huntington.

57. Joseph Holt to Vanda Vineyard Holt, January 13, 1894, Holt Papers, Huntington; *Washington Evening Star*, August 2, 1894, JHRS; *New York Times*, August 2, 1894; "Online Handbook of Texas," http://www.tshaonline.org/handbook/online/articles/fst41; unidentified, undated newspapers clipping, "Who Had Holt's Will," JHRS; unidentified newspaper clipping, "Adds to the Mystery," June 4, 1896, JHRS.

58. Joseph Holt's attending surgeon (name illegible) to the George D. Ruggles, August 1, 1894, H834 CB 1864, in RG 94, Records of the Adjutant General's Office, 1780s–1917, Letters Received by the Commission Branch of the Adjutant General's Office, 1863–1870, Roll 96, National Archives and Records Administration, Washington, D.C.; *New York Times*, August 2, 1894.

59. *Breckinridge News*, August 6, 1894; *Nelson County (Ky.) Record*, August 9, 1894; *Chicago Record*, August 2, 1894, JHRS; and the *Washington Evening Star*, August 2, 1894, JHRS. On postwar Kentucky, see Marshall, *Creating a Confederate Kentucky*.

60. *Washington Evening Star*, August 2, 1894, JHRS; George D. Ruggles to Com-

manding Officer, Fort Myer, Virginia, August 3, 1894; War Department Official Announcement of the Death of Joseph Holt, August 1, 1894, H834 CB 1864, in RG 94, Records of the Adjutant General's Office, 1780s–1917, Letters Received by the Commission Branch of the Adjutant General's Office, 1863–1870, Roll 96, National Archives and Records Administration, Washington, D.C.; *Breckenridge News*, August 8, 1894.

Epilogue

1. Joseph Holt "Will," February 7, 1873, Holt Papers, Huntington; unidentified, undated newspaper clipping, "Judge Holt's Will," JHRS; *Throckmorton v. Holt*, 180 U.S. 552 (1901), in *Supreme Court Reporter*, 21:474–88. See also *New York Times*, May 19, 1896; unidentified, undated clipping, "The Will Mystery," JHRS. The clipping entitled "Judge Holt's Will" (JHRS) lists, as Holt's "heirs at law," Thomas Holt's sons Washington Dorsey Holt and John W. Holt; Robert Holt's surviving children, Lockie, Robert, Thomas, James, and Sarah Holt; Elizabeth Holt Sterett's children, Billy Sterett and Margaret Bowmer; and one great nephew, Joseph Holt, living in Sherman, Texas.

2. Unidentified, undated newspaper clipping, "Judge Holt's Will"; unidentified, undated newspaper clipping, "Judge Holt's Servant"; unidentified newspaper clipping, "Adds to the Mystery," June 4, 1896; unidentified, undated newspaper clipping, "The Judge's Promise"; unidentified, undated newspaper clipping, "Who Had Holt's Will"; and unidentified, undated newspaper clipping, "Looking over Records," JHRS. See also *Washington Post*, May 29, 1896; Olds, "Memories of the Old Meigs Home," 89. In the context of the trial Billy Sterett testified that he had always felt a "high regard" for Holt, and that his mother, Elizabeth Holt Sterett, "thought the Judge"—her brother—"was the greatest man that ever lived." (Undated clipping, *Washington Post*, "Devlin's Clever Pen," JHRS.) And see *Throckmorton v. Holt*; Horatio King to Washington Dorsey Holt, June 26, 1896, HFPC.

3. Olds, "Memories of the Old Meigs Home," 92.

4. On the late nineteenth-century's contest over the memory of the Civil War see, for example, Blight, *Race and Reunion*; Creighton, *The Colors of Courage*; Fahs and Waugh, *The Memory of the Civil War in American Culture*; Gallagher, *Causes Won, Lost, and Forgotten*; Gallagher, *Lee and His Generals in War and Memory*; Silber, *Romance of Reunion*; Waugh, *U. S. Grant*. See also Bowers, *The Tragic Era*; Dunning, *Reconstruction*.

5. Yulee, "Senator David L. Yulee," 13–15, 17, 22. Perhaps the best early example of the trend toward caricaturing Holt's role in relation to the assassination was DeWitt's *The Judicial Murder of Mary Surratt*, which appeared the year after Holt died and whose title clearly reveals its perspective. Prior to the spring of 1865, DeWitt informed his readers early in the book, Holt had already "distinguished himself on many a bloody court-martial," a practice he eagerly carried forward into the trial of the assassins. See DeWitt, *The Judicial Murder of Mary Surratt*. DeWitt's characterization of Holt differs sharply from that presented by T. M. Harris in his slightly earlier study of the assassination. In his 1892 *Assassination of Lincoln: A History of the Great Conspiracy*, Harris—who had served on the commission—com-

mented that "a purer man, a truer patriot, a braver more intelligent and able officer than Gen. Joseph Holt never will grace the pages of American history" (282). That DeWitt's characterization held sway in the decades ahead is indicated by the fact that by the late twentieth century, books dealing with the assassination studies—even good ones—routinely depicted Holt as, at best, "vindictive and unforgiving." (Hanchett, *The Lincoln Murder Conspiracies*, 62.)

6. Joseph Holt Rose to Robert M. Mummey, May 9, 1956; and "Family Tree," HFPC; Finders Guide for the Papers of Joseph Holt, Library of Congress, Washington, D.C.

7. Joseph Holt Rose to Robert M. Mummey, May 9, 1956, in HFPC. See also the *Breckinridge County (Ky.) Herald-News*, March 23, 1988.

BIBLIOGRAPHY

Manuscripts

Gainesville, Florida
 David Levy Yulee Papers, Special and Area Studies Collections,
  George A. Smathers Libraries, University of Florida
Pasadena, California
 Holt Family Private Collection, held by Dr. Joseph Holt Rose
 Joseph Holt Rose Scrapbook, held by Dr. Joseph Holt Rose
San Marino, California
 Joseph Holt Papers, Huntington Library
Washington, D.C.
 Library of Congress
  Joseph Holt Papers
  Andrew Johnson Papers
  August V. Kautz Papers
  Abraham Lincoln Papers
  Edwin M. Stanton Papers
 National Archives and Records Administration
  RG 94, Records of the Adjutant General's Office, 1780s–1917, Letters
   Received by the Commission Branch of the Adjutant General's Office,
   1863–1870
  RG 153, Records of the Office of the Judge Advocate General (Army)
West Point, New York
 United States Military Academy Library, Special Collection
  Register of the Officers and Cadets of the U.S. Military Academy, 1835

Periodicals

Amherst (N.H.) Farmer's Cabinet
Baltimore American
*Baltimore Republican and Commercial
 Advertiser*
Baltimore Sun
Boston Courier
Boston Post
Breckenridge News
Breckinridge County (Ky.) Herald-News
Charleston Mercury
Chicago Record
Cincinnati Gazette
Daily Ohio Statesman
Detroit Free Press
Frank Leslie's Illustrated Newspaper
Galveston Weekly Journal
Greenville (Mich.) Independent
Hardinsburg (Ky.) Frontier News
Harper's Weekly
Journal of the Franklin Institute
Louisville Daily Journal
Louisville Public Advertiser
Milwaukee Daily Sentinel
Nelson County (Ky.) Record
New Albany (Ind.) Weekly Register;
 New Albany (Ind.) Ledger
New York Herald
New York Independent
New York Times
Philadelphia Inquirer

Richmond Enquirer
Scientific American
St. Louis Daily Commercial Bulletin
Vermont Phoenix

Washington Constitution
Washington Daily Chronicle
Washington Evening Star
Washington Post

Government Documents and Published Primary Sources

Address of Hon. James Speed before the Society of the Loyal Legion, at Cincinnati. Louisville, Ky.: John P. Morton and Company, 1888.

Annual Reports of the Secretary of War, 1865–1875. Washington, D.C.: Government Printing Office, 1865–1875.

Basler, Roy P. *Collected Works of Abraham Lincoln.* New Brunswick, N.J.: Rutgers University Press, 1953.

Burlingame, Michael, ed. *An Oral History of Abraham Lincoln: John G. Nicolay's Interviews and Essays.* Carbondale: Southern Illinois University Press, 1996.

Burnett, Henry L. *Some Incidents in the Trial of President Lincoln's Assassins and the Controversy between President Johnson and Judge Holt.* New York: D. Appleton & Co., 1891.

Chronicle of the Union League of Philadelphia, 1862–1902. Philadelphia: William F. Fell & Co., 1902.

Clous, J. W. "Judge Advocate General's Department." http://www.history.army .mil/books/R&H/R&H-JAG.htm.

The Collected Works of Abraham Lincoln. New York: H. Wolff Book Manufacturing Company, 1953.

Gienapp, William E., ed. *The Civil War and Reconstruction: A Documentary Collection.* New York: W. W. Norton & Company, 2001.

The Great Impeachment and Trial of Andrew Johnson, President of the United States. Philadelphia: T. B. Peterson & Brothers, 1868.

Graf, LeRoy P., Brooks D. Simpson, and John Muldowny, eds. *Advice After Appomattox: Reports for Andrew Johnson, 1865–1866.* Knoxville: University of Tennessee Press, 1987.

Graf, LeRoy P., and Ralph W. Haskins, eds. *The Papers of Andrew Johnson.* Knoxville: University of Tennessee Press, 1967.

Grant, Ulysses S. *Personal Memoirs.* New York: Penguin, 1999.

Holt, Joseph. *Digest of the Opinions of the Judge Advocate General of the Army.* Washington, D.C.: Government Printing Office, 1865.

———. *The Fallacy of Neutrality.* New York: James G. Gregory, 1861.

———. *Reply of J. Holt to Certain Calumnies of Jacob Thompson.* Privately printed, 1883.

———. *Speech of Joseph Holt Delivered at a Democratic Meeting Held at the Court House.* Louisville, Ky.: Harney & Hughes, Printers, 1853.

———. *Vindication of Judge Advocate General Holt from the Foul Slanders of Traitors, their Aiders, Abettors, and Sympathizers, acting in the Interest of Jefferson Davis.* 1866; reprint ed., Ithaca, N.Y.: Cornell University Library Digital Collections, 2010.

————. *Vindication of Hon. Joseph Holt, Judge Advocate General of the United States Army.* Washington, D.C.: Chronicle Publishing Company, 1873.

Impeachment Investigation: Testimony Taken before the Judiciary Committee of the House of Representatives in the Investigation of the Charges against Andrew Johnson. Washington, D.C.: Government Printing Office, 1867.

Johnson, Reverdy. *A Reply to the Review of Judge Advocate General Holt . . . in the Case of Major General Fitz John Porter.* Baltimore: John Murphy & Co., 1863.

Lincoln, Abraham. *The Truth from an Honest Man: The Letter of the President.* Philadelphia: King & Baird, Printers, 1863.

Louisville (Kentucky) City Directories, 1836–1857.

McChord, J. H. *The McChords of Kentucky and Some Related Families.* Louisville, Ky.: Westerfield-Bante, 1941.

Moore, Frank, ed. *The Rebellion Record: A Diary of American Events.* New York: G. P. Putnam, 1862.

Moore, John Bassett, ed. *The Works of James Buchanan.* Philadelphia: J. B. Lippincott Company, 1910.

Nevins, Allan, and Milton Halsey Thomas, eds. *The Diary of George Templeton Strong.* New York: Octagon Books, 1974.

Nicolay, John G., and John Hay. *Abraham Lincoln: A History.* 10 vols. New York: Century Co., 1904.

Niven, John, ed. *The Salmon P. Chase Papers.* Kent, Ohio: Kent State University Press, 1993.

Peterson, T. B. *The Trial of the Assassins and Conspirators.* Philadelphia: Peterson & Brothers, 1865.

Pitman, Benn, ed. *The Assassination of President Lincoln and the Trial of the Conspirators.* New York: Moore, Wilstach & Baldwin, 1865.

————. *The Trials for Treason at Indianapolis, 1864.* Cincinnati: Moore, Wilstach & Baldwin, 1865.

Poore, Ben Perley, ed. *The Conspiracy Trial for the Murder of the President.* Boston: J. E. Tilton, 1865.

"Reply of Hon. J. Holt to Hon. Montgomery Blair, Late Postmaster General." *Washington Chronicle*, September 13, 1865.

Review of the Decision of the U.S. Supreme Court. Washington, D.C.: Chronicle Print, 1867.

Simon, John Y., ed. *The Papers of Ulysses S. Grant.* Carbondale: Southern Illinois University Press, 1967.

Speech of Hon. C. A. Wickliffe, of Kentucky, on the Bills to Confiscate the Property and Free from Servitude the Slaves of Rebels, and other Matters, May 26, 1862, Washington, D.C. Frankfort: Kentucky Historical Society, 1862.

The Supreme Court Reporter. Vol. 21. St. Paul, Minnesota: West Publishing Co., 1901.

The Trial of John H. Surratt in the Criminal Court for the District of Columbia. 2 vols. Washington, D.C.: Government Printing Office, 1867.

United States Census, 1840–1890 (printed volumes).

Wakelyn, Jon L., ed. *Southern Pamphlets on Secession, November 1860-April 1861.* Chapel Hill: University of North Carolina Press, 1996.

War of the Rebellion: A Compilation of the Official Records of the Union and Confederate Armies. Washington, D.C.: Government Printing Office, 1880–1901.

Weichmann, Louis J. *A True History of the Assassination of Abraham Lincoln and the Conspiracy of 1865.* New York: Alfred A. Knopf, 1975.

Welles, Gideon. *Diary of Gideon Welles.* New York: Houghton Mifflin Company, 1911.

White, Andrew Dickson. *A Reply to the Hon. Reverdy Johnson's Attack.* Baltimore: Sherwood & Co., 1863.

U.S. Congress. House of Representatives. Executive Document No. 32. *Additional List of Pardons.* 40th Cong., 1st sess., July 19, 1867. Washington, D.C.: Government Printing Office, 1867.

———. Executive Document No. 47. *Albert M. D. C. Lusk.* 40th Cong., 2nd sess., December 16, 1867. Washington, D.C.: Government Printing Office, 1867.

———. Report No. 74. *Army Staff Reorganization.* 42nd Cong., 3rd sess., February 2, 1873. Washington, D.C.: Government Printing Office, 1873.

———. House Report No. 104. *Assassination of Lincoln.* 39th Cong., 1st sess., July 1866. Washington, D.C.: Government Printing Office, 1866.

———. Executive Document No. 90. *Awards for the Capture of Booth and Others.* 39th Cong., 1st sess., April 19, 1866. Washington, D.C.: Government Printing Office, 1866.

———. Judiciary Committee Report No. 7. *Impeachment of the President.* 40th Cong., 1st sess., November 25, 1867. Washington, D.C.: Government Printing Office, 1867.

———. Executive Document No. 36. *H. B. Sainte-Marie.* 40th Cong., 2nd sess., December 12, 1867. Washington, D.C.: Government Printing Office, 1867.

———. Executive Document No. 9. *John H. Surratt.* 39th Cong., 2nd sess., December 10, 1866. Washington, D.C.: Government Printing Office, 1866.

———. Executive Document No. 116. *Names of Persons Pardoned by the President.* 39th Cong., 2nd sess., March 2, 1867. Washington, D.C.: Government Printing Office, 1867.

———. Executive Document No. 16. *Pardons of the President.* 40th Cong., 2nd sess., December 4, 1867. Washington, D.C.: Government Printing Office, 1867.

U.S. Congress. Senate. Miscellaneous Document No. 42. *Articles of Impeachment Exhibited by the House of Representatives against Andrew Johnson, President of the United States.* 40th Cong., 2nd sess., March 4, 1868. Washington, D.C.: Government Printing Office, 1873.

———. Executive Document No. 11. *Letter of the Secretary of War.* 39th Cong., 1st sess., January 10, 1866. Washington, D.C.: Government Printing Office, 1866.

———. Executive Document No. 11. *Letter from the Secretary of War.* 42nd Cong., 2nd sess., January 8, 1872. Washington, D.C.: Government Printing Office, 1872.

Secondary Sources

Allen, Mary Bernard. "Joseph Holt: Judge Advocate General (1862–1875)." Ph.D. diss., University of Chicago, 1927.

Ambrose, Stephen A. *Duty, Honor, Country: A History of West Point*. Baltimore: Johns Hopkins University Press, 1966.

Anbinder, Tyler. *Nativism and Slavery: The Northern Know Nothings and the Politics of the 1850s*. New York: Oxford University Press, 1994.

Bartman, Roger J. "The Contribution of Joseph Holt to the Political Life of the United States." Ph.D. diss., Fordham University, 1958.

Baxter, Maurice G. *Henry Clay and the American System*. Lexington: University Press of Kentucky, 2004.

Benedict, Michael Les. *The Impeachment and Trial of Andrew Johnson*. New York: W. W. Norton & Co., 1999.

Bland, Thomas Keys. "Were the Lincoln Conspirators Dealt Justice?" *Lincoln Herald* 80 (1978): 38–46.

Blight, David, *Race and Reunion: The Civil War in American Memory*. Cambridge: Belknap Press, 2002.

Bowers, Claude. *The Tragic Era: The Revolution after Lincoln*. New York: Houghton Mifflin, 1929.

Chalmers, David M. *Hooded Americanism: The History of the Ku Klux Klan*. Durham, N.C.: Duke University Press, 1987.

Chamlee, Roy Z. *Lincoln's Assassins: A Complete Account of their Capture, Trial, and Punishment*. Jefferson, N.C.: McFarland & Company, 1990.

Clay-Copton, Virginia. *A Belle of the Fifties*. New York: Doubleday, Page & Company, 1904.

Collins, Richard H. *History of Kentucky*. Louisville, Ky.: John P. Morton & Co., 1924.

Coulter, E. Merton. *The Civil War and Readjustment in Kentucky*. Gloucester, Mass.: Peter Smith, 1966.

Creighton, Margaret. *The Colors of Courage: Gettysburg's Forgotten History*. New York: Basic Books, 2006.

Cumming, Carman. *Devil's Game: The Civil War Intrigues of Charles A. Dunham*. Urbana: University of Illinois Press, 2004.

Davis, William C. *Breckinridge: Statesman, Soldier, Symbol*. Baton Rouge: Louisiana State University Press, 1992.

DeWitt, David M. *The Judicial Murder of Mary Surratt*. Baltimore: J. Murphy & Co., 1895.

Dobyns, Kenneth W. *The Patent Office Pony: A History of the Early Patent Office*. Fredericksburg, Va.: Sergeant Kirkland's Museum and Historical Society, 1994.

Donald, David Herbert. *Charles Sumner and the Coming of the Civil War*. Naperville, Ill.: Sourcebooks, 2009.

———. *Lincoln*. New York: Simon & Schuster, 1995.

Dunning, William A. *Reconstruction: Political and Economic, 1865–1877*. New York: Harper & Bros., 1907.

Edgerton, Donald R. *Year of Meteors: Stephen Douglas, Abraham Lincoln, and the Election that Brought on the Civil War*. New York: Bloomsbury Press, 2010.

Egnal, Marc. *Clash of Extremes: The Economic Origins of the Civil War*. New York: Hill and Wang, 2009.

Engerman, Stanley L., and Robert E. Gallman. *The Long Nineteenth Century*. Vol. 2 of *Cambridge Economic History of the United States*. London: Cambridge University Press, 2000.

Etcheson, Nicole. *Bleeding Kansas: Contested Liberty in the Civil War Era*. Lawrence: University of Kansas Press, 2006.

Fahs, Alice, and Joan Waugh, eds. *The Memory of the Civil War in American Culture*. Chapel Hill: University of North Carolina Press, 2004.

Farber, Daniel. *Lincoln's Constitution*. Chicago: University of Chicago Press, 2004.

Faust, Patricia L., ed. *Historical Times Illustrated Encyclopedia of the Civil War*. New York: Harper & Row, 1991.

Fehrenbacher, Don E. *The Dred Scott Case: Its Significance in American Law and Politics*. New York: Oxford University Press, 2001.

———. *Lincoln in Text and Context: Collected Essays*. Stanford, Calif.: Stanford University Press, 1987.

Foner, Eric. *Free Soil, Free Labor, Free Men*. New York: Oxford University Press, 1995.

———. *Reconstruction: America's Unfinished Revolution, 1863–1877*. New York: Harper & Row, 1988.

Freehling, William W. *Prelude to Civil War: The Nullification Controversy in South Carolina, 1816–1836*. New York: Oxford University Press, 1992.

———. *The Road to Disunion: Secessionists Triumphant, 1854–1861*. New York: Oxford University Press, 2007.

———. *The South versus the South: How Anti-Confederate Southerners Shaped the Course of the Civil War*. New York: Oxford University Press, 2001.

Gallagher, Gary W. *Causes Won, Lost, and Forgotten: How Hollywood and Popular Art Shape What We Know about the Civil War*. Chapel Hill: University of North Carolina Press, 2008.

———. *Lee and His Generals in War and Memory*. Baton Rouge: Louisiana State University Press, 2004.

Glatthaar, Joseph T. *Forged in Battle: The Civil War Alliance of Black Soldiers and White Officers*. Baton Rouge: Louisiana State University Press, 2000.

Grimsley, Mark. *The Hard Hand of War: Union Military Policy toward Southern Civilians, 1861–1865*. New York: Cambridge University Press, 1995.

Grimsley, Mark, and Brooks D. Simpson, eds. *The Collapse of the Confederacy*. Lincoln: University of Nebraska Press, 2001.

Guelzo, Allen C. *Lincoln and Douglas: The Debates that Defined America*. New York: Simon and Schuster, 2009.

———. *Lincoln's Emancipation Proclamation: The End of Slavery in America*. New York: Simon & Schuster, 2006.

Hanchett, William. *The Lincoln Murder Conspiracies*. Urbana: University of Illinois Press, 1989.

Harris, T. M. *Assassination of Lincoln: A History of the Great Conspiracy*. Boston: American Citizen Company, 1892.

Harrison, Lowell Hayes. *The Civil War in Kentucky*. Lexington: University Press of Kentucky, 1987.

———. *Lincoln of Kentucky*. Lexington: University Press of Kentucky, 2000.

Haycraft, Samuel. *History of Elizabethtown, Kentucky, and Its Surroundings*. Elizabethtown, Ky.: Woman's Club, 1921.

Herbermann, Charles G., et al., eds. *The Catholic Encyclopedia*. New York: Encyclopedia Press, 1909.

Holt, Michael F. *The Political Crisis of the 1850s*. New York: W. W. Norton & Co., 1983.

Holzer, Harold. *Lincoln, President Elect: Abraham Lincoln and the Great Secession Winter, 1860–61*. New York: Simon & Schuster, 2008.

Huston, James L. *The Panic of 1857 and the Coming of the Civil War*. Baton Rouge: Louisiana State University Press, 1987.

Jampoler, Andrew C. A. *The Last Lincoln Conspirator: John Surratt's Flight from the Gallows*. Annapolis, Md.: Naval Institute Press, 2008.

Jermann, Donald R. *Fitz-John Porter: Scapegoat of Second Manassas*. Jefferson, N.C.: McFarland & Company, 2008.

Johnson, E. Polk. *A History of Kentucky and Kentuckians*. Chicago: Lewis Publishing Co., 1912.

Kauffman, Michael W. *American Brutus: John Wilkes Booth and the Lincoln Conspiracies*. New York: Random House Trade Paperbacks, 2005.

Keith, LeeAnna. *The Colfax Massacre: The Untold Story of Black Power, White Terror, and the Death of Reconstruction*. New York: Oxford University Press, 2009.

Kiddle, Henry, and Alexander J. Schem. *The Yearbook of Education for 1878*. New York: E. Steiger, 1878.

Kleber, John E., ed. *The Encyclopedia of Louisville*. Louisville: University Press of Kentucky, 2000.

———, ed. *The Kentucky Encyclopedia*. Lexington: University Press of Kentucky, 1992.

Klement, Frank L. *Dark Lanterns: Secret Political Societies, Conspiracies, and Treason Trials in the Civil War*. Baton Rouge: Louisiana State University Press, 1984.

———. *The Limits of Dissent: Clement L. Vallandigham and the Civil War*. New York: Fordham University Press, 1998.

Knobel, Dale T. *Paddy and the Republic: Ethnicity and Nationality in Antebellum America*. Middleton, Conn.: Wesleyan University Press, 1988.

Lankford, Nelson. *Cry Havoc: The Crooked Road to Civil War*. New York: Viking, 2007.

Leonard, Elizabeth D. *All the Daring of the Soldier: Women of the Civil War Armies*. New York: W. W. Norton & Co., 1999.

———. *Lincoln's Avengers: Justice, Revenge, and Reunion after the Civil War*. New York: W. W. Norton & Co., 2004.

————. *Men of Color to Arms! Black Soldiers, Indian Wars, and the Quest for Equality*. New York: W. W. Norton & Co., 2010.

————. "One Kentuckian's Hard Choice: Joseph Holt and Abraham Lincoln." *Register of the Kentucky Historical Society* 106 (Summer/Autumn 2008): 373–407.

————. *Yankee Women: Gender Battles in the Civil War*. New York: W. W. Norton & Co., 1994.

Levin, H., ed. *The Lawyers and Lawmakers of Kentucky*. Chicago: Lewis Publishing Company, 1897.

Little, Lucius P. *Ben Hardin: His Times and Contemporaries*. Louisville: Courier-Journal Job Printing Company, 1887.

Long, E. B. *The Civil War Day by Day: An Almanac, 1861–1865*. New York: Da Capo Press, 1971.

Lowry, Thomas P. *Confederate Heroines: 120 Southern Women Convicted by Union Military Justice*. Baton Rouge: Louisiana State University Press, 2006.

————. *Don't Shoot That Boy! Abraham Lincoln and Military Justice*. New York: Da Capo Press, 2002.

Lystra, Karen. *Searching the Heart: Women, Men, and Romantic Love in Nineteenth-Century America*. New York: Oxford University Press, 1992.

Marshall, Anne E. *Creating a Confederate Kentucky: The Lost Cause and Civil War Memory in a Border State*. Chapel Hill: University of North Carolina Press, 2010.

Martin, Asa Earl. *The Anti-Slavery Movement in Kentucky Prior to 1850*. Louisville: Standard Printing Company, 1918.

Mayer, Henry. *All on Fire: William Lloyd Garrison and the Abolition of Slavery*. New York: W. W. Norton & Co., 2008.

McGinty, Brian. *Lincoln and the Court*. Cambridge: Harvard University Press, 2009.

McPherson, James M. *Ordeal by Fire: The Civil War and Reconstruction*. New York: McGraw-Hill, 2001.

Neely, Mark, Jr. *The Fate of Liberty: Abraham Lincoln and Civil Liberties*. New York: Oxford University Press, 1992.

Neff, Stephen C. *Justice in Blue and Gray: A Legal History of the Civil War*. Cambridge: Harvard University Press, 2010.

Noel, Francis Regis, and Margaret Brent Downing. *The Court-House of the District of Columbia*. Washington, D.C.: Judd & Detweiler, 1919.

Oates, Stephen B. *The Fires of Jubilee: Nat Turner's Fierce Rebellion*. New York: Harper Perennial, 1990.

————. *To Purge This Land with Blood: A Biography of John Brown*. Amherst: University of Massachusetts Press, 1984.

Oertel, Kristen Tegtmeier. *Bleeding Borders: Race, Gender, and Violence in Pre-Civil War Kansas*. Baton Rouge: Louisiana State University Press, 2009.

Oldroyd, Osborn H. *The Assassination of Abraham Lincoln*. 1901; reprint ed., Bowie, Md.: Heritage Books, 1990.

Olds, May Meigs. "Memories of the Old Meigs Home and Historical Events in the Neighborhood, 1863–1913." *Records of the Columbia Historical Society, Washington, D.C.* 46/47 (1944/1945): 81–95.

Perrin, W. H., J. H. Battle, and G. C. Kniffin. *Kentucky: A History of the State.* Louisville, Ky.: F. A. Battey & Co., 1887.

Phillips, Jason. *Diehard Rebels: The Confederate Culture of Invincibility.* Athens: University of Georgia Press, 2010.

Potter, David M. *The Impending Crisis, 1848–1861.* New York: Harper Perennial, 1977.

Ranck, George M. *History of Lexington.* Cincinnati: Robert Clark & Co., 1872.

Remini, Robert V. *Andrew Jackson.* New York: Harper Perennial, 1999.

———. *Andrew Jackson and the Bank War.* New York: W. W. Norton & Co., 1967.

———. *Henry Clay: Statesman for the Union.* New York: W. W. Norton & Co., 1991.

Reynolds, David S. *John Brown, Abolitionist: The Man Who Killed Slavery, Sparked the Civil War, and Seeded Civil Rights.* New York: Vintage, 2006.

Robertson, James R. "Sectionalism in Kentucky from 1855 to 1865." *Mississippi Valley Historical Review* 4 (June 1917): 49–63.

Rudolph, Frederick. *The American College and University: A History.* Athens: University of Georgia Press, 1990.

Samito, Christian G., ed. *Changes in Law and Society during the Civil War and Reconstruction: A Legal History Documentary Reader.* Carbondale: Southern Illinois University Press, 2009.

Sears, Stephen W. *George B. McClellan: The Young Napoleon.* Cambridge, Mass.: Da Capo Press, 1999.

"The Secession Conspiracy in Kentucky." *Danville (Ky.) Quarterly Review* 2 (1862): 226–38.

Silber, Nina. *Romance of Reunion: Northerners and the South, 1865–1890.* Chapel Hill: University of North Carolina Press, 1997.

Sinha, Manisha. *The Counterrevolution of Slavery: Politics and Ideology in Antebellum South Carolina.* Chapel Hill: University of North Carolina Press, 2000.

Smith, William Ernest. *The Francis Preston Blair Family in Politics.* New York: Macmillan, 1933.

Stampp, Kenneth M. "The Milligan Case and the Election of 1864 in Indiana." *Mississippi Valley Historical Review* 31 (June 1994): 41–48.

Steers, Edward, Jr. *Blood on the Moon: The Assassination of Abraham Lincoln.* Lexington: University Press of Kentucky, 2005.

Swanson, James L. *Manhunt: The 12-Day Chase for Lincoln's Killer.* New York: Harper Perennial, 2007.

Thomas, Benjamin P. *Abraham Lincoln: A Biography.* New York: Alfred A. Knopf, 1952.

Thomas, Benjamin P., and Harold M. Hyman. *Stanton: The Life and Times of Lincoln's Secretary of War.* Santa Barbara, Calif.: Greenwood Press, 1980.

Tidwell, William A., James O. Hall, and David Winfred Gaddy. *Come Retribution: The Confederate Secret Service and the Assassination of Lincoln.* New York: Barnes and Noble Books, 1988.

Towne, Stephen E. "Dissent and Treason: Lambdin P. Milligan, Indiana, and the Civil War." Paper presented at Indiana Judicial Conference, Fort Wayne, Indiana, September 20, 2007.

Townsend, William H. *Lincoln and the Bluegrass: Slavery and Civil War in Kentucky*. Lexington: University Press of Kentucky, 1955.

Trefousse, Hans L. *Andrew Johnson: A Biography*. New York: Norton, 1989.

Trollope, Frances. *Domestic Manners of the Americans*. London: Whitaker, Treacher, & Co., 1832.

Turner, Thomas R. *Beware the People Weeping: Public Opinion and the Assassination of Abraham Lincoln*. Baton Rouge: Louisiana State University Press, 1982.

Van Deusen, Glyndon G. *William Henry Seward*. New York: Oxford University Press, 1967.

Van Holst, H. *The Constitutional and Political History of the United States*. Chicago: Callaghan and Company, 1892.

Vorenberg, Michael. *Final Freedom: The Civil War, the Abolition of Slavery, and the Thirteenth Amendment*. New York: Cambridge University Press, 2004.

Walther, Eric H. *The Shattering of the Union: America in the 1850s*. Wilmington, Del.: SR Books, 2003.

Waugh, Joan. *U. S. Grant: American Hero, American Myth*. Chapel Hill: University of North Carolina Press, 2009.

Webb, Walter Prescott. *The Handbook of Texas: A Dictionary of Essential Information*. Austin: Texas State Historical Association, 1952.

Weber, Jennifer L. *Copperheads: The Rise and Fall of Lincoln's Opponents in the North*. New York: Oxford University Press, 2008.

Wertz, Richard W., and Dorothy C. Wertz. *Lying In: A History of Childbirth in America*. New Haven: Yale University Press, 1989.

White, Jonathan W. "'Sweltering with Treason': The Civil War Trials of William Matthew Merrick." *Prologue* 39 (Summer 2007): 27–36.

Wyatt-Brown, Bertram. *Honor and Violence in the Old South*. New York: Oxford University Press, 1986.

———. *Southern Honor: Ethics and Behavior in the Old South*. New York: Oxford University Press, 2007.

Yulee, Charles Wickliffe. "Senator David L. Yulee." *Publications of the Florida Historical Society* 2 (July 1909): 3–22.

INDEX

Note: JH = Joseph Holt.

Badger, Margaret Rose, x

Bain, Cuthbert H., 57–58, 62

Bain, Elizabeth Harrison, 57

Bain, Patterson, 58

Bain, William P., 57

Bainbridge, E. T., 164

Baker, Lafayette C., 263, 289, 367 (n. 30)

Ballard, Frank W., 200–201, 229, 230, 257, 276–78

Banks, Jefferson, 288

Banks, Nathaniel P., 192

Baptist Church, 56

Bardstown, Ky.: during Civil War, 165; distance of, from Washington, D.C., 74; Harrison family in, 47, 62; JH's wedding to Margaret in, 63, 331 (n. 21); Margaret Holt in, following her marriage, 68, 73, 75, 102–4; Mary Holt's family home in, 47–49, 51, 53–54; population of, 62; St. Joseph's College in, 9–12, 17, 25, 34, 62, 63, 348 (n. 54); Wickliffe family home (Wickland) in, 62, 63, 76, 81, 84, 90–91, 102, 192

Barney, Hiram, 162–64

Bartee, Andrew, 175

Barton, Clara, 84, 87

Bates, Edward, 188–89

Beauregard, P. G. T., 43, 128

Beckham, John Crepps Wickliffe, 63

Beckham, Julia Wickliffe, 63, 102, 104

Beckham, William Netherton, 63

Belknap, William W., 296, 300, 370 (n. 6)

Bell, John, 13, 104

Bell, T. S.: on Civil War in Kentucky, 165, 185; and JH as judge advocate general, 222–23; and JH as secretary of war, 116–17, 125; JH's friendship with generally, 192, 308; on JH's self-defense in Conover scandal, 257; on Johnson, 257; and Lincoln assassination case, 213, 218, 296; on Lincoln's cabinet, 125; on Lincoln's firing of McClellan, 163; and military preparations in Kentucky, 154; on paroled Confederate soldiers in Kentucky, 218; on Porter case, 171; praise for JH by, 116–17, 125, 130, 145, 152, 223; on Stanton as secretary of war, 156; on Unionism of JH, 116, 125, 145, 152; on Unionism of Kentucky, 134, 145

Benham, Calhoun, 125

Benham, Henry Washington, 173

Benson, James, 353 (n. 25)

Bingham, John A.: and Fourteenth Amendment, 249; and impeachment of Johnson, 280–82; on Johnson's awareness of Mary Surratt petition, 293–94, 297, 311; photograph of, 208; and Reconstruction, 233; and trial of coconspirators in Lincoln assassination, 207, 212, 215

Black, Jeremiah, 97, 111

Black, John, 46

Blackburn, Luke, 214

Black codes, 233

Blacks: and Civil Rights Bill (1865), 237, 244, 245, 363 (n. 64); as Federal troops in occupied Texas, 240; and Fifteenth Amendment, 291–92; and Fourteenth Amendment, 249, 258, 261, 266, 284, 292; and Freedmen's Bureau, 237, 244, 292; future of freedpeople, 237–38; Holt family's former slaves, 239–40, 302; Johnson on, 280; and judge advocate general cases, 176–80, 220; in Kentucky, 234; military service by, 160, 161, 179–80, 185, 191, 222, 240, 244, 279, 291, 320, 360 (n. 31); murders of and other violence against, 220, 230, 254, 279, 288, 291, 292, 354 (n. 33), 362 (n. 49), 371 (n. 14); statistics on freedpeople, 237, 264; and Thirteenth Amendment, 189, 232, 233, 239, 266, 352 (n. 15); as U.S. congressmen, 291; voting rights for, 262, 267, 291–92, 363 (n. 64). *See also* Slavery

184–88; JH's retirement from, 299–302; judge advocates in, 252, 279, 284–85, 289, 365 (n. 12); and Lincoln assassination case, 201–2, 227, 263, 275; and military prisons, 290; organization and preservation of records and documents from, 277–78, 289; purpose of, 290; and sentencing practices of different military departments, 290; and Stanton, 184, 201–2, 227; statistics on, 190, 227, 259, 279, 284, 289, 370 (n. 7); understaffing of, 284–85, 289–90; and Wirz trial, 227. *See also* Judge advocate general; Lincoln assassination case; War Department, U.S.

Burnett, Henry L.: and Johnson's awareness of Mary Surratt petition, 311; and Lincoln assassination case, 205–6, 212, 215, 311; and Milligan case, 188, 205, 244; photograph of, 208, 212; praise for JH by, 257, 311; wedding of, 275

Burnside, Ambrose E., 182, 187

Burton, H. S., 268

Burwell, A., 226

Bush, Isaac, 8

Bush, Sarah, 8

Butler, Benjamin, 281, 282, 287

Calcoat, Wilson, 279

Calhoun, John C., 21, 22, 31

California, 64, 71, 75–76

Cameron, Simon, 128, 129, 130, 153, 155

Campbell, Hugh, 156, 164

Campbell, William (a.k.a. Joseph Hoare), 232, 247, 249, 250, 256

Camp Chase, Ohio, 175

Camp Dick Robinson, Ky., 148–49

Camp Douglas, Ohio, 191

Camp Jo Holt, Ind., 147, 148, 149, 161

Camp Wildcat, 153–54

"Canadian Cabinet" of Jefferson Davis, 202, 204–6, 212–15, 245, 263, 312, 361 (n. 38)

Caribbean, 304–5

Carrington, Edward C., 270, 283

Carrington, Henry B., 186

Carter, William. *See* Martin, John

Casey, Silas, 352 (n. 18)

Cash, Andrew D., 356–57 (n. 61)

Cash, Julia, 357 (n. 61)

Cash, Mary W., 193–96, 241, 242, 308, 356–57 (n. 61)

Cash, Rebecca, 357 (n. 61)

Cass, Lewis, 97, 110–11

Catholic Church: anti-Catholic sentiments against, 11, 77, 136; and execution of Mary Surratt, 221, 299; JH's conflict at St. Joseph's College, 9–12, 17, 25, 34; Know-Nothing Party as against, 77; and Lincoln assassination case, 231

Centre College, 12–14, 20, 63, 66–67

Chamberlin, Rev. Jeremiah, 14

Chandler, L. H., 268–69

Charleston Mercury, 84, 118, 129

Chase, Salmon P., 204, 214, 249, 259, 281

Cheatham, Benjamin, 293

Chilton, John M., 72, 333 (n. 28)

Cholera, 30, 53, 59

Churchill, John, 368 (n. 39)

Cincinnati, 66, 74, 139

Cincinnati Gazette, 276

Civil Rights Bill (1865), 237, 244, 245, 363 (n. 64)

Civil War: Americans' historical memory of, 320–22; Articles of War for U.S. Army during, 352 (n. 17); battles of, 147, 150, 153–54, 157, 160, 165, 168, 173, 180, 187, 188, 189; black soldiers in, 160, 161, 179–81, 185, 191, 222, 244, 320, 360 (n. 31); capture of Confederate capital at Richmond by Federal army, 197; casualties of, 3, 160, 165, 197, 269, 300; and defense of Washington, D.C., 126–27, 134, 140; deserters during, 173, 353 (n. 25); destruction of South by, 197;

and Emancipation Proclamation, 160, 162–66, 170, 176–79, 292, 352 (n. 15); end of, 197–98, 206, 219, 220, 237; Fort Sumter and beginning of, 133–34, 138, 160, 228, 230; future of U.S. following, 198–99, 237–38; "hard-war" approach to, 161–63, 170, 187, 222; JH on, 133; JH's family relations during and after, 190–92, 196–98, 238–41, 302–5; Johnson's proclamation of peace following, 244, 246, 264–65, 268; in Kentucky, 151, 153–54, 164–66, 351 (n. 13), 352 (n. 15); Kentucky's military preparations for, 138–39, 142–43, 147–49, 153–54, 156; Lee's surrender to Grant at end of, 198, 220; Lincoln's call for troops for, 133–34, 138, 139; military rule for states of former Confederacy following, 199; prisoners of war during, 191, 226–27; Proclamation of Amnesty and Reconstruction by Lincoln during, 185, 219; size of U.S. Army during, 133–34, 158; "soft-war" approach to, 161; spies during, 176, 353 (n. 30); and *Star of the West* expedition to Charleston Harbor, 118–22, 130–33, 228, 312, 313, 346 (n. 28); suspension of writ of habeas corpus during, 160–64, 182, 188, 351 (n. 6). *See also* Army, U.S.; Confederate States of America; Judge advocate general; *and specific battles and generals*

Clampitt, John W., 209

Clay, Clement C.: imprisonment of, 208, 223, 234, 236, 244, 246, 359 (n. 12); JH's attitude toward, 358 (n. 7); Johnson's parole of, 246, 268; and Lincoln assassination case, 204–5, 212–14, 234–37, 252; political career of, 204–5; reward for capture of, 205

Clay, Henry: and American System, 21, 26; cane as gift to, by JH, 335–36 (n. 48); and Compromise of 1850, 65;

death of, 70; influence of, on Kentucky, 135, 138, 347 (n. 42); James Harrison's friendship with, 45; and JH's trip to Europe, 58–59; in Lexington, Ky., 14; as National Republican/ Whig, 19, 20, 21, 26, 32, 44; and Nullification Crisis, 22, 31; portrait of, 15; and tariff compromise in 1820s, 22; as Transylvania University faculty member, 16; will of, 331 (n. 15)

Cleary, William C., 205, 212, 213, 214, 232

Clements, Judson C., 315

Clendenin, David R., 359 (n. 11)

Cleveland, Grover, 353 (n. 22)

Cobb, Howell, 97, 110, 121

Coleman, J. H., 334 (n. 41)

Colfax, Schuyler, 282

Collier, David L., 154

Command of the Army Act, 266, 281

Compromise of 1850, 65

Comstock, Cyrus B., 359 (n. 11)

Confederate States of America, 126, 127, 134, 136, 197. *See also* Civil War; Davis, Jefferson

Confederation, 125, 129

Confiscation Acts, 149–50, 160, 179

Congress, U.S.: and abuse of congressional franking privilege, 98; and Army Reorganization Act (1866), 251–52, 259, 279; boarding house for members of, 75; and Civil Rights Bill (1865), 237, 244, 245; and Command of the Army Act, 266, 281; and Compromise of 1850, 65; and Confiscation Acts, 149–50, 160, 179; and defense of Washington, D.C., 126; and federal judicial circuits, 259; and Fifteenth Amendment, 291–92; and Fourteenth Amendment, 249, 261, 266, 284, 292; and Freedmen's Bureau, 237, 244; gag rule on antislavery petitions in, 56; and Habeas Corpus Act, 188; Hawes's disappointment with, 24–25; and impeachment

of, as president, 285; inauguration of, 288; JH as judge advocate general under, 288–89; JH's retirement as judge advocate general under, 3; and JH's will, 319; Lee's surrender to, 198, 220; and Lincoln assassination case, 359 (n. 10); as presidential candidate, 282, 284; and Reconstruction, 266; and release of Clay and Yulee from prison, 246; as secretary of war ad interim under Johnson, 277

Gray, John F., 267

Gray, Thomas, 174

Green, C. C., 368 (n. 39)

Greenville (Mich.) Independent, 349 (n. 69)

Grimké, Angelina, 328 (n. 55)

Grimké, John Faucheraud, 328 (n. 55)

Grimké, Sarah, 328 (n. 55)

Gurley, Frank, 176

Gwin, William M., 44, 125

Habeas Corpus Act, 188

Hale, Charles, 264

Hanchett, William, 202

Hancock, Winfield Scott, 210, 217–18

Hardin, Benjamin, 19–21, 29, 47, 62, 326 (n. 32), 333 (n. 34)

Harlan, James, 258

Harpers Ferry raid, 100, 103

Harper's Weekly, 149, 300, 301, 313–14

Harris, Carey A., 43

Harris, Thomas M., 359 (n. 11)

Harris, T. M., 376–77 (n. 5)

Harrison, Burr, 47, 48, 53, 57, 332 (n. 25)

Harrison, Burton N., 233–34, 313–14

Harrison, James O.: on Buchanan, 110; and Clay, 45, 59, 331 (n. 15); and death of Margaret Holt, 106; on death of Mary Holt, 55, 57; and death of son Richard, 106; and financial problems of JH, 82; gifts from JH to, 55; and JH's appointment as postmaster general, 96; JH's sup-

port for, during Civil War, 192; as law partner of JH, 45; Lexington home of, 49; on Louisville home of JH, 49; and oath of allegiance after Civil War, 241; on problems in United States in 1859, 92–93; on religious beliefs of JH, 334 (n. 39); on secession, 110, 115; Unionism of, 93, 107

Harrison, Lowell Hayes, 351 (n. 13), 352 (n. 15)

Harrison, Mary Louisa. *See* Holt, Mary Louisa Harrison

Harrison, Richard, 106

Harrison, Sarah, 48, 58, 61–62, 80

Hartranft, John F., 210, 372 (n. 23)

Hawes, Albert Gallatin, 24–25, 29–33, 326–27 (n. 38)

Hay, John, 113, 117, 189, 297

Hayne, Isaac W., 126

Herold, David: arraignment of, in Lincoln assassination case, 207; burial of, 227; as coconspirator in Lincoln assassination, 202, 204, 271; defense lawyer for, 359 (n. 13); execution of, 218, 220; guilty verdict against and sentence for, 215, 218, 219; questions about, 211; reburial of remains of, 286; testimony against, 211

Heyl, Edward M., 279

Hickey, William, 126

Hitchcock, E. A., 352 (n. 18)

Hitchens, Owen, 159

Hoare, Joseph (a.k.a. William Campbell), 232, 247, 249, 250, 256

Holt, Ann (JH's sister-in-law), 54–55, 57, 97, 191, 270, 281

Holt, E. A., 88

Holt, Eleanor Stephens (JH's mother): birthdate of, 7; children of, 7, 8; during Civil War, 196; on Civil War, 239; death and burial of, 302–3; death of sister Mary Ann, 238; on emancipation of slaves, 239–40; finances of, 239, 302, 343 (n. 42); former slaves of, 239–40, 302; gifts to, by JH, 55;

and JH's appointment as postmaster general, 96; and JH's marriage to Margaret, 76; and JH's move to Mississippi, 44–45; JH's relationship with, after Civil War, 239–40, 302; on Lincoln, 239; and Margaret's failing health, 104, 343 (n. 42); marriage of, 7–8, 324 (n. 7); old age of, 281; and religious beliefs of JH, 55; and wedding between JH and Mary, 331 (n. 21)

Holt, Halaine, xi

Holt, James (JH's brother): birthdate of, 7; after Civil War, 240; clothing for, 13–14, 280–81; death of, 280–81; education of, 13; in Illinois, 39; as lawyer and judge, 39, 280; as supporter of Confederacy, 280; in Texas, 39, 57, 240, 280; and U.S.-Mexican War, 57; youth of, 19

Holt, James (Robert Holt's son), 376 (n. 1)

Holt, John W. (JH's father): advice to JH, 17–18; children of, 7, 8; death and burial of, 48, 303; family background of, 7; homes of, 37–38, 39, 329 (n. 2), 332 (n. 24); and JH's move to Mississippi, 44–45; land owned by and farming by, 7, 8; as lawyer, 8, 17, 33; marriage of, 7, 324 (n. 7); personality of, 8; as slave owner, 7, 323–24 (n. 4)

Holt, John W.(Thomas Holt's son), 139, 141, 142, 376 (n. 1)

Holt, Joseph: accomplishments of, 299–300; advice from family and friends and ambitions for, 5, 8–9, 12–13, 17–18, 20, 24–34, 37, 40, 44, 45–46, 74, 80, 91–92, 97, 254–55; and animals, 49, 51, 305–6, 334–35 (n. 41); avoidance of elective office by, 24–26, 43, 46, 70–71, 78, 96, 147, 330 (n. 9); bachelorhood and marriage prospects of, 28–29, 46–47, 327–28 (n. 47); birthdate of, 7; and California plan, 75–76; and chapel

project on family land in Kentucky, 303, 305, 318, 322, 373 (n. 32); children named after, x, 154, 234, 241, 270, 368 (n. 42), 375 (n. 56), 376 (n. 1); clothing for, 13–14, 18; courtship between Margaret Wickliffe and, 62–63; courtship between Mary Harrison and, 47–48; death and burial of, 316–18; and death of first wife Mary, 54–58, 73, 74, 304, 334 (n. 41); and death of second wife Margaret, 106, 192–93, 304; and deaths of family members, 27, 36, 37, 44, 45, 48, 88, 103, 190, 238–39, 269, 270, 280–81, 302–3, 305; education of, 8–14, 16–18, 20, 62, 66–67, 325 (n. 13); extramarital relationships of, 69, 93–94, 104, 192; family background and parents of, 6–9, 324 (n. 7); family relations of, during and after Civil War, 190–92, 196–98, 238–41, 302–5; finances of, 38, 66, 75–76, 82–83, 92, 184, 239, 302, 319, 343 (n. 42), 346 (n. 24), 350 (n. 78); gravestone of, 317; health concerns of, ix, 12, 17, 34–35, 48, 53, 80, 333–34 (n. 35); health problems of, 267, 275, 305, 314, 315–16; and health problems of wife Margaret, 73–77, 93–94, 102–4, 106; and health problems of wife Mary, 48, 53–55, 73; historians' neglect of, 1–2, 321, 322; homes of, 3, 49–52, 55–56, 68, 69, 76, 81–82, 97, 302, 332 (n. 23); honors and awards for, 33, 149, 154, 258, 366 (n. 20); as Jackson supporter and Democratic Party member, 21, 26–27, 30, 31–33, 40–46, 49, 53, 69, 71–73, 77–80; as Jefferson County commonwealth's attorney, 32–34, 44; law practice of, in Elizabethtown, Ky., 19–21, 23–25, 27, 29; law practice of, in Louisville, 30–31, 38, 44, 329 (n. 58); law practice of, in Vicksburg, Miss., 45–46, 48–49; and Margaret Crosby, 242–

Holt, Richard (JH's brother): advice to JH, 12, 26–27, 30; birthdate of, 7; death of, 36, 37, 40, 44, 45; and JH's move to Louisville, 30; medical studies of, 8, 12, 13; personality of, 36

Holt, Robert (JH's brother): admiration for JH, 39–40, 70; advice to JH, 74, 80, 91–92, 97; amnesty application of, after Civil War, 240; birthdate of, 7; children of, 54, 57, 74, 97, 191, 198, 239, 269–70, 281, 375 (n. 56), 376 (n. 1); during Civil War, 191; on Compromise of 1850 and sectionalism, 64–66; Confederacy's defeat and impact of Civil War on, 197–98, 239, 240, 302; Confederacy supported by sons of, 269–70; death of, 269, 270; on death of brother Richard, 36; and death of Margaret Holt, 107; and death of Mary Holt, 55, 57, 58, 107; defense of slavery by, 115; dislike of Ohioans by, 66, 74; education of, 38, 39–40, 328 (n. 55); finances of, 38, 66, 92, 97, 191, 197–98, 239; health problems of, 331–32 (n. 21); on JH as secretary of war under Buchanan, 114–15; and JH's appointment as postmaster general, 97; on JH's despondency, 35; on JH's enemies after Civil War, 254–55; on JH's move to Mississippi, 44–45; on JH's move to Washington, D.C., 80; on JH's speech at Democratic Party convention (1835), 43; and JH's trip to Europe, 59; on Kossuth, 70; law practice of, in Benton, Miss., 48, 50, 51, 53; on Lincoln's election as president, 107, 108; on Louisville home of JH, 49; marriage of, 54; move to Cincinnati by, 66, 74; and Nashville, 74; on Northerners, 109; on secession, 64–66, 107–9, 114–15; as slave owner, 66, 91–92; on Southern planter class, 91–92; on termination of JH

as Jefferson County commonwealth attorney, 35; on Thomas Holt's decision to leave home, 38–39; on Unionism of JH, 108–9, 114–16, 141–42; in Yazoo City, Miss., 80; youth of, 19

Holt, Robert S. (JH's nephew), 375 (n. 56), 376 (n. 1)

Holt, Rosina Board (JH's sister-in-law), 52, 59–60, 139, 281, 303–5, 373 (n. 31)

Holt, Sarah Ellen "Sallie" (JH's niece), 54, 97, 376 (n. 1)

Holt, Thomas (JH's brother): birthdate of, 7; children of, 54, 139, 141, 376 (n. 1); Confederacy's defeat and impact of Civil War on, 197–98; Confederacy supported by sons of, 139, 141, 142, 196; death and burial of, 303; and deaths of family members, 190, 280–81, 334 (n. 41); farming by, at family home, 39, 281, 303; former slaves of family hired by, 239, 281; guerrilla activities of, during Civil War, 191; and health of sister Elizabeth, 337–38 (n. 67); and JH's marriage to Margaret, 76; JH's relationship with, during and after Civil War, 303, 363 (n. 66); marriage of, 52, 54; as slave owner, 49–52; and wedding of JH, 331 (n. 21); will of, 303; youth and young adulthood of, 19, 38–39

Holt, Thomas (Robert Holt's son), 376 (n. 1)

Holt, Vanda Lee Vineyard (wife of JH's nephew Washington Dorsey Holt), 303–6, 308, 314–15, 318, 322, 323 (n. 3), 373 (n. 31)

Holt, Washington Dorsey (JH's nephew): birth and name of, 54; and chapel project on family land in Kentucky, 303; in Confederate army, 196; daughters of, 303–5, 322, 323 (n. 3), 373 (n. 31); death of, 322; and death of uncle James, 280; and funeral of JH, 318; health problems of, 314; and health problems of wife

226, 227, 231, 232, 235, 244, 246, 268, 285–88, 362 (n. 49); and patronage, 260; personality of, 311; photograph of, 256; presidency of, after Lincoln assassination, 3, 204; and proclamation of peace following Civil War, 244, 246, 264–65, 268; racism of, 280; Reconstruction policies of, 219–22, 226, 227, 230–38, 243–44, 246, 254, 261, 263, 266, 285, 292, 320; and release of Clay and Yulee from prison, 244, 246; suspension and later attempted firing of Stanton by, 276–78, 280, 282, 294; and treason case against Jefferson Davis, 223; vetoes by, 237, 245, 261, 262, 266; and writ of habeas corpus, 351 (n. 6)

Johnson, George, 373 (n. 34)

Johnson, Reverdy, 170–71, 209, 233, 367 (n. 36)

Johnson, Richard M., 41–42, 46, 59, 70, 330 (nn. 6, 9)

Johnson, Robert Ward, 70–72, 117

Johnston, Joseph E., 206

"Jo Holt Rifles," 147–48

Jolivet, Father Charles, 224

Jones, Eliza, 373 (n. 31)

Judge advocate general: and black soldiers, 179–81, 185, 191, 279, 360 (n. 31); and cases involving disobedience of orders, 166–73; and cases on slaves and former slaves, 176–80, 220, 230; and confinement of soldiers in state penitentiaries, 290; and Conover scandal, 247–52, 255–59, 268; and crimes committed by Confederate soldiers, 175–76; criticisms of JH as, 164–65, 170–72, 186–87, 227–30, 236–38, 263, 302; and deserters, 173, 353 (n. 25); digest of JH's legal opinions as, 182; Dunn as, 300; and Emancipation Proclamation, 162–64, 176–80; and executions, 173, 174, 175, 176, 188, 279; flexibility of JH in reviewing cases of, 173–74; and general courts-martial versus garrison and regimental courts-martial, 289, 370 (n. 7); JH as, under Grant, 288–89; and JH as brevet major general, 232; and JH as brigadier general, 184; JH's accomplishments at, 299–300; and JH's antislavery attitude, 162; JH's appointment as, by Lincoln, 2–3, 157, 159, 355–56 (n. 53); JH's refusal of attorney generalship under Lincoln, 189; JH's response to Conover scandal, 255–58; JH's retirement from, 299–302; and JH's support for Lincoln's policies, 162–64, 171, 188; JH's thoughts of resigning from, after trial of Lincoln assassins, 222–23; Johnson on JH as, 236–37; Johnson's charges against JH regarding Mary Surratt petition, 274–77, 293–99; and Lieber Code, 181–82, 216; and link between Jefferson Davis and Lincoln assassination, 223–24, 227, 230–34, 236, 237, 244–52, 254; and military prisons, 290; and military rule for states of former Confederacy, 199; and Milligan case, 187–88, 205, 207, 212, 219, 244, 364 (n. 74); and murder cases, 174–77, 220, 230, 279, 288, 360 (n. 31), 362 (n. 49); oath of office by JH as, 184–85, 232; organization and preservation of records and documents from, 277–78, 289; and policy on "incorrigible rebels," 354 (n. 40); and political prisoners, 354–55 (n. 42); and Porter case, 166–73, 182, 207, 209, 352 (n. 18), 353 (n. 22); praise for JH as, 163–64, 213, 218, 220, 223, 229, 230, 234, 236, 238, 242–43, 252, 257–58, 263, 275–79, 286, 288, 296–97, 300–301, 309–12, 376 (n. 2), 376–77 (n. 5); and rape cases, 354 (n. 33); and reorganization of army after Civil War, 251–52, 259, 365 (n. 12); responsibilities of, 158–59, 161, 350–51

Radical Reconstruction. *See* Reconstruction

Rainey, Joseph Hayne, 291, 371 (n. 12)

Randolph, John, 19–20

Rape, 354 (n. 33)

Rawlins, John A., 370 (n. 6)

Reconstruction: Americans' historical memory of, 320–22; congressional guidelines for, 265–66; Democratic Party and congressional Reconstruction, 290–91; and Fifteenth Amendment, 291–92; and Fourteenth Amendment, 249, 258, 261, 266, 284, 292; JH's criticisms of, 219, 243–44, 254, 261, 265; Johnson's policies for, 219–22, 226, 227, 230–38, 243–44, 246, 254, 261, 263, 266, 285, 292, 320; and John Surratt's trial, 274–75; Lincoln's plan for, 200, 219; negative impact of Johnson's policies on, 231–34, 243–44, 254, 265, 267, 278, 281–82, 284; and presidential election of 1868, 284; and Radical Republicans in Congress, 219–20, 222, 229, 232–37, 261–62, 265–66, 276, 281, 320; and Stanton, 266, 276; and state constitutions, 265–66; in Tennessee, 262, 265; and Thirteenth Amendment, 189, 232, 233, 239, 266, 352 (n. 15), 371 (n. 12); U.S. Army soldiers stationed in South during, 240, 266, 279, 288; violence undermining, 292

Redman, George, 177–78

Reed, William B., 249

Reede, Silas, 116

Reese, C. C., 362 (n. 49)

Religious liberty, 77–78

Reply of J. Holt to Certain Calumnies of Jacob Thompson, 312–13

Republican Party: and emancipation of slaves, 79, 108; formation of, 79; JH's criticism of "Black Republicans," 79, 90, 146; members of, 96, 100–101; and presidential election of 1860, 104; and presidential election of

1868, 282; Radical Republicans and Reconstruction, 222, 229, 232–37, 261–62, 265–66, 276, 281, 320; and South's secession threats, 109–10

Revels, Hiram, 291, 371 (n. 12)

Revolutionary War. *See* American Revolution

Reynolds, Rev. Ignatius A., 54, 59

Richardson, Anna, 373 (n. 34)

Rickets, James, 352 (n. 18)

Riddle, Albert G., 270, 287

Rives, William Cabell, 41

Robards, George, 52

Roberts, William (a.k.a. Joseph Snevel), 232, 247

Robinson, Alice, 373 (n. 31)

Rogers, Andrew J., 252–57, 262, 287

Rose, Catherine, x, 323 (n. 3)

Rose, Joseph Holt, Sr., x, 322, 323 (n. 3), 375 (n. 56)

Rose, Mary Holt, x, 303–5, 315, 322, 323 (n. 3), 375 (n. 56)

Rose, Walter Malins, 322, 323 (n. 3)

Rosecrans, William S., 165

Rousseau, Lovell, 147

Rucker, T., 57

Ruggles, George, 318

Russian czar, 71–72

Ryder, Rev. W. H., 213

Sailor, John W., 175

St. Albans, Vt., raid, 213, 214

Sainte Marie, Henri Beaumont de, 260–61, 271, 272, 366 (n. 25)

St. Joseph's College, 9–12, 17, 25, 34, 62, 63, 348 (n. 54)

Sanders, George, 205, 212, 213, 214, 232

Sandy (slave), 91, 340 (n. 17)

Sanford, John F. A., 170

Schoepf, Albin F., 153–54, 241

Schoepf, Julia, 241

Schofield, John M., 283, 318

Scientific American, 159

Scott, Winfield, 117, 118, 121, 127, 128, 130

Secession: Crosby on, 111; Democrats' attitudes toward threats of, 110; and Harpers Ferry raid by John Brown, 100; James Harrison on, 110, 115; Kentucky debate on, 134–49, 152–53, 349 (n. 69); Republicans' attitudes toward threats of, 109–10; Robert Holt on, 64–66, 108–9, 114–15; of South Carolina, 111, 117, 121, 136; and Southerners' attitudes toward Northerners, 109; of Southern states following South Carolina, 122, 134; and threats against JH as secretary of war, 116; and Yulee family, 107

Senate, U.S. *See* Congress, U.S.

Seward, Frederick, 294

Seward, William H.: and assassination plot against Lincoln before inauguration, 128; attack against, by Powell, 201, 202, 211, 214; death of, 294, 298, 309; and JH as secretary of war, 129; and JH on border-state affairs, 145; and Johnson's awareness of Mary Surratt petition, 293, 294; and John Surratt in Europe, 224–25, 260–61; and John Surratt's capture and arrest, 264; Montgomery Blair's criticisms of, 228; as possible presidential candidate in 1860, 93, 105; as secretary of state, 128

Seymour, Horatio, 284, 285

Shaffner, Tal P., 218–20

Shankland, Thomas, 286, 288

Sherman, Ellen, 319

Sherman, William T., 188, 189, 206, 222, 228, 319, 352 (n. 16)

Shiloh, Battle of, 157

Singleton, L., 327 (n. 39)

Slavery: anti-Lincoln activists' rumors on emancipation, 140, 144, 146, 148; charges of theft against female slave, 332–33 (n. 28); and Compromise of 1850, 65; Crosby on, 100; defense of, 23, 115; and *Dred Scott* case, 92, 170, 281; fears of slave rebellions,

108; and Frémont's emancipation order, 150–52; Fugitive Slave Act, 65, 105; and Harpers Ferry raid by John Brown, 100; harsh conditions of, 50–51; insurance on slaves, 91, 340–41 (n. 17); JH as slave owner, 2–3, 49–52, 57, 66, 67, 68–69, 90–91, 340–41 (n. 17), 341 (n. 18); JH's attitudes toward, 23, 66–67, 91, 101, 102, 113–14, 162; in Kentucky, 6, 7, 16, 19, 23, 29, 47, 49–50, 135, 137, 141, 332 (n. 25), 337 (n. 61); and Lincoln's Emancipation Proclamation, 160, 162–66, 170, 176–79, 292, 352 (n. 15); and Missouri Compromise, 66, 92; Nat Turner's slave rebellion, 22; Presbyterian Church on, 337 (n. 61); Republican Party and emancipation, 79, 108; Robert Holt's attitudes on, 66, 91–92; sale of JH's slaves, 51; sexual relations between white men and female slaves, 23, 41, 178; statistics on, 6, 23, 56, 135; in territories, 64, 92; U.S. Constitution on, 179–80; in Washington, D.C., 91. *See also* Abolitionism

Slough, John P., 352 (n. 18)

Smith, Caleb B., 122

Smith, Samuel, 360 (n. 31)

Snethen, W. G., 197, 230

Snevel, Joseph (a.k.a. William Roberts), 232, 247

Snowden, R. W., 33

Sociology for the South (Fitzhugh), 75

Soulé, Pierre, 78

South Carolina: Beauregard as Confederate military commander in, 128; black congressman from, 291; Federal troops in Charleston Harbor and *Star of the West* expedition to, 117–22, 130–33, 228, 312, 313, 346 (n. 28); Fort Sumter, 118, 120–21, 124–26, 128–33, 138, 160, 198, 228, 230; military preparations in, 118; and Nullification Crisis, 21–23, 31,

134–35; problems in reestablishment of civil government in, after Civil War, 218–19; secession of, 111, 117, 121, 136, 139

South Carolina Exposition and Protest, The, 21, 22

Spangler, Edman: arraignment of, in Lincoln assassination case, 207; arrest and imprisonment of, 204; as coconspirator in Lincoln assassination, 204; defense lawyer for, 359 (n. 13); guilty verdict against and sentence for, 215, 218, 219; Johnson's pardon of, 286; questions about, 211

Speed, James: as attorney general, 189, 207, 209; on Civil War in Kentucky, 165–66; death of, 310; education of, 348 (n. 54); and indictment against John Surratt, 225; and Johnson's awareness of Mary Surratt petition, 294–95, 297, 298, 310–12; as law professor, 309; and Lincoln assassination case, 207, 209; photograph of, 167; replacement for, as attorney general, 250, 255; on Schoepf at Battle of Camp Wildcat, 154; and treason case against Jefferson Davis, 223; Unionism of, 348 (n. 54)

Speed, John, 145, 149, 165

Speed, Joshua F., 143–45, 149, 150, 152–56, 278

Speed, Thomas, 312

Spies, 176, 353 (n. 30)

Spinner, F. E., 371 (n. 17)

Stanbery, Henry, 255, 259, 281

Stanton, Benjamin, 361 (n. 36)

Stanton, Edwin M.: and appointment of JH as secretary of war, 113, 155, 349 (n. 76); assassination plot against, 214; as attorney general under Buchanan, 111, 113, 116; and black soldiers in U.S. Army, 179; and Conover scandal, 255, 258; criticisms of, 228, 294, 371 (n. 17), 372 (n. 22); death of, 294, 298, 309, 371

(n. 17); JH on, 155, 349–50 (n. 76); and JH's appointment as judge advocate general of U.S. Army, 157; and JH's case against Jefferson Davis, 234, 237, 250, 314; on JH's performance as judge advocate general, 258; and JH's request for court of inquiry on JH's handling of Jefferson Davis investigation, 258; and Johnson's awareness of Mary Surratt petition, 293–94, 296, 372 (n. 22); and John Surratt in Europe, 225, 260; and Lincoln assassination case, 199–202, 255, 263, 358 (n. 4), 359 (n. 10), 367 (n. 29); and McClellan, 163; and Milligan case, 187; portrait of, 114; as possible presidential candidate in 1856, 78, 111; praise for, 371 (n. 17); and promotions for JH as judge advocate general, 184, 232; and Reconstruction, 266, 276; resignation of, as secretary of war, 283; as secretary of war under Lincoln, 154–56, 222, 229, 349–50 (n. 76); suspension and later attempted firing by Johnson of, as secretary of war, 276–78, 280, 282, 294; and treason case against Jefferson Davis, 223; and War Department's Bureau of Military Justice, 184, 201–2, 227

Star of the West expedition, 117–22, 130–33, 228, 312, 313, 346 (n. 28)

States' rights, 21–22. *See also* Nullification; Secession

Stephens, Alexander, 227, 232

Stephens, Ann "Nancy," 7

Stephens, Daniel Jennings (JH's uncle): advice to and ambitions for JH, 5, 9, 13, 18, 24, 26, 28, 29, 31, 32–34, 37, 40, 44, 45–46; birthdate of, 7; and Burr Harrison, 47; and clothing advice for JH, 13; criticisms of Stephen Douglas by, 88; death of, 103; and Democratic convention (1835), 40, 42–43; dueling by,

18; and education of JH, 14, 17; as
Jackson supporter, 20, 26–27; and
JH as Jefferson County commonwealth's attorney, 32–33; and JH as
Patent Office commissioner, 85–86;
and JH as postmaster general, 96,
99; and JH's marriage to Margaret,
76; on Louisville law practice of JH,
31; on public-speaking skills, 24;
and Robert Holt, 38; and secession
threats following Compromise of
1850, 65; on slaves owned by JH, 51;
in state legislature, 8

on Lincoln assassination case by, 308; fears about physical safety of, 260, 261; JH's friendship with generally, 308; and Johnson's awareness of Mary Surratt petition, 299; and John Surratt's capture, 264; and John Surratt's trial, 271–72; and Lincoln assassination case, 212, 214, 215, 217, 220–21, 260, 264; move to Indiana by, 374 (n. 42); patronage job of, at Customs House in Philadelphia, 231, 260, 299

Welles, Gideon: and Fort Sumter, 129, 228–29; on JH, 229, 236–37, 266, 276; on JH's refusal of attorney generalship, 355–56 (n. 53); and JH's request for court of inquiry on JH's handling of Jefferson Davis investigation, 258; and Johnson's awareness of Mary Surratt petition, 294; and Montgomery Blair's attack on JH, 228–29; on Stanton, 266, 276, 371 (n. 17); and suspension of Stanton by Johnson, 276

West, Lucy, 87

West, Nellie, 362 (n. 49)

Westcott, Gideon G., 98–99

West Point. *See* United States Military Academy at West Point

Whig Party: and Clay, 19, 21, 32; criticism of JH by, 43, 44; decline of, 79, 135; JH's criticisms of, 21, 32, 42, 71, 72; in Kentucky, 35, 44, 135; members of, 45, 46, 60, 62, 70, 72

White, Andrew Dickson, 170–71

White Brotherhood, 292

Wickliffe, Anne Dawson, 64

Wickliffe, Charles Anderson: and border-state convention (1861), 140; children of, 63–64; and daughter Margaret, 337 (n. 58); on Emancipation Proclamation, 162; and JH as Patent Office commissioner, 85; and military preparations in Kentucky, 149; as Peace Democrat, 184, 192;

political career of generally, 62, 184; portrait of, 61; as postmaster general under Tyler, 62, 74, 94; as slave owner, 91; in U.S. Congress, 62, 145, 162

Wickliffe, Charlie, 63–64

Wickliffe, Fannie Hill, 315, 319, 373 (n. 29)

Wickliffe, Margaret "Mag." *See* Holt, Margaret "Mag" Wickliffe

Wickliffe, Robert C., 14, 16–19, 28, 62–64

Wigand, H., 125

Wigfall, Louis T., 116

Wilding, Henry, 224–25

Williams, Thomas, 281, 368 (n. 39)

Wilson, James F., 245, 257–58, 281

Wilson, Joel B., 88

Wilson, Nathaniel, 270, 271

Wilson's Creek, Battle of, 150

Wintersmith, Charles G., 25, 327 (n. 39)

Winthrop, William, 277

Wirz, Henry, 226–27, 262, 286

Wisconsin, 64

Wood, Charles, 279

Woodbridge, Frederick, 368 (n. 39)

Woods, Charles R., 120–21

Work, George, 25, 28, 29, 32, 46

Wright, Farnum B., 232

Writ of habeas corpus, 160–64, 182, 188, 217, 268, 351 (n. 6)

Wylie, Andrew, 283

Yeaman, Harvey, 218

Young, Dr., 8

Yulee, C. Wickliffe, 321–22

Yulee, David Levy: betrayal of public trust by, before leaving Congress, 122, 124, 127, 131, 235; brother of, 87; death of, 321; imprisonment of, 235, 321, 363 (n. 59); JH's rejection of pardon for, 235–36; Johnson's parole of, 244, 268; loss of friendship between JH and, due to Civil War, 191, 321;

marriage of, 63, 81, 87, 107; photograph of, 123; resignation of, from U.S. Senate, 204; and secession, 107, 124, 127, 204, 235–36; as U.S. senator, 63, 81, 122, 124, 131, 235

Yulee, Elias, 87

Yulee, Nannie Wickliffe: children of, 337 (n. 58); and death of Margaret Holt, 106–7; and health problems of sister Margaret, 102–4; and JH as Patent Office commissioner, 90; marriage of, 63, 81, 87, 107; relationship between JH and, 106–7, 124; and Southern nationalism and secession, 107, 124; in Washington, D.C., 81, 87–88

Zolicoffer, Felix, 153